THE FONTANA ECONOMIC HISTORY OF EUROPE

General Editor: Carlo M. Cipolla

There is at present no satisfactory economic history of
Europe – covering Europe both as a whole and with
particular relation to the individual countries – that is
both concise enough for convenient use and yet full
enough to include the results of individual and detailed
scholarship. This series is designed to fill that gap.

Unlike most current works in this field the *Fontana
Economic History of Europe* does not end at the outbreak
of the First World War. More than half a century has
elapsed since 1914, a half-century that has transformed
the economic background of Europe. In recognition
of this the present work has set its terminal date at
1970 and provides for sixty contributions each written
by a specialist. For the convenience of students each
will be published separately in pamphlet form as soon
as possible. When all the contributions have been
received they will be gathered into six volumes as
The Fontana Economic History of Europe. A library
edition will also be available.

The Fontana Economic History of Europe

The Sixteenth and Seventeenth Centuries

Editor Carlo M. Cipolla

Collins/Fontana Books

First published in this edition 1974
Second Impression November 1976

© Carlo M. Cipolla 1974
© Roger Mols S.J. 1972
© Walter Minchinton 1974
© Hermann Kellenbenz 1974
© Aldo de Maddalena 1970
© Domenico Sella 1970
© Kristof Glamann 1971
© Geoffrey Parker 1974

Made and printed in Great Britain by
William Collins Sons & Co. Ltd Glasgow

Contents

Introduction

Carlo M. Cipolla

Conventionally the modern age is held to have begun at the end of the fifteenth century. Lines of demarcation – as everybody knows – are by their very nature arbitrary and artificial: but it is hardly contestable that the sixteenth century inaugurated a period that saw a dramatic change – or at least a dramatic acceleration of some basic developments that first appeared in previous centuries. The Europe of the eighteenth century is an utterly different place from the Europe of two centuries earlier.

Chiefly the reader will find in the chapters that follow examples and evidence of particular developments that took place in the technological and economic sphere. It is of the greatest importance to stress here that these phenomena can hardly be understood historically unless they are seen as an integral part of a far broader change comprehending simultaneous developments in the fields of thought, of the arts, of politics and social life.

By the beginning of the eighteenth century the city state and the petty principality had ceased to play any important part in the political life of Europe. In their place the nation state was growing from strength to strength. In the internal history of the different countries a parallel movement brought power to the central government at the expense of local jurisdiction. National armies and navies grew progressively larger and, as technology transformed the art of destruction as well as that of production, the economic cost of armies and navies increased in a proportion even greater than their size. Military expenditures absorbed by far the largest quota of governmental budgets. The ever increasing costs of armies and navies resulted in greatly increased taxation. A progressively larger proportion of the national product was drawn off and controlled by the central government. At the same time dominance of artillery and musketry, both on the high seas and on the battlefield, meant closer links between military power and manufacturing potential.

At the highest levels of thought the 'moderns' confronted the 'ancients'.[1] Practical experiment had won a reverence hitherto reserved for philosophical speculation. The description of phenomena began to be regarded as an equally respectable intellectual activity as formulating hypotheses to explain final causes. Mensuration of the phenomena observed became evermore widespread. As has been said, the 'virtuosi' and scholars of the seventeenth century 'overvalued observation and calculation . . . They continued endlessly and pointlessly to record, catalogue and count. The best minds of England squandered their talents in minutely recording temperature, wind and the look of the skies hour by hour.'[2] Much of this activity simply accumulated useless records. But the mental attitude that was behind the compilation of these records was one that favoured experiment and a systematic approach. Moreover this energy was turned also to the measurement of economic and social dimensions of various sorts. 'My virtue and vanity lies in prating of numbers, weight and measure' wrote Sir William Petty to his friend Sir Robert Southwell. As Professor Lawrence Stone has pointed out: 'One of the by-products of the revolution in human thought that took place in Western Europe in the sixteenth century was the growth of the statistical approach. To the educated layman as well as to the government clerk, numbers at last began to take on a form of reality. The attitude of mind that led medieval chroniclers to say *so many thousand* when they meant no more

1. On the history and significance of the struggle between 'ancients' and 'moderns' in the seventeenth century, see *Ancients and Moderns: a Study of the Rise of the Scientific Movement*, St. Louis 1961. This extremely learned work concerns itself particularly with England but it must be borne in mind that similar developments had taken place also in France, Italy and other parts of Europe.

2. W. Letwin, *The Origins of Scientific Economics*, London 1963, pp.99–100.

than *a very large number* began to die away.'[3] People progressively learned and realised that the value of mensuration
wholly depends on certain standards of accuracy in the
figures employed (a conquest of thought of which an
alarmingly large number of present day econometricians
and econometric-historians seem unaware).[4] The basic
concept of science was at least established. Thanks to the
application of mathematics, mechanics and physics took
their place on the frontiers of knowledge. The advances and
discoveries in these disciplines were in fact so dramatic and
impressive that their methodology was rightly or wrongly
adopted in an increasing number of different fields. From
this point dates what has been aptly called 'the mechanisation
of the world view' – a process which was to continue until our
own days.

On the level of general culture, the sixteenth and seventeenth centuries saw, particularly in the Northern countries,
an exceptional increase in literacy, an increase that was
nourished by the invention of printing and by the preaching
of the reformed religion. During the course of the seventeenth century even in a Catholic country such as France
the habit of reading became sufficiently common to make
the mass production of paperbacks an economic proposition.[5] At the end of the seventeenth century however, as
regards literacy, Holland and England were the two most
developed countries of Europe.[6] Its diffusion amongst ever
more extensive classes of society had an economic significance
that cannot be overstated. It must be kept in mind that the

3. L. Stone, Elizabethan Overseas Trade, in *The Economic History Review* ser. 2, vol. 2 (1949), pp. 30–58.

4. Every student of economics, econometrics and economic history ought to read and ponder O. Morgenstern, *On the Accuracy of Economic Observations*, Princeton 1963. It is the fashion nowadays to acquire the reputation for being a 'quantitivist', especially in the field of economic history, but a man is not necessarily a 'quantitivist' who makes an uncritical and inappropriate use of statistics just as he is not necessarily a 'qualitativist' if he objects to the glib and inexact use of figures.

5. Cf. R. Mandrou, *De la culture populaire aux 17e et 18e siècles*, Paris 1964.

6. C. M. Cipolla, *Literacy and Development in the West*, Harmondsworth 1969, p. 61.

real difference between a developed and an under-developed country consists not so much in the presence of a small number of cultural mandarins but rather in the more even diffusion of education among the population at large.

At the beginning of the eleventh century Europe was a backward area – nowadays we would say 'under-developed' – not only in comparison to the standards of our time but also by comparison to the levels of cultural, technological and economic developments of other places in that period. Europe was under-developed compared to the Byzantine Empire, to the Arab Empire and to the Chinese Empire. From the thirteenth century onwards the balance of economic potential and of technological scope moved progressively in Europe's favour. At the end of the fifteenth century Europe was unquestionably the part of the world that enjoyed the most advanced technology and her relative advantage continued to increase ever more rapidly. As regards numbers, the Europeans represented about 20-25% of the population of the world[7] and were inveterately divided amongst themselves, but a superior technology gave them a power far out of proportion to their numbers. It is inevitable that the nations with the most advanced technology must finish by getting the upper hand – peacefully or otherwise. The overseas expansion of Atlantic Europe and the expansion of Russia over the Steppes in the sixteenth and seventeenth centuries were the unavoidable result of a

7. As J. Mols has indicated in the chapter that follows, the population of Europe must have approximated to 82 millions about 1500, to 105 millions about 1600, and to 115 million about 1700. The population of China must have approximated to 100 millions round about 1500, and to 150 millions round about 1600. The Chinese population was drastically reduced by a series of disasters in the second quarter of the seventeenth century but recovered in the period that followed and must have again approached 150 millions about 1700. (Cf. Ho, P. *Studies on the Population of China, 1368–1953*, Cambridge Mass. 1959.) The population of America underwent a dramatic collapse between 1500 and 1650 (see on this the various studies of Cox and Borah) and in the middle of the seventeenth century it is doubtful if in the whole of the American continent there were more than 8 million people. It seems probable that about 1650 world population was somewhere between 450 and 550 millions.

balance of technological power that had already tipped too far in Europe's favour by the end of the Middle Ages. Amongst the by-products of this expansion the following at least demand notice.

1. The introduction into Europe of new products such as coffee, chocolate, china, tea, potatoes, tomatoes, maize, etc.
2. The import from the Americas of vast quantities of silver that brought with it a huge increase in international liquidity, and springing from it:
3. A vast increase in international trade.
4. A marked development in the ship-building and metal-working industries.

In particular, the development in international trade and of the various means of banking and exchange was such that, at least for Holland and for England during the period 1550–1700, it makes sense to use the term 'commercial revolution'. The commercial revolution helped to create much of the tinder that blazed up into the Industrial Revolution. It allowed a notable accumulation of wealth, it favoured the establishment and the growth of the middle classes, stimulated the expansion and diversification of demand and last but not least it nourished a school of entrepreneurship antagonistic to the traditional and the conservative, an attitude of mind and a standard of values favourable to economic growth.

While all these developments were taking place, England came to suffer from a severe shortage of timber. As a contemporary remarked:

'within man's memory, it was held impossible to have any want of wood in England. But such hath been the great expence of timber for navigation, with infinite increase of building houses, with great expence of wood to make household furniture, casks and other vessels not to be numbered, and of carts, wagons and coaches, besides the extreme waste of wood in making iron, burning of bricks and tiles, that at this present, through the great consuming of wood as aforesaid and the neglect of plant-

ing of woods, there is so great a scarcity of wood throughout the whole kingdom.'

The shortage of timber acted as a challenge. Ingenuity and
the abundant supply of easily available coal made possible a
positive response. The adoption of coal as fuel not only for
domestic heating but in a whole series of manufacturing
activities put England well on the road to the Industrial
Revolution.

It is fashionable today among economic and social
historians to speak of the sixteenth century as the golden age
in the economic and social history of Europe and to paint
the seventeenth century in sombre tones, muttering darkly
about 'the crises of the seventeenth century'. At the bottom
of every simplification there is always a grain of truth but
every simplification should be taken with a grain of salt. The
period 1500–1550 was not, in fact, a golden age for Italy. On
the contrary. Italy was then a battlefield fought over by
Frenchmen, Spaniards and Germans, and experienced wars,
plagues, famines and poverty beyond telling. The second
half of the century, for similar reasons, was not in fact a
golden age for the Southern Low Countries. To understand
the importance of these two exceptions, it must be remembered that the Southern Low Countries and Central and
Northern Italy were at the beginning of the sixteenth
century the two most highly developed areas of Europe. On
the other hand, the seventeenth century was a black century
for Spain, Italy and Germany and at least a grey one for
France. But for Holland it was *the* golden age and for
England, if not golden, at least silver.

These particularities are not brought in here purely for
the joy of pedantry. If the sixteenth century is to be considered as a period of general well-being and the seventeenth
century as a century of constant crises, this makes it the
harder to perceive and to understand one of the chief
facts in the history of Europe during the two centuries in
question. The disasters suffered by the Southern Low
Countries were the launching pad for the golden age of the
Northern. The fact that the seventeenth century was a
century of crises in Spain and Italy but a period of expan-

sion in the Northern Low Countries and for England brought about the decay of the whole Mediterranean world and moved the economic centre of gravity from the Mediterranean to the North Sea. Between 1500 and 1700 it was not only the balance of forces between Europe and the rest of the world that was upset: there was a revolution in the internal balances of Europe herself. If in the age of Leonardo, and Martini a European could have foreseen the Industrial Revolution, almost certainly he would have placed it in Italy. At the end of the seventeenth century it was obvious that every further economic development of any scale was only possible in the countries bordering the North Sea.

1. Population in Europe 1500-1700

Roger Mols S.J.

TWO CENTURIES OF DEMOGRAPHIC EVOLUTION

The question must be asked: do the two centuries between the reign of Henry VII and that of Queen Anne exhibit, as regards Europe, any clear and distinctive characteristics from the demographic point of view? How do they stand in the unfolding of the history of the population by comparison with, on the one hand, the Middle Ages and, on the other, the 18th century?

The answer is that the 16th and 17th centuries saw the first part of a transformation in the history of the European population—the first weakening of the medieval demographic pattern and the beginning of the contemporary demographic revolution. These changes did not have a very marked effect on the relationship between births and deaths: as far as one can judge, the figures and the trends were scarcely modified before the end of the 17th century. But changes occurred in substructures and environment without which the demographic revolution would never have taken the shape it did.

There are three distinctive features which help to give an identity to this crucial period.

1. Various changes took place in the geographical framework, in the ways in which people lived and in the ways in which they looked at life. These had profound and lasting repercussions in the demographic sphere. Let us consider the most important of them:

Between 1500 and 1700, the face of Europe was transformed; the main channels of trade shifted; modern states were consolidated. Europe had been shut in, Columbus and Vasco da Gama had only just peeped at the world outside and no one had as yet been round the world. Two centuries later, in an open Europe, the maritime nations were taking part in the exploration and exploitation of other parts of the world and the former Moscovy, now Russia, had staked its first claims in the conquest of the Siberian Far East. Europe, which had faced towards the Mediterranean and the Baltic in 1500, had become Atlantic Europe. Its sea-coasts had seen the growth of regions and ports interested in long-range commerce. It is enough to compare the fate of the old Mediterranean and Hanseatic centres with that of Lisbon, Seville, Antwerp, Amsterdam and above all London. The Europe of new-born monarchies had become the Europe of modern states. The rise of these states was accompanied by that of their capitals, large or small. The towns of princes and courts outdid the old urban republics. Dresden, Munich, Stuttgart and above all Berlin and Vienna expanded dazzlingly, while the free cities of the Empire could hardly hold their own. Madrid, a small and unimportant little town two centuries earlier, became the clear front-runner of all the Iberian towns. In the Low Countries, Brussels consolidated its position *vis-à-vis* its rivals and Amsterdam became fairly outstanding in the United Provinces. A similar contrast happened on a more modest scale to the Scandinavian capitals and, by comparison with Novgorod and Kiev, Moscow attained a higher rank. Even in Italy, the chief victim of this shift of activities, Rome was the only town, apart from Turin, to have tripled in size between 1500 and 1700. And who can doubt that the reigns of Francis I, Henry IV, Louis XIII and Louis XIV had a preferential effect on the rise of the French capital?

If the centre of gravity of the urban world shifted, that of the rural world grew firmer. There is no doubt that the peak reached by rural Europe was above all the achievement of the 18th century and of the first half of the 19th. But even before that, important changes had occurred or were in process: new uses of the soil, new rotation of crops, new farming techniques, new crops; development in the harnessing of energy (mills), in the exploitation of forest and mineral resources; spreading into the countryside of artisan and even industrial work; reduction in the former common lands for the sake of more intensive exploitation; reduction in those cereal crops least in demand for intensive cultivation, grazing and orchards; beginning of the modernisation of means of communications by roads and canals. Let us add a noticeable strengthening in the safety of the countryside. All this appreciably increased the demographic potential of the rural world.

Between 1500 and 1700, without being able yet to speak of an industrial revolution and even less of the centralisation of today, we also register real progress in the secondary and tertiary sectors. Side-by-side with the old manufacturing centres which are declining or only just holding their own, new centres develop, as do also new commercial and banking centres. The capitals often enriched their cultural life as they grew in administrative importance. In every respect the balance sheet for 1700 is noticeably different to that for 1500.

The development of experimental philosophy based on induction and the progress of a scientific way of thinking based on observation was bound to favour the practice of making demographic returns. This was the more so because the humanism of the Renaissance had increased interest in human values, because mercantilist tendencies gave a high place to population among the assets of nations and because the great discoveries had stimulated interest in all that could enrich geographical knowledge. The work of political arith-meticians would have been unthinkable and impossible of achievement in 1500. By 1700, it was quite naturally among the tendencies of the period and was assured of a promising future.

It is well known that the working and housing conditions of our ancestors, in the towns as much as in the countryside, were a continual violation of the most elementary rules of social hygiene. There is no question of speaking of the advent of an Eldorado at any date whatever of the period with which we are dealing. But is it certain that the environment in which our ancestors lived and worked towards the end of the 17th century had undergone no modification since the beginning of the 16th century? It seems, on the contrary, that the changes which had occurred in the ways of building or designing houses, in water-supply and other works of urbanisation, in the health inspection of towns, had resulted in certain demographic effects, even if these should not be overestimated.

It is no mistake to attribute an even greater influence to the changes affecting diet (for example, new foodstuffs and the respective proportion of the diet derived from animal and vegetal sources).[1] To this should be added various developments in bodily hygiene and clothing, certain changes in medical care and, for some regions, the putting-out (to nurse) of children in the country.

'The decline in the birth-rate', A. Landry has said,[2] 'has resulted from a change in moral attitudes, in the general way of looking at life.' Several elements of this psychological change of attitude can be seen in the period between the 16th and 18th centuries. They concern the family and the child. Family spirit and family life take on narrower, deeper, less tribal qualities. The child is more thought of as a person in his own right and in the context of the responsibilities of his upbringing.[3] Should we not look in this direction for an explanation of the 'European pattern of marriage' (see below) whose coming into being dates back to this period precisely?

Finally, it seems well established that a modification of the climate must be held responsible for a series of food crises which marked the whole period, from the end of the 16th to the middle of the 18th century. There were thus about 50 difficult years, of which several were very critical with considerable demographic repercussions.

2. There is another distinctive characteristic associated with the level of public health. This is still very mysterious and no satisfactory explanation has yet been found.

The Europe of 1500 had been suffering for more than 150 years from an intermittent series of epidemics. This series continued for more than another 150 years. But, from

1. W. L. Langer, Europe's Initial Population Explosion, in *American Historical Review*, 69 (1963) pp. 1–17.

2. A Landry, *Traité de Démographie*, Paris 1945, p. 636.

3. This aspect of the past was particularly emphasised in the work of P. Ariès. See, for example, Attitudes devant la vie et devant la mort du XVIIème au XIXème siècle, in *Population*, 4 (1949) pp. 463–70 and *L'enfant et la vie familiale sous l'Ancien Régime*, Paris 1960.

the middle of the 17th century, the frequency of these recurrent attacks decreased. There were many districts and
even towns in Europe which were not visited by the 'plague'
after 1660–1665. The fearful crisis of 1693–1694 and that of
the 'great winter' of 1709 brought together only the last
two horsemen of the Apocalypse, the first and most terrible
having to leave his horse in the stables. If this had not been
the case, the end of Louis XIV's reign would have been as
catastrophic as the Thirty Years War.

What caused a scourge that had become traditional to
abate? It has been claimed that in London the fire of 1666,
which came shortly after the terrible 'plague' of 1665 and
which reduced the greater part of the city to ashes, at the
same time purified the permanent breeding-grounds of in-
fection. It is possible, although not proved. But London was
not the only town where the plague did not reappear after
this period 1660–1665. And the other towns, e.g. Amsterdam, were not reduced to ashes. Something very mysterious
must therefore have happened in the field of public health,
at any rate in the last thirty years of the 17th century.

The Europe of 1700 was on the eve of witnessing the last
deaths due to the plague properly so-called. Only Central
Europe, from the Baltic to the Danube (1709–1714) and
Provence (1720–1721) were to be the victims of a last rear-
guard offensive. After this, the nosological history of Europe
—and, in a roundabout way, its demographic history—is
framed in quite new terms. No demographic revolution
would have been possible in a human environment
threatened 10 or 15 times a century with seeing itself
decimated by recurrent attacks of the plague.

3. Finally, a reference, not to the events, but to the
documentation which enables us to be better informed on
this subject. Our sources of information on the demography
of this period, despite their inadequacies, are better and less
scarce than for the autumn of the Middle Ages, to say
nothing of previous centuries. The following chapter will
deal explicitly with this question.

It is hardly necessary to add that the overall period
constituted by the 16th and 17th centuries forms, demo-

graphically speaking, a very heterogeneous background. The years 1500 and 1700 did not mark any clear break. The demographic position in the first decades of the 16th century was more like that at the end of the 15th century than that at the end of the 17th and the latter period was very like the early part of the 18th century. It was only gradually that the changes already mentioned took place, some above all in the 16th century, others in the 17th chiefly.

THE AVAILABLE SOURCES AND THEIR VALUE

DEMOGRAPHIC SOURCES OF A GIVEN DATE

These sources allow us to know the state of the population at a definite moment of the past.

For the period 1500–1700, our documentation shedding light on one particular point in time is similar to that for the end of the Middle Ages. But it is a little more direct, more abundant and more complete. We do not so often have to go 'round the North Pole to get to the South Pole'. It even begins to show a clumsy effort towards scientific qualities. Nevertheless, at no moment in this period, are we able to get a definitely accurate figure for a group of countries. Even for one country alone, it is very rare.

This gap can be explained by the different purpose which these sources had to fulfil and by the more limited means available of obtaining such data as they do contain.

Nowadays, official statistical enquiries are made for the purpose of general information, even if there may be additionally some less disinterested motive. It is the fruit of the spirit of scientific research, which attaches the highest value to an objective examination of facts and situations.

At the beginning of the modern period, the mental outlook of rulers was very different. Every demographic reckoning was subordinated to an essentially pragmatic final purpose, usually of a fiscal nature. A census foreshadowed a tax. It was meant to serve directly either to share out the tax (in currency or in the quantity of salt whose purchase was made compulsory) between collective units *pro rata* to their size, or to determine the number of people in each category liable to tax. As a result, everything considered irrelevant to the end aimed at was neglected, sometimes even including the listing of those citizens excused or exempted from the tax. As for the inhabitants who were listed, they were classified by non-demographic criteria. Some surveys were so little intended for purposes of information that the enumerators did not even bother to add up the numbers inscribed.

Apart from fiscal motives, other special purposes could also explain the setting-up, within a more limited framework, of arrangements to count certain particular human beings: to check on the destruction caused by a public disaster; to find out the number of citizens liable to a military or civil levy (muster rolls, *Eidregister*), the number of foreigners passing through, the numbers of a minority or suspect group, the number of dwellings on which troops could be billeted, the number of people to be fed in times of famine or during a siege and the food supplies at their disposal, the number of Christians old enough to receive Communion or liable to some other religious obligation.

This utilitarian concept of demographic statistics has survived throughout the modern period. But in the most advanced countries a change can also be observed, between 1500 and 1700, towards less old-fashioned and less simplistic practices.

The history of censuses in Venice is a good example of this evolution. It is probable that the administration of the Serene Republic drew its inspiration with regard to censuses from a Byzantine example. But there were numerous obstacles to overcome. The oldest official returns had been limited to a section of the populace; subsequently all had been included without distinction. In 1509, for the first time, the population enumerated was divided into two categories: 'useful persons' (male inhabitants between 15 and 60) and 'useless persons' (others). The results have been preserved for 3 *sestieri* out of 6. By using comparisons with later statistics, we can conclude the whole city contained about 100,000 inhabitants. It happens that two chroniclers of the period have written about this enumeration, Marin Sanudo and Fra' Marco. And here are the results as they have handed them down to us (errors included):

According to Sanudo:

Men, women, old people, boys and girls	300,000 souls
Men between 8 and 60 years old	160,000
Men of age for military service (*da fati*)	80,000
Women and children	48,346
Prostitutes	11,654

According to Fra' Marco:

All categories together	671,654
Old people, women and children	320,000
Men between 20 and 60 years old	160,000
Those liable for military service	80,000
Prostitutes	11,654

Such an example may enlighten us about the nature and worth of statistics handed down by ancient authors. Since data which can be checked can suffer such distorting transformations, what should be assumed where such data did not exist?

Between 1540 and the end of the 16th century, there were six further censuses in Venice. The later ones showed great progress in the presentation of results: the entire population was divided into the three socio-occupational categories: nobles, burgesses, craftsmen and shopkeepers (*nobili, cittadini, artegiani* and *bottegai*). For each category, the number of adults and minors is given; for the two former, the number of their servants (*servitori*). Each of these 8 groups was then subdivided by sex. Finally the religious of both sexes (*frati, monache*), the beggars (*mendicanti*) and their children (*putti*), the institutionalised poor (*poveri d'ospedale*) and the Jews (*ebrei*) were counted separately. In the 17th century, further progress: after 1607 those taking the census used printed forms and all they had to do was fill them in. After 1624 censuses should have taken place every 5 years, but this theoretical schedule could not be regularly kept.

This example of Venice shows how, in a favourable atmosphere, population statistics were able to make progress during the first two centuries of modern times. In the majority of the Italian states the story of Venice is repeated, almost down to details. Censuses affecting the whole population also took place at Naples and in Sicily, at Florence, at Sienna, in Piedmont and in several Duchies of the Po valley and in the states of the Church. At Rome, a plan for an annual census was accepted in 1591. It consisted of 22 headings whose ecclesiastical inspiration was very clear. Thus Italy is the sole country of which it has been possible to write a relatively complete history of the population for the period discussed in this chapter.[4] For the rest of Europe we have to be less demanding. More even than in Italy, the administrations were not able to tackle such a vast undertaking as a complete census of the inhabitants. A further obstacle everywhere was the general illiteracy of the population, preventing the distribution of forms to be completed personally by those concerned, as is done nowadays. Every table of figures therefore presupposed an itinerant enquiry carried out on the spot by investigators in whom being well-known took the place of professional training. This way of going about it excluded any possibility of getting synchronised operations and comparable and complete results, especially where the populace was considerably dispersed.

From this point of view the towns had an advantage. They had from far back geographical bounds and community traditions which could be used to carry out the necessary enquiries without hindrance and to make them apply more easily to the whole or almost the whole of the population. Thus the majority of the most reliable demographic statistics prior to the 17th century are urban statistics. They can be found above all in Central Europe, a region politically fragmented and with a greater range of urban autonomy. Referring to a particular time and place, their worth from a critical point of view, often exceeds that

4. J. Beloch, *Bevölkerungsgeschichte Italiens*, 3 vols. Berlin 1937–1961.

of more extensive surveys. Although difficult to compare with each other, they provide a valuable base for knowledge which seeks to go beyond the level of mere guesswork.

On the scale of whole countries, far-reaching demographic statistics are very rare. Some were produced in response to exceptional situations. Others owe their existence to a policy of centralisation or a passion for administrative efficiency.

The oldest in date was that occasioned by the contribution of the *Gemeiner Pfennig* (one pfennig for each inhabitant more than 15 years old) which the Imperial Diet imposed on 11 occasions, between 1422 and 1551, to finance operations against the Ottoman and Hussite threats. This was the only demographic act of measurement jointly affecting the whole of the German Empire properly so called. But the documentation which has been preserved contains too many gaps and presents too many critical problems to give us an approximation to the total population of the Empire in the period of Maximilian and Charles V.

The position is very different for the Spain of Philip II. Under the direction of Ambrosio de Morales, a vast descriptive enquiry, undertaken in 1574, produced, after seven years of work, the *Relaciones topograficas,*[5] which also included a part of the New World. It was a question of enumerating all the special features of each locality, among other things the number of houses, of families and of inhabitants. To keep this information up to date, two further enquiries took place before the end of the 16th century. The Spain of the Golden Century was thus the only great power with a relatively complete demographic documentation for the period.

In France, it was above all under Louis XIV that enquiries were on several occasions initiated to find out the general state of the Kingdom. The first was under the direction of Colbert and then, in the course of the last six years of the century, there were a number of censuses and inventories of which the most important were recorded in the *Memoires des Intendants,* rather like regional panoramas of all the economic and human resources. In fact the 32

5. Published (1950 and later years) by Viñas y Mey and R. Paz.

people in charge accomplished their task in a very different manner.[6] Vauban, the famous Marshal and economist, himself took part in this undertaking.

In about the same time in England the Act of Indemnity of 1694 arranged for a survey of the same kind, in which the arithmetician Gregory King collaborated. It seems, however, that this experiment did not give satisfactory results, as it was never undertaken again.

As to their real value these large-scale surveys often leave much to be desired. Their data are by no means beyond criticism. The good intentions of the enumerators were no substitute for technical skill. There is too wide a range of uncertainty about the way in which the basic figures were obtained at the local level.

The history of population in the 16th and 17th century cannot therefore do without either indirect or incomplete sources. The former contain numerical information other than population figures, such as, for example, the number of houses or hearths. The latter only deal with inhabitants in a definite category—those who pay taxes, those who receive Communion, those liable to military service. In both cases, to obtain a figure for the whole population, it is necessary to work out the gap existing between two categories: between houses or hearths and inhabitants, taxpayers and population, and so on. This calls for a calculation based on a prudently chosen 'multiplying factor'. Thus the result obtained can only be approximate.

In this field, surveys for fiscal objects are by far the most numerous. Hearth tax returns are found in most of the countries of Europe. For excessively ambitious demographic purposes, they run up against serious critical objections just like the personal tax rolls. As for the Poll Tax returns they were drawn up on quite a different basis, which complicates the way we can use them. For all these surveys, those nominal lists that have been preserved, whether of heads of households, of those liable to tax, or of all the inhabitants,

6. Critical study by E. Esmonin in *Bulletin de la Société d'Histoire moderne*, 55 (1956) 12–21. See also B. Gille, *Les sources statistiques de l'histoire de France*, Paris 1964, pp. 24–33.

are the most useful documents as regards demography at any one given moment.

Finally, there are the data derived from ecclesiastical sources. These are sometimes complete or partial lists of the inhabitants of a parish. In Catholic countries all the parish priests had to keep up to date a 'liber status animarum' from the beginning of the 17th century. But this rule seems only to have been observed very irregularly. Some Protestant countries were more fortunate. Thus Sweden has 'catechetical lists' from the 17th century onwards. These documents often deal with all the parishioners. To information about identity are often added details about where the person came from, his profession and the extent of his knowledge of the Bible. Württemberg has also kept an important series of 'Familienbücher' kept by the clergy. These documents, often scattered in private archives and not yet completely listed, can be made use of as can the nominal rolls drawn up by the civil authorities. The drawing-up of the latter was moreover more than once handed over to the parish priest.

Church documents very often contain numerical statistics, frequently brought to a round number, about the number of communicants in a group of places or parishes. These figures are normally given in the reports of diocesan visitations and other similar documents. Bringing them together and adding them up should help us know the demographic state of a diocese or of one of its districts. In fact these documents pose numerous critical problems. All one can derive from them is an order of relative sizes, especially for the larger parishes, where the lack of accuracy of the figures is the greater. Everything depends on the care taken by the priest to find out the number of his flock.

CURRENT DEMOGRAPHIC SOURCES

Two sectors must be distinguished: natural fluctuation and fluctuation due to migration. The latter is unsuitable for any complete numerical approach, both on a national and on a local scale. We will come back to this sector in the special chapter devoted to it.

Fortunately, the means of finding out the natural fluctuation is distinctly helped by the parish registers. These form at the present time the most copious documentary collection and the richest from the point of view of historical demography. Their existence transforms from top to toe our potential knowledge of the demography of modern times. For a long time the precious wealth of the registers was, with rare exceptions, exploited above all by genealogists. To be available for the systematic research of historical demography two preliminary conditions had to be fulfilled:

(a) to draw up a complete inventory of existing registers and determine their value.

(b) to work out a method of systematic analysis in a demographic perspective.

Today, thanks to the work undertaken by numerous archivists and historians, these two conditions have been satisfactorily fulfilled. Henceforth we know in its main outlines the history of the parish registers.[7] Almost everywhere a list has been drawn up of those which have survived to our own time.[8] Using them has been made easier sometimes by publishing them *in extenso*, sometimes by microfilming them, sometimes by card-indexing them. Their gaps and their critical value have been determined. A method of making use of them which meets the problems of the demographic historian has been established.

There is no worthwhile argument in favour of the opinion that these registers existed from the Roman period right through the Middle Ages. But it is certain that in several regions of France, Italy and Spain they appeared on the scene at least at the beginning of the 15th century and sometimes in the 14th. It is, however, in the 16th century

7. The most recent synthesis is that of H. Borsting, *Geschichte der Matrikeln von der Frühkirche bis zur Gegenwart*, Freiburg 1959. The best guide for England remains J. C. Cox, *The Parish Registers of England*, London 1910.

8. In 1958 and 1959 the review *Archivum* published a collection of monographs on this subject covering almost all the European countries.

that they become a source of information which can be exploited on a fairly large scale.

Of course, parish registers, even less than statistics of a given date, were not kept for purposes of demographic information. Worked out by Churchmen, their first purpose was pastoral.[9] To help the detection of impediments to marriage which could result for Catholics from ties of kinship contracted by birth or baptism. The oldest ordinance which is known on this subject, that of the Bishop of Nantes, Henri le Barbu, is explicit. It dates from 3rd June 1406 and inspired several others in the 15th and at the beginning of the 16th century.

To this first purpose a second was added which alone can explain why the civil authorities of the countries concerned never stopped legislating on this subject. This begins with Thomas Cromwell's ordinance in 1538 and that of Villers Cotterêts in the following year and goes on up to the secularisation of the civil status in contemporary times. It was a question of building up a documentary structure, which would be beyond challenge in any court of law, in any judicial dispute about the status of individuals. This went hand in hand with a transformation of legal procedure, by virtue of which proof by written documents began to surpass in value that of oral evidence.

Right up to the end of the Ancien Régime and beyond, the tasks carried out today by municipal authorities dealing with civil status were carried out by churchmen. There was no difference in this respect between countries which had remained Catholic and those which had gone over to Reformation. Various sacramental ordinances (*Sakraments-ordnungen*) legislated for the Lutheran Church from 1533 and 1535 onwards. Zwingli in 1526 and Calvin in 1541 did the same in Zürich and Geneva. So, in a very short time, did all the countries which had become Protestant. For Henrician England Cromwell's ordinance already referred to dealt directly with the Established Church, but it had

9. See my article, Les origines pastorales de quelques relevés demo-graphiques, in *Studi in onore di Amintore Fanfani*, vol. 5 Milan 1962, pp. 437–61.

the force of law throughout the Kingdom. It imposed the registration of baptisms, marriages and deaths. This was carried out more quickly and more thoroughly than on the Continent. About half of the English parishes have a series of registers beginning before 1600. In Scotland the initial dates are a little later, the order laid down by the Privy Council about registers dating from 1616. In the Roman Church more than 40 diocesan synods and provincial councils legislated about registers between 1406 and 1558 —that is to say before the intervention of the Council of Trent. But the complete series of three registers (baptisms, marriages, deaths) was not yet in current use. The Council of Trent itself, in 1563, did not give them the same status. It spoke of baptismal registers as an institution whose use was already familiar. It prescribed marriage registers. It said nothing about registers of deaths. Amongst the canonical texts of the Catholic Church, it is in the *Rituale Romanum* of 1614 that one first finds the three registers prescribed on the same footing as well as a series of others, with more exclusively religious objects, which were considerably less widespread.

This difference in date and legal patronage explains why, in many Catholic regions, the registers of deaths were often begun later and why there were more mistakes and gaps in the way they were kept. Especially the deaths of children were often not fully recorded before the 18th century. Great efforts and long delays were also needed before a regular way of keeping the registers was found which fitted in all respects the guide-lines laid down. Even more time and trouble was needed to ensure that the registers were kept in duplicate with one copy to be preserved in a safe place.

Nevertheless, taking account of all these rules, of the checks made and of the penalties incurred by those who broke the rules, it seems reasonable to conclude that from different dates in the 17th century there were parish registers wherever there ought to have been.

Were all these registers preserved right up to our own time and do they contain in full all the information enabling us to reconstruct the natural fluctuation of population? These are two further questions which deserve a careful answer. Let us deal with the main points.

It is certain that heavy losses have decimated the collections of old registers, particularly amongst the oldest in date. Too many causes, general and particular, have worked together to cause their disappearance: carelessness, rats, fire, theft and the devastation of war. Finally one is astonished to realise how many registers have escaped them and have remained in good condition.

In all the Western half of Europe (the geographical province of the Eastern Churches presents in this respect a special situation about which very little is known) there still exists, except in special circumstances (for example the Catholics in Ireland and certain religious minorities), series of registers which can be made use of for the large majority of parishes. But it is vital each time to check whether there are gaps, and to take account of the difference between the initial dates of each series. For these reasons a full and consecutive collection of current statistics becomes fairly hard to achieve for a large part of the 17th century and almost impossible for the 16th. It is also more difficult in districts where several denominations lived side by side. If each of these kept separate registers, one runs a greater risk of finding gaps (without speaking of the difference between parish boundaries). If they did not, there is an obvious risk of too few people being registered. One must therefore always test the registers from the point of view of their completeness. Generally they come out of it very well, except for troubled periods and for the deaths of children.

Besides the registers kept by the Churches, there existed also, but on a local basis, a collection of registrations, sometimes even a separate record of certain demographic phenomena, organised directly by the official secular authorities. At Sienna, the municipality for 436 years (1381–1817) had an official copy of the registers prepared which it has preserved in its entirety. A similar, though not so ancient, arrangement existed in several Italian and German towns. In Venice there were even two specialist departments which shared the work. Holland also had a municipal department to register marriages and a register of deaths prepared by the burial departments of cemeteries. Finally, everyone knows about the Bills of London and other English districts established from the end of the 16th century by the Company of Parish Clerks.

The parish registers and other similar books are just a series of registrations, kept from day to day more or less regularly and their uncertain lacunae are compensated for by miscellaneous information. They do not however contain, in the strict sense of the term, any statistics. But they provide the materials which should allow the historian to establish them. This forces him to undertake a work of analysis which becomes harder as he refines his statistical enquiries.

He can confine himself to simply adding up, year by year, the baptisms, marriages and deaths, written down in these registers and to an arithmetical comparison between the figures obtained. Thereby he establishes the crude numerical material which expresses the natural fluctuation of the population studied. Many historians have gone no further.

He can add to this a work of simple addition by several subdivisions, in so far as the contents of the registers allow him to: by sex, age, the season of the year, matrimonial status, by the regions of origin of married couples. This notably enriches our knowledge of how these fluctuations were made up.

Finally, he can even try to arrive, with the help of the registers of one or several localities, at the demographic reconstruction of families or of cohorts born or married in certain specific years. To achieve this result is only possible with the most meticulously prepared technique of analysis. This was established, for the first time, in 1956, by Messrs. Fleury and Henry, whose Manual[10] has become the classic guide in this field and served as an example for the first publication of the 'Cambridge Group for the History of

10. M. Fleury and L. Henry, *Nouveau manuel de dépouillement et d'exploitation de l'état civil ancien*, Paris 1965.

Population and Social Structure'.[11] Over the last few years, some results obtained by the application of their method to France and to other countries of Western Europe have begun to be published. They already enable us to reject certain over-imaginative assertions and to tighten the limits within which the value of the demographic phenomena of the past can be found. They will soon allow us to reconstruct the movement of population for geographic units on a more than local scale and, thanks to techniques which refer to demographic models, to determine a number of their characteristics.

THE AWAKENING OF DEMOGRAPHIC CURIOSITY

Generally speaking, the Middle Ages were very little concerned either with the facts or with the theories of population. Economic Science was still in its swaddling-clothes and administrations were not able to undertake real demographic censuses. To this was added a superstitious fear derived from a literal interpretation of the passage in the Old Testament[12] telling how David was chastised by Jehovah for having undertaken the numbering of his people. The chroniclers and other medieval writers are usually very sparing of statistical data: they content themselves with vague and qualitative expressions: 'well-peopled', 'a multitude of people'. When they go so far as to give 'exact' numbers, for example the number of victims of some epidemic or some catastrophe, their information is only valuable as manifest proof of their lack of statistical sense.

In this respect, the 16th and even more the 17th century saw the first steps towards our position today. It was the joint achievement of four different groups: humanists, geographers, politicians and economists. On these four fronts, the Italians led the way. They were followed all over Western Europe, especially after the development of

11. *An Introduction to English Historical Demography* ed. E. A. Wrigley, London 1966, pp. 44–159.

12. 2 Samuel 24, vv. 1–17; 1 Chronicles 21, vv. 1–17.

'university statistics' in Germany, and, even more, after the impetus given by the 'political arithmeticians' of England towards a better understanding of demographic situations and laws.

By nature, the humanists were people with curious minds, anxious for knowledge. Their interest in the ancient world encouraged them to enlarge their horizons, but it also led them to adopt a distorting vision of the values of their own period. Moreover they were habitually credulous in scientific matters; they had no idea of the most elementary laws of demography nor of the diversity of social and historical climates. Like the painters of their times, they attributed to every society the landscape familiar to themselves. They were never interested in demography for its own sake. But, considering Classical Antiquity as a Golden Age unsurpassable in every respect, they were above all preoccupied with establishing a comparison between the population of the Ancient World and that of their own time. For these unconditional admirers of Antiquity, this comparison redounded to the greater glory of the Ancient World, whose population must have attained astronomic grandeur. Since then the world had become notably depopulated; by the same token it would soon become a desert. Others, more moderate or more realistic, did not share these pessimistic views. But they were no better informed about the real dimensions of the problem.

Certain demographic legends of mysterious origins long continued to survive. The most famous attributed to France 1,700,000 church towers. Another, beginning to be more modest, spoke of 120,000 well-inhabited places, 25 million hearths, 2 million merchants and other corresponding splendours. Similar evaluations were also passed on for other European countries. Only the triumph of experimental philosophy relegated this nonsense to the limbo of things outgrown.

Experimenting! In a period when scientific curiosity and the inductive method were beginning to assert themselves, we notice the appearance on the scene of people interested in noting down demographic facts. Such as, for example,

Felix Platter, a doctor of Basle, who, when an epidemic occurred in 1610, kept detailed numerical records and had even, two years later, made a complete census of the population.

In the 17th century people became more and more intent on numerical accuracy. One very characteristic episode is the bet made before a lawyer by two middle-class citizens of Ghent after a conversation in a tavern in which they argued about the size of the population of Antwerp without succeeding in reaching an agreement. This episode shows at least three things:

(a) that curiosity about demography had penetrated the middle-class section of society,

(b) that this curiosity was no longer satisfied by vague generalisation or figures depending on 'they say',

(c) that there must have been some source of information capable of settling a bet made before a notary in a way which could prevent any argument.

Geographers had the best reason in the world to be interested in everything affecting population. It is well-known how the period of great discoveries everywhere stimulated interest in geography. We see the publication of compilations of regional geography, which aimed at accumulating 'real' facts, among which the figures given, including those for population, became more and more important. Thus in 1517, Charles le Clerc tells the story of the Neapolitan censuses in giving the list of localities with the number of hearths. Agostino Giustiniani (died 1536) deals with Genoa and Liguria, Tommaso Fazello (died 1570) with Sicily, Francesco Sansovino (1567) with the principal towns everywhere in Italy, Luigi Guicciardini (1581) with all the Low Countries. Giuseppe Moleti (1580) tries to classify the five principal empires of the whole world in order of importance, Pierre Davity publishes (1614–1637) a general description of the four quarters of the world and, in 1661, there appears the *Geographia et Hydrographia reformata* of G. B. Riccioli whose appendix bears a suggestive title: '*de Verisimili hominum numero superficiem terrae inhabitantium*'. We meet again among the geo-

graphers of this very period the first person to use the term
'statistics': Helenus Politanus published in 1672 his
*Miscroscopium statisticum quo status imperii Romano-Germanici
repraesentatur*. This work was also one of the first of a new
literary form: the statistical repertory. Books like the
Población general de España by Rodrigo Mendez Silva (1645),
the *Teutscher Fürstenstaat* of V. L. von Seckendorf (1656) and
the *Index Villaris* of John Adams (1680) soon found a
readership in every country in Europe.

The point at which all this movement finally arrived was
the appearance on the scene of what has been called 'university statistics' whose first representative, Hermann Con-
ring, in his *Thesaurus totius orbis quadripartitus* (1675) did not
hesitate to write: 'Pertinet ad cognitionem hominum ut
sciamus eorum numcrum sivc quantitatem; multum enim
interest Reipublicae an numerus civium sit magnus vel
parvus.'[13]

About a century later, this phrase was an echo of a
doctrine already solidly laid down and defended by the
Economists. Let it suffice to quote Jean Bodin's adage,
'Il n'cst forcc ni richesse que d'hommes' (Men are the only
strength and wealth). This attitude became an essential
article of the gospel of the mercantilists, for whom the
'populace' constituted one of the fundamental sources of
the wealth of nations. Therefore, it was of the greatest
importance for anyone interested in the well-being of his
country to be as well-informed as possible about this item
in the balance-sheet. But information was sometimes notably lacking. Skill was then needed in getting better information, sometimes by organising sample-censuses, sometimes by using fiscal documents, such as the Hearth Tax
Returns which were used as a basis by Charles Davenant
and John Houghton for demographic calculations. Humanists, geographers and economists were also powerfully
supported by politicians. The administrators and diplomats of the Italian republics, the great book-keepers of

13. 'It is part of the understanding of any human situation that we
should know the number or aggregate of people involved. For it matters
a great deal to a state whether it has a large or small number of citizens.'

the centralised monarchies tried hard to collect useful data about population and to ensure their diffusion in scientific circles. Thus, on Colbert's orders, the *Journal des Savants* published from 1672 onwards, the monthly state of baptisms and deaths in Paris. Several years later, the Great Elector Frederick William himself ordered the publication of the annual *Populationslisten* for Berlin and Brandenburg. Similar lists were published on the initiative of municipal authorities. Those for Leipzig (from 1676) even include a triple classification of current demographic facts: chronological, topographic and sociological.

Whatever were the merits of humanists, geographers, economists and politicians, they must give place to those to whom history has given the name of 'political arithmeticians'. These are not yet professional statisticians but amateurs from all sectors of administration and the liberal professions. They had to find everything out by themselves.

For them, figures dealing with population were more than the object of collection or of a regional or local description. They formed the basis of a calculation. This was an entirely new idea, as was the attention they paid to current data. They were the first to realise the importance of the latter. They can fairly be called the 'self-made men' of statistics.

In the 18th century their type will be spread to almost every country of Europe. But in the 17th century, their true and only home was England. Their pioneer was a teacher of music, John Graunt (1620–1674).

By what chance did Graunt happen to interest himself in the Bills of Mortality published regularly in London from the end of the 16th century and giving the natural fluctuation of the population for each year? The fact remains that he had an inspiration of genius about the Bills, which one of those who followed him, the clergyman Süssmilch, compared to that which sent Christopher Columbus on the discovery of America. He said to himself that these 'miserable little scraps of paper' could become a valuable store-house of information if used for study and calculations. Even if he got no personal profit from them, he would be like a miner who extracts diamonds from the earth for the benefit of his employer. He therefore set to work to study, to calculate and to compare and from all this activity there resulted a book: *Natural and political observations upon the Bills of Mortality* (1661).

For the first time, a series of numerical reports about births and deaths were put forth: that 14 boys were born for every 13 girls, that more men die than women, that there are four times more births than marriages, that there are relatively more births in the country and deaths in the towns, that London is like a cemetery-city with an ever increasing death-rate, that its centre is moving towards the West and that the town is growing three times faster than the rest of England.

A contemporary of Graunt, William Petty (1623–1687) shares with him the honour of having traced out the road towards political arithmetic. This thinker, whose economic works were well known, composed *Five Essays in Political Arithmetic*. He also used data taken from the Bills of London to determine the rate of growth of the English capital and to establish comparisons with about ten other European towns.

Gregory King (1648–1712), who was younger by a generation, wrote, right at the end of the century, a more general study based primarily on statistics of a given date: *Natural and Political observations upon the state and condition of England*. He tried to work out a way of using the hearth-tax records as evidence of the numbers of population. As a starting point and a control for his calculations, he collected statistical materials from his native town, Lichfield, and from some other places throughout the kingdom.

With political arithmetic the century of enlightenment found a basis for a useful initiation into the problems of population.

THE OVER-ALL POPULATION

For the period 1500–1700, the over-all population for all the European countries together can only be estimated on the basis of partial or indirect data. These data often pose numerous critical problems. In the most favourable cases, these estimates leave a possible margin of error of at least 10%. Under several headings, the figures put forward by different historians of population vary from once to twice (without the cases where they prefer not to mention any figures at all). One can also apply a method of working backwards from the first contemporary censuses. But this does not allow us to go further back than 1700.

In the table below we have used the figures which have seemed the most plausible. To avoid discussing problems arising from boundary changes we have confined ourselves to considering the twelve most characteristic European geographical areas:

Population in Europe (estimate, in millions)

	In about 1500	In about 1600	In about 1700
Spain and Portugal	9.3	11.3	10.0
Italy	10.5	13.3	13.3
France (incl. Lorraine and Savoy)	16.4	18.5	20.0
Benelux countries	1.9	2.9	3.4
British Isles	4.4	6.8	9.3
Scandinavian countries	1.5	2.4	2.8
Germany	12.0	15.0	15.0
Switzerland	0.8	1.0	1.2
Danubian countries	5.5	7.0	8.8
Poland	3.5	5.0	6.0
Russia	9.0	15.5	17.5
Balkans	7.0	8.0?	8.0?
Total for Europe	81.8	104.7	115.3

One cannot go far wrong in giving Europe from between 80 to 85 million inhabitants in about 1500; from 100 to

110 million in about 1600; from 110 to 120 million in about 1700. We know that there were about 190 million inhabitants in about 1800.

The period from 1500–1700 was thus one of demographic expansion, attributable chiefly to the 16th century. Nevertheless, despite the terrible crises which wracked it, the 17th seems also to have experienced a slight gain in population. It is only in Spain and in numerous regions of Northern Italy and Central Germany that the change in population, even on the scale of the whole century, must have shown an adverse balance. As for the Balkans, the 8 million put forward for 1600 and 1700 seem to us to be a minimum. But for lack of information it is impossible to know if the increase of the 16th century was only slowed down or was actually halted. The growth of Europe was achieved above all by the new countries and by those which were relatively untouched by the demographic disasters. All in all, the growth remained modest (about 40% in two centuries), only reaching half that of the 18th century, but very largely exceeding what it can have been in the Middle Ages.

The over-all figures given above correspond in fact to very noticeable divergences in the population density for different regions. For Italy, in about 1600, this divergence could mean that one region had a tenfold population density of another. The most thickly populated regions (Lombardy, Massa-Carrara, Malta) had 100 to 120 inhabitants per square kilometre. The rest of the plain of the Po, Liguria, Tuscany and Emilia had between 50 and 80. The most densely inhabited parts of Naples and Sicily had between 40 and 60. The most mountainous provinces of the interior had from 25 to 40. Only the unhealthy coastal districts, Corsica, Sardinia and some Alpine valleys had less than 15. Similar divergences, though on a smaller scale, existed in other regions of Europe. Thus the average density for France may have been between 35 and 45.

The Europe of this period was a rural Europe. The majority of the towns of today already existed, but their size was much smaller. Moreover, the scale of urban magnitude was at that time quite different from today. In the period of Charles V, a town of 20 to 30,000 inhabitants was a large city. A German geographer[14] has calculated that in around 1600 out of about 75 million Europeans some 3½ million lived in about 100 'large cities', which means not even 5% of the total. At least seven out of 10 Europeans were living in the country and two more in small country towns. The spread of important urban centres on a map of Europe was very uneven. Northern Italy and the coastal plain of the North Sea had the brightest constellations. But the majority of these towns were comparatively little developed during this period.

The most noticeable increase in size occurred in towns which benefited from the setting-up of new activities and the change in channels of trade. London must have increased in size tenfold in two centuries, despite the considerable losses which it suffered from epidemics. Amsterdam, Berlin, Vienna, Moscow, Madrid may have grown four- or five-fold. A limited but still more rapid growth can be noted in certain smaller localities. One would like to know how fast Versailles, the creation of Louis XIV, grew. We know that there were mining boom-towns like Jachymov (Joachimsthal) in Bohemia, whose population grew in ten years (1516–1526) from 1050 to 14,072 inhabitants.[15] But this was an ephemeral glory. Half a century later it was in the Harz mountains that the mining districts were expanding. At Wildemann, 44% of the population were by origin from the Joachimsthal region.[16]

For lack of sufficiently extensive and precise data, it is not possible to reconstruct in numbers the evolution of this urban population between 1500 and 1700. We will confine ourselves to a list in which the principal towns are shown in categories of size (see Map 1).

14. K. Olbricht, Gedanken zur Entwicklungsgeschichte der Grossstadt, in *Geographische Zeitschrift*, 35 (1929), p. 474. The author excludes from his study Eastern and South-eastern Europe.

15. P. Jancarer, *K problematice demografickeho vyvoje Jachymova v dobe piedbelohorske* (The question of the demographic development of Joachimsthal before the battle of the White Mountain), in *Historicka Demografie*, vol. 2 (1968), p. 18.

16. E. Keyser *Bevölkerungsgeschichte Deutschlands*, Leipzig 1941.

Population	c.1500 ·	c.1600	c.1700
under 40,000	Dublin	(nil)	•
40–60,000	*Ghent*	———	△
60–100,000	GENOA	———	●
100–150,000	**PARIS**	———	□
150,000 and above	(id)	═══	■

Map 1 European towns of more than 40,000 inhabitants

Towns of more than 40,000 inhabitants

Categories	Early 16th century	End of 16th - early 17th century	End of 17th century
more than 400,000			London Paris Constantinople
200–400,000	—	Constantinople Naples Paris	Naples
150–200,000	Constantinople Paris Naples	London Milan Venice	Amsterdam
100–150,000	Venice Milan	Rome Seville Amsterdam Lisbon Palermo Antwerp (1560)	Moscow Rome Venice Milan Madrid Vienna Palermo
60–100,000	Cordoba Seville Grenada Florence Genoa	Messina Florence Genoa Bologna Grenada Valencia Madrid Lyons Rouen Moscow (?)	Florence Genoa Bologna Seville Lisbon Valencia Lyons Marseilles Rouen Toulouse Brussels Antwerp Hamburg Berlin
40–60,000	Valencia Lisbon Barcelona Palermo Bologna Rome Brescia Cremona Lyons Rouen	Cordoba Barcelona Valladolid Verona Cremona Toulouse Bordeaux Marseilles Ghent Brussels	Barcelona Cordoba Grenada Messina Turin Verona Lille Bordeaux Strasbourg Montpellier(?)

Towns of more than 40,000 inhabitants (contd.)

Categories	Early 16th century	End of 16th - early 17th century	End of 17th century
40–60,000	Toulouse	Bruges	Amiens (?)
	Ghent	Leyden	Dublin (?)
	Antwerp	Haarlem	Ghent
	London	Hamburg	Liège
	Augsburg	Danzig	Leyden
	Cologne	Augsburg	Haarlem
		Vienna	Danzig
		Prague	Breslau
		Nuremberg	Prague
		Cologne	Cologne
			Copenhagen
			Stockholm

This list may be incomplete. Constantinople and Moscow were perhaps not the only towns with more than 40,000 inhabitants in Eastern and South-eastern Europe. We should doubtless add Salonika and Kiev, perhaps also Adrianople, Sofia, Novgorod and Smolensk (?).

Speaking from a demographic point of view these large towns were made up of very different quarters. The old commercial hub, the quarters for a long time inhabited by the working classes, had a density frequently as great as 300 to 500 inhabitants per hectare.* At the very highest this could reach almost to saturation level, even over 1000, notably in the Mediterranean and Danubian countries, but only over very small areas. In London, half the parishes 'within the walls' had more than 500 inhabitants to the hectare in 1695. In Paris, in all the sections of the city within the walls of 1370, the density was never less than 400; in some districts it was over 800.

Nevertheless, except in special cases explicable by geographical factors, such high figures cannot have applied to any urban area taken as a whole. Even taking account only of the built-up area, one would be wrong to think that the average density was much more than 300 inhabitants to

* hectare — 2.74 acres

the hectare. The real figures are often much less. In all North-western Europe, except in Scotland, they only just reach half this figure.

Finally, the differences in density also reflected differences in the vertical dimensions of the town which, in turn, depended on techniques of construction. These were transformed in the course of this period. The average size of buildings increased noticeably, especially in districts where the material hitherto used, wood, was replaced by more resistant materials which made it possible to raise tall buildings and thus absorb a part of the increase in population.

The average number of inhabitants per house (which must not be confused with the number per household) was never stable. It varied very considerably, especially in the towns, as a result of geographic, psychological, technical, economic and historical factors.

Nevertheless urban growth was above all horizontal. Many towns had in the 14th century built boundary-walls so spacious that they could develop within them completely at their ease. Others spread beyond their former limits, forming ever more wide-spreading suburbs.

New neighbourhoods were thus built in all the developing centres, especially in the capitals. Nowhere are these stages so clearly marked as in Amsterdam, with its series of concentric canals around the old commercial hub.

This led even to problems of conurbation. Hamburg, a free city, grew up side by side with Altona, in the duchy of Holstein. A first Greater Berlin was formed, between 1688 and 1709, by the joining-up of five adjacent localities whose expansion had made an urban unity. In London, the area included in the register of the Bills grew ever further outside the City, increasing from 750 hectares in 1600 to 9,160 in 1726.

PROBLEMS OF DEMOGRAPHIC STRUCTURE

The classification of a population in terms of the different groups and sub-groups of which it is composed can take a very great variety of forms. Amongst the criteria of division one can distinguish the strictly demographic criteria (sex, age, matrimonial status) and those whose nature is primarily cultural, social or professional (e.g., educational attainments, language, religion, wealth, profession).

Before the 18th century, the personal circumstances recorded in population lists were ordinarily limited to those of identity. These particulars were very rarely complete and there was no uniformity about the principles of classification. Any comparative study in this field of research comes up against considerable obstacles. It is possible to draw up a theoretical list of different 'items' about which the old lists sometimes give information.[17] But it is chimerical to rely on complete answers for the greater part of them. In this field and for this period, the history of population can only be carried forward by sampling, these samples being provided by the chance which has presided over the conservation of documents and by their exploitation by authors of useful monographs. Only the reconstruction of numerous demographic cohorts, on the basis of a systematic investigation of parish registers, will help us to get, from the 17th century onwards, a clearer answer to the different structural problems, above all those which envisage strictly demographic criteria.

Meanwhile the following reflections will help to place the problems in their context.

17. P. Laslett, The study of social structure from listings of inhabitants, in *An Introduction to English Historical Demography* ed. E. A. Wrigley, pp. 189–91 (for the strictly demographic criteria see also the same author's size and structure of the household in England over three centuries, in *Population Studies*, 23 (1969), pp. 199–223. Several studies are being prepared on the socio-professional sector.

STRICTLY DEMOGRAPHIC CRITERIA

Any examination of the structure of an entire population should logically and as its first priority envisage simultaneously the three explicitly demographic classifications (age, sex, matrimonial status), divide the population according to these three and adopt the same divisions for each item.

It must be admitted that, for the centuries which interest us, the classifications which we have or could reconstruct are far removed from this logical hope.

The divisions of age used are often different for boys and girls and sometimes also for adults. The division between male and female is often omitted for servants and for children. Entries concerning civil status are normally given for widows and married women, more rarely for widowers; the other categories have to be worked out from the context. On the lists of names, some privileged persons are known of in detail; the rest are reduced to the most simple terms. As for indications of age, they show such a predilection for certain numbers, above all round numbers, that the diagrams which they could be used to construct have more resemblance to a battle-ship than a pyramid.[18]

The lack of homogeneity in these classifications has not only affected the different listings, one as against another; one also notices it, for the same account, between different localities and even between the different parishes of the

18. The following table shows the division by age, in 1561, of the inhabitants of Sorrento aged 30 and upwards (from J. Beloch, *Bevölkerungsgeschichte Italiens*, I, pp. 29–31):

Ages	Number	Ages	Number	Ages	Number	Ages	Number
30	122	45	92	60	95	75	19
31–34	74	46–49	10	61–64	6	80	6
35	107	50	94	65	58	81	1
36–39	71	51–54	12	66–69	2	85	4
40	139	55	70	70	16	87	1
41–44	29	56–59	4	71–74	–	90	2
						100	2

same locality, as was the case with Cologne in 1574 and Louvain in 1598. This lack of homogeneity can go so far that the same person may have been listed by two enumerators with different personal particulars. This was the case in Rome in 1526 with a cardinal.

Because of a higher masculine mortality rate very noticeable at all ages (except that of childbirth) the balance between the sexes was frequently upset. The 16th and 17th centuries saw the continuance of the *Frauenfrage* whose existence Karl Bücher pointed out with reference to urban society at the end of the Middle Ages. For the population taken as a whole, the numerical balance between the two sexes seems to have been normal. But extreme situations were much more frequent and in numerous urban populations the excess of women among adults was considerable. Socially, this disequilibrium found its compensation by the very great frequency of remarriages among men, by a high proportion of widows forming part of a household as grandmothers and aunts and, in certain Catholic countries, by the development of institutions such as beguinages. Statistically this excess easily reached 20% to 30%. In particular cases (immediately after epidemics, in troubled periods, in neighbourhoods with chiefly female employment), it could well surpass 50%. The opposite phenomenon, a considerable male preponderance, can also be noticed in garrison, church or university towns and in ports at the time of prosperity and expansion. Thus Rome in 1592 had only 58 women for 100 men. In Venice we see that the excess was the other way round: more men than women in the 16th century, more women than men in the following century. The explanation is obviously, at least in part, a reversal of economic circumstances.

In the towns, unmarried persons often constituted 50% to 60% of the population, sometimes more. Adults who had remained unmarried constituted at least one third, sometimes more than half. In the countryside, the proportion was reversed: in some places as many as two thirds were or had been married.

The same contrast between town and country can be

seen in division by ages. But, for lack of precise figures, the old records often leave us frustrated. This detail is often only mentioned in connection with the fiscal, military, religious and civil impositions which were linked with it. Or it may come directly from special surveys of those liable to mobilisation, of communicants or of citizens who had come of age. Local statistics dealing with communicants are fairly frequent. In England and in Wales they were twice (1603 and 1690) extended to the whole country. The notion of a communicant did not everywhere correspond to a very exact age-limit. But generally speaking one can say that in Roman Catholic countries the young Christian became a communicant in his 13th year. Other surveys distinguished between children and adults. But there was no exact or agreed age-limit to childhood. It could go on until a man left his father's house.

A comparison between the ecclesiastical surveys of Grötzingen in Württemberg, from 1654 to 1703, is interesting because the population was divided into 3 groups[19]:

	1654	1676	1684	1687	1690	1693	1703
Communicants	65.8	72.1	69.7	61.0	61.6	60.2	64.7
Catechumens	14.8	13.4	16.2	18.7	18.4	23.7	19.2
Children	19.4	14.5	14.1	20.3	20.0	16.1	16.1
Total	100	100	100	100	100	100	100

One can see immediately that certain age groups must have been particularly numerous, for example those born immediately after the Thirty Years War and those born between 1685 and 1690.

Several surveys, especially in Italy, divided the inhabitants into three or four age classifications, corresponding to the seasons of life. When comparison is possible between a town and the surrounding territory, one notes that the proportion of adults is appreciably higher in the town (difference of between 5% and 13%); on the contrary, the proportion of children and sometimes of old people is higher

19. H. Höhn, Geschichte der stadt Grötzingen . . . bis 1700, in *Württembergische Jahrbücher für Statistik und Landeskunde* (1906–12), p. 12.

in the country. From the very limited data available it seems that for every 100 male inhabitants one could reckon on 30 to 35 boys in a town. This percentage was well over 40 in the country. Being comparatively handicapped at birth and being more rapidly counted as adults, girls were at least 5% less numerous. Inhabitants over 50 represented from 10% to 15% of the population. Those over 65 were a negligible proportion. In most cases, this category had a fairly noticeable female surplus, especially in the towns.

Some very rare censuses made before the 18th century divided the population into regular age-groups. They sometimes distinguished between men and women. Elsewhere, they counted a town and the surrounding countryside separately. Here are two[20] examples which it would be easy to show as an age-group graph (see Figure 1):

Ages	Carpi Men	(Emilia) 1591 Women	Pesaro Town	(Marche) 1689 Country
81 and over	0.3	0.1	0.5	0.7
71–80	0.6	0.4	2.4	2.7
61–70	1.8	1.4	5.9	5.9
56–60	3.1	3.5	3.9	3.8
51–55	2.8	2.4	6.7	5.4
46–50	5.1	5.7	5.8	5.5
41–45	4.1	4.1	8.2	6.6
36–40	7.1	8.7	6.0	5.0
31–35	5.9	5.9	7.1	6.6
26–30	8.1	9.1	8.4	7.7
21–25	8.2	8.6	10.4	8.2
16–20	9.8	11.0	9.1	9.5
11–15	14.4	12.5	8.7	9.7
6–10	15.5	13.8	8.2	10.4
0–5	13.0	12.8	8.7	11.3

A systematic analysis of parish registers (where they are complete!) makes it possible to reconstitute the age-groups of the population and thus to work out the changing structure of age-groups. We note that this structure was

20. For Carpi, see Beloch, *op. cit.* pp. 24–5. For Pesaro, C. Mengarelli, La popolazione di Pesaro dal 1628 al 1839, in *Rivista internazionale di scienze sociali*, 42–5 (1934), pp. 675–6.

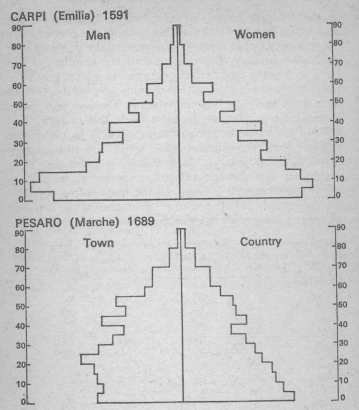

Fig. 1. Distribution of population by age-groups: Carpi 1591 and Pesaro 1689

considerably affected by epidemics and natural disasters, as can be seen from the strong variations in age-groups.

D. Beltrami has undertaken such a reconstruction with the help of the registers of 17 parishes in Venice.[21] He has worked out the decennial average of age-groups each composed of a 10-year range. As far as the 17th century is

21. D. Beltrami, *Storia della popolazione di Venezia dalla fine del secolo XVI alla caduta della Republica,* Padua 1954, appendix, table 4.

concerned, his data has enabled us to draw up the three following tables:

(a) percentage of age-groups within a 10-year range. Average numbers over a 10-year period.

Period	0–9	10–19	20–29	30–39	40–49	50–59	60–69	70–79	80+	*Total*
1601–10	*22.3*	16.7	*17.4*	13.6	10.6	8.8	6.1	2.7	1.9	100
1611–20	18.5	*18.2*	15.4	*15.7*	11.0	8.3	6.5	3.9	2.5	100
1621–30	20.0	14.2	*17.0*	13.7	*13.2*	8.8	6.2	4.1	2.9	100
1631–40	*26.7*	15.4	13.4	*14.0*	10.7	*9.6*	5.2	3.4	1.6	100
1641–50	*23.4*	*19.0*	12.4	11.2	*12.2*	8.8	*7.2*	3.6	2.1	100
1651–60	21.8	*19.2*	*16.8*	10.4	9.4	*9.7*	6.2	*4.3*	2.1	100
1661–70	*24.2*	17.2	*16.6*	*13.9*	8.3	7.3	*6.5*	3.7	*2.2*	100
1671–80	*22.9*	*19.1*	14.9	*13.9*	*11.4*	6.6	5.4	*3.7*	2.0	100
1681–90	18.8	*19.4*	*16.9*	13.7	*12.1*	*8.7*	5.1	3.3	*2.1*	100
1691–1700	20.3	14.8	*17.2*	*14.5*	11.8	*9.8*	*6.5*	3.2	1.9	100

Notice the persistence of demographic waves across the 10-year periods (the figures in italics). The first two waves show, respectively, the direct revival after the plague of 1576-7 and its consequence in the next generation. The following pair show the same phenomena after the plague of 1630.

(b) destiny of each 10-year age group.

Ten-year period	*Ten-year period of origin*									
	1601–10	*1611–20*	*1621–30*	*1631–40*	*1641–50*	*1651–60*	*1661–70*	*1671–80*	*1681–90*	*1691–1700*
1601–1610	100									
1611–1620	81	100								
1621–1630	69	70	100							
1631–1640	45	52	62	100						
1641–1650	44	50	56	80	100					
1651–1660	37	43	48	73	84	100				
1661–1670	26	36	41	65	78	84	100			
1671–1680	16	28	35	56	69	77	83	100		
1681–1690	7	17	26	42	59	69	72	83	100	
1691–1700	1.5	8	17	32	48	60	63	75	80	100

(c) index of survival for each 10-year age group.

	10–19 0–9	20–29 10–19	30–39 20–29	40–49 30–39	50–59 40–49	60–69 50–59	70–79 60–69	80–89 70–79	90+ 80–89
1611–20 ——— 1601–10	81	90	89	80	78	73	62	74	29
1621–30 ——— 1611–20	70	85	81	77	73	68	57	50	35
1631–40 ——— 1621–30	62	75	66	63	58	46	44	20	20
1641–50 ——— 1631–40	80	91	94	99	92	85	80	55	50
1651–60 ——— 1641–50	84	91	87	87	81	73	61	47	28
1661–70 ——— 1651–60	84	92	89	86	83	72	63	43	30
1671–80 ——— 1661–70	83	91	88	87	84	77	60	46	26
1681–90 ——— 1671–80	83	87	90	85	75	76	61	45	25
1691–1700 ——— 1681–90	80	90	87	88	82	76	62	47	21
1701–1710 ——— 1691–1700	81	92	89	88	84	81	68	52	23

DEMOGRAPHIC CRITERIA IN A BROAD SENSE

Though less important in itself from the point of view of strictly demographic history, the division of the population according to social, occupational or tax-paying criteria is of the greatest interest from the point of view of economic history.

In a good many localities and regions scattered across Europe, surveys have been made which can give us information about these criteria.

For example:

– the division of tax-payers according to the tax-paying category to which they belong by virtue of their wealth or taxable income;

– the division of agriculturists according to the way in which their land is exploited;

– the division of working people according to their occupation;

– the division of heads of households according to those working for them, male or female;

– the division of lodgings by rentable value (for example, in Venice);

– the division of tax-payers into property-owners, owners of personal chattels and non property-owners.

Each of these surveys provides material for a very suggestive and interesting study. The difficulties begin when one tries to compare them.

Since the majority of surveys had a fiscal objective, a survey of heads of households according to characteristics linked directly or indirectly to wealth stood to reason. The only exceptions were surveys which treated all households and inhabitants on the same basis.

From the demographic point of view, the principal interest presented by these surveys is that they allow us to compare certain characteristics of marriage, birth and death (for example, age at marriage, births per marriage and infantile or epidemic mortality) with the division into fiscal categories. Among the latter, the distinction between the poor, beggars, the indigent, those excused from any contribution and those paying at a reduced rate, often poses very delicate problems of interpretation whenever there is a question of comparing different surveys or different localities in the same survey. Any comparison involving time or region must of course also take into account the real value of money.

Unless it had some fiscal significance, division by occupational categories was of no interest. In old documents therefore this information was only rarely totalised. But since the profession was a normal element of personal description, the old local lists often include this way of categorisation. Since the nearly one hundred year old study by Bücher on Frankfurt, quite a number of studies have tried to reconstruct the socio-occupational composition to be derived from such lists. Their interest depends on the abundance of details mentioned in each document and on the competence of the historian who has undertaken their exploitation. One trap which must be, but has not always been, avoided is to force all the old designations into an up-to-date codification. It is better to keep as far as possible the nomenclature of the period and to classify according to the working conditions of the time. Working conditions have changed too much to allow us to do otherwise without damage.

To start with there was a much greater distinction between the urban and the rural environment, from a professional point of view.

Except in centres of specialised manufacturing production, urban activity was more artisan than industrial. It worked with limited means for a limited market. The typical form was the family business. From this resulted the considerable proportion of townspeople belonging to household staff—one twelfth of the population, children included, is a minimum; in commercial centres, it is sometimes more than a fifth, even a quarter of the population. Their number was then greater than those of all other working people put together.

This household staff is principally female. It can be

found in all professional circles. At Heidelberg, in 1588, under the heading 'Food supply' there were as many as 72 female servants for 100 households. Even for 'textiles' there were still 22 for 100. Male domestic servants, normally less numerous, often constituted from 3% to 7% of the population. But apprentices were often included in this category. The statistical analysis of this important fringe of the population of the past has not yet been done as it should have been.

In the country districts surveys enabling us to make a division by occupations are more rare. They are also less interesting, because, apart from the mining and forestry regions, agriculture is everywhere the principal sector of activity. Here the most important criterion of division is the socio-economic level of those who have a share in the land (farmers, cottagers and those paying rent in kind) or of wage-earning agricultural workers (permanent, seasonal or casual workers).

In several surveys we find also headings of cultural classification, such as nationality of region of origin, ethnic group and above all religious denomination and membership of a special group (soldiers, university graduates, prisoners, those in hospital, monks and religious). Thus at Vienna, in 1654, one survey dealt exclusively with the non-Catholic population; at Antwerp in 1582, a general survey of heads of household indicated their religious adherence by means of conventional symbols; at London, in 1573, one census dealt only with the foreign population.

These references are too diverse and too widely scattered to allow an overall study on a European scale.

MIGRATORY FLUCTUATION

Statistical analysis of the migratory fluctuation in past epochs comes up against an insurmountable obstacle: the lack of original sources. Administrations, national as well as local, were not capable of preparing them. For this reason the best studies of the past abstain from any overall numerical evaluation for periods prior to the 19th century.

In one country alone, Sweden, a current registration existed on the local level, from the latter half of the 17th century: in their 'catechetical lists' the clergy equally noted certain facts about migration. But these lists are far from being complete and it is hard to interpret them within a national framework.

The fragmentary documentation which we have for other countries is even less satisfactory, except for certain aspects of the regular emigration across the Atlantic Ocean which was also, in principle, the easiest to supervise and hence to record. The most valuable collection of documents in this file concerns the emigration from Spain for the countries of what is today Latin America. Legal regulations submitted every embarkation to very strict rules including the preparation of a list of passengers to be sent to the Council of the Indies. The Gonzalo Fernandez Institute has reconstructed and published these catalogues of passengers. Unfortunately, a considerable number of annual lists were lost, especially for the more remote period. Since there were considerable numerical fluctuations, these gaps make any serious attempt at an overall evaluation very difficult. Canadian demographers and genealogists have also carried out successful research about the regional French origin of their earliest immigrants. For the 17th century the numbers involved are very small. For the United States also similar research has had a certain amount of success. But this research has been more valuable from the point of view of American immigration than from that of European emigration which could choose other destinations.

Amongst local sources of documentation, mention must be made of the valuable collections of registers of burgesses. They must be used with great care in any study of migratory movement: they did not exist in every town and did not take account of the countryside (except indirectly through the non-resident burgesses); many of the registers have disappeared and inclusion in them does not have the same meaning: everywhere in a large number of towns they include the sons of burgesses who have reached their civil coming-of-age; elsewhere they include non-resident burgesses. Moreover, the enrolments only refer to the names inscribed, neglecting totally the outward movement; they refer in the same way to a bachelor and to a head of household, who has come with all his children. Women only rarely appear on the list. And, even amongst the men, there is no record of immigrants who preferred not to attach themselves to the burgesses. We know, moreover, that there were never candidates for the status of burgess among the non-qualified migratory population and that there were not many among immigrants of average status, the advantages of becoming a burgess being to a degree outweighed by its inconveniences and snags. Moreover, the burgesses who already enjoyed this status operated the principle of 'numerus clausus' (limitation of number) in admitting new applicants.

A further category: local surveys. Several had as their object to determine the number of persons who had immigrated or emigrated. Others made a separate calculation of the number of foreigners, often specifying the region of origin, the date of their arrival and even their age at the time. These surveys took place particularly at periods and in regions especially affected by migrations caused by religious motives (for example, the Huguenots who emigrated after the Revocation of the Edict of Nantes). Some parish lists also made a note of new arrivals and struck a line through those who had emigrated. But these additions and subtractions may have been made once and for all after long delays. We know that lists of the same kind were kept in certain towns by ward officials from the end of the 15th century onwards. All seem to have been lost.

These different categories of documents teach us only a little about the whole scale and rhythm of inward and outward migration.

Theoretically, the scale of a migratory movement can also be worked out by an indirect arithmetic method. If one knows the total population for two different dates and the number of births and deaths for the intervening period, the difference between the increase shown and the balance of natural fluctuation shows the extent of the migratory fluctuation. We can, of course, only find out the balance between immigration and emigration and not the extent of these two separately.

A particularly interesting example, showing also how this migratory balance was able to alter the components of a given population, comes from Augsburg. This old free Imperial city had gone over to the Reformation at the time of Luther, but was surrounded by a countryside which had remained Catholic. From 1627 to 1635 Augsburg faced the most terrible period of its history: six epidemics of plague causing 29,865 deaths. Two demographic surveys were made there, in 1635 and in 1645, which counted Catholics and Protestants separately. The results were as follows[22]:

Survey	Total population (incl. foreigners)	Catholics (not incl. foreigners)	Protestants
1635	16,432	3,721	11,980
1645	21,018	6,170	13,790
Increase	4,586	2,449	1,810
Percentage	28%	66%	15%

Such an increase exceeded clearly the natural possibilities of the local population.

By natural increase of a normal level (7.5‰) the town could have gained about 1,250 inhabitants (950 Protestants and 300 Catholics) and perhaps twice these figures, if we allow for an increase of 15‰ owing to demographic revival. The excess by immigration came to a minimum of 2,000, most of them being Catholics. It is therefore wrong to ascribe only to the Counter-Reformation a religious change which was also due to statistical causes.

With such gaps in the documentation there can be no question of attempting an evaluation of migratory fluctuations. We must be content with drawing some general

22. From the data of A. Schreiber, Die Entwicklung der Augsburger Bevölkerung vom Ende des 14. Jahrhunderts bis zum Beginn des 19. Jahrhunderts, in *Archiv für Hygiene*, 123 (1939–40), pp. 139–46.

impressions derived from varied and fragmentary data which are nevertheless valid except for isolated regions.

Immigration to the towns was vital if they were to be preserved from extinction. But there was a great difference between the small regional centres and the large towns as regards the hinterland from which they derived their migration. While the former gained numbers from the surrounding countryside, the latter had extended their zone of attraction over the whole economic or cultural region. But, outside a radius of a bare hundred kilometres or so, it was from the towns that the great centres attracted their immigrants. In this way a cosmopolitan, inter-urban milieu was created. An analysis of the locality of origin on university registers leads to the same conclusions. The great majority of marriages, on the other hand, took place within a much narrower range.

A comparison of fiscal lists (or of urban surveys giving lists of names with a few years' interval between them) shows a rapid turnover in surnames, sometimes as much as two-thirds of those noted down. Even in the countryside, the changes of surnames were numerous. A considerable proportion of our ancestors were affected by instability in their place of domicile. Not at all demanding in matters of comfort, often possessing only what they could stuff into a small bundle, they perhaps found it easier to change their place of residence than their shirt. They could also be ready at any moment to face the necessity of their last journey. The insecurity of the times, famines and wars chased them out in their thousands on to the main roads. Every town was an obvious refuge to the hard-pressed countrymen. To this endemic mobility were added the large-scale displacements resulting from great crises or measures of collective expulsion. Attempts have been made to calculate the numbers involved in the main displacements. But, as always in similar circumstances, the estimates diverge greatly. But it is certain that those displaced are numbered in several hundreds of thousands during the following crises: the expulsion of the Jews and Moriscos in Spain; the emigration of the Protestants of the Spanish

Netherlands; the departure of the Huguenots after the Revocation of the Edict of Nantes. Moreover, the whole of Central Europe, especially at the time of the Thirty Years War, and all Eastern and South-eastern Europe were involved in numerous migrations caused by wars and the settling of colonies.

The various migratory fluctuations therefore showed very great geographical and social selectivity. For example: in the survey at Zürich, in 1637, the division of non-native inhabitants according to their place of birth was as follows[23]:

Social categories	Canton of Zürich	Rest of Switzerland	Germany	Other countries	No. given
New Burgesses	67.60	25.80	4.10	6.05	2.45
Independent non-burgesses	53.90	19.80	21.10	5.20	—
Journeymen, apprentices	34.10	31.70	29.50	4.00	0.70
Women servants	63.30	22.80	6.80	5.10	—
Independent women	70.70	20.20	9.10	—	—

In Prague, in the 16th century, there was a great difference between city-districts[24]:

Districts	Dominant profession	Percentage of Germans among every 100 immigrants	
		1527–1570	1571–1621
Stare Město (Altstadt)	commerce	24	48
Nové Město (Neustadt)	crafts	7	22
Mala Strana (Kleinseite)	luxury articles	55	69
Hradčany (Hradschin)	administration	58	74

23. Z. Daszynska, Zürichs Bevölkerung im 17. Jahrhundert, in *Zeitschrift für Schweizerische Statistik*, 25 (1889) p. 407.

24. Th. Mayer, Zur Geschichte der nationalen Verhältnisse in Prag, in *Aus Sozial—und Wirtschaftsgeschichte*. A volume in honour of Georg von Below, Stuttgart 1928, pp. 259–60.

In three towns in the Netherlands, there is an equally large difference as to the origin of their new burgesses[25]:

Origin	1590–94			1655–59		
	Amsterdam	Leyden	Middleburg	Amsterdam	Leyden	Middleburg
Netherlands	50.4	15.5	18.0	53.5	41.2	43.9
Belgium	34.3	53.3	72.1	5.0	15.2	30.5
France	1.8	26.8	5.8	3.7	18.2	13.6
Germany	11.2	3.1	1.9	28.8	21.6	3.3
others	1.8	1.3	2.2	6.9	3.2	8.7
Total	100.0	100.0	100.0	100.0	100.0	100.0

This difference was connected with the difference in job opportunities. A world port like Amsterdam attracted above all workers in tertiary occupations; a single-industry centre like Leyden offered a source of employment to refugees coming from the similar cloth-weaving towns of Flanders. We notice this when we compare[26] the list of ten centres which provided them with the largest number of new burgesses, in the period of large-scale immigration (see Map 2).

Amsterdam (1578–1606)				Leyden (1575–1619)			
Antwerp	780	Alkmaar	121	Hondschoote	276	Bruges	80
Deventer	186	Utrecht	110	Ypres	154	Delft	72
Haarlem	156	Kampen	109	Bailleul	132	Renaix	71
Emden	131	Hoorn	106	Antwerp	108	Neuve-Eglise	70
Zwolle	129	Groningen	106	Ghent	86	Lille	64

Nevertheless modifications in general circumstances are also shown by differences between the migratory currents of successive periods and by very great fluctuations from one year to another.

25. N. W. Posthumus, *Geschiedenis van de Leidsche Lakenindustrie*, vol. II, The Hague 1939, p. 892.
26. From the data of J. G. Van Dillen, *Bronnen tot de geschiedenis van het bedrijfsleven en het gildewezen van Amsterdam*, vol. I (1512–1611) The Hague 1929 pp. LVII–LXXX and from Posthumus, *op. cit.* II, pp. 48–59.

(a) The origin of burgesses of Leyden during three successive periods covering the two centuries under study[27]:

Periods	Neighbour-hood of Leyden	N. & S. Holland	Rest of Low Countries	Belgium	France	Germany	Other Countries
1500–74	24.6	43.6	17.1	7.2	—	6.4	1.5
1574–1619	6.1	9.8	9.1	38.4	24.5	7.6	4.5
1620–99	10.8	21.7	16.9	14.6	13.7	18.8	3.5

(b) Number of registrations of new burgesses in Amsterdam in the course of 15 very hectic years[28]:

1566	60	1571	81	1576	5
1567	0	1572	27	1577	0
1568	65	1573	3	1578	170
1569	117	1574	13	1579	155
1570	129	1575	14	1580	57

Finally there was, especially in certain poor and relatively over-populated districts, one particular type of emigration: enlistment as mercenaries in the armies of the major powers. In the Swiss cantons, this was officially organised. Demographically, it helped to modify the equilibrium between the sexes, to lower the marriage and birth-rate and to increase the death-rate (250,000 to 300,000 deaths in the 16th and 17th centuries).

NATURAL FLUCTUATION

THE THREE COMPONENT FACTORS: BIRTHS, MARRIAGES, DEATHS

Their monopoly as factors in the natural evolution of the population is undisputed and solidly established. For information about this subject, parish registers have a similar indisputable monopoly. Where they do not exist we know nothing. We have seen earlier on that, for the 16th century and the first half of the 17th, they enable us slightly to draw aside the veil of our ignorance. With some exceptions, the series of registers for that period lack the frequency, the

27. Posthumus, *op. cit.* p. 886.
28. Van Dillen, *op. cit.* p. XXXII.

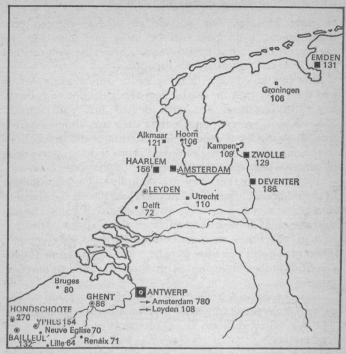

Map 2 Sources of principal migrations to Amsterdam (1578-1606) and Leyden (1575-1619)

The numbers refer to the new burgesses supplied by each town

regularity and completeness of those of later periods. Historical criticism must be more cautious in making use of them. The method of analysis used by Fleury and Henry is less easily applicable to them, although it can be used more often for those of the last decades of the 17th century. Any particular research in this field can only give us a sample, whose representivity it would be risky to guarantee. But to the extent that the research at present being undertaken in several universities, following a scientifically predetermined programme, succeeds in cross-checking for the principal countries the sectors for which we shall be able to have samples, our knowledge of the demographic development of the past will be more and more sure. In the course of the last fifteen years, noticeable progress has already been made in this direction.

One fundamental critical difficulty which must not be lost sight of is that the parish registers deal not with births but with baptisms, not with deaths but with burials. Nevertheless, we can accept that they are almost equivalent, allowing for a slight delay in time, some precautions in the analysis of the registers and more serious reservations in places where several religious denominations co-existed.

To the extent that they are complete, a rapid analysis of the registers allows us to know the change in the absolute number of births, marriages and deaths. We know already that the chief difficulties come from the registers of deaths: in many cases they are more behindhand and less complete. Their graph can therefore only be traced again from a more recent date in comparison with those for births and marriages.

The graphs which result from studies made up to the present time show numerous and considerable oscillations. The way they oscillate is simultaneously determined by four factors:

(a) A general orientation over a very long period (the secular trend). For the whole of Europe the three graphs, if it were possible to retrace them, would doubtless show a slightly rising tendency in the 16th century and an almost stationary one for the 17th century, the impact of a slight demographic increase being neutralised by a slight contraction in the rates. In fact, from the 17th century onwards, the secular demographic trend began to feel the effect of the appearance of the 'European marriage pattern' (see below).

(b) cyclical fluctuations, whose waves spread over several years, under the effect of a combination of particular circumstances and the general demographic and economic situation. This last point is particularly important. The number of births, marriages and deaths, does not depend chiefly on the total number of inhabitants but on the size of those demographic groups from which the bulk of births, marriages and deaths are to be expected. This figure itself is subject to cyclical variations according to the growth and decay of particular classes.

(c) (for graphs drawn up month by month) seasonal fluctuations showing how vital statistics are affected by the periods of the climatic, agricultural, civil or religious year.

(d) besides this more or less regular triple fluctuation, a final factor arose unexpectedly from time to time and upset everything completely to a degree which would seem incredible if it had not been historically proved: namely, epidemics, crises and catastrophes of different kinds. These events so destructive to the human race occurred on a very uneven scale. They will be dealt with in the following chapter.

The effects of this factor were often very much a question of the possibility of getting enough to eat. Economic historians have therefore suggested setting out the data of natural fluctuation, not only in the context of calendar years but in the context of harvest years. Moreover they think that graphs of conceptions, derived in the first place from graphs of births, would better enable us to elucidate certain connections of cause and effect.

FREQUENCIES—DISTRIBUTIONS—SEASONAL VARIATIONS

The frequency of the three phenomena was very uneven: one crude, single rate, worked out for one year by itself has no significance, especially if it deals with a thinly populated locality. Only 5 or 10 year averages have any value. To get these averages the registers have to be complete for the period under study and the total for the whole population has to be known. The first condition is not always fulfilled, the second almost never. This is why the administrations of the Century of Enlightenment, under the influence of political arithmeticians, took a great deal of trouble to work out a list of multipliers enabling them to proceed from a knowledge of the number of births, marriages and deaths, to a calculation of the number of inhabitants. Applied to 'ordinary' periods not too remote from the base periods, this procedure can provide us with some order by size. But the periods were very rarely 'ordinary'. There was no decade completely isolated, either from an epidemic, or a famine, or a war, or a phenomenon of revival after a catastrophe, or from one of the successive waves resulting from the effect of troughs and peaks some thirty years previously.

Having made these reservations, what can we establish?

For the 17th century we can establish that the 'ordinary' marriage rate was usually between 8‰ and 12‰. In favourable circumstances it could easily exceed 15‰. This high level of the marriage rate is explained by a large proportion of remarriages, resulting from a high death rate affecting families still in the prime of life. The remarriage of young heads of families was usual. As against this, divorce, not recognised by the majority of churches, was almost non-existent.

The birth-rate was very often between 35‰ and 45‰. Rates between 25‰ and 35‰ were also not uncommon. The rural rate was higher than the urban rate because of a more favourable composition of the population with a higher proportion of married people among young adults.

The rate of male to female births showed a fairly small difference: usually between 103 and 108 boys to every 100 girls. The frequence of illegitimate births was very variable. It depended on local customs or exceptional circumstances. In some places there was more than 1 illegitimate birth in 10, in others less than 1 in 100.

The abandoning of newborn infants was partly a result of these illegitimate births. It was a very widespread custom and sometimes a very rapidly increasing one, especially in the large towns, where institutions looked after foundlings coming from the whole surrounding countryside. In Paris, the annual average of admissions to the Foundlings Home increased as follows[29]:

29. *Annuaire statistique de la Ville de Paris*, 1880, p. 470.

1640–49	1650–59	1660–69	1670–79	1680–89	1690–99
305	360	453	688	1027	2115

As to the 'ordinary' death-rate, it was between 25 ‰ and 35 ‰ in the country; between 30 ‰ and 40 ‰ in the towns. But a slight crisis was enough to push it up by half. There were also noticeable differences in health conditions, in the towns as well as in the country. Some poor town neighbourhoods, some suburbs, some marshy districts, were antechambers of death. In this respect particularly we must beware of the 'ordinary'. Some serious historians have considered the whole of the 17th century as a period of crisis.

The higher rate of male mortality was a well-established phenomenon. It was found in every age group, except sometimes those with frequent maternities. For the period which concerns us, there is no question of dividing deaths by their causes. This particular point is almost never mentioned in the registers. But it does appear in the Bills of London after 1629. John Graunt has made use of them in his work. He drew up a statistical table in which 81 causes of death are listed in alphabetical order with the number of victims over a period of 20 years.[30] As a matter of curiosity, these are the ten leading categories: consumption and whooping-cough 44,487; new-born babies and young children 32,106; intermittent fever and fever 23,784; plague 16,384; deaths from old age 15,759; illnesses of the teeth and worms 14,236; smallpox and confluent smallpox 10,576; dropsy and tympanitis 9,623; convulsions 9,073; abortions and still-births 8,559. The classification was done by the 'sworn searchers'. It reflects the medical knowledge of the period.

For the 16th century the available data are too rare for us to be able to generalise. It seems as if marriages and births were a little more frequent, deaths a little less. But this point is made with reservations.

Each of these three phenomena was subject to very

30. J Graunt, *Natural and political observations upon the bills of mortality*, p. 452.

marked seasonal variations. The variations for marriages showed the joint influence of three factors: the yearly rhythm of agricultural work (a low period in the summer); religious and psychological occurrences (a Jump in December and March, a slack period in May in the Mediterranean countries); the rigour of the climate (a low period in the winter in the Northern countries). The result was that there was a big build-up of marriages in the late autumn (October–November) and around the Lent period (February–April).

Births were more numerous in the winter months corresponding to conceptions in the spring and at the beginning of summer. There is a noticeable decline in births at periods corresponding to Lenten conceptions.

As to the annual graph of deaths, it usually showed two peaks: the first at the end of the winter and the beginning of spring, the second at the end of the summer and the beginning of autumn. The latter was due to infant mortality, the former to deaths of adults and the aged.

AGES AND DURATIONS

Let us begin with deaths, because there can be found the key to the demography of the pre-statistical period.

The arithmeticians, the statistical essayists and their followers were first interested in the sub-division of deaths according to age. Fortunately, even the elementary data to be found in the registers were sufficient to draw up a first table of calculations, from which it was clear that average life-expectation was increasing and that every baby coming into the world could reckon on a longer life than his predecessors. On this point a Geneva doctor, E. Mallet, and the celebrated clergyman T. R. Malthus are entirely in agreement[31]:

31. E. Mallet, Recherches historiques et statistiques sur la population de Genève, son mouvement annuel et sa longévité, depuis le XVIe siècle jusqu' à nos jours (1549–1833), in *Annales d'hygiène publique et de médecine légale*, vol. 17 (1837), pp. 35–6.—T. R. Malthus, *An Essay on the Principle of Population*, new edition, London 1803, II, c.5.

	Average length of life		Expectation of life at birth	
	Mallet	Malthus	Mallet	Malthus
mid-16th cent.	21 years 2 months	18 years 6 months	8 years 7 months	4 years 10 months
17th century	25 years 8 months	23 years 4 months	13 years 3 months	11 years 7 months
18th century	32 years 9 months	32 years 3 months	27 years 9 months	27 years 2 months

If these figures are somewhat dissimilar, it is because they are derived from different environments. The study quoted by Malthus deals with a more exclusively urban population. We can notice moreover that this difference gradually declined. The fact remained that the majority of children coming into the world were condemned to die without having been able to make anything of their lives.

Out of the 1,000 parishioners who died in a Florence parish in the course of six years in the second half of the 17th century, the division by age-groups was as follows[32]:

Ages	Number of deaths	Ages	Number of deaths
0–1	367	10–20	36
1–5	285	20–30	25.5
5–10	58	30–40	33
0–10	710	40–50	49
		50–60	50
		60–70	43.5
		70–80	38
		80+	15

Three quarters of the parishioners buried were children or young people. And of these half were children less than one year old.

Infant mortality thus reached considerable proportions. For the six districts of Venice, its victims represented from 25% to 37% of the total of births between 1620 and 1629; from 24% to 29% between 1631 and 1696 and from 42%

32. P. Pieraccini, Note di demografia fiorentina, la parochia di S. Lorenzo dal 1652 al 1751, in *Archivio Storico Italiano*, 7th series, vol. 4 (1925), p. 67.

to 61% in 1630 (a year of epidemic).[33] Research undertaken in France, thanks to the method of Fleury and Henry, enables us to put forward the following percentages for the last third of the 17th century: healthy rural regions, between 20% and 25%; large market towns, between 25% and 30%; unhealthy rural areas, working-class districts, manufacturing areas, between 30% and 40%. In all the large towns, more than half the children coming into the world had only a short time to live.

Parallel to the prolongation of the average length of life we can see the building-up, in the course of the 17th century and in the majority of Western European countries, of what has been called the 'European marriage pattern'.[34]

This resulted simultaneously from an increase in the average age at marriage and from a reduction in the matrimonial frequency of each age-group.

Whereas, everywhere else in the world and at other periods in history, four-fifths of the girls were married before they were 25 and the rest almost all ended by finding a husband, Western Europe began to be unique in this respect: between 10% and 15% of girls remained permanently unmarried, and amongst those who got married, almost half did so after 25 years of age.[35]

The cause of this singular phenomenon has not yet been found. But its demographic importance is clear.

Every year by which the conclusion of a marriage is deferred has a direct repercussion on the possible number of children. To defer one's marriage by some years thus has very different consequences in a human environment where the average life expectation is about 70 years and

33. Details in Beltrami, *op. cit.* pp. 162–63.

34. J. Hajnal, European marriage patterns in perspective in Glass and Eversley, *Population in History*, London 1965, pp. 101–46.

35. According to L. Henry's pilot-study on the bourgeoisie of Geneva, the average age of marriage for girls rose by five years in a century and a half:

22 years old for girls born in			1550–1599
24·9	„	„	1600–1649
25·2	„	„	1650–1699
27	„	„	1700–1849

in another where life expectancy varies between 20 and 30 years, as was the case in the pre-statistical period. In the first case, there will always be enough years of fertility to guarantee a substantial increase in the population. In the second, the demographic equilibrium is directly threatened, because more than half the girls coming into the world run the risk of not reaching the age of marriage and those who do reach it can only rely on a limited period of matrimonial life. In these circumstances, it becomes very difficult to achieve a rate of reproduction sufficient to do more than maintain the population.

A fine French historian, P. Chaunu,[36] discussing this situation has recently been able to say quite rightly that the age of marriage was the key to fecundity in the old demographic structure; that it was 'the real contraceptive weapon of classical Europe'.

THE DEMOGRAPHIC RHYTHM OF THE 16TH AND 17TH CENTURIES

ENDEMIC DISEQUILIBRIUM AND UPHEAVALS CAUSED BY EPIDEMICS

In one generation, every normally constituted household is easily capable of doubling and even considerably more. If then, over a period of two centuries, from 1500 to 1700, Europeans were far from doubling in number, it was because the normal rhythm of their increase was disturbed. It was so disturbed both in an endemic way and by epidemics.

Endemically, as a result of a very high rate of child mortality and a high rate for adults. This caused an average length of life, which, taking account only of 'normal' years, scarcely exceeded thirty years and a life-expectancy at birth which was even shorter. This diminished by more than a half the period of fertility due to every new-born girl. This diminution was further increased by the fact that the average age at marriage gradually got

36. P. Chaunu, *La Civilisation de l'Europe classique*, Paris 1966, p. 204.

closer to 25. Such a situation was full of threats to the demographic equilibrium of the population.

It would in fact be a mistake to imagine that, under the Ancien Régime, families could normally expect one live birth every year. The extension of the period in which the mother breast-fed her baby, the frequency of miscarriages and still-births, the abstention from sexual relation at penitential seasons for religious motives and sometimes also the fairly long absences of the husband—these were all factors which combined together to space out births without any element of birth control.

It has been calculated that a marriage lasting for 25 years of fertility was responsible for between 8 and 10 births; there were 6 or 7 for 20 years of fertility; 4 or 5 for 15 years. Studies based on reconstructions of families have shown that marriages entered into at about the age of 25 could expect an average duration of about 15 years with 4 or 5 children. On the other hand, of every 100 children born into the world a good half were destined to die before reaching the average age of marriage. Out of every 4 or 5 children, only 2 or 2.5 were to replace the two parents.

The normal demographic pattern for years in which nothing special happened, consisted therefore of a slight favourable balance in rural districts and a situation beneath equilibrium in urban areas. The thin rural surplus was almost wiped out by emigration to the towns and towards 'new lands' to be colonised.

But how many times in a century did nothing happen? First of all, towards the end of summer and in a strictly narrow regional context, very frequent epidemics affected the younger generation. The mortality rose then sharply and this was sufficient to upset the demographic balance of the district affected, to diminish several age-groups dangerously and thus to reduce proportionately the reproductive possibilities of the following generation. On the national scale, the graph for deaths was not affected, unless the epidemic had affected a fairly wide geographical area. The effect on the other two graphs was almost non-existent.

Then there were what may be called crises. Crises of

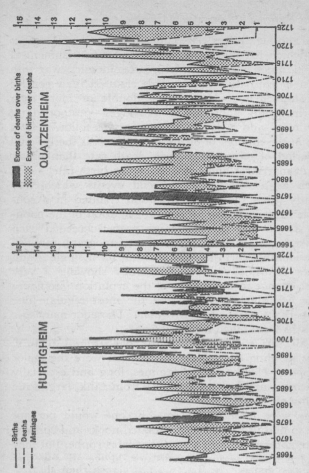

Fig. 2 Crises of Subsistence 1660–1725: irregularities of the following demographic curves exemplified in two Alsatian villages

Source: J. P. Kintz, Etudes alsaciennes, in *Annales de démographie historiques* (1969), p.287

supplies and high prices, especially as regards the necessities of life, which led inevitably to the under-nourishment of the poor; minor but fairly widespread epidemics; war with its train of ruin and misery. This resulted in a general death-rate which could easily be double or more than the normal rate, a decline in marriages—postponed till better times—and a decline in conceptions followed by a decline in the number of births. After the crisis there would be a period of recovery: a lower death rate than usual, plenty of marriages and finally a higher birth-rate.

Taken as a whole, these special events which very frequently upset the normal situation resulted in a considerable irregularity in the general evolution of the population. Above and below average years succeeded each other like waves, reminding one of a seismograph registering considerable earth-tremors. Set out on a single graph the lines continually intersect, thereby showing a very frequent change in the rhythm of the evolution (see figure 2). The line showing births was the most regular (one should perhaps say the least irregular). Those for marriages and deaths were much more irregular.

But all this only made up the background picture. Sharply standing out against this pattern were the major catastrophes: clearly marked famines, long and especially devastating wars and, in the very front rank, large-scale epidemics of 'plague'.

If one were to search thoroughly, one would perhaps be able to find in Europe a few isolated nooks and corners, which remained sheltered from every catastrophe. But they cannot have been very numerous nor, above all, covering a large area. Fairly often one notices two or three catastrophes in a century, but there were sometimes more.

The evidence of the registration documents, tragic in its very conciseness, obliges us to accept certain conceptions of scale which no historian would have accepted simply on the strength of some narrative sources. But the evidence of their day-by-day inscriptions is eloquent and overwhelming. In talking of populations being literally decimated, we are understating the truth. It is no longer a question of an ordinary death-rate of 30% to 40%, nor of a death-rate due to crisis which might reach double this. The ordinary death-rate was in fact multiplied five, ten or fifteenfold.

On the graphs, these catastrophes make such sharp peaks that they give the impression of wanting to go through the ceiling (and, in fact, they sometimes succeed, the scale in use not being large enough). Marriages and births are seriously affected by the rebound. They begin by falling to an almost nil level, then, if there are still people of marriageable age, one notices a boom in marriages and a noticeable rise in the level of births, while that of deaths becomes particularly low. Thus a part of the loss is recovered, thanks also to a new migratory inflow.

The London Bills of Mortality are, from this point of view, especially valuable evidence. They give us information from the last third of the 16th century onwards about the ordeals experienced by the English capital.[37] Taking into account only occasions when the death-rate exceeded 10%, we can find five in one century: in 1563 23,660 deaths (27%); in 1593 25,886 (18%); in 1603 42,945 (26%); in 1625 63,001 (25%); in 1665 97,306 (28%). From 70% to 90% of these deaths were caused by plague. Proportionately to their population, English towns of the second-rank were no less severely hit.

Holland and Germany also suffered very heavily: in Amsterdam, eight years of epidemic in one half-century (1617–1664) with a total of 110,000 deaths; in Leyden, more than 40,000 deaths in four 'severe' outbreaks of plague; in Breslau, 35,000 deaths in the four principal outbreaks of plague, as well as 10,000 in others; in Danzig and Königsberg, 86,000 and 56,000 during the 17th century alone. In Augsburg, where the number of deaths is known year by year, there were, between 1500 and 1549, eight years of plague with 38,405 deaths; between 1550 and 1599,

37. N. G. Brett-James, The London Bills of Mortality in the Seventeenth Century, in *Transactions of the London and Middlesex Archaeological Society*, 6 (1933), pp. 284–309. W. G. Bell, *The great plague in London in 1665*, 2nd ed. London 1951.

seven years with 20,680 deaths; between 1600 and 1649, nine years with 33,928 deaths. With such a balance sheet is it surprising to discover that by 1650 the 'normal' death-rate was only one-third that of 1500? In addition, the first half of the 17th century was marked, for almost the whole of Germany, by the ravages of the Thirty Years War. On both sides of a diagonal line between Basle and Stettin, for about 100 kms, in width, every province lost between 60% and 75% of its inhabitants and many rural communities disappeared from the map.[38]

In Italy, attacks of the plague were as frequent and even more deadly than in Germany. Northern Italy, already severely put to the test in 1576–77 (more than 100,000 deaths in the four chief towns) became the principal victim of the 1630 epidemic. Most towns, of large and medium size, suffered the death through plague of between 25% and 70% of the population; in country districts the average was 30%. In 1656, it was the turn of Liguria and the Peninsula. Naples and Genoa lost at least half their population. Rome could consider herself lucky with a loss of 10%. For her, the terrible date was that of the sack in 1527. Three years later, the town still had only 60% of its population before the ordeal.

A general survey of other countries would only complete the picture of devastation. For some of the more exposed regions, such as the Balkans, one is confined to guess-work. But it is certain that, for each of these two centuries, the 16th and the 17th, the European victims of plague alone are numbered in millions, without counting the victims of other disasters. The ravages caused by the most deadly were such that recovery could only take place after a delay of more than a century.

THE FECUNDITY OF MARRIAGES

In historical demography, we have to be content with available existing tools and not stray in search of data for which the surveys of today are barely sufficient.

38. G. Franz, *Der Dreissigjährige Krieg und das Deutsche Volk*, Jena 1940.

To find out the average number of children for each marriage in the 17th century, the only method applicable on a large scale is the most elementary: to divide, period by period, the number of inscriptions in the baptismal registers by the number of inscriptions in the marriage registers. It is a far from satisfactory method, since it often registers in reverse the variations produced by changes in natural circumstances: in certain years of recovery after a demographic catastrophe, marriages were more numerous than births and deaths!

We must therefore carry out a survey over a period of several years. This question did yet formerly interest the arithmeticians. Gregory King claims a difference of 8% between London and the country. In other very varied regions, the proportions shown by contemporary studies are between 3.0 and 4.5 for the main towns and between 4.0 and 5.5 in the countryside. A distinction must also be drawn between marriages and re-marriages. Because of the latter, the average number of children per marriage is noticeably different from the number per married man. According to a genealogical study in Basle, this difference was more than two children up to the last quarter of the 17th century. Other studies have shown that the relationship of births to marriages was higher for bourgeois and peasant families than for artisans and day-labourers. This can of course be explained by a higher death-rate leading to an earlier break-up of families.

A more thorough sifting of certain series of parish registers and the reconstruction of families will soon give us less summary information about certain aspects of fecundity in marriage: revised figures for the birth-rate and fecundity, a division of births according to social status and the age of the mother, and the interval between births in the same family.

So far we can consider it certain that the normal interval between two births was two years or more and that the rate of fecundity varied with the age of the mother, whatever might be the duration of the marriage and the number of children already born. This proves that there was no general practice of birth control. Birth control may however have crept in in some restricted circles at the end of the 17th century.

THE NATURAL SURPLUS

To arrive at this, we must limit ourselves simply to the districts where births and deaths were registered in full. Elsewhere it is impossible.

From one district to another, the situation varied considerably because of the varied effect of endemic factors (the usual sanitary situation) and epidemic factors (infections, famines, wars).

The main towns usually showed a deficit. In the course of a century this deficit could equal the figure for the whole population. Immigration therefore wholly or partly filled the gap and even finished by making up the losses due to catastrophes.

The small towns were often similar to the large. But since their numbers were much smaller the balance could more easily be restored.

In normal times, the healthy country districts showed a modest surplus. But the great disasters fell on them twice as heavily: both through death and through emigration to make up for the urban deficit.

No over-all balance can therefore be drawn up for an entire country nor even for an entire region. Only the following observation seems logical. Since the 16th and 17th centuries produced a certain increase in population and since Europe's balance of migration was certainly not favourable, this increase must be attributed to a natural surplus.

BIBLIOGRAPHY

There is no work devoted entirely to the history of the European population in the 16th and 17th century. The synthesis coming nearest to it is K. F. Helleiner's *The Population of Europe from the Black Death to the Eve of the Vital Revolution* in *The Cambridge Economic History of Europe*, vol. IV, Cambridge 1967, pp. 1–95.

It is also worth consulting the chapters dealing with these two centuries in works on demography and in general histories of population. The two best known titles are: M. Reinhard, A. Armengaud, J. Dupaquier, *Histoire générale de la population mondiale*, new edit., Paris 1968 – E. W. Bucholz, *Raum und Bevölkerung in der Weltgeschichte*, new edit., vol III: 1100–1750, Würzburg 1966 (Bevölkerungs-Plötz, III). These are two very different works. The Plötz is essentially a collection of facts. It continues brilliantly the old tradition of works of statistical indexing and deals above all with statistical data but without criticising them. The new Reinhard aims above all at being an up-to-date synthesis, bringing together the results of the most recent research and concerned above all with the dynamic elements of demography. These two works should usefully be used in conjunction with other older works, such as H. Westergaard (1932), P. Fortunati (1934), A. M. Carr Saunders (1936), F. Burgdörfer (1940), E. Esmonin in *La Statistique* (1944), R. von Ungern-Sternberg and H. Schubnell (1950). Two recently issued works should not be neglected: P. Guillaume and J. P. Poussou, *Démographie historique*, Paris 1970 (Collection U) – E. A. Wrigley, *Population and History*, New York, Toronto 1969.

The heuristic, critical and problematical aspects of demographic history are particularly dealt with in: T. H. Hollingsworth, *Historical Demography*, London 1969 (Coll. The Souces of History)—*An Introduction to English Historical Demography*, ed. E. A. Wrigley, London 1966 (dealing with the method of analysing old documents: lists of household, parish registers)—R. Mols, *Introduction à la démographie historique des villes d'Europe du XIVe au XVIIIe siècle*, 3 vols.,

Gembloux-Louvain 1954–56 (only for Western Europe).

These works also give a bibliography which can be supplemented by that of *Population Index*. Since 1964, the Société de démographie historique française has published in its *Annales de Démographie Historique* several articles, reports and bibliographical notices which provide the best up-to-date information in this field. A good popular work is also J. Thirsk, *Sources of information on population* in *Amateur Historian* IV/4–5 (1959) 129–33, 182–5.

The following will help to place the history of the population in a more general context: P. G. Ohlin, *The positive and preventive check: a study of the rate of growth of the pre-industrial population*, Harvard 1955—H. Mauersberg, *Wirtschafts—und Sozialgeschichte Zentral-Europäischer Städte in neuerer Zeit*. Göttingen 1960 (very well documented)— B. H. Slicher van Bath, *The agrarian history of Western Europe*, London 1963—C. T. Smith, *A Historical Geography of Western Europe before* 1800, London 1967.

Recently, on the initiative of D. V. Glass and D. E. C. Eversley, a series of articles in reviews which have been amongst the most worthwhile contributions to different aspects of general demographic history, British, European and American, have been brought together in one volume with the title *Population in History, Essays in Historical Demography*, London 1965.

Studies written within a national or regional framework must also not be neglected.

FOR GREAT BRITAIN:

J. Brownlee, The History of the Birth and Death Rates in England and Wales taken as a whole from 1570 to the present time, in *Public Health*, Cambridge 29 (1915–16), 211– 22, 228–30.

E. E. Rich, The Population of Elizabethan England, in *Economic History Review* 2 (1949–50), 247–65.

G. S. L. Tucker, English Pre-Industrial Population Trends, ibid, 16 (1963), 205–18.

L. Owen, The Population of Wales in the 16th and 17th

Centuries, in *Transactions of the Honourable Society of Cymmodorion*, 1959, 99–113.

J. G. Kyd, *Scottish Population Statistics*, Edinburgh 1952.

K. H. Connell, *The Population of Ireland*, Oxford 1950.

FOR CONTINENTAL EUROPE:

Sufficiently recent demographic histories exist for several countries to be indispensable guides. The following deal with the 16th and 17th centuries:

J. Nadal, *Historia de la poblacion española*, Barcelona 1966.

J. Nadal and E. Giralt, *La population catalane de 1553 à 1717*, Paris 1960.

K. J. Beloch, *Bevölkerungsgeschichte Italiens*, 3 vol. (See especially the final synthesis, vol. III, Berlin 1961, pp. 339–85).

W. Bickel, *Bevölkerungsgeschichte und Bevölkerungspolitik der Schweiz seit dem Ausgang des Mittelalters*, Zürich 1947.

E. Keyser, *Bevölkerungsgeschichte Deutschlands*, Leipzig 1943. See also the articles (under the name of each district) in the *Deutsches Städtebuch*, edited by Keyser since 1939.

D. Placht (The population and social structure of the Czech State from the 16th to the 18th century) (in Czech), Prague 1957.

J. Kovacsics and others (Demographic history of Hungary) (in Hungarian), Budapest 1963 (see especially pp. 115–42).

For other countries one had to rely on articles in reviews. Their value is uneven and their authors write from different points-of-view. But the reader has no choice.

FRANCE:

R. Mousnier, in *XVIIe siècle* (1952)—J. Dupaquier, in *Revue Historique* (1968)—P. Goubert, in *Population in History* (supra), pp. 457–73.

BELGIUM:

R. Mols, in *Vierteljahrschrift für Sozial—und Wirtschaftsgeschichte* (1959).

NETHERLANDS:
    J. A. Faber and others, in *A. A. G. Bijdragen* (1965).

PORTUGAL:
    J. T. Montalvao Machado in *Jornal do Medico* (1950).

SCANDINAVIA:
    E. F. Heckscher, in *Economic History Review* (1950).
    H. Gille, in *Population Studies* (1949–50).
    G. Utterstrom, in *Population in History* (supra) pp. 23–548.

POLAND:
    E. Vielrose, in *Kwartalnik Historii Kultury Materialny* (1957).

RUSSIA:
A. I. Kopanev, in *Istoricheskie Zapiski* (1959).

BALKANS:
    D. F. Barkan, in *Journal of Economic and Social History of the Orient* (1957).

2. Patterns and Structure of Demand
1500-1750
Walter Minchinton

Concerned with the two hundred and fifty years between 1500 and 1750, this chapter deals with the question of demand in what should perhaps be called the age of commercial Europe, the age which lies between that of feudal agricultural Europe and industrial Europe. The period opens with the expansion of Europeans across the oceans of the world, a movement which was in time to expand the range of foodstuffs and raw materials available to them; it begins with a further forward movement in population growth and with an upward movement of prices. The period closes just as the pace of industrialisation, which was to make England the first industrial nation, was about to quicken; it ends with both population and prices once more moving upwards and, by its terminal date, famine had ceased to be endemic in Europe. After 1750 only 'submerged' famines – almost bearable ones – continued to occur.

This chapter deals with the classical period of absolute monarchy, of aristocratic Europe, of noble conspicuous display, of growing bourgeois pretensions, of persistent peasant poverty. But such broad generalisations should not cloak the fact that although Europe is clearly to be marked off from the other continents at this time, some experiences like price movements and demographic trends were shared to a lesser or greater degree. Further, the greater part of the trade in which people engaged was within Europe and so served to link its constituent countries together, yet at the same time the sub-continent possessed a fundamental, if narrowing, diversity. In part this was a reflection of geography and climate and of factor endowment, in part of economic, social and political organisation, in part of technology and spirit. Europe was not yet, as it was to become by the end of the eighteenth century, a region in which men travelled easily or frequently or migrated from one country to another. Differences between regions, between classes and over time need to be borne in mind throughout the ensuing discussion.

THE SOURCES

Compared with production and trade, the study of consumption in early modern times is greatly handicapped by the difficulty of obtaining source materials. Even in a mature economy where a major part of the provision of goods and services occurs through the market, it is still difficult to obtain a complete picture of the patterns of consumption. To the extent that people grow their own food, paint and repair their houses, provide their own entertainment and so on, the situation becomes harder to depict because little information in quantitative terms is available. And a most important contemporary gap is information about the services provided by wives and other members of the family for their husbands, children and relatives. The provision of some goods and services too may disappear from the national accounts when small firms are merged into big. If these are problems in dealing with a developed economy, *a fortiori* the problems of dealing with a less-developed economy are much more serious. The performance of services and payments in kind instead of money payments make for great difficulties. Many consumers, too, are small users of a wide range of products who keep no record of their consumption. The majority of the population of Europe in the sixteenth, seventeeth and eighteenth centuries consisted of peasants who kept no accounts.

Evidence about consumption for this period is of two main kinds: direct evidence and indirect evidence. As far as direct evidence is concerned, most is known about how the wealthier members of society disposed of their incomes. Estate records show how they spent their incomes on consumer goods or durables, invested them or gave them away.

In some instances the records of less wealthy members of the community have survived. So, for example, we know something about the expenditure of an English yeoman farmer in the early seventeenth century from Robert Loder's farm accounts.[1] Diaries such as Pepys' or Evelyn's provide evidence in general descriptive terms of the patterns of consumption – what food was eaten, what clothes were bought – together with evidence about services, domestic servants, coachmen, etc.

For England the study of inventories attached to wills has cast considerable light on the changing scale of expenditure of a much wider range of the population. Especial use has been made of the inventories of farmers. These records are of particular importance because they permit us a glimpse into the lives of less well-to-do members of the community whose consumption patterns it is not easy otherwise to document.

Legal records are a further type of document which enables us to obtain a fitful and intermittent glimpse into the scale of income and the ways in which individual members of the community in Europe spent their income. Bankruptcy records are particularly important for the information they contain but other legal proceedings can also provide information for our purposes. For example, in the course of law suits in France relating to appeals against over-assessment for the taille, experts gave a complete analysis and valuation of the real estate (whether owned or leased), the livestock and the debts and credits of the peasants concerned.

Part of the picture of demand consists of the demand of traders, farmers and industrialists for goods not only on current but also on capital account and these survive to some degree. The records of the great merchant princes, like the Fugger, have not yet been fully exploited but in various parts of Europe the records of other merchant firms, of industrial enterprises and of some farmers survive.

Consumption can be studied in a second respect from

1. George E. Fussell, ed. *Robert Loder's farm accounts, 1610-1620* (Royal Historical Society, Camden 3rd series, LIII, 1936).

the records of institutions and administrative bodies. Government purchases for the armed forces, the army and the navy, state and local provision for the poor, the purchases of hospitals, almshouses, schools and the like give some indication of the pattern of demand, the range and quantity of foodstuffs and materials consumed and some evidence about the prices paid. Traditionally, however, institutional purchases were made on long-term contract so that the prices do not fluctuate to the same extent as prices in the market place. In like manner, the records of the church, of bishops, of dioceses, of cathedral and abbey churches and of monasteries and convents, help to bring life to our discussion of what goods and services were consumed in particular places at particular times and what capital investment took place.

In the case of many commodities, demand is a reciprocal of supply. To the extent that we can compile production figures and also take account of stockholding and external trade, we can obtain some estimate of consumption. Such figures are available, for example, when the state, the responsible government, imposes a tax on an article: so (to the extent they were not evaded) taxes on salt, wine, spirituous liquors and bricks and the records they produced provide us with some indication of the consumption of these items. Much of government revenue in this period was raised not by internal taxes but by tariffs and imposts on imports. With the proviso that some part of the customs duty may be evaded by smuggling, such duties provide an index of the quantity of a particular commodity imported. In the case of some commodities, such as cane sugar, Indian cottons or tobacco, imports accounted for the entire supply of the commodity. When an appropriate adjustment is made for re-exports, the import duties give some indication of the total amount available for consumption. But in the case of many products, such as cloth and some foodstuffs, imports were only a proportion of the total quantity available and so to that extent are less informative. In a similar fashion to customs records, transport tolls, such as Voltaire complained of when he crossed France, the machinery for the supervision and regulation of the internal market in foodstuffs, the assizes of bread and ale, etc provide some information about the foodstuffs available for consumption. Tax assessments, local or national, provide evidence about the structure of income.

Contemporary or later estimates of the outputs of particular industries provide us with another type of aggregate information. The growth of political economy in the later seventeenth century gave rise to some estimates not only of trade but also of production and of the structure of society. Gregory King's assessment of the size of the different classes, for example, gives some picture of the structure of demand in late seventeenth-century England. So the records of government, customs returns and taxes on production together with the writings of political arithmeticians provide us with some evidence to assess aggregate demand in early modern Europe.

Then, descriptive and literary accounts provide some information about patterns of consumption. Examples of accounts by visitors are Andrew Boorde's guide to travelling in Europe, *The fyrst boke of the introduction of knowledge* (1550); Owen Feltham's *A brief character of the Low-Countries under the States* (1652); William Carr's *An accurate description of the United Netherlands, and of . . . Germany, Sweden, & Denmark* (1691); William Bromley's *Remarks in the Grande Tour of France & Italy* (1692); and Daniel Defoe's *A tour through the whole island of Great Britain* (1724-7). Once they appear, newspapers and journals can also be drawn on.

Finally, and very impressionistically, painters provide a visual record of the styles of life prevailing in early modern Europe as they move from a preoccupation with religious subjects to depicting men, women and children not only in special sittings but either formally or informally at work and play. Thus Breughel provides a somewhat idealised and bucolic picture of sixteenth-century peasant activities and the Dutch painters illuminate bourgeois life in the Netherlands in the following century. The conversation pieces of English early eighteenth-century painters give a stylised impression of some aspects of English social life while Hogarth provides a more vigorous and earthy insight into others.

If by class structure, by socio-economic group, the source material available for the study of consumption in these two and a half centuries is uneven, so it is by geography also. It will be obvious from the foregoing account that some parts of Europe can be much better documented than others. At present, more material is available from Sweden, France, northern Italy, Russia and England than is available for some of the other countries, particularly those in eastern Europe. The picture that can be given is therefore fuller for some parts of Europe than it is for others just as it is easier to portray in detail the patterns of expenditure of the nobility than it is of the peasantry.

DETERMINANTS OF DEMAND

In aggregate terms the stock of goods and services available both for current consumption and for investment depends on the current level of production less exports and hoarding and with the addition of imports and dis-saving. With information difficult to obtain, any account must of necessity be impressionistic. In this chapter the various determinants of demand will be first examined. Among the factors which affected the pattern of consumption were geography and climate; production and technology; the components of aggregate income, its level and distribution between public and private consumers, between classes, between countries and over time; the demographic trend and the growth of cities; the methods of articulating demand; the role of fashion and social custom; and finally the functions and activities of the state. Then, secondly, the components of demand will be looked at: the demand for food, clothing and other consumer goods, for heating, lighting and shelter, for labour and services and for capital and capital goods.

Throughout the sixteenth, seventeenth and eighteenth centuries Europe enjoyed a predominantly subsistence economy and the greater part of the population had little if any income available for purchases beyond their basic needs. What was bought – most foodstuffs, clothing and furnishing – was produced in the immediate locality and capital projects were carried out predominantly with local materials. To a considerable extent production was performed for personal consumption without the intervention of the price mechanism. The effective market demand for goods and services formed therefore only a small portion of total demand. But to the extent that the better-off sections of communities were unable or ceased to be content with what could be produced locally, there was a wider market for goods.

GEOGRAPHY AND CLIMATE

First, geography and climate were not without their effect on demand. The needs of those who dwelt in northern and central Europe and had to cope with long dark winters differed in some degree from those of the inhabitants of Mediterranean Europe, just as the requirements of those who lived in the mountains were not entirely coincident with that of those who lived on the plains. And those who lived on the coast and won their livelihood from the sea required articles of which their compatriots who dwelt far from water had no need. And the reciprocal of these differing situations was that for purely geographical and climatic reasons, the stock of goods available for consumption varied to a substantial degree from one part of Europe to another. Then longer-run climatic variations affecting both rainfall and temperature had a deleterious influence on agricultural yields and thus operated adversely against the standard of living of many people in Europe. Nor are we dealing with natural limitations alone. Europe still had a considerable diversity and man's response to similar circumstances differed. While many might keep cows, the animals which they owned were of varying breeds, the meat they obtained and the cheese which they made from the milk like the beer which they brewed and the bread which they baked, was not of a standard sort. A similar variety was visible in clothing and other manufactures such as textiles, leatherwork, metalwork and carpentry. The geography of vernacular architecture reflects to a considerable degree the availability of building materials: stone, brick, cob or timber were employed because they were the materials to be had locally. To a large extent factor endowment imposed a control on what could be done and difficulties in transport which were reflected in price prevented the use of raw materials which were not available in a particular locality but the individual or collective skills of different communities gave their products a distinctive local, regional and, where the term is appropriate, national appearance.

Conditions of work also modified patterns of consumption. The agricultural worker required a different diet from the clerk, the muscular and the mental, the active and the sedentary. They took different amounts and sorts of nourishment. They also needed different clothing, tools and equipment and involved different types of capital expenditure. Their patterns of work also differed and so did their leisure hours and needs. These and other considerations need to be taken into account in any discussion of patterns of consumption.

PRODUCTION

On the supply side there were influences which need to be considered. The factor endowment of different parts of Europe varied, the level of technology changed and the ability to supplement European resources by external trade varied from place to place and over time. The needs most easily satisfied were those for agricultural products. An overwhelming proportion of the population was engaged in farming, forestry and horticulture while fishing provided a livelihood for many along the seaboard of Europe and some on the inland lakes and waterways. Like the harvests, geographical conditions varied so that, in good times as well as in bad, there was a considerable trade in grain, in meat, in fish, in dairy products and in fruit. But the absence of improvement in agricultural productivity in most of Europe exercised a restraint on demand. Low seed ratios of the order of 1:3 and 1:4 which were the rule in many parts of Europe, not only in the middle ages but also in the sixteenth, seventeenth and eighteenth centuries, meant that a substantial part of the harvest had to be kept to provide next year's seed. And since scarcely one-third of the farmland was used each year for bread grains, the limitation imposed on consumption by low yield ratios becomes even more evident. To raise the seed ratio from 3 to 4 – that is by one-third – added significantly to food supplies. Conversely, a lowering of yield ratios had a catastrophic effect on supplies available for consumption.

Whereas agriculture was widely distributed throughout Europe, the extractive industries were more specifically located. Men did what they could with the materials available locally and tools as well as buildings reflected the availability of local resources but if minerals such as tin, copper or iron were not to be had in the immediate neighbourhood, they had to be obtained from a distance as metals or as finished goods. Other raw materials, such as wool, timber, salt and alum, were bought in if local supplies were not available in sufficient quantities. And there was a trade in manufactured products, in textiles, in metalware and in luxury products. To some extent the products of these industries changed over time, the new textile industries, for example, producing lighter fabrics. New industries, too, were developed; clockmaking, printing and the manufacture of soap expanded. Some industries became more capital-intensive but there were no major technological developments in the sixteenth, seventeenth and early eighteenth centuries, and apart from a few limited developments, much industrial activity continued as it had done for centuries before. Overall the manufacturing capacity of Europe increased somewhat in these two and a half centuries and the variety of products was certainly extended and, as the products of European industry changed and developed, so did their demand for raw materials.

To the resources available from local growth and manufacture must be added those which could be obtained by trade. Since climatic conditions and factor endowment varied, such differences gave rise to an exchange of goods. The cereal, wine and cattle areas commonly exported their surpluses, a trade in textile yarns and fabrics, in metalware, in coal, in timber, in paper and in other raw materials and manufactures was carried on. With the changing geography of industry in the course of these two and a half centuries there was a change in the pattern of trade, the Mediterranean declining in importance relatively to the Atlantic seaboard of Europe.

While the bulk of trade was Euro-centred, a new and significant development which, while it may not have greatly increased the stock of goods available for consumption, widened the range was the expansion of extra-European trade. With the discoveries and colonisation, Europe imported the products of tropical and semi-tropical lands: sugar, coffee, tea, spices and other groceries, raw materials such as dyewoods, cotton, timber and naval stores, manufactured products such as Indian cottons and other commodities such as tobacco and luxury articles as well as gold and silver. Some of these goods were imported in small quantities but by 1750 a significant volume of sugar, tea and Indian cottons were being brought into Europe.

A second addition to current consumption was dis-saving which provided in certain cases a once-for-all addition to supplies. The dissolution of the monasteries in England in the sixteenth century may have increased the stock of goods available as well as altering their distribution while the conspicuous display of the nobles at the court of the sun king, Louis XIV, some have argued, was achieved by dis-investment. But dis-saving affected the pattern of consumption only to a negligible degree. Moreover, since both agricultural production and industrial production expanded and non-European imports grew, both a wider range and a greater quantity of goods was available to satisfy the needs of the European consumer by 1750.

This stock was to some extent reduced by the export of goods from Europe. The greater part of these consisted of manufactures – woollen textiles, metal work, leather goods, furniture, glassware, paper, as well as luxury articles such as silks and lace. To the Americas went wine and beer while to Africa were sent cotton goods, firearms and metal trinkets. Most of these exports which helped to balance the trading account were European products but some non-European imports such as Indian cottons were re-exported. While discussions have concentrated on the commodity movements and the way in which they were organised by shipowners and trading companies, little attention has been paid to the gains from trade. No adequate information is available about the terms of trade, about the relative movement of the prices of European and extra-European goods, so that it is impossible to generalise at this point in time. Certainly the most articulate of Europe's overseas customers, the inhabitants of the English mainland colonies, gave no indication that they thought they were being exploited by the trading nexus until the 1760s when the particular political conditions of the time gave rise to complaints. But if imports only compensated for exports (some of which, at the prevailing level of prices, were surplus to European requirements), they nonetheless served to extend the range of raw materials and foodstuffs available for European consumption.

Consumption can be increased not only by a rise in incomes but also by an extension of supply. The demand for some products is inelastic, as it was by and large for working clothes in this period; some products, such as bread, have a backward-sloping demand curve since as incomes rise, people tend to reduce their consumption of bread and to consume a wider variety of other foodstuffs. But the demand for many other goods was price-sensitive. Particularly was this so for imports. While the price of tea and sugar remained high, consumption was limited but when greater supplies became available and prices fell in consequence, a change in taste occurred and larger amounts of sugar were consumed and tea drunk. So the pattern of demand in early modern Europe, as at other times, was affected by changes in price. Many other examples could be cited but enough has been said to make the point. Further, it should be noted that supply and demand are not independent variables but are related. There can be no effective demand for a commodity until it is available. Of such, the book provides a vivid example in our period. Until the invention of the printing press, the application of a multiple production technique to the manufacture of books, printed books were not available and manuscript books were scarce and expensive.

Finally, the pattern of immediate consumption was to some degree affected by investment. In the main, agricultural and industrial demand was for working rather than fixed capital though the development of trade involved the improvement of port facilities and warehousing and the growth in size of merchant fleets. Building provided the largest claim on resources on capital account for these two and a half centuries saw a significant amount of rebuilding for the middle ranges of society while the rich were provided, by the creation of parks, palaces and theatres, with a more splendid stage upon which to strut. As with most countries in a stage of commercial capitalism, it was current consumption rather than investment which made the predominant claim upon resources.

INCOME

As far as income is concerned, three aspects need to be considered: the level of income, the social distribution of private income and the division of income between the public and the private sectors.

Because productivity was low due to the limited nature of technology, the shortage of skill and the lack of market opportunities, incomes were low and individual producers had little incentive to increase output. In consequence the growth of wealth occurred only slowly and intermittently when it occurred at all between 1500 and 1750. Kuznets sets the possible (and perhaps the maximum) long-term rate of growth of output per head in the developed countries of western Europe between 1500 and 1750 at about 0.2 per cent per year, giving a total rise in per capita product over the period of about 65 per cent.[2] As population growth during the same years occurred at the rate of 0.17 per cent per annum there was some slight overall increase in per capita income between 1500 and 1750 in western Europe but the benefits of this growth were very unevenly distributed both over time and between places. Moreover, in the rest of Europe increase in average per capita income did not reach the level of the countries of western Europe – England, France and the Netherlands – which were preindustial rather than underdeveloped and in some places the standard of living may actually have declined during the early modern period.

To the extent that they were affected by the movement of prices – and those who produced their own food or clothing or received payment in kind could to some extent insulate themselves against price movements – the living standards of the people of Europe depended on the relationship between the course of prices and the movement of money wages. Overall in the sixteenth century, with the pressure of growing population on food supplies and several though not more frequent famines, agricultural prices rose, influenced by the fact that farming was subject to diminishing returns. At the same time, since there were some cost-reducing developments, the prices of industrial products rose less rapidly. Yet, although the greater part of the European labour force was employed in agriculture, it benefited little from the upward movement of prices of farm produce since agricultural productivity was low and many lived close to subsistence. For England, Thorold Rogers contrasted the golden age of the peasantry in the fifteenth century with a picture of growing exploitation in the next hundred years. While the purchasing power of the agricultural labourer was thus restricted, high food prices meant that the industrial worker had little to spare after meeting his needs for food in order to buy industrial products.

2. Simon Kuznets, 'Capital formation in modern economic growth and some implications for the past', *Third International Conference of Economic History* (Paris, 1968), pp. 30-1.

But the course of events did not follow the same pattern throughout Europe. In the Low Countries, it has been said, prices and wages were happily related between 1500 and 1520, that they then parted company for thirty-five years but that during the last 40 years of the sixteenth century the position of the workers recovered so that the reign of Philip II saw conditions improve compared with those during the reign of Charles V.[3] And for Venice, Dr Pullan has suggested that the period between the two great plagues of 1575-7 and 1630-1 was not one of unrelieved gloom and growing despondency.[4] In the middle of the seventeenth century the sustained inflation of the previous century and a half in Europe came to an end and was followed by a period of stable prices for a century or so. With slackening population growth and, in some countries, agricultural improvement, food prices tended to fall while wage rates held their own or did not decline to the same extent. 'During the last forty years of the seventeenth century and the first twenty of the eighteenth', wrote Thomas Malthus, 'the average price of corn was such, as compared with the wages of labour, would enable the labourer to purchase, with a day's earning, two-thirds of a peck of wheat. From 1720 to 1750 the price of wheat had so fallen, while wages had risen, that instead of two-thirds, the labourer could purchase the whole of the peck of wheat with a day's labour.'

The distribution of income in Europe in this period was largely determined by the institution of private property, the laws of inheritance and the fact that surpluses, when generated, accrued largely in the hands of those who owned capital. There was, in consequence, a marked inequality in the distribution of wealth. In sixteenth-century Spain the higher income groups (including the nobles, bishops and professional classes who amounted to between 5 and 7 per

3. Charles Verlinden, Jan Craeybeckx and E. Scholliers, 'Mouvements des prix et des salaires en Belgique au XVI siècle', *Annales: Economies, Sociétés, Civilisations*, X (1955), pp. 173-98.

4. Brian Pullan, *Rich and poor in Renaissance Venice: the social institutions of a Catholic state to 1620* (Oxford: Blackwell, 1971), pp. 20-1.

cent of the population and the skilled artisans who accounted for a further 10-12 per cent) formed about one-fifth of the population with the poor comprising the other 80 per cent. At the end of the seventeenth century Gregory King presented a more detailed picture of the distribution of wealth in England (summarised in the following table). Again the rich formed a small proportion of society and the poor about 50 per cent, half of whom lived in conditions of dire and chronic poverty. At the same time, according to

TABLE I: Income distribution in late seventeenth-century England

Family income (pa)	Total no. of persons	No. of families	Percentage of total no. of persons	Percentage of total families	Occupations, etc
Over £200	209,520	23,586	4	2	Peers, baronets, etc; greater office holders; eminent merchants, etc.
£70–£199	440,000	65,000	8	5	Lesser office holders, merchants; clergy; lawyers; navy officers; better freeholders.
£38–£69	2,026,000	412,000	37	30	Artisans, tradesmen; lesser clergy; farmers, lesser freeholders, etc.
£14–£37	1,495,000	449,000	27	33	Labouring people and out-servants; soldiers and seamen.
Under £14	1,330,000	400,000	24	30	Cottagers, paupers, vagrants, etc
TOTALS	5,500,520	1,349,586	100	100	

Source: Maurice W. Thomas, ed. *A survey of English economic history* (Blackie, 1957), p. 216, derived from Gregory King, *Natural and political observations and conclusions upon the state and condition of England* (Lancaster, 1696) reprinted in George E. Barnett, ed. *Two tracts by Gregory King* (Baltimore: Johns Hopkins Press, 1936), p. 31.

Vauban, five-ninths of the population of France lived in poverty. In the early eighteenth century it was estimated that in the German ecclesiastical estates fifty clergy and 260 beggars were to be found in each thousand of the population while Cologne then had, by report, 20,000 beggars in a population of 50,000. Poverty persisted for a number of reasons but amongst them was the fact that much of the population had a high leisure preference and a lack of acquisitiveness, sanctified by Roman Catholicism.

F.E.H.E.—D

Because of religious celebrations it was said that the Carinthian iron industry operated only 100 eight-hour shifts per year in the seventeenth century while in 1660 103 holidays were celebrated a year in Paris. In the late seventeenth century, French intendants frequently complained of the idleness of the poor while in England commentators reported that there were thousands miserably poor yet who would not work – though such complaints can be found at other times and therefore need to be viewed sceptically.

But there were important developments which affected the distribution of income in Europe in this period. Firstly, there was a shift in the structure of rural society and particularly the re-enserfment of the peasantry in eastern Europe and the growth of commercial and urban artisan classes in the towns of the developing centres of western, central and southern Europe. In the developing agricultural areas of Europe – England, the Netherlands, Scandinavia and France to some extent – the commercialisation of agriculture proceeded apace. The extreme position is in England where many landlords ceased to farm their land directly but leased it to tenant farmers who cultivated it with the aid of wage labour. But while serfdom disappeared, the commercialisation of agriculture operated against the peasantry who suffered from the diminution of common rights. In the later seventeenth century, which saw the growth of large estates, pressure on the land became apparent. There was a growth in the rural population at a time when the number of separate holdings was not growing. In those parts of Europe where inheritance was by primogeniture, division of holdings was not the custom, those who failed to find land to cultivate were forced to move to the towns, to wander about the countryside in search of a livelihood or to turn to crime. In eastern Europe – Europe east of the Elbe – the late sixteenth and seventeenth centuries saw a reassertion of serfdom. For Russia it has been said that before 1550 the peasants were free men, a hundred years later they were serfs. A similar process took place in Poland and Lithuania. The gap between rich and poor widened.

Then secondly, as ever, one effect of inflation on incomes was a redistributive effect. In the developing parts of Europe the upward movement of prices together with the expansion of commercial activity served to enhance the income of the commercial classes – merchants, industrialists and landowners – who by the end of the period began to challenge in wealth the lower reaches of the aristocracy.

But the shape of the wealth pyramid varied from country to country. The poor are always with us but by the end of the seventeenth century, England was distinguished from the societies of the continent by the large part of the national income which accrued to people with moderate incomes. In the other developing parts of western Europe there may also have been some narrowing of social distance. By and large, however, the European situation between 1500 and 1750 was that purchasing power was concentrated in the hands of a wealthy few who were able to direct a high proportion of surplus resources to meet their ambitions for conspicuous consumption or other ends. And by contrast the great majority of the population had extremely limited purchasing power which was used almost entirely to meet their immediate basic needs for food, clothing and shelter.

The third question is the division of income between the public and the private sectors. To assess this, little information is available. For England at the end of the seventeenth century, Gregory King suggested that private consumption of goods and services amounted to about 91 per cent of total demand, government consumption of goods and services to between 4 and 5 per cent and domestic capital formation to between 3 and 4 per cent. In the following table are to be found estimates for consumption, taxes and saving per head in three west European countries, England, France and Holland, in 1688 and 1695. These suggest that in 1688 England had a relatively high level of consumption and a relatively low rate of taxation compared with either France or Holland and a relatively low rate of capital accumulation compared with Holland. As a result of war, by 1695 all three countries had increased their rate of taxation and reduced their levels of saving and consump-

TABLE 2: Estimates of consumption, taxes and saving per head of the population, 1688 and 1695

	England 1688 £	s	d	England 1695 £	s	d	France 1688 £	s	d	France 1695 £	s	d	Holland 1688 £	s	d	Holland 1695 £	s	d
Consumption	7	4	0	7	3	0	5	0	9	4	18	2	5	0	0	4	13	9
Taxes[1]		7	3	1	4	0		15	0	1	5	0	2	3	2	3	1	7
Saving[2]		6	8		−11	0		7	0		−8	10		18	4		7	7
	7	18	0	7	16	0	6	3	0	5	18	0	8	1	4	8	2	9

[1]Including local government taxation, the English average would be in the region of 10s per annum.

[2]King sets off poor relief against total savings by the private sector in arriving at these estimates of net saving per head. His estimated total saving in England, ie before netting out poor relief, amounts to about 8s 9d per head.

Source: Phyllis Deane, 'The implications of early national income estimates for the measurement of long-term economic growth in the United Kingdom', *Economic Development and Cultural Change*, IV (1955-6), 12, derived from King, *Natural and political observations*, p. 55.

tion.[5] No doubt two propositions which can be derived from this table – first, that public expenditure formed only a small proportion of total expenditure and, secondly, that public expenditure was higher in times of war than in times of peace – were more generally true of European countries in the early modern period.

POPULATION AND URBANISATION

Basic to a consideration of our subject is the demographic picture. Although there is still some argument about details, the consensus of opinion now suggests that after the serious check in the later middle ages, European population grew in the sixteenth century from about 82 million in 1500 to 105 million or so in 1600 and reached a peak in the early seventeenth century. Then the Malthusian dragon roamed the land and war, famine and plague brought about a check to the growth of European population. Despite a recovery in most parts of Europe in the later seventeenth century, European population had only reached a figure of about 115 million in 1700. Thus whereas the most recent

5. Phyllis Deane, 'The implications of early national income estimates for the measurement of long-term economic growth in the United Kingdom', *Economic Development and Cultural Change*, IV (1955-6), pp. 11-12.

scholarship suggests that there was a 25 per cent increase in European population in the sixteenth century, the comparable change in the seventeenth century was only 15 per cent. Thereafter growth was more rapid and by the middle of the eighteenth century about 140-150 million people were living in Europe. In these two and a half centuries the overall picture is that European population approximately doubled and for much of the time it was pressing severely on resources.

Then there was the geographical distribution of the population. In the overall picture of growth the population of some countries of Europe grew less rapidly than that of other areas. Growth appears to have been general in the sixteenth century but in the seventeenth century the population of Spain and Portugal declined while that of Italy, Germany and probably the Balkans stagnated. Between 1660 and the end of our period the population of regions such as Languedoc also declined. Accompanying the broad picture of demographic expansion was the greater mobility of the population. The outstanding development was on the urban scene. These two centuries and a half saw the growth of cities to a new order of magnitude. London, which by 1600 John Stow called a great wen, grew from 50,000 to half a million and the rise of metropolitan centres could be seen elsewhere in Europe. Whereas in 1500 there were only four cities (Paris, Milan, Naples and Venice) with populations over 100,000, by 1700 there were eight such cities (Rome, Venice, Milan, Madrid, Lisbon, Vienna, Seville and Palermo) with populations between 100-200,000, two (Naples and Amsterdam) with between 200-100,000 and another two (London and Paris) with populations in excess of 400,000. And urban growth continued in the eighteenth century with the large cities becoming notably larger.

The growth of towns was a response to the expansion of old purposes as well as the growth of new demands. Towns developed as ports, as markets, as manufacturing or mining centres, as the seat of secular governments or of ecclesiastical princes. But there were significant developments between

1500 and 1750 and particularly after 1600. First there was the growth of many cities and towns, but particularly those performing a metropolitan function, as centres of conspicuous consumption. The creation of an active and civilised social life with assembly rooms, theatres, opera houses, pleasure gardens and other places of recreation and entertainment was a feature of these years. Then there was the beginnings of the spa town or seaside resort. And finally there was the rise of fortress towns as in eastern France and Sweden and the establishment of naval bases such as Brest, Lorient, Rochefort and Devonport (Plymouth).

With the expansion of the towns to their new order of magnitude came a changing pattern of urban demand. Food supplies, for example, could no longer be obtained with relative ease from the surrounding countryside; they had to be organised with great deliberation from further afield. Best documented is the growth of the London food market, which already by the end of the sixteenth century had stretched its tentacles of demand widely through England, but market gardening also developed around Paris and other large European cities. The provision of some commodities had to be done on a larger scale. Before the end of the seventeenth century large town dairies had developed in London with as many as 300 cows in one dairy to meet the metropolitan demand. In other directions the growth of towns with a mixed population gave rise to a more varied and cosmopolitan demand for goods and services. The provision of water and the disposal of refuse and excrement, human and animal, also posed new problems and their inefficient solution made the early modern towns great killers of people. But the growth of the towns was not only a consequence of the widening range of functions they performed; it also reflected problems in the countryside. Excess population, sometimes forced off the land by changes in tenure and farming, moved into the towns in search of employment and shelter. A minimum of subsistence, whether by employment or charity, appeared to have been more easily obtained both in normal times and in emergencies in the towns than in the countryside.

And in the towns people usually had greater safety from the periodic wars and uprisings of these years.

THE ARTICULATION OF THE MARKET

For demand to be effective, the appropriate instruments must be available. One of the clichés of economic history is the rise of the money economy but this development was particularly influential in the early modern period. The deficiencies of a barter economy are commonly recognised since the difficulties in achieving a coincidence of wants places a serious brake on effective demand. While barter still prevailed in parts of Europe, as in Beauvais in the seventeenth century, in most of the developing sectors of Europe a money economy became more fully developed. It was the virus which, Tawney argued, led to the European economy incurring the disease of capitalism. Money came to be used for a growing range of payments, customary obligations to perform services in kind came to be replaced by money payments and facilities for credit transactions developed. Merchants' drafts, letters of credit and bills of exchange came to be more widely accepted and the volume of credit trading grew. But price determination did not become fully rational, the notion of the 'just price' persisted and, as in underdeveloped countries today, a good deal of haggling on a personal basis went on.

Then there were improvements in distribution. For perishable commodities the market, held weekly or more frequently depending on the size of the area and the volume of trade, performed an important function. Held more infrequently, the fairs provided a way of breaking into the ordinarily closed and inward-looking regional economies and helped towards the establishment of a national or even international market. But here there was change: while a number of fairs continued to serve a regional or national function, the growth of business at Antwerp transformed the fair from a twice-yearly event to almost continuous session by the middle of the sixteenth century. But the effectiveness of trading there was cut short by war which also greatly reduced the importance of the Lyons fair in the following decades. Frankfurt then was of importance until 1648 when Leipzig replaced it, while trading at Novgorod grew. With the growing volume of trade in western Europe came the need for more regular arrangements so that fairs declined in importance as markets, except for particular purposes such as the sale of cloth, while their role as places of entertainment became more obvious. The major cities, whether London, Paris, Lyons or Nantes, came to fulfil the function of permanent fairs. Trading was then carried on more directly between merchants, their factors and agents. Wholesale trading, particularly for food, moved from the market place to the closed market, whether the warehouse, the corn exchange or the inn. To meet such needs, many hostelries in England, for example, were extended in the seventeenth and eighteenth centuries. At the same time the number of alehouses increased to cater for the growing traffic in livestock. For particular goods, commodity exchanges grew up and sale by sample rather than by complete consignment became accepted as a preferable way to trade in homogeneous commodities such as grain or cloth. Military provisioning went a stage further by adopting the contract system. Particularly in foreign trade, the auction sale, a transitional form between the intermittent fair and regular wholesaling, was used for the disposal of goods. By the eighteenth century auctions were established practice in the major trading centres such as Amsterdam, Copenhagen, Hamburg, Leipzig and London. These factors tended to lead to the decline of the smaller trading centres and to the concentration of dealings in larger towns. As the period wore on, the scale of wholesaling increased and became more complex and the numbers of factors and middlemen proliferated. As they did so they specialised by function, becoming known as coal merchants, Hamburg merchants, Carolina merchants or East India merchants. At the same time the wholesaler or 'mere merchant' became clearly differentiated from the retailers. As Defoe reported in 1727, retailers in the provinces no longer buy their goods of the manufacturer, 'they correspond with the wholesale dealers in London, where there are particular shops or warehouses for all these'.

The increase in the range of consumer goods, the development of wholesaling and the spread in the use of money had two effects on retailing. First, it led to the development of the shop. In this process of evolution, the seventeenth century was a crucial period with consumers, notably in western Europe, feeling a new authority in their purses and a new confidence in the exercise of choice, beginning to be wooed by retailers. Specialisation of shops also gained ground, first in the great cities of Europe (and in London earlier than in Paris) and later in the smaller towns. But customers still loved to see the master face to face in the shops. More attention was paid to decoration and display and by the eighteenth century shops came to be found in the more elegant parts of the major European cities. Meanwhile peddling increased in significance, particularly for the tea trade, small hardware, watches, glass, millinery and textile goods. Peddlers, the milliners of farmers' wives, helped to develop a demand for new goods in the remoter parts of Europe.

Postal services were improved. Venice had had a postal system since 1300 and state postal services appeared in Spain, France and England at the end of the fifteenth century. By the beginning of the seventeenth century the principal towns of Europe were connected, though not always directly, by a mail service. A private messenger service became available in Paris in 1653 and in London in 1685. And with growing facilities came greater speed and frequency. In the fifteenth century a letter took from 18 to 22 days from Genoa to Paris. A century later one from Antwerp to Amsterdam took 3 to 9 days while in 1666 the estimated speed of mail in England was 3 to 4 miles an hour. But at the same time the cost remained high. In England, by the tariff of 1657 letters were carried within a radius of eighty miles from London for 8d an ounce, to Scotland for 1s to 1s 6d an ounce, to Constantinople for 3s 9d and to Stockholm and Copenhagen for 4s an ounce. From the late 1620s two couriers set out from Paris every week for Lyons, Dijon, Bordeaux and Toulouse. In the later seventeenth century there was a daily service between London and the coast.

The methods of commercial intelligence were also improved. The Strasburg *Zeitung* appeared in 1609. In England the first newspapers were established in London in the seventeenth century while the early years of the eighteenth saw the foundations of a provincial press, first in Norwich and soon after in Bristol, Exeter and elsewhere. By 1753 it was estimated that the total sale of newspapers in Europe had reached over 7 million. Notably the development of the newspaper provided both a means of commercial information and of advertisement. To take just but one example, once the 'Letter from London' in the *Kentish Post* gave a hint of shortage of barley in the capital, some of the crop would move coastwards to the waiting ships on its way to the metropolis.[6] And an enormous range of goods and services was advertised in the seventeenth- and eighteenth-century newspapers. An analysis of the *London Gazette* shows that houses could be purchased, leased and furnished, books and musical instruments bought, food obtained, remedies for ills made available and many other articles and services obtained.[7] In some cases newspaper offices acted as information bureaux. Calendars also came to be published which gave information about fairs: and directories whose main purpose was to provide commercial intelligence. Printed bills of advertisements also appeared in London in the seventeenth century and in France by the early eighteenth century. Market lists began to be published and 'Prices current', as these sheets came to be known, were offered for sale in London and Amsterdam before 1700. But these aids to knowledge which stimulated competition were not universally approved. In 1745 the

6. See Dennis Baker, 'The marketing of corn in the first half of the eighteenth century: north-east Kent', *Agricultural History Review*, XVIII (1970), p. 133.

7. See Harold C. Whitford, 'Expos'd to sale: the marketing of goods and services in seventeenth-century England as revealed by advertisements in contemporary newspapers and periodicals', *Bulletin of the New York Public Library*, LXXI (1967), pp. 496-515, 603-13.

Compleat English tradesman complained that 'this underselling practice is grown to such a shameful height that particular persons publicly advertise that they undersell the rest of the trade' and advertising was regarded as 'mean and shameful'.

In general, however, improvements in transport were comparatively limited. Throughout this period the advent of winter slowed down and disrupted traffic or brought it to a halt. Roads were often impassable and seas hostile. Sea or river carriage was cheaper, more comfortable and often quicker and safer than by land. Overland transport was often exorbitantly expensive, particularly for bulky goods. In the sixteenth century a last of grain could easily double in price between Cracow and Vilna. There were the same boats, the same pack animals, the same vehicles and so neither by water nor by land was there much increase in speed though there was a marked increase in the volume of traffic. In the sixteenth century, it normally took 10 days by road from Venice to Brussels, 12 from Venice to Paris, 24 from Venice to London and over a month from Venice to Constantinople. In the seventeenth and early eighteenth centuries there was some improvement of roads, particularly in France, a few canals were built and some ports were improved. The 18 lighthouses existing in west European waters in the sixteenth century were augmented by 35 in the following hundred years and by a further 29 by 1750. For those who travelled by land there were improvements in staging facilities for horses, coaches became slightly more comfortable and a growing number of inns and hotels catered for the traveller whether on pleasure or business.

But as late as 1750 there were still important restraints on the articulation of the market. A money economy had not yet been fully established, there were a variety of weights and measures, there were considerable transport difficulties, there were still a multitude of states in Europe and local tolls within countries provided a limitation on the free movement of goods as did tariffs between countries. Purchasing power was still concentrated in the hands of a small minority and demand was still largely for goods unmade. As yet manufacturers were by and large unable to anticipate demand.

FASHION AND SOCIAL CUSTOM

The popular market for food, drink, clothing and shelter was not greatly affected by fashion though tides of taste which lapped at the coasts of demand for these goods did not ebb and flow without leaving their mark. The degree to which consumer tastes are socially determined is often ignored. Over the two centuries and a half, for example, there was some slight shift in the consumption of beverages: tea, beer and spirits made ground in some countries. Not only the style of noble houses, castles and châteaux was affected by fashion but so were the dwellings of the urban middle class, the merchant or professional man and the wealthier farmers in the countryside. The rebuilding of farmhouses to separate man from beast and to give greater privacy to the individual owed something to function and efficiency but not a little to fashion. Furniture, too, was to some extent involved.

But clothes were most vulnerable to the fickle jade of fashion. Monarchs, princes and their wives, dukes and duchesses, set the pace in this pursuit of the ephemeral. These two hundred and fifty years were the apotheosis of conspicuous display by the rich as wigs soared to dizzy altitudes and clothes reached new heights of extravagant display. In the sixteenth century Spanish influence affected fashions. Though in England Elizabeth I had an extensive wardrobe, in general women's fashions were slow to change. But men sought to emulate the dress of the victorious soldiery, first the Swiss and then the Spanish. One innovation, the knitted stocking, spread from England. From about 1630, however, largely as a result of urbanisation and particularly the growth of large cities such as Paris and London and the emergence of a bourgeois society, fashion affected women's dress more quickly. There was a move against Spanish fashion and by the mid-century the leadership had passed to France. There was a reaction against the sixteenth-century stiffness of dress and an elaboration of clothes, wigs and hats. A sharper differentiation between male and female attire occurred. The increased mobility of certain groups of European society, soldiers, financiers, diplomats, merchants and artists, provided a means of dissemination of the new fashions. But other more deliberate means were also adopted. From 1680 dolls dressed in the latest style were sent from Paris to the main capitals of Europe from London to St Petersburg. Also influential were the French fashion magazines, the earliest of which, the *Mercure Galant*, was founded in 1672. Arbiters of fashion, like Beau Nash, also were of some effect. The excesses of the rich did not pass unnoticed and function was of some significance lower down the social scale. Nevertheless, service in a household of high social standing must have helped to create, especially amongst women, a standard-conscious group. A market in second-hand clothes also developed. And there was some interaction between classes. While some fashions were transmitted downwards, the long-run movement had already started by which the sports clothes or working clothes of one generation became the formal clothes of the next. In 1739 the *Gentleman's Magazine* scornfully reported that it had become fashionable for men to dress 'like Stage-Coachmen, Jockeys, and Pick-Pockets'. And amongst women, prostitutes and mistresses were commonly amongst the most fashionable and even the initiators of fashion. By the mid-eighteenth century, the absurd but fruitful notion was entrenched that 'one had as good be out of the world as out of fashion'.

Resistance to the tides of fashion came from custom, nationalism and religion. 'If the inconstancy of modes shortens the term of consumption of certain articles, the taste of the beautiful in the arts', it has been said, 'prolongs that of some others.' Custom, as evidenced in costume, uniform or livery, may withstand change for centuries. Of this the English beefeaters or the Vatican guards provide illustrations. In England in the days of the first Elizabeth, every street 'from the Tower to Westminster alonge' was full of French and Italian shops displaying goods 'able to make any temperate man to gaze on them and to buy somewhat, though it serve to no purpose necessarie'. And more than a century later Defoe wrote 'Tis better for England that we should all drink turnip wine or any wine than that we should drink the best wine in Europe and go back to France for it'. To ape the French was not only improvident but also unpatriotic.

As a counterblast to the siren calls of fashion, the ethical preaching of the Protestants against conspicuous display had in some circles a limited degree of success. The Quakers and some other nonconformists in England became renowned for their sober mode of dress and their disdain for ostentatious display. And from the sixteenth to the eighteenth centuries economists inveighed against luxuries. As Heckscher has argued, at the heart of the discussions about the role that the state should play in economic matters in early modern Europe was the conflict between the notions of power and notions of plenty.[8]

But what effect did such exhortations have on the pattern of demand? Did restraint provide the source of investment funds and in consequence lead to claims on capital rather than current account? To what extent did fasting impose a curb on avaricious appetites? The religious and social context of demand deserves fuller consideration than it has so far received. Further, to what extent were there variations in different parts of Europe?

Nor should attention entirely concentrate on the provision of goods and services. The Puritan doctrine of work was a pervasive and persuasive one but the leisure preferences of the aristocracy were not seriously inhibited by such teachings. Moreover, low wage levels and irregular work patterns did not encourage application. Much later the creation of a disciplined regular work force had to meet the challenge of Saint Monday. When the range of goods and services was limited, more leisure might indeed seem preferable to more income from more work.

8. See Eli F. Heckscher, *Mercantilism* (revised ed. 2 vols., Allen & Unwin, 1955).

THE STATE AND CORPORATE DEMAND

But total demand was not just a summation of the needs of individual consumers, it also had an institutional component. The forms of social organisation which Europeans established, their governmental arrangements, their religious denominations, their economic and social organisations also exercised a claim, albeit small, on resources. Most important of all in these years was the growth of the national state and the emergence of the concept of absolute monarchy. Rulers and their ministers, officials and parliaments had to be provided with appropriate buildings and coronations and royal weddings as well as the pomp and ceremony of government were surrounded by a blaze of aristocratic display. In 1542 the luxury expenditure of the king of France amounted to 3.275 million livres and under Louis XIV to 28.8 million livres. Diplomatic occasions such as the Field of the Cloth of Gold also provided opportunities for conspicuous expenditure. The costs of administration and of justice had also to be met and a small amount was spent on local government.

The heaviest if intermittent example of the changing scale and character of public expenditure came with the institutionalisation of war. Between the late sixteenth and the first decade of the eighteenth century, expenditure by the English crown in time of war rose from £500-600,000 to £6 million a year, of which two-thirds was military expenditure. From being a casual and spasmodic business, war grew in scale and increased in complexity. So its demand on resources – on food and equipment – expanded. Standing armies and navies were established, the number of men under arms increased and their demands for equipment grew. Fortifications, barracks and dockyards were built, warships grew in size, uniforms, weapons and supplies were required on a hitherto unprecedented scale. From the sixteenth century attempts were made to supply standard weapons; uniform clothing for soldiers emerged in the following century; and appropriate organisations were created for supplies and billeting. It was the Spanish government which first developed a system of providing food and shelter for troops through government functionaries, quartermaster or *servis*, instead of leaving such matters to the individual soldier. And war also provided a stimulus to the advance of technology.

Then legislative action by governments affects consumption. To a slight degree legal restraints affected the pattern of demand. Sumptuary laws were frequently passed to restrict competitive emulation. After 1604 England had no formal clothing ordinances though under the woollen acts the dead had to be buried in woollen cloth. But many other European countries had sumptuary legislation until late in the eighteenth century. Governments attempted to control expenditure and consumption for varied motives: to encourage savings or domestic industry, to maintain class distinctions, to prevent the moral decline it was alleged to induce, to strengthen the balance of payments or for fear of things foreign. In the sixteenth century the city governments of Basle, Berne and Zürich went as far as to prescribe the length of certain garments, the number of flounces, the length of shoe points or the height of bonnets. And sometimes such legislation extended beyond clothes. In eighteenth-century Venice, to prevent rivalry and so safeguard public order, it was ordained that gondolas could only be painted and upholstered in black and as a result wedding processions no longer swept down the Grand Canal in a line of decorated gondolas, christenings were less splendid but funerals remained as stately as ever. Such laws were fitfully enforced and were eroded by the growth in wealth and political importance of a widening section of the population. Although often disregarded, in some cases this legislation was of economic importance. The clothing ordinances of Sully and Colbert, for example, helped to foster the manufacture of luxury goods in France and were a factor in making Paris the centre of European fashion in the seventeenth century. Colbert himself commented 'fashion is to France what gold mines are to the Spaniard'.

More important were tolls and taxes which affected

patterns of expenditure by raising the price of the goods involved relative to others. A particular instance was the English differential tariff on Portuguese and French wines which served to increase the consumption of port in England to the detriment of French wines. How far internal taxation affected the pattern of demand is not a question to which historians have turned their attention though sometimes duties were used to restrict consumption. Moreover, it should be noted that indirect taxes are usually regressive in effect. When imposed on goods widely consumed, they limited the purchasing power, particularly of the poorer classes. In some countries attempts were made to discourage the importation of luxuries by placing heavy duties on them.

Since competition was often limited in practice and it was felt necessary to control the activities of middlemen, in a number of instances the government attempted to protect the consumer. The first method was control of marketing. As the staple diet of the people and vulnerable, given free market operation, to considerable fluctuations in price, bread was often subject to control by government. The price of beer was also supervised in England and attempts were made to regulate the foreign trade in corn in the interests of consumers and to control the activities of middlemen in both home and foreign trade. Local authorities also sought to control prices. In 1549, for example, the Court of Aldermen of the city of London ordained that certain commoners should be appointed 'to peruse the flesshe shambles and fish market weekly . . . that the people may have reasonable penniworthes for their money'. A second method of consumer protection was to control methods of manufacture. In England efforts to control the production of tanned leather and footwear continued until 1604 but fell into disuse later that century. Controls on textile manufacture, however, were longer lived. In a series of acts in 1708, 1725 and 1738 the government tried to impose regulations on the manufacture of woollens and worsteds in Yorkshire. Licences were yet another method employed to control manufacture.

Governmental action was also important in other directions: in checking the monopolistic activities of gilds, in imposing limits on usurious transactions, in encouraging industry and improving transport facilities. To provide the cloth, weapons, powder and ships and to make his country independent of imports, Peter the Great 'formed the determination to have all the factories in his own state which were necessary for the army, the artillery and the fleet'. The attempts of the French crown under Louis XIV to develop manufactures such as the Gobelins tapestry works and the Sèvres porcelain works are but two examples while government assistance in the construction of roads and bridges was of some significance in a number of European countries. Then governments also influenced the market for labour by enacting wage regulations. In order to employ the able-bodied poor, both municipal authorities and governments provided stocks of materials or inaugurated workhouses. Forced labour was used in some circumstances. And countries competed for skilled labour to develop new industries or processes.

While the state grew in power, the church though challenged was not without importance. Churches, cathedrals and other ecclesiastical buildings were erected and through alms and bequests a proportion of European purchasing power was diverted to expand the financial resources of the church. Gilds and trading companies also exerted their claims on both capital and current account while corporate forms emerged in industry as well as in trade and need to be considered. This said, what was the effect of such institutional claims on the pattern of demand? To what extent were such corporate needs met at the expense of individual demand? Was expenditure on war at the expense of civilian consumption? Was the wealth of the church a reciprocal of the poverty of the faithful? Or did the mobilisation of demand in such ways provide a stimulus to production and lead to a wider generation of income which in its turn was reflected in more widely diffused demand? Did corporate demand have a beneficial multiplier effect or not? In the present state of knowledge, alas, such questions are easier to pose than to answer.

THE COMPONENTS OF DEMAND

The components of private and of public demand will be considered separately. Of private demand there were five components: food, clothing and shelter were of importance for all: and beyond that some had a surplus for conspicuous consumption, for luxuries, for personal services, for entertainment, for education and for travel: and some were able to save, hoard or invest. More recent discussions seem to confirm Engel's law that the proportion of income spent on food falls as income rises. Since a substantial proportion of the population of Europe had little in the way of money income in this period it is difficult to allocate expenditure. Though there were changes, by far the greater number of the inhabitants of early modern Europe were poor. Family budgets are lacking but Phelps Brown has done some calculations for England and for France, which, although they may be little better than well-informed guesses, suggest that 80 per cent of the income of the poor was spent on food, 10 per cent on clothing and approximately 10 per cent on housing, furnishings, etc and so they had virtually no surplus available for other expenditure.[9] Both the consumption and capital aspects of institutional demand will also be considered.

FOOD

While Adam Smith held that 'the desire of food is limited in every man by the narrow capacity of the human stomach' and varies in quality rather than quantity, such a view underestimates the range of consumption in the early

9. Ernest H. Phelps Brown and Sheila V. Hopkins, 'Seven centuries of the price of consumables compared with builders' wage-rates', *Economica*, new series, XXIII (1956), p. 297; 'Wage-rates and prices: evidence for population pressure in the sixteenth century', *Economica*, new series, XXIV (1957), p. 293.

modern period. Although the thesis of low income elasticity for food can be accepted in general terms, there were times in Europe in the sixteenth and seventeenth centuries when the gluttony of the rich provided a marked contrast to the restricted dietaries of the poor. The dominant fact about food supplies was that they were extremely variable over time, between places and between classes. In the normal run of events the plenty of the harvest home gave way in due course to the short commons of the spring. Lent was as much an economic necessity as a religious obligation. Those – perhaps the minority – for whom the rotting meat of winter had been made more palatable by a lavish addition of spices needed little compulsion to restrict their diet of fish in March while the majority eked out their dwindling supplies of grain till the new harvest. As feasts punctuated with gluttony the tedium of a more restricted dietary, so fasts gave official sanction to curbs on consumption which would nonetheless have been necessary. Good harvests ensured a prospect of reasonable food supplies through the winter: bad harvests meant stringency and malnutrition for many and starvation for some.

Food supplies were further affected by a secular climatic trend which was responsible, as a colder period set in, for a series of poor harvests between the second half of the sixteenth and the first half of the eighteenth century, altogether about fifty years being affected. The growth of towns and money incomes in them provided a stimulus to agricultural specialisation. The market gardens surrounding Amsterdam were famous by the fifteenth century; the influence of the London food market on English agriculture in the sixteenth and seventeenth centuries has been described in some detail and the impact of other urban areas, such as Paris, on their hinterland resulted in the extension of market gardening. Further, the effect of harvest failure began to be offset to some extent by the expansion of European commerce and shipping which facilitated the movement of grain between areas of plenty and scarcity.

In the long run the pressure of population still threatened

to outstrip food resources in Malthusian fashion and had an influence on dietaries. Although all the evidence does not point in the same direction, for much of Europe in the late sixteenth and early seventeenth centuries the food situation appears to have become more acute. If food budgets from the sixteenth century are compared with those of the seventeenth, an unmistakable decline appears. The average decrease in per capita food consumption has been estimated at one-third. And the general trend was punctuated by years of abundant harvest and years of famine. In England, from whence had come reports of how well people fed in the early sixteenth century, come complaints that the poor now had to eat black bread. In 1590-1 famine occurred in Italy, Spain and parts of France. In the Udine cheaper maize, which became the staple food of the poor, appeared in official price lists from 1622. And in Sweden, it has been argued, the peasants fared less well. Whereas in the manor of Gripsholm in 1555 daily consumption of calories had amounted to 4166 calories per head, in the years 1638, 1653 and 1661 it amounted to only 2480, 2883 and 2920 calories respectively although in composition the diet remained almost exactly what it had been a century earlier.

Experience in the later seventeenth century is contradictory. Conditions in Beauvais worsened in these years as they appear to have done in Italy, Poland, Sweden and Finland. As late as the last decade of the seventeenth century the great famine of 1693-4 brought heavy mortality in France; in one Finnish province one-third of the population died in the great famine of 1696-7 and in 1698, after a serious crop failure, death rates in Sweden rose to 9 and 16 per cent in certain provinces. In the Udine mixtures of grains and pulses – a sign of distress – were officially quoted. Death and starvation in this decade stalked the land from the Mediterranean to the Baltic, from Scotland to Austria. In England, however, with improving agriculture and slackening population growth, dietaries improved. By 1698 Charles Davenant held that 'there is no country in the world where the inferior rank of men were better . . . fed' than in England.[10] Thus food supplies not only varied over time but also from place to place.

In the early eighteenth century slackening population growth relieved the pressure on food supplies. But still there were years of difficulty. The exceptionally long and hard winter of 1708-9 caused widespread crop failures which led to serious famine in France and less disastrous shortages in other countries; harvest failures in Beauvais in 1725 caused localised hardship, there were food shortages in Silesia in 1730 and the Scandinavian countries suffered a subsistence crisis in 1737-43. The seriousness of these harvest failures and shortages of foodstuffs, however, was reduced by the growing trade within Europe and with the rest of the world which meant that no area was entirely dependent upon its own output. Although famine continued to threaten the people of Europe into the nineteenth century, by the mid-eighteenth century it was no longer the scourge it had been in earlier centuries.

Throughout this period, the dietary of the poor was predominantly grain-based though the grains consumed varied. Rye was predominant in northern Europe, wheat was much grown in southern Europe, while in England barley, used for beer as well as bread, was the chief cereal crop. In many parts of Europe wheaten bread was what the gentry ate and other people as they prospered. In some countries, as in France, Italy and Spain, wheat was often mixed with other grains while in eastern Europe, which became the granary of the continent at this time, the peasant producer himself ate rye bread and the nobles did not always have white bread at their tables. In the same way the farmers of Provence sold the wheat they grew and themselves consumed inferior wheat from the Levant or Barbary. In England Harrison reported in 1577 that:

'The bread throughout the land is made of such grain as the soil yieldeth; nevertheless *the gentility commonly provide themselves sufficiently of wheat for their own table*, whilst their

10. *Discourses on the publick revenues* cited in Jack C. Drummond and Anne Wilbraham, *The Englishman's food: five centuries of English diet* (revised ed. Cape, 1957), p. 101.

household and poor neighbours are forced to content themselves with rye or barley, yea and, in times of dearth, many with bread made either of beans, peas or oats, or of all together and some acorns among.'[11]

Whiter wholemeal bread was commonly eaten in the towns in England, while in the countryside darker rye and brown flours were used although one distinguishing feature between the yeoman and the husbandman was said to be the former's consumption of white bread. In 1665 captured Dutch seamen imprisoned in Chelsea College, London, complained that the bread they were given was too fine and they wanted to have coarser loaves more like those they were accustomed to at home.

As there were class differences in bread consumption, so there were changes over time. In England, with the agricultural inprovements from the later seventeenth century, there came a marked shift in the relative importance of bread grains. In the 1690s Gregory King estimated that wheat accounted for 38 per cent, rye for 27 per cent, barley for 19 per cent and oats for 16 per cent of the bread grain used in England whereas according to Charles Smith (*Tracts on the corn trade*, 1764) wheat had sharply increased in importance to furnish the bread corn for 62.5 per cent of the population, rye of 14.8 per cent, barley of 12.3 per cent and oats of 10.4 per cent.[12] At the same time regional differences persisted. Broadly speaking, more wheat was eaten in southern England than in northern and in Scotland oats remained the staple into the nineteenth century. If the evidence of the Sound Tolls, which show a rising proportion of wheat in relation to rye exported from eastern Europe in the seventeenth century, can be relied on, this same phenomenon of white bread must also have occurred in other parts of Europe.

If cereals dominated the dietary of early modern Europe, meat was less important and its consumption appears to have declined since, for a number of reasons, meat produc-

11. Cited in William Ashley, *The bread of our forefathers: an inquiry in economic history* (Oxford: Clarendon Press, 1928), p. 58.

12. *Ibid.*, p. 8.

tion did not keep pace with demand. The conquest of Hungary by the Turks cut off a meat-producing area, the growth of towns prevented townsmen keeping as many pigs as they had previously done, the shrinkage of oak and beech forests caused a decline of pig keeping in some parts of Europe while on some grassland it became more profitable to keep horses. Further, the pressure of population led to the conversion of land from pasture to arable to meet the growing demands for grain. Such trends were not equally apparent, however, throughout Europe and again there were regional differences. But the consequence was that less meat was eaten per head in these years, a trend which appears to have been part of a long decline from the fifteenth to the eighteenth century. In the German towns, according to Abel, the yearly consumption of meat declined from an average of 100 kilograms or more per person (a sort of biological maximum) in the fifteenth century to not more than 14 kilograms per person in the nineteenth. What was true of Germany, Braudel and Spooner assert, was sooner or later true, to a lesser or greater degree, of other parts of Europe.[13] Yet there were exceptions. Visitors to England commented that the more substantial English peasant ate a great deal of meat, particularly mutton and beef, and were surprised at the large numbers of butchers' shops in the towns. In 1598 Otto Hentzner wrote that the English ate less bread but more meat than the French but even here the rise in prices in the second half of the sixteenth century caused complaints of a decline in meat consumption. Bacon remained widely available and brawn was a popular dish. The workers in the town seem to have eaten more meat than the rural poor. Much meat was dried or salted in order to preserve it. Of a total meat consumption of 101.6 kg per head among the inhabitants of royal castles and estates in Sweden in 1573, 99 kg was dried and salted.

13. Fernand P. Braudel and Frank Spooner, 'Prices in Europe from 1450 to 1750' in Edwin E. Rich and Charles H. Wilson, ed. *The Cambridge economic history of Europe*, vol. IV. *The economy of expanding Europe in the sixteenth and seventeenth centuries* (Cambridge UP, 1967), p. 414.

One way to make the best of the meat and other food available is to make it into soup and this seems to have been a popular dish. In 1542 Andrew Boorde said that 'potage is not so moch used in al Crystendom as it is used in Englande' and it has also played a part in the dietaries of other countries, in some cases remaining a traditional dish to the present day. The national dish of Venice, a soup made from the sea-louse, a kind of mussel found in the lagoon, was bought ready-made from those who specialised in its preparation. In the sixteenth and seventeenth centuries many unemployed and vagrants in Spain lived on the soup provided by convents and broth or potage features frequently in institutional diets.

In many parts of Europe fish from river, lake or sea played an important part in the dietary although its market was restricted because it was very perishable and could only be carried short distances. Fresh fish was therefore much less important than dried or salted fish. In the sixteenth century the London fishmongers dealt mainly in dried cod, haddock, pollack and ling from Norway and Iceland and salted and pickled herrings, cod, eels, whiting and mackerel from the east coast of England or Holland and the Baltic. Barcelona was supplied with Atlantic cod by Breton fishermen and with sardines and tunny from Africa via Portugal. During the sixteenth century the typical workman's midday meal there was said to consist of a chunk of bread, a herring and a head of garlic. As noted earlier, during certain religious seasons it was obligatory to eat fish and in England legislation aimed at encouraging the development of the navy ordained the consumption of fish on certain 'fish days' during the week. And as time wore on, a transatlantic supply of fish from Newfoundland helped to augment the dietaries not only of north-western but, since the Mediterranean fisheries provided only a modest yield, of southern Europe too.

The consumption of fruit and vegetables varied within the different regions of Europe and though limited everywhere, on the whole, was higher in southern than in northern Europe. In the later sixteenth century in England, writers commented on the rapid increase in the amount and variety of vegetables grown in both estate gardens and cottager's plots, many of them introduced from other parts of Europe, but the only vegetable which seems to have been widely eaten was the onion which was popular because its strong flavour helped to hide the tainted taste of stale meat. Cabbages were sometimes boiled with meat or soup. Seventeenth-century books mention the growth of cabbages, parsnips, carrots and other garden vegetables in England. Market gardening expanded, to some extent due to the imported skill of the Dutch who were growing lettuces and other salad plants for the Amsterdam market by the fifteenth century. In London, the famous fruit and vegetable market at Covent Garden was established about 1630. But the urban working class seem to have scorned vegetables which they considered the standby of the rural poor when times were hard. In France vegetables were more popular and were frequently eaten as a separate dish. In the eighteenth century, Venetians bought vegetables ready-cooked from itinerant greengrocers. By the first half of the eighteenth century they were also playing a more important role in the English diet. In 1751 it was reported of Nottingham that carrots, turnips, parsnips, cabbages, savoys and potatoes were 'immediate necessaries' for the working class and there were complaints of food dressed 'in the French style'. But vegetables were still an optional extra rather than a dish on their own, at least for the middle classes. In many parts of Europe the consumption of fruit was limited by a widespread belief that it was unhealthy and caused fevers. The quantity and variety of fruits available in England increased in the seventeenth century and to supplement supplies, orangeries and hothouses for exotic fruits were built by many landowners but fruit largely remained a luxury except in southern Europe where it was plentiful.

During this period the butter which was available was always very salt and often rancid and in a liquid state. Despite this there was a market for it in the towns of northern Europe in the sixteenth century and in the seventeenth century the amount consumed in English towns grew, spread on bread by the poor and used for cooking by the wealthy. In southern Europe, pork fat, lard or olive oil was used. Cheese formed an important part of the English farm labourer's diet in the sixteenth century and probably provided the only fat and protein in the meals of the poorest. It was also popular in other parts of Europe and there was an extensive trade, particularly in Dutch cheeses. On a Polish manor in 1560-70 the per capita daily consumption of dairy products was 100 grammes of cheese and 25 grammes of butter. In English towns the consumption of cheese grew during the seventeenth century due to the growth of cow herds on the enlarged country estates. But at the same time, the growth of a profitable urban market for dairy goods meant a decline in their consumption by the rural poor. The countryman may have had plentiful supplies of milk to drink, in some areas sheep's or goat's milk, but there was little demand for it in the towns. Many people considered whey a more healthy drink than milk. Eggs were cheap and in plentiful supply throughout Europe.

If fairly crude assumptions are made about the characteristics of diet, then four Europes can be discerned in this period. First, north-western Europe – Great Britain and Scandinavia – which had a high protein, low cereal diet; then southern Europe – Portugal, Spain, Italy and Greece – which had a predominantly cereal, low meat diet with olive oil, wine, goats and sheep: thirdly, in an intermediate position between north-western and southern Europe, was central Europe – France, Belgium, Germany and Austria – with a dietary which included porridge, beer, sausages and potatoes with medium reliance on meat and less cereal than southern Europe: and finally, eastern Europe – Poland, Russia, Rumania and Bulgaria – which, like southern Europe, had a low meat, high cereal dietary but the cereal base was different. Whereas southern Europe was predominantly wheat, eastern Europe relied on the hardier grains, oats and rye together with some maize.

For drink there were three Europes, of wine, of beer and

of spirits. The drinks commonly available, whether wine, beer, cider or spirits, were important as nourishment as well as stimulants since they provided some vitamins not otherwise available in the dietary. The least expensive calories the Polish peasant obtained in the eighteenth century were what he absorbed from grain liquor. All the evidence appears to point to an increase in the consumption of wine, beer and spirits between the fifteenth and the eighteenth centuries and there were changes in their distribution and popularity. The considerable quality of salt and spices used to make food palatable gave rise to an oceanic thirst and in many parts of Europe, notably in England, there was an increase in the numbers of inns and taverns. Wine ceased to be made in England at about the time of the dissolution of the monasteries as these were the last stronghold of the art in that country but it remained an important native and therefore mass drink in many continental European countries. In the middle of the sixteenth century the inhabitants of Valladolid consumed 100 litres of wine each per year. It was also imported for the use of the wealthy into those countries where it was not made. In England claret, burgundy and Rhenish were drunk with meals and afterwards large quantities of madeira and particularly port were consumed. All wine in this period had a short life and vintage wines do not appear until the eighteenth century.

Beer, and in some parts cider, was the drink of the mass of the population in Holland, England and other parts of northern Europe. Beer was largely home-brewed but in some countries, as in England, there was some restriction on its sale for which a licence was required and attempts to control its quality. In the sixteenth century the consumption of beer per head in Sweden was about forty times higher than today and in a Polish manor in 1560-70 the average daily consumption was 3 litres a head.

Probably the most notable aspect of the consumption of alcoholic drinks during this period was the rise of spirit-drinking. Spirits first appeared commercially in the sixteenth century and grew rapidly in popularity in the next two hundred years. In France, brandy was distilled from wine. Gin was introduced into Holland by German soldiers serving in the war of liberation against Spain and from thence it spread to England and Ireland. By 1621 there were 200 establishments distilling aquavita in the cities of London and Westminster and a Distillers Company, to maintain standards in the industry, was established in 1638. There was also a large importation of Dutch genever into England during the seventeenth century and this was encouraged at the end of the century by the accession of William of Orange to the English throne. In the following century, as Hogarth portrayed, gin-drinking became a social menace in England as cheap spirits, often made from very suspect ingredients, were available, it was said, at every fourth or fifth house in some of the worst slums. The consumption of dutiable spirits in England rose from half a million gallons in 1700 to over 5 million gallons in 1735 and more than 7 million gallons in 1751 and even this figure did not include the worst illicitly distilled spirits.

Apart from the shifting importance of bread cereals, the declining consumption of meat and the increased consumption of drink, there were other changes in the European dietary. Perhaps the most widespread change was the partial decerealisation of the dietary with the bean, the pea and the potato making their appearance. The potato first reached Spain from South America about 1570 and spread from there to Italy then to France and through Burgundy to Germany. It took many years before it became a field crop but by the mid-eighteenth century it was widely grown in Europe. As well as the potato, the effect of the growth of contacts between Europe and the wider world had other influences on food supplies. Maize was brought from the Americas to Europe at the beginning of the sixteenth century and spread through southern France, Italy and the Balkans but it made little headway in northern Europe where the climate was unfavourable. It was mostly eaten in the form of a porridge called *polenta* and was also used as cattle feed. Rice, known in Spain since the eighth century, was introduced into Italy in the sixteenth but its spread in Europe, particularly to satisfy the hunger of the poor, was severely limited by the growing conditions it required.

Tea, coffee and chocolate became fashionable drinks in many parts of Europe although their popularity varied from country to country. By the end of the seventeenth century in England, a light breakfast of coffee or chocolate and rolls had replaced the traditional heavy breakfast among the fashionable upper class. Tea was first brought to Europe from China by the Dutch East India Company in 1609. By 1636 it was drunk in Paris and the English East India Company was importing it by 1646. By the end of the seventeenth century its price had fallen considerably although it was still a luxury drink and was often taken for its medicinal properties. In 1689 about 20,000 lb were officially imported into England and legal imports remained at this level until 1700 and then rose rapidly. But there was also much illicit trade. The first retail shop specialising in tea was probably that opened by Twinings in 1713. In Italy, France and Germany, coffee was preferred to tea. Coffee was first harvested in Ethiopia in 1450. It reached Venice in about 1615 and Paris in 1643 and by the end of the century there were about 250 coffee houses in the latter city. In England the first coffee house was opened in Oxford in 1650 and it was quickly followed by similar establishments in London, Cambridge and other cities. Sweden first used coffee in the 1670s. Chocolate was brought from Mexico to Spain in 1520 and reached Flanders and Italy early in the next century. The first chocolate house in London was opened by a Frenchman in 1657.

As supplies from the East reduced its price, in England from 1s 6d at the beginning of the seventeenth century to 4d–6d at the end, the consumption of sugar grew. In 1700 English retained imports amounted to about 15,000 tons or an annual consumption of 5 lb per person. One reason for this increase was its use in the new hot drinks and its growing employment in cooking, particularly in pies, puddings and fruit tarts. Apart from Newfoundland fish the one addition to meat supplies from the new world was the turkey, introduced from Mexico about 1520, which had become common Christmas fare by the early seventeenth century.

In some countries, tobacco became the solace of all classes during this period. At first used for its supposed medicinal qualities, tobacco was grown in 'physic gardens' in western Europe in the first half of the sixteenth century and reached England about 1565. Its growth in Europe began in Spain and spread to Italy, the Balkans, Russia and England. But imports were more important than home production. By 1750 more than 50 million pounds a year were brought into Europe from north America. Originating in Portugal in the mid-sixteenth century, snuff-taking spread through Europe in the following decades.

From the foregoing account it can clearly be seen that as well as changes over time there were marked differences between countries and regions, between towns and the countryside, depending on the immediate availability of foodstuffs and the ability to supplement these supplies by trade. To some extent, too, custom and convention determined both the pattern of meals and the kinds of foodstuffs consumed. Contemporaries were certainly conscious of national and regional differences. According to a saying current in mid-seventeenth century England which may have contained an element of national pride: the Spaniard eats, the German drinks and the English exceed in both.

Class differences in food consumption were also marked. If the dietary of the poor was limited, monotonous and almost devoid of meat (unless they were able to keep a pig or obtain fish or meat by trapping or poaching), for the rich the situation was entirely different. Professor Stone has painted a vivid picture of the lavish way in which the English aristocracy fed, with boards groaning with a variety of meat, fish and game.[14] And of sixteenth-century Sweden, Heckscher has written that at court the sin of gluttony can scarcely ever have been absent. If Heckscher's calcula-

14. See Lawrence Stone, *The crisis of the aristocracy, 1558–1641* (Oxford: Clarendon Press, 1965), Appendix XXIV.

tions are to be accepted, those who fed at the royal court consumed 6400 calories a day, those at the court of the deposed king Eric, 6500 calories a day, while Duke Magnus and his court enjoyed 7400 calories a day[15] compared with today's norm of 3000-3300 calories per day. And such hospitality was enjoyed by a wide circle. But those who ate in this style inevitably paid the penalty. High mortality and poor health were certainly related to the gluttony of the age. But again there was change. As patronage of the arts and of music, the acquisition of books, the building of splendid houses and so on became a mode of life, as it was possible to signal one's wealth and standing in such ways, there was in some respects a decline in hospitality. While ostentation and gluttony continued, no longer was a person's wealth and position necessarily to be correlated with the size of his household or the amplitude of his table.

A last category of the demand for food was the institutional demand. And here there were two important changes. With the Reformation, the role of the church in ministering to the poor and indigent was checked in some countries but it continued in others and secular bodies for the relief of paupers were established. There were too the requirements of hospitals, schools and other institutions for food. If the case of the Collegio Borromeo in Pavia, where the meals provided 5000-7000 calories daily in 1609-18, is in any way typical, the diets in such institutions gave more than adequate nourishment: the real poor were those who got no such help. Cereals played an important part in the menus, 81 per cent of the food supplied to the hospital for incurables in Genoa and 58-63 per cent of the provisions of a hospital in Pavia, but this was a feature of all diets in this period. In 1588 the dietary of the Bury House of Correction in England provided two meals a day, each consisting of 8 oz rye bread, 1 pint of porridge, $\frac{1}{4}$ lb meat and 1 pint of beer. A hundred years later the daily allowance at St Bartholomew's Hospital was $1\frac{1}{2}$ oz cheese, 1 pint milk porridge, 4 oz beef or mutton, 1 pint

15. Eli F. Heckscher, *An economic history of Sweden* (Cambridge, Mass: Harvard UP, 1954), pp. 69-70.

broth, 1 oz butter, 10 oz bread and 3 pints beer. The children of Christ's Hospital received a similar diet in 1678. In the early sixteenth century soldiers lived off the country eating what they could get and armies were usually disbanded in the winter as food was not available. Navies, too, were only intermittently in commission. But in the following century the situation changed. Permanent camps and barracks were established and so victualling had to be arranged more systematically. Moreover, the numbers of hangers-on who moved around with the army further increased the numbers who had to be fed. Supplies came to be organised by traders and porters under the direction of state administration. The great increase in supply services in the hundred years preceding the War of the Austrian Succession was an important factor in industrial expansion from the midseventeenth century. In England a soldier's daily ration in the Tudor period was 24 oz wheat bread, $\frac{2}{3}$ gallon beer, 2 lb beef or mutton, $\frac{1}{2}$ lb butter and 1 lb cheese with a quarter of cod or ling or 7 or 8 herrings instead of the meat on fish days. An analysis of food supplied to soldiers in the later seventeenth century suggests that while great efforts were made to furnish meat, only bread, biscuit, salt and some kind of beverage were regarded as 'absolutely necessary' provisions. Armies marched, worked and fought, it has been calculated, on 1700 calories a day.[16] No wonder disastrous epidemics befell armies, especially at the end of summer. Seamen appear to have fared better. In the midsixteenth century the diet of the Spanish fleet provided 3000-4000 calories a day, about 72 per cent of the rations consisting of cereals. In the Danish navy cereals were also most plentiful, the rations in 1680 being just over 3 lb pork and beef, 2 lb fish, 1 lb butter, 1$\frac{1}{4}$ bushels barley groat,

16. G. Perjés, 'Army provisioning: logistics and strategy in the second half of the 17th century', *Acta Historica Academiae Scientiarum Hungaricae*, XVI (1970), p. 12-14. See also Fernand Braudel who accepts that 'official menus were always without exception *officially* good' and adds in comment that this 'may simply mean that galley slaves and soldiers were servants precious enough to have their health cared for' (*The Mediterranean and the Mediterranean World in the Age of Philip II*, vol. I (Collins, 1972), p. 460).

2½ bushels peas, 6 lb 'hard bread' and 70 quarts of ale a week. By 1736 the meat allowance had increased while fish had declined, butter and bread had increased and the other items had declined. The British navy ration in 1745 was 12 oz cheese, 4 lb salt beef, 2 lb salt pork, 8 oz butter, 7 lb biscuit, 2½ lb oatmeal, 2 pints pease and 7 gallons beer per week.

CLOTHES

The second basic human material requirement, clothing, is at the same time a physical need and a manifestation of personality. In fact Veblen, to underline this point, made the distinction between clothing and dress. Throughout this period the satisfaction of the needs of the poor peasant and town worker remained extremely modest. Most of the needs of the majority of the population, who wore durable clothing, were met by domestic production. Eve spun and wove the cloth, Adam tanned the leather and a small amount of textiles was purchased. In his calculations for England, Phelps Brown provided for the purchase of ⅔ yard of canvas, ½ yard of shirting and ⅛ yard of woollen cloth in 1500 and for ½ yard of woollen cloth in 1725.[17] The effective demand of the greater part of the community for clothing was therefore small. The typical dress of the English countryman was a loose belted garment buttoned across the chest with an open knee-length skirt, made of canvas, fustian, leather or cloth. He wore hose on his legs. By the end of the sixteenth century he had adopted breeches, often left loose below the knee for ease of movement, with stockings. In Russia the working man wore a fur overcoat, kaftan and cap and his womenfolk had wide gowns, belted at the waist, and a kind of diadem on their head to which a veil was attached. The urban working class wore more varied clothes but they were mainly of coarse woollen material in dark or dull colours and black predominated for the women. By the end of the seventeenth century

17. Phelps Brown and Hopkins, 'Seven centuries of the prices of consumables', p. 303.

industrial progress was bringing a wider variety of cloths and colours within the reach of the working class. Domestic servants usually dressed in a more fashionable style. Some of them received clothes as part of their wages or wore livery and the upper servants often had their employers' clothes passed on to them. There was little specialisation of dress for particular occupations during this period but there was increasing use of protective clothing. One of the earliest tradesmen to wear an apron was the miller; the butcher wore protective sleeves as well as an apron; workers such as smiths, coopers, metal workers, tanners, slaughtermen and sometimes carpenters wore leather aprons. Sailors had tarred petticoats to protect them from the wet. There was an extensive market in discarded clothes since most working people expected as a matter of course to obtain their clothes second-hand. They also made them last a long time and, like other classes, seldom bothered to wash them. It has been said of a working-class woman in eighteenth-century London that 'a pair of leather stays, a double-quilted horse-hair petticoat, a stuff gown and a linen shift would keep the wearer and her fleas warm for several years before they rotted away'.[18]

The great demand for textile products in a commercial sense came from the urban middle class, the nobility, the church and a few other institutions and the state, predominantly for the armed forces. With the rise of the nation state, clothes became one means of pronouncing distinctive nationhood but among the wealthy there was also a strong tendency to follow the styles of the country which was considered fashionable at the moment. In the sixteenth century the most influential country was Spain although in northern Europe the Dutch and German influence remained greater. Spanish fashion introduced the farthingale and tight-fitting bodices for women. Rich materials in dark colours with much heavy embroidery were popular although in England the Elizabethan period was one of great variety and brightness of colour. In the

18. Dorothy Davis, *A history of shopping* (Routledge & Kegan Paul, 1966), p. 219.

seventeenth century the Dutch and French replaced Spanish styles. There was a smaller farthingale, a greater use of lace and a less rigid outline for women's clothes. Changes in fashion became more frequent. The influence of art on fashion increased and the Italian baroque taste was reflected in costume, more so in France, Flanders, Spain and central Europe and less so in the Low Countries, England, north Germany and Scandinavia. The other factor affecting fashion during this period was the introduction of new fabrics. Lighter woollen cloth, the new draperies, was manufactured in the Low Countries, England and other parts of Europe; cotton fabrics, often delicately printed, were brought from Egypt and India; and silks came from Persia, Iraq and Syria. There was a general trend away from the hard-wearing medieval woollen cloths to lighter and less durable fabrics which lent themselves to greater variety and changes of style. Throughout the period the clothes of the wealthy and fashionable were designed more for display than for comfort.

Particularly for the well-to-do, accessories played an important part in completing the picture. The ruff was popular during the sixteenth century and at times reached remarkable dimensions. Richly decorated leather gloves, often perfumed, were much prized. Women wore jewelled girdles and clothes were often heavily encrusted with jewels. In the sixteenth century these had to be precious stones and were the privilege of the most wealthy but in 1644 a merchant in the Temple district of Paris discovered a process for colouring crystal to imitate jewels; and paste stones were invented in Strasbourg at the end of the century. These 'Temple diamonds' and paste jewels spread rapidly and came within the reach of the less affluent. Ornate buttons were also popular, particularly for men's clothes; on one occasion Sir Edmund Bacon had 138 gold buttons on a suit. Wigs came into fashion after 1633 when Louis XIII lost his hair during an illness. Many of them were exported from France and they became larger and more elaborate towards the end of the century, often being built up with lace and ribbons for women. The women's own hair was also dressed in similar styles when it was thick enough to do so. Shoes, similar for both men and women, were usually light-weight and dainty though from 1570 fine leather replaced satin for men. Other materials included silk, brocade and velvet. In the sixteenth century they were generally flat-heeled but in the following century heels became higher. Men also wore boots. Soft overshoes with cork soles, often thicker than necessary, known as pantouffles were worn outdoors to protect shoes but as they became themselves more ornate they developed into slippers for indoor wear. Another protection from mud and dust worn over ordinary shoes were pattens which had raised soles or were elevated from the ground by metal rings. Foreign goods were particularly prized. As Ben Jonson wrote:

'I would put on
The Savoy chain about my neck,
The cuffs of Flanders, then the Naples hat,
With the Rome hat band and the Florentine agate,
The Milan sword, the cloak of Geneva set
With Brabant buttons; all my given pieces,
My gloves the natives of Madrid . . .'

The middle classes imitated the fashions of the wealthy as best they could within the resources they had available and often spent considerable sums on clothes. In 1660 Pepys paid £4 5s for a beaver hat, a sum nearly equal to six months' wages for a skilled mason. Despite sumptuary laws which aimed to restrict the wearing of the new fancy fabrics to the upper classes, they spread down the social scale and by the seventeenth century it was no longer possible to tell a person's social rank from his clothes. When the wealthy tired of their latest extravagantly expensive garments they would sell them on the well-organised second-hand clothes market or pass them on to less wealthy relations. As they passed from hand to hand down the social scale, they would be altered and adapted many times. Even those who could only afford the traditional woollen cloths trimmed their clothes with the fashionable velvets and laces.

During this period there was little development of specialised clothes for particular purposes. The earliest seem to be riding clothes. In the sixteenth century men wore breeches, stockings and jerkin with a long cape or overcoat and boots. Women wore a large cloak to protect their dress. From the mid-seventeenth century coat and waistcoat replaced the jerkin and doublet for men and riding clothes were made of plainer cloth than normal dress. Women began to wear specially-designed dresses with a close-fitting bodice and flaring skirt, protected in bad weather by a 'safeguard' or overskirt or a dust coat. Racing colours were in use by the sixteenth century and other sports required special equipment. For hawking a glove and a pouch to hold hoods, leashes, etc, both often very ornate, were needed. The archer, who traditionally dressed in green, had a belt to hold the arrows and gloves and bracers to protect his arm from the string of the bow. Mourning clothes began to appear in the sixteenth century and were governed by strict rules by the following century.

For clothes, too, there was an institutional demand. The church had for centuries provided a major market for fabrics, white, black or brown according to the order and scarlet for the dignitaries of the church. A few companies and institutions provided uniforms for their employees in this period. As early as 1590 the Aberdeen post carrier wore 'a livery of blue cloth with armorial bearings of the town worked in silver on his right sleeve'. In England the fire insurance companies which developed in the seventeenth century provided uniform for their firemen. In 1683 the Friendly Society had about twenty men in livery with silver badges. About 1710 the Sun Fire Office dressed its firemen in blue with silver badges and about the same time the Royal Exchange Assurance livery was yellow. In the Catholic countries many hospitals were run by convents and the nurses wore the usual habit. When St Bartholomew's Hospital in London was re-established as a secular institution after the dissolution the nurses were issued with a regulation dress. This was russet frieze in 1544 and in 1555 it was changed to blue and has remained that colour ever since. But this would appear to be the only example of uniform for nurses in this period.

To such institutional demand must be added an expanding demand from the armed forces. While a considerable proportion of an army wore armour there was no point in providing uniform for it; and even when armour was dispensed with, finally disappearing in the seventeenth century, the mercenary's habit of changing sides by enlisting overnight under the standard of the victor would have made uniforms more confusing than distinctive. At the beginning of the sixteenth century there had been little standardisation but as the century wore on a more determined effort was made to provide clothing for the troops. In 1562 the Danish troops were equipped with black hats and coats and red trousers. In 1588 the contract for the supply of clothing for the English army in the Netherlands amounted to £12,000 for the winter season and £8000 for the summer season. By the early seventeenth century military clothing had become, as the term implies, more uniform. Some of the soldiers of Mansfield or of George William of Brandenburg can be said to have worn real uniforms. Both Maximilian of Bavaria and Kristian of Denmark made serious attempts to clothe their armies on a distinctive standard pattern but it was Gustavus Adolphus of Sweden who was the first to attempt, not altogether successfully, to put the whole of his native army into uniform. In England, too, in the course of the Civil War the Cromwellian government put its soldiers into uniform. Standard dress was first used in the French army in 1660 and in 1670 the entire army was put into uniform consisting of a full tunic-shaped coat, which later became more tight-fitting, over a long sleeved waistcoat. Each unit had its own colour, the infantry pale grey, the artillery royal blue and the cavalry divisions more varied. In 1698 the officers were compelled to dress in the colour of their regiments. By the end of the seventeenth century this practice had made general headway and in most European nations, blouses, coats, trousers and often shoes were manufactured to government specifications for issue to troops.

There is little doubt that soldiers were better clad in 1750 than in 1500, the princes and priests of the church maintained their standards, the nobility and court dressed to changing standards of elegance. The dress of the professional and commercial middle classes was affected by religious considerations, the Puritan movement in the seventeenth century bringing greater simplicity of dress, but whether flamboyant or sombre was of a reasonable quality while the clothes worn by the mass of the people was to some extent affected by changes in taste and availability. Leather was of declining importance. But as most people continued to make their own clothes and tan their own leather, it is not easy to decide whether there was any improvement in the clothes worn by the masses in this period.

HOUSING

Housing, the third major need, was also required in some form by everyone. Throughout this period the dwellings of the poor remained, for the most part, miserable hovels constructed from local materials. In England, the houses of the poorest in the country had walls of earth or wattle, roofs covered with turf, heather or straw, few partitions, no windows and scarcely any chimneys other than a hole in the wall or roof, possibly a barrel or basket with the bottom knocked out, to let smoke out. This habitation was often shared with the animals. In the towns the houses of the poor were subdivided and overcrowding increased as the population grew. This had become a serious problem in London by 1593 when an act of parliament noted that 'great mischiefs daily grow and increase by reason of pestering the houses with diverse families, harbouring of inmates, and converting great houses into several tenements'. About the same time most of the new inhabitants of Madrid still occupied squalid housing which contrasted sharply with the palatial dwellings of the nobility. The slums of Naples were proverbial.

But in the housing of other classes of the community there was definite improvement. Beginning in Italy in the late fifteenth century, the building and rebuilding of houses both in town and countryside made possible by prosperity spread north and west through France, the Netherlands, central Europe and England in the course of the sixteenth century. In England, the century between 1540 and 1640 was a period of great rebuilding. 'The ancient manors . . . of our gentlemen', William Harrison noted in 1577, 'are yet, and for the most part, of strong timber . . . Howbeit such as be lately builded are commonly either of brick or hard stone, or both.' As the rebuilding spread geographically north and west from Italy, so it spread socially down the pyramid from the richer merchants and the country gentry to townspeople and farmers of more modest means. In England between 1570 and 1640 most yeomen, a great number of husbandmen and probably a few cottagers found themselves in new or enlarged houses and a similar process in the rehousing of the wealthier citizens was visible in the great cities such as London and in provincial towns such as Shrewsbury or Totnes.

The new or remodelled houses provided more specialised facilities and greater comfort than their predecessors. Ceilings were inserted in medieval halls to make bedrooms on the first floor. At first these were just loose boards laid on joists but then the wooden panelling which came to line the walls was continued across to 'seele' the room. Later plaster ceilings, often elaborately moulded, replaced wooden and plaster and then wallpaper took the place of wainscot. With affluence the height of ceilings was raised so that the ambience of living became more spacious. On the ground floor partitions were erected to separate the kitchen from the living-room and the dining-room and the scullery from the kitchen and to create rooms for other purposes while the upper floor was divided into individual bedrooms. Then as the movement towards privacy continued, corridors were constructed so that the rooms did not lead from one to another. The habit of confining the kitchen and other domestic offices to the basement began to spread from France to England. Staircases had to be built to allow access to the upper rooms. Originally these were merely ladders in many cases but they gradually progressed to a spiral stone staircase and then to a wide and handsome wooden flight, or marble in the grandest houses, which became an architectural feature. Small windows protected by parchment, pigskin, paper, linen or heavy shutters began to be glazed and could consequently be enlarged. In the Tudor period the diamond-paned window became established for domestic use in England and at the end of the seventeenth century the sash window spread to England from Holland under the influence of William III. During the later sixteenth, seventeenth and early eighteenth centuries these new notions became more widely diffused. In England glaziers were at work at King's Lynn in the 1540s but they did not appear in Leicester until the 1570s and in Leicestershire villages until 20 or 30 years later.

The insertion of an upper floor made a chimney necessary to carry away the smoke from the fire which had previously been allowed to escape through the windows or a louvred hole in the roof. Harrison commented on the growing number of chimneys in England in 1577. The central fire was moved to the wall. Handsome cast iron firebacks were made to protect the house wall from the heat of the fire and ornate hoods and mantles made the fireplace an important decorative feature. In the kitchen the open fire was replaced by a range. Then, with the introduction of the closed tile stove, there was more improvement of conditions in those parts of Europe which had a long hard winter than in those which had more variable winters. These stoves, which gave great heat without smoke, were favoured over the open fire in the German-speaking countries and in the sixteenth century they were often very elaborately decorated, particularly in Switzerland. By the early eighteenth century it was better to pass the winter in Cologne or Warsaw than in Milan or Toulouse.

From the later sixteenth century coal made headway as a fuel for domestic heating and its effect was soon apparent. Already in the early seventeenth century John Stow was complaining of the fog caused by its use in London. With lighting as with heating there was again an enormous range. The shuttered and windowed hall illuminated by glittering candelabra and warmed by a log or coal fire was the privilege of the few made possible by wealth and the availability of cheap glass and cheap coal. In such conditions it was possible to be less constrained by changes in the climate or the shortening of the days. And the spread of the oil lamp provided better illumination for the great houses and the commercial and professional middle classes. But for the majority of the population heating and lighting were rudimentary. The peat or wood fire or brazier whose smoke permeated the living space before escaping and a candle or rush-light provided fitful illumination at some cost. Although much fuel must have been collected by the country dweller at no cost other than the labour involved, Phelps Brown suggests that between $7\frac{1}{2}$ and 9 per cent of the ordinary budget was spent on fuel and lighting.[19] And as there were marked class differences in comfort, so there were considerable differences between town and country and between different parts of Europe.

Sanitary conditions seem to have declined rather than improved during the period. Baths, which had been in use in the medieval period, disappeared during the sixteenth century. In Frankfurt the number of bathmen fell from 29 in 1387 to none in 1530. In the seventeenth century Turkish or Russian baths were opened in a number of cities but they were regarded more as pleasure haunts and places of assignation than as a means to cleanliness. At the beginning of the period some of the larger houses continued to use the medieval garderobe, an upstairs closet with a stone or wooden seat over a chute which carried the waste outside the building. These started to go out of use in the early seventeenth century and were replaced by the close

19. Phelps Brown and Hopkins, 'Seven centuries of the prices of consumables', p. 297; 'Wage-rates and prices', p. 293.

stool, a box with a pierced seat which contained a pot. Invented by Sir John Harington in 1596, the water-closet was adopted very slowly and until the invention of the trap and the ventilating stack the backing-up of sewer gas into the house meant that it was not always an improvement. And none of these conveniences would have been available in the great majority of houses.

Building materials differed in various parts of Europe according to what was available locally and to some extent due to the dictates of fashion. There were also changes over time. In England, most of the timber cottages were built between 1558 and 1625 and it has also been suggested that in rural areas such as the Cotswolds and north Yorkshire stone was replacing timber as a building material during the sixteenth century while in towns such as Northampton the opposite trend was visible. In the south-eastern counties of England and East Anglia brick became popular during the sixteenth and seventeenth centuries due to a shortage of natural building stone in these areas and from 1660 it became a fashionable material in other areas.

While the lower orders made a relatively limited impact on townscape and countryside, nobles, princes and the more affluent middle classes built themselves more splendid houses in both town and countryside. By the beginning of the sixteenth century Gothic architecture had gone out of fashion in Italy and Italian architects were turning to Roman buildings for their inspiration. In France, where Gothic architecture was much more firmly rooted, Roman or Renaissance influence began to be felt in the sixteenth century. It did not reach England until the following century, at first in the form of ornamental details and then in the work of Inigo Jones, the first architect as distinct from builder to emerge in England. In the seventeenth century Baroque architecture became fashionable in Italy and spread from there to the other Catholic countries. In the Protestant countries the Baroque style never became popular and less ornate buildings remained dominant to the end of the period. Styles of buildings varied between areas. During the sixteenth century in England the fortified

house built around a courtyard gave way to a new plan in
the form of an E or an H with a principal block and additional wings in order to give greater spaciousness and privacy
and allow a freer circulation of air. The great hall became
smaller and the long gallery replaced it as the focal point of
the house, the first example being built at Ingatestone Hall
in 1530. On the continent the fortified *château* or *schloss* remained more popular. In England the country house, often
designed more for display than for comfort and convenience,
remained the principal home of a wealthy family but in
France it declined in importance after 1660 as the life of the
ruling class centred on the court in Paris. Here they lived
in detached and elegantly varied *hôtels*, carefully designed
to be both functional and spacious. In London and other
English cities the noblemen and wealthy merchants preferred to live in almost standardised terraced houses, often
arranged around squares or in crescents, with the service
rooms in the basement and two large rooms on each floor.
The size of buildings increased and they extended over a
greater area rather than growing in height so that the
density of urban housing increased and the problem of
the conurbation was already emerging.

As transport costs were very high, the cost of building
depended considerably on the availability of the necessary
materials. For a large project it might be worthwhile to open
a small quarry on the site rather than transport the stone
from an established quarry some distance away. Some
examples of cost are available for England and it is clear
that over the two and a half centuries, even if account is
taken of the falling value of money, the cost of building
rose. Hengrave Hall was built in the 1530s at a cost of
£3000, Longleat in the 1570s at a cost of £8000 and Hatfield
in the 1620s at a cost of £40,000. Of more modest houses,
a substantial stone church house, 60 ft by 19 ft and 16 ft
high, at Great Sherston in Wiltshire cost £10 in 1511. A
probably finer than average farmhouse was constructed
near Oxford for Merton College in 1516 for £29. If the
necessary materials were available near at hand, an
average-sized farmhouse of three bays (about 39 ft wide)

could probably have been built for £6-15 in the early sixteenth century; by the end of the century this had risen to £20-30 and in the next fifty years it rose to about £40.

But not only growing wealth and the desire for conspicuous display led to building and rebuilding in town and countryside. Since houses were often constructed of combustible materials and fire-fighting resources were limited, considerable numbers of houses were often burnt down. Most spectacular was the Great Fire of London in 1666 when 13,200 houses were destroyed but other towns also had severe fires. To take only English examples, 214 houses were destroyed at Marlborough in 1653 and 400 families were rendered homeless at Blandford in 1731.[20] These disasters led to attempts to regulate building in the interests of safety. For example, timber building was prohibited in the city of London after the Great Fire.

The Great Fire provided an opportunity for the systematic replanning of the city of London, an opportunity of which full advantage was not taken. A number of plans were submitted and discussed at length but eventually rejected due to the cost involved and individuals were left to rebuild on their original sites. In other parts of Europe the sixteenth and seventeenth centuries saw much activity in planning new towns: in Malta, Valetta; in Italy, Palma Nuova, planned as a fortified nine-pointed star in 1593; in France, Vitry-le-François (1545), Charleville (1606), Henrichemont (1609) and Richelieu (1631-8); in the Netherlands, Coeworden; and in southern Poland, Zamosc. Not only were new towns built but old towns were replanned. Rome and Venice provide the finest examples in Italy; Amsterdam is an instance of an old town north of the Alps being replanned on a spider's-web plan with houses lining the many canals; and parts of Paris were replanned and new areas laid out on a grid-iron pattern. This new concern for town planning was influenced to a large extent by the desire on the part of both individuals and municipalities for ostentatious display but

20. See Eric L. Jones, 'The reduction of fire damage in southern England, 1650-1850', *Post-Medieval Archaeology*, II (1968), pp. 140-9.

other factors also played a part, notably the changing methods of warfare which rendered medieval defences obsolete and the growing problem of traffic congestion.

And this rebuilding movement may have had some effect on the demographic trend. The sequence in England, it has been suggested, seems to be: savings – rebuilding and enlargement – decreased mortality and perhaps higher fertility – rise of population – new building and development of congestion – rise of mortality rates. But this thesis has not been fully investigated. The building of this period may also have had an importance beyond the physical. As Lewis Mumford has written, 'the first radical change, which was to destroy the form of the medieval dwelling house, was the development of a sense of privacy.'[21] Bedrooms became private, the boudoir and the study provided privacy for master and mistress and this new privilege gradually spread to others as a shift from the communal to the individual took place. This move originated among the wealthy Italians and French and spread at the courts and among the nobility and then among the wealthier members of the rising middle class who aped their betters in other countries as well.

OTHER EXPENDITURE

Along with changes in housing, heating and lighting went improved furnishings. Here too the same trends towards greater sophistication and from communal to individual living were evident. In the houses of the well-to-do, walls were hung with tapestries and rush mats or carpets replaced loose rushes on the floors. Furniture became more elaborate. The main pieces, owned by all but the poorest, were the refectory table, sometimes with draw-leaves, some chairs and stools, a coffer or chest and the four-poster bed, usually the most expensive item. Individual chairs took the place of the common bench first for the head of the household and then for others as well. In the seventeenth century

21. See Lewis Mumford, *The culture of cities* (Secker & Warburg, 1938), p. 40.

furniture-making began to develop as a specialised craft and styles evolved which meant for the wealthy the need to keep up with the latest fashion. The growth of trade with the Far East brought an interest in chinoiserie. The number of ornaments and the amount of furniture found in houses grew in quantity as it diversified in function. The communal bowl or cup was replaced by individual items. Tin or pewter platters were used instead of wooden or earthenware. Fine glass spread from Italy across the continent as far as Sweden and England in the sixteenth century and glass drinking vessels became common about 1650. Cutlery came into use and by the end of the period was becoming very elaborate and was often made of silver. The use of the spoon spread quickly in the sixteenth century and in the seventeenth century the Italian fashion of using a three- or four-pronged fork, previously a serving tool and usually two-pronged, to convey food to the mouth was adopted. In 1651 food was still eaten with the fingers at the Austrian court but forks and table knives had become fashionable, in imitation of French manners, by 1750. The change from an open fire to a kitchen range involved a change in cooking vessels. Bronze cauldrons suspended over the fire on tripods or chains were replaced by copper pans. In the same years bedding became more elegant and comfortable as the blanket cast over straw was superseded by feather beds, pillows, sheets and counterpanes. Writing of the English in 1598, Otto Hentzner said 'their beds are covered with tapestry, even those of the farmers'. Table linen also appeared. More cushions became available and padding was transferred from the seats of dresses and trousers to the chairs. With the invention of printing the republic of letters was enlarged and the acquisition of a library became an object of ambition for the educated and the well-to-do. Many of the early books were on religious topics but there were also works on practical subjects such as gardening and cookery and many of them were intended for use in schools. As the period wore on the range and number increased substantially and books could be bought to suit all tastes and to answer most questions. During the

Renaissance the artist rose markedly in status and one competitive outlet the rich found for their wealth was to commission portraits or to acquire other works of art, whether painting or sculpture. In this patronage they were joined by crown and municipality. But despite the range of household and luxury goods which became available, their market was largely restricted to the wealthy classes and the possessions of the lower middle class and the small landowners remained very few. The possessions of a typical English farmer who made a comfortable living without gaining great wealth are illustrated by those of a Worcestershire husbandman who died in 1613: a framed table, a form and a fixed bench, two chairs, three bedsteads, a press and a coffer. He also had some cooking equipment and table ware, two spinning wheels and painted cloths on the walls.[22]

Throughout Europe many of the rich divided their time between town and country. By the mid-seventeenth century a clearly-defined London season which lasted from October to June had become an essential part of the social round of the well-to-do. Other European capitals, whether Moscow or Paris, were also deserted in the summer. For some at least, hunting and the chase, which Machiavelli commended because of their value in the training of princes, formed part of the career of pleasure. In Venice, too, the winter was a period of prolonged carnival while to escape the summer heat Venetians went to their villas in the country. Near the villa the patrician could shoot hares or waterfowl. In the villa he could study or drive away the almost inevitable boredom with chess or cards, parlour games or practical jokes.[23]

But the great opium of the rich was gambling, the corruption of an idle and exhibitionist society whose most extravagant manifestations were confined to court circles

22. Maurice W. Barley, 'Rural housing in England' in Joan Thirsk, ed. *The agrarian history of England and Wales*, vol. IV. *1500-1640* (Cambridge UP, 1967), pp. 751-2.

23. Peter Burke, 'Patrician culture: Venice and Amsterdam in the seventeenth century', *Transactions of the Royal Historical Society*, 5th series, XXIII (1973), p. 139.

but whose contagion was European in extent. In the six-teenth century Venetians bet on elections in the Great Council: in the seventeenth on cards in the Ridotto which opened as official gambling rooms in 1628. Heavy betting on cards, on games of chance or on more random objects spread in the seventeenth century and became more open in the eighteenth. Organised gambling was a feature of the Bath of Beau Nash till it was checked by legislation in 1745. Originating in Italy, both private and state lotteries became popular in many European countries. And gambling was also an out-of-doors activity. Newmarket racecourse was opened in 1640 and received royal patronage from the Restoration and other racecourses were founded in England in the following years. Betting also took place on prize-fights and cock-fighting. Gambling, as Sir John Harington pointed out, was the product of the triple vices of idleness, which created boredom and therefore a demand for palliatives; of pride which made men play for higher stakes than they could afford in order to give an impression of magnanimity and carefree opulence; and of avarice which fed on hopes of a killing.[24] But while idleness might be killed and pride satisfied, in this habit-forming pastime no one ever really seemed to win.

While informal entertainment of friends continued, the trend was towards more organised and institutionalised entertainment. In the major cities of Europe the rich began to manifest a taste for parks and pleasure gardens and for public entertainments. By the reign of Charles II, Hyde Park, for example, had become a parade ground for the coaches of the fashionable. Though they still continued to visit the homes of the nobility, before the end of the sixteenth century, the wandering troupes of players began to find permanent homes in theatres especially built for the pur-pose. Renaissance courts and noble houses also patronised the masque which fathered two new art forms, ballet and opera. The germ of ballet, linking the virtuosity of the acrobat with the grace of the courtier, was brought from Italy by Catherine de Medici, for whom 'Le ballet comique

24. Stone, *Crisis of the aristocracy*, p. 568.

de la Reine' was performed in 1581. But the real impetus to the growth of the ballet came from Louis XIV, himself an expert dancer, who created a number of roles between 1651 and 1669. When he founded L'Académie National de la Danse in 1661 under the leadership of Lully and Beauchamp, he made ballet professional. An unbroken line of dancers and teachers can be traced from this company to the present day. From France the ballet spread to other countries. With the encouragement of Peter the Great, it had taken root in Russia before the end of the seventeenth century.

The forerunners of opera can be traced back to the thirteenth century and the art form developed slowly in the form of musical interludes between the acts of tragedies. The first true opera was a performance of Peri's *Dafne* in Florence in 1597 and Monteverdi's *Orfeo* was performed in Mantua in 1607. This form of entertainment then spread to other Italian cities and later to Paris and Vienna, the German princedoms, England and Scandinavia. By the end of the seventeenth century the opera had become a popular aristocratic diversion.

With the political and religious changes of the sixteenth and seventeenth centuries came changes in the patronage of music. While the Roman church generally strove to subordinate its liturgical music to the spoken word, its music was affected by the general development of the art and plainsong gave place to the polyphony of Byrd or Palestrina. In their turn, the reformed churches also provided an opportunity for musicians, a Bach or a Purcell, to display his talents. Musicians also found employment in courts and noble households.

The demand for secular entertainment in the theatre, whether by drama, ballet or opera, had a number of consequences. As rising expenditure elsewhere, on clothes or housing, led to an expansion of employment in a wide range of occupations, so the growth of interest in the arts gave employment to actors, dancers, singers and musicians and to all the ancillary staff necessary to enable a theatre or opera house to function properly. It provided commissions for playwrights, composers and ballet masters. It was also a stimulus to musical and artistic education.

So much for the entertainment of the rich and well-to-do; what of the majority who also in pre-industrial Europe often enjoyed a great deal of leisure or suffered enforced idleness? For them there was the constant conviviality of the inn or hostelry. Then there were the periodic fairs which were not only places of business but were also the occasion for public entertainment. Gypsies, tumblers, acrobats and other performers wandered from fair to fair amusing their varied public with their capers and contortions. Holy days were also holidays and the opportunity for communal enjoyment. Then there were the public ceremonies, semi-public orgies and sadistic displays provided by state or municipality. Hangings were occasions of public entertainment while in some cities, such as Naples and Palermo, there were annual festivals of prostitutes. And finally there was the popular culture of folk song, legend, superstition and oral tradition which provided more informally and casually for the leisure hours. But the history of popular entertainment is still a neglected subject.

Those who had lived ostentatiously were also accorded elaborate last rites which are so much better described by the French term 'pompes funèbres' than by the English 'funeral'. As Professor Stone has written: 'so grandiose in scale and portentous in style were the funeral arrangements of the nobility that the most contemptible of human beings on earth could hardly fail to be ushered out of it to universal admiration. Of many could it be said that nothing became them so much as their going; it was the last tribute of a deferential society to the dignity of a title'. The opulence rose to a peak in the 1570s and by 1631 the epitaph of the stately funeral was written by John Weaver when he said: 'funerals in any expensive way here with us are now accounted but a fruitlesse vanitie', largely a result of the realisation that the cost incurred was out of all proportion to the prestige earned. The demand curve of the great figured tomb followed a rather different pattern, rising to a peak between the middle years of Elizabeth and the death of

James. Expenditure on both funerals and tombs was thus declining well before the Civil War gave the process a further impetus. In the second half of the seventeenth century, the number of tombs with figure sculpture erected per decade had fallen to less than a third of the peak total.[25] Such was the course of events in England but the question remains to be asked how far this was typical of the experience of other European countries.

As well as the demands of individuals, there was the demand of agriculture and industry for goods for immediate consumption. Some of these markets are as yet hardly recognised by historians. Throughout these centuries Europe remained predominantly agricultural and subsistent. In normal times most of a farmer's needs were met from his own resources or from those of his lord. The arable farmer saved seed from each harvest for the next year's crop. Similarly the pasture farmer bred his own sheep or cattle and dried his own hay to feed his livestock. They both made their own tools with the assistance, where necessary, of the village blacksmith who also shoed the horses and made iron implements. Wooden articles – ploughs, harrows, pails and presses – were usually made by the farm worker. In other ways also the village was largely self-sufficient, relying on the craftsmen available locally, the mason, the carpenter, the baker, the glover and the leatherworker as well as the blacksmith. The fisherman made his own equipment, his nets, baskets and traps. Good neighbourly assistance was usually available in times of individual misfortune so that it was only when the crop failed or murrain struck the cattle that seeds or breeding stock had to be obtained from elsewhere. In any case the majority of peasants had very little if any surplus available to extend their holdings or expand their herds or flocks even if such growth were possible. But agriculture was by no means completely unchanging in these two centuries and a half. New crops began to be sown such as the turnip, improved grasses and later the potato and attempts were made to

25. This paragraph derives from Stone, *Crisis of the aristocracy*, pp. 572-81.

improve stock by selective breeding. So a market in seeds and breeding cattle grew up. According to Duhamel de Monceau 'both the English and the French have most of their flax seed from Flanders. . . . Cauliflower seed was for a long time brought from Malta, melon seeds from Italy and the seed of lucerne from Languedoc'. There was a trade in breeding cattle across the Irish Sea and the Dutch exported livestock for this purpose. A market in plants and seeds also resulted from changes in husbandry. Portugal, for example, shifted from the cultivation of grain to that of olives and vines.

Industry also had requirements for tools, raw materials and fuel. In the main the needs of individual artisans and businesses were met from their own resources or by the local carpenter or blacksmith but some foundries were established and a market in specialist tools began to emerge. Most of the raw materials for many industries were obtained locally but this was not always the case. As the market for woollen textiles changed and lighter fabrics became fashionable, different wool staples were required. The English, the Flemish and the Italian woollen textile industry obtained wool from Spain to meet these new needs. Indeed many branches of the textile industry – flax, silk, hemp and the emerging manufacture of cotton – came to depend on trade for their raw materials. Mordants and dyes were also imported. Although the Portuguese named their new-found land on the continent of South America Vera Cruz, it soon became known as Brazil from the dyewood which it produced which was its earliest product to win a European market. Like cotton, sugar and tobacco were new industries using imported raw materials from the wider world of the discoveries. Hides, too, were imported from Algeria as well as Spain to meet the demands of fashionable Europe for leather articles. Because metals were not everywhere available, there was also a significant trade in lead for roofing and piping, in copper for a range of purposes including coinage, roofing and vessels and containers and in tin, with the market for tinplate wares and utensils expanding as the use of tin for armour declined.

In iron rods and bars the market grew, with Sweden dominating the trade by the early eighteenth century. With the spread of printing, paper too became an article of international trade. Then there was a demand for building materials, for stone and bricks and timber. In the seventeenth century houses at Topsham (near Exeter) were built from Dutch bricks brought as ballast in ships which returned to the Netherlands laden with English woollen cloth. And there was a widespread trade in timber, not only for shipping and building purposes and for use in mining but as a fuel for both domestic and industrial needs. The main impact of Abraham Darby's successful employment of coke for smelting iron falls outside our period but for a range of industries such as brewing, sugar, soap, salt and glass, coal came to rival wood as a fuel in some countries and so led to an expansion of coal production. Coal, wrote a French observer in 1738, is 'the soul of English manufactures'. And, as with clothing, the major institutional demand was from the armed forces, in this case for weapons of war. The long pike of the Spanish infantry in the sixteenth century provides the first example of uniform weapons issued in quantity by a government. The demand of the navy for armament was also substantial. English naval vessels carried 8396 cannon in 1700 compared with 2087 in 1548 while under Colbert the demand of the French navy for guns expanded seven-fold.

LABOUR AND SERVICES

In relation to other factors of production, labour was plentiful and cheap and most activities carried on in early modern Europe were labour-intensive. By 1750, as the process of industrialisation began to gather momentum in England, it has been estimated that 45 per cent of the labour force was employed in agriculture, 30 per cent in manufacturing and the remaining 25 per cent in services but in the rest of Europe the proportion employed in agriculture generally was much higher. By the sweat of men's brows – and women's and children's too – crops were grown and harvested and livestock was tended. The demand of animal husbandry for labour was steady and unremitting while that of arable farming followed its own rhythm of periods of intense activity in seedtime and harvest alternating with less time-demanding periods. And climate and geography imposed their own restraints on the chronology of labour within the farming year. As the days shortened and the frosts and snows of winter set in, the length of the working day out-of-doors inevitably contracted. When work on the land was impossible, not required or did not suffice to give them a living, many peasants engaged in bye-employments such as spinning and weaving, leather work and carpentry, largely to meet their domestic needs. In most industries, manufacturing and extractive output was directly related to employment and most industries were labour-intensive, notably mining and quarrying, textile manufacture, metal working and building. As with agriculture, geography and climate affected the demand for labour. At a time when the sources of internal illumination were limited and expensive, the hours of daylight largely limited the working day and the pattern of the working year. Nor were agriculture and industry distinct occupations. Particularly at harvest time, extra labour was pressed into use. And in some parts of Europe farming or sometimes mining were combined with fishing. Other climatic restraints also controlled the employment of labour. Mills could not work when streams froze in winter or diminished to trickles during the summer. Before the impersonal insistent demands of the steam engine and the factory hooter required the creation of a disciplined working force, the rhythm of industrial production was less regular and more spasmodic. Similarly the demand for labour for the sea, for trading vessels and the fisheries, paid regard to changes in the weather and the climate. Though underemployment rather than unemployment was typical of early modern Europe, a new feature of these years, in the advanced sectors of the European economy, was the emergence of cyclical unemployment. In the textile industry, notably in the 1540s and the 1620s in

England, spinners and weavers were thrown out of work as the market for their products slumped. In the face of this new situation which was beyond the scope of local resources, the English state was forced to attempt remedial action by wage regulation and poor relief.

To a considerable degree the demand for agricultural and industrial labour could be met locally. The farm worker had a range of skills, which often go unregarded, which were called into service with the changing demands of the farming calendar. Industrial needs were met by training labour through apprenticeship though such requirements were sometimes used rather as a restraint on labour mobility than as a means of imparting skills. The fisheries were commonly regarded as a nursery for seamen. Some intermittent or seasonal needs were met by wandering artisans such as masons or by itinerant harvest workers. Skills were jealously guarded and were not easily susceptible to widespread diffusion thus imposing a restriction on the pace of technical change. In such conditions when the mystery of trades lay in the hands and the heads of skilled workers, migration provided the means by which specialised skills could be transferred. Governments or industrialists attempted to lure artisans to enable them to develop new industries or processes. So German metal-workers were invited to England to establish copper, brass and zinc working on a commercial basis. Religious persecution also served to diffuse skills. Flemish cloth workers with their knowledge of the new draperies and Huguenot glass and paper makers in the seventeenth century gave a welcome impetus to these industries in England. One way or another the migration of skilled labour provided the means by which the geography of European industry was transformed between 1500 and 1750.

The spread of the money economy meant that a growing proportion of the European labour force, particularly in the developing trades, was recruited as wage labour. The market for labour remained relatively primitive and as Adam Smith pointed out, 'in many places the money price of labour remains uniformly the same sometimes for half a century together'. But the concept of the sale of labour is a comparatively recent one in human history and not all labour in early modern Europe was paid wages. Particularly in eastern Europe, the sixteenth and seventeenth centuries saw the re-enserfment of the peasantry and the tightening of obligations. Here labour was performed under duress. In southern Europe slavery continued to reach its highest peak of 100,000 slaves in Spain at the end of the sixteenth century. In this part of Europe there were still considerable numbers of Berber, Circassian, Levantine and negro domestic slaves in the eighteenth century. Mediterranean warships were powered by galley slaves which led to a particularly brutal trade in convicts. And slavery continued within the Ottoman empire.

Besides those who had employment, there were a large number of vagrants who won for themselves a precarious existence on the margins of society and periodically threatened its peace.

'Hark hark the dogs do bark,
The beggars are coming to town'

was no innocent nursery rhyme for town dwellers of early modern Europe.

The wealth and standing of men in modern society is frequently signalled by their possession of goods – automobiles, aeroplanes, yachts and other products of modern technology. In the sixteenth and seventeenth centuries, where the cheapness and availability of labour contrasted with the scarcity and dearness of goods in Europe, status was to a considerable degree correlated with the size of one's personal retinue. Personal services were a major item of demand among the well-to-do. Paralleling the structure of society at large, there was a hierarchy of domestic service, of butlers, footmen, valets, cooks, chamber maids, scullery maids and so on and outside the house there were gardeners, ostlers, coachmen and the like. The rich also had other employees of higher status, a surgeon or a priest. The size of some households was considerable. In England in the sixteenth century the Berkeley estate kept 150 servants and the Derby 140 while the much more modest middle-class household of Sir William Petre employed 21 servants in 1580. A century later Gregory King gave the average size of a peer's household as 40 while in eighteenth-century Spain the nobility maintained an 'eastern multitude' of servants and hangers-on as a form of conspicuous expenditure demanded by position. And the demand for personal service inevitably involved a need for accommodation, for clothing and for food. If personal service was a sign of standing, it was also the subject of competitive emulation. From a considerable way down the social ladder came a demand for servants. Small farmers or well-to-do artisans could employ one or two servants.

Inevitably female domestics sometimes found themselves fulfilling sexual roles. But there was also more deliberate provision to meet man's sexual needs. Courtesans earned themselves a place in the highest ranks of society but prostitutes were in demand by many. How numerous they were it is not easy to discover but one example can be given. In Venice in 1509 prostitutes were separately enumerated in a census and numbered 11,654 – the only precise figure given in this account! – out of a total population, according to one chronicler, of 571,654 or approximately 2 per cent. Prostitution was certainly a feature of the major cities in these centuries and the existence of brothels was openly recognised. 'If they don't like brothels', Charles II is reported to have tartly retorted, 'they need not go to them.' But such provision was not confined to the large towns: Colyton (Devon), which has earned itself a place in the history of English demography, apparently had two brothels in the later seventeenth century. Periodically an attempt was made to limit the activities of prostitutes though not with marked success. In 1690 Frederick I of Prussia ordered all the brothels in Berlin to be closed with the result that the prostitutes moved from the area where their activities had been concentrated more widely through the capital. Prostitution was a function of social forces as well as of individual needs.

One respect in which personal and corporate demand for labour became more diversified in these years was in the demand for services, for medicine, for education, for legal and other professional services. As far as medicine was concerned, the onset of the scientific revolution with the work of Harvey and others provided a better understanding of the functioning of the human body. Notable progress was made in the accurate description of diseases such as rickets, diabetes, gout and tuberculosis in the later seventeenth century so that they could more accurately be recognised by physicians. Medical training was improved and there was a wider use of chemical remedies and exotic drugs but these benefits were only slowly diffused to the population at large. The prevailing standard of competence can perhaps be best summed up by a quatrain about a noted physician:

> 'When any sick to me apply
> I physics, bleeds and sweats em.
> If after that they chose to die
> Why verily I lettsom.'

But only a minority fell into the hands of the doctors. It was not the physician but the local wise woman who delivered, physicked and laid out the peasant masses of Europe.[26]

Then there was a growth of educational provision to meet the obviously expanding needs of society as well as individual aspirations. Education benefited from the concern of the state, the municipality, wealthy philanthropists, religious reformers and the eager entrepreneur. In Denmark the state laid down a policy for schools in 1539; four years previously the municipality of Bordeaux had founded the College of Guyennon; the Reformation in Germany and elsewhere brought a substantial reorganisation of education; numbers of schools were founded or their endowments were increased by wealthy businessmen. There was, too, a growth of schools for the sons of the gentry and nobility – and sometimes for their daughters too. Not every town experienced such increases in provision as

26. Alfred Rupert Hall, 'Scientific method and the progress in techniques' in Rich and Wilson, ed. *Cambridge Economic History of Europe*, IV, p. 139.

York where the six functioning grammar schools of 1480 had become 106 schools with adequate endowments and another 38 living from hand to mouth by 1660 but undoubtedly there was improved formal provision for education. The universities continued to provide a training for the professions and they too grew while in England the Inns of Court strove to meet the increased demand for lawyers. Much industrial and commercial training was carried out through apprenticeship but there was also the growth of private schools and academies to provide seamen and merchants with the skills necessary for their business. Military academies – the Accademia Reale (Turin) and Woolwich – were established. And handbooks such as the *Marchant's Aviso* – an English commercial guide – were published to meet the demand for knowledge about business methods. Thus education in a formal way became available to a growing though still inconsiderable section of society. The scientific revolution, too, brought with it a desire for institutions to foster and promote learning and science and learned societies came to be founded. Such was the Royal Society, established in 1660, which in its first century devoted itself very much to the application of science to particular practical projects.[27]

With the growth of a contractual society, with the spread of commerce, the commercialisation of agriculture and the growth of a land market, there came, certainly in the more developed parts of Europe, a demand for a wider range of professional services. These were litigious times and lawyers or notaries were much in demand. For the improvement of land, the services of a surveyor were required, buildings needed an architect, the sale of goods or property an auctioneer, the control of income and expenditure an accountant, the supply of credit or the transfer of funds a banker or scrivener, the limiting of risks at sea or from fire an insurance broker who in time came also to engage in life insurance. For the landowner, the merchant, the

27. See Edgar A. J. Johnson, *Predecessors of Adam Smith: the growth of British economic thought* (P. S. King, 1937; New York: Kelley, 1960), Appendix A, pp. 387-401.

tradesman and the manufacturer, specialised services developed to meet changing business needs.

Although the majority of the peasants and urban labourers never travelled far from the places where they were born, transport was necessary for the richer classes for both entertainment and business. Once dressed in their finery, the noble peacocks and popinjays had to be transported in fitting style. Great detail is not required to make the point and a single instance will suffice. In the year before the Civil War in England a luxurious town coach for a nobleman, exclusive of horses, cost up to £200. In addition to this showy contraption, a nobleman needed a less elaborately fitted and lighter travelling coach costing about £45 to take him down to the country and back and another £25 would probably be spent on a sedan chair for private visits in town. Travel was not cheap in the sixteenth and seventeenth centuries but the increase in the size of towns and the growing needs of the commercial classes led some enterprising individuals to try to fill the gap. From the middle of the seventeenth century coaches plied for hire in Paris and in other cities it became possible for people of relatively modest means who occasionally wanted to enjoy the prestige and comfort of wheeled transportation to hire coaches or carriages. For longer distances between towns, the majority of those who travelled in the sixteenth century did so by hiring horses at staging posts. In the sixteenth century Rome was the centre of some sixty-nine posts. By the middle of the seventeenth century when London, for example, was connected by stage coach with 'remote places' of the kingdom, stage coaches began to operate on regular schedules. By sea, too, increased traffic led to more systematic provision. By the seventeenth century there were regular sailings from Amsterdam to various parts of Europe and by 1700, regular services from England both to continental and transatlantic ports had been established.

Finally, a growing if intermittent demand for labour in early modern Europe was for war. Warfare had been endemic in medieval Europe and kings, lords and princes had kept their private armies, largely recruited for the occasion from their retinue and supplemented as the need arose with mercenaries. But the emergence of the nation state made war a more persistent and professional affair and led to the formation of standing armies and navies. Most states developed some form of compulsory service. Although the officer class was recruited from the high-born and well-to-do, since exemptions favoured the better-off, the lower ranks of the armed forces tended to consist of the dregs of society supplemented by mercenaries. Of 133 Spanish infantry battalions in 1751, 28 consisted of foreigners. As a source of mercenaries, Switzerland was particularly notable. At any time in the first half of the eighteenth century, it has been estimated that 50-60,000 Swiss soldiers were serving foreign princes. The size of armies also grew. During the Thirty Years War the effective strength of the armies involved was 100-120,000 men whereas in the War of the Spanish Succession 450-500,000 soldiers took part on both sides. Navies, too, grew in size.

CAPITAL AND CAPITAL GOODS

The majority of the European population had no effective demand for capital on any scale. And the scope of money transactions was not all-pervasive. In times of individual difficulty good neighbourliness was encouraged by the church but in hard times all suffered. For a substantial range of society the moneylender provided a necessary if unpopular function but his activities attracted loud condemnation as usurious. In the more advanced areas of Europe his activities became less important as other institutions developed and the greater availability of capital led to a fall in interest rates. To rescue the poorer sort from the clutches of the moneylender, *montes pietatis* were set up on a public basis while in the seventeenth century the pawnbroker emerged as a source of small and temporary loans. In 1746 a British Parliamentary Committee recognised the importance of the pawnbroker as a source of credit in a working class community. For the commercial community loans were made on a short-term basis and those who for some reason or another were often in temporary possession of funds, such as tax collectors, turned this accident to good account and out of some of their activities private banks emerged. By the end of the sixteenth century business firms such as the joint-stock company had emerged to meet the needs of enterprises whose capital needs and degree of risk were beyond the resources of the individual or partnership. Organised at first on a temporary basis, like the East India Companies whose joint-stock was initially concerned with a single voyage, they later developed into continuing concerns. The richer sort often raised money by pledging goods but more frequently obtained access to larger sums by mortgaging their estates. By increased indebtedness of this kind, the nobility were able to live ostentatiously.

Much of the provision of finance, at whatever level of society, was on a personal basis but to meet the needs of government or the commercial community for finance, banks were established. The older public banks such as the Banco di San Giorgio in Genoa or the Banco dello Spirito Santo in Naples were followed by the Bank of Amsterdam in 1609, the Banco Giro in Venice in 1619, the Nürnberg Bank in 1621 and eventually the Bank of England in 1694. Out of the activities of the scrivener, the goldsmith or the tax collector, who made advances to farmers, merchants or industrialists in the need of short-term accommodation, the English country bank emerged in the course of the eighteenth century.

But circumstances limited capital formation in the early modern period. The great majority had no surplus available while the nature of European society gave the rich a high consumption preference. The slow and intermittent growth of the market and the slow rate of technical change provided little incentive to save or invest. Then, despite the beginnings of banking and share-dealing, there was for many an absence of safe and productive outlets for investment which were hampered in the third place by the impact of calamities. The physical life of a great deal of investment, too, was short. Large gross savings were there-fore needed to secure small net capital formation.

One direction in which the spread of the commercial spirit in early modern Europe was particularly evident was in the growth of a land market. In England the dissolution of the monasteries led to a great redistribution of landed property and the supply of land coming onto the market was augmented in the century before 1640 by the sale of crown lands. The demand for land was fed from two sources: the growing commercial outlets for agricultural produce and the search by the rising wealth of the middle classes for land as a source of status. Similar considerations to a greater or lesser extent, powered the growth of land markets in other European countries. In many parts of Europe, too, landholdings were consolidated into great estates.

Much economic activity was carried out in the early modern period with little in the way of fixed equipment but capital investment became increasingly necessary in many directions. In agriculture, one way in which the pressure of population on food supplies was relieved was by the extension of the cultivatable area by drainage. Particularly in the mid-sixteenth century and in the first forty years of the seventeenth under the stimulus of rising food prices, considerable reclamation of land both from the sea and from lakes took place in the Netherlands. But, as is well-known, Dutch engineers also helped in the drainage of the Fens in eastern England. In Italy and Spain the construction of irrigation canals enabled more land to be tilled. The control of the rivers in the Po valley and attempts to drain the Pontine marshes were based on river-training and regulation which developed on a scientific basis in seventeenth-century Italy. In France, where the marshy areas were not concentrated as in England or Italy, attempts at drainage were carried out in widely scattered areas including Normandy, Languedoc and Provence from the later sixteenth century.

Other farm activities required some capital investment. In the arable areas there was greater emphasis on the barn

TABLE 3: Reclamations from the Sea in the Netherlands, 1540-1715 (acres)

	Reclamations by dyking				Reclamations by draining lakes	Total reclamations	Yearly a'age
	Friesland[1]	Holland	Zeeland[2]	Total			
1540–1565	34,592	31,195	23,232	89,019	3,372	92,391	3,685
1565–1590	–	10,105	8,485	18,590	1,525	20,115	802
1590–1615	7,980	30,770	28,660	67,410	22,872	90,282	3,610
1615–1640	18,925	11,347	33,485	63,757	47,650	111,407	4,457
1640–1665	5,910	9,900	54,315	70,125	2,597	72,722	2,907
1665–1690	2,275	5,460	18,195	25,930	5,020	30,950	1,237
1690–1715	2,732	3,147	23,855	29,734	1,602	31,336	1,252
Total	72,414	101,924	190,227	364,565	84,638	449,203	2,567

[1]'Friesland' includes the present-day provinces of Friesland and Groningen.
[2]'Zeeland' includes the present-day provinces of Zeeland and Noord-Brabant.

Source: Paul Wagret, *Polderlands* (Methuen, 1968), p. 79.

and the granary and in the livestock areas on stock buildings round some version of the great open courtyard which was typical of large farms in many parts of Europe where cattle were more important than corn. Pigeon houses and dovecotes – there were some 26,000 in England in the seventeenth century – had to be provided. For drying barley and hops, maltkilns and oasthouses were built and poundhouses were erected for crushing apples for cider. From the sixteenth century, lime, to produce which limestone was burnt in limekilns, came to be used to reduce the acidity of some soils. Like the town dairies developed in London in the seventeenth century as the capital outran its local milk supply, the need for the maltkiln, the oasthouse, the poundhouse and the limekiln were all evidence of the growing commercialisation of farming.

Much of industry required little in the way of fixed equipment and much expansion was based on the multiplication of existing productive units. But in some directions development could only take place by investment in fixed capital. A growing range of industries required greater power than could be supplied by men or animals. Windmills spread for corn-milling and drainage while water power was used for paper-making, cloth manufacture, iron-making and other manufactures as well as for corn-milling. To provide the water supply, dams and reservoirs had to be built, leats and water-courses constructed and wheels, gearing and shafting made and erected. This development led not only to an expanded demand for engineering skills and equipment but also to an enlarged demand for timber, stone, bricks and other building materials. With its forges and foundries, its blast furnaces and slitting mills, the iron industry was an outstanding example of an industry where the demands for capital equipment grew but it did not stand alone. Copper was in demand for vats for salt-making, sugar-refining and brewing as well as for roofing. And other industries such as carpet-making and porcelain developed on a more capital-intensive basis. As the demand for coal increased for industrial as well as domestic purposes and metal-mining grew, mines increased in depth, a development which increased the problems of transport, ventilation and drainage. Some of these were only very inadequately solved before the middle of the eighteenth century. Most pressing was the problem of drainage which stimulated the development of the steam engine by Savery and Newcomen. In consequence, by the middle of the eighteenth century mining had become a much more capital-intensive activity. But, as well as some successes, there were also false starts, such as the attempts of people like William Stumpe and Jack of Newbury to shift the woollen textile industry into factories before this move was imperative either on technological or management grounds.

The growth of trade led to a pressure for the improvement of transport facilities. In the construction of new roads and the amelioration of old, France led the way but roads were also improved in other countries as well. For land transport there were two Europes – southern Europe, the land of mule-trains, and northern Europe where carts and carriages were used. But there were exceptions to this. Far from towns where roads were bad, in the north it might also be necessary to use pack animals. And in the mountainous regions sledges might be used for winter transport. The growth of land transport also meant an increased demand for stable accommodation and fodder for the animals. By water, navigation by river was made easier as weirs were by-passed and river courses were straightened. But where river improvement was difficult canals were built. A small start was made in the sixteenth century when canals were constructed in England (the Exeter canal, 1560-6), Flanders (the Brussels canal), Germany and Italy but more was done in the following century. By 1688, for example, Germany had 185 kilometres of canals and 330 kilometres of canalised rivers. Following the construction of the Briare canal linking the Seine and the Loire, the crowning achievement of the seventeenth century was the building of the Canal du Midi (150 miles long with 100 locks), linking the Atlantic and the Mediterranean, in 1692. Further river improvement and canal construction was carried out in the early eighteenth century.

The growing needs of trade also had other consequences. Barges were required to carry goods along the canals and rivers and an increasing volume of shipping was needed both for coastal and for oceanic trade. The largest merchant fleets in this period were that of Holland which in 1700 totalled 900,000 tons and that of Great Britain which grew from 50,000 tons in 1560 to 340,000 tons in 1686. These centuries saw some advance in ship design, particularly the emergence of the Dutch fluit, and they witnessed the growth of shipbuilding, one of the earliest industries to become capital intensive. At the same time there was some improvement of ports. Quays and breakwaters were constructed. The breakwater at Portugalete, the outer port of Bilbao, was begun in 1530 and that at Barcelona in 1616. More navigational aids such as lighthouses were provided, some on medieval sites, for example Genoa (1543) and Cordouan in the Gironde (about 1584) and some entirely new like the Eddystone (1697-8). In the early eighteenth century the first attempts to build wet docks were made. To accommodate goods, warehouses were constructed and to facilitate trading, exchanges and market halls were erected. Gresham's Royal Exchange, for example, was built between 1566 and 1571 and the Corn Exchange in

Bristol between 1740 and 1743. In the early seventeenth century, John Abel built a series of timber market halls at Brecon, Hereford, Weobley, Kingston and Leominster.

The growing towns and self-consciously aspiring nations strove to make their architectural mark. To take but a few examples at random: the Kremlin was built between 1485 and 1516, the old chancellory at Bruges between 1535 and 1537, the library of St Mark in Venice in 1536 and the new town hall at Amsterdam in 1645. Palaces, courts of justice, bourses and prisons were also erected. And on capital account the new artistic flowering was not without effect. The Teatro Olimpico was built in Vicenza in 1584 and the first opera house in Venice in 1637. Libraries, museums and concert halls were also constructed. So architects and builders shared in the interest in these new artistic activities. Of church building there was comparatively little in the sixteenth century as the Reformation had its effect. While the reformed churches initially provided a much more limited and restrained demand for church buildings, the new buildings of the Roman church blossomed into rococo and provided ample opportunity for the architect, the sculptor and the glazier to give their exuberance free rein. Not only in Florence but in Mantua and in Rome with St Peters and Il Gesu, new styles of church architecture emerged and this influence spread to other parts of Europe such as Poland. Between 1660 and the middle of the eighteenth century the baroque flourished in Roman Catholic countries, in Toledo, in Granada, in Turin, in Württemberg and in Munich as well as in Rome. Monasteries were built at Klosterneuberg, St Florian and Melk. In England there was little church building before 1660 but the Great Fire of London gave Wren the opportunity to point the London skyline with the spires of his parish churches and the dome of St Paul's. A further burst of church building occurred in England between 1711 and 1736. The welfare services and education also had to be housed. Some almshouses and workhouses were built in the sixteenth century and hospital construction, started in the seventeenth century, gained pace in the eighteenth as the importance of cleanliness and fresh air in medical treatment came to be recognised. Schools, colleges and universities were housed or rehoused to meet the expanding need for education. In Cambridge, Trinity, Gonville and Caius and Emmanuel provide examples of sixteenth-century collegiate building and St Johns and Wadham in Oxford of the seventeenth century and both had considerable additions in the early eighteenth century. The new mood of scientific enquiry also required accommodation. Greenwich Observatory was built in 1675. And then there was investment in public display, in statues, ceremonial arches and fountains.

The growth of large cities posed new problems of water supply, street lighting and the disposal of refuse. The need to improve the social infrastructure became more insistent. Towards the end of the sixteenth century some towns in Italy and the Netherlands began to organise regular cleaning of the streets and the removal of refuse while an act for the better paving and street lighting of London was passed in 1671. Street lighting was introduced into Venice in 1732. Drake's leat was constructed in 1591 to supply Plymouth with water and in 1613 the New River proposal for providing London with water was implemented. Iron pipes for water distribution were first used there in 1746, three years after the Chelsea Water Company had installed an atmospheric steam engine to pump water to its customers. Amongst the earliest towns to take active precautions against fire was Nurnberg where fire engines were introduced in 1623.

With the introduction of artillery, the question of the defence of cities attracted some of the best minds of the age. Machiavelli, Leonardo and Dürer all concerned themselves with the problem which seemed to demand a geometrical solution with bastions constructed to provide as wide a range of fire as possible. Such new fortifications were extremely expensive and so by no means all fortress towns were modernised in this way. Amsterdam, which had been fortified with towers in 1481-2, acquired a more elaborate system of bastions in 1593 and a barrage was erected in the Ij to protect shipping. As a precaution against foreign attack, Henry VIII erected a number of fortresses on the new plan at Gravesend and Tilbury on the Thames, Sandown, Deal, Walmer and Sandgate in Kent, Camber and Rye in Sussex, Southsea, Calshot and Hurst in the Solent, Sandsfoot in Dorset and Pendennis and St Mawes in Cornwall. In the late seventeenth century the principles of fortification were elaborated by the Dutchman Coetoorn and the Frenchman Vauban. Many of the fortresses built in France in Vauban's time still survive. With the rise of standing armies, accommodation had to be built. In the sixteenth and early seventeenth centuries tents were carried for use when billets could not be found but later in the seventeenth century, as armies on campaign spent increasing lengths of time waiting about, huts replaced tents. At home, with the rise of standing armies, extensive barracks were erected for the first time and were sometimes large enough to form small towns of their own. For the navy, dockyards were built, at Brest in 1665 and at Devonport later in the century, while at sea the trend was towards differentiating the warship from the merchant vessel and increasing the tonnage and armament of ships. Under James I, a medium-sized war vessel could be built for £3-4000; in the early eighteenth century the cost had grown to £15-20,000. Armament and clothing factories were also built to meet the needs of war which provided the first sizeable demand for products.

CONCLUSION

It is difficult to assess or quantify the effect of all the changes set out in the foregoing paragraphs. While the scale and the pace of change appears small to modern eyes, it is incontestable that Europe in the middle of the eighteenth century was in many respects a different place from what it had been in 1500. It was a Europe in which the demands for goods and services was expanding. It was a Europe in which this expansion was held back not only by limitations of technology but also by a shortfall in effective demand, even though particularly in western Europe there had been a slight increase in per capita income. Bearing in mind there were in all probability significant regional differences, a few generalisations may be hazarded:

First, it was better to be rich in 1750 than in 1500. The range of provisions had increased and living conditions had significantly improved with warmer and more comfortable houses. For those who needed them, a wider range of professional services were available and a considerably augmented range of professional entertainment could be had. Travel was more easily possible. All in all it was easier to indulge the new tastes for luxury and ostentation.

Second, particularly in the more developed parts of Europe there was a larger and more substantial urban commercial and professional middle class who were also better fed, better dressed and better housed.

Third, for an intermediate group of skilled artisans and small farmers conditions were also better, a consequence of the growth of towns, the spread of money wages, the growing supply of imported products and a wider range of manufactured goods. The fairly ordinary man as a consumer was beginning to emerge as a person of importance in the demand picture.

Fourth, generally town workers enjoyed more assured conditions but in southern Europe particularly urban wages appear to have been kept down by continued immigration from the countryside.

Fifth, the gulf between rich and poor widened. This trend was most marked in eastern Europe where the rising living standards of the rich appear to have been not so much a result of greater productivity as of increased exploitation by landlords of the re-enserfed peasantry.

Sixth, some changes in agriculture, industry and commerce gave rise to new demands for seeds and raw materials, for tools, for power supplies and for other capital equipment.

Seventh, the demands of public display and war shifted to a new level.

But, lastly, for the mass of the population, whose major endeavours were to keep body and soul together, to feed themselves, to clothe themselves and to obtain some degree of protection from the elements for themselves and their families, the degree of change may well have been much less perceptible. 'Was a cottar', Sir John Clapham once asked, 'better housed, or fed, or clothed' in 1745 than in the 1550s? 'The statistician cannot say'. At the latter date society in Scotland 'was stabler, safer, more law-abiding. Whether its lower strata had become any more comfortable may certainly be doubted, but cannot be demonstrated'.[28] And what can be said of Scotland can no doubt be said for other parts of Europe as well.

In all this discussion it is necessary to underline the fact that as there were considerable differences between different classes of society, so there were significant variations over time and between regions. There were decades when conditions were better, decades when they were worse. Though in some sense Europe had a degree of unity, it was nevertheless distinguished by a fundamental diversity. One example, relating to France, must suffice. Although Pierre Goubert's study of Beauvais and René Baehrel's of Provence cover the same time period – the long seventeenth century – and each divides this 120 years into four almost identical periods, the only coincidence is in dates.[29] For when a period of prosperity reigned in Beauvais, Provence was depressed. And when Provence once again began to expand, Beauvais was plunged into catastrophe. Improvement where it occurred was neither steady nor sustained but episodic and fitful.

There is as yet no consensus about the changes in the patterns of demand which took place during this period, the age of the commercial revolution, the period *par*

28. John H. Clapham, *A concise economic history of Britain from the earliest times to 1750* (Cambridge UP, 1949), p. 216.

29. See Pierre Goubert, *Beauvais et le Beauvaisis de 1600 à 1730: contribution a l'histoire sociale de la France du XVIIe siècle* (2 parts, Paris: Sevpen, 1960); René Baehrel, *Une croissance: la Basse Provence rurale de la fin du seizième siècle à 1789: essai d'économie historique statistique* (Paris: Sevpen, 1961).

excellence of aristocratic display in Europe. To the *Cambridge Economic History of Europe*, IV, a volume entitled 'The economy of expanding Europe in the sixteenth and seventeenth centuries', Braudel and Spooner contribute a chapter in which they make by contrast the striking generalisation that 'from the late fifteenth century until well into the beginning of the eighteenth century, the standard of living in Europe progressively declined'.[30] To an assessment of this statement, this chapter may perhaps make a contribution.

30. Braudel and Spooner, 'Prices in Europe from 1450 to 1750', p. 429.

BIBLIOGRAPHY

Demand has been a neglected subject both because the source material is not easy to handle, particularly with respect to individual consumers, and because economists and historians have tended to be more interested in production, in supply rather than in demand. The consumer has been little discussed except by:

Elizabeth W. Gilboy, 'Demand in the industrial revolution', *Facts and factors in economic history: articles by former students of Edwin Francis Gay* (Cambridge, Mass: Harvard UP, 1932), pp. 621-39; reprinted in Ronald Max Hartwell, ed. *The causes of the industrial revolution* (Methuen, 1967), pp. 121-38.

Simon Kuznets, 'Quantitative aspects of the economic growth of nations, VII. The share and structure of consumption', *Economic Development and Cultural Change*, X (1962), pp. 1-92.

Ada E. Levett, *The consumer in history* (Benn, 1929).

General works of relevance include the following:

Fernand Braudel, *Capitalism and material life, 1400-1800* (Weidenfeld & Nicolson, 1973) (first published in French, 1967).

Pierre Chaunu, *La civilisation de l'Europe classique* (Paris: Arthaud, 1966).

Ragnhild M. Hatton, *Europe in the age of Louis XIV* (Thames & Hudson, 1969).

Eli F. Heckscher, *Mercantilism* (2 vols., Allen & Unwin, 1935; revised ed. 1955).

Pierre Jeannin, *L'Europe du nord-ouest et du nord aux XVIIe et XVIIIe siècles* (Paris: Presses Universitaires de France, 1969).

Henry Kamen, *The iron century: social change in Europe, 1550-1660* (Weidenfeld & Nicolson, 1971).

Frédéric Mauro, *Le XVIᵉ siècle européen: aspects économiques* (Paris: Presses Universitaires de France, 1966).

Roland Mousnier, *Le XVIᵉ et XVIIᵉ siècles: la grand mutation intellectuelle de l'humanité, l'avènement de la science moderne et l'expansion de l'Europe* (5th ed. Paris: Presses Universitaires de France, 1967).

Frederick L. Nussbaum, *A history of the economic institutions of modern Europe: an introduction to* Der Moderne Kapitalismus *of Werner Sombart* (New York: Crofts, 1937; New York: Kelley, 1969).

Edwin E. Rich and Charles Wilson, ed. *Cambridge economic history of Europe*, vol. IV. *The economy of expanding Europe in the sixteenth and seventeenth centuries* (Cambridge UP, 1967).

Clifford T. Smith, *An historical geography of western Europe before 1800* (Longmans, 1967).

For Great Britain, see in particular:

John Burnett, *A history of the cost of living* (Harmondsworth: Penguin Books, 1969).

Leslie A. Clarkson, *The pre-industrial economy in England, 1500-1750* (Batsford, 1972).

Peter Laslett, *The world we have lost* (Methuen, 1965; revised ed. 1971).

Sidney Pollard and David W. Crossley, *The wealth of Britain, 1085-1966* (Batsford, 1968).

For other European countries, see:

Fernand Braudel, *La Méditerranée et le monde méditerranéen a l'époque de Philippe II* (revised ed. Paris: Armand Colin, 1966).

Fernand Braudel, *The Mediterranean and the Mediterranean world in the age of Philip II*, vol. I (Collins, 1972).

Jerome Blum, *Lord and peasant in Russia from the ninth to the nineteenth century* (Princeton UP, 1961).

Pierre Goubert, *Louis XIV and twenty million Frenchmen* (Allen Lane, 1970).

Pierre Goubert, *Beauvais et le Beauvaisis de 1600 à 1730:*

contribution à l'histoire sociale de la France du XVIIe siècle (2 parts, Paris: Sevpen, 1960).

Eli F. Heckscher, *An economic history of Sweden* (Cambridge, Mass: Harvard UP, 1954).

Hajo Holborn, *A history of modern Germany, vol. I. The Reformation; vol II. 1648-1840* (Eyre & Spottiswoode, 1965).

Robert Mandrou, *La France aux XVIIe et XVIIIe siècles* (Paris: Presses Universitaires de France, 1967).

Brian S. Pullan, ed. *Crisis and change in the Venetian economy in the sixteenth and seventeenth centuries* (Methuen, 1968).

Brian S. Pullan, *Rich and poor in Renaissance Venice: the social institutions of a Catholic state to 1620* (Oxford: Blackwell, 1971).

Jaime Vicens Vives, *An economic history of Spain* (Princeton UP, 1969).

Most attention has been paid to food and food supplies, see:

Wilhelm Abel, *Agrarkrisen und Agrarkonjunktur in Mitteleuropa vom 13 bis zum 19 Jahrhundert* (Berlin: Paul Parey, 1935: revised ed. Hamburg and Berlin: Paul Parey, 1966).

William J. Ashley, *The bread of our forefathers: an inquiry in economic history* (Oxford: Clarendon Press, 1928).

Bernard H. Slicher van Bath, *The agrarian history of western Europe, AD 500-1800* (Arnold, 1963).

Noel Deerr, *The history of sugar* (2 vols., Chapman & Hall, 1949-50).

Jack C. Drummond and Anne Wilbraham, *The Englishman's food: five centuries of English diet* (Cape, 1939; 2nd ed. revised by Dorothy F. Hollingsworth, 1957).

Jean-Jacques Hémardinquer, ed. *Pour une histoire de l'alimentation* (Paris: Armand Colin, 1970).

Redcliffe N. Salaman, *The history and social influence of the potato* (Cambridge UP, 1949).

André L. Simon, *The history of the wine trade in England* (3 vols., Wyman & Sons, 1906-9).

Joan Thirsk, ed. *The agrarian history of England and Wales, vol. IV. 1500-1640* (Cambridge UP, 1967).

Abbot P. Usher, *The history of the grain trade in France, 1400-1700* (Cambridge, Mass: Harvard UP, 1913).

For marketing and services, see:
Dorothy Davis, *A history of shopping* (Routledge & Kegan Paul, 1966).
John D. Marshall, ed. *The autobiography of William Stout of Lancaster, 1665-1752* (Manchester UP for the Chetham Society, 1967).
Ray B. Westerfield, *Middlemen in English business, particularly between 1660 and 1760* (New Haven, Conn: Yale UP, 1915; New York: Kelley, 1968).
Thomas S. Willan, *The English coasting trade, 1600-1750* (Manchester UP, 1938).
Neville J. Williams, ed. *Tradesmen in early-Stuart Wiltshire: a miscellany* (Wiltshire Archaeological and Natural History Society Records Branch, XV, 1960).

For clothes and consumption goods, see:
François Boucher, *A history of costume in the West* (Thames & Hudson, 1967).
Caroline A. Foley, 'Fashion', *Economic Journal*, III (1893) pp. 458-74.
Alfred Rive, 'The consumption of tobacco since 1600', *Economic History*, I (1926), pp. 57-75.
Werner Sombart, *Luxury and capitalism* (Ann Arbor: University of Michigan Press, 1967).
Thorstein B. Veblen, *The theory of the leisure class: an economic study in the evolution of institutions* (New York: Macmillan, 1899).
John M. Vincent, *Costume and conduct in the laws of Basel, Bern and Zurich, 1370-1800* (Baltimore, Md: Johns Hopkins Press, 1935).

For building and the growth of towns, see:
Ronald Brunskill, *Illustrated handbook of vernacular architecture* (Faber, 1970).
Lewis Mumford, *The culture of cities* (Secker & Warburg, 1938).

John Summerson, *Architecture in Britain, 1530-1830* (revised ed. Harmondsworth: Penguin Books, 1969).

For wages and the standard of living, see:
Ernest H. Phelps Brown and Sheila V. Hopkins, 'Seven centuries of building wages', *Economica*, new series, XXII (1955), pp. 195-206, reprinted in Eleanora M. Carus-Wilson, ed. *Essays in economic history*, vol. II (Arnold, 1962), pp. 168-78.

Ernest H. Phelps Brown and Sheila V. Hopkins, 'Seven centuries of the prices of consumables, compared with builders' wage-rates', *Economica*, new series, XXIII (1956), pp. 296-314, reprinted in Carus-Wilson, ed. *Essays in economic history*, II, pp. 179-96.

Ernest H. Phelps Brown and Sheila V. Hopkins, 'Wage-rates and prices: evidence for population pressure in the sixteenth century', *Economica*, new series, XXIV (1957), pp. 289-306.

Mary E. Finch, *The wealth of five Northamptonshire families, 1540-1640* (Northamptonshire Record Society, XIX, 1956).

Elizabeth Gilboy, *Wages in eighteenth century England* (Cambridge, Mass: Harvard UP, 1934).

Richard Grassby, 'The rate of profit in seventeenth-century England', *English Historical Review*, LXXXIV (1969), pp. 721-51.

Richard Grassby, 'English merchant capitalism in the late seventeenth century: the composition of business fortunes', *Past and Present*, 46 (1970), pp. 87-107.

Richard Grassby, 'The personal wealth of the business community in seventeenth-century England', *Economic History Review*, 2nd series, XXIII (1970), pp. 220-34.

Alan Simpson, *The wealth of the gentry, 1540-1660: East Anglian studies* (Cambridge UP, 1961).

Poul Thestrup, *The standard of living in Copenhagen, 1730-1800: some methods of measurement* (Copenhagen: Institute of Economic History, 1971).

For other topics, see:
George N. Clark, *War and society in the seventeenth century*

(Cambridge UP, 1958).

Michael Foss, *The art of patronage: the arts in society, 1660-1750* (Hamish Hamilton, 1972).

Wilbur K. Jordan, *Philanthropy in England, 1480-1660: a study of the changing pattern of English social aspirations* (Allen & Unwin, 1959).

Emmanuel Le Roy Ladurie, *Le paysans de Languedoc, XV-XVIIᵉ siècles* (2 vols., Paris: Sevpen, 1966).

John U. Nef, *War and human progress: an essay on the rise of industrial civilisation* (Routledge & Kegan Paul, 1950).

Charles Singer, Eric J. Holmyard, Alfred Rupert Hall and Trevor I. Williams, *A history of technology, vol. III. From the Renaissance to the industrial revolution, c 1500-c1750* (Oxford: Clarendon Press, 1957).

Lawrence Stone, *The crisis of the aristocracy, 1558-1641* (Oxford: Clarendon Press, 1965).

Gladys Scott Thomson, *Life in a noble household, 1641-1700* (Cape, 1937).

3. Technology in the Age of the Scientific Revolution 1500-1700

Hermann Kellenbenz

INTRODUCTION

If we consider the European economy from the fifteenth century to the beginning of the eighteenth century, and compare it with the dynamic forces generated by the industrial revolution, we cannot help being aware of essential differences between the two.

An initial phase of territorial discoveries, that followed one another in astonishing succession, led to overseas expansion by the nations of Europe. This in turn has to be seen in the context of the new upswing in population that started in the middle of the fifteenth century following the bad harvests of the fourteenth century and the subsequent plague epidemics. The overseas expansion brought in its train an expansion of international trade, while the rise in population and other factors also stimulated home markets. The resultant upward trend of economic growth lost its impetus in the course of the seventeenth century. We have become accustomed to speak of the ensuing period as a phase of crisis, stagnation and recovery that lasted for decades and did not finally give way to a new upward movement until about 1740.

But to return to the initial phase. Expanding markets called for increased production. This was dependent on a number of factors, the most important of which seem to have been new technical procedures that made it possible to increase production and productivity in various branches of the economy.

What does productivity mean? Formerly it was understood to mean simply the ability to produce. Modern economists, in defining it, stress first and foremost the relationship between production and production factors, between output and input: accordingly they speak of the productivity of capital, labour, the soil, etc. Productivity as a whole, therefore, is the sum of the results obtained from dividing production by the various production factors.

The western world is indebted to the Middle Ages for a series of important technical achievements, in particular for the mill and the various uses to which it can be put. The possibilities of the cam were also discovered, while as early as the thirteenth century experiments had been made with the spring and the pedal; finally, in the fifteenth century, the crank, the connecting-rod and the regulator were invented, thus enabling continuous rotary motion to replace reciprocating motion. Important achievements followed in shipbuilding and navigational techniques. Within a comparatively short time western man had succeeded in raising considerably the technical level of performance. This level was not surpassed until the decisive advances of the industrial revolution.

The intervening period can show few, if any, technical achievements to compare with those of the preceding age, let alone with those of the eighteenth century.

The process of mechanisation, on the other hand, continued to develop, and this is a fact that needs to be emphasised. As the art of printing spread, technical knowledge could be disseminated more rapidly and widely. But the problem must be seen in a broader context and not merely from the technical angle. Non-technological factors could also cause productivity to rise, the stimulus coming from an increase in population, for instance, or from increased consumer purchasing power in the home market due to wider credit facilities and higher incomes, or finally from opening up new markets abroad. Or again, productivity could rise if the businessman thought on new lines and acted more rationally than hitherto, if he took the risk of producing more for stock, thus reducing production costs and hence the price at which he could sell, or if he canvassed for new customers or exploited foreign markets. This often led to new capital expenditure, and this in turn forced him, from the costs angle, to increase productivity. Finally, and especially since the fifteenth century, increased business competition was a spur to increased productivity. But it was not only new business initiatives and organisational measures in the private sector of the economy that encouraged the process; state institutions also developed new forms that enabled them to use technical means to get a firmer grip on the economy and bring about increased productivity.

It must not be forgotten that in the early days technical knowledge was mainly in the hands of practical men; it was also they who extended it. It was in this sense that Leonardo da Vinci described himself as unlettered, and Tartaglia insisted that his knowledge came from new inventions, and was not taken from Plato or Plotinus. Only from the time of Galileo, Torricelli and Redi, and then increasingly after the middle of the seventeenth century, did scholars show any great interest in this sort of practical knowledge. Fausto Veranzio, with his *Machinae Novae*, exemplifies the transition; with him the combination of humanistic knowledge and technical skill appears in a new form. The purpose of what follows is to establish and record the most important technical achievements during the two centuries between the discovery of America and the introduction of Newcomen's steam engine, and the extent to which they influenced the various sectors of the economy.

THE MOST IMPORTANT TECHNICAL ACHIEVEMENTS BETWEEN THE END OF THE FIFTEENTH AND THE BEGINNING OF THE EIGHTEENTH CENTURIES

PRINTING AND THE DISSEMINATION OF TECHNOLOGICAL KNOWLEDGE

Printing, and the results of printing, are the first things that come to mind when we ask ourselves what technical advances were made in Europe between the fifteenth and the beginning of the eighteenth centuries. Printing made it much easier to pass on information about new technical discoveries than it was in the days when everything had to be written by hand. No one could foresee the consequences of this, how far-reaching they were to be or how great an effect they might have on western civilisation.

The story of how printing with moveable type was invented does not concern us here; what matters for the purposes of this study is that the Mainz printing works was unable to keep its original monopoly and that before long the art of printing had spread throughout Europe. By about 1500, when twelve countries already knew the secret, forty thousand editions of books had been printed, over two-thirds of them in Germany and Italy; before the middle of the sixteenth century the art had spread to America.

Moreover by the middle of the sixteenth century the tools and methods used in type-founding and printing had reached a stage at which they remained virtually unchanged until the era of industrialisation. The first account of type-founding is contained in Vanoccio Biringuccio's *Pirotechnia*, published in 1540; in 1567 Christoph Plantin gave a fuller description, and a year later Jost Amman included printing in his illustrations to Schoeffer's work. But the first really detailed description of the tools and methods used in type-founding is contained in Joseph Moxon's *Mechanick Exercises* of 1683, which shows that an improved type-mould, permitting a reduction in the manual work, had been developed. According to Moxon the type-foundry and cutter could turn out four thousand types a day, a boy being employed to break off the jags. In the course of this development the original tin and lead alloy had been replaced by one containing antimony and several other metals; the antimony made the type harder.

The trade in printing-type had already started in Peter Schoeffer's day. Printing works will normally have had their own type-founding equipment throughout the sixteenth century; other users, however, bought their type. From the middle of the sixteenth century Holland, in particular, became a centre of this trade in type, although as the century progressed other European countries also specialised in type-founding. As was to be expected, this resulted in a tendency to standardise the height of the type. The development of the printing-press, which was originally made of wood, was another factor. With Willem Janszoon Blaeuw's Dutch press a new phase began.

Riccobaldi, the Ferrara chronicler, reports that these early printers could turn out three hundred pages a day. By the end of the sixteenth century this figure had risen to over a thousand for large-scale high-quality work. At the beginning of the eighteenth century the daily production of types was between two thousand five hundred and four thousand; working from six in the morning till eight at night in the summer, or from seven till nine in the winter, two printers could print two hundred and fifty single-sided pages an hour, or three thousand a day. Thus between Gutenberg's time and the beginning of the eighteenth century productivity had increased three or four times.

An exceptionally important element in book making was illustration, because many things could be expressed much more clearly visually than was possible in words. Woodcuts and metal engravings had been in general use as printed illustrations since the 1460s; before long, diagrams, plans, maps and music were added – by the German Ratdolt in Venice, for instance, in the 1480s. Albrecht Dürer's drawing-mill (Drahtziehmühle), done between 1495 and 1500, is the first pictorial record of mechanical wire-drawing. Printing was intimately connected with paper-making. The stamping-mill, used to pulverise the raw material, had been known since shortly after the introduction of paper-making in Spain in the twelfth century; the watermark came in during the next century. With the innovation of printing the paper market expanded considerably, which is shown by the growing number of paper mills. However, the most important subsequent innovation was not introduced earlier than about 1670. It was the 'hollander' which pulverised the raw material by means of knives set into a cylinder, which rotated within an oval container; its daily output exceeded the weekly output of eight stamping-mills.

So far as we are concerned here, the most important consequence of the discovery of printing was the dissemination of technological information through books. *Das Mittelalterliche Hausbuch* of about 1480, in which the various furnaces of importance to metallurgy were illustrated, being a manuscript had only a very limited circulation. The same was true of other manuscripts, such as that produced by Martin Löffelholz of Nuremberg in 1505, which contains the first illustration of a wooden vice with iron jaws, or that of the *Mendelsche Zwölfbrüderstiftung* (a Nuremberg charitable foundation) for the year 1528, which also shows a vice. No use was made of Leonardo da Vinci's wealth of technical ideas because they remained unprinted and so unknown. Technical journalism began with the *Bergbüchlein* and *Probierbüchlein* – practical handbooks on mining and the working of precious metals; Rülein of Calw described the copper smelting process in *Ein nützlich Bergbüchleyn*, which was published in Augsburg in 1505 and ran through several editions, Vannoccio Biringuccio's special distinction is that in his *Pirotechnia*, published in Venice in 1540, he gave the first systematic and comprehensive account of metallurgy, based on practical experience which he had gathered in Germany and Austria. His account is particularly valuable for casting technique and for its description of how several machine tools could be operated simultaneously by means of a water-wheel.

But in the fields of mining and metallurgy, Biringuccio was soon superseded by Georg Agricola's *De re metallica*, published in Latin at Bâle in 1556, a German edition appearing the following year. About this time Jost Ammann of Zürich settled in Nuremberg, as being the best place to study the seventy-six craftsmen whom he portrayed in the one hundred and fourteen woodcuts of his *Eygentliche Beschreibung aller Stände auf Erden*, which he published in Frankfurt in 1568. The series of great technical manuals, with copperplate engravings, on machine construction began in 1578 with the publication in Lyons of Jacques Besson's *Théâtre des Instruments*; a German edition appeared in 1595. It contained illustrations of dredges, hoisting apparatus, rammers, a calender operated by a horse-driven whim, pumping plant, polishing and grinding machines, a builder's crane, a conveyor chain, a lathe for cutting screws and so on. In 1588 Agostino Ramelli published his *Le diverse e artificiose machine composte in lingua italiana et francese* in Paris; it was the most comprehensive illustrated work of the day and showed more complicated driving-gear than Besson's book. A German edition followed in 1620. The third great book on machines and machinery, by Jacopo de Strada of Rossberg, was published in two parts by his grandson Oktavio de Strada in 1617/18 under the title *Künstliche Abriss allerhand Wasser – Wind – Ross – und Handt Mühlen, beneben schönen und nützlichen Pumpen* (Artistic compendium of all sorts of water – wind – horse – and hand – mills, together with fine and useful pumps). Published simultaneously in French, it contained the following new material: a cable transmission for operating a large grindstone, a post-windmill with rotating roof, a tilt-hammer and a similarly operated fulling-mill for cloth makers.

In his *De subtilitate*, published in 1550, Geronimo Cardano mentions a bolting machine for refining flour that had been invented within the previous three years. Giambattista della Porta's *Magiae Naturalis*, first published in 1558, enlarged in 1589, and containing noteworthy material on the natural and technical sciences, also has a place in this group of books. The first book on glass-making was Antonio Neri's *Arte Vitraria*, published in Florence in 1612. Other books on mechanical appliances were written by Zonca, de Caus, Veranzio and Branca; they contained illustrations of hoisting apparatus, mills, stamping-mills, devices for lifting water, sawmills and calenders, together with the appropriate driving-gear worked by man, beast, wind, water and even hot air. But compared with Leonardo's sketchbooks they contained nothing very original, although Zonca's *Novo teatro di machine et edificii* of 1607 showed a twisting-machine and a chamber-lock. German names are conspicuously absent from this list of authors; north of the

Alps people were content with translations or collections of extracts such as the six-volume *Theatrum machinarum* published by Zeising, Gross and Megiser between 1607 and 1614. Salomon de Caus, a native of Dieppe who laid out the gardens of Heidelberg Castle, wrote *Raison des forces mouvantes*, a work in three parts that appeared in French and German in 1615.

In 1597 the physician Andreas Leibau published his *Alchemia*, the first comprehensive manual of chemistry; it remained the standard work for many years. In the middle of the seventeenth century Johann Rudolf Glauber, known as the first chemist to interest himself in technical matters, published his findings in *Des Teutschlandts Wohlfahrt*, a series of technical writings that appeared in Amsterdam between 1656 and 1661.

Dud Dudley's *Metallum Martis*, published in England in 1665, set out his experiences in using coal in the preparation of iron. Robert Boyle, in his *Sceptical Chymist* of 1661, subordinated chemical research to experience, as the supreme arbiter, and maintained that mere speculation, while a valuable aid, could never be the real goal of economic endeavour. In the second half of the seventeenth century the vogue of the illustrated book declined again. Andreas Böckler's *Theatrum machinarum novum* of 1661 strikes one as already out of date; the publications of Kircher, Mersenne and Schott contained less original than extraneous material, and were forerunners of the scientific journals, which started to appear in the last third of the seventeenth century. These were reinforced by the new technical dictionaries, of which Conrad Dasypodius's *Lexicon mathematicum*, of 1599, was the first; Jacques Ozanam's *Dictionnaire mathématique* followed in 1691. Promoters of schemes and projects, to whose activities Bacon's essay 'On Innovations' to some extent formed a prelude, were a characteristic phenomenon of the age; some of the inventions announced in their publications turned out to be sterile. An exception was Denis Papin, who published his studies in the *Journal des Savants*, in the *Transactions* of the Royal Society and in the *Acta Eruditorum*

Lipsiensia edited by Mencke; he made significant contributions to the research that led to the steam-engine. Johann Kunkel, one of the best glass-makers of his day, demonstrated in his *Ars vitraria experimentalis oder Vollkommene Glasmacherkunst*, of 1679, how far the experience of an expert craftsman had diverged from the speculative thinking of many of the sixteenth-century writers. Jakob Leupold's nine-volume *Theatrum machinarum*, published in 1724 and the first completely factual description of engineering as it existed in his day, marks the end of an epoch.

The books on agriculture, partly still written in Latin, must not be left out; while some of these relied to a great extent on the classical authors, others gave useful hints on technical improvements. The most important German writer was the Silesian Johan Coler; with his *Oeconomia ruralis et domestica*, published between 1593 and 1601, he founded the household book. The authors of these works advised farmers 'to make better use of manure, change the crop more frequently and plough deeper'. One of them, Abraham von Thumbshirn, was chief steward of the electoral domains in Saxony, and in his *Oeconomia*, or 'instruction and guidance on how a whole household can be best and most usefully . . . employed,' made use of his experience to advise his readers on questions of estate management. Among English writers two must be singled out: Thomas Tusser, whose *Five hundreth good points of husbandry*, of 1573, described among other things the tools and implements needed by a farmer, and Walter Blith, whose *English Improver Improved*, of 1652, described those needed for drainage.

To these must be added works on architecture, town-planning, and the construction of dykes and canals. In 1561 Philibert de l'Orme published his *Neue Erfindungen*, or new inventions to aid good and cheap building. Simon Stevin's treatise *Nieuwe maniere van sterctebou door spilsluysen*, of 1617, was probably the first work published on the construction of sluices. In Italy, during the second half of the sixteenth century, Antonio Lupicini published books dealing with, among other things, hydraulic problems that arose in connection with safety works on the Po and the Arno; in the following century hydraulic techniques were further developed by Cornelis Janszoon Meijer, Benedetto Castelli, Domenico Guglielmini and Giovanni Battista Barattieri. In France H. Gautier tackled the problem of improving road-building technique in his *Traité de la construction des Chemins*, published in 1695.

Mention must also be made of the books on commercial arithmetic, book-keeping, and other aspects of business technique that appeared after the end of the fifteenth century.

As already indicated, the practical value of these publications varied considerably; it was greatest when the author knew his subject from practical experience. This occurred most frequently in writings on mining, metallurgy and dike-building; the authors of books on machinery borrowed extensively from one another. Clearly some records were deliberately left unpublished precisely because of their practical value: the *vade mecum* on workshops, by Vavřinec Krička of Bityšky, is a case in point; compiled in the 1560s it dealt with problems of casting and pump-making.

We have, moreover, only a vague idea of the influence exerted by this printed literature on technological matters, how widespread it was or how profound. We know, for instance, that six German editions of the *Bergbüchlein* of 1505 were printed between 1518 and 1539. Brunschwygk's *Liber de arte distillandi de compositis*, of 1512, passed through five editions, together with an English and two Flemish ones. By the beginning of the eighteenth century Coler's *Oeconomia* had been reprinted some fourteen times, while eight thousand copies of Biringuccio's *Pirotechnia* were printed in the first hundred years of its existence. One must also be careful to distinguish between an inventor's idea and the actual use made of it as an 'innovation', to use Schumpeter's expression, in the economic process. But it was not enough for a trader, or group of traders, to introduce a new technical device into the economic process. For such an innovation to be fully effective, a series of conditions of an institutional nature had to be fulfilled, and this depended not only on the interested traders but also to a considerable extent on political or military decisions on the part of the country concerned.

Against a background of technical knowledge, that had become increasingly widespread through the agency of the printed word, one has to imagine a growing class of specialists who could not only write but who were capable of making technical drawings and of seeing that they were carried out in practice. Others had to know something of accountancy and bookkeeping. The overseer, as business manager of a mining company, kept the accounts of one or more mines, as well as the shift records, and rendered an account to the owners – the Saxon ore-mining industry at the end of the fifteenth century was run in this way. Overseers with a working knowledge of *Wasserkünste*, or devices that employed water power, were highly paid, and sometimes formed their own trading syndicates; *Meister* Peter of Feltisheim did this in Danzig, with Johann Boitzenburg and Dietrich Wiko of Lübeck. As early as 1477 Paulus Eck of Sulzbach proudly announced that he was a 'surveyor and astronomer of long standing', who considered himself far superior to the 'common layman'. One of the best known of these new specialists was Blasius Dalmaticus of Ragusa.

The names most frequently given to these experts were architect and engineer. Salomon de Caus called himself 'engineer and architect to the Elector of the Palatinate'.

The name engineer – already used in Lombardy and France as *inzignerius* during the thirteenth century – probably spread to central Europe from France and the Netherlands in the beginning of the seventeenth century. In 1630 Johann Faulhaber of Ulm called one of his technical works on constructing fortifications a 'school of engineering'. In his *Tractatus de natura et studium ingeniariae* of 1649 (German edition 1658), Christian Jacobi described an engineer as a man who combined a knowledge of mathematics with mechanical proficiency, and classed him, as distinct from the craftsman, with the representatives of the liberal arts. According to Christoph Weigel's *Hauptstände*, or principal vocations, published in 1698, an engineer had 'to have thorough knowledge and practical experience of geometry, geodesy and surveying', as well as of matters connected with building and warfare, and to be able not merely to draw up plans on paper but to lay out and direct everything on the site and, if necessary, do the work adequately himself. It is also worth noting that the names 'undertaker' and 'entrepreneur', as forerunners of the later 'contractor', had their origins in the sphere of public building, where the organisation necessitated the use of technical resources.

ACHIEVEMENTS IN THE FIELD OF ENGINEERING

The biggest problem was how to produce the power to operate mechanical appliances. The water-wheel, as a source of power, made slow progress, but at least it is possible to trace this progress during the sixteenth and seventeenth centuries. The horizontal water-wheel,[1] referred to as a step forward by an anonymous engineer of German origin about 1430, was introduced into Europe without undergoing any further technical improvements, its principal users being peasants in the mountain regions. In the Toulouse area a horizontal water-wheel with compartments into which the water flowed, thus facilitating the forward movement of the wheel, was developed; in this improved form, which anticipated the idea of the turbine, it had wider applications and could be operated by a smaller flow of water. In Renaissance times it led engineers to consider new improvements, which took the water-wheel a stage further on the road to the turbine; Francesco di Giorgio, Leonardo, Besson, Ramelli, Veranzio, Turriano all described the '*molino regolfo*', an invention which effected some increase in power but found only sporadic acceptance;

1 The older type of the water wheel has a vertical axe. The water falls either from above on the paddles and thus moves the wheel by its weight or it flows below the wheel and presses on the paddles according to the strength of the drift.

The water wheel with a horizontal axe could be driven by paddles or by vanes or buckets which later were developed to the turbine.

evidently the water supply was too complicated and, generally speaking, people were content to rely on the power provided by the vertical water-wheel. But so long as there was no transmission, the possibilities of this were also limited. By and large a water-wheel was constructed to operate a set of millstones, a hammer, a rammer and so on, its size being adjusted accordingly worked along these lines.

Whether these water-wheels were undershot, overshot or side-driven, they were made of wood until into the eighteenth century, a fact that automatically limited the power they could generate.

Iron would have made them more cumbersome; moreover it rusted and was too expensive. Normally it was used only for smaller and more important parts. The performance was determined by the volume and speed of the water. In the fourteenth and fifteenth centuries the average diameter was between two and three metres. A water-wheel with twenty-eight floats, known to have existed in Toulouse in 1489, seems to have represented the upper limit; this was equivalent to a diameter of between two and three metres. From the sixteenth century onwards the diameter was increased, but not beyond twice the previous size; Agricola mentions one of ten metres, which raised the energy generated to ten horse-power. According to Fernand Braudel, until into the eighteenth century a total of five to six hundred thousand flour-mills generated one and a half to three million horse-power, an increase that can only be described as modest in view of the increase in population. Generally speaking the seventeen kilograms of flour per hour, which is the estimated figure for the twelfth century, was increased by only thirty-three per cent, although Makkai gives an upper figure of thirty-seven kilograms per hour for Hungary in 1693. The traditionalist agrarian structure was a main obstacle to the greater increase in production that technical skills would meanwhile have made possible. In the industrial sector much greater use was made of technical opportunities.

The advance that resulted from the increased size of the mill-wheel is a factor that cannot be ignored. It has been calculated that the power generated by a mill-wheel was five times greater than that produced by two men operating a hand-mill, or twice as much as that of a whim-driven mill. Where there was no water with sufficient fall, a situation that was particularly apt to arise in flat country, other sources of power had to be found. Where wind-power was available, principally in coastal areas, windmills were used. The older type of windmill, with a tower, came from the Mediterranean area. The next development was the post-mill, in which the wooden cage was moveable; it was already in use in the Middle Ages on the flats bordering the North Sea. It is clear that the Dutch had invented the *Wipmolen*, in which only the tower-cap needed to move, as early as the fourteenth century: Agostino Ramelli published a drawing of it showing details of the mechanism. The power was increased from ten to thirty horse-power, or by twenty to forty per cent, which was a marked improvement on the water-wheel. But, except in Holland, windmills were not as widely used as water-wheels; they were also more expensive and the wind to drive them was not available every day.

A significant innovation was the use of a windmill to drive a saw, the first combination of the sort being set up in Holland in 1592 by Cornelius Cornelisz. Windmills were used for many industrial purposes in Holland, particularly on the banks of the Zaan, where sometimes as many as nine hundred were in operation; they played an especially important part in drainage work.

The level attained by machines and appliances, and it had risen still further in the fifteenth century, first became known to a wider public through works like Agricola's *De re metallica*, published in 1556; the stimulus given by such publications led to new improvements and yet more illustrations. It was in the improved use of driving-gear and screws that the sixteenth and seventeenth centuries made their special contribution. A characteristic feature of those days was that wood was still largely used in the construction of machinery and equipment, metal being employed only for parts that needed to be more durable.

The most remarkable machinery recorded by Agricola is that for extracting and dressing ore. The part played by the pump was more important than it had been in the Middle Ages, and the equipment was more varied. Pumping installations in the mines and for supplying water were larger than hitherto, the suction pump in particular undergoing further development. Agricola describes and illustrates various types of pump. Both he, and to a still greater extent Ramelli in 1588, make it clear that the suction pump was already known and used in the sixteenth century. As time went on more of the component parts were made of lead, copper and iron, instead of wood; in the second half of the seventeenth century cast iron cylinders were used. The pump at the *Pont Notre Dame* in Paris was representative of the level of achievement reached by 1670: used to draw water from the Seine, it was a combination suction-and-plunger-pump; it was illustrated by Belidor in 1737. The continuing and expanding use of the suction-pump led men like Galileo, Torricelli, Guericke and Pascal to apply themselves to the problems of the vacuum; their work created the necessary conditions for developing the steam-engine. But although the history of this started with Papin's experiments at the end of the seventeenth century, it was not until the beginning of the eighteenth century that Newcomen succeeded in producing a model that could be employed practically.

The making of tools and equipment is closely connected with the screw and its uses, and we owe to Leonardo da Vinci the first pictorial record of how screws were employed in tool making and mechanical engineering. Da Vinci, and later Besson, both worked on the problem of making screws by machinery; but for the time being both wooden and metal screws were cut with the chisel or the file. Another possibility was the lathe, first illustrated in 1568 in Hartmann Schopper's book of handicrafts, but even in Plumier's day (1701) it was still a very limited one. Screws could doubtless have been cast in bronze; the coarser iron-casting presumably gave still more unsatisfactory results.

One of the most important applications of the screw was

the screw-press, for printing and for minting coins. About
1550 Daner, in Nuremberg, replaced the wooden screw
with a copper one and was thus able to obtain a finer
image.

The screw-press is said to have been first used by
Bramante, to produce Pope Julius II's lead seal; the pope's
medals were also stamped in this way. The next stage was
the coin-press, first used by Cellini to stamp medals for
Pope Clement VII. The introduction of this press was
understandably opposed by the minters; but attempts to
get it accepted continued. Augsburg and Zürich were
centres of the new process. At the beginning of 1552 a
coin-press, bought from the Augsburg goldsmith, Max
Schwab, was installed in the Louvre; coins were stamped
mechanically in the Louvre until 1585, when the *Cour des
Monnaies* succeeded in limiting the Louvre's activities to
medals and copper. Another version of the story says that
the production costs were too high. In the 1560s Rudolf
Rordorfer of Zürich was minting coins by machine in Hall
(Tyrol); from 1566 Hans Vogler, also of Zürich, was doing
so in Mühlau. The equipment then made its way to
Segovia, Bohemia and Graz. Nicholas Briol developed a
similar process, which was adopted by the Scottish mint in
1639. A French process, using water power, was introduced
into England in 1561, but the French expert, Mesrell, was
sentenced to death for counterfeiting; in 1649 Peter
Blondeau reintroduced this process into England, where he
further improved it. There was also the balance-press, the
extremities of whose arms were weighted with leaden balls;
in 1651 the Royal Mint in London was using a press of
this kind.

A significant development was the use of the roller for
purposes other than minting. Eoban Hesse, in 1532,
describes an early application of it in processing iron; it
was used by the Nuremberg wire-drawers and nail-makers.
Zonca (1607), de Caus (1615) and Branca (1629) all
describe rollers used to flatten out gold and silver, copper
and lead. The stage reached by the roller in the early
decades of the eighteenth century can be seen from the

Political Testament, dated 1746, of the Swede Christopher
Polhem, who set up a workshop for processing iron and
other metals in Stjärnsund in 1704. Polhem's first concern
was to use water power to the greatest possible extent. In
addition to the older hammer technique, he favoured the
roller; by using a water operated roller, he could turn out
ten or twenty times as much strip-iron as he could with a
hammer. Polhem also said that, compared with the widely
used hammer, the roller was still very little known in
Sweden, the reason, in his view, being that it was too
difficult to make.

In spite of various achievements in the field of engineering,
the possibilities of machinery remained restricted by the
limits set by the power of wind and water, and water
power still had not reached the efficiency of the later turbine.
But the next development of engineering lay not towards
the turbine but towards steam power. In 1711 the blacksmith
Thomas Newcomen built an engine that was actually used
for pumping water out of the workings of a mine in War-
wickshire. It was – as we mentioned – based on the driving
force of steam power condensed in a cylinder.

THE CHEMICAL PROCESS

Just as engineering, the whole apparatus of machinery, forms
one side of the technological efforts of our period, so the
other side includes all what we today term the chemical
process. Chemistry in our modern sense did not yet exist.
What people were interested in was much more the al-
chemist part of the whole complex, to find the stone of the
wise man, to discover the 'arcana' which could produce
gold and other precious things in an artificial way. Anyway,
tradition gives to Paracelsus (1493–1541) the honour of
being the founder of scientific chemistry with his statement
that chemistry was the science of transformation of the
'materia'. Transformation meant changing all kind of stuff,
especially minerals, into metals by casting, distilling,
subliming, finding new combinations by the method of
assaying.

The handling and treatment of metals culminated in the assayer's art, which was pursued on an experimental basis. From Biringuccio, Agricola, and especially Ercker, we can see that this art reached its zenith in the sixteenth century. Metals were assayed to determine the uses to which they could be put and what alloys were possible. The empirical knowledge of the assayer was first linked to chemical theory by Cramer in the seventeenth century. One of the most important discoveries in this field was the combination of coal, saltpetre and sulphur to gunpowder which, already known by the Chinese, came in use in Europe during the thirteenth century and led to the development of fire weapons. Another important achievement was made in the field of metallurgical methods. Surely, no spectacular new inventions were made during the sixteenth and seventeenth centuries with the exception of the patio process in Latin America (see next paragraph); however important, too, was the large scale application of the new metallurgical methods by better mechanisation and organisation.

The method of separating silver ore from copper by liquation goes back to the early fifteenth century. The problem was to combine copper with lead. The brothers Allenpeck, who came from a Nuremberg family, and Georg Thurzo of Cracow had been working on the process since the middle of the fifteenth century. The new expansion of silver and copper production in Europe was connected with their work.

Of the greatest importance to the European silver mining industry was the amalgamation of silver ore with mercury; the process, which had already been described by Biringuccio, was further developed by Bartolome de Medina in Pachuca (Mexico), and was in large scale use from 1566 onwards. Pero Fernandez de Velasco introduced the process into Peru in 1571; it became known in Europe through the accounts given by Antonio de Ulloa and Alonso Barba (1640).

Biringuccio and Ercker described the manufacture of brass. A new method of making brass from copper by fusing the latter with charcoal and calamine was invented by

Ebner, a Nuremberg patrician. Savot was the first to write about the production of brass by combining zinc with copper.

Tin and tin compounds were needed to manufacture sheet metal from copper and iron. Here again the Nurembergers and Saxons distinguished themselves as innovators. In the first half of the seventeenth century bismuth was also added. Printing type was originally made of material from the tin-foundries; later, as Moxon tells us, lead and antimony compounds were used, which were both stronger and cheaper.

Extensive work was done on the production of steel, Biringuccio's account of it being the first we have. In the seventeenth century several patents were granted in England for new methods of making steel; one new method of this sort was proposed by Anton Zeller of Aschhausen in 1608. The first description of fusing iron bars with charcoal to make steel was given by Robert Plot in 1686, in his *Natural History of Staffordshire*. Robert Hooke mentioned cast steel in his diary, and two years later Joseph Moxon compared cast steel to Damascus steel; but it was the method discovered by Huntsman in 1740 that first made it possible to market this cast steel. The tempering of steel must have been understood and practised in the Middle Ages, and a booklet published in 1532 gave instructions on how to make steel and iron soft and hard. The best description we have is that given by della Porta in his *Magiae Naturalis* already alluded to.

Chemical knowledge played a particularly important part in improving and refining the art of glass making. The Venetian skills of glassmaking, especially the cristallo, were mostly kept as secrets but then Antonie Neri's *Arte vetraria*, published in 1612, remained a standard work throughout the seventeenth century. Red glass had been successfully made in the sixteenth century by adding gold; Andreas Cassius, in Hamburg, and Johann Kunkel developed ruby glass by adding a mixture of gold chloride and stannic chloride. A further German innovation was the production of opaline and opaque white glass by the addition of horn or bone substance. George Ravenscroft seems to have been the first to make lead crystal in the 1670s.

The problem of increasing the heat involved a special aspect of chemistry. Blowing-furnaces for melting soft non-ferrous metals had been known in late medieval times. Larger furnaces were needed for iron. The open-hearth furnace developed into the 'Stückofen' and then into the blast furnace, which towards the end of the seventeenth century was twice as large as that used in the middle of the sixteenth century (see below).

The intensity of the heat also depended on the fuel used; the higher temperatures were easier to obtain with coal than with charcoal or peat. A particularly important discovery was that coal could be used for smelting in metallurgy. In 1612 and 1613 Simon Sturtevant and John Ravenson published papers in which they advocated coal-fired blast-furnaces; but they could not get their inventions accepted. The substitution of coal for charcoal in glass making was also found possible at this time. The London brewers started to use coal, someone having hit upon the idea of drying malt with coke, in other words with coal from which various impurities had been extracted. During the civil war coke-dried malt was produced in Derbyshire; the beer made from it became famous. Towards the end of the seventeenth century it was discovered that coke could be used for smelting lead ore; later it was used for tin and copper ore as well. In 1707, in Brosely in Shropshire, coke was used for the first time to smelt iron.

TECHNICAL ACHIEVEMENTS IN THE INDIVIDUAL SECTORS OF THE ECONOMY

This complex of questions has been approached from the technological angle with a view to establishing where innovations occurred and what form they took.

In what follows an attempt is made to explain what effect these technical innovations had in the individual sectors of the economy, in agriculture, in mining and processing, and in distribution.

Technical aids in agriculture and fishing

In the twelfth and thirteenth centuries, agricultural implements, including those used for harvesting, reached a standard that remained essentially unchanged in quality for several centuries.

The one-way frame plough was already fully developed in the fourteenth century. Its construction was subsequently strengthened, but this also made it heavier and a powerful team was needed to pull it; gradually more and more of its parts were made of iron, so that it became lighter again, and a single pair of horses or oxen was sufficient. The harrow, in the form of the frame-harrow and, like the plough, made of wood, was also perfected in the fourteenth century. In the sixteenth century harrows with up to three frames were in use.

The usual harvesting implement was the sickle, of which various types were known in the Middle Ages. Since the fifteenth century the scythe, which had long been used for hay and low-growing crops like oats, barley and peas, began to replace the sickle for cutting grain as well. The scythe used for cutting grain was provided with a special grill that threw the grain to one side. In some parts of Europe grain continued to be cut mainly by the sickle until into the eighteenth century. Rakes, and forks for hay or grass with two wooden prongs, also reached their traditional forms in the Middle Ages. Threshing continued to be done on the threshing-floor with a flail consisting of a handle and swipple. Braking flax and hemp were also traditional rural occupations, as were carding or combing, by means of a comb stuck with iron nails, spinning on the distaff and, later, on the spinning-wheel; the changes that took place in these will be dealt with in another context. In gardens and vineyards the two-pronged hoes and iron shovels or spades still familiar in our own day were used, as well as the traditional rakes. Gardening-knives were curved like a sickle, which made grafting easier. The wooden presses used for pressing grapes and other fruit have not changed in form since the Middle Ages. Butter-churns, on the other hand, were improved: Bohemian illustrations of the end of the sixteenth century show a revolving, barrel-shaped churn. Bee-keeping literature in circulation in the sixteenth century tells of the part played by apiculture and of the increasing use of bee-hives made from plaited straw.

The tackle, casting-nets, trawl-nets and baskets used by fishermen already existed in the Middle Ages. In the sixteenth century the thriving Newfoundland fisheries called for special measures to process dried cod. Because the fishermen had to sail great distances to catch the cod, these had to be salted and stored in the hold; when the ship reached port the fish was turned into dried cod. As the fishing industry expanded – the waters off Norway being one of the most important new fishing-grounds – the ancient method of the hand-line was replaced early in the seventeenth century, on the initiative of the Dutch, by the tow-line. In the seventeenth century, too, the rising whale industry demanded, and devised, new methods not only for catching but for processing the whales.

Another important development was the expansion of the pond fisheries, by creating whole systems of ponds joined by canals. In the sixteenth century Bohemia became a sort of nursery for the pond fisheries of Europe, a valuable stimulus being provided by the *Libellus de piscinis* of Jan Dubravius, published in 1547; through it a wider public became familiar with the problems of breeding carp and the need to segregate the fish in different containers according to age – a procedure already known in the fifteenth century.

Technical aids in mining and smelting

Mining. Because the deposits were more extensive, iron, generally speaking, could still be obtained without resort to the deep-level mining, with its complicated equipment, that was sometimes necessary in the case of precious metals, copper and, to a lesser extent, tin and lead. Nevertheless in the Eifel shafts reached depths of 8–10, and 15–20 metres, while even in medieval times shafts and galleries requiring the simultaneous installation of drainage equipment had been dug in the Upper Palatinate. In the early days this equipment was driven by 'man and beast', but in time these gave way to mechanical means. In the Upper Palatinate mining was done at a depth of about 100 metres, although bills of enfeoffment were issued for twice this depth.

In mining for precious and non-ferrous metals, the value of the output was an additional incentive to dig deeper, which increased the difficulties of extraction and drainage. On the Schneeberg, in Saxony, the richest mines had already reached a depth of 200 metres in 1480, and two years later, after a gallery – the *Fürstenstollen* – had been built to drain away the water, 200 metres below that. The *Fürstenstollen* ran 70 metres under the Stadtberg, so that individual pits in the silver mines were already some 270 metres deep; about 1500 the *St Georg* pit, of about 300 metres, seems to have been the deepest.

The problem of draining was thus solved by constructing galleries; another solution was to haul the water up through shafts. Sometimes a combination of both methods was used. A few years after ore had been discovered on the Schneeberg, thirteen galleries had been constructed there. The first of these draining-galleries to be built was the *Fundgrüblerstollen* mentioned in 1471. The *Fürstenstollen*, clearly built with assistance from the ruling prince, was 24 metres deeper; thanks to it the mining operations thrived again after 1476. A few years later a still deeper gallery was needed to overcome the water problem, and in 1481 an order was placed for the *Markus-Semlerstollen*; but years passed before it was completed.

Water could be hauled up through the shaft by means of a windlass, but this was possible only from small depths; the shafts were also narrow, which limited the number of windlasses that could be erected. At greater depths water-powered devices were necessary; these could drain the water down to depths of 200 metres, but below that windlasses had to be used again. Paternoster-pumps, consisting of an iron cable to which buckets were attached, could drain water at a depth of 70 metres; another device using leather pouches, was effective at depths of 160–180 metres. *Meister* who could operate these devices were highly paid. The device with leather pouches is said to have come from Slovakia. *Meister* Peter of Feltisheim who lived in Danzig installed a number of these in the Carpathians and later in Ilkusch near Cracow, before he contracted to work for the Schneeberg mines; but while his devices could drain more water, they could not operate at greater depths. At first 200 metres was the extreme limit for such devices. On the other hand technical progress resulted in increased productivity and a saving in manpower.

In the Schneeberg mines six to eight men worked in each pit, which means that operations were on a small, or very small, scale. The same was true of Marienberg, which began to flourish in 1519/20. Here the workings were shallow, unlike those at Freiberg, on the Schneeberg and in Tyrol, and gallery construction and drainage presented no comparable problems. One mine employed fifty-eight men, two others fourteen men, three others twelve men, and so on.

In the Bohemian tin mining industry, whose great days were in the first half of the sixteenth century, seams were worked by deep-level mining to a depth of 200 metres. Initially the ore was brought to the surface by a whim driven by a team of animals; working at an average depth of 150 metres, each shift produced up to thirteen tons of material. Later, using a water-wheel instead of a whim, it became possible to extract more, but then the question of profitability arose. In the 1550s and 1560s the Bohemian tin-mining industry considered using water-power to raise the ore to the surface, but the plan was never put into effect, probably because it was too expensive. Haulage equipment of this sort paid its way in silver mines, in those in Tirol for example, but was too expensive to use in the English coal mines.

In the middle of the sixteenth century, paternoster-pumps installed in the Bohemian tin mines raised 150 hectolitres an hour from a depth of 60 metres, or 5700 hectolitres a day. Improvements in ventilation, which are known to have been introduced in the second half of the sixteenth century, also helped to increase output and working efficiency.

In Tyrol there were mining areas round Schwaz and on the Röhrerbühel. In 1515 a total of 274 pits, employing more than 10,000 men, were in operation in the Falkenstein area, which was part of the Schwaz region. In the same year work was started on the construction of shafts in the *Erzherzog Sigmund* draining-gallery; eventually these descended in nine workings to a depth of 240 metres below the surface of the valley. A force of 600 men was employed to haul up the water. In the year 1535 the costs of this work amounted to about 14,000 florins, although the total costs of the mine were not supposed to exceed 7,700 florins. In 1538 eight large handpumps were installed, which could be operated by 240 men working in three shifts. In 1554 Wolfgang Leuschner constructed a reversible water wheel, which became famous; an overshot water wheel, about ten metres in diameter, it hauled up the ore in buckets, and the water in big leather pouches each holding 1,400 litres, through a distance of 218 metres. This machine, which needed only two men to work it, could raise 100 cubic metres of water in eight hours, a performance equivalent to that of 629 men or 35·5 horse-power.

On the Röhrerbühel, near Kitzbühel, mining operations did not start until 1540/41. The seams ran at an angle of eighty-five degrees, or almost vertically, which meant that the sinking of shafts was an expensive affair from the very beginning. Mining regulations, issued in 1543, provided for a combined ore-raising and drainage operation in nine vertical shafts, thus ensuring the prosperity of the Röhrerbühel mines for the next fifty years. The shafts were sunk a further 16–31 metres each year, a remarkably impressive performance considering the difficulties of ventilation and drainage. In 1618 the six most important of the shafts had reached depths of from 645 to 886 metres. The 886 metres of the deepest shaft, the *Heiliger Geist* shaft, took it to a depth of 144 metres below sea level; more than seventeen sections had already been completed in 1597. For some three hundred years it remained the deepest shaft in the world; not until 1872, in Pribram in Slovakia, were greater depths achieved. It cost so much to drain that in 1570 thirty per cent of the whole labour force was engaged in this work. In this *Heiliger Geist* shaft the pressure of water at a depth of 540–550 metres was already so great in the 1550s that in 1554 a wooden device by Wolfgang Leuschner had to be installed; consisting of eight parts, it was at first driven by hand and later by horse-power. In 1587 a water supply was completed which brought water a distance of six and a half kilometres to drive a reversible wheel; this operated the cable to raise the ore and also the drainage system. In its early days the output of the Röhrerbühel mine was exceptionally high: the figures for 1552 were 6,430 kilograms of silver and 361 tons of copper, and for the years 1570–96 28,231 kilograms of silver and 5,688 tons of copper. But the annual running costs for the same period were 72,277 florins. In 1597 2,002 workers were employed in the Röhrerbühel mine, only one eighth of whom were actually engaged in mining.

In the lead mines of Upper Silesia and Poland drainage was particularly difficult because, although the pits were only 40–80 metres deep, they were situated to a greater extent in low-lying country. The pumping apparatus used in the fifteenth century was driven by teams of twelve, and even up to sixteen, pairs of horses, which had to be changed every few hours. In the course of the sixteenth century, and more particularly during the second half, a draining plant with a length of up to 50 metres was installed. The capital costs were defrayed by a joint stock company with an issue of sixty-four shares; the citizens of Cracow, people living in the mining towns, the nobility and the king all contributed.

The next important technical advance was blasting. Fire-setting had been known in late medieval times, but because of the smoke given off, and other problems, its use was limited. Blasting was first introduced in 1627 in Schemnitz (Banska Stiavnica), but some time elapsed before it resulted in increased production. In Neusohl (Banska

Bystrica), where it was introduced in 1629, there was initially no marked increase in production; but the market was bad at the time and there was no great demand. It was only at the end of the seventeenth century that blasting found wide acceptance.

Drilling-machines brought new opportunities for increasing production, but they did not come into use until the beginning of the eighteenth century: they could clear more rock in less time than four men working by hand.

Transport of the ore from the pit to the dressing plant could also be a factor in increasing production; but improvements in this department were only effective if the ore was carried away as quickly as it was raised. An improvement of this sort occurred in the sixteenth century when the 'dog' (*hund*), a truck that ran on wheels, was introduced as a means of transport. The name 'Hungarian dog' indicates that one type originated in the Slovakian copper mines, while in all probability another, central German, type was first used in the Harz and from there found its way to the English coal mines and later to the early wooden railways.

Dressing the ore. Since only pure and easily reducible ore could be smelted, dressing the ore was more important in the Middle Ages and early modern times than it was later. Agricola described the dressing process in detail. First the ore was sorted by hand and the 'gangue' knocked off with a hammer; ore that was covered with clay or mud had to be washed. After it had been cleaned, the ore was roasted in walled 'sheds'. Deleterious ingredients like sulphur could be leached away with water afterwards. Sometimes the ore, instead of being roasted, was left out in the open for years: oxidisation turned the sulphides into sulphates and the rain leached the ore. Finally the ore was stamped and sieved, to make sure that the 'mixing' was even.

In the fifteenth century the hand-mill, as a means to crush the ore, was gradually replaced by stamping-machines that used a dry process; but the loss of metal through pulverisation was still considerable. Wet-stamping reduced the loss of metal through pulverisation, and in addition crushed the ore more finely. In spite of this, according to Mejer, the loss of metal in tin mining amounted to between twenty and twenty-five per cent.

The connection between mechanisation and increased production can be established in the case of tin-ore dressing. In the sixteenth century the dressing plants became more complicated. Washing, by means of various types of sieve and rinsing trough, was combined with stamping and roasting; according to Mejer 'the powdered ore thus produced had a high degree of homogeneity'. In the course of the sixteenth century ninety-one of these complicated dressing plants were installed in the Schlaggenwald and Schönfeld areas, seventeen in Sangerberg and a number in Lauterbach. The performance of the stamping-machines was improved by providing each machine with three or four individual stamps; the machines were also coupled, so that, for example, three water-wheels served three different stamping machines. A machine with three stamps could crush 450–750 tons of ore; one with four stamps could crush 650–1,000 tons. The smaller plants employed two to seven people, the medium ones eight to eleven, and the large ones twelve to twenty-nine. In the sixteenth century Schlaggenwald and Schönfeld had thirty large dressing plants.

Smelting: Iron. As far as the fourteenth century the direct process of smelting iron ore was dominant: in a primitive furnace a mixture of charcoal and iron was heated intensely for several hours, with the aid of wind or bellows, until the iron was reduced into a glowing ball, whereas the remainders of the minerals and the charcoal ash were sintered into a kind of slag. The process being finished the furnace was broken and the lump or pig of metal, in German called Luppe from lupus, was hammered in order to separate remainders of slag and to obtain a more or less coherent mass of metal.

Wrought iron produced in this way was nearly free from impurities. In order to obtain steel wrought iron bars had to be packed with charcoal in clay boxes or jars and heated for several days during which the iron absorbed the quantity of carbon which was necessary for the hardness typical for steel.

In the various regions of Europe there were various types of furnaces or forges in use. In Germany they were called Rennfeuer or *Zerrenfeuer*: local varieties were the Hessian forest forge (*Waldschmiede*), the Corsican forge and the Catalan forge. A transitional type of furnace, the forerunner of the shaft-furnace, or *Stückofen*, was common in Sweden, Finland and Russia until into the eighteenth century; in the absence of lime they were built into a framework of beams. They were used mainly for converting bog-ore into Osmund iron.

The bellows which were used to increase the temperature originally were worked by hand; later they were worked by treadmills driven by men or animals; when water power was introduced, water-wheels were used. For the sixteenth century Biringuccio and Agricola show various forms of water-driven bellows.

The next stage in development was the Stückofen or shaft-furnace, which even in the Middle Ages was built of stone to heights of between four and six metres. The *Stückofen* was used in Styria, Carinthia, Carniola, in the Schmalkalden district and in the near east. In the Alpine regions it was also known as the *Pla-, Bla-* or *Blauofen*; from the resulting *massa* such excellent forged steel was obtained that its reputation remained unrivalled for a very long time. Styrian and Carinthian steel held its own until after the middle of the eighteenth century, and that from Schmalkalden until the year 1840.

The development of the *Stückofen* shows how the growing demand for iron made it necessary to build bigger and bigger furnaces. These furnaces needed a much stronger blast in order to obtain the equal heating of the charge. During this process of conversion the pig iron which resulted absorbed carbon to the degree that it became liquid. Later this impure pig iron had to be transformed in various processes into wrought iron; on the other hand it could be used for casting iron articles. On behalf of the transformation of pig iron into wrought iron the whole process is called 'indirect' process and the furnace which was developed especially for pig iron was called blast furnace (*hautfourneau, Hochofen*). Being continuous the indirect process consumed less fuel than the 'intermittent' *Stückofen*; on the other hand, more fuel was needed to refine the pig-iron, and for this reason the refining plants were transferred to districts with adequate supplies of wood and water.

The earliest description of a blast-furnace is that given by St Bridget in her revelations. According to her there must have been blast-furnaces in Sweden round about 1320, the idea being suggested by the copper-furnaces; they were about five metres high and had a special device for eliminating the slag. In the mid-fifteenth century there were blast furnaces of this sort in Sweden, the Siegerland, Belgium, the Bergamo area and in Tuscany; about 1500 they were to be found in France as well. German and Walloon workmen brought the innovation to England. About 1500 pig-iron was being produced in central Germany, and thirty years later in Carinthia. From there the innovation spread to the other alpine regions, individual countries developing their own typical forms.

In the early days, that is to say in the sixteenth century, the German blast-furnaces must have had a very high reputation, because Gustav Wasa sent from the north for German blast-furnace designers. But the furnaces consumed a relatively large quantity of wood. Meanwhile an advance was made in France and Belgium with a type that Louis de Geer introduced to the northern countries; these furnaces were seven metres high and gradually ousted the older models. In the second half of the seventeenth century blast-furnaces in England reached a height of over eight metres, while at the beginning of the eighteenth century still larger ones of up to thirteen metres were built in the Urals.

For a long time the limit imposed on these furnaces by the charcoal firing was insurmountable. The turning-point came with the substitution of coal for charcoal, and the resulting increase in iron production. It was Abraham Darby who in 1713 for the first time produced a kind of coke with which he operated a blast furnace in Coalbrookdale. A further consequence of this revolutionary change was that the focal point of the industry switched from the alpine regions and Sweden to England and the rest of Western Europe. Hitherto density of population and a correspondingly high level of culture, as well as a large output of iron, had been mutually exclusive; from now on they rose together.

Up till this point the process had been unsatisfactory because the sulphur in the coal passed into the iron and spoilt it. Good quality iron from a coal fired furnace was first produced in the 1620s at Pensnet in Worcestershire by Dud Dudley, working in the ironworks he had taken over from his father. But he kept his method secret. Abraham Darby, who came from the same district, invented a special process for making cast-iron and in 1709 acquired the disused Coalbrookdale works in Shropshire, where he produced castings; after 1713 he used coal mixed with charcoal and peat for smelting.

Non-ferrous metals. Copper smelting in central Europe, as described by Agricola about 1550, had a long tradition behind it. The fact that the furnaces used, in Falun for example, for smelting copper led to the invention of the blast-furnace for smelting iron has already been mentioned. The copper-smelting furnaces themselves underwent no further significant development, because copper was easier to smelt than iron. This made the liquation process all the more important; just how important it was can be seen from the fact that the finished products, refined copper and silver, cost some two-thirds more than the earlier black copper. Unfortunately we know very little about either the technical installations or the production of the smelting-works. At Eisfeld the production was probably between 1,000 and 2,000 hundredweight; after 1500, when the smelting technique underwent constant improvement, the production rose too. The equipment was complicated and expensive. Before long, however, there were smelting complexes capable of turning out 7,000 hundredweight of copper a year: one of these comprised eight smelting-furnaces, ten liquation-furnaces, three refining-hearths, three cupelling-hearths and two drying-ovens. The Leutenberg smelting-works took several years to build and cost more than 10,000 florins. In the 1550s a large smelting-works was built at Neusohl; it was intended to replace the smaller works at Stare Hory and Harmanec, which were no longer profitable to run because of the shortage of wood. Here there were sixteen shaft-furnaces for smelting the ore and fifty roasting-hearths; 9,000 tons of ore could be smelted annually, giving a yield of 10,000 hundredweight or more of good copper. Several smelting processes were tried out, in order to discover the most profitable; the best proved to be the Jörger furnace, with which the costs were one gulden ninety-three denarii less than with the smaller furnaces. A Jörger furnace could take up to 254 *Par* of ore, the smaller type only 60.

We know the exact yield from a report on a trial smelting operation in 1633, when smelters from Tirol and Carniola competed for a wager. 100 *Par* (13,000 kilograms) of black *Herrngrund* ore were treated. The Tyrolese smelters lit the furnaces at six o'clock on Monday evening and worked in shifts until three o'clock on Saturday afternoon; from the 100 *Par* of crude ore they obtained 30 *Par* or 93 hundredweight of metal extract and burned a total of twenty-seven loads of charcoal. The Carniolese smelters worked only two at a time and burned only fourteen loads of charcoal. Thus they worked more economically. In each case a hundredweight of ore yielded 14 pounds of copper and 75 grains of silver.

In tin smelting the productivity was not so clearly apparent. Here, too, the process consisted of a series of operations: there was a domed furnace for roasting, a rinsing trough, an ore mill, a further milling process, and finally the smelting proper in four-sided furnaces between 2·5 and 2·7 metres high. Above the furnaces were compartments in which the metal, released by the action of smoke and steam, was deposited by cooling. In Schlaggenwald and Schönfeld there were thirty-two smelting works, the proportion of smelting-plants to dressing-plants being one to three.

The main centres of copper production and smelting were Slovakia, the Harz and Thuringia, Tyrol and Carinthia; it was here that the liquation method was concentrated and developed. The main centres of tin production and smelting were the north and south sides of the Erzgebirge and England. The main centres of lead production and smelting, of great importance in the liquation method, were the Harz, Poland and Carinthia.

Technical aids in other branches of industrial production

Forging: Iron. Heavy tilt-hammers were needed to compress the lumps of metal; they had an effective weight of 1,500–1,600 kilograms. The hammers used for hammering out the metal delivered quicker, lighter blows. A 300 kilogram tilt-hammer delivered 60–120 blows a minute; the lighter slitting-hammer, which weighed 70–80 kilograms, delivered 200 blows a minute.

The improvements that came with the wire-drawing mill, the slitting-mill and the rolling-mill must also be mentioned here. The mechanisation brought by these inventions naturally resulted in a much greater output than was possible with a purely manual process or with previous forging methods. The rise in productivity from the end of the sixteenth century to the first half of the eighteenth century is shown by studies of G. Hofmann and A. Paulinyi. Hofmann tried to find out how much wrought-iron one worker could produce during one day in 1575 at the Stara Hut works near Beroun in Bohemia and how much the average output with the hammer was. With the same method A. Paulinyi tried to find out how much the output of the Hronec works in Slovakia was in 1747. The comparison between the two calculations is shown overleaf.

Stara Hut works 1575		Hronec works 1747	
Output of wrought iron during a year with 35 working weeks	460 qu[9]	Output of a year with 15 working weeks	476 qu
Output of a day	220 kg	Output of a day	257·6 kg
Employed men	8	Employed men	5
Daily output per man	27·5 kg	Daily output per man	56 kg
Daily output per hammer	73 kg	Daily output per hammer	126 kg

[9] 1 qu=100 kg.

In Stara Hut 100 kilograms of wrought-iron represented the 3·64th part of a working shift, in Hronec only the 1·8th part, that is, productivity had about doubled.

In another calculation Hofmann tried to show how in Bohemia blast furnace output rose during the seventeenth century. These, of course, are selected cases; further research is needed to supplement and, if necessary, correct the above figures.

Non-ferrous metals. Forges in the non-ferrous metal sector, as well as in the iron sector, were already producing articles for the trade that were often finished off elsewhere. In Neusohl the copper obtained was cast and hammered into certain standard forms, such as square discs, circular discs, hemispheres, 'granular' copper for the mints, and hollowed-out finished articles like pots and pans. This industrial undertaking, which was one of the most modern of its day, thus produced a large and varied range of wares including work done by the hollowing-hammer. This method of production, which was very advanced compared to the more time-consuming hand-work, was also introduced in the Aachen area in the first half of the sixteenth century. Hitherto the guild regulations here had permitted only sheet-brass and plate to be produced by means of flattening – or longshafted – hammers; any further processing had to be done by hand. The ban on hammer-mills is first mentioned in a decree issued in 1510; with these hammer-mills several brass discs could be hollowed out into bowls simultaneously. A plant equipped with hollowing-hammers could turn out more in one day than ten other plants in

Bohemian blast furnace

Beginning seventeenth century

Output of pig iron per man per shift	83 kg
1·2 days needed for	100 kg

Second half of the seventeenth century

Output of wrought iron per man per day	47 kg
2·13 days needed for	100 kg

Included the pig iron process
3·18 days were needed

Assuming miners, woodmen, charcoal burners, etc., to be employed in the proportion one to two 12 working days were needed for each 100 kg of wrought iron

Middle of the eighteenth century

Output of pig iron per man	120–125 kg
1·5 days needed for	100 kg
Output of wrought iron a day	67 kg
1·5 days needed for	100 kg

Pig-iron and wrought iron process

Taken together 2·7 days were needed for 100 kg

ten days; it also used less calamine. The final product, however, was not as good as that made by hand. Because of the Aachen ban, the first hollowing-hammers were set up outside Aachen on land belonging to the Duke of Jülich and under the jurisdiction of Stolberg. This was the beginning of Stolberg's rise to prosperity; later it became Aachen's rival. Guild regulations also made it difficult to introduce the hollowing-hammer in the country bordering the River Meuse; the privilege granted by Philip IV to the batteurs of Bouvines in 1625 contained a ban on using hammer-mills. Namur and Bouvines only received permission to install copper-mills in 1643.

Mention must also be made here of the rationalisation that took place in the minting of coins. At first the coins were hammered out by hand, a process involving relatively high labour costs. Machine stamping reduced these; thanks to the mill-wheel, and the power it generated, the labour force could be reduced, the running costs lowered, and the performance improved. This new process, as we have seen, was adopted by the Habsburg mints and in Segovia; but attempts to introduce it in France and in England were short-lived.

Casting. Significant discoveries, resulting in increased productivity, were made in both bronze – and iron – casting in the later Middle Ages. The incentive came from the technique of arms production. The early cannon were cast over a core, the barrel being re-bored later. Increased output was made possible by boring-machines, driven by whim or water-wheel; Biringuccio records one driven by water. By the seventeenth century these boring-machines had reached a remarkably advanced stage of development. Casting iron cannon balls was another very important activity. The early moulds with a single cavity were later replaced by moulds with several cavities, thus permitting several balls to be cast simultaneously. A further rise in productivity came with the expansion of the blast-furnace industry; indeed the development of this industry, with its yield of liquid pig-iron, has to be seen in conjunction with the manufacture of cannon balls. Some of the most spectacular progress was made in Sussex where, about 1570, eight blast-furnaces, together with one in Kent, had a total annual output of five to six hundred tons of iron, whereas by the turn of the century it had risen to a thousand tons, or a little less. An important landmark in casting grenades and bombs was the method, introduced in the sixteenth and seventeenth centuries, of casting them over a core of clay in partitioned sand-boxes.

In those days increases in productivity were connected with improvements in casting methods because these meant greater rationalisation. The older method, in which a wax mould was used, had the disadvantage that the mould had to be made afresh for each casting. If an object had to be produced in large quantities, wood or metal moulds were prepared and then divided, so that the individual sections could be removed. According to Biringuccio this was the procedure used about 1533 by a foundry in Milan that made brass objects in everyday use, such as fittings, rings and clasps; the moulds were of brass and tin. One workman had from six to eight forms in hand at the same time, which meant that the firm could keep the whole of Italy supplied with these articles. Wooden moulds, impressed in an even bed of sand, were used to cast decorated iron plates for stoves and fireplaces. In Hesse, where in the sixteenth century plate-casting reached its zenith and supplied a European market, the casting was done by a more advanced process in which closed sand-moulds were used, together with wooden moulding- and casting-boxes.

After about 1500 a method was devised of casting pots, like bells, by means of clay moulds that consisted of a core and a cope. With this development cast-iron entered an important sphere of everyday life. The next stage came with pig-iron smelted in a coke-fired furnace; this iron, which was rich in silicon, was especially suitable for making thin castings. In 1707 Darby obtained a patent for a method of casting pots and pans 'in sand only without loam or clay'.

Wire-drawing: rolling and slitting. During the Middle Ages wire was drawn through metal dies by hand and various means were used to augment the strength of the wire-drawer. In general only copper and other soft metals allowed the drawing of larger wire. Large-diameter wire from iron and other harder metals had to be hammered. Here mechanisation by water power opened new ways which in the fourteenth century already was introduced in the Sauerland (*Drahtrolle*) and in the Nuremberg region. The first illustration of a *Drahtziehmühle* such as it existed near Nuremberg is given by Albrecht Dürer in the ninth decade of the fifteenth century.

At about the same time, about the year 1495, Leonardo da Vinci made sketches for rolling mills. The development of the rolling process in connection with minting has already been mentioned. In 1532 there is mention of an ironworks in Nuremberg that was driven by a water-wheel and was probably connected with a rolling-mill. The further development of rolling and slitting techniques took place in Central Europe; there is a description of a German iron-slitting-mill in 1683. In the eighteenth century a new phase was ushered in by John Payne in England and the Swede Christopher Polhem.

The production of sheet metal. Black sheet-iron was made in Nuremberg in the fourteenth century; the men who made it had business connections with the tin mines in the Fichtelgebirge. This suggests that the production of tin-plate, made by alloying iron and tin, also dates from this time; its origins are to be found in the Fichtelgebirge, and especially in Wunsiedel, as well as in Nuremberg. The industry long remained a German monopoly, centred in the Nuremberg area, the Upper Palatinate, the Fichtelgebirge and Saxony. In the middle of the sixteenth century, however, tinned sheet metal was being produced in Styria; Sweden and the Netherlands followed suit in the seventeenth century, when beginnings were also made in Russia. The English gained possession of the secret in 1670 but the French, in spite of repeated attempts, had no real success until 1726.

The textile sector. During the two centuries under consideration various innovations were introduced in the textile industry to overcome difficulties in the working-process; other innovations were aimed at improving the quality of the goods produced. A new appliance was devised for fulling the wool; it was bigger than the earlier models and was often suspended. In order to increase production the size of the carding-machines was increased until finally carding by hand was replaced by a piece of equipment that corresponded to the system used in flax-braking (*chevalet de cardage*). The next step, the invention of the rotary machine by Daniel Bourn of Leominster, did not come until the eighteenth century. The Dutch had the best tools for braking flax. In the second half of the seventeenth century attempts were made in England to brake flax by mechanical means; similar attempts must also have been made in Holland. It was not until decades later, however, that any marked success was achieved, and then it was in Scotland. Another step forward was the use, in both Holland and England, of long steel teeth for carding; there is evidence of this at the beginning of the eighteenth century.

The silk-mill was used industrially in medieval times: it wound the fine silk strands of the cocoon into organzine. In Florence in 1581, so Montaigne tells us, one woman, using this machine, could supervise five hundred '*fuseaux*'. It evidently spread to Belgium and Holland from Italy in the sixteenth and seventeenth centuries, although in England it remained unknown until the brothers Lombe introduced it in 1717. In Bologna a special type of mill was developed to produce *orsogli*; during the seventeenth century the Venetians succeeded in gaining control of it. For the rest, the spindle and distaff still remained in use for winding the thread, especially in outlying districts; they survived because, though slow in operation, they were simple and particularly suited to flax and hemp yarn. The spinning-wheel, which was better suited to spinning wool, had been known since the thirteenth century. The next significant step was the spinning-wheel with a flyer; it is first mentioned in the Waldburg-Wolfegg house-book of 1475–80, but without a pedal. The foot-mechanism is illustrated in the Glockendon Bible of 1524; it may have been improved in Lower Saxony, where a tradition, dating back to 1530, exists of a stonemason named Jürgen in

Wolfenbüttel. It was at this time that the Wuppertal yarn trade banned the innovation; in spite of this, however, it spread throughout Europe. The spun yarn was wound on a spool by means of a hand-wheel. Once again it was the silk industry that provided the incentive for improvements, of which the warping-mill in the seventeenth century was one.

In weaving, progress can be traced from the fourteenth century, the stimulus again characteristically coming from the silk trade. The old vertical loom was replaced by a horizontal one. A loom for weaving designs, at which a boy was employed to hold the threads taut, was already in use in Italy in the Middle Ages; the form came from the east, and from Italy found its way to France, where it was improved in the second half of the seventeenth century (1687) by Galantier and Blache. In the same year Joseph Mason's invention was introduced in England. At the beginning of the seventeenth century Claude Dangon, a weaver in Lyons, attracted notice with an invention that enabled the number of threads to be increased to two thousand four hundred; this made it possible to reproduce large designs in several colours. Further contributions to mechanisation were made by the French in the first quarter of the eighteenth century, but again these can only be touched on here.

A number of inventions since the sixteenth century had helped to pave the way for the mechanical loom. Anton Möller of Danzig is said to have invented something of the sort in 1586, but the city council forbade him to use it. In 1604 there is confirmation of a *moulin à rubans* invented by the Netherlander Willem Dierickzoon van Sonnevelt; in the following year the States General granted him a patent for ten years. The use of these looms, which caused disturbances in Leyden in 1620, was authorised by decree in 1623 and by subsequent directives. From the Netherlands the ribbon looms spread to England, France, Switzerland and Germany. Eventually these 'Dutch' looms were able to weave up to twenty-four threads simultaneously. This led to new regulations forbidding the use of these innovations;

but in fact they continued to be employed in numerous centres of the textile industry within the Holy Roman Empire, such as Deutz, Mülheim, Solingen, Elberfeld, Barmen and Radevormwald. In 1685 an imperial edict banned all the mechanical looms; in 1719 the city of Augsburg succeeded in getting the ban renewed. Although outside the scope of this book, it is worth mentioning that the hydraulic gear for operating ribbon looms, invented by Hans Hummel in Bâle about the year 1730, was also banned by the authorities.

Certain improvements also took place in other sectors of the textile industry. Fulling, for instance, was originally done by foot, but even in the Middle Ages beaters operated by water-wheels had started to replace the older method. In the Netherlands, it is true, manpower was still preferred for high quality work, but in England mechanical fulling became general in the sixteenth century; France and central Europe adopted it too. In Holland windmills were used.

Equipment for teasing cloth existed in the fifteenth century. In England the use of such 'gigmills' was forbidden by Act of Parliament in 1551; in spite of this they were used in Gloucester in the first half of the seventeenth century. The stirrup-grip was used for napping the cloth up till the end of the seventeenth century, after which a rotary lifting device took its place. In Paris the wooden plate had already given way to the calender, a cylindrical press, in Colbert's day; pressing the cloth under heat increased its lustre. This was known in the late Middle Ages, but was prohibited everywhere at first. In the seventeenth century, however, it became an integral part of the finishing process, like crimping and teasing; in the second half of the century the French made increasing use of special machinery for this last process. These and other pieces of textile machinery were used in conjunction in the business run by Sieur Guillaume Véron at the end of the century.

In the field of linen production, 'clear' linen or lawn, a new type developed in the Netherlands, spread to Westphalia and other countries. The Dutch also developed the best technique for bleaching hemp – and flax-linen; the bleaching was done with buttermilk, and the whole dressing process took six months. It was not until the 1750s, and the introduction of chemical agents, that the bleaching-time could be reduced.

The technique of knitting, which went back to the Middle Ages, was perfected by the Florentines in the sixteenth and seventeenth centuries. About 1589 an English clergyman named William Lee designed the first stocking-frame, but he received no support in England and approached King Henri IV of France. The hand-knitters raised such difficulties, however, that the machine made only slow headway in the seventeenth century, England finally being the first to take it up; in the 1650s the French followed suit, especially in the southern part of the country. The Italians developed a loom for making figured designs which was adopted in Lyons.

To sum up, one can say that the textile industry manifested a certain tendency towards technical improvements, and that generally speaking the stimulus for this came from the silk trade, in other words from Italy, where its origins are hard to trace. Following the appearance of the flyer spinning wheel at the end of the fifteenth century, various new pieces of equipment were added during the seventeenth century whose purpose was to improve the finish and make the products more uniform. But the manual process still predominated, the mechanical innovations relating only to parts of the whole procedure. For the decisive innovations, that were to be of importance in industrialisation, the trade had to wait until the 1730s.

Other branches of industry; glass and pottery. In the early days of glass making Italy was technically the most advanced country, particularly the island of Murano, off Venice, where a highly specialised glass technique was practised. Two processes that went back to late medieval times were enamelled glass and colourless, so-called crystal, glass. One result of the Italians' pre-eminence in this field was that the other European countries tried to copy them. By threatening severe punishments the Venetian authorities did their utmost to prevent the Murano glass makers from leaving the country and giving away the secret of the '*façon de Venise*', but those in Altare, near Genoa, were not so closely watched. At all events, in the middle of the sixteenth century the Italian art of glass making spread to other parts of Europe as far as to Sweden. It reached even England before 1570 and Denmark about 1572. According to Biringuccio and Agricola, the Italian glass-men worked with one, others with two, others with three furnaces. The last gave the best and cleanest glass. Those who used three furnaces smelted the mixture of the material in the first, recooked it in the second in order to prepare it for the elaboration and cooled the glass articles off in the third furnace. A better construction of the furnace was used in England from the beginning of the seventeenth century. In order to facilitate ventilation the heating space (furnace room) was put on a grille.

Glassmaking by the gaffer's chair was a technique probably developed by Italians working in the Netherlands towards the end of the sixteenth century from where it spread to other parts of Europe.

An event of importance to English glass making was a proclamation issued in 1615 which forbade the use of wood for heating glass furnaces; coal was to be used instead. But coal produced higher temperatures. This seems to have been instrumental in leading to the invention of a 'covered pot' for making clear glass, whereas open pots were used as earlier for green bottle glass. Another English invention was the 'one-shaped' glasshouse, which made it possible to concentrate the air current and to increase the calorific value of the fuel.

Engraving on glass, adapted from stone-cutting, was known before the end of the sixteenth century; the foot-operated wheel, which was used for this, gave way, in the seventeenth century, to water-power. The invention of coloured, opaline and opaque glass, as well as of lead crystal, has been noticed in another context.

The production of stained glass was greatly stimulated

by the Gothic style of architecture, with its many and varied opportunities for inserting glass windows. These opportunities were seized and further exploited by Renaissance builders, those in the Netherlands being technically the most advanced.

As far as plate glass was needed glass centres such as Venice and then Nuremberg developed casting sheets which in the beginning remained small. Large sheets of clear glass such as for mirrors were cast for the first time in Normandy. A Norman glassmaker, Lucas de Nehou, introduced the method in the famous Saint-Gobain works in the second half of the seventeenth century.

In the middle of the sixteenth century it became possible, by using a combination of convex and concave lenses, to see distant objects magnified. At the end of this century a telescope was built in Italy, and then copied by Dutch experts; but Galileo's telescope, and the microscope, were improvements on this. Further improvements continued to be made until about 1680. In addition to the professional instrument makers, numerous scientists also specialised in making lenses.

Pottery techniques, like the glass maker's art, made their way north from the Mediterranean south. The art of making pottery vessels in Italy owed a great deal to the potteries round Valencia and Malaga; from the early 'majolica' vessels, first made at Florence, Urbino and Faenza, came the 'faience' of the Italian Renaissance. Levantine influences spread by way of Venice. North of the Alps, cobalt blue from Saxony made possible the rise to fame of the pottery known as Delft blue. Meanwhile Chinese porcelain had captured the market, and, spurred on by the growing fashion for chinoiserie, the Saxon Tschirnhaus and Johann Friedrich Böttger eventually succeeded in re-inventing the important Chinese hardpaste; with their invention as a basis, the first European porcelain was manufactured at Meissen.

Coal mining and salt production. Coal had been mined in the Aachen–Liège area and the Ruhr since the Middle Ages, but the industry received a boost of decisive importance in the sixteenth century, when flourishing trade conditions made the shortage of wood fuel more and more apparent. A vital step forward came with the discovery that coal could be used for smelting. In 1612 and 1613 Simon Sturtevant and John Rovenzon published papers in which they advocated the use of coal fired blast-furnaces; but their inventions did not catch on. Simultaneously, however, it was found that wood could be replaced by coal in glass-furnaces. Coal was also used by London brewers in making beer. According to J. U. Nef, the processes of drying malt, and obtaining coke from coal – that is of freeing coal from its impurities – could be combined. This was done in Derbyshire during the Civil War; beer brewed from malt that had been roasted with 'coaks' proved to be particularly sweet and pure, a discovery that made Derbyshire beer famous. Towards the end of the seventeenth century it was found that charcoal could be replaced by coke in cupola-furnaces; originally used for smelting lead ore, this type of firing was later used for smelting tin and copper ore as well. In 1706 iron was successfully smelted with coke for the first time at Brosley in Shropshire and then – we mentioned it (p. 207) – Abraham Darby operated a furnace with coke in Coalbrookdale in 1713.

Another obstacle to the industrial use of coal was the problem of draining the mines from which it was obtained. Pumps of various sorts were already known and used for drainage purposes, especially in the tin and copper mines; but they were too expensive to install in coal mines. There was no significant new impetus to production until the steam-engine – at first in the form invented by Newcomen – was introduced.

In salt mining, the *Sinkwerksbau*, which had been known in the mountain regions since the eleventh century, was replaced after 1562 by the more rational *Wehrbau*. The *Sinkwerksbau* was a method of mining salt in which water was introduced into specially sunk shafts; the water dissolved the saliferous rock and could then be pumped out as brine – in the early days it was drawn up in buckets. In the

Wehrbau method, dams or *Wehre* were built in the mine to collect the brine, which could then be drawn off. Where rock-salt existed in a more or less pure state the *Weitungsbau* method continued to be used virtually unchanged: this was a procedure by which the saliferous rock was excavated from the mines and turned into salt. To strengthen poor quality brine rough wooden frames, or graduation-houses, were used; the process of boiling in large pans also continued more or less unchanged. In the sixteenth century the production of common salt by boiling and refining sea-salt or bay-salt was a profitable business, run in competition with home-produced salt.

Further technical achievements; arms production. J. U. Nef and latterly Carlo Cipolla have both stressed the importance of war as a factor in technical development. One cannot help being struck by the way in which this development proceeded little by little, with the great land wars of the sixteenth and seventeenth centuries, the overseas expeditions, the naval wars, and those responsible for them, all contributing to it.

Since explosive weapons first appeared, about the year 1330, guns had gradually improved, developing on the one hand into large pieces, like bombards, howitzers and mortars, for siege warfare, and on the other into small and medium calibre pieces for open warfare. Since the end of the Middle Ages, the mobility of field-pieces had been increased by supplying them with wooden mountings and wheeled gun-carriages. The solid stone cannon-ball had been supplemented, since the fourteenth century, by balls made of lead and wrought-iron, and, since the middle of the fifteenth century, by cast-iron ones. Since the sixteenth century the manufacture of cannon had passed increasingly into the hands of specialist cannon-founders, who also cast bells. Since Maximilian's time, artillery had been further subdivided, according to calibre and use, into mortars and howitzers, cannon-royal (a short barrelled, large calibre cannon), and lighter but longer barrelled field-pieces known as culverins, falcons and falconets. About 1504

Georg Hartmann of Nuremberg invented the calibre-rule; gun-carriages were improved at the same time. Hollow projectiles filled with explosive, cartridges made of paper and leather, grapeshot, in the form of hollow canisters filled with lead shot, came into existence; *Orgelgeschütze* – cannon composed of several small calibre barrels ranged horizontally and vertically, that could fire with great rapidity – were manufactured. The seventeenth century saw further improvements in artillery organisation and tactics, Prince Maurice of Orange and King Gustavus Adolphus of Sweden playing prominent parts in this. In small arms the match-lock had been joined since the beginning of the sixteenth century by the superior wheel-lock; this was used pre-eminently for horse-pistols, which thus became weapons of war for the first time. In the middle of the sixteenth century Spanish troops used the spring flint-lock for the first time. From the second half of the seventeenth century the flint-lock ousted all other systems of firing; to this period also belongs the crucial innovation of the paper cartridge.

The building sector. Progress in the technique of war exercised a strong influence on building. Those responsible for defence demanded special fortifications, with suitably thick walls, bastions and redoubts; this culminated in France in Vauban's system of fortifications, which extended along every frontier of French territory. New walls, with towers and gateways, were needed to encircle the towns, the most costly defence systems being constructed by towns like Nuremberg and Hamburg; Amsterdam expanded concentrically.

As the Gothic gave way to the Renaissance a new wave of building activity spread from Italy, bringing with it elements of classicism, and featuring the dome, which reached its zenith in St Peter's Cathedral in Rome and St Paul's Cathedral in London. The princes and aristocrats left their castle strongholds for city palaces and country estates; this resulted in new building schemes and finally in the splendid buildings of the baroque princes, modelled on Louis XIV's château at Versailles.

To a great extent this whole field has been studied only from the standpoint of architectural history and not from that of its importance to the building industry; this is unfortunate because, in addition to hundreds and thousands of workmen, these building schemes called for technical improvements and feats of organisation that for the first time give clear evidence of the existence of the building contractor as a type of entrepreneur.

To some extent associated with these building schemes was the great dike-building and land reclamation work carried out in the Netherlands, in England, on the North Sea coast of Germany, on Amager, in France and in Italy; in the plains of Western Europe this work could only be done with the aid of extensive pumping installations and windmills.

The construction of dwelling-houses and ships gave impetus to the timber trade. Saw-mills driven by water-power, known in Germany since the fourteenth century, spread in the sixteenth century to Scandinavia, where they were needed to produce cut timber for Western Europe. Frame-saws had been in use in Regensburg since the second half of the sixteenth century. Efforts were also made at this time to produce an automatic feed mechanism. The high level of cabinet-making in Augsburg encouraged the development of the veneering-saw; there is mention of a veneering-mill there in 1588.

Technical achievements in transport, trade and credit

Transport. The discoveries made during the fifteenth century would not have been possible without the improvements that took place in shipbuilding and navigation. In order to round the dreaded Cape Bojador in the Atlantic, the Latin triangular sail, used in the Mediterranean, was needed in addition to the square sail; this made it possible to sail close to the wind. It also necessitated a second mast. The more northerly countries of Europe began to adopt this two-masted type of ship in the 1430s, which was when the Portuguese took the lead in Atlantic travel with their 'caravels'. These caravels had two or three masts and so could be sailed both 'with the wind' and 'into the wind'; in the weather conditions prevailing in the South Atlantic, this made it possible for them to make the return journey. It was this assurance that enabled Bartolomeu Dias to make his second voyage to South Africa, Christopher Columbus his American discoveries, and Vasco da Gama, in 1498, his voyage to India, and to do so with large ships capable of carrying adequate supplies, weapons and crew.

Experience gained in the small caravel led to the construction of a larger type of ship called *nau, năo, nave* or *vaisseau*. During the sixteenth century these three-masted ships underwent further development as freighters. They carried square sails fore and amidships and a lateen (i.e. Latin) sail aft; they had a capacity of between four and six hundred tons. These large freighters made it possible to trade between the Baltic, the Atlantic, and the Mediterranean, and to pioneer the new routes to America, the East Indies via the Cape of Good Hope, and even to risk the passage through the Straits of Magellan. The method of building the caravels was another important development that came from the Mediterranean: the timbers of the ship's hull being placed flush against each other, its displacement was less than that of the clinker-built cog. This new method of construction, which spread to the waters of northern and north-western Europe as early as the fifteenth century, also made it easier to pierce the ship's side to make the gun-holes. By the beginning of the sixteenth century the Baltic ports, and above all Danzig and Lübeck, had taken the lead in building large caravel-type ships. Henry VIII increased the size of his fleet mainly by buying from the Baltic shipbuilders; these ships served as models for new ones built in England. Later England went on independently to construct three-decker men-of-war, until in Queen Elizabeth's day it had outstripped every other country, although the Dutch and Hanseatic shipbuilders retained their supremacy in merchant-shipping.

More was learnt about handling the sails: better use could thus be made of the wind, and a wind slightly from the quarter was found to be better than one from dead astern. With several smaller sails the work was reduced and fewer crew were needed.

In the Baltic ships of one hundred and fifty tons were not uncommon, and in Spain and Portugal still larger ships were built; in these great attention was paid to the upper-works, as the passenger traffic was heavy. The celebrated *Madre de Deus* is said to have been a ship of sixteen hundred tons. But these galleons were not very manoeuvrable: a Portuguese galleon, seized by the north Netherlanders in 1605, could not be accommodated anywhere in the Netherlands and had to be sent on to the Ems.

Because of the poor navigability of the German North Sea waters, ships could not exceed a certain size. Ships of fifty tons could not sail up as far as Bremen; they could navigate the dreaded *Stade* sandbanks in the Elbe only at high tide. Great difficulties were also experienced in the Netherlands, where lighters had to ply between the ship and the port itself.

To overcome these problems a new and more practical – because smaller – type of ship was devised, which could navigate the shoals and shallows that abounded in these waters. This was the Boyer, which carried the typically Frisian sail with a diagonal sprit. In the 1520s the Hamburg sailors, using these ships, made their first trips to places as far afield as Zealand, England, Scotland, Norway and the Baltic. Towards the end of the sixteenth century these Boyers had conquered a good part of the route to the Iberian peninsula, while the entire Netherlands traffic with French and English ports was based on Boyers and Hoyers, a type developed in Zealand.

The advantage of these ships, now mostly built with two masts, was that they were economic to run. A three-master of fifty tons required a crew of fourteen, whereas a Boyer of twenty-five tons could be sailed with a crew of only five or six. A Netherlandish square-rigged ship made either one trip a year to the Baltic and combined it with a tramp run, or else made two trips to the Baltic; a Boyer could make three Baltic trips a year. Although less seaworthy than a square-rigged ship, it could be loaded and unloaded more rapidly as it could berth right alongside the quay wall.

Ships of the Boyer type were built only on the North Sea coast of Germany and in the Netherlands, and contributed to the seafaring supremacy of this region; the English took over the Hoyer from the Zealanders.

In the 1570s there appeared a type of boat that undermined still further the supremacy of the square-rigged ship, and at the same time limited the wider use of the Boyer. The idea was taken from the dogger-boats, used for cod fishing off the Dogger Bank, but its development has to be seen in relation to herring fishing, for which special herring-boats were used in the North Sea as early as the first quarter of the sixteenth century; in all probability the new 'boats' were evolved from these herring boats. Starting in the 1570s ships of this type were built for exclusive use as freighters, the main centres being places the major part of whose trade passed through the '*Vlie*'; for this reason they were also known as *Vlie*-boats, generally anglicised as 'fly-boats'. While, generally speaking, Boyers did not exceed twenty-eight tons, the Emden boats used for the Baltic trip were of twenty-five to thirty-five tons. These boats possessed roughly the same advantages as the Boyers; they probably drew less water than the square-rigged ships, and they were faster than either these or the Boyers because they had better sails. In 1565 a Netherlandish 'boat' made four trips to the Baltic; in 1585 there were already twenty-five of these 'boats', six of which made as many as nine or ten Baltic trips. This tendency to build smaller ships was also evident in the Mediterranean.

Before the turn of the century another new type, the fluit, had been added; first built in 1595, it combined the advantages of the 'boats' and the square-rigged ships. At first the length of these ships was four times as great as their breadth; later it became five and even six times as great. Some twenty years passed before this type of ship attained its optimum form, but then it held its place for almost a century. In addition to the change in proportion of the hull, the rigging was substantially improved. Because they were slimmer, these ships were much faster than their predecessors; they could also sail closer to the wind. They had taller masts but shorter yards, and their sails were still smaller and therefore still easier to handle. The result was that they also needed a smaller crew than the large vessels previously in use. It was thanks to these ships that, following the armistice of 1609, the Dutch were able to start their triumphal progress as a freighting nation. The Hanseatic League and the Scandinavians took the lead in adopting the fluit. In about 1618 Lübeck started to build them; the English and French took up the idea, too, but in doing so preserved their national characteristics. The Spaniards were among the most resistant to the innovation.

The technical development of sea warfare made possible by the emergence of naval artillery is also of importance in this context. By the middle of the fifteenth century most large European men-of-war carried cannon; these were small moveable bronze pieces, housed in the bow and stern superstructures. Towards the end of the century the ships' sides were provided with openings to fire through; this suggested a new possibility, that of side armaments. The future belonged to the 'broadside'. These broadside armaments affected not only fighting tactics but ship construction as well. A large number of heavy cannon mounted along the sides of a ship exerted great pressure on those sides; because of this, the parts of the sides that housed the cannon were set back.

At the same time the expensive bronze cannon were replaced by cheaper iron ones; after being rebuilt in 1540, the *Mary grace à Dieu* had one hundred and twenty-two pieces of artillery, of which nineteen were bronze and the rest iron. There was also a growing tendency to mount long-barrelled cannon (*couleuvrine*): in 1588, when the English fleet fought the Spanish Armada, the proportion of short-barrelled to long-barrelled cannon in the Spanish ships was 43·5 to 56·5 per cent and in the English ships 5 to 95 per cent; it was the English who determined the future development. They were also responsible for the increasing use of four-masted men-of-war. In 1618 one half of the English fleet consisted of four-masters; by 1640 it was composed entirely of them.

During the second half of the seventeenth century the French took the lead in naval warfare, and its mathematical aspects acquired increasing importance. The ships were divided into five classes according to type; the flagship class, of from sixteen hundred to two thousand two hundred tons and with a displacement of over three thousand tons, had an armament of one hundred bronze cannon, while all other ships had iron cannon.

The top deck was correspondingly narrow amidships and broad in the bow and stern. This made boarding difficult and ships had to rely as much as possible on the effectiveness of their artillery.

The Portuguese seem to have been the first to recognise and fully exploit the superiority of cannon to infantry: while the latter could board an enemy ship and engage its crew in combat, the former could sink an entire ship. The first engagements in which cannon were used to sink an enemy ship took place, not in the Mediterranean, but in the Indian Ocean. The Moslems were inferior to the Portuguese because the latter understood these new tactics. The Battle of Lepanto in 1571 was the last great naval battle in which boarding played a decisive part. The victory of the English over the Spanish Armada in 1588 was the first time the new tactics were used in a naval battle in the Atlantic.

These more advanced fighting techniques also had the effect of increasing the activities of privateers, especially of the Barbary pirates in the Mediterranean, the danger from whom had diminished after the Battle of Lepanto. When ships started to sail in convoy, as a protection against pirates and privateers, large, well-armed ships came into their own again at the expense of the Boyers, 'boats' and unarmed fluits. The three-master still predominated, but at the beginning of the eighteenth century its name was changed from pinnace to frigate.

As improved charts replaced the old *portolanos* and *roteiros*, and as navigational instruments were improved, navigational technique also developed. The progress made in charting the seas by the end of the sixteenth century is well illustrated by Wagenaar and Blaeuw, who compiled whole atlases of charts. In the course of the seventeenth century the nautical instruments hitherto in use – the astrolabe, the quadrant, the cross-staff – were replaced by John Davis's 'back-staff', which could be used with one's back to the sun. At the beginning of the eighteenth century the steering-wheel was introduced, and refinements were made in the plane chart, the theodolite and the level.

Advances were also made in land travel, but they were less important. In the sixteenth century the clumsy disk-wheel gave way to the lighter spoked-wheel. At the end of the fifteenth century Galiot, an artillery expert, improved the wheel's action by slanting it inwards. From Italy came the coach and the carriage, which shortly afterwards were suspended on frames instead of, as formerly, being attached directly to the wheels; since the end of the sixteenth century they had been provided with windows. A significant improvement was made by shifting the harness attachment from the animal's neck to its shoulders; this increased its drawing power by 3·6 times.

With coaches and carriages came the need for more solidly constructed roads and stronger bridges. In France Henri IV created the post of *Grand Voyer* and appointed Sully to fill it; but during his reign and that of Louis XIII the programmes could be carried out only to a limited extent. In 1669 Colbert appointed commissioners for bridges and highways to assist the provincial administrators, and by the time he died in 1683 a very considerable amount of road-building had been done in the Paris area, along the eastern border and in the *Massif Central*. From the fifteenth century onwards the construction of stone bridges increased in Italy, the Rialto bridge in Venice being among those built in the sixteenth century. The *Pont Notre Dame* in Paris was built by Fra Givendo in 1513 and Androuet du Cerceau, who learned the art from him, created a tradition which, though it remained chiefly in his own family, enriched the city of Paris in particular with stone bridges; the *Pont Neuf* was one of these. But it was not until the eighteenth century that the problems of vaulting were mastered and work could be carried out on an economic basis.

Organised transport was extended. Following the introduction of wheeled traffic in the Alps in the Middle Ages, large forwarding businesses came into existence in the sixteenth century; among these were Annoni in Milan, Della Faille in Antwerp, as well as Kleinhans, Enzensperger and others which originated, significantly, in the Füssen, Reutte, Kaufbeuren area. Extensive overland connections were organised from Frammersbach and Schmalkalden, the former reaching as far as Antwerp.

Progress was also made in mapping the land routes. Printed itineraries or traveller's guides were used. The quality of the maps in these itineraries can be seen from the traveller's map of central Europe published by Erhard Etzlaub, a Nuremberg compass maker, in 1501. As time went on traveller's guides became more and more popular. Among historico-geographical handbooks the *Itinerarium Germaniae Nov-Antiquae*, of 1632, and its supplementary volume the *Itinerarii Germaniae Continuatio*, of 1640, were epoch-making.

Printing made it possible to reproduce the maps in quantity. In 1554 Mercator published a map of Europe, and in 1595, the year after he died, his collected work was published under the title *Atlas sive cosmographicae meditationes de fabrica mundi et fabricati figura*. In the seventeenth century the Dutch maintained their supremacy as cartographers, with Hondius and Blaeuw as their leading representatives.

Considerable progress was also made in canal building, although this was of only limited assistance to international overland travel. A system of canals designed to connect the Elbe with Silesia was started in 1548 and completed in 1669. The canals in the Southern Netherlands were extended. The Briare canal, connecting the Loire and the Seine, was opened to traffic in 1642; the Orleans canal, built between 1682 and 1692, further improved the water-way communications between the two rivers. The Langue-doc canal or Canal du Midi, built in 1661–81 under the supervision of Colbert and Paul Riquet to connect the Garonne near Toulouse with the Mediterranean, by way of the Aude, became of great importance to southern France. With it canal building reached a peak from which the eighteenth century gained inspiration but which it could not surpass.

The postal and news services were also improved to some extent. In France and Spain the post had been developed on a national basis since the end of the fifteenth century. In the Holy Roman Empire the important task of main-taining postal communications between Upper Italy and places as far away as the Netherlands was undertaken by the Taxis family of Bergamo. The seventeenth century brought frequent rivalry between the postal services of different countries; in 1695 Hamburg, for instance, had ten post offices representing various national and city postal authorities. Towards the end of the seventeenth century, passenger-carrying mail coaches began to supersede post-riders. Throughout the sixteenth century the communica-tions system maintained by the merchant traders played a dominant part, alongside the postal services, in transmitting news. The advices sent out by the merchant houses, and above all the Fugger news-sheets, were a primary source of information. Since the beginning of the seventeenth century news-sheets had been printed, but they still continued to appear only weekly until 1702, when the first daily news-paper was published in England.

Trade and credit. In an enquiry of this kind, technical improvements in trade and credit have also to be con-sidered, and in this sphere two questions are relevant: to what extent was the organisation of business undertakings improved, and to what extent was it possible to operate them more efficiently. The first of these questions is discussed elsewhere; here it is primarily the technical side that is of interest. The improvement that took place in school education and business accounting was of great importance. Since the end of the fifteenth century printed booklets, giving instruction in business accounting, had supplemented the work of schoolmasters and teachers of arithmetic. The first time the general public was given any details of business technique, which hitherto had been a closely guarded professional secret, was in a work published by Lorens Meder of Nuremberg in 1558.

Particular stress has been laid on the expedient of double-entry bookkeeping as a factor in the inner workings of business undertakings; it had been developed in Italy in medieval times and found its way across the Alps before 1500, in 1494 to be precise when Luca Pacioli described it practically for the first time in his theoretical work *Summa di arithmetica*.

The essence of the new technique was that it made possible an integrated system of classification; it took various forms both inside Italy and outside it – in Upper Germany for instance. While Pacioli spoke of the memorial, journal and hauptbuch, the Genoese Angelo Pietra, in 1586, mentioned only the journal and ledger, Mathhäus Schwarz, one of Fugger's agents, taking the same view; in the special form of 'German bookkeeping' the *Güterbuch Kapus*, or goods ledger, had a place alongside the journal and account-book. To these important books must be added others, which varied according to the particular circumstances of the business: the costs-book, for example, the bill- and rent-book, or the journeymen's-book. Altogether it was a complex of innovations in the field of business management, a complex, needless to say, that did not find expression in a rigid, uniform system but left plenty of room for such variations as arose in individual practice. Admittedly the importance of double-entry bookkeeping has often been exaggerated – even by Werner Sombart – especially the profit and loss accounting, credit accounting and capital accounting, or in other words accounting in terms of assets and liabilities, which it made possible. Others, and especially Yamey, have stressed the point that, for the purpose of making day to day decisions, it was of no importance to know exactly what the total profits of a business amounted to – this was important only when it came to dissolving or selling the business; and according to Yamey double-entry bookkeeping was of no real help to a businessman in deciding between a number of alternatives. The value of double-entry bookkeeping for the day to day management and control of a firm's assets was simply that it made it easier to marshal and keep an eye on facts relevant to running the business. And the new system certainly made it easier for a business like the Fuggers to control their network of agents than it had been, let us say for the Veckinghusens, a century earlier with a less highly developed system. Subsequent to this development, which continued into the sixteenth century, and the further expansion of the new Italian system by way of Antwerp, London and Hamburg, nothing was added until the eighteenth century.

A further important contribution to the economic process was the continuing change-over from trading in kind to a money economy and, attendant on it, the extension of outstanding cash assets or their replacement by credit instruments. This was of special significance in the development of banking and bills of exchange.

In this sphere, too, a great deal had already been accomplished in medieval times. Bills of exchange had long been known, as had cheques, and deposit moneys in the form of payment orders with the great private banking houses. Negotiable securities also existed in a rudimentary form. Indorsed bills of exchange came into use at the beginning of the fifteenth century. It is above all in Florentine banking that these advances are known to have taken place, and its declining role in international credit transactions, together with the increasing one played by the bankers of Upper Germany in particular, may have had something to do with the fact that these beginnings were not followed up in a logical manner. Compared to what had been achieved in Italy in the Middle Ages, the innovations introduced at Antwerp, the leading money market in the sixteenth century, were limited in scope. The practice of indorsement, first used, so far as we know, in Spain in

1575, does not seem to have existed in Antwerp before 1610 or in Lyons before 1618, although Blockmanns has established the existence of an indorsed bill of exchange in 1571. Van der Wee has found discounted bonds for the year 1536 as well as a discounted bill of exchange for 1576. The transfer of deposits from one trade fair to another also goes back to the Middle Ages. The *cambio con la ricorsa*, closely connected since 1524 with the practice of 'aval', or guarantees, was a new form of the old *recambio*, which, according to Heers, was in common use in Genoa in the fifteenth century.

During the seventeenth century the credit instrument was enlarged in a number of ways. The private banker, usually a trader, adapted himself increasingly to the practice of indorsing and discounting bills of exchange. Then, with the banks at Amsterdam (1609), Hamburg (1619) and Nuremberg (1621), a type of giro bank came into existence that facilitated payments between these trading centres. New means for the satisfaction of the growing need of circulating money and of credit, offered the 'notes accountable' of the London goldsmiths and the 'notes' issued by the Swedish Riksbank and finally by the Bank of England (1694). The latter, a privileged joint stock enterprise, at the same time served the financial requirements of the Crown. The rising stock exchange speculation in Amsterdam in the shares of the East India Company also became an active force in credit business; it was later extended to include state bonds. The first loan in the form of bonds, issued at par and carrying an annual rate of interest, was arranged in 1695 by the firm of Deutz in favour of the ruling House of Austria.

This gives an indication of the new technical resources that came into existence. The reduction of risks, especially in merchant shipping, was a spur to marine insurance, whose origins also went back to the Middle Ages; it was now developed in Antwerp and Amsterdam, a special feature being the formation of insurance companies. The system of trade fairs at regular intervals in south-west, west and central Europe was reorganised in the seventeenth century following the decline of the Spanish fairs and the crises in Antwerp. Bourses on the Antwerp pattern as markets for bills of exchange, shares and stocks were opened in Cologne, Hamburg, Frankfurt, Amsterdam and London; for some time the Piacenza fairs maintained their role dominated by the Genoese. Avisos, printed news-sheets and lists of prices supplemented the sources of information gained through the trade fairs and bourses. The beginnings of propaganda and publicity are also to be seen at this period.

TECHNICAL ACHIEVEMENTS IN THE SUPPLY NETWORK OF THE VARIOUS SECTORS OF THE ECONOMY

The first part of this enquiry has considered the most important technical achievements effected between the end of the fifteenth century and the beginning of the eighteenth century. The next task is to consider how these achievements were turned to account in the individual sectors of the economy, to what extent they were accepted and to what extent they were opposed. Only if they are viewed within this institutional framework will a clear picture emerge of the full historical relevance of these technical innovations.

NON-TECHNOLOGICAL FACTORS INFLUENCING PRODUCTION OR PRODUCTIVITY

The role of authority

The economy could only evolve in the measure that it was protected, and promoted, by the institutions which we call collectively authority. In the open country this might be a nobleman or monastery in the capacity of landlord. In the market place, the small town or the city, it might be the guild and above this the town or city council. And above all these was the head of state, the duke, the elector, the king, the signory, the states general or, in the Holy Roman

Empire, the Reichstag and the emperor – in other words authority in various forms.

Of primary interest for the purpose of this study is the part played by the guilds within the framework of the manufacturing process. Speaking very generally it can be said that the principle of subsistence stood in the way of intensifying production by means of concentration, rationalisation and new techniques. The inventions of Lobsinger of Nuremberg, and the introduction of the ribbon loom in the textile industry, are famous examples when the guilds or city authorities, and indeed the supreme authority of the Holy Roman Empire itself, intervened in favour of the principle of subsistence. But often the latter may have served as a pure pretext for competition.

If, in general, it is true that city authorities were anxious to defer to the interests of the guilds, and to organise home production and marketing conditions in such a way as to balance, as far as possible, opposing interests and avoid the danger of unemployment, the examples of Hamburg and Frankfurt show that efforts were also made to introduce new production techniques with the help of outside experts. National politics were two-faced, a state of affairs that continued until into the 'mercantile' era. During the period of the Reformation and Counter-Reformation, on the one hand, specialists were forced to leave their homes for religious reasons, and had to do so again after the Edict of Nantes was revoked. On the other hand, within the framework of the economic concepts of the day, and of the principality in particular, 'political interests' and 'reasons of state' asserted themselves increasingly, with the fiscal and military aspects of these playing a prominent part; and as the authorities of the territory or state expanded their organisational network, and mercantile thinking became more widespread, a corresponding degree of specialisation developed in the supervisory bodies, through the creation of mining and commercial colleges for example. The mining industry received a powerful impetus from the financial policies of the ruling princes, who were anxious to open up new seams of precious metals. The intervention of the authorities was particularly apparent in the mining regulations that governed the working of the mines, the legal position and questions of working-hours; and while these regulations applied in the first instance to precious and non-ferrous metals, iron was added later. There were also important timber and forestry regulations controlling the consumption of timber. In Sweden steps were taken, under the regency acting for the young Queen Christina, to reserve the woods round mining sites for mining and smelting, and to transfer the forges to more densely wooded areas, a move that was of special benefit to Värmland. In smelting and further processing, state intervention was important in times of crisis, in the Styrian iron industry, for instance, or when competition threatened to become critical, as in the case of the tin-plate cartel in the Upper Palatinate. The authorities could intervene in the sales organisation, too: an early example of this occurred when attempts to gain a monopoly were made in the Electorate of Saxony; and in Styria the authorities also intervened over the question of sales.

Every imaginable means was employed to turn new inventions to account and bring in specialists from abroad. These latter were granted privileges and monopolies that enabled them to disregard local and regional rights and privileges; and, starting in England, patent-laws were evolved that secured proprietary rights to the inventor.

The extension of systematised defence also had its effect on technical development. The development of the cannon and the arquebus into new weapons of attack and defence, or the expansion of naval artillery and its influence on shipbuilding, are unthinkable without the part played by power politics among the nations of Europe and overseas. One of the most significant consequences was the fight against piracy and the development of the convoy system, which made it possible to reduce the costly armament of merchant ships as well as their crews. This applied especially to voyages in the Baltic, the North Sea and the north Atlantic; piracy in the Mediterranean and the Indian Ocean still remained a danger. The form taken by state initiative naturally varied from region to region; it was less in evidence in the more highly developed countries, such as the Republic of the Netherlands, than in the continental monarchies. It was seen in its most pronounced form in the France of Louis XIV, with Colbert as the central figure, as well as in Denmark, Sweden and Russia.

The role of the individual business initiative

The driving force of private enterprise varied in intensity in the different sectors of the economy. The resistance of traditional structures was particularly stubborn in the agricultural sector. On the manorial estates the system of taxation in kind or money rents was to a large extent retained. The prevailing three-field system of cultivating the land did not change very much either; nor could the splitting up of the serfs' messuage, which was based on division of inheritance and connected with this system, result in more than a limited increase in production, by specialising in the cultivation of fruit and vegetables, for instance, or of plants for which there was a commercial demand. A way out of these fossilised structures was provided by large privately owned agricultural holdings or by the system of holding land on tenure; in this latter case the tenant, because he had the use of the land for only a limited period, felt bound to 'get as much out of it' as possible, and this he could do best by using rational methods, fertilising the land better, specialising in certain lines such as dairy farming, employing paid labour, seeking more and better outlets for his produce, and so on. But there were limits to the system as such; it spread to any great extent only near large cities, like Paris or Cologne, and in the coastal areas from the Netherlands to Schleswig and Mecklenburg, which were largely given over to cattle farming. It was here, too, that most of the large privately owned agricultural holdings were to be found. As early as the sixteenth and seventeenth centuries, the labour used in the Dithmarschen countryside was provided largely by paid free workers, who combined this work with business and seafaring activities. A more dynamic attitude was to be found east of the Elbe, in the sphere of demesne farming, which was in the process of expanding. Here the independently run manor farm was developed in conjunction with the 'outlying' farms, expropriation of land from the peasants, and a more or less extensive system of bartering, selling and buying, making it possible to round off the estate and thus simplify its management. The use of peasants who had been enserfed and 'bound to the soil' did not, it is true, make for increased per capita output, and hence increased productivity; on the other hand the use of trained stewards was of great benefit on the organisational side and resulted in special attention being given to marketing opportunities, particularly overseas. Added to this was a more thrifty attitude on the part of those of the nobility who had turned Protestant and had been influenced by the teachings of the Reformation; this attitude was not confined to the agricultural sector but led these men to exploit favourable sites, available mineral resources, water power and supplies of timber in order to develop, with the aid of mills, business activities that in some respects were very far reaching. Exceptionally clear evidence of this attitude and its practical application was to be found in the area between Hamburg and Lübeck, and later on the estates of the Habsburg monarchy.

This aristocratic entrepreneurial activity had a parallel in the sixteenth and early seventeenth centuries among some of the Protestant ruling princes; in their case, however, the whole principality, and not merely their private domains, was made the basis of a more thorough-going economic development that exhibitied many of the features of private enterprise. Early examples of this were the entrepreneurial interests of Gustav Wasa of Sweden, the Elector August of Saxony, Duke Julius of Braunschweig-Wolfenbüttel and, later, Duke Jakob of Kurland.

In the field of industrial production and distribution, the organisational activities of the large-scale trader deserve special attention. Improvements in technical aids and resources can be traced back to the thirteenth century; they culminated in double-entry bookkeeping and the credit system. Of even greater importance, however, was what had been done on the organisational side, thanks to a markedly rational approach that put an end to the ban on interest. Using the general partnership, and the system of sleeping partners and moneys held on deposit, as a basis, and with the help of the factory system, it had become possible, particularly since the resurgence of the mining industry at the end of the fifteenth century, to combine trade in goods, and especially in metal, with credit transactions, and by this means to break into mining and other branches of production. This was the distinctive accomplishment of the Upper German trading companies, whose attempts to dominate the market through cartels and monopolies also illustrated this practice in its clearest form.

The capital investment required for mining in particular, but also for other branches of production, occasioned a greater use of existing possibilities for obtaining outside capital. The principal means available for this were deposits and limited liability interests. Capital procurement by means of deposits was not new, and efforts to obtain limited liability shareholders had been made in Florence in the early fifteenth century; an imperial privilege for Nuremberg, dated 1464, had a similar purpose. Individual business houses observed a policy of letting the outside world know as little as possible about all this, and thus it is really never possible to establish how much outside capital was employed by, say, the trading companies of Upper Germany, or how it was divided between deposits and limited liability interests. The example of Bishop (later Archbishop) von Meckau of Brixen shows the role played by outside capital, in the form of deposits, in the house of Fugger during Jakob Fugger's day, when the firm was making its name; we can see the same thing happening in the house of Höchstetter. Very little is yet known about the system of limited liability interests. Federigo Melis claims to have discovered the first clear example of a *compagnia d'accomandita's* agreement among the Strozzi papers held by the firm of *Francesco di Giovanni Lapi e compagnia* in Seville;

it is dated 1552. In the second half of the century the limited partnership is mentioned in the legislation of Italian trading towns, and became firmly established in French commercial legislation in 1673 under the same *Société en Commandite*; Germany kept the name *Stille Gesellschaft*, or undisclosed partnership, which indicated better its development in that country. Nevertheless, for the time being, the general partnership, with full liability on the part of those concerned, remained the prevailing form. An interesting extension into the important copper, silver and tin mining sector was the *Saiger*, or metal processors', trading company, which provided the capital for the costly smelting works.

In comparison the part played by the mining company in *Gewerkschaft* form – that is a company with shares of no par value called *Kuxe* – has received less attention. It first came into prominence with the revival of the Saxon silver mining industry: by splitting the *Kuxe* first into thirty-two parts, and later on the Schneeberg into as many as a hundred and twenty-eight, it became possible not only to obtain capital over the wide area bounded by Magdeburg, Zerbst, Leipzig, Nuremberg and Augsburg, but also for those in comparatively poor financial circumstances to take part; this led to the first clear case of speculation in shares of this sort. The usual price of a *Kuxe* was from five to twenty florins, but some cost as little as one florin; half *Kuxe* were also dealt in.

This line of development ended in the joint stock company. Its beginnings go back to the co-operative system of medieval times, which spread from the field of agriculture to the mining industry and the trading activities of the guilds, and with which institutions like the *Maone*, the *Compere* and the *Casa di San Giorgio* were associated. The ship-owning partnership also belongs in this context. Other lines of development lead in the direction of the chartered companies in England, the *Saiger* trading companies and the general partnerships, in so far as they embodied transferability of share certificates, limitation of liability and recognition of the body corporate. A new stage, decisive for further development, was reached with the privileged overseas trading companies, of which the first large ones were the British East India Company of 1600 and the Dutch East India Company of 1602. In order to carry out the difficult task of opening up overseas areas commercially, they secured state guarantees in the form of privileges and monopolies, and political and sovereign right. While results were achieved, especially by the Dutch and British, in increased trade with Asia, Africa and America, many companies in other countries, in trying to copy the Dutch and the British, came to grief at the outset. The part played by private enterprise – in the role of interloper for instance – should, therefore, not be over-looked.

The organisation of industrial production in particular

The development of industrial production in Europe depended to a large extent on how well organised it was. Throughout the phase under consideration many branches of production were still based on handicrafts, that is to say they were in the hands of small master craftsmen, their families, perhaps as many as three trained craftsmen and one or more apprentices. Generally speaking, large-scale production was the exception. In most parts of Europe the guilds assumed responsibility for production; they were usually situated in the cities and small market towns. In western Europe they had undergone a similar development, though with many special features in individual cases: special features of this sort were to be found in Italy, Spain, England, France, Germany, and countries influenced by them.

As has already been seen, the guilds always did their utmost to hold on to what they had. They defended the interests of their members against outsiders, and these included the inventors, who, with their new equipment and techniques, threatened to disturb their members' economic status. They were thus against progress. But their importance came from the political role they played in the community and the State; in general it is true to say that this importance waned as absolutism grew. Monarchies used the guilds to extend the influence of the state; they granted privileges to the existing guilds and created new ones with privileges of their own, often for purely fiscal reasons.

In England this phase lasted from the reign of Elizabeth to that of Charles II, after which the 'corporations' became less and less powerful; it is thought that this was one of the reasons why the industrial revolution was able to establish itself so decisively in England. In France, on the other hand, the system of *métiers* advocated by Colbert, and maintained after his death for fiscal reasons, impeded development. The same thing happened in Spain, where the formation of new corporations continued, as well as in Italy and parts of central Europe. In northern and eastern Europe the guild system enabled the state to raise the economy to the level of that in central and western Europe, and Czar Peter I characteristically tried to establish guilds on the western model in Russia.

In spite of this a large sector of handicraft production remained outside the control of the guilds: this consisted of new branches like the printers, and the numerous specialists in textile techniques and luxury articles. There were also the privileged master craftsmen, the so-called free masters, and there was the rural production, which mostly was organised by the entrepreneurs of the towns with the means of the putting out system.

The entrepreneurial system. When a craftsman had no market for his goods near at home, and the raw materials he required came from great distances, he needed to be in touch with a trader who, by virtue of his long-range trade connections, had the necessary market and sales contacts. He was thus in a position to supply the craftsman with the wool, cotton, silk and metal he needed, and at the same time to find the best outlet for his finished products in the markets of the world. As a result the craftsman often found himself in a position of dependence that might take various forms, because the trader-entrepreneur was in the stronger position and could dictate his terms.

This entrepreneurial system encouraged the process of differentiation. Organised and independent workers were employed at the same time. Generally the rougher work was done in the country, while the final stages were carried out in the towns by specialised workers. Often the processing – sorting the raw materials, washing and combing the wool, and so on – was begun in the trader's workshop, the spinning, weaving and dyeing were done outside, and the finishing was carried out in the workshop again. There was a whole chain of debtor-creditor relationships between the big trader, the middleman and the worker, whether in the town or in the country. If some branch of production developed into an export industry, the craftsmen who had control of the raw materials, or were responsible for the final process in the chain of production, were often able to become entrepreneurs themselves.

Manufacture. When special knowledge and techniques were required, it was in the trader's interest to have the production processes concentrated under one roof in the form of a manufactory. In Tuscany and the Netherlands there had been a tendency in this direction in medieval times. John Winchcombe's manufactory in England at the beginning of the sixteenth century is famous. But in the early days concentration on this scale proved impossible, because it was opposed by the guilds and ran counter to state policy. At the end of the sixteenth century the tendency reasserted itself; it became more marked in the second half of the seventeenth century, when it received strong state support, especially in France under Colbert. Generally speaking, centralised manufacture established itself in branches of production that required special technical skills: Gobelin tapestries were an example, so were calico printing, glass making and the manufacture of porcelain. 'Decentralised manufacture', centralisation and entrepreneurial organisation were often combined. A special type of manufacture existed in Protestant orphanages, prisons and other places of correction which had equipment for this purpose.

Large-scale production involving advanced technical equipment. An important feature of the manufactory was that it was a focal point for handicrafts. Many branches of production, on the other hand, used technical equipment involving pumps, furnaces and machinery. This was very much the case with mining, smelting and the further processing of metals. In these capital costs played a substantially bigger part. The cost of individual pieces of equipment of this sort has been referred to elsewhere; here it is the organisational side that needs to be stressed. The trading companies of Upper Germany were prominent in exploiting the presence of non-ferrous metals in central Europe; a special form of company adapted to this task was the *Saiger Handelsgesell-schaft*, or metal processing and trading company, which provided the capital for the costly undertakings of the processing-sheds and other installations. From this it was not a very far step to participation in mining itself, especially when new technical aids became necessary to overcome operational problems.

The labour market. The employment of new or additional technical devices made demands on the labour market, for specialists in particular – there was never any lack of unskilled labour. In some cases skilled workers were in such demand that cartel agreements were made, like those between Saxony and Bohemia in the mining industry. A favourite method of obtaining skilled labour was to import it from abroad; Gustav Wasa of Sweden was one of those who did this. In other respects the attitude in the sixteenth and seventeenth centuries to these specialists was contradictory. Religious convictions were often uppermost, provided one ignores advantages that would have accrued on purely rational grounds: hence the many skilled workers who migrated for religious reasons, and, consequent on this, the movement away from existing centres of production and distribution into new and increasingly prosperous ones.

But in spite of this adverse factor, which was to become strikingly apparent in the emigration of Upper Austrian Protestants and later when the Edict of Nantes was revoked, it is true to say that the state, as it became stronger and pursued a conscious economic policy, also gave special attention to the advisability of acquiring, or restraining the movement of, skilled labour.

Sales and consumption. Sales could be stimulated by a suitable sales policy and organisation. The great trading companies, which maintained both production and sales in their own hands, and combined these with a well developed intelligence service, acquired an optimal knowledge of the market. The beginnings of what later became advertising policy also existed. Princely businessmen did not hesitate to solicit new customers by drawing attention to the excellence of their wares. When, on the other hand, sales were fostered by population increases, or wider overseas markets, this brought in its train a greater demand for luxury goods and corresponding changes of fashion.

In all this, producer, distributor and consumer often worked hand in hand. One should beware of seeing the tendency for consumption to increase too one-sidedly from the standpoint of 'Renaissance man's' need for luxury, because the upheavals caused by the Reformation and Counter-Reformation also resulted in great changes in ownership. The classes that benefited from secularisation – the princes, the nobility, members of the new and prevailing political movement in Protestant Sweden and Denmark, for instance, and in the Holy Roman Empire and England – used their increased purchasing power, which in fact they often exceeded by obtaining credit, to demonstrate their new status by building houses and adopting a modern style of living worthy of them. At least until the early years of the seventeenth century, this whole complex of questions has to be considered in relation to the general rise in prices stimulated by the increased production of precious metals: wage-earners and those living on private means, of course, could buy less; but all those riding the wave of increased prices, such as producers and distributors, received a corresponding increase in purchasing power which they were able to turn to account. Stimuli of this sort did not end here. In the seventeenth century war and fashion increasingly stimulated sales, thus continuing a trend that had started in the previous century. War, whose influence on the armaments market and the supply of foodstuffs was particularly great, also created groups of war profiteers, who acquired for themselves possessions lost by others; the clearest examples of this were in Bohemia at the beginning of the Thirty Years War. They, too, swelled the customer class, which included in particular those who traded in war, with men like Wallenstein and the Mansfelds at their head.

Fashion emerged in the sixteenth century as a factor that contributed to increasing sales and expanding markets, and not only in the luxury trade but also among a wide range of purchasers, who were attracted above all by the catchword *nouvelle draperie*, by the tendency, strongly in evidence since the middle of the sixteenth century, to reject the heavier wool cloth in favour of the new mixed weave, which was lighter, cheaper and above all 'more fashionable'. Typical new 'fashionable' materials were bays, says, cloths, as well as materials made of grosgrain, mercerised cotton and mixtures of the two. At the end of the sixteenth century Spanish fashions set the tone, bringing with them a boom in lace making. The new French trend, whose *à la mode* role had been clearly evident since the 1630s, greatly benefited the silk trade; without this new trend the fashion for *passementerie* would scarcely be conceivable. This brought new classes of purchasers into the field. Beginning in the second half of the seventeenth century, a growing preference for calicos, prints and fashionable cotton articles asserted itself in a similar way, and this in turn helped to pave the way for the chinoiseries of the eighteenth century.

EFFECTS OF TECHNICAL ACHIEVEMENTS IN
INDIVIDUAL SECTORS OF THE ECONOMY

The agricultural sector

The scope of the enquiry needed to assess correctly the
range and significance of the technical innovations has now
been traced out.

Improvements in agricultural implements, as we have
seen, were of relatively small importance. Those made to
the plough, which in any case date back to the Middle
Ages, enabled it to plough deeper; but even this advance
was of no benefit to the Mediterranean area because,
generally speaking, the ground there was not suitable for
ploughing. Machine sowing made possible a more even,
and possibly also a more extensive, harvest than hand
sowing. What place, then, did ploughing and sowing
occupy in the peasant's total programme of work?

According to one estimate – admittedly produced in the
eighteenth century – ploughing and sowing were completed
in twelve days; harvesting the hay and corn, and threshing
the latter, took much longer. But in view of the fact that
the peasant could call on his whole family to help him, and
that there was never any real shortage of labour, the
amount of labour required was of relatively small importance.

More discouraging was the fact that productiveness, the
relation of what was sown to what was reaped, could
obviously be improved to only a limited extent and only in
certain particulars. From 1500 to the eighteenth century
this relation was, in general, 1 : 4·5; in certain parts of
England, Belgium, the northern Netherlands and France
it reached 1 : 7. The figures for rye and barley were a little
better, for oats they were still worse. This method of
calculating the productiveness has been disputed on the
grounds that both soil conditions and climatic influences
varied so enormously; it has been pointed out that the
figures for Poland were also 1 : 7.

The information available on productiveness in cattle farming is also inadequate. According to Slicher van Bath a cow gave 450–650 litres of milk in one milking-period, the amount of butter obtainable from it being not more than 30 kilograms. On the other hand, a case is known in Friesland, about 1570, of cows yielding 1,350 litres of milk; from this 42 kilograms of butter and 28 of skim-milk cheese could be made. The reason we are so starved of figures is that the agricultural world of those days clearly knew very little about bookkeeping. One of the few examples of a farmer who kept books was Robert Loder of Harwell, near Oxford, at the beginning of the seventeenth century; in his accounts he included the interest on capital invested in seed and cattle, and was aware that his own labour, together with that of his wife and other women who worked for him, had to be reckoned as labour costs.

Seen from this angle the opportunities for determining productivity figures in the agricultural sector are also extremely limited. Until the Norfolk plough was introduced, a man could not plough more than 0·3–0·4 hectares a day. It took a man using a sickle 5–6¼ days to cut a hectare of wheat; this was equivalent to 130–160 litres of wheat a day. With a scythe the results will have been considerably better. There was also an improvement in threshing: in the thirteenth century a man could manage a total of 72 litres of wheat or 300 litres of oats in a day; at Harwell in 1613 the corresponding figures were 120 litres of wheat or 380 litres of barley. There is another method of calculation which attempts to measure the number of people who could live off the produce of a farm. In the twelfth century it took from fifteen to thirty peasant families to feed a knight and his family; this figure seems to have remained more or less constant until the eighteenth century.

The first thing necessary in order to increase the productivity of an agricultural concern was to consider how to make improvements in the organisation and to seek ways and means to raise the small per capita productivity.

The soil could be enriched by planting leguminous crops like peas, beans and clover, instead of leaving it fallow, or else by using more cattle dung and other fertilisers. The former system was used to some extent in the Netherlands and Upper Italy, where the most progressive farms were to be found; on large farms, like those in Denmark for example, cattle food in the form of mast provided a better means of fertilising the arable land. Another way to increase production was to specialise in fruit and vegetables if one lived near heavily populated areas, or in hemp, flax, woad, madder, hops, tobacco, flowers, seeds and young trees for commercial purposes, or in stock-breeding. In the sixteenth and seventeenth centuries it was once more in the Netherlands that this was most highly developed, as well as in the marshlands along the North Sea coast between Friesland and Schleswig, where Netherlandish influence was strong. In the duchies the *Holländerei*, or leasehold dairy farm, came into existence during the seventeenth century. Of Denmark it was said that young aristocrats went abroad to gain experience, and in the second half of the sixteenth century introduced fallow conditions at home.

The three-field system, and this is the crucial point, still prevailed everywhere; alongside it traditional methods of cultivation like the system of alternate husbandry, the *Eschwirtschaft* or continuous cultivation of a single field, the four- and five-field systems, continued to hold their own. The system of crop rotation, which ushered in a new and decisive phase did not emerge clearly until the eighteenth century. For the rest the production of grain, so vital to western Europe, was assured by the domains and estates. On these the aim was to produce on as large a scale as possible; under certain circumstances, in order to round off an estate, peasants' land was expropriated, and the management put into the hands of a steward who had not only experience of bookkeeping but the necessary marketing knowledge. Thus here again it was a question of organisation rather than technique. The same was true of the tenant farmers, in the vicinity of Paris, for example, or on dairy farms in Schleswig-Holstein, who cultivated their land to the utmost.

It is important not to overlook the fact that the overseas

expansion brought an additional flow of foodstuffs to Europe. Beans, cultivated in Peru, spread to Europe in the sixteenth century and became an important item of food in the Iberian peninsula. In the sixteenth century, too, the Portuguese started to grow American corn, which produced an abundant crop; it was called *milho*, a name given to several plants in the Middle Ages, while the Haitian name *maiz* spread to the rest of Europe from Spain. Tomatoes and paprika also came from South America. Potatoes, of which numerous varieties were cultivated in Peru, had been grown in Europe since the seventeenth century, although they did not establish themselves in regions with temperate climates until the eighteenth century. Equally important was the rising prosperity of the Newfoundland fisheries which, at a time of growing population pressure, provided a welcome addition to basic foodstuffs, especially in western Europe and the Mediterranean area.

Finally, the possibility of increasing per capita output and creating additional means of income must also be seen in conjunction with the rural crafts. Especially in areas mainly given over to cattle breeding, where labour was less in demand than it was in agricultural areas – in England, Belgium and Switzerland, for instance – we know that every member of the peasant families, from the children to the grandparents, earned money by spinning, and sometimes by weaving. Apart from this there were opportunities to earn money by felling trees, transporting coal, performing other cartage services, or by quarrying.

In forestry, the loss of trees caused by thriving trade conditions led people to consider ways and means of speeding up re-afforestation. From Nuremberg came the solution of seeding the land with conifers, a method that had been used since late medieval times. In the Memmingen district attempts were made to find new ways of felling and restocking. In the royal forests replanting with the quicker growing poplar and willow was advised. Once again these were processes that belong to the sphere of organisation rather than to that of technology.

Mining, smelting and other industrial production

Technical advances made a much greater impact on mining, metal processing and the other branches of industrial production than they did on the agricultural sector.

In these sectors, too, it is important, however, not to see the technical facts in isolation; what matters is the place they occupied within the economic process. Organisation played a part in extracting the ore, in processing it, and in marketing it. An important feature of iron-mining was that it was less affected by the royalty regulations than the non-ferrous metals: iron-stone belonged not to the crown, or ruling prince, but to the landlord. Thus it was the landlord who, in the first instance, had the chief say in exploiting iron deposits, permission to do so being granted, in the form of fiefs, to competent interested parties. The peasants were strongly represented in mining, mining and smelting forming secondary occupations for them; they frequently combined to form co-operatives. When deep-mining was necessary to extract the iron, as in the Upper Palatinate, and a corresponding amount of capital was required, larger associations were formed, such as the *Gemein Gesellschaft* of the Amberg iron mines in 1464; the same thing occurred in the Fichtelgebirge. The *Hauptgewerkschaft*, or mining company, that took over the Innerberg ironworks in 1625, combined mining with processing and retail sales.

In processing, the specialised activities of the wheel-wrights, cutlers and smiths had exerted an influence in medieval times. Forging required a whole complex of equipment, with one or more smithies, refining hearths and water-driven bellows. Because capital was needed to set up a forge, the entrepreneur, or the iron merchant in larger towns like Nuremberg, Amberg, Steyer, Leoben, Cologne, Liège and Stockholm, had the opportunity to step in and offer credit.

Processing was done largely by individual craftsmen organised into bodies not unlike guilds, that is to say it was in the hands of small master-craftsmen working with their families and a few assistants and apprentices. Here again specialisation gave the entrepreneur an opportunity to step in: he could supply the half-finished product, advance capital and provide tools, and assume responsibility for sales. The Nuremberg piece-work trade was a typical phenomenon of these entrepreneurial activities.

Processing benefited not only by being split up into numerous branches of the smith's craft, but also by the availability of special forging hammers and other equipment, such as the wire-mill, cutting-mill and wire-drawer.

Nor must one lose sight of the fact that smelting and processing involved other groups of workers who did outside work, like the charcoal burners and carters. When the landlords kept the business in their own hands, and rented none of it out, the workers were dependents obliged to do forced labour; this occurred in Bohemia, Moravia, Hungary, Poland, and also in the Dillenburg area.

With non-ferrous metals the connection between increased productivity and business organisation, or concentration, was still clearer. The work could be organised better and planned more expertly when the business was large; the larger operators were in a stronger position when the need arose to invest in new technical equipment. In the sixteenth century a paternoster-pump cost 300–400 gulden, a piston-pump between 200 and 700 gulden, a system of guiding-rods between 500 and 1,000 gulden, an animal-operated whim a similar amount, a reversible water-wheel up to 3,000 gulden, a stamping-mill 1,200–1,500 gulden, smaller smelt-houses for tin 100–400 gulden, smelt-houses for silver and larger smelting-works over 1,000 gulden. Small concerns could not afford such sums; only financially strong mining companies, or syndicates, could do so. The Leutenberg smelting-works took several years to build and cost over 10,000 florins.

Large undertakings were also prepared to engage in drastic rationalisation by closing down businesses that had become unprofitable, as the Fuggers did in Slovakia and Carinthia. Equipment was devised for using up rich waste, poor ore and slag; in this way earnings could be increased without having to invest large sums in the mine itself. In Slovakia there was fierce opposition to the Fuggers' rationalisation measures both from the town of Neusohl and from the workers themselves; it reached a climax in 1540.

But again there were also limits to the degree of concentration possible. It necessitated a corresponding increase in the administrative and clerical apparatus. In the 1580s, for instance, Neusohl employed an administrative and clerical staff of fifteen.

Specialisation among the working personnel

The above suggests an important negative effect of technical improvements. The positive side was specialisation. Work in the mines, as we have seen, was often seasonal, and because of this pay was still low. In most cases this work was additional to work on the land, especially in the iron sector. Where quantity was the first consideration, piecework or contract work was the rule; where quality was more important, a daily wage was preferred. As the use of technical equipment in mining became more widespread, a whole range of specialised workers came into existence. In Bohemia in 1578 an ironworks employed eight men: five with different functions at the Stückofen; and three at the forge. Neusohl was one of the places where this specialisation was most marked: in 1581, of the 592 people employed there, only 233 were engaged as pickmen in the actual mining operations, whereas 359 were engaged in constructing the adits, hauling and transporting the excavated ore, and in the necessary carpentry and other auxiliary activities; by 1629, when blasting was introduced, 51 more people had been added for work in connection with the bellows and the whim, and other operations – included among them were two carters and an innkeeper. To these must be added the personnel already mentioned. The pay also varied with the specialisation. Specialisation received a boost in the dressing and smelting processes, as it did in the underground working, when stamping-mills, *Stücköfen*, and blast-furnaces were introduced and use was made of bellows, water-driven forges, casting equipment, drilling-machines and apparatus for producing sheet metal and wire.

In all this the proportion of inside workers to miners and woodworkers must be borne in mind; these last often formed a considerable part of the whole. In the Gmunden iron mines in Carinthia, there were 39 miners and smelters to 120 woodworkers and charcoal burners.

Although the productive capacity of the *Stücköfen* and blast furnaces is a known quantity, the weekly number of runs varied greatly; and apart from this one needs to know whether a six- or seven-day week was worked: Hofmann assumes a seven-day week for the smelters and a six-day week for the pickmen. Finally the holidays: there were constant complaints that too much time was taken off for holidays, feastdays and the eves of such days, with the result that there were twice as many holidays as working days in the year.

Limits to attainable productivity

The above already suggests severe limitations to the productivity that was attainable. But there were other obstacles as well. Increase in productivity often had to be bought at the price of a corresponding rise in the consumption of timber.

The Slovakian smelting works at Stare Hory and Harmanec were forced to close down to a large extent about the year 1560 because of the shortage of timber in the neighbouring forests. In 1564 two forestry experts were appointed to see that the stocks of timber in the forests were used economically and at the same time protected. At that time 57,000 cubic metres of wood a year were floated down the River Gran to the collecting points at Neusohl, where the smelting works consumed 24,000 loads of charcoal a year; an additional need for mine timber must not be forgotten.

The disastrous effects of cutting down the forests to feed the mines and smelting works are well known from Mexico, where it took scarcely more than forty years to destroy the forests over a radius of almost fifty kilometres round the mining and smelting district of Zacatecas. The situation there was eased by the introduction of the *patio* process, which only required fuel to distil the mercury from the amalgam. The silver mines in Freiberg consumed more than 60,000 cubic metres of timber a year, those in Hüttenberg and Joachimstal probably taking a similar quantity; the consumption of the tin mines was on the same scale. In the 1580s, when production had already fallen off, the Schlaggenwald and Schönfeld districts used almost 76,000 cubic metres of timber a year. The rising consumption of timber was reflected in a corresponding rise in price: in central Europe a small rise in price took place about 1470, and by about 1535 the upward trend was general, reaching a peak in the *Kipperzeit* of 1621–3. Attempts had already been made in the fifteenth century to check the excessive consumption of timber by means of regulations governing timber, timber floating and forestry. A special type of rationalisation of timber consumption is to be seen in the associations formed to cultivate trees in coppices (*Haubergenossenschaften*), which are known to have existed in the Siegerland from the end of the fifteenth century. In order to ensure the supply of fuel, long-term supply contracts were entered into.

A few figures will show what a high cost item timber consumption was. In the Hüttenberg iron district of Carinthia, in about 1570, fuel represented some 70 per cent of the costs and the ore about 25 per cent, the remaining 5 per cent being divided between wages and other necessities. Similar figures are provided by the Gmunden mines about eighty years later.

Four cubic metres of wood were needed to produce a ton of pig-iron, and a further nine cubic metres for a ton of wrought iron. In the face of these problems, attempts were made to rationalise charcoal production: in the Brdy area, at the beginning of the eighteenth century, they had succeeded to the extent of producing seventeen, as against the former fifteen, tons of charcoal from each fathom of wood.

Quite early on coal and peat were tried as substitutes. In the Aachen district and in the Ruhr coal had been used for forging in medieval times; in the sixteenth century it was used in Saxony as well. In England peat had been widely used since the end of the sixteenth century, but it was not suited to blast furnaces. Coal, too, had been used in England since the end of the sixteenth century, but only that from Oakmoor in Staffordshire and only in the refining furnaces called chaferies. The result was that it would 'hardly sell above £10 the tonne'. The process did not come into general use until about 1700, and in the fineries charcoal had to be used until 1783/84, when Cort was granted his patent. Attempts had been made to use coal in blast furnaces since the end of the sixteenth century. At first, however, the only significant result was the development of the cupola furnace; this was constructed in two parts, so that the ore did not come into direct contact with the coal but was melted by the flames. John Robinson (1613) played an important part in this development. But final success only came with the introduction of the coking method.

Distribution and consumption

This review of increased production, an increase especially noticeable in mining, metal processing and textiles, leaves one other question to be considered: that of distribution and consumption. How big was the market? Was it capable of absorbing the supply that technology had now made possible?

There is no doubt that during the two centuries under discussion the market expanded enormously. The penetration of the Turks in the south-east during the fifteenth and early sixteenth centuries, it is true, blocked long-standing marketing outlets and opportunities; but this was offset by the territorial discoveries and conquests made by Europeans overseas, even if at first, as in the case of the Portuguese in west and east Africa and the East Indies, these were confined to isolated strongholds and coastal strips. In Brazil, on the other hand, the thriving plantations, and above all the sugar trade, started to attract the import of African slaves in the middle of the sixteenth century; and once they were baptised, these slaves had to be clothed. In the territories occupied by the Spaniards the system of government they imposed, and the diseases they brought with them for Europe, caused devastating losses among the Indian population, a state of affairs that continued until the middle of the seventeenth century. Unfortunately the figures provided by research vary so greatly that it is still impossible to get a clear picture of the decline that started about 1500 and the resurgence that followed in the second half of the seventeenth century. Were there thirteen million inhabitants in the middle of the seventeenth century or only eight million? At any rate both emigrants from Europe and slave ships from Africa continued to arrive; after the middle of the seventeenth century an increasing number of the latter went to the Antilles.

The growing importance of the American continent to the European market emerges particularly clearly from the figures worked out by P. Chaunu for the period up to the middle of the seventeenth century. In the meantime the other European nations, led by Holland, England and France, had made headway overseas and opened up additional markets. Once again, the clearest evidence of this is provided by the increase in these countries' maritime traffic; moreover their ships carried a constant stream of European emigrants travelling as crew and mercenaries, among them many Germans in the service of the Dutch, and they, too, helped to swell the overseas market. As the Portuguese and Spaniards lost more and more of their original monopoly, their rivals extended and intensified the ramifications of world trade until they reached into eastern Asia. Nevertheless, the market's centre of gravity still remained in Europe, if we include in this the Mediterranean, with the opportunities it offered for trade with the Levant and North Africa, and the new route to Archangel, with its connections to Russia and Siberia. One also has to remember that the home market was growing, as the result of rising population and consumption. Recent calculations give the population of Europe in the middle of the fifteenth century as about fifty-five million, rising to some hundred million in 1600. Allowing for various restraining factors, and losses, due mainly to the Thirty Years War, the figure will probably again have been about a hundred million in 1680. Among factors stimulating sales must be reckoned first and foremost the growing demand for weapons on land and sea, and the growing demand for ships; added to these was the Renaissance taste for increased luxury at the courts of the princes, among the nobility, and also among the upper middle classes. The social changes brought about by the Reformation, especially secularisation, also stimulated consumer activity, as did fashion, particularly the vogue of the *nouvelle draperie*, Spanish fashions and, starting in the 1630s, the growing demand for French fashions. At this period, too, as we have seen, various departments of the tertiary sector had developed a remarkable productive capacity, above all shipping. Technical improvements in ships contributed in large measure to better connections with the important markets for raw materials in the Baltic and other parts of northern Europe; and inasmuch as each ship could now make more journeys, western and southern European ports were supplied more quickly with ship-building materials.

But the movement of goods was speeded up only when use could be made of seagoing ships and the technical advances they incorporated, that is to say in the neighbourhood of the sea – in the Baltic and North Sea regions, on the Atlantic seaboard, and in the Mediterranean; apart from better organised dispatching arrangements and a certain amount of road, bridge and canal building, there had been no spectacular advances in river and overland traffic. The organisation of the post-services had certainly improved communications, although overseas communications were entirely dependent on the speed of the ships: in transactions with America and the East Indies much more than a year was needed to get an answer to a letter. About the year 1600, when Dutch penetration into Portuguese colonial territories had reached its decisive phase, an interesting attempt was made by a Netherlandish–German trading group to build up a quicker communications system with Goa. But it did not last. In the seventeenth century it still took a year and a half to get an answer to a letter from Batavia.

The organisation of the trading companies, and the modernised credit system that came with it, made it possible to install expensive equipment to stimulate and improve the mining industry and metallurgy; the overseas companies, which were organised on a share-holding basis and supported by the state, enabled the Spanish–Portuguese trade monopoly to be broken and more European interests to participate directly in overseas trade. But because of the bad communications, the credit terms had to be adjusted to the long handling times – in Seville the periods were twelve, fifteen and eighteen months.

The factors that caused markets to expand, in a phase that lasted until the beginning of the seventeenth century, have now been indicated. But the markets did not expand sufficiently to prevent the increase in production, made possible by the new organisational and technical resources, from soon overtaking them.

The copper market was a particularly clear example of this. An initial sales crisis, especially noticeable in Venice, occurred at the end of the fifteenth century, at the very moment when the Fuggers were loading the market with more Neusohl copper. Further similar crises followed in the 1520s and 1540s. Here again there was a clear connection with the overproduction that resulted from the investments of the great *Saiger*, or metal processing, companies. In the mid-1520s Christoph Fürer of Nuremberg tried to form a syndicate of copper producers, but failed owing to the opposition of Hans Welser. In the mid-1540s Anton Fugger gave up the 'Hungarian business' because of marketing difficulties. At the beginning of the seventeenth century there were renewed difficulties of this kind, when a glut of Swedish copper came on the market and the Swedes, as intermediaries, had the great Amsterdam and Hamburg traders in their power. More copper was needed than formerly, for the copper and brass industry, for ship-building, and for coins during the *Kipper* and *Wipper* period of debased coinage, when copper coins were minted in Spain and copper coins were exported from the Elbe and the Amstel to Poland and Russia. In spite of the increased sales, however, Swedish production, itself increased by the use of new technical equipment, was faced with difficulties, because copper was also mined in the Mansfeld area and in Slovakia, although the Tyrol production had dwindled to insignificance. Subsequently the wars in Bohemia and the Palatinate, and other military events, had a very damaging effect on the market for copper from central Germany and Slovakia, from which the Swedes profited. And so it went on until the Spanish edict of 1626. When Spain stopped minting copper coins, the stocks of copper in the Baltic ports, Hamburg and Amsterdam rose. Thus one reason why Sweden intervened on the mainland of Europe was to gain control of the copper market, so that it could unload the stocks it held. The Thirty Years War, by disorganising copper production in Mansfeld, Bohemia and Slovakia, was instrumental in bringing about a new balance between production and sales, to the advantage of Sweden. Although Sweden's copper production fell towards the end of the seventeenth century, it was still able to dominate the market to a great extent, from which one is justified in concluding that saturation point had been reached internationally.

It was now iron's turn to assume the leading role in the metal sector. Europe's iron production continued to increase until into the second half of the sixteenth century; then, because the seams were becoming exhausted and charcoal was getting scarcer and scarcer, stagnation set in, with the result that no particular difficulties were experienced in finding a market. During the Thirty Years War iron production and processing suffered in various parts of central Europe, but Sweden, in the context of its war economy, was able to increase both production and sales. Its export figures rose from 7,000 tons in, or about, 1620 to 15,000 tons in 1641. Western Europe was the main outlet for these exports, but after 1716, when Russian iron came on the market, the owners of the Swedish forges found themselves in difficulties and were faced with the choice of restricting production or seeking new markets in the Mediterranean area. Thus once again an upper limit to the international market's absorptive capacity was in sight; it was not to take a new upward turn until the coke-fired furnace came into widespread use.

The textile market also underwent a series of crises and changes. The day of heavy, high quality cloth was nearing its end. Since the second half of the sixteenth century buyers had shown a growing interest in kerseys, bays, says, cloths, grosgrains and other materials. Sometimes political developments closed down markets: the Turkish expansion in the south-east made sales difficult for producers in Nuremberg, and probably elsewhere in Upper Germany; the difficulties experienced in selling English goods in Antwerp forced the Merchant Adventurers to seek new sales outlets in the North Sea area. In addition the Muscovy, Eastland and Levant companies were looking for new markets. The English sales crisis that occurred about 1620 showed up in particularly clear relief the marketing obstacles that faced producers. On the continent the North Netherlands led by Leyden, and Southern France, together with places like Amiens in the north, were able to fill the market gaps caused by the political difficulties under which the South Netherlands textile producers were labouring. There was also increasing competition from Switzerland. In eastern Europe the market was growing for both the simpler local things and the more expensive ones from western Europe, while overseas the plantation market for linen and cotton goods had been gaining in importance since the middle of the seventeenth century.

Although the transport system was fairly well geared to the new tasks of marketing, land transport lagged considerably behind, with particularly serious consequences for the transport of raw materials and other heavy goods in areas that were not near the coast, a river, a large stream or a canal. This was one of the main reasons why it was so difficult to get supplies to these districts when they were hit by drought or some other disaster. Thus it is evident that the relationship between technology and the economy was also subject to conditions imposed by distribution and consumption, and that these conditions lent a dynamic force of their own to the economic process. While the picture of expanding markets during the sixteenth century fits well into the framework of the long rhythmic period that extended from the second half of the fifteenth century to the beginning of the seventeenth century and beyond, the recurrent sales recessions show clearly the barriers that faced increased production under the economic conditions of the day. The signs of stagnation in production, traceable since the end of the sixteenth century, were strongly emphasised after the end of the second decade of the seventeenth century by the effects of the war, even though the war in its turn benefited sales in certain fields of production. Nevertheless it is a remarkable fact that the markets for copper and iron continued to move within relatively narrow limits until into the eighteenth century.

CONCLUSION

If our judgement on the relationship between technology and the economy in the two centuries between 1500 and 1700 is to be comprehensive, it must take into account their role as a bridge between the innovations introduced in the high and late Middle Ages and the violent changes that came about with the industrial revolution. Technologically speaking, the age to which the great scholars Copernicus, Galileo and Newton belonged was not stamped by science and learning but by the work of practical men. The most important innovations had come in the preceding centuries; the problem now was to turn them to better practical use. The true significance of the age lay not in great spectacular innovations, but in countless small technical advances, in the spread of technical knowledge by means of the printed word and illustration, in the training of men technically skilled in the various departments of industrial activity, above all in the industrial regions north and south of the Alps.

The most striking advances were made in mining and the processing of metals, and to some extent in the textile field; agriculture and building lagged behind, while transport shows a striking contrast between the upsurge in shipping and the relative stagnation of land transport.

Fascinating though it is to see economic growth resulting from economic progress, and 'innovations' from inventions, one must not overlook the many obstacles that repeatedly stood in the way of full realisation of the new technical possibilities.

One of the main reasons for not using, or using to a greater extent, the new machinery in the mining industry was the high cost in relation to yield. Expensive extraction and drainage equipment could be used profitably in mining precious metals, copper and tin, at least up to a certain point which was determined by, among other things, the competition of American silver; but, generally speaking, such equipment was too costly for iron and coal mining.

A further obstacle was the growing shortage of fuel, especially charcoal. The use of coal in the industrial process spread only slowly: it is true that coke – in other words coal from which certain impurities had been eliminated – was used for malting (in beer production), glass making and processing lead; but it was not until the eighteenth century that coal came into its own as an ingredient in the immensely important indirect method of smelting iron. Until then shortage of fuel had limited the smelting process to the specific period of the 'run' of the furnace. The frequent holidays were also an obstacle to increased production: at the beginning of the eighteenth century, the working year in the iron works in the Austrian alpine regions was 161 days; the other 204 days were holidays.

Another reason why businesses were not more go-ahead

was that it sometimes paid to postpone introducing technical improvements, because for the time being older processes were more profitable: hence the hesitation in introducing the indirect method in districts like Styria, where the iron ore was of a higher quality. Finally the workers' opposition to the introduction of technical innovations must be seen against a wider social background. The introduction of innovations that cut down on manpower disturbed the social equilibrium. This could be restored if the earnings shortfall could be made good by new opportunities for earning; generally speaking, however, the instruments of economic and social policy in the sixteenth and seventeenth centuries were not sufficiently sensitive for such opportunities to be created quickly. The introduction of innovations was therefore forbidden as need arose in individual cases, this, in the eyes of the authorities concerned, being the best temporary solution. And it was not only in Nuremberg and other cities, and not only in the Holy Roman Empire, that this was done; at appropriate moments the Tudor regime was also guided by such general considerations.

If these matters still require further scientific clarification, none needs it more than the problem of calculating productivity. The definition of productivity, as last given by Fourastié, shows how difficult it is to make such a calculation for the pre-statistical era. Taking as a starting point the various relationships from which the total productivity is derived, it has so far proved possible to complete only part of the picture. Great as were the merits of Slicher van Bath's computations of yields, the fact remains that they embraced only a portion of the agricultural sector – and in the light of more recent research this has been still further reduced. Slicher's studies on the productivity of labour are also interesting, as are the calculations of Hofmann and Paulinyi, whose work should be followed up. Continuing on the lines laid down by Fourastié, that is using the auxiliary calculations suggested by him, Philippi attempted to obtain at least approximate figures for linen and brick production, by taking as his basis the Elsas price indices and dividing the wages index by that of the prices of the products. But linen and brick production were activities in which there were no significant technical innovations in either the sixteenth or the seventeenth century. More convincing are the calculations made by North, who established that there was a rise in productivity in shipping subsequent to 1600; but on the basis of Hagedorn's and A. E. Christensen's work it ought also to be possible to establish a rise in productivity in, let us say, Baltic shipping for the sixteenth century.

Select Bibliography

GENERAL WORKS

The seminal work on the interrelationship between technology and the economy is W. Sombart, *Der modern Kapitalismus*, 2 vols. (Munich and Leipzig, 1922). One of the best recent books on this topic is J. U. Nef, *La naissance de la civilisation industrielle* (Paris, 1954) (English translation, *The Conquest of the Material World* (London and Chicago, 1964)). D. S. Landes in *The Rise of Capitalism* (New York, 1966) deals with the technological questions and F. Braudel, *Civilisation materielle et capitalisme XVe-XVIIIe siècles* (Paris, 1967) (English translation, *Capitalism and Material Life 1400-1840* (London, 1973)) looks at the international aspects. A still more recent contribution to these questions is H. Kellenbenz, 'Les industries dans l'Europe modern (1500-1750)' in *L'industrialisation et typologie*, ed. P. Léon *et al* (Paris, 1972).

There are several recent publications on the history of technology: in English; *A History of Technology*, eds. C. Singer, E. J. Holmyard *et al*, 5 vols. (Oxford, 1954-58) and A. R. Hall, *The Scientific Revolution 1500-1800* (London, 1962); in French, *Histoire générale des techniques*, ed. M. Daumas, 4 vols. (Paris, 1962), of which the 3rd volume with contributions by Daumas himself is especially relevant; in German, F. M. Feldhaus, *Die Technik der Antike und des Mittelalters* (Hildersheim, 1971) and F. Klemm *Technik, eine Geschichte ihrer Probleme* (Freiberg, 1954) (English translation *A History of Western Technology* (London, 1959)). Finally there are two bibliographies: E. S. Ferguson, *Bibliography of the History of Technology* (Cambridge, Mass., 1968) and K. R. Rider, *History of Science and Technology, a Select Bibliography* (London, 1970).

PRINTING AND THE DISSEMINATION OF TECHNICAL KNOWLEDGE

There are many publications on the history of printing among them: H. Barge, *Geschichte der Buchdruckerkunst*, 2 vols. (Dresden and Berlin, 1928–41), S. H. Steinberg, *Five Hundred Years of Printing* (London, 1959) and J. Carter *et al*, *Printing and the Mind of Man* (London, 1959). On the dissemination of technical knowledge see: U. Troitzsch, *Ansätze technologischen Denkens bei den Kameralisten des 17. und 18. Jahrhunderts* (Berlin, 1966).

ENGINEERING

The best book on this subject is A. P. Usher, *A History of Mechanical Inventions* (Cambridge, Mass., 1954) and by the same author see: 'Machines and mechanisms', in C. Singer, *A History of Technology*, vol. 3. In French there is B. Gille, *Les ingénieurs de la Renaissance* (Paris, 1964) and in German, W. Treue and R. Kellerman, *Die Kulturgeschichte der Schraube* (Munich, 1962).

THE CHEMICAL PROCESS

G. Lockemann, *The Story of Chemistry* (London, 1960) and J. R. Partington, *A History of Chemistry*, 4 vols. (London, 1960–67), both deal with general problems in the history of chemistry. On the topic of chemical processes there is C. Singer, *The earliest chemical industry, an essay in the historical relations of the economics and technology illustrated from the alum trade* (London, 1948) and C. Stanley Smith, 'Metallurgy and assaying' in C. Singer *et al*, *A History of Technology*, vol. 3.

TECHNICAL AIDS IN AGRICULTURE AND FISHING

V. Husa *et al*, *Traditional Crafts and Skills* (London, 1967) gives a good survey of the technical aids used in agriculture. On the history of agriculture in Western Europe see: B. H. Slicher van Bath, *The Agrarian History of Western Europe A.D. 500–1850* (London, 1963). On national agrarian histories see: J. Thirsk (ed.), *The Agrarian History of England and Wales*, vol. 4 *1500–1640* (Cambridge, 1967) and W. Abel, *Geschichte der deutsche Landwirtschaft* (Stuttgart, 1962).

TECHNICAL AIDS IN MINING AND SMELTING

The most comprehensive general study on the subject is: O. Johannsen, *Geschichte des Eisens* (Düsseldorf, 1953). Good national studies are provided by: H. R. Schubert, *History of the British Iron and Steel Industry* (London, 1957); B. Gille, *Les origines de la grande industrie métallurgique en France* (Paris, 1947). On coal mining and its effects see: J. U. Nef, *The Rise of the British Coal Industry*, 2 vols. (London, 1932) and 'Coal mining and utilization' in Singer's *A History of Technology*, vol. 3 by the same author.

TECHNICAL AIDS IN OTHER BRANCHES OF INDUS-TRIAL PRODUCTION

On technical aids in the textile industry see: R. Patterson, 'Spinning and weaving', in *History of Technology*, *op.cit.* vol. 3; J. Norberg, 'A note on knitting and knitted fabrics', *ibid.*; J. F. Flanagan, 'Figured fabrics', *ibid.* For a more general study see: W. Endrei, *L'évolution des techniques du filage et du tissage du Moyen Âge à la révolution industrielle* (Paris, 1968).

TECHNICAL ACHIEVEMENTS IN TRANSPORT, TRADE AND CREDIT

For medieval achievements in transport see: R. S. Lopez, *The Commercial Revolution of the Middle Ages, 950–1350* (Englewood Cliffs, 1971). For the years 1500–1700 see: J. H. Parry, 'Transport and trade routes', *Cambridge Economic History of Europe*, vol. 4 and K. Glamann, 'European trade' on p. 427 of this book. R. Davis, *Rise of the English Shipping Industry in the 17th and 18th Centuries* (London, 1962) and C. M. Cipolla, *Guns and Sails in the Early Phase of the European Expansion, 1400–1700* (London, 1965) both provide good studies on the shipping industry.

NON-TECHNICAL FACTORS INFLUENCING PRODUC-TION AND PRODUCTIVITY

Douglass North in his article 'Institutional change and economic growth', *Journal of Economic History*, 1971 stresses the point that technological questions should be seen within an institutional framework. There are two good books which look at the subject in the context of French history: H. Hauser, *La pensée et l'action économique du cardinal du Richelieu* (Paris, 1944) and B. Gille, *Les origines de la grande industrie métallurgique*, and C. Wilson, 'Trade, society and the State', *Cambridge History of Europe*, vol. 4 gives a good synthesis of the problems involved. See also H. Kellenbenz, 'Les industries dans l'Europe moderne', *op.cit.*, on the role of the government.

ENTREPRENEURSHIP

J. Streider, *Studien zur Geschichte kapitalistischer Organisationsformen* (Munich, Leipzig, 1914) deals with the question of private entrepreneurship in Central Europe and H. Kellenbenz in 'I grandi mercanti e la mobilità sociale nell'Europa dal Cinque al Settecento', *Annali*, Facolta di Economia e Commercio, Verona, 1967–8 treats the subject in the wider European context.

ORGANISATION OF INDUSTRIAL PRODUCTION

For this question see Domenico Sella's article on pp. 354–426 of this book and H. Kellenbenz, 'Les industries rurales en Occident de la fin du Moyen Âge au XVIIIᵉ siècle', *Annales: Economies, Sociétés, Civilisations* (1963). On the factory system see: R. Forberger, *Die Manufactur in Sachsen von Endes des 16. bis zum Anfang des 19. Jahrhunderts* (Berlin, 1958) and again B. Gille, *Les origines de la grande industrie métallurgique*, is the best book using the French material.

SPECIALISATION AMONG THE WORKING PERSONNEL

For more information on this subject see: W. Sombart, *Der moderne Kapitalismus*, and F. M. Ress, 'Unternehmungen, Unternehmer und Arbeiter im Eisen – bergbau und in der Eisenverhüttung der Oberfalz von 1300–bis 1630', *Schmollers Jahrbuch* (1954).

LIMITS TO PRODUCTIVITY

This question was analysed by Gustav Hofmann and Akos Pauliny at the *3rd Settimana di Studi* (not yet published). See also H. Kellenbenz, 'Les industries dans l'Europe moderne', pp. 108–12, which has a good bibliography on the subject and J. Fourastie *Die grosse Hoffnung des zwanzigsten Jahrhunderts* (Köln, 1954).

For the interesting problem of the Swedish iron market and Russian competition see: Erik Astrom, *From Cloth to Iron, the Anglo-Baltic Trade in the Late Seventeenth Century* (Helsingfors, 1963–6) and K. Hildebrand, 'Foreign markets for Swedish iron in the 18th century', *Scandinavian Economic History Review*, VI, 1958.

4. Rural Europe 1500–1750

Aldo De Maddalena

*Note: The statistical tables for this contribution have been printed as an
appendix to this volume.*

INTRODUCTION

From the sixteenth century to the middle of the eighteenth
rural Europe experienced the effects of the radical political
and economic changes that went hand in hand with the
profound spiritual and cultural transformation that characterised the period. The upheavals caused by a number of
very important developments — geographical discoveries,
changes in the direction of maritime trade, the formation
of the big unified States, the religious Reformation and
Counter-Reformation, to mention only a few — had their
effects on agriculture too, and aroused aspirations towards
reform and innovation in the rural societies of Europe.

Developments in agriculture were, however, only modest
as compared with those in other economic spheres, especially trade, and for the most part did not alter the pattern
that had emerged during the late Middle Ages and the
Renaissance. The new ideas and aims of public or private
operators in the other economic spheres in general con-
flicted with the interests and aspirations of the country
people. We need only recall how 'mercantilism', both in its
doctrinal propositions and its concrete application, made
the merchant-capitalist the main figure in economic activity,
propounded the development of industrial activity and,
except for a particular Catholic trend of Cameralism[1] in
Germany, left agricultural problems on one side. It was
said, with justification, that industry and trade, especially
foreign trade, were the 'children' in whom were placed the

[1] Cameralism was the German branch of 'Mercantilism': it included
both a Catholic and a Protestant current.

highest hopes and expectations. Old agriculture, though it continued to be the basic factor in the production, distribution and consumption of wealth, offered small possibilities for applying the law of increasing returns. Most people thought that the undeniable and in some ways revolutionary agrarian changes at the end of the Middle Ages, which in part were still operative, constituted an epilogue rather than a prologue.

On the other hand, expansion of the monetary and commercial economy, even when, as in some cases, it partook of feudalistic involution, spilt over into the rural world and influenced its values, both human and practical. For example, the so-called 'price revolution', which occurred more or less everywhere, caused landowners and farmers to seek new solutions both in agrarian contracts, by modifying the economic clauses in such agreements, and in agriculture itself, by changes in methods of cultivation. Changes in monetary values also had their effects on the property market, where at times a real upheaval was caused by waves of speculation.

In short, some changes were undoubtedly at work even in these centuries; but, given the traditional conservatism of the rural world, such changes came about only very slowly, and their rate, extent and effects differed from place to place. Consequently, great caution is needed in attempting any synthesis of agricultural developments in Europe during the modern era. Duby's exhortation to avoid generalisations, given in his section on medieval agriculture, applies even more to the period we are dealing with here. True, improved communications, wider markets, and even the aggressive spirit that pervaded international life and often found expression in prolonged wars, all created easier exchanges and contacts between areas, populations and rural communities. But regional differences persisted, and even in some cases became accentuated, after the breakdown of that Christian-Latin unity which, despite all its shortcomings, had imprinted uniform features upon medieval European civilisation. The definite collapse of the principle of universality maintained by Catholicism; the opposition, political as well as doctrinal, between the Reformation world, with its various confessional manifestations, and the world of the Counter-Reformation; the germination of a new economic mentality and the growing adherence of Protestant society to the precepts of utilitarianism (the utilitarian principle gaining the upper hand over the principle of equity, which had constituted the essence of medieval thought and education) — all this furthered the rise, even in country districts, of antagonisms between different classes and communities. Moreover, in the countryside of the modern era local interests revived which, though differing in aim and features from the medieval counterparts, militated against that process of assimilation and homogeneity which the new conditions might have promoted. At the same time those regional differences in agricultural structures, forms, conditions and experiences, to which Duby refers in relation to the Middle Ages, still persisted, making any attempt at generalisation both difficult and dangerous.

(a) Geography and climate still profoundly influenced rural activities and their results. '*L'Europe est multiple*'; and each geographical sector of Europe had its corresponding agricultural countryside. Improvements in farming methods, or such modernisation of technique and implements as occurred in places, were still on too small a scale to enable European agriculture to free itself from subjection to natural constants and variables. Manual labour was still by far the most important factor in the exploitation of the soil and was bound to adapt itself to local conditions. Recent studies have established that definite climatic variations occurred during the sixteenth and seventeenth centuries; variations which, in the Mediterranean area, accentuated the recurrent phases of dryness, and in the intermediate zones affected the degree of humidity and precipitation cycles, thus making agricultural yields even more uncertain.

(b) Differences arose also from the degree of economic and social development and the particular incidence of events and circumstances. European history is a mosaic of histories, at the economic and social level too; and the rural world bears witness to that fact.

Between the sixteenth century and the middle of the eighteenth various interwoven trends combined to alter the relative positions of the different economic areas of Europe. Some regions hitherto in the forefront, though putting up a stout resistance, lost ground. For example, economic depression in the seventeenth and eighteenth centuries overtook and impoverished the once flourishing centres of the Italian peninsula even in areas free from foreign domination. In other countries, such as England and, even more, the Low Countries, economic development was impressive, in spite of temporary setbacks; while in yet other countries a phase of tumultuous expansion was followed by a disastrous decline, as in the case of Spain. These different trends can partly be accounted for by the more or less skilful exploitation of the immense resources placed at the disposal of European economic operators through the conquest of new territories overseas; but the determining factor was the tremendous and disparate development of commercial capitalism. This, in some countries (e.g. Central and Northern France), remained aloof from agriculture; but in others (the Flemish regions, Britain, small areas of Northern Italy and Southern France, and even in Eastern Europe) it intervened more or less directly to regulate the rate of agricultural activity, contributed towards developing the framework of the agricultural world (it had an undeniable influence in accentuating the feudalistic character of land ownership east of the Elbe), and in short played a part in changing the agricultural character of some regions and altering the status of the rural population. In addition, political and military vicissitudes had their varying effects in the different rural regions of Europe (the wars of religion in France, the Thirty Years War in Germany, Sweden's war in the central and eastern regions, the revival of peasant unrest, especially in the German principalities). The rate of population growth and the incidence of epidemics in the sixteenth and seventeenth centuries, varied greatly in the different rural areas of Europe. Taxation pressure on rural incomes and capital also varied, both geographically and in time. Finally, technical innovations, meagre though they were, distinguished certain agricultural areas from others, even within the same country. From all this it can easily be seen that it is virtually impossible to treat the agricultural development of Europe in the sixteenth and seventeenth centuries as a whole.

(c) That task is made still more difficult by the heterogeneous nature of the studies so far done on the subject. In recent years there has been an encouraging and widespread revival of interest and initiative in the study of modern agrarian history, hitherto notoriously neglected. But the multiplication of studies (some of them of considerable importance and originality of treatment and method) makes any attempt at synthesis even more difficult and risky. Such studies are conditioned by the extent and quality of the documentation available; they tend to concentrate on periods or manifestations regarded as fundamental and typical in the context of a particular region's agricultural development; the criteria governing them may be strictly agronomic, mainly economic, or purely sociological, according to the taste, training, ideology or particular 'school' of the author. The result is that all these works photograph or film, from a variety of camera angles, particular situations, dissociated fragments of the many-sided entity that is European agriculture. To recapitulate them under a common denominator is an impossible undertaking, if we are to avoid distortion. In order to judge the true significance of the individual regions' characteristics it is therefore always necessary to go back to the various analytical studies. Moreover, the profound differences among these recent and meritorious researches leaps at once to the eye if we compare those by Eastern and by Western European scholars. The former, it will be seen, tend to emphasise the social and cultural aspects of the rural world, and especially the class interaction, whereas the latter are inclined for the most part to examine the agricultural landscape and the problems of marketing. Different subject-matter is also naturally suggested by the respective historical experiences of any given countryside. This, once again, merely serves to emphasise the variety of situations and experience that have influenced the agricultural history of modern Europe.

SOURCES

There is no need to repeat what Duby has said in an earlier chapter of this work. But it is necessary to revert to the subject.

The greater extent of documentation, both in quantity and variety, available from the fourteenth and fifteenth centuries is merely the prelude to an even more abundant wealth of sources for the subsequent centuries. The morphology of the rural world, the system of land ownership, the relations between landowners and peasantry, the agronomical and social framework of the countryside, the structure and system of the agricultural produce market, the supply and demand of agricultural products, and the attitude of the public authorities towards rural activities can be more thoroughly investigated thanks to copious evidence from various sources, both public and private. With all the caution prompted by a critical sense and a sense of history, it is certainly possible to extract from this variety of sources a series of statistical data which are much wider in scope and more reliable than those provided by the memoirs of the preceding centuries: many investigations have, advisedly, been framed and conducted on the basis of quantitative data. But there is also a good deal of significant qualitative information to be found. Nor must we underestimate the fact that, by comparison with the Middle Ages, the documentation for the modern era seems to be more consistent in all countries, so that the disadvantages mentioned earlier by Duby would appear to be much less serious. This does not, however, alter the fact that certain countries, and in particular England, are able to profit in their studies of agricultural history from their more careful and accurate preservation of valuable fundamental sources.

As far as concerns documents of public administration, in addition to rate valuations, many more details, especially in the Latin countries, are provided under the registers of landed properties (*catasto*), of which the most outstanding example, a model still today, is probably that of Milan (inventory, measurement and tax assessment of landed property, concluded under Maria Theresa, went on for decades during the first half of the eighteenth century). Population censuses also became more frequent, and these, supplemented by much more careful and systematic anagraphical annotations, not only provide valuable indications about the movement of population, both urban and rural, but also enable interesting conclusions to be drawn about the professional composition of the various social classes.

Of great interest, too, are the documents relating to public finance (State Budget estimates and accounts, Treasury accounts, and such like) which enable us not only to estimate the extent, variations and effects of fiscal pressure on the country areas, but also to get some indications about privileges and fiscal immunity, and about the import and export of agricultural produce (foreign trade in these goods was always more or less strictly controlled and subject to taxation).

In addition to the traditional legislation on food supplies, to which fresh items were added, another important source is the surveys regularly carried out by the offices charged with the supervision and regulation of the internal market in foodstuffs, in order to ascertain the amount of foodstuffs available, arrange purchases of grain and suchlike and calculate the prices to be fixed and decreed on the basis of current market prices.

Midway between public and private documentation comes the evidence concerning the administration of agricultural properties belonging to princes and sovereigns. At a time when a certain confusion still existed between private property of the Crown and public State property (the respective limits of which were still not clearly separated), considerable interest attaches to the papers registering variations in the composition of landed property administered by the Court, periodical assessments of the value of rural properties, types of cultivation practised there, annual incomes (in cash and kind), legal and economic relations with dependent personnel, and so on. Legal, administrative and accounting sources of this kind (some of them already used) are to be found everywhere from Poland to Spain, from Italy to Germany and England.

Also of great importance as a source of information on agrarian history in the modern era are the immense files of lawyers' documents. Yet another very valuable source is private memoirs, becoming richer and more numerous as time goes on. Family archives and the archives of ecclesiastical and secular organisations owning rural property provide a great deal of material, very little of which has so far been used (the sources relating to the vast landed properties of the bishoprics have, however, been widely investigated by Eastern European scholars). This most interesting material provides all kinds of significant evidence. The inventories, often drawn up at the time of succession to property and its division among the heirs, are not confined to bare catalogues of property but also indicate the quality of the land, its productive capacity and yield in income, and its market valuation. The contracts signed between the landowner and the farmer, and the various records of assignment and reassignment made when a contract was signed or renewed, reveal changes both in the power of one of the contracting parties vis-à-vis the other and in the criterion of estate management, variations in the amount and quality of livestock and other stocks, and the increase or reduction in the various types of cultivation. Bailiffs' books, estate accounts of incomings and outgoings (in money and kind) and the balance-sheets drawn up from time to time to provide an overall survey of a property's administration over several years (such balance-sheets were regularly drawn up when a property was ceded or divided), all these documents provide valuable sources of information about harvest yields, the economic progress of a property, price movements in agriculture and in rural industries, the values of different types of farmland, technical innovations, numbers employed, and so on. Useful information can also be gleaned from the immense 'dossiers' covering the legal,

judicial and administrative records concerning disputes between private individuals and the authorities (disputes
about boundaries, serfdom or feudal rights, lawsuits and
appeals about taxation, and so on). Details about food consumption are also quite often to be found in family archives,
and such information is of course extremely valuable for
any study of agrarian history.

So far barely the surface of these private archive sources
has been scratched, and they will repay much more
thorough investigation by historians of the modern rural
world. One thought, however, deserves to be borne in mind.
The family archives that have come down to us belong to
representatives of the highest and wealthiest ranks of society:
on the one hand the aristocracy, whose fortunes were by
tradition closely linked with the land, and on the other
those who, having enriched themselves through trade,
manufacturing, banking or financial activities or through
acquiring high and remunerative public positions, tended
to invest a good part of their wealth in land, especially from
the last decades of the sixteenth century onwards. The evidence that these documents provide inevitably therefore
relates to the larger and, in general, better-run landed
properties. Only indirectly can we deduce from them information about the real conditions of life, the incomes and
the consumption of lesser people in the rural world who
have left behind less lasting traces of themselves.

Finally, an important source, valid also for the modern
era, lies in archaeological discoveries, portrayals in pictures
and artefacts (intelligent use of which has been made
in some recent studies of developments in the agrarian
countryside) and bucolic treatises or manuals which, while
not wholly discarding their literary flavour, now tend to
become more 'scientific', especially those by some Italian,
French or English authors, as if with them those classical
reminiscences beloved of the technically ill-equipped
writers of the humanistic period were gradually being left
behind.

DEMOGRAPHIC, LEGAL AND SOCIAL ASPECTS OF RURAL EUROPE

RURAL POPULATION

As an account of the demographic development in modern Europe appears elsewhere in this history, we shall confine ourselves here to considering the number of people living and working in the various agricultural regions of the Continent.

The population growth became apparent in the second half of the fifteenth century and accelerated during the sixteenth century. The seventeenth witnessed instead a stagnation; but towards the end of this century the population started to increase again. If taken as a generalisation, however, all this may lead to deceptive inferences: for population development varied considerably from place to place.

First of all, it is important to remember that population increase was registered mainly within the orbit of the towns. From London to Antwerp, Paris to Cologne, Lübeck to the Castilian towns, Venice to Sicily, urban population increase reached very high levels. This applies especially to the sixteenth century. Wars, epidemics and the crises of the next century brought about drastic reductions even in some urban populations. But, except for some important urban centres caught up in an apparently insuperable economic recession (e.g. in Spain), the towns gradually became repopulated, especially after the beginning of the eighteenth century. Roughly speaking, it can be said that town-dwelling was more pronounced in Mediterranean Europe in the sixteenth century and more intensive in Central and Northern Europe in the seventeenth. It is tempting to account for the denser urban populations of the depressed or backward Southern areas by the plethora of tertiary activities there, and to explain the urbanisation of the North by the gradual development of an 'industrial' economy.

But we must also ask ourselves whether town-dwelling

may not also have been caused by over-population of the countryside, at least in relation to local means of support. Here, too, any generalisation is liable to produce distortion, for the situations, and hence the explanations, are manifold, both in space and time.

There is no doubt that especially, though not solely, in the sixteenth century population fell in the mountain regions, where previously it had risen considerably (hence the extensive clearing of land and deforestation that took place then). When local resources became impoverished the mountain people came down into the valleys to settle in the more fertile areas of the hillsides and plain: the Mediterranean hillsides, the undulating countryside of Burgundy, the plains of Campania and Southern Germany. These large settlements in restricted areas soon produced a rupture in the balance between production and consumption of the means of sustenance. The inevitable consequence was an exodus of surplus population to the towns, hungry hordes seeking employment, whether stable or precarious. Quite apart from the moral aspect, is not banditry, both rural and urban, a symptom of overpopulation, or at least of an over-rapid increase in population?

Elsewhere the incursion of people from the country into the towns was largely due to changes in the system of land tenure and farming, accompanied generally by growing incentives towards manufacturing and trading activities in the towns. In Tudor England, and especially during Queen Elizabeth's long reign, side by side with a perceptible natural increase in the population we find a fall in the rural population as a result of the continuing practice of enclosures and the higher rate of production of industry in the towns. Such internal migrations, which far exceed the quite appreciable influx of foreigners into several urban centres of England, not only London but also, for example, Norwich, Colchester, Ipswich or Halstead in Essex, were equally by no means fortuitous in France, although on a much smaller scale, in the enclosed farm-property areas (*bocages*) of Normandy, Picardy and part of the Ile-de-France. Even in the Mediterranean basin the enlargements of the seigneurial domain and the inclusion of common lands in enclosed properties had a negative effect on the density of rural population in some places.

To set against this there was some movement in the reverse direction, mainly for two reasons. First the growth of rural industries which re-absorbed the urban under-employed, a development which becomes discernible from the sixteenth century onwards in England, Sweden, some parts of Flanders and Germany and certain districts of the Po Valley. Second the desire, not at all uncommon among the rich bourgeois, to invest in land which compelled them to live, if only for a few months of the year, outside the city walls. This is particularly notable in Mediterranean France, e.g. Languedoc and Lower Provence, and again in the Valley of the Po.

In other regions the town–country dichotomy, with all its social and economic implications, was ambiguous, not to say artificial. Broadly speaking, the Flemish region affords proof of this: there the integration of the rural world with that of the towns reveals many different and sometimes surprising aspects. The combined pressure of economic, political, administrative and ethico-religious factors some-times produced quite contradictory effects on population. Bruges and Antwerp, for example, demonstrate two opposite patterns: the former becoming gradually depopulated, the latter increasing in population. In the modern era, however, population increase in the Flemish urban centres became an established fact: by the end of the sixteenth century a third of the inhabitants were already town-dwellers. Con-sequently, in certain areas there was a serious shortage of rural labour, and big rewards were even offered (e.g. in Costemarcke and Aertrycke) to citizens who resumed culti-vation of the land they had occupied before moving into town. But in other country regions (e.g. the Flemish Franc district) there were vast uncultivated and uninhabited areas which only gradually began in the seventeenth century to be once more tilled and repopulated. In the not far distant area of the 'polders', on lands rescued from the sea and at once cultivated, human settlement was rapid and intensive.

But apart from the outflow of human capital from country to town, the rural populations in general suffered more from adverse circumstances and economic crises. Within the city walls it was usually easier than in the countryside to make and carry out arrangements, both in ordinary times and in emergencies, to ensure a minimum of subsistence. In particular, the periodic crises arising in agriculture caused more immediate and deeper changes among the rural population (which does not, however, alter the fact that for particular reasons, as has been shown, the relationship between the birthrate and varying phases of the economic cycle was sometimes the opposite of what might have been expected).

Numerous proofs exist of the greater vulnerability of country-dwellers. The most impressive is provided by the German states in the seventeenth century, where the Thirty Years War raged most fiercely and caused terrible devastation: at the war's end, in not a few rural districts, the population was literally decimated.

But the prostrating effects of disastrous economic situations, not infrequently assuming epidemic manifestations (often aggravated or actually caused by wars), did not spare even the most populous and flourishing country districts. We recall the dramatic events which, at the very end of the sixteenth century, presaged a more than century-long period of decadence for Spain's agricultural economy; or the stormy experiences of the 1620s–30s in the Lombard countryside, which became rapidly depopulated and had to wait for decades before regaining its former enviable position; or the startling population decline in Languedoc (the same phenomenon, though less marked, was also to be found in nearby Lower Provence) between 1660 and 1740, coinciding with the serious economic recession which particularly affected agriculture. Other examples could be mentioned, but these will suffice.

With the exception of Spain, whose decision, once the first stages of pillaging were past, to exploit the conquered new lands overseas necessarily involved the transfer thither of a good deal of agricultural labour, colonial enterprises abroad do not seem to have subtracted much manpower from the countryside in the old Continent. Only about half a million Dutchmen in more than a century left their motherland to settle in the colonies. A more important point is how far colonisation, by absorbing almost exclusively males, and young men at that, altered the numerical proportion between the two sexes and thus influenced the birthrate. This question has been recently tackled in the case of Spain, with very interesting results.

Much more serious and immediate, however, were the repercussions on the rural population of certain provisions by the public authorities. The expulsion of Jews and Moslems from the Mediterranean countries, which occurred frequently in the second half of the sixteenth century and the first decades of the seventeenth, and, in particular, the eviction of the Moriscoes from Spain by Philip III, rapidly denuded of manpower agricultural areas that had till then been densely populated and highly productive. Similar effects were produced in France by Louis XIV's eviction of the Protestants after the revocation of the Edict of Nantes. But it is open to question whether these measures merely reflected the exacerbation of religious antagonisms or had also the subsidiary aim of reducing local population pressures.

The growth of rural population itself was also influenced by ethical and religious factors, becoming more apparent as the Reformation movement achieved a stronger hold on men's minds. In places where Protestantism became established, the rate of marriages and births tended to increase with the removal of moral restraints and canonical inhibitions. On the other hand, by the beginning of the eighteenth century in certain regions, for example parts of North-Western France, an inverse process set in: the rate of births and marriages fell, as a result, it would seem, of a crude application of Malthusian principles.

Finally, rural populations in the centuries under consideration showed a high degree of mobility. In addition to the reasons already mentioned, the actual increase in population also provided a justification for seeking new pastures.

This development, which had already begun to emerge in the late Middle Ages, could be clearly observed in Eastern Europe and particularly in the western provinces of Russia. Mobility of population in some regions brought about a levelling-up of density. But in others it merely accentuated the existing differences, for example, in the Iberian peninsula, where there was a tremendous contrast between the deserted areas of Aragon and the populous countrysides of the Valencia plain, or between Entro-Douro-e-Minho, in Northern Portugal, and Alentejo and Algarve in the south.

LAND OWNERSHIP, FARMING AND RURAL CLASSES

The variety of aspect that characterised rural Europe in this period is nowhere more clearly demonstrated than in the profound differences in the legal and social structure of land ownership, in methods of farm administration and in the diversity of class systems. These fundamental variables of agricultural economy and society must be constantly considered in any discussion of the subject. For the sake of convenience, we shall divide agricultural Europe into two parts, taking the Elbe as the line of demarcation: the eastern regions, distinguished by the definite prevalence of *Gutherrschaft* (direct administration, at his own risk, of an entire, or practically entire, property by the overlord), and the western regions, characterised by the preponderance of *Grundherrschaft* (where the management of properties is entrusted by the owner to others in exchange for leases, rents, payments in cash or kind, etc.).

In Central and Eastern Europe, that is to say, in the *Gutherrschaft* area, from the beginning of the sixteenth century the landowners (sovereigns or secular or ecclesiastic overlords) strove methodically by more or less legitimate means to extend the boundaries of their possessions. They took from the peasants lands to which the overlords claimed rights, only rarely paying a small price for them, and so in effect enlarged the *pars dominica*, or, to use a less medieval term, the *réserve seigneuriale*.

A significant illustration of this occurs in the vast

domains of the Polish sovereigns, in Ruthenia and the region between the Vistula and the Bug, and within the orbit of other great properties owned by nobles. By the end of the sixteenth century the quantitative composition of the various rural classes had already undergone great changes. The *zagrodniki* and *chalupniki* (the poorest classes among the rural population, the former corresponding roughly to the French *closiers* and having a tiny farm, while the latter lived in wretched huts with only a small patch of land) considerably increased in numbers, whereas the number of *rolniki* fell (these were better-off tenants who, unlike the other two categories, were not obliged to do heavy manual work for the overlord but had only to place their farm implements, carts and ploughs at his disposal). The degradation of the peasant class became worse during the seventeenth century. The high profits obtained by exporting large stocks of cereals enabled the landowners to add to their properties, which became vast *Latifundia*, surrounded by the remaining few miserable farms of the tenants and *zagrodniki* and what was left of the dismembered possessions of the lesser nobility. These last provided some of the hated bailiffs who, in the service of the overlords, directed work on the land, superintending the gangs of enslaved peasants, recruiting the necessary paid workers (who increasingly came from *zagrodniki* and even *rolniki* families) and controlling the regular execution of services imposed on tenants of land not directly administered by the overlord. Contracts, which were short-term, were usually renewed under the most harassing conditions: the tenant in effect lost the right to leave the domain and he, too, became virtually a serf.

Increase in the *dominium utile* and in the land directly exploited by the owners, greater numbers pressed into service, and greater severity of the feudal régime were, in short, related phenomena which, favoured by the recurrent wars, grew more conspicuous not only in Poland but also in the German territories east of the Elbe and in Bohemia, Silesia, Livonia, Hungary and Rumania. In all these regions there were more or less frequent protests and revolts among the peasants, by now little more than slaves of the overlords, who arrogated to themselves the right to sell lands without the serfs or serfs without the lands. Serfdom was even revived by law — after 1518 King Sigismund of Poland refused to consider peasants' complaints against their landlords, and in 1595 Michael the Brave in Rumania issued a solemn decree about peasants' obligations to remain on the land. Legal rights were re-transferred from the sovereign to the great feudal lords, whose power extended so far that they succeeded in preventing the application of the radical reforms voted by the enlightened princes in the middle of the eighteenth century, as happened in Prussia under Frederick II. In East Prussia in the eighteenth century tributary services ('corvées') still often amounted to five or six days a week; in Pomerania peasants were still regarded as estate property, as capital invested in the running of the estate of which they were deemed to be a part; and in Bohemia the saying went: 'To till the land with paid day-labour is like pouring water through a sieve.'

The peasants' status also deteriorated from the middle of the sixteenth century, and especially after the advent of Amurat III, in the Balkan regions subject to Ottoman rule. The big estates there had been somewhat reduced in the fifteenth century (when the Turkish nobility replaced the Christian, the system of land tenure was reformed and the land redistributed under a new form of ownership, the *timar*, freed from hereditary obligations); but in the sixteenth century they began to revive. *Latifundia*-type estates belonging to the nobility and clergy (the *vakoufs*) reappeared, absorbing common or freehold lands (the *melk*), which became increasingly incorporated in the seigneurial domains. Feudal rights became wider and more effective; the area under cultivation increased (for higher prices encouraged here, too, the production and export of cereals); the population grew, especially in the sixteenth century; and at the same time the legal and economic situation of the Balkan land-labourers became steadily worse. Indeed, by the seventeenth century serfdom had come back even in the region south of the Lower Danube.

In Russia, with the strengthening of the central authority

at the end of the fifteenth century, big seigneurial land-ownership weakened. The *votchina*, or vast aristocratic domain, was replaced by the *pomestye*, a smaller estate, usually assigned by the sovereign to his most faithful military or civilian subjects as a reward for services rendered. The composition of the landowning class changed: the old rural nobility became a small minority, and instead a composite collection of new landowners emerged — bourgeois, merchants or big farmers — lacking political power or real feudal rights, but nevertheless increasingly despotic masters in the administration of their newly-acquired properties. The new *pomeshchik* realised more readily than the *boyar* the shortage of agricultural labour and therefore tightened up the land contracts. Payment in kind (*obrok*) or cash came more and more to be replaced by services and work done on the land (*barshchina*): thus the balance between services and rent, which had characterised the relations between landowner and farmer in the *votchina*, was destroyed. Between the beginning and end of the six-teenth century the time that the peasant spent working for the landowner doubled, amounting to as many days a year as he could devote to his own land. Stipulations in the text of the contract were of no help to him. His hard state and the hope of finding better conditions with another master induced him to flee (in the course of a century the number of abandoned villages in the central provinces of Russia increased tenfold). But his illusions were soon destroyed: with the new master he had to take on even more onerous obligations, and that meant definite surrender and accept-ance of serfdom. The laws of 1497 and 1550 recognised the peasants' restricted right to leave the farm; but in 1649 that right, already suppressed in practice, was officially repealed.

The unhappy situation of the rural population became even more wretched in the seventeenth and eighteenth centuries, especially under Peter the Great and his successors down to Catherine II, when the Tsars, in the course of a series of exhausting military campaigns, brought to fulfil-ment their determination to centralise political and ad-ministrative authority. By drawing on Crown lands and land confiscated from opponents, the Court succeeded in re-creating huge *latifundia* which it distributed to military leaders, ministers and favourites. The character of the land-owning aristocracy changed yet again. And the new pro-prietors, invested with legal, administrative and jurisdic-tional powers over whole villages or groups of villages, and free to condemn their dependents to forced labour and deportation irrespective of family ties, reduced the peasants to mere chattels. Properties came to be valued according to the number of serfs there rather than by acreage or fertility. In 1730 only 13 per cent of the peasants, or something over 5 million, were free; and their liberty was merely relative, for in order to have the use of State lands and their produce they had to pay a tax. Of the 4,400,000 serfs, 70 per cent were dependents of the nobility, and that percentage in-creased during the following decades as the number of free smallholders and of serfs working on church lands fell. The land reserved by the overlord for his own direct use absorbed most of the territory inhabited by the rural communities. The smallholder had only restricted possibilities for farming the land left him by the overlord for his own use against payment (usually in kind), for on four days a week or more he was compelled to work on his master's land. On these immense properties such work involved not only farmwork but anything else the overlord might require for his family and the community under him. Thus in Russia, as Bücher has said, a type of natural economy, a 'closed' domestic economy, was revived and remained in force right up to the first half of the nineteenth century. In short, the big Russian landowners restored the legal, economic and social organisa-tion which had characterised the great feudal domain of the late Middle Ages and which had since completely dis-appeared in Western Europe.

South-west of the Elbe, the agrarian pattern of *Grund-herrschaft* became more or less uniformly established. From Germany to France, in the sixteenth century, the process of dissolution of the old seigneurial properties accelerated. The impoverishment of the landowning aristocracy caused by monetary devaluation, wartime devastation, civil and religious strife, and peasant revolts (e.g. the revolt of 1524 which spread to Swabia, Thuringia, Alsace, Franconia, the Tyrol and Salzburg) helped to erode feudal rights and prerogatives and to make landed property more easily transferable. Though revolts were suppressed, as was the peasant rising of 1524, the *status quo* was restored only in appearance: down to the end of the sixteenth century, when here and there feudal pretensions were reasserted, in France and in Central and Western Germany seigneurial rights steadily waned and, though publicly they still retained some significance, at the private level and in practice they became reduced to recognition of the eminent domain over lands transferred to the 'possession' of the smallholders. With a few rare exceptions, now that the extent of land reserved to the overlord for his own administration had been much reduced, compulsory peasant labour on it practically disappeared or at most amounted to two to four weeks a year, being replaced instead by small tributes. Despite the theoretical opinions of the stricter 'feudalists' (e.g. the jurists Cujas and Dumoulin), lands not farmed directly by the overlord were virtually expropriated — indeed, in many of the small principalities and baronies of North-west Germany such expropriation was sanctioned by law. Peasants possessing plots of land were, in practice, allowed to make what use they pleased of them and even to bequeath them to their heirs. Much of the land hitherto locked up by the rigid restraints of seigneurial ownership could now be freely sold or divided up. In this way small peasant farm ownership became more widespread in France and Germany than elsewhere.

In the seventeenth century, after some preliminary attempts at the end of the previous century, properties again increased considerably in size when the landowners, adducing '*urgens et improvvisa necessitas*', proceeded to confiscate farms formerly owned by peasants. This attack on peasant property was mounted in the middle of the century mainly by the new bourgeois landowners who had profited from the enfeeblement of the old landed aristocracy by speculating in landed property and now aimed to extract

the maximum advantage from the rise in prices by extending the areas they farmed themselves. But they went about
it circumspectly, since the incorporation of peasant farms
meant assuming the tax obligations that went with them.
Nor does small and medium farm property seem to have
been seriously threatened by the reconstitution of big
landed estates by the nobility and clergy after the Thirty
Years War, when the inhabitants of the countryside, decimated and terrorised, abandoned lands left devastated and
uncultivated. Even where, as in North Hanover, this
phenomenon was so widespread as to suggest that the
Gutherr might replace the *Grundherr*, the imposition of compulsory labour seems to have been kept within strictly
defined limits; and smallholding continued to be of considerable importance. In any case, the very fact that the old
overlords were little concerned to resist the dispersal of
their properties contributed to prevent a repetition here
of the agrarian pattern that had developed east of the
Elbe.

It is also worth noting that it was not so much the landowners but the farmers themselves who strove to join up
and centralise farming properties, so as to make their
management more rational and profitable. This can be
seen from the beginning of the seventeenth century in
various districts of France north of the Seine, where quite a
number of farmers with scattered holdings, mindful of
England's profitable example, made a point of grouping
together their leased lands, if necessary exchanging one
farm for another. This concentration, based on the business
of farming rather than on actual land ownership, does not
appear on the registers or plans of landed property (*catasti*)
and has consequently caused some confusion among
scholars of European post-medieval agrarian history when
dealing with the juridical and administrative aspects.

The tendency of French and German *Grundherren* to keep
their properties subdivided did not, however, check the
expansion of seigneurial properties. Landowners could not
but realise from the sixteenth century onwards, as prices
for farm produce rose, that a way out from an economically

onerous situation had to be found: they realised, in other words, how costly their situation was as mere *rentiers du sol*. The case, recently documented for the Poitevin Gâtinais, of a *réserve* enlarged through the overlord's patient policy of purchase and exchange of land does not seem to have occurred frequently. But the attack on communal, village lands was certainly much more widespread and of longer duration. Favoured by the heavy indebtedness of the rural communities to the overlord, and formally justified by presumed and often arbitrary property rights, the expropriation — it might be better termed usurpation — of a third of the communal property (hence the term 'triage') did not, indeed, directly attack smallholdings, but it did damage and cause hardship to the rural communities because of its drastic reduction of the areas on which rights of pasturage, woodgathering, and so on, were customarily exercised. Hence the peasants' protests and rebellions, and hence the interventions by the public authorities to declare the 'triages' null even when effected by formally regular transactions, agreements or legal pronouncements (see, for example, the French ordinances of 1575, 1659 and 1667). The very reiteration of the prohibitions, moreover, suggests that, notwithstanding the subjects' repeated protests and the Sovereign's apprehensions about the enlargement of property belonging to the nobility, clergy or bourgeoisie, the dividing-up of communal lands encountered little effective opposition. In fact, it continued up to the second half of the eighteenth century when, with changes in circumstances and points of view, it even came to be regarded as desirable and was regulated by law, with the result that conditions improved for the poorer classes in the countryside.

In any case, in France and Western Germany the enlargement of the *réserves seigneuriales* never got out of hand; nor did it destroy small and medium peasant landownership, which on the whole, rather, increased. It did not, moreover, check the steady transformation of farm tenancies towards some form of leasehold or share-cropping. These two forms of tenancy, apart from the numerous local variations and the different kinds of payment involved, were especially characterised by the regulations governing live and dead stock. Under a leasehold tenancy dead and live stock (*cheptel*) were provided by the farmer, who ran the whole farm himself and made a payment in cash or kind to the landowner. Under the share-cropping system, of which *métayage* was the most widespread version, the landowner owned at least part of the stock and took a share in the risks of the enterprise, also sharing the harvest with the *métayer*. Both these two types of tenancy were very popular (*fermage*, or farm-leasing, was especially frequent in the rich cultivated areas of the middle Seine valley), because they allowed of periodical adaptation of cash-or-kind payments to market conditions. Contracts were, in fact, signed for short terms: generally three to four years in the sixteenth century and the first half of the seventeenth, and later on six to nine years at most. As can be seen, the duration of contracts became longer as the century-long process of rising prices drew to an end.

There was, however, no clear-cut demarcation line between the *Gutherrschaft* and *Grundherrschaft* areas. Certain regions, running from Prussia to Bavaria, Austria, Mecklenburg and Holstein, included simultaneously both these opposite types of agrarian enterprise, with what implications can be readily imagined. This was, in fact, an intermediary area, containing landed properties almost resembling *latifundia* in their size and method of management, and at the same time farms left to peasants' ownership during their lifetime (*Leigedinge*), side by side with others on which the farmer retained the right to pass on the farm to his heirs (*Erbstift*), and yet others on which the overlord exercised the right to terminate the farmer's contract every year (*Freistift*). In this area, too, *Bauernlegen*, or the joining-up of small farms to the *latifundium*, was customary, and tributary labour, if in attenuated form, was legally recognised (even as late as 1756 the Bavarian civil code devoted a whole chapter to serfdom). In short, it was a rural world in transition, in which the farmer's relationship of personal dependence on the overlord seems to have been much more strictly observed than was the case in the West German territories and, in general, in France.

In concluding this survey of continental Europe a word must be said about the Low Countries. In their southern regions the agrarian situation in general reproduced approximately the forms and characteristics found in Western Germany and Northern France. In the north, on the other hand, especially after it became independent in 1579, there were noticeable innovations. In the internal provinces large properties belonging to the nobility and clergy were by no means rare, and they did not disintegrate, although there was also considerable ownership of medium and small properties, and this became more widespread especially in the eighteenth century. Leasehold tenure for a fixed period (of from three to twelve years) and perpetual or very long (up to 99 years) leases with the obligation for the tenants to improve the plot of land (*emphyteusis*) were further supplemented by hereditary leasehold; direct management of large properties by their owners was almost non-existent. In the new United Provinces, and especially in the western ones of Zeeland, Holland and Friesland, political and social changes following the successful conclusion of the Reformation movement and the struggle for independence led to the general suppression of seigneurial rights and to an extensive parcelling-out of land, much of which came into the hands of the rich bourgeoisie. This resulted in the introduction of modern and remunerative methods of management of farms, which were by preference leased for short terms so as to make it easier to adapt to the changing economic conditions. Numerous villas and gardens also grew up around the towns, representing not only a sop to their owners' social ambitions, but also a sensible policy of investment and agronomic innovation. At the same time considerable capital was spent on reclaiming new land through the drainage of marshy areas and estuary lands.

In the Mediterranean area the great variety of conditions already observable in the Middle Ages, as Duby has clearly described earlier, became in certain respects accentuated in the modern era.

In the Italian peninsula, consisting of a number of different states, there were very wide regional differences in the types of land tenure, in methods of farm management and in the conditions of the rural population. For this reason it is worthwhile to examine the Italian situation rather more closely.

In Piedmont, for instance, the land, even in places where a few big properties still remained in the hands of nobles or the church, was increasingly divided up into small farms entrusted to share-tenants, for the most part descendants of serfs emancipated by Emmanuel Filibert. But at the other end of the peninsula, in Sicily, the agrarian system still remained based on feudal patterns, which strengthened in the seventeenth century and lasted right up to the laws abolishing them in the nineteenth century. A target of popular hatred was the *gabellotto*, or bailiff, a big tenant farmer who was also the loathed intermediary between the rapacious landowner, the sub-tenants and the impoverished rural proletariat. In the mainland provinces of the Kingdom of the Two Sicilies, *latifundia* belonging to the Church, the municipalities or, above all, to the decadent feudal nobility, scattered and isolated estates in the interior enjoying fiscal privileges, contrasted sharply with the small, dynamic peasant properties or remunerative sharehold farms along the coastal strip. At the beginning of the eighteenth century Charles III furthered the breaking-up of the land by means of a sensible reorganisation of land taxation, and soon after the middle of the century Ferdinand suppressed serf labour on the mainland.

The Papal States included both the huge properties of the Latian Campagna, which became even more extensive after the sixteenth century, owned by Roman patricians and mostly used for grazing and let out to shepherds, and also, by contrast, the little farms of the Umbrian hillsides, where the types of tenancy, among which *mezzadria*, or share-cropping, predominated, resembled those in nearby Tuscany. In the Church's territories in the Po valley the picture, a complex one, deteriorated during the seventeenth–eighteenth century. In general, the big properties belonging to the Church, the aristocracy, or occasionally to the new bourgeoisie, gradually stifled the small farms variously held under share-cropping or short-period leasehold contracts or under emphyteusis (see above).

Emphyteusis, on the other hand, tended to disappear among the fertile Mantuan lands of the Gonzaga family which by the end of the sixteenth century were all leased out for short and medium periods. Leasehold tenancy also became widespread in the neighbouring State of Milan, especially in its south, both on the big properties of the nobles and the Church and on the growing number of estates owned by rising merchants and business men. These properties in general were well run, but they suffered from the adverse economic trend in the seventeenth century, and this was also largely responsible for the impoverishment of the peasants who, however, reacted, in the long run successfully, against the revival of feudal practices. The *mezzadria* system prevailed even then in the Lombard hillsides, where parcelling-out of the land into small plots, though it did exist, was much less frequent than in the poor mountain areas which clung tenaciously to the emphyteusis system.

Big estates were much more in evidence in the Veneto, but they were divided up into a great many small farms. This system was furthered by the absenteeism of the landowners who, from the end of the sixteenth century onwards, came increasingly to think of their country properties merely as places for recreation and to satisfy their prestige, and who therefore left them in the hands of the all-powerful bailiffs to be let out on lease or to impoverished sharecropping peasants.

Joint farming by landowners and farmers in association, on the other hand, reached a high point and proved very profitable in Tuscany, especially in the hilly country in the north-west of the Grand Duchy which was the *mezzadria* area *par excellence*. But even in this region, especially in the south-west, from the seventeenth century a decline set in, with concentrations and extensions of the big properties, lack of interest on the part of the owners and progressive depopulation. It was not until the Grand Duke Leopold's reforms, anticipated in 1739 when corn was freed from taxation in the Maremma, that the wretched situation of the rural population improved.

Along the Mediterranean coast of France the agrarian pattern in the modern era resembled in its components and development that of Central and Northern Italy. Share-cropping tenancy, especially *métayage*, was definitely more frequent than leasehold, and rural estates were often much fragmented, especially up to the 1620s. After this date, rural districts here, too, began to be affected by a serious depression which lasted for more than a century and brought about a concentration of landed properties in the hands of mainly bourgeois speculators, thus veering back towards feudal exploitation and poverty.

In Spain, the sixteenth century witnessed a strengthening of seigneurial landownership, both secular and ecclesiastical. The urge to expand the properties so as to profit by the prosperous economic situation not only caused encroachments on communal lands and grazing grounds but also, which was even more serious, prompted the landowners to lay claim to peasant farms under conditions highly favourable to themselves. By the system of land obligations (*arrendamiento*) which they introduced, they in effect brought back in all their old oppressiveness those feudal rights which had gradually come to assume a purely symbolic value. Moreover, from the early decades of the seventeenth century, as the period of relative prosperity resulting from the regular rise in prices for agricultural produce came to an end, peasants found themselves running into debt. Then the *censos al quitar*, or quitrent system, by causing the town-dwelling bourgeoisie to recall their capital from the countryside and encouraging speculative operations on the property market, brought about a heavy increase in the mortgages on peasant property and so both worsened the economic situation of the rural classes and accelerated the concentration of agricultural property. The only bright spot in this dark picture was in Andalusia. For the Andalusian plain contrived, at least in part, to escape the deterioration in agrarian structures despite the serious repercussions of the Moriscoes' eviction at the beginning of the seventeenth century. Throughout the whole Guadalquivir basin, although some big properties did exist there, the parcelling-out of the land and the more rational and humane methods of farm tenancy on a particularly fertile soil enabled the peasants to lead a life which, if not comfortable, was at least free from actual poverty.

To cross the Channel signifies coming into a rural world which, even before the revolution of the eighteenth century radically transformed it, appears much more highly developed and dynamic than that of continental Europe (with the exception of the Low Countries), both in respect of landed property and tenure systems and in its social configuration. This applies, of course, to the countryside in England, for in Ireland backward rural conditions prevailed throughout the modern era because of the survival of a system based on large estates where much of the land remained under the landowner's management and where heavy labour requirements were imposed on the rural communities — in short, a wellnigh feudal system which in many ways resembled that in the *Grundherrschaft* territories east of the Elbe.

In England, up to the first decades of the seventeenth century, the process of land tenure reorganisation continued which had begun when the combination of the two systems typical of the medieval rural world — the large landed estate, or 'manor', and the village community — had come to an end. With the break-up of feudal superstructures, changes in landownership had become more frequent and farming more remunerative, and these developments were furthered by the growth of town markets and of interregional and foreign trade, by the rise of a monetary economy, by the expansion of the wool industry and by the birth of a capitalist class. The practice of enclosures, though confined in those centuries largely to the central counties and restricted to a tenth of the agrarian area (some half-million acres between 1455 and 1607, or less than 3 per cent of the total area), together with the confiscation of properties of the monastic communities suppressed after the Reformation, certainly brought about an increase in the extent of big landed properties and an alteration in the relations between landowners and peasants. But can it be categorically stated, as Marxist interpretations have claimed, that the transformation of rural landownership (due basically to the appropriation of common lands and the expropriation of farmlands by the landlords and the better-off and more enterprising peasants), the usurpation and abolition of certain rights enjoyed by the country people, the renewal of agrarian contracts on conditions unfavourable to the working-farmer, and the conversion of cultivated land to grazing, were reasons which, by making 'primitive accumulation' possible, contributed to the progressive impoverishment of the peasant class and its gradual disappearance? Some recent and perceptive opinions have given fresh weight to the traditional thesis.

It cannot be denied that, whereas in continental Europe the peasant had gradually made ground in his relationship to the landowner (indeed, by now peasant farms were becoming the keystone of the agricultural edifice), in Britain the small owner-farmer was gradually disappearing except in a few marginal Celtic areas. Ever since the end of the Middle Ages, and increasingly in our period, rural society was tending towards a three-tier structure: the landlords who owned their land; the tenant-farmers who rented their farms without owning them; and the agricultural labourers who owned no land. Nevertheless, the dissolution of the peasantry cannot be attributed solely to more or less arbitrary expropriations and incorporations of land from the small peasant farms. The sale of rural properties also played an important part in modifying the agricultural and social structure of rural England. In this process there were two distinct periods: the period of more than a century up to 1660, and the eighty years after 1660.

In the fifteenth and roughly speaking the first half of the sixteenth century, only tenants who held their farms for a fixed term or for their lifetime, without the possibility of renewing their contracts, ran the risk of losing their farms. Freeholders (holders, in effect, in perpetuity), copy-holders on inheritance (holders with the right of succession from father to son) and copyholders for a term of years (holders with an option to renew their contracts) were completely guaranteed against having their holdings taken from them. Thus only 35 per cent of the peasants were at the mercy of anyone who might, more or less unjustly, deprive them of their plots. Expropriation could therefore have caused the disappearance of, at most, only one-third of the peasant class (and that hypothesis is certainly a long way from what actually happened).

But purchases and sales of farms must also be taken into account. Everything points to the supposition that market conditions (rise in prices and increase in production) caused the old aristocracy to sell land rather than buy it. Thus the ranks of the 'gentry' increased with the advent, first of all, of the new capitalist bourgeoisie (mainly merchants, professional people and civil servants who might eventually expect to receive a title), but also of quite a number of peasants who, through favourable circumstances, managed at the expense of noblemen in difficulties, and in competition with the bourgeoisie, to secure a good deal of land.

There seems to be no doubt about the fact that up to about the middle of the seventeenth century there were fewer expropriations of peasant holdings than there were sales of seigneurial lands to the peasants: thus the peasantry secured a net gain.

The crisis of 1640 and the civil wars that followed led to a sharp rise in taxation which increased still further towards the end of the century — the land tax of 1692 was extremely heavy; prices oscillated violently and between 1680 and 1720 fell, causing agricultural incomes to contract; and the increase in manufacturing and professional activities attracted people from the country into the towns. All these factors brought about a radical change in social and economic conditions in the countryside and consequently in the legal conditions of landownership. Thus a chain development set in, which can be tabulated briefly as follows: (a) a growing number of small landowners moved into the towns, leaving their farms in the hands of bailiff-lessees; (b) peasant owner-farmers showed a greater tendency to mobilise their capital so as to invest it more profitably in other ways; (c) a similar tendency was shown by the lesser gentry, whose incomes, derived solely from rents, inevitably fell as incomes from agriculture diminished; (d) the better-off became less inclined to sink their capital in large landed properties, preferring to invest most of it in profitable mortgage deals and public loans and reserving only a small portion for the purchase of land sold — and quite often undersold — by the peasants and gentry; (e) the landlords began once more to expand their properties by purchasing peasant farms.

Why this change of conduct on the part of the landlords? The reasons were both economic and social, plus the fact that their purchasing-power was now greater, if only in relative terms, given the difficulties with which the owner-farmers and gentry had to contend.

From the economic standpoint, the indisputable advantage of large-scale leasing prompted the landlords to purchase land from the peasants and lease it out to bailiff-lessees to whom the landowner, in order to increase the yield from his property, granted a considerable amount of capital at a high rate of interest. Thus as time went on the number of mortgages on farm property increased (for a loan obtained on the security of a farm could, if skilfully employed, bring in more than could be derived from running the farm) and more and more credits were opened in favour of 'bailiff-lessees'.

As to considerations of a social nature, it must be remembered that by the end of the seventeenth century, given the radical changes that had taken place in the political structure, to be a property-owner had become almost an essential in order to enter public and political life; whereas in the past activity in politics had been the premise for achieving a higher position among the ranks of the landed proprietors.

Thus by the end of the seventeenth century the big estates ceased to be sold, and the new rich who wanted to acquire landed property as a basis for their social prestige and political ambitions had to content themselves with purchasing small properties from the peasant farmers and the gentry. The rise of the oligarchy, in other words the increase of the really extensive landed estates, marks the beginning of that process of gradual dissolution of the English peasantry which was to become fully manifest in the second half of the eighteenth century (when enclosures were actually favoured by law) and the following century (by which time the agrarian revolution had come to an end in England).

THE AGRICULTURAL LANDSCAPE:

TYPES AND METHODS OF CULTIVATION:

STOCKBREEDING

Agrarian production, in the widest sense of the term, constituted even in our period by far the most important branch of supply. Pre-industrial economy, essentially agricultural, was conditioned by the geography, morphology and climate of the various European territories, quite apart from such influences as local institutional, social and cultural factors or the general state of the economy. The various regions, though they show certain overall similarities, will therefore be treated separately.

Under the heading of *Northern Europe* we may include the Franco-German continental belt extending from east of the Armorican massif and north of the central massif to the curve in the Elbe, and having on its southern boundaries the northern Rhineland and Westphalia. In this vast region, in the period under consideration here, there was a sharp distinction between a predominantly forest and livestock economy in the mountainous or hilly northern areas and an economy mainly devoted to cultivation in the plains, the lower plateaux and slopes, and the valleys. The considerable differences in climate between the Scandinavian territories and those south of the Baltic produced variations in crops and in rural landscape.

In Norway and Sweden by far the most widespread crop was barley, which grew quite far north, especially along the shores of the Gulf of Bothnia. In the southern plains it was often accompanied by rye. Livestock breeding, of which there was very little in the south (though after 1720 merino sheep began to be introduced there), appeared more conspicuous and widespread near the borders of the immense forest that covered much of the northern part of the Scandinavian peninsula. This typical thick vegetation led to the formation of numerous so-called 'forest colonies', little oases of habitation established particularly beside rivers. Amid land cleared of trees and bushes these dwellings arose one after the other in regular succession, approached by a single road. Behind them stretched in uniform rows the fields of cultivated land. This was an agricultural landscape that retained its characteristic features throughout the seventeenth and eighteenth centuries and was also not infrequently encountered in Denmark and North-western Germany.

There, however, as in North-eastern France, the rural dwellings usually centred round the church. The farms, lying outside and around the villages, produced various cereals: wheat in calcareous, rye in siliceous soil; barley and oats were also usually grown as part of the regular cycle. In these areas, which were much more intensely cultivated than the Scandinavian plains, agriculture underwent little change. The most obvious advances seem to have been made in Alsace and Thuringia as a result of the development of two important industrial crops: hops in Alsace and woad in Thuringia. Farming also seems gradually to have spread along the sides of the valleys, especially those with southern slopes, at the expense of woodland. Woods, however, continued to dominate the hilly or mountainous land farther up, and besides providing timber for building and firewood for heating the houses in the few scattered villages, their oak trees and chestnuts afforded abundant food for the numerous pigs. Cattle also grazed in the mountain regions providing good pasture, and there was quite a lot of dairy produce. In the plains the soil was more fertile and therefore more intensively farmed, in the German and French provinces near the Rhine. The northern plains and the undulating lands along the Baltic's southern shores, mainly sandy and arid alluvial land, were not much good for cultivation. On the plains livestock was kept mostly for farmwork and consisted largely of oxen and draught-horses. But in the north-western regions, especially in Jutland, animal husbandry was widely and successfully practised, modelled on the experience of nearby Flanders. Denmark in the sixteenth–seventeenth century exported an average of from 30 to 50 thousand head of livestock a year, sometimes even reaching 70–80,000; the farmers specialised in cattle-fattening, especially when grain prices fell heavily. The high price of butter caused the Danish farmers in the second half of the seventeenth century, and even in the eighteenth, to move over from breeding meat cattle to dairy cattle, and this led to a considerable import of dairy cows from Holland.

From the sixteenth to the eighteenth century in Nordic Europe, as defined here, it was mainly a subsistence agriculture, based on crops which would satisfy the basic food needs of the local populations. Nevertheless, under the stimulus of rising prices and up to the outbreak of the disastrous Thirty Years War, in Norway and, more particularly, in North-western Germany there was a temporary increase in land ploughed and sown to cereals and a considerable export of grain. Methods of cultivation, with a few sporadic exceptions, remained anchored to the traditional pattern of the Scandinavian peninsula: free and regulated rotations continued almost everywhere with a year of fallow and, particularly in Sweden, so-called 'temporary cultivation' (*Feldgraswirtschaft*) was practised. These methods were also generally followed on the Continent. But long before the second half of the eighteenth century when, following results secured in Flanders and on the insistent advice of well-known agronomists, notably von Moltke and von der Lühe, other successful rotations were introduced on the lines of convertible husbandry, some interesting experiments had already been made in the sixteenth century, especially in Schleswig-Holstein, Mecklenburg, Denmark and Alsace. To meet the growing needs of livestock, big farms introduced a two-course rotation alternating oats with grass. When, towards the end of the seventeenth and the beginning of the eighteenth century, the transition to cattle-fattening and dairy-farming began, the rotation came to cover an eleven-year period (in Holstein, a year of fallow was followed by a year each of wheat, barley, rye, two years of oats, and then grass from the seventh to the eleventh years; in Mecklenburg a year of fallow was followed by five years of cereals and five of grass). As a general rule, on good land in northern continental Europe in the sixteenth century the fallow period fell between the fourth and the eighth year, while three-course rotation was used on poorer land. That last type of rotation was, however, widely revived after the devastation of the Thirty Years War when de-population of the countryside made intensive exploitation of the land difficult, and neglected lands needed more frequent fallow periods and plenty of manure. But once these difficulties had been overcome there was a general tendency to reduce the fallow area. For example, in the south-eastern corner of Nordic Europe, in the Harz and Saxony, fallow as a percentage of the total arable area was as follows:

Schmatzfeld estate		Lohmen estate		Wasserleben estate		Ilsenburg estate	
1592	37·3%	1590	53·0%	1655	32·6%	1705	33·3%
1606	28·4%	1632	46·0%	1711	5·3%	1722	21·4%
1740	20·8%	1680	55·0%			1747	6·0%
		1713	29·0%				

Throughout continental Nordic Europe, wherever the quality and humidity of the soil made it suitable, hemp and flax were grown. In the eighteenth century cultivation of coleseed was extended to the coastal fringes of North-western Germany, apparently with excellent results. Along the Rhine, and especially in Alsace, vine-growing was widely resumed from the end of the seventeenth century. This development, also met with in Switzerland, especially in the cantons of Aargau, Vaud and Zürich, seems to have been fostered by the fall in cereal prices, which made it advisable to revive a more remunerative branch of agriculture.

In the vast territory of plains and gentle hills stretching from Central Germany east of the Elbe to the Russian provinces, the agricultural landscape in certain respects resembled that of Nordic Europe. The huge extent of the afforested area prompted the populations of *East-Central Europe* to cut down timber and create large open spaces where the fertile soil yielded good crops. Thus the same kind of 'forest colonies' grew up which have already been mentioned earlier in connection with Nordic Europe.

This sort of land lent itself to large-scale cultivation of cereals, and in particular rye. Industrial crops, especially textile fibres, were also quite important in the type of 'enclave' economy characteristic of the rural areas in those regions. Livestock rearing was practised only to a modest extent except for some isolated pockets in Hungary, Moravia and Southern Poland. In those regions, moreover, grazing grounds and natural pasture tended to become more confined after the second half of the sixteenth century, especially in the Polish plains and between the Vistula and the Bug. Such land was increasingly turned over to cereal cultivation as the international demand for cereals intensified and (up to the middle of the seventeenth century) as cereal prices rose. The influx of precious metal into Poland caused the price of agricultural produce to soar more than in the other areas of Central and Eastern Europe. This produced the agrarian and social effects that have been mentioned earlier: expansion of seigneurial properties and a reversion to serfdom.

However, as recent studies have shown, the profitability of an estate did not increase in proportion as the seigneurial *réserve* expanded (calculations referring to the end of the sixteenth century show that an expansion of the *réserve* by

126 per cent produced an increase in income of only 39 per cent). This is perfectly comprehensible, for the difficulties of procuring sufficient and apt labour must alone have been considerable; but it may have had a beneficial effect in restraining the expansion of estates. The average extent of a seigneurial domain at the end of the sixteenth century was about 130 hectares (*c.* 320 acres), of which 44 per cent belonged to the overlord's *réserve*, the average being higher in Masovia (the big province with Warsaw as its centre) and lower in Central-Eastern Poland; production of the main crops on the *réserve* in normal years reached about 500 hectolitres (*c.* 1,420 bushels), rye accounting for some 38 per cent, wheat and barley each 10 per cent, and oats 42 per cent. Over 70 per cent of the wheat produced was sold, rather more than half the barley when not used for making beer, and half the rye and oats. Half the oats went to feed the livestock, which on an average consisted of three draught oxen, two horses, ten cows, a score of pigs and flocks of sheep, the latter being especially numerous in Central Poland. 70 per cent of the annual income of an average nobleman's property was derived from vegetable produce and 30 per cent from animal produce. On small seigneurial properties the *réserve* accounted for 94 per cent of the annual income, while on the big estates its contribution was about 70 per cent of the total.

It would seem, however, that the phase of expansion of agricultural production began to wane in Poland even before prices reached their highest point, and before the war with Sweden (1655–60) had seriously damaged the country's economy, which recovered only very slowly during the subsequent decades. Researches carried out over a good number of *réserves* in Masovia show that on an average in each *réserve* there was considerable variation, both in harvests and in the proportions of the various crops, between 1569 and 1660, as can be seen from the table on p. 310.

The decline is striking: in 1660 sowings fall to a third, and harvests to less than a fifth, of the 1569 figures. Moreover, the percentage of rye and barley cultivation shows an

Years	Sowing of cereals	Harvest of cereals	Rye	Barley	Wheat	Oats	Total harvest
1569	100	100	50·3	6·1	5·0	38·6	100·0
1616	78	71	54·2	11·9	3·4	30·5	100·0
1660	34	17	55·2	20·0	2·8	22·0	100·0

increase, which is tantamount to saying that the fall lies with the more significant grain-crops. Another figure further demonstrates the impoverishment of the agricultural economy: in 1660 only 15 per cent of the land under crop rotation appears to have been sown, while 85 per cent lay fallow. This unsatisfactory situation is also borne out by documentation relating to the huge royal estate of Rebkov. Here sales of cereals plummeted from about 3,000 boisseaux in 1569 (the boisseau equals about 12½ litres, or one-third of a bushel) to 1,700 in 1616 and 200 in 1660; and in 1660 there were only 55 head of livestock as compared with 155 in 1569. Other researches carried out in respect of domains belonging to the bishoprics of Wloclawek and Gniezno and some 160 estates scattered throughout the six provinces of Poland merely confirm that agricultural production expanded up to the end of the sixteenth century, remained stationary for some decades and after the middle of the seventeenth century contracted sharply. Hence the gradual impoverishment and subjection of the peasant class to which reference has already been made.

Poland's experience is symptomatic of the agricultural trend in East-Central Europe, and for that reason we have considered it at some length. It should, however, be noted that the influence of rising prices and increasing demand for cereals in the Western countries was less marked in Bohemia, Moravia, Hungary, Bulgaria, Austria and Slovenia, where progressive expansion of the area under cereal cultivation also occurred side by side with an extension of seigneurial *réserves*. We need only compare the rise in prices in the Polish towns with those in the regions just mentioned: by comparison with prices in Danzig, prices in Prague, Vienna and Ljubljana, etc., rose less rapidly and their maximum levels were 30–50 per cent below those in the Baltic port. But the undoubted increase in regional demand (partly due to the population increase) and the spread of a 'mercantile' mentality among the landowners explain the increase of cereal cultivation in the sixteenth century. 'Est mihi animus,' wrote a big Hungarian landowner in 1542, 'ut emam unam navem, quae mille metretas ordei et tritici ferre potest. Ordeum, farinam et alia victualia mecum ducam.' ('I intend to buy a ship which can carry a thousand *metretas* of barley and wheat. I shall bring barley, flour and other supplies with me.') Among the 'alia victualia' in which the big Hungarian entrepreneurs traded extensively with their neighbours were wine and meat, most of which went to the Viennese market. In short, up to the end of the sixteenth century agricultural production in the Danubian and Carpathian countries increased considerably — for example, in the domains of the fortress of Gyula, in Hungary, profits from the sale of wheat multiplied thirteenfold between 1519 and 1557. But in the seventeenth century progress was checked and a drastic reduction in grain harvests ensued. Maize-growing was introduced and did well in the Balkan and Danubian plains, especially in Bulgaria and Rumania, but even that was unable to compensate for the losses sustained or improve the wretched lot of the rural populations at the end of the sixteenth and during the seventeenth century.

In the boundless Russian provinces, too, after a considerable increase during the first half of the sixteenth century in the area cultivated and in new lands reclaimed from forest or grazing, the changes in landed tenure recorded above, the dispersal and impoverishment of the country-people, and frequent military campaigns, all combined to restrict the area under cultivation and extend the pasture-land and wooded areas while bringing no increase in live-stock rearing. Here, too, especially in the eighteenth century, maize made a tentative appearance and acclimatised well in the central plains.

Changes in the Central-Eastern European agricultural scene in general arose from the great variations in the quantity of production and the revival of serfdom among the peasants. They did not depend on variations in the type of crops grown, still less on changes in agricultural technique. In fact, in these regions the three-course rotation, with a year of fallow, was the method universally and continuously employed — a method which, as has already been stressed, besides being well adapted to a mainly cereal production favoured the landowners' aim of binding the labour force to the land.

To the west and south-west of the two big geographical regions described above lie the regions approaching the northern side of the Alps, the southern slopes of the Central Massif, extending westwards beyond the Garonne basin to include the whole North Atlantic seaboard of the Iberian peninsula. This region, which we may term *Atlantic Europe*, at its higher latitudes reproduces some of the characteristics of the agrarian countryside of Nordic Europe, while at its lower latitudes it shares some of the salient features of Mediterranean agriculture. The continental and insular (i.e. the British Isles) portions of this region present considerable differences with regard to agriculture, and during the centuries we are dealing with here the agrarian landscape underwent some important changes. It will therefore be useful to divide this Western-Atlantic region of Europe into three agricultural sub-areas.

The territory lying between the Franco-Flemish coasts of the North Sea and the North-Rhine-Westphalia region was well farmed and prosperous. Agriculture here was affected in much the same way as other regions of Europe by economic and other influences such as rising prices and wars; but it developed a particular trend of its own which occurred elsewhere only in England, and there less markedly. This trend might be termed the 'Dutch agricultural cycle'. In other continental regions, the agricultural expansion of the sixteenth century was followed by a serious depression in the seventeenth century which lasted almost everywhere until around the 1750s. In the Low Countries, on the contrary, after a preliminary setback in the 1560s and 1570s, agriculture flourished throughout the period from 1590 to 1670; it then suffered a decline and remained stagnant until the middle of the following century. This general trend is borne out by statistics concerning the drainage of land reclaimed from the sea. Taking the area thus reclaimed (the so-called 'polders') in 1715–39 as 100, figures for the previous 25-year periods are as follows:

1540–64	346	1615–39	419	1690–1714	118
1565–89	75	1640–64	273	1715–39	100
1590–1614	340	1665–89	116		

There can be no doubt that land reclamation was carried on vigorously when prices of agricultural produce were rising and was allowed to lapse as they fell (this is confirmed in East Friesland, where areas reclaimed for cultivation amounted to 6,000 hectares in 1633–60, nothing in 1661–1735 and about 2,750 hectares in 1735–46).

Of course, expansion and recession in agriculture cannot be explained simply by the movement of prices — least of all in the case of Holland. Market values for agricultural produce may have suggested a certain line of conduct to the Low Countries farmers, but only in the short term. In the long term the essential influence on development or contraction must be, as Pareto teaches, the level of incomes. And where could an intelligent policy of investment in land operate more successfully than in Holland, a country especially rich in personal capital, open to the trends of international trade and free from preconceived political and economic ideas, in a word 'anti-conformist' (or 'anti-mercantilist') ? How can we ignore the relationship between the remarkable development of Dutch agriculture and the pre-eminence of the Low Countries in the seventeenth-century international economic scene? Dutch capitalists at the beginning of the seventeenth century even advanced finances to French farmers to drain the marshes and establish monoculture, finances which represent one of the earliest examples of the application of capitalist methods to agriculture.

Other events outside the economic sphere also had a considerable influence on changes in the type of farming in the Low Countries. For example, between 1637 and 1648 Harlingerland in East Friesland moved over from animal to arable husbandry: this was quite simply because under military occupation the war-levy was based on the number of head of livestock that a farmer owned. On the other hand, east of Liége, in the district of Herve, the ban on export of cereals (introduced in order to satisfy the needs of the densely populated South Netherlands) caused farmers, in view of rising prices, to convert their land from its formerly prosperous cereal cultivation to pasture and go in for animal husbandry, which they pursued successfully throughout the century after 1650 when livestock prices remained high. In Herve, indeed, arable land, which in the sixteenth century represented 66 per cent of the total area, fell to 19 per cent in the following century and to only 2 per cent in 1740 (in the nearby districts of Henri Chapelle and Montzen over the same period the percentage of arable area to the total fell, respectively, from 76 to 14·4 and from 56 to 15 per cent). This is not, of course, to say that market conditions did not act as a stimulant to certain types of agricultural production or influence changes in farming. Such was, in fact, the case in Salland, where in the seventeenth century reafforestation was undertaken simultaneously with a rise in the price of timber; also in Overijssel and Twente, where meadows and hay fields expanded afresh towards the end of the seventeenth century and many farms went over to animal husbandry because of the rise in meat prices.

The importance which the Flemish farmers attributed to livestock farming as compared with arable farming is a testimony to their wisdom and rapid reflexes (a similar attitude among farmers occurred on a smaller scale and, somewhat later, after the middle of the seventeenth century, to the south of Flanders, in a region running through France from Thiérache — in the Aisne department of today — to Burgundy and thence across Switzerland to Germany and Austria). Flemish farmers were real entrepreneurs, who knew how to make the most of both natural possibilities and market conditions. In the polders area fodder crops became the most important, and they provided the necessary basis for establishing a sound livestock economy such as would provide the impetus for connected dairy production (yields of milk per head were much higher than elsewhere, reaching figures not far off the averages for the beginning of the present century, and the Low Countries were in a position to export nine-tenths of their cheese production over and above domestic needs). Cultivation of fodder crops also gained a footing in the inland Flemish provinces, side by side with a restricted but rational cultivation of cereals; expanding animal husbandry ensured greater supplies of manure and so made possible here a much more effective fertilisation of the soil than in other countries. Industrial textile plants (hemp and flax) were also increasingly grown in these areas, and at this time madder, woad and pastel were successfully introduced, responding to the demand for dyestuffs from the expanding local textile industry. Another industrial crop was hops, grown side by side with barley, the main cereal, and important for the development of the brewing industry. Tobacco-growing gained some footing in the second half of the seventeenth century, especially in Veluwe, east of Utrecht, and in the Hainaut, district of Belgium. Various experiments were made in introducing plants from the colonial territories, among which the most successful were potatoes, especially after the serious crop failure of 1740 prompted the introduction of new types of crops. Flemish growers' enterprise and interest in specialisation can also be seen from the fact that from the end of the sixteenth century onwards much money and labour was invested in flower-growing: in the seventeenth century tulip-bulbs were regularly quoted on the Amsterdam exchange, and tulip-cultivation became so popular that it was quite justifiably described as a 'tulip-mania'.

This trend towards specialisation was both a cause and an effect of constant modernisation of the cultural cycles which, in accordance with careful planning to maintain the fertility of the soil, included fodder crops and pulses. On the model farm of Hemmema, at Hitsum in Friesland, innovations in crop rotation were introduced from the middle of the sixteenth century (in the first and third year peas and beans, in the second year winter grain — wheat or barley — and in the fourth year spring grain — barley or oats — with a much smaller area, about an eighth of the total, left fallow) and in combination with rich manuring produced very high yields; but in general methods of cultivation on all farms were well thought out and proved profitable. Such methods included the infield-outfield system practised in the interior regions around Namur, continuous cultivation of rye in the eastern Low Countries, the four- to six-course rotation combined with extensive cultivation of pulses in Friesland (a system also adopted in Alsace), convertible husbandry in the Groningen area of Flanders, rotation of cereals with fodder-crops as catch crops in various parts of the Netherlands and the alternation of cereals with fodder-crops in the rest-year. A single example will suffice to give an idea of the variety of crops used in rotation: at the end of the period under review, in 1750, in some farms in the neighbourhood of Klundert (Netherlands) 58·3 per cent of the soil was sown with eight different types of cereals, while 41·7 per cent carried pulses, industrial crops (rape, colza, flax, madder) and potatoes.

The Flemish regions, and more especially the Low Countries, achieved the highest agricultural development in this period. But in England too, and also to a lesser extent in Northern and Central-western France, considerable progress was made, due partly to the inspiration derived from Holland's example, whose innovations were made widely known by the English agriculturalist Sir Richard Weston (1591–1652). The influence of Flemish experiments in agriculture do not, however, appear to have penetrated to South-western Europe, which fell rather within the Mediterranean orbit. For this reason we shall consider these three geographical areas separately.

Agriculture in the *British Isles*, subject to a damp but relatively mild climate owing to the Gulf Stream, was influenced by the changes in legal and social institutions and in technical practice which had been going on there since the Middle Ages. Scotland and the more northerly areas of Britain were in general more isolated and backward, and agriculture there concentrated mainly on exploiting the rich forestry resources and on livestock-rearing. Animal husbandry developed more intensively as the demand for meat grew in the expanding urban centres of England, especially London. The traditional transfer of livestock from Scotland to pastures in Southern England increased: in the eighteenth century some 40,000 head of livestock were driven south each year, fattened in the green fields of Norfolk and finished up in the Smithfield meat market. Crop cultivation in Scotland was mainly cereal, especially barley, though some beans were also grown in rotation. The infield–outfield system, together with temporary culti-vation, was the method most generally used. The infield, usually occupying a third of the arable area, was kept constantly under crop, with a rotation of spring barley and two years of oats and summer barley. When pulses formed part of the cycle, rotation covered two years (spring barley and pulses), three years (peas or beans, summer barley, oats), or four years (peas, wheat, barley, oats). The outfield was reserved for oats as long as the yield was remunerative; thereafter it was left to pasture. Where livestock was kept as well, part of the outfield (in Aberdeenshire, about a tenth) was reserved for the animals, who stayed there night and day. When the land was sufficiently manured it was sown to oats for five years and then left again as pasture. Waste land beyond the outfield was quite often burnt (at that time ashes were widely used as a fertiliser) and then sown to oats for several years. But despite improvements Scottish agriculture did not reach the same level as in England.

Agriculture in Ireland was even less advanced, being based up to the early eighteenth century on poor cereal cultivation with a little forestry and livestock. The Irish peasantry, oppressed by a system of land tenure and farm-ing resembling that of the European *Gutherrschaft* regions in their perpetuation of feudal practices, lacked the energy to react against tyranny. At most, fear of losing their jobs prompted them after about 1630 to demand government intervention to restrain the landowners' attempts to transform arable land into grassland in order to increase their livestock and secure more regular profits from the higher prices for meat and dairy produce. The changeover from tillage to animal husbandry was in any case a slow but inevitable process: between 1723 and 1776 Ireland had to import considerable quantities of cereals and the government even exhorted farmers to revert to arable farming. The fall in grain production was one reason for the development of potato-growing in the eighteenth century, which with improved techniques became a model to be copied elsewhere. Some scholars have even maintained that potatoes, by becoming the nation's staple food, contributed decisively to the population increase in Ireland. But up to the eighteenth century the productivity of the Irish soil remained at a low level because of the persistence of antiquated methods based chiefly on temporary cultivation and on free three-course rotation with a year of fallow.

In England it was a very different story. Changes in the system of land tenure and farm management and in rural society were accompanied by changes in methods of cultivation, farming techniques and economic output of the farms. The interest in agricultural problems is demonstrated by the number of works which, as early as the sixteenth century, dealt in detail with various aspects of farming, often bringing to bear a new approach. Works by Plat, Maxey, Markham, Fitzherbert, Plattes, Hartlib and Weston (already mentioned earlier) were frequently reprinted and widely plagiarised — though not, however, those of Tull, whose daring and revolutionary theories only came to be applied much later. But the importance of agriculture in the country's economic development was recognised even by the most ardent defenders of mercantilism (who in this respect differed markedly from their more rigid and shortsighted counterparts in other countries) and was fully accepted by the merchant-capitalists and the new bour-

geoisie. In consequence, business methods were introduced
into farm management; constant efforts were made to adjust
production to market conditions; considerable capital was
expended on improvements to farm property such as irrigation channels, better byres and stabling, etc.; and great
interest was shown in the fruitful experiments being made
in Flanders, which English farmers aimed to copy. In this
last respect, indeed, farmers in England readily adopted
some of the new types of plants imported from America and
already tried out in Holland, such as the turnip, introduced
around 1565 near Norwich by Flemish immigrants, as well
as the fodder-crops lupin and clover.

The introduction of fodder-crops into the farming
routine, and the creation of irrigated pasturelands, were by
no means infrequent even in the sixteenth century (in the
reign of Elizabeth water-meadows covered a considerable
area of Herefordshire and Dorset, and probably Shropshire); by the second half of the seventeenth century they
had become generally accepted methods of contributing to
agricultural development. By that time the fall in cereal
prices had intensified the trend towards animal husbandry,
stimulated by the growing demand of the wool industry;
and a strong movement towards a system of crop rotation
better suited to convertible husbandry culminated in the
Norfolk system. It is not surprising, therefore, that the
farmers' own enterprise, the efforts to modernise agricultural techniques and equipment (progress in agricultural 'technology' is described elsewhere in this history)
and the fortunate combination of improved standards in
both arable and animal husbandry should have prepared
the way for that 'new husbandry' which reached its highest
expression in England and became a prime factor in the
agricultural revolution of the second half of the eighteenth
century. That revolution followed a serious depression in
1730–50, largely the result of a long series of good harvests
(the crop failure of 1740 and the cattle plague of 1745 were
sporadic disasters which had little effect on market conditions) which produced an imbalance between supply and
demand and thus aggravated the fall in prices, reduced

agricultural incomes and imposed serious financial sacrifices in an attempt to subsidise by means of a crop bounty the export of farmers' surplus stocks. But, as in the case of the Low Countries, the progressive rise in the general level of incomes, over and above transitory oscillations in prices and market conditions, went far to account for the basically favourable trend in English agriculture up to the revolution. Recent researches in respect of, for example, Lincolnshire demonstrate the influence exercised by the growth of personal wealth on the agricultural economy.

In the favourable agricultural conditions of the sixteenth and early seventeenth centuries arable husbandry undoubtedly held out attractions for farmers despite their awareness of the advantages of increasing livestock, as the following instances can testify. In the Midlands there was a general trend towards expanding arable land at the expense of grassland; in certain districts the increase in arable land was very high indeed, as for instance at Bittesby in Leicestershire, where in 1640 the arable area was fourteen times as large as in 1572. Despite some opposition, important land reclamation works were carried out during the seventeenth century in the eastern counties, partly under the direction of Dutch experts, with a view to transforming pasture land into arable land sown to cereals and coleseed. This move was fully justified in view of the higher income to be derived from arable land as compared with pasture: in Norfolk between 1600 and 1640 rents from it increased sixfold, whereas rents from pasture merely doubled. Up to the middle of the seventeenth century there was little or no transformation of arable land to pasture on enclosed land; but enclosure tended to intensify with the fall in cereal prices. In Leicestershire 52 per cent of the enclosed area was registered between 1607 and 1730; but by far the greatest number of enclosures was carried out after 1660.

With an agricultural economy more dependent on livestock-rearing, livestock farming itself became better organised and more remunerative. The yield of wool from sheep improved, cattle increased in numbers and weight and the milk yield rose; but the number of horses fell, partly because there was less land to be ploughed. At the same time a greater variety of crops was cultivated, with an increase in fodder-crops and tubers that favoured soil conservation. Even before this, however, the productivity of the soil had been increased by means of more efficient crop rotation and a greater use of fertilisers, both animal and mineral, and by improvements in farm equipment. As early as the sixteenth century, side by side with the traditional three-course rotation, two-course rotation had been introduced, and in combination with extensive use of fertilisers had produced greatly increased yields, as for example at the Loders' farm at Harwell near Oxford, where over a four-year period corn alternated with fallow and then corn or barley once again with fallow. A prelude to convertible husbandry was the rotation of four to six or even more courses combined with extensive cultivation of pulses. Statistics compiled from a number of farms in Leicestershire in the sixteenth century show that, comparing the data for 1500–30 with those for 1588, the area sown to winter grain (mainly wheat) fell from 18·8 to 12·5 per cent, while the area sown to spring grain (mainly barley) and pulses (peas and beans) rose by, respectively, 38 to 41·5 and 43·2 to 46 per cent. Even higher percentages were shown at Wigston: there the area under pulses was 49·5 per cent of the total, that under barley 43·5, under rye 1, and under wheat 6 per cent. An early form of convertible husbandry was practised even before the seventeenth century in the west of England: in Cornwall with a rotation of two years of wheat, two of oats and then seven or eight years of pasture, and in Devonshire with wheat, two years of barley, then oats, peas, oats again, and lastly some years of pasture. In those particular districts sea-sand and crushed seashells mixed with seaweed were used as fertilisers: the typical Devonshire fertiliser, a mixture of burnt grass-ash and seaweed known as 'Denshiring', seems to have been particularly effective and was also used elsewhere. But the form of convertible husbandry most widely adopted and favoured by the experts in the first half of the seventeenth century was the ten- or twelve-year system. This system had three variations according to the type of soil involved, clay, sand or fenland. On clay soil, two years of wheat or rye were followed by a year of barley, three years of oats, one year of pulses and then at least three years under grass. On sandy soil, wheat or rye was sown for the first three years, then a year of barley, three years of oats, a year of lupin or vetch and three or four years of grass. On fenland, three years of wheat were followed by a year each of barley and rye, three years of oats, one year of peas and three of grass. After 1650, at the suggestion of Sir Richard Weston, the admirer of Flemish farming, fodder-crops became widespread, with a complicated succession of crops culminating at the end of the century in the celebrated Norfolk system, the prototype of the 'new husbandry'. This system involved two variations: a four-course rotation of corn, turnips, barley and clover, and a six-course rotation of wheat, barley or oats, turnips, oats or barley together with clover, grazed clover till 21st June and then sown to winter wheat, and lastly winter wheat. The Norfolk system is rightly claimed to have proved so successful not only because of its method of rotation but also because its introduction coincided with the progress of marling and enclosures, with expansion of farms and with longer leases. It came fully into its own in the second half of the eighteenth century.

To sum up, the agricultural face of England underwent profound changes between the sixteenth and the eighteenth centuries. To realise this we need only to compare descriptions of Leicestershire in the seventeenth and eighteenth centuries: in the 1600s a countryside characterised by extensive cornfields contrasting with wide grasslands, in the 1700s a mainly pastoral countryside dominated by vast green meadows pasturing herds of cattle and flocks of sheep.

In *Northern France*, in the stretch of country extending, roughly speaking, diagonally from the Somme to the Vendée and the Charente on the Atlantic coast, the undoubted resemblances to the agricultural scene in Flanders and England become less marked as we approach the central-western regions. English and Dutch influence is shown especially in the growing importance given to animal farming and hence to fodder cultivation.

This is not to say, however, that the Ile-de-France regions felt the need to specialise in livestock, despite the great demand for meat and dairy products emanating from the ever-growing population of Paris and its surroundings. On the contrary, the major and continuing preoccupation of farmers in those areas was how best to overcome local conditions adverse to cereal cultivation. In other words, it was not a question of differentiating between areas of arable or animal farming, but between areas suitable or otherwise for cereal-growing; and the agricultural landscape itself seems to have reflected this particular attitude of the farmers.

In fact, wherever climate and the nature of the soil favoured arable farming, livestock represented a purely secondary source of income and was treated as such. So much so, indeed, that there was a serious shortage of protein foodstuffs for the ill-nourished local population: this was the case, for example, in the Limagne valleys of the Auvergne, where, despite their natural advantages, an obstinately short-sighted policy of cereal cultivation was maintained at the expense of livestock-rearing. In areas less suited to cereal-growing, on the other hand, livestock-rearing represented the main activity for the rural population and the means of promoting a market economy: for the head of livestock or the dairy product became the unit of exchange for procuring the stocks of grain needed to satisfy local needs. Thus hilly or mountainous areas, such as the Auvergne, were generally found to be more commercially aware than the plateaux or plains, where the cereal-growing 'vocation' tended to obsess the farmer, blinding him to other possibilities. This explains why live-stock-rearing was relatively insignificant in the rich fertile areas around Paris, and why in Picardy and the Soissons and Beauvais regions the land was scoured by the plough to receive, in accordance with the wellnigh universal practice of triennial rotation, rye and wheat, with the

addition of pulses on the better soils. A large property south
of Paris provides an example: in the sixteenth century 91·2
per cent of its total area was ploughland, 8·8 per cent vineyards and 0·4 per cent pasture; of the arable area, 34·5 per
cent was sown to winter grain, 36·9 per cent to summer
crops (22 per cent oats, 10·5 per cent barley, 4 per cent
beans, peas and vetch, and 0·4 per cent hemp) and 28·6 per
cent left fallow. A perfect example, in fact, of three-year
rotation. The little meadows along the river-banks were
gradually taken away from the village populations by the
noblemen and bourgeoisie and enclosed to become ploughed
fields; consequently, the only pasture available for the livestock was the third of the total area left fallow during the
rotation cycle and the stubble remaining after the harvest.
In these regions where cereal cultivation predominated
livestock-rearing, in fact, played a subsidiary part in the
agricultural picture. There were far more sheep than cattle
(in a 300-acre farm regarded as 'good' in the neighbourhood
of Soissons in the 1620s, out of 163 head of livestock there
were 150 sheep and only 13 cattle), and a cow weighing
200 kg. (440 lbs.) was considered 'prime fat'.

That weight would not have been thought satisfactory,
however, on farms in Normandy, Brittany, the Boulogne
area, Limoges or Poitou, where favourable climate and soil
produced good natural pastures and where greater interest
in livestock-rearing led to its becoming the main farming
activity; though there, too, cereal cultivation was of considerable importance, especially in periods of rising prices.
Throughout Central and North-western France, particularly in the regions just mentioned, there was relatively
little interest in corn-growing, as can be seen from the fact
that on the numerous enclosed farms much of the land
(*bocages*) was often not cleared but left instead in its natural
state to provide food for the animals.

Livestock consisted mainly of carefully selected and reared
cattle which gave good yields of meat and milk. Unlike the
other regions near Paris mentioned earlier, these districts
were extensive suppliers of the capital's demand for those
products. Farmers here had not completely abandoned the

old traditions: it must not be forgotten that in France the agricultural treatises of Palissy, Estienne and de Serres, written in the sixteenth century and based on antiquated methods of cultivation, were constantly republished and even in the eighteenth century were still regarded as fundamental works (the much more modern treatise of Duhamel du Monceau, for example, appeared only after the middle of the eighteenth century). But some revision of technical and economic standards of farm management was nevertheless creeping in, if only slowly. In these predominantly livestock-rearing areas the customary three-course or two-course rotation was gradually moving over to more complex and more suitable systems, with the inclusion of other plants and pulses as well as grains, until finally in the eighteenth century, when sainfoin and lucerne became widely grown especially in Normandy and Brittany, fodder-crops came to be included as a regular part of the rotation. The numerous livestock provided quantities of manure, thus promoting easier and more rapid soil regeneration and a gradual reduction of the fallow area. At the same time the right of free pasturage was more strictly controlled: it came to be suppressed altogether on land destined for cultivation by rotation and was confined to certain parts of the fields after the second crop of hay had been cut.

In all these regions from the Pas-de-Calais to the Charente, particularly during the sixteenth and seventeenth centuries, there was increasing cultivation of buckwheat and spelt, graminaceous plants that acclimatised easily and produced good yields even on poor soil. In Picardy and the neighbouring areas coleseed was widely grown, especially towards the end of the period under review. Hemp and dyestuffs were grown to some extent everywhere, with woad prevailing especially in Picardy and Normandy, where it had been sown for centuries. Maize, potatoes and tobacco, however, did not appear until some decades later in these areas. During these centuries vine-growing continued to decline in these regions, which in any case were not particularly suited to it, except in certain districts of the Ile-de-France, Poitou, the Charente and the Basse-Loire.

Specialised high-quality vine-growing was confined to other parts of France. Export demand fell (Rouen and La Rochelle were no longer the main ports for exports), but production of low-quality wine still went on, chiefly for local consumption, in the more populous areas such as the surroundings of Paris. Prices contributed to the decline in vine-growing between the sixteenth and seventeenth centuries. At a time of rising prices the market value of agricultural products rose more rapidly than that of wine — between the end of the fifteenth century and the early 1700s prices for cereals in France increased tenfold, for meat eightfold and for wine five or sixfold; farmers therefore tended, for instance in the Maine district, to replace their vineyards by cornfields. All this caused a change in the aspect of the countryside and the outward appearance of the farms grouped around the rural buildings, among which windmills were often to be seen, especially in Normandy and Brittany.

In *South-western France*, the region to the south of the area described above and extending westwards towards the Pyrenees and the Atlantic, there was a great variety of cultivation. In the sixteenth century farms were small in size, but they subsequently tended to expand as changes took place in the countryside as a whole, and many crops were grown so as to spread the risks as widely as possible. For climatic conditions in these regions approaching the Mediterranean were not such as to give farmers an easy life. Sudden incalculable changes in temperature and humidity made the land unsuitable for olive-growing, and nut-trees, better able to stand up to the caprices of the weather, were usually grown instead.

In the regions near the interior, in the valleys of the Adour, the Gave, Armagnac, the Garonne towards Bordeaux, and the Dordogne towards Bergerac, vines were already widely grown in the sixteenth century, and after a pause during the seventeenth century their cultivation expanded afresh in the 1710s. Vine-growing was fostered by the export trade: Bordeaux became the main port for the export of wine. This export trade was carried on mainly by Dutchmen, who besides supplying their own market brought the finest French wines to the rest of Northern Europe, from Scandinavia to Germany. The revocation of the Edict of Nantes in 1685 had some significant effects on viticulture and the wine trade. In addition to the temporary hindrances to the trade resulting from confusion following this drastic measure, the transfer of tens of thousands of Protestants (some 59,000 families) to countries outside France, and especially to the Low Countries, brought a considerable part of the trade in French wines into new, international channels. This led to specialisation, often specifically expressed by name, among certain types of vine-growing: for example, the classification of Monzibillac as *Marque Hollandaise* — specially grown for the émigré market — dates back to this period. In South-western France, as in Burgundy, though in different climatic and market conditions, the cultivation of vines proved on the whole remunerative, despite occasional setbacks.

All kinds of cereals were grown in these regions; but agricultural technique was somewhat rudimentary, and farmers clung to the customary two-year rotation of crops. Maize began to appear only late in the seventeenth century; besides bringing a new crop into the cycle, it also indirectly encouraged livestock-rearing. This had developed considerably in the Landes and Périgord as a result of export of animals to Spain, but it suffered a serious setback at the turn of the seventeenth-eighteenth century through the wars of 1688–97 and 1702–13 which then ravaged South-western France. War operations, including the Anglo-Dutch naval blockade and requisitioning of food for the French army, together with a number of bad harvest years between 1690 and 1720, caused cereal prices to rise sharply, and this induced many farmers to reduce their pastureland in order to increase cereal production, thus causing a further setback to animal husbandry. During this period adverse conditions brought about a reduction in the hitherto considerable exports of chestnuts, walnuts, plums, linseed, turpentine, resin and timber; but cultivation of tobacco and hemp increased. This region also produced a particularly remunerative industrial crop, pastel or woad, a dyestuff in wide demand on international markets which represented a considerable source of income for Toulouse merchants up to the middle of the seventeenth century.

Beyond the Pyrenees, in the western regions of the *Iberian peninsula*, more closely associated than South-western France with the Mediterranean, the rural world was not entirely static. During the centuries under review the agrarian scene underwent some changes, though not in the direction of modernisation. On the contrary, the landed-property régime if anything accentuated its traditional characteristics during the period of Spanish and Portuguese economic decadence. It was in the sphere of agriculture itself that changes arose.

The main forms of cultivation were cereals, mainly wheat and rye, of poor quality and easily subject to the vagaries of the weather, together with olives and vine-growing. Olives and vines had been cultivated there for centuries; much of the produce was exported to northern countries of Europe and represented a rich source of income for the farmers. In the adverse social and economic conditions of the seventeenth century, however, cereal cultivation proved disappointing, and was made more so by a succession of bad harvests. Partial compensation was provided by maize, introduced here at the end of the sixteenth century and thus earlier than in other European countries, which became firmly established particularly in Central and Northern Portugal and in Galicia. This new cereal, imported from America, soon became widely grown and thus brought a fresh element into the hitherto traditional three-course rotation. Lands left fallow were reduced and almost disappeared by the end of the seventeenth century, being replaced by arable land ploughed to the new crop. But the advent of maize did not solve the fundamental problems of this difficult farming area. Its introduction into the normal rotation further impoverished the soil, and its harvests did not make up for the loss of the more valuable crops it replaced.

Mediterranean Europe. The lands adjacent to the northern

shores of the Mediterranean, like an immense amphi-
theatre into which the Italian peninsula projects, present
great differences in types of farming and cultivation, due
both to the structure of the soil and to the considerable
diversity of climate and geography between the higher,
more northerly regions and the flatter regions in the south.
In no other agricultural area in Europe, indeed, do we find
so great a variety of produce or such great differences
between one country district and another only a few miles
away. This composite rural world, which can nevertheless
be grouped together under the single denominator of
'Mediterranean', developed in various different ways in the
course of this period some places showing signs of vigorous
agricultural revival, while others reverted to systems already
thought to be outworn. For this reason considerable and
unexpected changes are to be found in the agricultural
scene.

The agrarian economy of the Mediterranean mountain
areas, however, between the sixteenth and eighteenth centuries showed no particular tendency to alter a way of life
that was essentially based on forestry and extensive natural
pastures. In the higher regions of the Alps, the Apennines,
the Pyrenees and the Sierras the main activity of the population was pastoral, rearing cattle and sheep. But possibilities of gaining a livelihood were limited, and as a result
of population increase many of the inhabitants found themselves forced to leave their native places and seek their
fortunes in the valleys. This emigration corresponds to the
dynamic character of a mountain population and economy.
The same characteristic can be seen in the regular seasonal
migration of flocks and herds from the hillsides to the plain.
A pendular movement, this change of grazing (transhumance) which was so much a part of the agricultural
scene that it dictated the rhythm of economic and social
life and in the places where it occurred on a large scale
became regulated on definite lines. This did not, however,
entirely succeed in smoothing out the inevitable differences
between the stable farmers and the nomadic herdsmen, for
the farmers worried about vagrant animals while the herds-

men were constantly seeking wider areas on which to exercise the right to pasture their flocks. This happened, for example, in the transhumance between the Italian Alps, especially the Upper Adige area, and the central-eastern plains of the Po valley. It happened, to give a better-known and more striking example, with the migrations between the Castilian plateaux and the green plains of Andalusia: along the two famous routes, the 'Leonesa' and the 'Segoviana', between two and three million sheep belonging to the powerful Mesta sheep-breeding organisation travelled each year in this colossal transhumance.

In speaking of the Castilian plateaux we have already descended from the lofty mountain regions to the still quite high tablelands which, separated from the sea by mountain ranges, are characterised by a continental type of climate moderated by the altitude. This area presents agrarian characteristics of its own, differing both from the mountains and from the hillsides and plains. These tablelands of New and Old Castile indeed afford an example almost unique in the Mediterranean region, and in any case the only one of significance from the agricultural point of view, of a countryside which combined at the same time both extensive corn-growing and equally vast areas left practically wild and used for grazing. Here the *Mesta*, the sheep-breeders' combine, pastured their vast flocks, deriving huge profits from it at least as long as they enjoyed the King's protection. That situation came to an end, however, in 1550–60, when in the face of increasing pressure from farmers anxious to profit by the rising price of cereals, which had gone up considerably since the import of precious metal from America started in 1535, pasturelands were encroached upon and transformed into ploughland. Thus up to the middle of the seventeenth century animal farming declined (falling from a maximum of three million sheep in 1516–20 to two million in 1556) while arable farming increased. The Castilian plateaux, traversed by viable roads and dotted about with villages, intensified their character of a privileged European corn-producing area. But they did not escape the unhappy fate that overtook Spain's economy in the seventeenth to eighteenth centuries. With the fall in cereal prices much of the arable area was reduced and reverted to pasture. Sedentary and unregulated sheep-grazing, extremely harmful to arable farming, was resumed, but it failed to bring the country the same profits as in the past. Cultivation of maize was introduced with some success, though results here were not so good as in the Atlantic regions of the Iberian peninsula. But it served to vary the crop rotation, which still adhered to the three-course system.

The hillsides and foothills of the Mediterranean countries enjoyed a particularly fortunate climate. During the six-teenth and early seventeenth centuries these regions with their varied types of farming presented on the whole a flourishing picture. From the farm-plots (*starze*) of Calabria, the Tuscan hillside criss-crossed by fields, the Euganean hills cultivated across the slopes (whereas the usual method in Central Italy was to follow the line of the contours), the coastal lands with their typical methods of cultivation by terracing or curved gradations as in Sicily, the Amalfi coast, Liguria, around Lucca, on the hillsides above Lake Garda, and round Mantua, to the 'garrigue' of Mediter-ranean France in Lower Provence and Languedoc and the indented coasts of Valence and Catalonia, the garden of the Mediterranean seemed to be well-cared-for and profit-ably conducted. Against a background of typical Mediter-ranean vegetation (the *macchia*) from the Iberian peninsula to the Peloponnese, along the hillside slopes with a good exposure grew vines, olives, mulberries and almond-trees, and increasing areas took to fruit-growing (peaches, pears, cherries, etc.). Where temperatures were higher, in the south of the peninsulas and the islands, citrus fruits were widely grown, experiments were made in cotton-growing and attempts were made to extend the area under sugar-cane. But the hillsides were being increasingly ploughed (as, farther north, in the Veneto), and cereal cultivation occupied the most important place in the rural economy, with wheat as the chief crop, in combination and alter-nation with poorer quality corn, rye, barley, spelt, vetch,

Italian millet, millet, and so on. In some areas such as the Abruzzi saffron was grown, and the higher slopes of the hillsides produced chestnuts. Towards the middle of the seventeenth century, however, dark clouds appeared on the agrarian scene. The worsening of the economic situation, the recrudescence of feudal pretensions in certain regions such as Southern Italy and some parts of Mediterranean France, the shortcomings of the public administration, for example, in the Papal States, all contributed to alter conditions; there was a return to antiquated methods of cultivation (e.g. the 'fields-and-grass' method in Central-southern Italy), causing a gradual reduction in the arable area and an expansion of uncultivated land left for pasture or afforestation. Thus even on the hillsides there was a relapse towards combining forestry and agriculture; sheep-rearing was revived even in the wooded areas, and the transhumance of flocks increased.

This decline was particularly noticeable in Central-southern Italy, but it was also to be found elsewhere in the plains, where during the sixteenth century undoubted advances had been made in agriculture. In the Roman Campagna, especially the Pontine marshes, in the lower Rhône valley, in the Durazzo plain and in much of the Apulian Tavoliere, desolate, unhealthy and marshy areas developed, infested with malaria and subject to floods which washed away the poor soil. In such regions the wretched population concentrated in small scattered localities where they tried to make a living by keeping a few animals and growing whatever they could. However, during the sixteenth and early seventeenth centuries some land reclamation works were resumed which had already been started earlier on. Agriculture benefited temporarily therefrom, especially in the lower Rhône valley, but the improvement did not last. In the second half of the seventeenth century and the early 1700s conditions in these low-lying regions grew steadily worse, cancelling out previous progress. Much of the redeemed land reverted to its earlier abandoned state, desolation spread and by the beginning of the eighteenth century dominated the landscape.

Attempts at reclamation had also in some cases produced disappointing results, as in the Adige valley, where the marshes drained at the end of the sixteenth century under the Venetian Republic proved unsuited to cultivation and became choked with reeds.

Even those areas which natural conditions or human endeavour had made suitable for productive farming suffered after the flourishing period of the sixteenth and early seventeenth centuries. The plain of Languedoc, for example, up to the middle of the seventeenth century had made considerable advances, combining traditional crops with the new plants, maize and beans, imported from America; but after 1660 it fell into decline. In Narbonne district and the Comtat deterioration in the economy compromised the hopeful results obtained in the preceding decades from the cultivation of lucerne. Beyond the Pyrenees, in the little plains of Catalonia and Valencia and the fertile lowlands of Andalusia and Southern Estremadura which enjoyed a combination of Atlantic and Mediterranean climates, mixed farming, a source of considerable profits from exports, encountered a serious setback, especially in cereal cultivation, from the beginning of the seventeenth century, when the peasants felt the pinch even more after the expulsion of the Moriscoes. Only the vine and the olive continued, on the whole, to be grown profitably. New species of plants brought back from the colonies did not suffice to improve the system of cultivation, which in general was based on a three-course rotation with two years of fallow. The Po valley, which had profited from the innovations introduced, especially in Lombardy, on the principle of balancing fodder and other crops, aroused the admiration of Montaigne in the sixteenth century and, later on, of Arthur Young in the eighteenth; but after 1620 it too suffered a decline which in certain regions, notably round Cremona and in parts of Emilia, came near to destroying its agricultural economy. But despite the serious difficulties created by the economic crisis and the decline in population, the Po countryside, and especially lower Lombardy, succeeded to a great extent in preserving the progress it had achieved. True, Emilia stuck firmly to an economy based on 'pane e vino' (bread and wine), as preached by the shrewd but traditional-minded Bolognese agronomist Tanara. But north of the Po farming techniques tended increasingly to embrace livestock-rearing as well: the capitalist basis of the exploitation of the land was not, on the whole, undermined. But for the time being little notice was taken of the ambitious plans advanced by the Brescian agronomist Tarello; people preferred to follow the more elementary advice of another Brescian, Gallo, well known in the same field.

PRODUCTIVITY IN AGRICULTURE:

CROP YIELDS AND ECONOMIC RESULTS

The numerous studies of small agricultural units — private farms or farms belonging to princes, rulers or the Church — which have been undertaken in recent times have made possible the accumulation of considerable data about agricultural yields. But we still have little information about the economic results of farming in general.

The ideal thing would be to be able to compare yields for equivalent areas, the hectare, the acre, etc. Unfortunately, it has seldom been possible to estimate yields in this way, given the difficulties nearly always encountered in establishing the exact extent of arable farms and according a precise significance to the measures of area, weight and capacity in use locally. Consequently, the only way of ascertaining variations in agricultural productivity has been to compare the relationship between the amount of seed sown and the quantity harvested. Such a comparison provides a measure of the soil's generative capacity and of the influence exercised on that capacity by innovations introduced into agricultural techniques, such as fertilisation, new crop rotation, the use of new types of farm implements, and so on.

Fortunately a few years ago, thanks to Professor Slicher van Bath, surveys were drawn up showing the seed/yield ratios of the various crops in each country from the Middle Ages onwards. In this valuable work we find condensed the 'average' yields, whose significance is bound to be dubious since they relate to farms differing widely in size, ownership and type of management. Nevertheless, these averages help us to build up points of reference in time and space; in other words they help us, if used with caution, to arrive at an interpretation of the facts. The compiler of the surveys has rightly pointed out that the rate of yields enables us to make a more reasonable estimate of the food-producing possibilities and the general conditions in which farms were conducted. An increase in the ratio between sowing and harvest (for example: if seed sown = 1, an increase of from 4 to 5 in the amount harvested) signifies, after setting aside the seed for the coming year, a larger stock of corn or rye for food consumption. Other things being equal, a greater area can be reserved for the production of human and animal foodstuffs. *Vice versa*, a reduction in the yield ratio inevitably means that the area growing foodstuffs must be reduced, since a larger portion of the total area must be reserved to produce seed for the coming year. To try to get over the fall in yields by enlarging the area under cultivation would raise a number of problems. More draught animals would have to be used because of the greater area to be ploughed and manured; the ratio of arable to pastureland (meadows, hayfields and wasteland) would have to be changed; and that would mean a change in the whole way of running the farm, both in the scheme of crop rotation and in livestock-rearing. Changes in yield ratios are, in fact, indices which demonstrate the favourable or adverse effects of both immediate and more long-term influences — the general fall in agricultural yields in the seventeenth century can be accounted for in a number of ways, from the exhaustion of the soil to a series of bad weather years, the *latifundia* system and the consequent tightening of bondage, war conditions and climatic variations. But these changes in yield ratios also serve to remind us of the farmers' constant struggle to adapt his methods to his production and of the anxieties of a rural population fearful of the slightest fluctuation in yield because the productivity of farming still remained at so low a level. A fall in yield which to our eyes might seem insignificant might spell catastrophe, while a modest-seeming increase could seem an immense boon.

What, then, were the rates of yield of the main crops grown in the various countries of Europe during our period? On the basis of the geographical areas described earlier, data covering yield ratios in each of those areas have been summarised in four tables, from which it should be possible to get a clear picture of developments in agricultural productivity in respect of cereal cultivation.

In *Northern Europe*, as will be seen from Table 1*, against the background of a general trend applying to every type of cereal cultivation, certain significant differences can be observed.

For *rye*, yields similar to those for *wheat* were recorded in Sweden, and yields more than 10 per cent higher than those for wheat (in extreme cases as much as 100 per cent higher) in continental Europe. The tendency to fall was more marked: even in the early 1700s yields of rye fell below those of wheat by as much as 15–20 per cent. The ratios for *barley*, which were lower in Sweden and Norway than in Germany, in the sixteenth century were roughly similar to those for rye, but in the next century they fell considerably, recovering sharply in the eighteenth century, when they were only 10 per cent below those for wheat.

As to crops not included in the table, it should be mentioned that *buckwheat* achieved yields approaching those of wheat in the sixteenth–seventeenth centuries; towards the middle of the eighteenth century the ratios rose considerably, averaging around 10 in France and 9 in Germany. The few available data for *mixed corn* suggest that its yields pursued a course similar to that of the other cereal crops.

Beans and *peas* seem to have produced higher yields in France than in Germany, but the data are insufficient to enable us to say definitely. Yields of *hemp* and *flax* are equally difficult to estimate.

* For Tables 1 to 5 see Appendix pp. 595–622.

Taking into account the yields obtained in the central-southern states of Germany and in Switzerland, which on the whole resemble those just given for Northern Europe, overall average data (or figures) have been calculated for the Scandinavian countries and Central Europe which give some idea of the difficulties that farmers were still encountering in the first half of the eighteenth century following the serious crisis of the century before. In respect of the four main cereals grown, yield ratios between the first half of the sixteenth century and the first half of the eighteenth show the following falls:

Crops	1500–1549	1700–1749	Percentage fall
wheat	4·6	4·3	− 8
rye	5·0	3·7	−32
barley	5·1	4·0	−27
oats	4·0	3·2	−27

The percentage fall is calculated on the ratios allowing for a deduction of one unit (i.e. the seed sown each year): it thus indicates the reduction in the amount of cereals available for consumption. The trend of wheat yields, as can be seen, differs markedly from that of the other less important cereals. The fact that productivity of wheat fell less sharply (or rather recovered more quickly after the decline of the seventeenth century) suggests that this most important cereal was especially favoured as regards both production and consumption as agricultural techniques improved.

As can be seen from Table 2, yield ratios in *Eastern Europe* do not differ appreciably from those found in the areas of average productivity in Northern Europe, as far as Poland and the Danubian countries are concerned. In Russia and the Balkans, however, yields are very low. Data for Poland are particularly abundant, thanks to the valuable work done by Polish scholars.

It should be noted that yields for *rye*, somewhat lower than those for *wheat* (in the sixteenth century on an average 15 per cent below), fell only slightly during the long period of agricultural depression, and in the first half of the eighteenth century reached the same levels as those for wheat. The trend for *barley's* ratios was similar to that for wheat, but with yields about 10 per cent higher. Yields of *oats* were originally midway between those for rye and for wheat, but in the seventeenth century they fell to the lowest figures shown for any cereals in Europe.

Yields of *buckwheat*, which was quite widely grown in Eastern Europe in the sixteenth and seventeenth centuries and then almost disappeared, varied considerably according to the area, averaging around 3–5 throughout the period. At the same levels were the yields for *peas*, which were widely grown in Poland in the sixteenth and seventeenth centuries and also in Russia in the eighteenth, though there the ratios were lower. Yields of *vetch* were small, except for an occasional good year, falling to little over 2 in the seventeenth–eighteenth centuries. *Millet* yields are known only for Poland; they varied greatly both in area and in time, but were much higher than those for wheat (from one-and-a-half to four or more times as much).

The yields of *hemp* and *flax* in Poland and Russia in the sixteenth century followed the same trend of those for wheat, being, of course, higher in Poland. The average changed very little throughout the whole period under review.

For the first half of the sixteenth and of the eighteenth centuries overall average yield ratios for all the Eastern European countries show the following falls in respect of the four main cereals:

Crops	1500–1549	1700–1749	Percentage fall[a]
wheat	4·7	3·6	−30
rye	3·9	3·6	−10
barley	5·2	3·9	−31
oats	4·1	2·4	−55

[a] One unit of the ratio deducted for seed.

Comparing these figures with those given earlier in respect of the Scandinavian countries and Central Europe, we find that the respective falls in yields of wheat and rye are practically reversed here, while the fall in the ratios for oats is twice as large in the Eastern European countries.

These facts bear witness to the very serious decline in agriculture and farming in Eastern Europe: the big drop in oats yields suggests that in the face of increasing difficulties cultivation of a cereal basically intended for horse fodder was neglected in view of the reduced number of horses. The fall in cereal prices led to less growing of wheat, the grain most generally exported when market prices were high. Some attempt was made to check the fall in yield of rye, the cereal which probably represented the basis of the low-level consumption of the rural population.

In *Atlantic Europe* a distinction must be made between the yields in the agriculturally advanced countries (the Low Countries and, further behind, England) and the less far advanced (in effect Atlantic France, since precise information is lacking in respect of Atlantic Spain and Portugal). Unfortunately, as will be seen from Table 3, the data concerning these regions are somewhat meagre. It is to be hoped that in the future further and more complete series of yield ratios may become available from which it will be easier to evaluate the trend of agricultural productivity.

A superficial glance at Table 3 will suffice to demonstrate the high yield of cereal crops, especially in the Low Countries. The yield ratios appear on an average far superior to those found in other regions of Europe even in the seventeenth century when a regression in agricultural productivity was taking place in those usually favoured areas.

Further proof of the high productivity of agriculture in Holland and, to a lesser extent, in Britain can also be seen from the data concerning *beans* and *peas*. At Hitsum in Friesland the average ratio for beans was 6·6 and those for peas were 12·1 (maple peas) and 15 (blue peas); two centuries later the average figure in Friesland for both beans and peas was 10. As to Great Britain, the yield of beans was around 4 (Gloucestershire) and that of peas was around 6 (Cuxam in Oxfordshire) in the sixteenth century, but the peas yield rose to 7 and more in the seventeenth century (Gloucestershire and Berkshire) to approach 12 (and beans 10) in many districts by the mid-1700s.

Unfortunately no data are yet available about the yield ratio of English industrial crops (coleseed, linseed, etc.). In 1765 the yield ratio of *coleseed* in Friesland reached 160. Comment seems superfluous here.

Cereal yields in England, though in general a good deal higher than those recorded in continental Europe, are distinctly below those of the Flemish territories where, too, yields of pulses were higher. However, the decline in cereal yields was less marked than elsewhere between the sixteenth and eighteenth centuries. This phenomenon is to be accounted for by the progressive trend away from mainly arable farming to a type of farming in which livestock predominated. In the other European regions the decline in agricultural productivity represented not only a loss in itself but a symptom of a long and exhausting crisis; whereas in Holland and England it was not so much a manifestation of agricultural depression but rather the consequence of 'growing pains'. England's agricultural system possessed a sounder basis, and when market conditions proved favourable in the second half of the eighteenth century it was able to resume that expansion of arable farming which was shortly to secure very high returns.

Taking together the ratios for Holland and England, overall average yields of the four main cereal crops appear to have fallen between the first half of the sixteenth century and the first half of the eighteenth as follows:

Crops	1500–1549	1700–1749	Percentage fall[a]
wheat	8·7	7·0	− 22
rye	8·1	7·2	− 13
barley	6·4	5·3	− 20
oats	4·4	2·9	− 44

[a] One unit of the ratio deducted for seed.

The larger fall in the oats yield is significant: the transition to animal farming inevitably meant a reduction in the number of horses, a smaller demand for oats and, consequently, a progressive reduction in the cultivation of that cereal, which was replaced by fodder-crops in the rotation cycle (compare the rotations carried out under the Norfolk system with those practised in earlier types of convertible husbandry described earlier).

For the areas of France that fall within the confines of Atlantic Europe unfortunately few data are available, and such as there are concern mainly the eighteenth century. It is therefore not easy to obtain a precise idea of agricultural productivity there, and it can only be hoped that researches in this particular field may be intensified, as also in the fields of Atlantic Spain and Portugal.

In the light of the meagre data available it seems reasonable to infer that yields of the main crops lie more or less half-way between those averaged in Holland and England and those of Nordic Europe. In particular, for wheat the yield would seem to correspond to the overall ratios calculated synthetically for France as a whole. They were 6·8 for the first half of the sixteenth and 5·8 for the first half of the eighteenth century, denoting a fall (with the deduction of one unit for seed) of 17 per cent. This percentage fall compared with that for Holland and England (22 per cent) and with that for Scandinavia and Central Europe (8 per cent) confirms France's midway situation in respect of agricultural productivity.

Lastly we come to yields in the *Mediterranean* countries, data for which are given in Table 4.*

As will be seen, information about Spain is practically nil, amounting at present, so far as we are aware, to only a single item. Information about yields in Mediterranean France is also far from adequate, in spite of some recent studies of importance for rural history. Italy is the Mediterranean country about which we have the most rich documentation on agricultural productivity; and it is curious that in the overall surveys referred to above the yield ratios for Italian crops are barely mentioned.

The figures given in Table 4 clearly demonstrate the serious recession in agricultural productivity which occurred also in the areas of the Mediterranean basin during the seventeenth century. Are the high levels of productivity

* For Table 4 see Appendix pp. 616–19

achieved for minor cereals (rye, barley and oats) during the first half of the eighteenth century to be regarded as proof that the crisis had been overcome? If, in fact, we apply here the same comparison as was made in respect of other regions of Europe, between average ratios for the principal cereal crops in the first half of the sixteenth century and the first half of the eighteenth, we find that while, as elsewhere, there is a fall in the yield of wheat, there is instead an increase in the ratios for rye, barley and oats. The figures are as follows:

Crops	1500–1549	1700–1749	Percentage variations[a]
wheat	5·4	4·3	−25
rye	4·5	7·1	+74
barley	5·1	7·0	+46
oats	5·5	7·1	+36

[a] One unit of the ratio deducted for seed.

Even if these values are regarded as merely approximate (the analytical data are meagre and refer mainly to Italy), the considerable increase in yield of the minor cereal crops is nevertheless fully established. One cannot but think that the long and exhausting crisis must have caused farmers to concentrate more on cereal crops which, because of their lower cost, could more readily satisfy the nutritional needs of a population which had seen its purchasing power reduced. But another reason for the greater attention given, especially in Italy, to cultivation of the lesser cereals may well lie in the changed methods of utilising the soil and, in particular, in new and more complex crop rotations.

It should also be emphasised that, side by side with the traditional cereals, cultivation of rice gained ground in North Italy between the sixteenth and eighteenth centuries. This new cereal, the 'corn of the marshes', gradually inserted itself into the crop cycle, thus contributing towards the development of agronomical techniques. Yields for rice continued to increase as a result of the constant improvement in methods of cultivation: the rice yield was about

seven to nine times the seed sown in the sixteenth century and as much as fifteen to eighteen in the eighteenth.

The fall of yield ratios for the principal cereals between
the sixteenth and eighteenth centuries is a remarkable
phenomenon. Explanations — not always convincing —
have been put forward: changes in climatic conditions;
changing methods of cultivation (e.g. the higher economic
yield obtained by fodder-cultivation may have led to the
withdrawal of human capital, investments and fertilisers
from land intended for cereal-growing); the use of less fertile
land in highly populated areas (thus reducing yield ratio
averages); changes in rural population resulting in a
decrease in working capacity; the restoration of feudal
structures. Further research is needed if there is to be an
answer to this important question.

In respect of Italy it has been possible to collect a good
deal of data about production per area unit, i.e. per one
hectare of cultivated land. These unit yields are summarised
in the following table:

Production of cereals per one hectare (quintals)		
Como region	4·0–4·5	(16th century); 6·0 (2nd half 16th century)
Portalbera (Lombardy)	3·4	(*c.* 1550); 9·0 (*c.* 1650)
Upper Milanese	4·5	(1579–88)
Corbetta (west of Milan)	4·5	(1577–96); 5·5 (1600–03); 5·7 (1606–08)
Adda plain (east of Milan)	3·8	(1600–04); 3·9 (1605–29); 3·5 (1634–47)
Gonzagas farms (Mantua)	3·5	(average 1578–87: min. 2·0 and max. 5·0)
Montaldeo (Piedmont)	2·1	(2nd half 16th century); 3·2 (2nd half 17th century); 3·7 (beginning of 18th century)

Rice in general gave higher yields from the sixteenth to the
eighteenth century. The unit yields shown above in any
case demonstrate that the productivity of the soil was still
low: in the same areas today the yield for rice per hectare
in normal years is between 25 and 35 quintals.

Although quite considerable documentation on the subject exists, no attempt will be made here to give figures for productivity of Italian vineyards; the data available refer to vines that differ too greatly in quality, age and variety and also refer to widely different types of land and cultivation (specialised or carried out promiscuously in combination with cereal-growing), so that no correct estimate can be formed.

Calculation of yields becomes even more difficult when we move on from arable to animal husbandry. The afore-mentioned recent surveys provide only meagre data, which are given in Table 5* with some additions.

An obvious feature is the considerable difference in weight of the animals in the different regions: the agri-culturally more advanced countries produce animals that are heavier and therefore economically more profitable. As compared with the present day, however, the weight per head of livestock seems low, especially in the case of cattle: for instance, in the hilly region of Piedmont referred to in the table, the normal weight of an ox or cow today would be over two or three times the weight registered three cen-turies ago.

The sharp difference, from the agricultural point of view, between well-developed and under-developed areas is further confirmed by the daily yield of milk per cow. While the daily yield of milk per cow barely reached an average of 2 litres, yields could amount to six times that figure in

Daily milk yield per cow (litres)

Place or country	Year	Average	Maximum
Hitsum, Friesland	1571–73	4·5–5·0	
Lombardy, Italy	end of 16th century	7·0–9·0	12·0–13·0
Harwell, England	1618	4·0	5·0
Schleswig-Holstein, Germany	1740	3·0	6·0
Lombardy, Italy	c. 1750	9·0–12·0	15·0–18·0
Friesland	1760		15·0–20·0

* For Table 5 see Appendix pp. 620–22.

regions particularly specialised in rearing milk-producing cattle, as the above figures show.

Butter and cheese production also varied considerably from one agricultural region to another, but in general yields seem to have increased between the sixteenth and the eighteenth centuries. However, the data given in the afore-mentioned overall surveys leave room for doubt, since the quality of the products varies according to the different areas and periods reviewed. In any case, all these data go to show that, but for a few exceptional cases, yields of animal husbandry between the sixteenth and the eighteenth centuries were considerably lower than those of today.

Lastly, we give some data concerning the economic results achieved on particular farm properties. Unfortunately these are too few to enable us to work out an overall trend of agricultural economy during our period. But they are nevertheless of interest. It is to be hoped that they will induce scholars to carry out further research and secure more information of a similar kind.

Let us first consider the results of management of farm properties as shown in their income and expenditure balance-sheets.

Between 1569 and 1573 the Hemmema farm property at Hitsum (Friesland) realised on an average consistent annual profits, despite a loss in 1572 due to war conditions. Taking 100 as the average annual income, annual expenditure was 72·4, thus producing a surplus of 27·6.

An even higher average annual surplus was obtained by the Loders at their farm at Harwell (England) in 1612–20, a period not disturbed by unfavourable events. Taking 100 as the average annual income, average expenditure was 36·6, giving a surplus of 63·4.

Results were lower, though still fairly good, on a Belgian farm in Klundert (N. Brabant) in 1750. Here, taking income as 100, expenditure was 83·5, giving a surplus of 16·5.

The longest series of data of this kind, so far as we know, concerns the estate of Ambrogio D'Adda, a Milanese nobleman, owner of a large property in the Lombard plain along the River Adda. The data are given in the following table, taking as equal to 100, for each eight-year period, the total annual income, and also indicating, for each period, the percentage of profits secured between 1600 and 1647.

Farm property of Ambrogio D'Adda (Lombardy)

Years	Income	Expenditure	Surplus or deficit	% of profits 1600–47
1600–07	100	44·4	+55·6	35·9
1608–15	100	53·0	+47·0	31·8
1616–23	100	57·2	+42·8	28·6
1624–31	100	89·2	+10·8	6·4
1632–39	100	95·1	+ 4·9	2·3
1640–47	100	111·6	−11·6	−5·1 (loss)
1600–47	*100*	*71·5*	*+29·5*	*100·0*

These balance-sheets of the D'Adda property and the percentage of profits there over the six eight-year periods bear clear witness to the decline which after 1624, and more especially after 1632, gradually affected the flourishing and well-equipped Lombard countryside. Its causes were various: the economic depression permeating the whole Italian peninsula, the rapid increase in land taxation and a series of disasters including wars, passage of troops through the country, epidemics and adverse climatic conditions.

This decline is also demonstrated by another index figure relating to the profitability of an estate: the net remuneration on invested capital. This remuneration, in the case of the D'Adda farm property, averaged around 1·5 per cent during the years 1600–47: in the first twenty years it fluctuated around 3 per cent (with maxima of around 4 per cent between 1604 and 1610), but after 1624, when the property showed an adverse balance, it barely reached 1 per cent.

A considerably higher return on capital was achieved by another Lombard property, situated in the western plain towards the River Ticino (an irrigated and particularly fertile area), which belonged to a Milanese, Gottardo Frisiani. There the percentage return was 3·8 in 1580, 4·5 in 1590, 6·5 in 1600 and around 8·5 in 1608. The high profits secured by Frisiani were also made possible by the considerable rise in prices at the time.

Moving from Lombardy to nearby Piedmont, we encounter the longest series of data concerning net profits, calculated as percentage of the capital invested in a farm property. The property in question is that of the Dorias at Montaldeo, a hilly place situated in an area considerably less fertile than the Lombard plain. Profits between 1572 and 1751 were as follows:

1572–80	5·3	1658–63	3·2	1700–04	4·1
1588	6·8	1664–68	3·8	1707–08	4·2
1595–98	6·4	1672	6·0	1722–26	3·5
1599–1602	6·9	1675–82	4·7	1735–39	2·7
1611	6·7	1683–86	5·6	1742–44	2·7
1632	8·0	1687–90	6·2	1747–51	3·1
1642–50	3·5				

It will be noted that in the sixty years up to 1630 — the period of rising prices which came to an end with the plague — profits were well above 5 per cent, reaching as much as 8 per cent in some years. The effects of the plague and various other disturbances then reduced the incomes until a little after the middle of the seventeenth century. Profits increased in the second half of that century, when the Dorias resumed direct control of the estate, introduced stiff contracts for farm tenancy and skilfully exploited the favourable market conditions (in the last decade of the century prices for corn and wine rose considerably). But in the first fifty years of the eighteenth century, owing to difficulties in exporting grain from Genoa, falling prices, lower production of wine and fruit, and revision of farm contracts, profits fell again, returning only at the end of the century to satisfactory levels.

These few examples should suffice to show how a study of the balance-sheets of some farm properties can be of great use in helping us towards a better understanding of the evolution of European agrarian economy in the modern era.

Bibliography

If this bibliography were to include all the studies that have been published, especially in the last few years, on the subject of European agrarian history in the sixteenth to eighteenth centuries, the result would be a very long list indeed, numbering some hundreds of titles. The main works must nevertheless be mentioned, and these also provide full and up-to-date bibliographical information for anyone wishing to pursue his studies further. For obvious reasons this bibliography has had to be confined to works in Western languages; this is a serious limitation, for historiographical production in the Slav, or at any rate Eastern European, countries, has been both abundant and of great value, especially in recent years. This defect can, however, be remedied by recourse to the very full bibliographies given in the works mentioned here.

For anyone embarking on a study of European agriculture during our period, a useful first approach is the short article of B. H. Slicher van Bath, 'Survey on the activities in agricultural history in various countries', *Agrártörténeti Szemle* (*Historia rerum rusticarum*), published by the Magyar Tudományos Akadémia Könyvtára in Budapest, IX, 1967 (Supplementum). For more recent historiography a valuable bibliographical source comes from another Hungarian cultural institute: the *Bibliographia Rerum Rusticarum Internationalis*, edited by P. Gunst and published by the Museum Rerum Rusticarum Hungariae Budapestini (Vol. I, 1964, to Vol. V, 1969, covering works published in the various countries between 1960 and 1966). Another important source is the *Zeitschrift für Agrargeschichte und Agrarsoziologie*, published from 1953 onwards.

Among general works, both descriptive and dealing with fundamental problems, old works that still remain useful are: R. H. Tawney, *The Agrarian Problem in the Sixteenth Century*,

London, 1912; N. S. B. Gras, *A history of agriculture in Europe and America*, 2nd ed., New York, 1940; and in particular W. Abel, *Agrarkrisen und Agrarkonjunktur in Mitteleuropa vom. 13. bis zum 19. Jahrhundert*, Berlin, 1935. In addition to these, of oustanding importance, also for their extensive bibliographies, are the essays of J. Meuvret, B. H. Slicher van Bath and W. G. Hoskins, 'L'agriculture en Europe aux XVIIe et XVIII° siècles', in *Relazioni del Congresso Internazionale di Scienze Storiche*, Rome, 1965, Vol. IV (Meuvret deals with general aspects, Slicher van Bath with 'Agriculture in the Low Countries, *c.* 1600–1800', and Hoskins with 'English Agriculture in the 17th and 18th Centuries'), and the fundamental work of B. H. Slicher van Bath, *The Agrarian History of Western Europe, A.D. 500–1850*, trans. from the Dutch by O. Ordish, London, 1963; unfortunately no work of similar significance has hitherto appeared on the agrarian history of Eastern Europe. On the influence of meteorological and economic cycles on agricultural activity during our period, works to be consulted are M. Deveze, 'Climat et récoltes aux 17e et 18e siècles', *Annales. Economies, sociétés, civilisations*, 15, 1960, and J. Sirol, *Le rôle de l'agriculture dans les fluctuations économiques*, Paris, 1942 (the emphasis on France in no way detracts from the general interest of the problems dealt with). Following the appearance of the first volume of records of the Third International Congress of Economic History, held in Munich in 1965, publication of further volumes is still awaited and we therefore cannot give a precise citation for the important Report presented there by B. H. Slicher van Bath on questions relating to agricultural history in the pre-industrial period. An Italian translation of this report has, however, been published: 'Problemi di storia dell'agricoltura in Europa nell'età preindustriale,' *Quaderni storici delle Marche*, no. III, 1966. See also the important collection of studies by several authors on Agricoltura e sviluppo del capitalismo, *Studi Storici* 3/4, 1968.

Bibliographical indications on demographic evolution and related problems will be found in another section of the present volume.

For the Eastern European countries the only recent general work on rural history concerns Russia: J. Blum, *Lord and Peasant in Russia from the ninth to the nineteenth century*, Princeton, N.J., 1961; the extensive bibliography contained therein renders it superfluous to cite other works on agricultural evolution in Russia. For the other countries, recourse must be had to a vast number of works, mostly in local languages. The few publications mentioned here, besides dealing with essential aspects of agricultural history in these countries, also contain valuable bibliographies: J. Ochmanski, 'La grande réforme agraire en Lithuanie et en Ruthénie Blanche au XVIe siècle', *Ergon*, II, 1960; J. Topolski, 'La régression économique en Pologne du XVIe au XVIIIe siècle', *Acta Poloniae Historica*, VII, 1962; A. Wyczanski, 'Le niveau de la récolte des céréales en Pologne du XVIe au XVIIIe siècle', *Contributions – Communications* de la Ière Conférence Internationale d'Histoire Economique Stockholm, 1960, Paris, 1960; *idem*, 'En Pologne: l'économie du domaine nobiliaire moyen (1500–1800)', *Annales E.S.C.*, 18, 1963; J. Valka, 'La structure économique de la seigneurie tchèque au XVIe siècle', *Actes* de la IIe Conférence d'Histoire Economique, Aix-en-Provence, 1962, Vol. II, 1965; Z. P. Pach, 'Ueber einige Probleme der Gutwirtschaft in Ungarn in der ersten Hälfte des 17. Jahrhunderts', *Ibidem*, Vol. II; T. Stoianovich, *L'économie balkanique aux XVIIe et XVIIIe siècles*, Paris 1961; F. Maksay, 'Ungarns Landwirtschaft zür Zeit der Türkenherrschaft', *Agrartröteneti Szemle Historia rerum rusticarum*, Budapest, IX, 1967 (Supplementum).

For German-speaking countries an extensive literature exists on the evolution of the rural world; we can only mention here the most recent works and those of a general character with good bibliographies. Besides the work by W. Abel, already cited, other volumes by this author are *Geschichte der deutschen Landwirtschaft vom frühen Mittelalter bis zum 19. Jahrhundert*, Berlin, 1962, and *Die drei Epochen der deutschen Agrageschichte*, 2nd ed., Hanover, 1963; also F. H. Riemann, *Ackerbau und Viehhaltung im vorindustriellen Deutschland*, 1953; R. Krzymowski, *Geschichte der deutschen*

Landwirtschaft, 2nd ed., Stuttgart, 1951; S. Frauendorfer von, *Ideengeschichte der Agrarwirtschaft und Agrarpolitik in deutschen Sprachgebiet*, Berlin, 1957; F. Luetge, *Geschichte des deutschen Agrarverfassung vom frühen Mittelalter bis zum 19. Jahrhundert*, 2nd ed., Berlin, 1966.

For the Scandinavian countries, no general work on agricultural developments exists, and for a general conspectus we must therefore refer, and for Sweden alone, to E. F. Heckscher's standard work, *An Economic History of Sweden*, trans. by G. Ohlin, London, O.U.P., 1954. For the (broadly speaking) Flemish countries in addition to the essay of Slicher van Bath, Meuvret and Hoskins, cited above, a virtually exhaustive bibliography is provided in two other articles, one also by Slicher van Bath, 'Zwanzig Jahre Agrargeschichte im Benelux-Raum, 1939–1959', *Zeitschrift für Agrargeschichte und Agrarsoziologie*, VIII, 1960, and the other by A. Verhulst, 'Les recherches d'histoire rurale en Belgique depuis 1959', *Agrártörténeti Szemle (Historia rerum rusticarum)*, Budapest, IX, 1967 (Supplementum).

For England, too, there is a long list of works on agricultural history, especially of recent publications. Here it will suffice to mention, in addition to Hoskins's essay cited above, the standard and still valuable work of Lord Ernle (R. E. Prothero), *English Farming Past and Present*, 6th ed., London, 1961, which includes an extensive bibliography, as does also C. S. Orwin, *A History of English Farming*, London, 1949. Leaving aside works of local interest several of which are of great importance, also to be mentioned are: G. E. Fussel and C. Goodman, 'Crops husbandry in 17th-century England', *Agricultural History*, XV, 1941; H. J. Habakkuk, 'La disparition du paysan anglais', *Annales E.S.C.*, 20, 1965; W. G. Hoskins, 'The rebuilding of rural England, 1570–1640', *Past and Present*, IV, 1954; H. J. Habakkuk, 'England Landownership, 1660–1740', *Economic History Review*, X, 1940; A. H. John 'The course of agricultural change, 1660–1740', *Studies in industrial revolution*, L. S. Pressnell (ed.), London, 1960; *idem*, 'Agricultural productivity and economic growth in England, 1700–1760',

Journal of Economic History, XXV, 1965; S. Shina, 'Le XVIᵉ et le XVIIᵉ dans l'histoire agricole de l'Angleterre', *Nogyo Keizai Kenkyu*, 28, 1956; R. Trow-Smith, *A history of British livestock husbandry*, 2 vols., London, 1957–59; F. M. L. Thompson, 'The social distribution of landed property in England since the XVIth century'. *Economic history review*, XIX, 1966. E. L. Jones, *Agriculture and Economic Growth in England 1650–1815*, London, 1967. See also bibliography in Section 8 of Volume 3 of this history.

For France, quite a number of works on rural history have appeared in recent times. On general problems, M. Bloch, *Les caractères originaux de l'histoire rurale française*, new ed., 2 vols., Paris, 1960, remains fundamental. Also still useful is G. Roupnel, *Histoire de la campagne française*, Paris, 1932. Interesting examples of the new methods of research and current methodological solutions are, among others, R. Baehrel, *Une croissance: la Basse Provence rurale (fin seizième siècle – 1789)*, Paris, 1961; P. Goubert, *Beauvais et Beauvaisis de 1600 à 1730*, Paris, 1960; E. Le Roy Ladurie, *Les paysans de Languedoc*, XVI–XVIIᵉ siècles, Paris, 1967. R. Dion's two works, *Essai sur la formation du paysage rural français*, Paris, 1934, and *Histoire de la vigne et du vin en France des origines aux XIX siècle*, Paris, 1959, still remain of interest.

For the Iberian peninsula, an overall picture of rural conditions can only be obtained from the general works on economic history. Still valuable, though dealing with only a particular aspect of rural economy, is J. Klein, *The Mesta: a study in Spanish economic history, 1273–1836*, Cambridge, Mass., 1920. Among more recent works touching on particular aspects of Spain's agrarian development, a valuable bibliography will be found in J. Gentil da Silva, *En Espagne: développement économique, subsistance, déclin*, Paris, 1965. On Portugal, a remarkable study is V. Rau, 'Large-scale agricultural enterprise in post medieval Portugal', *Contributions – Communications* de la Ièrᵉ Conférence Internationale d'Histoire Economique, Stockholm, 1960, Paris, 1960.

On the agricultural history of Italy, sources and problems are discussed in A. de Maddalena, 'Il mondo rurale nel Cinque e nel Seicento. Rassegna di studi recenti', *Rivista storica italiana*, LXXVI, 1964. A recent work of considerable methodological interest is G. Doria, *Uomini e terra di un borgo collinare dal XVI al XVIII secolo*, Milan, 1968.

On the evolution of yields and agricultural productivity, fundamental works in addition to those already cited are B. H. Slicher van Bath, 'Die europäischen Agrarverhältnisse im 17. und der ersten Hälfte des 18. Jahrhunderts', *A.A.G. Bijdragen*, 13, 1965; *idem*, 'Le développment de la productivité des travaux agricoles', *ibidem*, 14, 1967, and in particular *idem*, 'Yield ratios, 810–1820', *ibidem*, 10, 1963. To supplement the very extensive bibliography contained in that work, mention should also be made of G. Doria's book cited above and of C. Rotelli's article, 'Rendimenti e produzione agricola nell' Imolese dal XVI al XIX secolo', *Rivista storica italiana*, LXXXI, 1968.

5. European Industries, 1500-1700

Domenico Sella

The two centuries roughly comprised between Columbus's
first voyage of discovery and the creation of the Bank of
England form a distinct period in the economic history of
Europe, and the economic historian, conscious though he
may be of the risks involved in periodisation, feels comparatively few qualms in carving those two centuries out of
the flow of human events and in presenting them as a
distinct segment of our past. For the two hundred years
that witnessed the discovery and opening up of a new continent, the emergence of new economic powers on the
shores of the North Sea, the penetration of the market
economy into eastern Europe and Scandinavia, the harnessing of resources and manpower to the unprecedented needs
of the absolute monarchy, clearly have a claim to a separate
place in the annals of mankind.

Once such a place has been granted, however, there still
is the danger of making too much of change and novelty
while losing sight of all that represented mere continuity
with the preceding age. The danger is especially real in the
case of industry: it is tempting, for instance, to assemble
such information as we possess on the growth of English coal
mining, Dutch shipbuilding, or Swedish iron output, and
then portray the sixteenth and seventeenth centuries not
only as an age of considerable industrial expansion, but as
one indeed during which mining and manufacturing moved
to the forefront of Europe's economic life and replaced
agriculture as the leading sector of its economy. This would
be grossly misleading: for all the changes and the progress
experienced in those two centuries, Europe's industrial
sector as it stood in 1700 bore far greater resemblance to its
medieval antecedent than to its nineteenth-century successor.

Around 1700 industrial technology, in spite of some significant innovations, was still very much what it had been in the late medieval period, with its limited array of power-driven machines — fulling mills and paper mills, mechanical bellows and tilt hammers — and its dependence on manual effort at the loom and the anvil, in the glassmaker's workshop and the shipyard. In the days of Colbert and Newton, moreover, most manufacturing continued to be carried on in diminutive units — the weaver's cottage, the village smithy, the paper-mill manned by a handful of workmen. Finally, and more importantly, there was continuity with the preceding age in the range of goods produced as well as in the relative importance of individual industries.

In terms of the size of the work force employed in them, the top-ranking industries were probably those catering to such basic human needs as shelter and clothing. Construction has been too much neglected by economic historians as a field of study except perhaps for its most conspicuous and lasting products — the churches, castles, and mansions which over the centuries, came to stud and to adorn the landscape of Europe. It is easy, however, to overestimate the importance of that particular branch of the construction industry in terms of the resources and the manpower actually allocated to it,[1] and to ignore, because it has left fewer traces and escapes our measurement, the far more important construction activity involving the building, rebuilding, and repair of the countless common houses and cottages in which the population of Europe lived and worked. It is obvious, however, that here was a major field in which Europe's resources were used. As regards the manufactures connected with clothing, they are far better known and have, in fact, long been a chosen object of historical investigation. This is especially true of the several textile industries — wool, linen, cotton, and silk: the conspicuous place they occupy in the annals of medieval and early modern economic history may, to some extent, reflect

[1] Cf. H. T. Johnson, 'Cathedral Building and the Medieval Economy', *Explorations in Entrepreneurial History* (1967), for a stimulating, if controversial, approach to the subject.

the greater survival rate of documents bearing on them; yet their predominance on the industrial scene cannot be doubted as it was not by contemporary statesmen and political writers when they equated industrial prosperity and progress with the spread and success of textile production. Not only did the making of textiles employ in given areas thousands and even tens of thousands of people; in one form or another it was also carried on nearly everywhere in medieval and early modern Europe, from the banks of the Arno to those of the Scheldt, from the hamlets perched on the slopes of the Alps where coarse cloth was woven for local use to the cottages of the English Midlands where production was geared on the demand of foreign markets.

Few other industries could compete with construction and textiles in terms either of their contribution to the national product or in terms of geographical diffusion. No doubt leather-making was widely practised in an age in which leather found an incredible variety of uses not only in footwear and garments, but also in the making of harness, bellows, containers, chests, and furniture, but it certainly could not take precedence over textiles. Neither could the metal trades. The range of metal goods that were produced at the time as well as the demand for them continued to be, by our standards, very limited. Nails, pins, needles, chains, wire, locks, cutlery, and tools of all kinds were indeed common items in the shops and households of Europe around 1700 much as they had been two or three centuries before; their production, as will be seen, was a major source of livelihood in certain areas, and we may well agree with that sixteenth-century writer who claimed that 'for the everyday necessities of life (. . .) iron is as essential as bread.'[2] For all that, it must be borne in mind that the demand for iron goods was kept low by the absence of elaborate machinery in the production process as well as by the fact that in such machinery as was used at the time, more parts were made of wood than of iron and steel; and

[2] G. Botero, *The Reason of State* (1589) ed. D. P. Waley (London 1956), p. 152.

the same remark applies, of course, to ships, carriages, and farming implements.

The primacy of construction and textiles and the limited scope of iron metallurgy were not the only features which the industrial sector had inherited from the Middle Ages. Possibly the clearest element of continuity between the medieval and the early modern economies (as well as the sharpest elements of contrast with the world we live in) is afforded by the smallness of the industrial *vis à vis* the primary sector of the economy. That the majority of the European people were engaged in agriculture even in the most advanced and economically sophisticated nations is a fact too well-known to require much elaboration. What needs emphasis, if our survey of the industrial sector is to be set in proper perspective, is rather the fact that in 1700 Europe was not only a predominantly agrarian world, but also one in which stark poverty continued to be the lot of the greater part of its people. Although overall conditions may have been somewhat better in the days of John Locke than in the days of Machiavelli, the fact remains that at the close of the seventeenth century a good half of the population of Europe lived close to what, in normal times, must have been a physiological minimum. Gregory King was able to express this grim fact in quantitative terms when he showed that roughly half the population of England fell under the poverty line;[3] shortly after, Vauban, the disgruntled minister of Louis XIV, drew an even darker picture for France as he reckoned that five-ninths of its people lived in utter destitution;[4] even Holland at the zenith of its commercial prosperity was reportedly swarming with beggars and vagrants;[5] and what modern research has been able to find about the average workman's earnings and diet fully supports the sombre conclusions drawn by eye-witnesses.

---

[3] Cf. D. C. Coleman, 'Labour in the English Economy during the Seventeenth Century', *Economic History Review* (1956).

[4] Vauban, *Projet d'une Dîme royale* (1707) ed. E. Coornaert, pp. 6-7.

[5] C. R. Boxer, *The Dutch Seaborne Empire, 1600-1800* (New York 1965), pp. 54 ff.

The roots of such widespread poverty need not detain us here: it will suffice to say that in the past the low level of technology forced most human effort to be expended on the production of basic foodstuffs, while the rudimentary state of transportation in general and of overland transportation in particular severely restricted the scope of trade and specialisation. The consequences of poverty, on the other hand, are of special interest in the present context as they help us preserve a sense of proportion in our discussion of the industrial sector in early modern times. Low income levels plus the fact that the peasant family often produced itself such simple textiles and crude implements as it needed, placed severe limitations on the size of the market for manufactured goods; at the same time a still backward technology obviously meant small markets for producer goods.

Much as in previous centuries widespread poverty, of course, stood in sharp contrast with the wealth and affluence of a restricted minority — the kings and rulers and their courts, but also the noblemen, churchmen, officials, and financiers who clustered around the seats of power or held sway in the provinces. While the destitution of the many severely restricted the scope of industries producing common, inexpensive consumer goods, the wealth of the few — whether Spanish grandees or English peers, Roman prelates or Dutch regents — presented unique opportunities to a variety of luxury manufactures. Although it is difficult to subscribe to Sombart's view on the decisive role played by luxury in the rise of the modern economy, there is no denying that conspicuous consumption at the hands of a wealthy minority caused a remarkable amount of resources and skills to be channelled into the making of non-essential goods. Every student of urban history is familiar with the long lists of craft guilds in which city authorities and local chroniclers seem to have taken so much pride, and he is duly impressed by the number and diversity of highly specialised trades (jewellers, embroiderers, leather-gilders, lace-makers, tassel-makers, woodcarvers, and what not) which are found even in towns of modest size in the late medieval and early modern periods. Their existence and number is proof that, in spite of the moralist's tireless reprimands and the lawmaker's barrage of sumptuary laws, the demand for luxuries continued to be a major force behind a good deal of industrial activity. The connection between lavish spending at the hands of the rich and the prosperity of the artisans was, of course, clearly perceived by political writers and publicists long before *The Fable of the Bees* went to press. And it appeared rather obvious even to casual observers such as the Duke of Rohan who, after commenting on the Italian aristocracy's astonishing taste for luxury and display, went on to state that:

> 'this has caused the artisans to devote so much care to good workmanship that they have achieved excellence each in his own trade (. . .) with the result that anyone who wishes to secure exquisitely wrought arms, fabrics, harness, all sorts of embroidery, and, in short, all the fine things a man may wish, must seek them in that country.'[6]

Similar remarks could have been made in medieval times. Then as later, a large portion of manufactured goods was intended for the insatiable appetite of a narrow, but rich clientele.

Limited markets, a technology still heavily dependent on the artisan's knowhow and manual dexterity, the puny size of enterprise, the predominance of construction and textiles in the industrial spectrum, all this suggests that the secondary sector, in sixteenth- and seventeenth-century Europe, still bore the marks of an earlier age. And yet, for all such continuity, things were far from static between 1500 and 1700: new markets were found for manufactured goods; industrial output became more diversified and sophisticated as a result of both changing consumer tastes and improved technology; a few new industries developed vigorously thus broadening the range of choices open to consumers; lastly, the geographical distribution, if not the basic structure, of

[6] Rohan's quotation in A. Frumento, *Imprese lombarde nella storia della metallurgia italiana* (Milan 1958), vol. II, p. 86.

industry was deeply altered. It is to this changing scene that we must now turn.

The first section of this chapter will be mainly devoted to a discussion of the changes that occurred in the size and nature of the market for industrial goods; the second will deal with the production; the third with the changing geography of European industry.

THE DEMAND FOR INDUSTRIAL GOODS

OVERSEAS EXPANSION

The most dramatic event in the economic history of early modern Europe was no doubt the discovery and colonisation of the New World. And yet, while its impact on trade, shipping, and the stock of precious metals has received extensive treatment at the hands of a host of historians, its significance for Europe's industries has been comparatively neglected. We know a great deal more, in fact, about what the Old World received from the New than about what the former sent to the latter; we have more accurate information about the dyes, the sugar, and the bullion that poured in increasing and truly astonishing amounts into Seville, Lisbon, Antwerp, and Amsterdam than about the cargoes that sailed out of those ports bound for the West Indies, the Spanish Main, and Brazil. Our lopsided knowledge reflects in part the nature of the available information. Unlike later colonialists and empire builders, the explorers, conquerors, and statesmen of the Renaissance looked on the New World primarily as a source of exotic commodities and of bullion rather than as potential markets for their countries' manufactures, and this may explain why better records were kept of incoming than of outgoing shipments. The historians' concern with the Price Revolution and the rise of modern capitalism, moreover, has resulted in one particular branch of the new colonial trades, namely that involving precious metals, being thoroughly investigated, while other trade currents have been largely ignored.

Such neglect is serious indeed, for all the silver and gold, dyestuffs and sugar that reached Europe in the sixteenth and seventeenth centuries did not represent unilateral flows, but were largely matched by exports from Europe in the form of either commodities or shipping and commercial services. In point of fact, the importance of the American colonies as outlets for European goods did not escape contemporaries altogether, although the main emphasis lay on what Europe received from, rather than on what it sent to, the New World. In the 1540's, for example, considerable concern was voiced in Castile over the export trade to the Indies: internal prices, it was claimed, were rising dangerously and the blame was often laid at the door of the great Sevillian merchants who purchased vast quantities of foodstuffs and manufactures for shipment overseas; and requests were set forth that such shipments be curbed — a revealing, if perverted, recognition of the impact of colonial demand on the metropolitan economy and its strained resources. Some fifty years later the opportunities which the New World seemed to offer to the merchants of the Old were extolled in a more optimistic vein by the anonymous English compiler of a *Direction for divers trades*. In his view,

> 'for the trade of the West Indews belonginge to Spaine all these wares following ar very good: oyles ar very well sold (. . .), lookinge glasses of chrystall and others; knyfes of all sortes very well sold; taylors sheres and sissars for barbors; linne clothe of divers sort; (. . .) some quantities of wyne, but it must be singular good; also pines, pointes, and such other like small wares . . .'[7]

The enumeration is interesting and indicative of the variety of manufactured goods that could find a market overseas. Nor was the export of commodities from Europe a mere trickle at the time the anonymous *Direction* was written. Working on some detailed trade statistics for the early

---

[7] R. H. Tawney and E. Power eds., *Tudor Economic Documents* (London 1924), vol. III, p. 206.

1570's (at a time, that is, when the torrent of American bullion was nearing the high levels it was to maintain for the next fifty years), Dr Jose Gentil DaSilva[8] has been able to show that about half that bullion was spent in Seville on the purchase of return cargoes, while the remaining half went to pay for shipping and commercial services or was absorbed by taxes and profits. The return cargoes themselves included Andalusian wines and oils as well as a nondescript assortment of manufactured goods made in Spain or abroad. We are, unfortunately, in the dark as to the exact amounts and the kind of manufactures involved, but it is safe to say that American bullion, while it may not have been, any more than Calvinism, the parent of modern capitalism, did act as a powerful stimulant on Europe's industrial production.

It certainly stimulated Spanish industries, at least in the first half of the sixteenth century, when the making of woollen cloth in Segovia and Valladolid, of silks in Valencia, of metal goods and ocean-going vessels in the Bilbao area all enjoyed a long spell of prosperity and expansion that largely reflected a brisk and expanding colonial demand. After mid-century, as the volume of American trade climbed to new heights, the pull of overseas demand apparently outstripped Spain's industrial capacity and new sources of supply had to be tapped abroad, eventually leaving for Spain herself little more than the role of a funnel through which manufactured goods produced beyond her border found their way to their final destination in the Caribbean, in Mexico, and in the highlands of New Granada.

'The Spaniards, whose living wholly depends on France, being compelled by inexorable circumstances to secure from us grain, linens, cloth, woad, paper, books, even carpentry and, in short, all manufactures, sail to the end of the world to fetch for us gold, silver, and spices.'[9]

So wrote Jean Bodin in 1568 as he probed the effects of

---

[8] J. Gentil DaSilva, *En Espagne: développement économique, subsistance, déclin* (Paris-The Hague 1965), p. 65.

[9] Quoted in R. Carande, *Carlos V y sus banqueros* (Madrid 1965), p. 167.

American treasure on the European, and particularly the French, economy. His recognition of the importance of the American market for French industries was echoed, at the opening of the seventeenth century, by the Rouen city council as it asserted that 'linen fabrics are the true gold and silver mines of this realm (France) because they are shipped to the lands from which gold and silver are brought to us.'[10] This was no mere rhetoric, for we know that linen fabrics, either as sail canvas or as clothing, formed one of the major articles demanded in the colonies and that Normandy itself was at the time and long remained one of the chief suppliers of linen. Flanders was another, at least until the outbreak of the Revolt against its Spanish rulers: as Etienne Sabbe has brought out, the remarkable surge of linen output in the Low Countries during much of the sixteenth century can be largely ascribed to the opening up of the new American markets, while the temporary slump in the last quarter of the century reflected the breakdown of normal trade connections with Spain. It was then that Normandy and Brittany managed to engross much of that tempting trade, only to be forced to yield to Flanders once again in the first half of the seventeenth century when Flemish linen enjoyed a privileged position in the Spanish empire. After the Peace of Westphalia of 1648, Flemish textiles lost in the face of foreign competition as several countries were allowed to trade in the Spanish colonies; Dutch and Silesian linens made substantial inroads, but in the 1680's, when annual shipments of French linen reached a summit of 75,000 pieces, Bodin's homeland was once again in the lead. At any rate, whether made in France, Flanders, Holland, or Silesia, linen loomed large in the American-bound trade It also found a not negligible, if much smaller, outlet in West Africa where it was used alongside silks, firearms, and trinkets to secure slaves for the sugar plantations of Brazil and the West Indies. We know, for instance, that linen was shipped from Normandy to Africa in the late sixteenth century[11] and that in the late seventeenth century the Royal

[10] H. Lapeyre, *Une famille de marchands: les Ruiz* (Paris 1955), p. 502.
[11] *Ibid.*, p. 523.

African Company traded large shipments of Dutch-made linen sheets on the Guinea Coast.[12]

In the tropical and subtropical regions of the New World the demand for linen far outdistanced that of other textiles, but in the uplands and mountains of the interior a respectable market was found for woollen cloth and the opportunity was seized upon, at first, by the Castilian clothmakers and, later on, by such great and thriving centres of the wool industry as Hondschoote, Lille, and Amiens. A close study of the output curves of the Lille cloth industry has, in fact, revealed a significant correlation with the ups and downs of the Spanish American trade; the impressive rise of the industry in Hondschoote between 1530 and 1570 has been ascribed in good part to growing exports to the New World; and so has been the growth in output which the Amiens manufacture experienced in the second half of the sixteenth century.

For all their importance in the new ocean trades, linen and cloth did not exhaust the colonists' shopping list. A large assortment of other manufactured goods were, in fact, shipped to America and to West Africa — from luxuries to firearms, from small hardware to paper and books. In the absence of precise statistical information we cannot, of course, try to estimate the magnitude of those exports. Something, however, can be said about the chief commodities involved and their place of origin, for we know, for instance, that iron bars, nails, knives, and tools of all sorts made in Barcelona, in the Forez, in Liège and Dordrecht were shipped from Seville to the colonies in quantities large enough to have left a trace in historical records. It is also known that small firearms and gunpowder manufactured in Spain, the Low Countries, and Germany were important articles in the African slave trade alongside more peaceful goods such as Venetian glass beads and French silks. By the late seventeenth century, moreover, New Spain and its dependencies are known to have developed a strong appetite for such luxuries and comforts as English and Italian stockings, French hats, and, above all, silk fabrics,

[12] K. G. Davies, *The Royal African Company* (London 1957), p. 172.

ribbons, and lace. In the days of Colbert, French silk-makers sold some 2 million *livres* worth of silks to Spain and nine-tenths of that hefty figure were ultimately intended for the overseas market. Even then, however, French officials and merchants had to acknowledge the fact that they had secured but a fraction of a handsome market on which their Italian, and notably Genoese, rivals were still leading.[13]

The Spanish colonies saw the French and the Genoese pitted against each other in the paper trade as well. Hundreds and even thousands of reams of paper were normal items in the cargoes that sailed from Seville and Cadiz in the seventeenth century, and so were large consignments of legal and devotional books. Much of that reading material came from the printing presses of Lyons and Paris, one of their specialities being precisely the production of books intended for the Spanish metropolitan and colonial markets. Paper, on the other hand, came from both France and Italy: up to the middle of the seventeenth century, France had been the chief supplier of paper to the Spanish colonies; in the later part of the century and well into the next, however, the Genoese succeeded in capturing most of that trade and reportedly each year 200,000 reams of paper produced in some fifty papermills strung along the Riviera were shipped to Spain and her overseas possessions.[14]

POPULATION AND URBANISATION

If the stimulus imparted by the opening up of new markets in America is clearly discernible, albeit not measurable, it is much more difficult to tell whether in Europe itself the size of the market for industrial goods was substantially affected, in the two centuries under discussion, as a result of changes in either the size of population or income levels.

Regarding the former, it is possible to say, in spite of considerable uncertainties, that from the late fifteenth century and for the next 150 years Europe was the stage of an im-

[13] A. Girard, *Le commerce français à Séville et Cadix au temps des Habsbourgs* (Paris-Bordeaux 1932), pp. 375, 379.
[14] *Ibid.*, p. 384.

pressive demographic upswing at the end of which a number of countries had scored gains of the order of 50 per cent. It is also known that in the period from about 1620 to 1660 severe losses were registered in the Italian peninsula, in Spain, and in Central Europe, while in the north and west the earlier rapid rate of increase gave way to stagnation or, at best, slowed down markedly. Ultimately, however, it would seem that in 1700 Europe had a population larger than in 1500, although probably somewhat below the high mark which had been reached at the beginning of the seventeenth century. Given this overall increase and the sharp contrast between a dynamic sixteenth century and a sluggish seventeenth century, one would be inclined to assume, on the basis of the historical experience of the last 150 years, that industrial production surged vigorously during the great demographic upswing of the sixteenth century only to stagnate at a comfortably high level in the following century.

Such simple correlation between demography and economic growth, however, is probably misleading when applied to the early modern period. As P. Bairoch has convincingly argued,[15] before the Industrial Revolution, increasing numbers, far from being translated into larger effective demand for industrial goods, were likely to leave things basically unchanged. Much depended, of course, on whether food supplies kept pace with population: should they lag behind, living standards would deteriorate and, on the average, a smaller proportion of per capita income would be spent on commodities other than basic foodstuffs.

Such apparently was the case in sixteenth-century Europe. What research has been done on real wages in that period points to their erosion in much of Europe as food prices rose faster than money wage-rates, with but a few fortunate areas escaping the inexorable effects of population pressure on an inelastic food supply. In the second half of the seventeenth century, on the other hand, the situation was reversed as food prices tended to fall while wage-rates held their own or failed to drop to quite the same extent. In

[15] P. Bairoch, *Révolution industrielle et sous-développment* (Paris 1964), ch. 2.

summary, one is led to believe that the potential effect of rising numbers on the size of the market for manufactured goods was cancelled or, at best, dampened until about 1650 by lower per capita incomes, while the latter's improvement after mid-century may have been offset in part by sagging population figures. What is true of aggregate demand need not, however, apply to the demand for specific goods, for while rising food prices forced consumers to reduce expenditures on non-farm goods, they also brought larger earnings to food producers — the landowners, the tenants, and the farmers with a surplus to sell. In other words, the scissors movements of food prices and wages effected a redistribution of income among different social groups and this may well have caused shifts in the demand for individual commodities.

If changes in the sheer size of European population are not likely to have profoundly affected aggregate demand, changes in the distribution of population between country and town certainly did. That a redistribution of considerable magnitude did occur is beyond doubt: around 1500 only four cities in western Europe had over 100,000 inhabitants and none reached the 200,000 mark; by 1700 as many as twelve cities had crossed the 100,000 threshold and four of them had a population of over 200,000.[16] Even granting that by the latter date the total population of western Europe was larger than it had been two centuries before, it is clear that it had not grown to quite the same extent as its urban segment. We can safely assume, in other words, that in the course of two centuries a significant townward drift had occurred as immigrants from the countryside and smaller towns had come to live in the larger cities.

The transfer of substantial numbers from their traditional residence to such sprawling capitals as Naples, Rome, Paris, Madrid, or London obviously called for heavy investments in housing and in public facilities, whether city walls or churches, new town-halls or hospitals or bridges. No doubt, part of the increase in numbers was absorbed by packing

---

[16] R. Mols, *Introduction à la démographie historique des villes d'Europe du XIVe au XVIIIe siècle* (Louvain 1955), vol. II, p. 47.

more people in existing dwellings rather than by the addition of new ones. But, even by the very tolerant standards of the time, there were limits to overcrowding. In his study of sixteenth-century Rome, J. Delumeau[17] has called attention both to a rising density in the old popular districts of the papal city and to the appearance of whole new blocks of low-cost houses designed after a common pattern and intended to accommodate part at least of a population that doubled in size in the course of the century. The 'explosion' experienced by Madrid after it became the permanent residence of the royal government around the middle of the sixteenth century resulted, too, in appalling conditions of congestion, but also in a great deal of new constructions however hastily and cheaply put together; the city's central area 'was divided and subdivided *ad infinitum* into smaller and smaller plots' to make room for new dwellings; the total area covered by the city expanded fourfold between 1500 and 1700 while its population rose from 10,000 to 150,000.[18] In the heart of seventeenth-century London many great houses which had formerly served as aristocratic residences were minutely subdivided into small, separate dwellings and turned into unhealthy tenements; at the same time whole new districts were built to the north and west of the old urban core.[19]

In Renaissance and Baroque Europe urban construction was further stimulated by forces other than mere increase in size. On the one hand, the architect and the mason were called upon to satisfy the new grandiose taste for display and ostentation that obsessed popes, monarchs, noblemen, and *nouveaux riches* at the time; on the other hand, governments and municipal authorities began to develop a keen interest in the layout of their towns as well as in the quality and structural features of new constructions: wider streets and spacious squares were carved out of the congeries of

[17] J. Delumeau, *Vie économique et sociale de Rome dans la seconde moitié du XVIe siècle* (Paris 1957), vol. I, pp. 280-86.

[18] E. A. Dutkind, *International History of City Development*, vol. III: *Urban Development in southern Europe* (New York 1967), p. 404.

[19] H. C. Darby ed., *An Historical Geography of England before 1800* (Cambridge 1961), p. 528.

medieval houses, while timber and thatch were often discarded in favour of more durable building materials such as
stone, brick, and tiles. This fresh interest in urbanism, it
must be pointed out, reflected only in part a better and
keener appreciation for symmetry, perspective, and beauty;
it was also prompted by two practical problems that came to
confront the European town in the early modern period.
One problem arose from the changing methods of warfare,
and notably from the improvement in the efficiency of
artillery: not only did this make the old medieval walls
obsolete and call for stronger and far more elaborate
defensive structures; the increased vulnerability of towns to
enemy shelling during a siege also encouraged the substitution of brick or stone for the old building materials. Another
problem was posed by urban traffic: the very growth in size
obviously resulted in greater congestion at the centre of
towns; from the late sixteenth century, however, the problem of urban traffic was compounded by the appearance
and the rapid diffusion of the great coaches and sumptuous
carriages as indispensable status symbols among the well-to-
do. In spite of repeated attempts to curb what legislators
considered an objectionable and wasteful trend, wheeled
traffic became a serious problem for municipal authorities
and city planners; and when we read that in a city of
120,000, such as Milan was in the late seventeenth century,
something like 1,400 coaches jammed its narrow streets, we
find it easier to understand why contemporaries became so
much interested in redrawing the map of their cities.[20]

Rome certainly set a record of architectural splendour,
urban planning, and fabulous spending with 54 churches
(and St. Peter's among them), some 60 sumptuous palaces,
20 stately villas, 3 aqueducts, and 35 public fountains
either built or totally renovated and enlarged in the course
of the sixteenth century. Alongside the construction activity generated by the addition of 50,000 new residents
and by the opening of 30 new streets that cut across the
tangle of tightly packed medieval houses, this astonishing

building programme imparted a peculiar character to the economy of the papal city as construction came to represent by far its largest single industry in terms of the size of the labour force employed.[21] Elsewhere the new taste for urban magnificence and geometric order was no doubt on a smaller scale, but still impressive enough. Naples, Palermo, and Genoa were caught, in the sixteenth century, in a 'frenzy of demolition and reconstruction' as new port facilities were developed and palaces and churches came to line the spacious thoroughfares newly opened across the welter of their old, dilapidated urban centres. Venice, of course, owes much of its present charm to the builders and patrons of the Renaissance and Baroque periods and its two northern rivals, Antwerp and Amsterdam, still bear, both in their layout and in their architecture, the mark placed on them by the city planners and the private architect in the sixteenth and seventeenth centuries respectively. In Paris such well-known sights as the Place des Vosges and the Tuileries bear witness to the taste and ambitions of the first Bourbon king, while in Germany a host of princely capitals were either rebuilt or thoroughly redrawn and embellished after the destruction wrought by the Thirty Years War.

From the towns the search for architectural splendour spilled over into the countryside. Palladio's villas in Venetia were the harbingers of a new fashion that was to sweep Europe in the first centuries of the modern age as monarchs, noblemen, and wealthy upstarts developed the habit of spending part of the year in a country mansion built to exude prestige, grandeur, and impeccable taste. At the hands of kings and statesmen the new fashion could attain astonishing proportions. The Spanish Habsburgs spent on an heroic scale on their numerous residences outside Madrid — El Pardo, Aranjuez, El Escorial — while at least one of their favourites, the Duke of Lerma, vied with his royal masters in lavishness and magnificence when he had a whole town designed and built around his country residence as a tangible symbol of his power and influence. On the opposite side of the Pyrenees their French rivals,

[21] Delumeau, *op. cit.*, pp. 359 ff.

whether Valois or Bourbons, left an equally impressive architectural legacy and in the late seventeenth century one of them was to overshadow every other ruler in Europe with that unique monument of human vanity that was Versailles.

Unlike art historians and modern tourists, economic historians have seldom been kind to the rulers, churchmen, and tycoons of the past who invested enormous fortunes in palaces, country mansions, and churches; they have, in fact, repeatedly accused them of squandering vast resources instead of channelling them into productive investments. That sweeping indictment, of course, rests on the implicit assumption that had it not been for their prodigality the factors of production that were in fact buried in the great architectural achievements of the Renaissance and the Baroque would have found their way into other and more useful undertakings; and, if this was the case, it follows that economic growth was retarded or impeded by what looks very much like a flagrant misallocation of resources. But was this, in fact, always the case? It all depended, of course, on whether or not at a given time and in a given area the economy was operating at or near full-employment levels; for if it was not, then even the building of useless mansions and sumptuous palaces could, as Lord Keynes argued long ago, contribute to the general welfare by activating factors that would otherwise have remained idle thereby generating new rounds of income.

Much detailed research will have to be done before final judgment can be passed on the economic impact of the huge investments that were locked up in brick, stone, and mortar by the extravagant ruling classes of early modern Europe. The final verdict need not always be unfavourable. It will probably be so in the case, for example, of a Philip II who spent on a stupendous scale on his Escorial residence at a time when the resources of Castile were notoriously strained to the point of disaster. In other cases, however, the verdict may well turn out to be different. In his discussion of 'conspicuous expenditure' by the English aristocracy in the late sixteenth century, Lawrence Stone has spoken of its 'critical importance in galvanising into activity the sluggish Tudor economy'[22]: in view of what is known about the slow-down of economic activity in that period his remark does not seem unwarranted. Much the same could probably be said of Germany after the Thirty Years War, when its numerous princes embarked on great works of urban reconstruction and renewal: in times of prolonged depression lavish spending on construction could no doubt act as a powerful stimulant of income and employment. The more so on account of the strong linkages the building industry had with a wide penumbra of related trades and crafts. The point was made, with understandable enthusiasm, by Nicholas Barbon, a London contractor and land speculator who had waxed rich in the wake of the Great Fire of 1666, when he wrote:

> 'Building is the chiefest promoter of trade. It employs a greater number of trades and people than feeding and clothing: the artificers that belong to building, such as bricklayers, carpenters, plasterers, etc. employ many hands; those that make the materials for building, such as bricks, lime, tile, etc. employ more; and with those that furnish the houses, such as upholsterers, pewterers, etc. they are almost innumerable.'[23]

Urbanisation did more than just promote construction. As an increasing, if still modest, proportion of the population of western Europe came to live in large towns and thus ceased to be engaged in the growing of foodstuffs, agriculture was called upon to step up its production of a surplus for the market; in the process, the area of commercial farming was broadened at the expense of subsistence farming and food producers, whether great landowners, tenants, or (more rarely) small freeholders, received income that could be spent on manufactured goods. What dimensions the process actually reached it is impossible to say. The widening of the area of commercial farming generated by

---

[22] L. Stone, *The Crisis of the Aristocracy, 1585-1641* (Oxford 1965), p. 585.
[23] Quoted in W. Letwin, *The Origins of Scientific Economics* (New York 1965), p. 64.

urban growth has been traced in detail in the case of London's agricultural hinterland in a well-known article by F. J. Fisher several years ago;[24] and something has been written on the stimulus imparted in the course of the sixteenth century, by the growth of Seville and of Venice on their respective countrysides.[25] What these and similar developments meant in terms of the demand for industrial goods has not, however, been adequately investigated as yet.

In but one case, and a rather spectacular one at that, is the creation of a whole new market for industrial goods clearly traceable to the spread of commercial agriculture. This is the case of Poland. It is well-known that in the course of the sixteenth century that country was drawn into the mainstream of international trade as it became a major source of food supplies to the urban masses of western Europe. As early as the 1530's a Flemish envoy in Danzig noticed the changing pattern of the Polish economy.

'In the past — he reported — the great landowners did not know what to do with their grain and left their lands uncropped (. . .) In the last twenty-five years, however, they have found it possible to ship their grain to Danzig down the rivers and to sell it in the said town. Accordingly the kingdom of Poland and the great lords have grown very rich.'[26]

The new trend gained momentum decade after decade and by the early seventeenth century, when as many as 70,000 tons of rye left Danzig each year westbound, Polish grain exports were nearly ten times as large as they had been at the close of the fifteenth century; and increasingly that swelling flow was reinforced by exports of raw materials

[24] F. J. Fisher, 'The Development of the London Food Market, 1540-1640', *Econ. Hist. Rev.* (1935).
[25] Cf. R. Pike, 'Seville in the Sixteenth Century', *Hispanic American Historical Review* (1961), p. 22; and D. Beltrami, *Saggio di storia dell'agricol ura nella Repubblica di Venezia* (Venice-Rome 1955), pp. 30 ff.
[26] Quoted in P. Dollinger, *La Hanse: XIIe-XVIIe siècles* (Paris 1964), p. 520.

such as timber, tar, potash, and flax.[27] In the process, Poland became an ever more attractive outlet for western commodities: Biscayan salt, French wines, Dutch cured fish, English and Dutch woollens. Before the sixteenth century was over some 30,000 'cloths',* mainly from England, entered the Baltic each year; by 1630, at the zenith of the Polish grain trade, England and Holland together sent there twice that amount.[28]

The opening up and the rapid expansion of the Baltic trade, involving as it did bulky cargoes, must also be accounted as a major stimulant of one of the few 'heavy industries' of the early modern period, namely ship-building. The number of ships clearing the Sound rose from about 1,000 at the beginning of the sixteenth century to nearly six times as many in the early seventeenth century. Although inaccurate registration, changes in the average size of ships over time, and considerable uncertainty as to the number of voyages the average freighter could effect in a year require caution in the interpretation of these figures, there can be little doubt that the Baltic trade played a decisive role in the growth of the shipbuilding industry in general, and particularly of that of Holland, the country which by 1600 controlled three-quarters of the carrying trade in that area.

The colonial trades, too, added considerably to the world's demand for tonnage, the crucial factors being here both the mileage to be covered and the relatively high rate of replacement caused by frequent shipwrecks as well as by losses inflicted by privateers and pirates. For all that, the demand for tonnage in the colonial trades fell far short of demand in the Baltic: in the late seventeenth century the Dutch merchant marine, by then unquestionably the largest in the world, employed less than one tenth of its 560,000

* A unit of measurement probably equivalent to 24 yards.

[27] M. Malowist, 'The Economic and Social Development of the Baltic Countries from the 15th to the 17th Century', *Econ. Hist. Rev.* (1959), p. 184.

[28] R. W. K. Hinton, *The Eastland Trade and the Common Weal in the Seventeenth Century* (Cambridge 1959), pp. 226-30.

tons in the American trade as against 200,000 in the Baltic.[29]

LUXURY, COMFORT, AND LEISURE

The new taste for luxury and ostentation which, as will be recalled, found expression in the construction of stately palaces and handsome country houses, affected the whole style of life of the European upper class. It was reflected in the use, referred to above, of sumptuous coaches, but also in the growing refinement of interior decoration with its profusion of silk hangings, tapestries, and carpets, its increasingly elaborate and ornate furniture, the substitution of silver plate and ceramics for pewter and common earthenware on the table of the rich. Their wardrobe, too, came to reflect a change in taste: the extravagant display of silks, lace, ribbons, and embroidery in seventeenth-century paintings stands in sharp contrast with the more austere dress of an earlier age.

Stimulated by a swelling stream of conspicuous spending, luxury industries prospered throughout Europe. The making of silk fabrics, once chiefly confined to a few Italian towns, spread to other countries — Germany, Holland, England, and, above all, France. By the late seventeenth century, 8,000 looms were reportedly at work in Lyons alone and by then French silk fabrics and fashions were eagerly sought and imitated abroad. The making of finely painted, glazed pottery, had, by that time, reached unprecedented standards of workmanship in Delft, while in Augsburg and Nuremberg the trades of the gold- and the silver-smith had risen to new prominence after the eclipse caused by three decades of war. Early in the century the tapestry industry had brought new blood to the Antwerp of the Archdukes; in Venice the making of finely-carved and inlaid furniture added fresh strength to a declining economy.

Most of the luxury productions which in those days

[29] J. H. Parry, 'Transport and Trade Routes', in *Cambridge Economic History of Europe*, vol. IV (Cambridge 1967), pp. 171, 206.

formed the pride of individual towns throughout Europe and specimens of which are today the cherished possession of museums and art collections were, of course, intended for the restricted minority which commanded a disproportionate share of the existing wealth. Some luxuries and comforts, however, did come within the reach of a larger clientele especially during the seventeenth century. At this point one could recall the substitution of glass for waxed canvas or paper on the windows of private homes, better heating such as the large tiled stove, the use of bed and table linen, or even the renting of coaches and carriages by people of modest means who occasionally wanted to enjoy the prestige and the comfort of wheeled transportation. But possibly the strongest evidence of changing and more exacting consumption standards among the 'middle class' is provided by the history of clothing. Two developments are clearly discernible here. On the one hand, in spite of a flood of sumptuary laws aimed at restricting the more costly fabrics to the top echelons of society, silk garments did find their way into the wardrobes of 'ordinary people' whose immoderate spending habits and 'excessive luxury' moralists and political writers denounced with admirable perseverance.[30] On the other hand, in country after country, an equally deplorable trend was noticed: consumers tended to shun traditional woollen fabrics that were well-known for their fine quality and durability, and increasingly turned to more attractive, although flimsier, ones simply because the latter came in a variety of ever changing patterns and colours; the demon of fashion allegedly lured people away from judicious spending and made them reckless and vain.

The spreading use of silks and the tendency to follow the capricious turns and twists of fashion by renovating one's wardrobe more frequently would seem to indicate that, even among the middling group of European consumers, incomes were perceptibly rising. It is also possible, however,

[30] Cf., for example, L. Zuccolo, *La Repubblica di Evandria* ed. R. De Mattei (Rome 1944), pp. 37, 51; A. de Montchrétien, *Traicté de l'économie politique* ed. T. Funk-Brentano (Paris 1889), p. 72; also *Early English Tracts on Commerce* ed. McCulloch, pp. 421-2.

that the satisfaction of the new frivolous taste for display and ostentation was made easier by reductions in the relative price of textiles or by a wider range of fabrics so priced as to suit a broader spectrum of consumers. On these points our knowledge is admittedly still very limited. In the case of silk, some broad developments referred to elsewhere in this chapter should be borne in mind: the industry's diffusion in Europe; the increasing differentiation of local products; the adoption of improved equipment such as the silk-mill, the draw loom, and the ribbon frame. These developments all point to a growing aggregate output, to efforts to cut production costs, and to a widening range of products; the implication seems to be that at least some silk goods became accessible even to consumers who had to reconcile their vanity and social ambitions with the constraints of a modest budget.

In the case of woollen textiles the role played by an expanding and cheaper supply in creating its own market is more easily discernible. The chief development here was the emergence and the remarkable success of a whole, proliferating family of worsted fabrics (bayes, sayes, perpetuanas, etamines, etc.), commonly known in the Walloon country as *nouvelle draperie* and as 'new draperies' in Britain. This new branch of the textile industry had its birthplace in the southern Low Countries in the late fifteenth century and its early progress occurred there: by the 1550's Lille, and, to an even greater extent, Hondschoote had acquired a towering position as centres of the *nouvelle draperie*; at that time Hondschoote reached its zenith with an output of nearly 100,000 pieces a year, most of them for export to other European countries as well as to the new, promising markets of the New World. The trials and tribulations which beset the Low Countries in the later part of the century played havoc on the Flemish worsted manufacture, but the remarkably successful example set by Hondschoote and Lille proved contagious and imitators were soon to emerge in various parts of Europe — in Liège and Amiens, in the Leyden area, in Württemberg and East Anglia — wherever the Flemish artisans found refuge from persecution, oppression, and hardships. When normalcy was restored to their homeland under the rule of the Archdukes, many of them, or rather their children, did return and in the early decades of the seventeenth century once again the worsted industry loomed large in the economy of the Spanish Low Countries. The earlier summits, however, were not to be reached again: in 1630, with an annual output of about 60,000 pieces, Hondschoote was still unquestionably an impressive textile centre, but by then it had to share an expanding market with a number of powerful competitors: Calw in Württemberg had already outdistanced Hondschoote, while England and Holland were rapidly catching up with, and were soon to leave behind, their Flemish masters. By mid-century the aggregate output of new draperies in Europe was certainly several times as large as it had been a century before.

The success of the worsted industry rested both on the wide variety of fabrics it produced and on their comparatively low price. As such, worsteds competed with and partly displaced the traditional textiles made of carded wool which had long satisfied the less frivolous tastes of earlier generations. True enough, the new fabrics were flimsier and less durable than the old, heavy woollens which had been the pride of Florence, York, Arras, and Valenciennes in late medieval times: tradition-minded authorities and guild officials, obsessed with the decline or the stagnation of the 'old draperies', were tireless in pointing out that the new substitutes, for all their 'outward appearances and attractive prices', ultimately were a fraud wrought on consumers. The latter, however, must have felt otherwise, for they went on buying more and more worsteds; clearly, as E. B. Supple has suggested,[31] short-term obsolescence presented no problem to consumers who were anxious to keep up with rapidly changing fashions — the more so as the relatively low price of the 'new draperies' made replacement easier in one's wardrobe.

The range of goods available to consumers of even

[31] B. E. Supple, *Commercial Crisis and Change in England, 1600-1642* (Cambridge 1959), p. 154.

moderate income was further widened, in the course of the sixteenth and seventeenth centuries, by the development of two industries of recent vintage which succeeded in expanding their sales thanks to lower prices: one such industry was printing, the other was clockmaking. Both were rooted in the late medieval period, but both came of age and prospered in the first two centuries of the modern period; both started on a diminutive scale as the work of a restricted élite of highly skilled craftsmen and artists, but both by 1700 had spread far and wide and were in a position to offer large quantities of standardised goods to a substantial consumer market.

The story of printing from movable types is too well-known to require retelling here. It will suffice to say that from its modest beginnings in the Rhineland around the middle of the fifteenth century, the book industry made rapid headway in the first century of its existence and became firmly established not only in Germany but also in Italy and France; over the next century and a half the map of Europe became covered with printing presses, large and small, long-lived and ephemeral, while a position of clear supremacy was gradually achieved by the Low Countries, with France, Italy and, later, England, trailing not far behind. The geographical distribution and the multiplication of printing shops is, of course, easier to trace than the progress of aggregate output. It may be useful, however, to recall that in the second half of the fifteenth century an estimated 35,000 editions (or something like 15 million books) were produced in 236 localities scattered throughout Europe, while in the course of the following century Paris and Lyons alone had a combined output of some 40,000 editions — and, of course, the two French cities were by no means the largest printing centres in sixteenth-century Europe, but were certainly outranked, for instance, by Antwerp and possibly by Venice. Progress continued in the seventeenth century when the older centres of the industry were overtaken by new ones, and notably by Amsterdam, Leyden, and London. It is instructive at this point to notice that the catalogues of the largest European book fair, that of

Frankfurt, totalled nearly 20,000 entries in the second half of the sixteenth century and twice as many in the second half of the seventeenth century.

In view of this remarkable record, it is clear that the printing industry could count from the start on a buoyant and indeed expanding demand for its products. Admittedly, neither the sixteenth nor the seventeenth century witnessed a dramatic change in the literacy rate, but some progress certainly did take place even among artisans and small tradesmen. More importantly, among the well-to-do and the educated minority reading habits and the appetite for books spread as a result of a renewed interest in religion, the law, and secular culture. The Reformation, the Counter-Reformation, and the great religious debates that stirred the Protestant and Catholic camps alike in the seventeenth century unquestionably acted as powerful stimulants of the book trade: before the end of the fifteenth century, 99 editions of the *Imitation of Christ* had left the presses; during Luther's lifetime, 430 editions of his translation of the Bible or parts of it appeared in print; the great Antwerp printer Plantin, while he is chiefly remembered today for his fine editions of the classics, made in fact most of his profits and indeed supported his thriving business by producing tens of thousands of missals, breviaries, and devotional books;[32] ironically enough, in Protestant Amsterdam John Blaeu, in the late seventeenth century, was able to defray the cost of his magnificent world atlas by printing under assumed names vast numbers of missals and other religious works intended for the German Catholic reading public.[33]

If, however, religious literature continued to represent a major segment of the printer's output and Bibles, prayer-books and doctrinal works were long at the top of the best-seller lists, secular works steadily gained ground as time went by. The works of the humanists and the editions of classical authors, however important for the history of

[32] R. M. Kingdon, 'Patronage, Piety, and Printing in Sixteenth-century Europe', in *A Festschrift for Frederick B. Artz* (Durham 1964), pp. 19-36.
[33] W. G. Hellinga, *Copy and Print in the Netherlands* (Amsterdam 1962), p. 37.

European culture, never had more than a restricted aud-
ience, and Erasmus was certainly an exception among the
scholars of his time in that he could impose his own terms
on publishers who were only too anxious to have his immensely popular works in their list of titles.[34] Unlike most
classical and literary books, on the other hand, legal
treatises and compendia became quite popular in an age of
increasing litigation when even the old feudal nobility
ceased to regard horsemanship, military training, and
physical exploits as the chief ingredients in a gentleman's
education and began to send their sons to law school. The
new interest in the law was paralleled, moreover, by a
taste for secular subjects in general — political treatises and
tracts, scientific works, plays, essays, and that new child of
the Baroque age, the periodical press.

The printing industry, for its part, effectively contributed to making more books available and accessible to
its public by paring costs, expanding output, and improving marketing practices and methods. In the first century of
its history printing had mainly been the business of adventurous pioneers who often spent their lives moving from
town to town in search of a generous patron or a promising
local clientele. Such men combined the roles of type-
founders, printer, publisher, and bookseller; after the mid-
sixteenth century, however, the small itinerant printer was
gradually superseded by larger established firms and the
various functions in the book trade tended to become
highly differentiated. Type-founding, for instance, evolved
into a separate trade, individual printers hiring the services
of a type-founder whenever a new set of type was needed;
subsequently, the cutting and casting of type came to be
handled by specialised firms and by the late seventeenth
century an estimated fifty firms controlled the business in
the whole of Europe and supplied thousands of printing
shops with movable type. This trend towards specialisation
and concentration, resulting as it did in more durable
types, greater uniformity, and greater simplicity in the

[34] S. H. Steinberg, *Five Hundred Years of Printing* (rev. ed., Penguin Books
1966), p. 142.

design of typographical signs, must have led to substantial reductions in costs.

Specialisation affected other phases of the printing industry as well: increasingly the owner of a printing shop confined himself to management and proof-reading while entrusting to educated and highly trained employees the actual composition of the page; the operation of the press itself was left to workers who were often illiterate but whose astonishing manual dexterity and physical endurance could turn out as many as 3,000 printed pages in one day. The benefits of an increasing divison of labour extended to the marketing process, too. Here two developments are discernible: one is the emergence of the large bookseller who acted as entrepreneur securing author's manuscripts, contracting work with the printers, and attending to the diffusion and sale of books; the other development is the establishment of the great book fairs where printed materials from all over Europe were made available to an international clientele.

Thanks to the invention of printing from movable types, reading materials ceased to be a luxury and the exclusive possession of a few churchmen and scholars. By the seventeenth century, if not earlier, the printed book had become a fairly common item in the homes of at least such people as enjoyed a measure of economic well-being and the privilege of at least some years of formal schooling. By that time, moreover, their homes were as likely as not to include, alongside a small assortment of books, a new and much admired gadget, namely the clock.

Mechanical time pieces had, of course, a long history behind them. Clocks based on the verge escapement, an oscillator activated by weights, go back to the thirteenth century; in the next two centuries they were produced in a wide variety of shapes and designs and with mechanisms of increasing complexity that could show not only the hours of the day, but also the passing of months and seasons as well as the movements of planets and stars. Those admirable clocks, however, were large in size and expensive to build and maintain; as such, only prosperous cities and

wealthy churches could afford them. Only with the advent
of some important technical innovations did time pieces
come within the reach of private individuals. The first
major breakthrough occurred in the fifteenth century: the
invention of the coil spring as motive power, in fact, made
possible the manufacture of portable clocks; and in course of
time improvements in design and workmanship further
helped reduce their size. Mechanical clocks thus ceased to
be exclusively huge public facilities and could find their
place in private households. Around 1650, moreover, the
invention of the pendulum as time-setter, by greatly adding
to the precision and dependability of clocks, made them
even more attractive to people.

It is hard, for lack of precise evidence, to follow the progress of clock-making in the sixteenth and seventeenth
centuries. That the industry made great strides in that
period is, however, beyond doubt and is attested by the
sheer diffusion of the industry throughout Europe — from
Augsburg and Nuremberg to Paris and Geneva, from
London to the villages of the Black Forest — and by what
is known about the size of its output in some centres of clock-
making. By 1680, for instance, Geneva alone reportedly
produced 5,000 pieces a year, while its great rival, London,
probably had already topped that figure. The growth of
the industry is further illustrated by the changes that
occurred over the years in its organisation and structure.
While the great medieval public clocks had been the work
of individual craftsmen who were responsible for every stage
of production from the making of parts to their assemblage,
the domestic clocks of the seventeenth century drew upon
the skills of several groups of specialised workers, each of
them attending to a specific task such as the making of
wheels or coils, the assemblage of the mechanism, or the
manufacture and decoration of dials and encasements.
The process of differentiation of skills and functions in the
clockmaking industry closely resembles, of course, a trend
of affairs which is discernible in the printing industry as
well and it reflects here, too, the growing size of the market.
And so does the emergence, in the seventeenth century, of

the clock merchant who placed orders for parts or for complete clocks with a host of specialised artisans, advanced funds to them, and took care of marketing the finished product.

WARFARE

Our survey of the forces and stimuli impinging on the industrial sector in the early modern period would be seriously incomplete without a discussion of warfare, for in an age that witnessed the creation of vast overseas empires and the ensuing struggle for seapower, the division of Europe into hostile religious camps vying for supremacy, and the long-drawn conflicts between the great absolute monarchies, a rising and unprecedented amount of resources was channelled into military use. Whether this was done entirely or primarily at the expense of civilian consumption; whether, in other words, the war effort shouldered by individual nations at one time or another was wholly matched by a proportional curtailment of production in the industries that catered for civilian uses rather than by mobilising otherwise unused factors is, of course, impossible to tell with any degree of accuracy, given the present state of knowledge. What can be said with considerable confidence however, is, first, that between 1500 and 1700 the scale of warfare as measured by the sheer size of armies and navies increased very substantially and, secondly, that warfare gained in complexity to an even greater extent with the result that the amount of resources embodied in armaments, equipment, and fortifications rose at a faster pace than did the size of armed forces.

The first point is firmly, if not precisely, established.[35] The size of armies exhibited a crescendo from the days of Louis XII when the French crown could muster 30 to 40,000 soldiers to the days of Louis XIV when the French army numbered nearly 300,000 men. Nor was this trend confined to one country only: in the 1560's the Duke of

[35] Cf. G. Clark, *The Seventeenth Century* (2nd ed., New York 1961), pp. 98-100.

Alva could still hope to subdue the Low Countries with 10,000 men; forty years later Ambrogio Spinola, the Spanish commander in Flanders, failed to accomplish the task with five times as many. In the Thirty Years War, armies 50,000 strong were fielded and Wallenstein at one point reportedly set a record with 100,000 soldiers under his command; the English Civil War may have seen as many as 150,000 men under arms on the two sides together, a far cry from earlier times. Much the same holds true of naval forces. In 1588, England mustered nearly 16,000 men against Spanish naval forces; some eighty years later, when she was locked in combat with Holland, twice as many men were serving at sea. At the time Richelieu took power, France had no navy worthy of that name; within a decade the Cardinal had built up its strength to 21 galleys in the Mediterranean and 35 ships of the line in the Atlantic seaports; and Colbert, on his part, was to raise the number of ships of the line to over one hundred.[36]

By 1700 armies and navies were not only larger than before; they also used a far more elaborate and costly equipment. At the opening of the modern period land warfare basically rested on the infantry formation armed with the long pike and drilled in the Swiss order; armour clad cavalry was at the time on its way out as a key instrument of warfare, while firearms (both heavy ordnance and small handguns) were still playing a secondary supporting role on the field of battle. At sea hand-to-hand fighting was still considered normal and gunfire, if used at all, was directed not so much at sinking enemy ships as rather at inflicting losses on enemy crews prior to boarding. Before the end of the sixteenth century, however, large numbers of infantrymen were equipped with light firearms, the pikemen's main role being now that of providing protection to the arquebusiers and musketeers during reloading; as for naval warfare, drastic changes were introduced after Lepanto (1570), the last great battle to be fought according to traditional methods: henceforward the core of naval forces would consist of large

[36] C. W. Cole, *Colbert and a Century of French Mercantilism* (2nd ed., London 1964), vol. I, p. 194.

sailing ships bristling with long-range cannon and artillery duels, rather than man-to-man mêlées, would provide the main decisive act in the cruel drama of battles at sea.[37]

The armament race gained momentum in the seventeenth century. At sea the trend was towards increasing the size of navies, differentiating the warship from the merchantman, increasing the tonnage and the armament of individual vessels. On land three main developments must be recalled besides the increasing use of light firearms at the hands of infantry: first, a revived role for cavalry as the latter was equipped with pistols and carbines; secondly, the appearance of lighter, highly manœuvrable field artillery; and thirdly, in response to quantitative and qualitative improvements in gunfire, an entirely new conception in the layout of fortifications as these came to be based on an interlacing system of polygonal defences calculated to provide maximum concentration of crossfire and maximum protection against enemy shelling.[38]

The above developments were made possible by scientific and technological progress in a variety of fields. The new system of fortifications owed much to advances in mathematics and geometry; the widespread use of artillery was facilitated by the substitution of iron for bronze in the casting of ordnance, a substitution which to some extent sacrificed quality and performance to lower costs and large-scale production; the adoption of firearms by cavalry, on its part, was made possible by significant improvements in the making of thin-walled gun barrels as well as by the invention of self-igniting mechanisms, such as the snap-lock and the flint-lock, that replaced the less practical matchlock previously used in hand-guns.

The combined effects of large-scale warfare and of a more sophisticated military technology on European industries are, of course, hard to gauge with any degree of precision.

[37] On the evolution of naval warfare in the late sixteenth century see M. A. Lewis, *The Spanish Armada* (London 1960), ch. 5, 'The Changing Face of War at Sea'.

[38] A. R. Hall, 'Military Technology', in *A History of Technology* ed. C. Singer and others, vol. III (Oxford 1957), p. 371.

There is little doubt, however, that in the age of Stevin and Vauban, of Tilly and Louvois enormous sums were spent on the construction of impregnable defence works, on the creation by the state of naval yards, arsenals, and gun foundries, and on the purchase of ships, military hardware, and ammunition from private manufacturers. Predictably enough, war contractors and arms manufacturers built vast fortunes for themselves and in many cases their names have survived in the annals of history as early examples of entrepreneurial talent and success in business — from John Browne, the gunfounder of the early seventeenth century whose reputation was as great in his English homeland as it was abroad, to the famous dynasties of the De Geer, the Tripp, and the De Beche who controlled the booming Dutch and Swedish arms industries during much of the seventeenth century, to the Klett family of Thuringia who rose to prominence as war contractors during the Thirty Years War, and to Daliez de La Tour, the purveyor of ordnance on whom Colbert relied to refurbish the French army and navy. We also know that some districts in Europe came to harbour an unusual concentration of arms and munition industries and became heavily dependent on the growing needs of war-like rulers for their economic prosperity. Such was, for example, the Bishopric of Liège, famous since the early sixteenth century for its small firearms, gunshot, cannon balls, and gunpowder and a major source of supply to the Spanish monarchy from the days of Charles V to the days of Charles II. The Brescia province in Venetian territory had an equal reputation for its carbines and muskets and although its craftsmen are chiefly remembered today for their superb, custom-made sporting pieces, down to the end of the seventeenth century their main business and source of livelihood consisted in the production of large quantities of common service firearms or unmounted barrels that were shipped by the thousands to the armouries of Spain, Bavaria, and the several Italian states. In France, Saint-Etienne, Sedan, and the Forez district were important centres of the armament industry, and so were, in Germany, Augsburg and Nuremberg in the sixteenth century and Suhl (Thuringia), Solingen, and Essen in the seventeenth.

The making of bronze cannon had its earlier and most renowned centres in the Low Countries (Namur and Malines), in southern Germany (Augsburg and Nuremberg), and in Italy (Venice, Brescia, and Milan) during the sixteenth century. In the 1540's, however, the casting of iron ordnance made a promising start in the Weald of Sussex and before the close of the century English iron cannon was much in demand at home and abroad on account of its attractive price; in spite of repeated export restrictions, it had found a market on the Continent, particularly in the United Provinces, but occasionally even in Spain. The seventeenth century saw a marked slowdown in the production of English cannon as the industry was increasingly faced with a fuel shortage as well as with stiff foreign competition; eventually England herself became a net importer of cannon. Among her numerous rivals, one must recall the Dutch towns of Utrecht and Amsterdam, Marsberg and Asslar in Westphalia, and the French provinces of Périgord and Angoumois. All of these centres of gun making, however, were soon to be outdistanced by the rapid progress achieved by Sweden. Wrought and cast iron cannon had been produced in Sweden since the 1530's, but for a long time the scale of production had remained trivial, locally made cannon being chiefly intended for the still limited needs of the Swedish crown. Early in the seventeenth century, however, Dutch gun makers and arms merchants brought improved casting techniques as well as their superior organisational and financial power to bear upon Sweden's vast, but still largely untapped, iron and timber resources. The fruits of foreign entrepreneurship and technology were not late in coming: annual exports of cast-iron cannon from Sweden rose from a paltry 20 metric tons in the 1620's to nearly 1,000 tons in the 1640's and to twice that amount in the 1660's.

EXPANDING OUTPUT

When the growth of cities, the opening up of new markets overseas, the increasing diversification and sophistication of production are taken into account, it is hard, even in the absence of aggregate output data, to escape the conclusion that the period from 1500 to 1700 was one of industrial expansion and advance for Europe as a whole. This broad conclusion admittedly runs counter to the view now held by a number of historians which portrays those two centuries as comprising a long upswing from 1500 through the second quarter of the seventeenth century and a subsequent period of depression and contraction that lasted until the early decades of the next century. During the period of 'general crisis', it has been argued, not only did aggregate output of goods and services fall dramatically, but a widespread process of involution set in in which older and backward forms of economic and social organisation were revived and came to exert a stifling influence on the European economy thus, in fact, retarding by a century or so the advent of a genuinely modern, industrial economy such as the buoyant, dynamic sixteenth century had seemed to herald.[39]

Without embarking upon a detailed discussion of the 'general crisis' thesis, it must be said that, while there exists a good deal of solid evidence that would seem to support it, other facts can and should be recited which simply do not fit the sombre image of a great downturn and a prolonged debacle. True enough, one major branch of the wool industry — the making of carded fabrics — suffered severe setbacks at the time; but, as will be recalled, the making of worsteds and of linen fared quite differently. No doubt the Spanish-American trade did contract sharply after about 1620, but the Brazilian and West Indies sugar trade went on expanding. In the Baltic trade a contraction is clearly

---

[39] Cf. E. J. Hobsbawm, 'The Crisis of the Seventeenth Century', *Past and Present*, nos. 5 and 6 (1954). For a recent critique of the 'general crisis' thesis cf. A. D. Lublinskaya, *French Absolutism: the Crucial Phase, 1620-1629* (Engl. transl., Cambridge 1968), ch. I.

discernible in the second half of the century, but it reflected mainly a reduction of grain exports to the West: export of industrial raw materials, on the other hand, tended to rise.[40] In various parts of Europe, and notably in England and Germany, iron mining and metallurgy probably contracted in the course of the century, but in Sweden the opposite was true. And while Italian silk-makers encountered increasing difficulties and even suffered heavy losses, their younger French rivals made steady headway. The enumeration could be prolonged on both sides of the balance sheet, but enough has been said to suggest that the seventeenth century was not so much a time of 'general crisis' as rather one of profound changes in the composition of Europe's economic spectrum and of dramatic shifts in the geographical distribution of economic activity.

We shall come back to the question of geographical shifts at a later point in this chapter. What must be done now is to consider the overall record of Europe's industrial progress from a new angle, namely that of the supply of factors. For if a measure of industrial progress was indeed achieved during the sixteenth and seventeenth centuries in response to new demands and new opportunities, it was obviously because no insuperable obstacle or bottleneck, in terms of either natural resources, manpower, technology, or capital, stood in the way.

NATURAL RESOURCES

So far as natural resources were concerned, the most common way to meet the growing needs of industry was, of course, that of tapping previously unused sources of supply. Examples of this are as numerous as they are well-known. In the case of industrial crops, for instance, one could recall the spread of the cultivation of flax and hemp in the Low Countries, Poland, and Silesia, of the mulberry tree from Sicily and Calabria to the Lombard plain and, at a later

[40] P. Jeannin, 'Les comptes du Sund comme source pour la construction d'indices généraux de l'activité économique en Europe', *Revue historique* (1964), pp. 336-7.

date, to southern France, of woad in Languedoc and Piedmont and of indigo in the New World. In the case of hides
and leather there are reasons for believing that their supply
in western Europe seriously lagged behind demand especially in the sixteenth century when population pressure
caused arable farming increasingly to encroach upon
pastureland; the shortage, however, was relieved in part by
enormous shipments of hides from Spanish America and
from eastern Europe. Fresh sources of supply were also
tapped to meet the rising demand for mineral resources.
The opening of new silver mines in Saxony and Tyrol in
the early sixteenth century is a case in point, and so is the
extraordinary surge of silver output in the New World. But
more significant, if less spectacular, were the efforts undertaken to step up the production of other, and humbler,
minerals.

Such efforts are discernible in iron mining: in all of the
districts where iron-working had traditionally been practised
— the Alps, the Basque provinces, the Rhineland, the Low
Countries, England — the sixteenth century witnessed an
expansion of output in response to the growing demand for
tools, small hardware, and weapons; in the following
century, as further expansion was checked as a result either
of diminishing returns in the operation of mines or of a
shortage of fuel for the processing of the ore near the mining
pits, new iron fields were sought and exploited. Examples
could be quoted for the Alps as well as for Ireland, but the
most remarkable case is beyond question that of Sweden
where iron production, on the upgrade since the early
sixteenth century, attained impressive results in the course
of the seventeenth: in the 1620's exports of iron from
Sweden amounted to about 6,600 tons per annum; at mid-
century over 17,000 tons were exported; in the 1690's, with
an estimated annual output of some 33,000 tons, Sweden
was probably the largest producer of iron in Europe.[41]
Sweden also made a major contribution to industrial
growth as a supplier of copper, a metal increasingly de-

[41] B. Boethius, 'Swedish Iron and Steel, 1600-1955', *Scandinavian Econ.
Hist. Review* (1958), pp. 149-51.

manded for both monetary and industrial uses: the output of Swedish copper kept rising at least until mid-seventeenth century when nearly 3,000 tons were annually shipped abroad.

While new supply sources of iron and copper were being tapped to offset shortages in the older mining districts and to feed the buoyant metal trades of western Europe, a similar development was under way in the case of alum, a basic ingredient in the dyeing industry and one which in medieval times had been mainly secured from the Levant. From 1462 and through the next hundred years a new and plentiful source of supply was represented by the alum works of Tolfa in the Papal States: for nearly a century the great textile centres of Italy, Flanders, and England came to depend on Tolfa for their needs. At the same time efforts were being made to find alternative sources of supply: both in the Low Countries and in England the processing of native alumstones was undertaken before the close of the sixteenth century; by the middle of the next century the new alumworks of Yorkshire and Durham, with an estimated output of 1,000 tons per year, were not only in a position to meet domestic needs, but successfully competed with their Italian rivals on third markets.

In the case of no other raw material were the pressure of demand and the need for fresh sources of supply so strongly felt as in the case of timber. This is understandable in view of the indispensable role played by timber and its by-products in practically every industry of the time: construction and shipbuilding were obviously among the chief consumers of forest resources, but it must be borne in mind that wood entered to a greater extent than iron or steel in the making of tools and mechanical devices, whether ploughs or cranes, watermills or carriages, looms or tilt hammers; and, of course, charcoal or firewood remained throughout this period the most common source of thermic energy in furnaces, forges, kilns, and domestic hearths, while wood ashes were a basic ingredient in the making of soap and glassware. Not surprisingly, the sixteenth and seventeenth centuries, with the manifold and rising de-

mands placed on Europe's woodlands by a growing population and an expanding industrial sector, witnessed local
scarcities of a very serious nature, the more easily so as the
high cost of transportation of timber and firewood relative
to their value placed severe limitations on the actual use of
potential forest resources, unless they be located near the
seashore or in the proximity of navigable rivers.

A shortage of timber was certainly felt before the close
of the sixteenth century in much of southern Europe: it
was a major concern of Venetian shipbuilders and acted as
a powerful brake on their activity before the century was
over; in the same period shipbuilding in the Bay of Biscay,
after several decades of expansion generated by the opening
of the Atlantic sea routes, ran into a similar bottleneck;
before the end of Philip II's reign, the supply of firewood
and charcoal was reportedly running short in much of
Castile as well as in north Italy. The problem, however,
was not unknown north of the Alps and the Pyrenees. By
the late seventeenth century, for example, deforestation had
become a major concern in Dauphiné and the blame for it
was squarely placed on the local forge masters whose insatiable appetite for charcoal allegedly drove up prices and
led to reckless felling. In the Liège district, too, iron metallurgy had resulted in extensive deforestation by the opening
of the seventeenth century, while in early Stuart England
urban construction, the growth of the iron and shipbuilding
industries, and the expansion of sheep raising combined to
eat deeply into the country's timber resources and to bring
about a 'national crisis' of alarming proportions.[42]

The response to the timber shortage basically took two
forms: either new and more distant sources of supply were
tapped or, but less frequently, substitutes were adopted.
The Baltic countries with their seemingly inexhaustible
forest resources represented, of course, the largest and most
promising source of timber supply from the late sixteenth
century onwards: not only was the largest merchant marine

[42] Cf. P. Léon, *La naissance de la grande industrie en Dauphiné* (Paris 1953),
vol. I, p. 19, and C. Wilson, *England's Apprenticeship, 1603-1763*
(Oxford 1965), p. 80.

of the time, that of Holland, totally dependent on Polish and Scandinavian timber for its growing needs, but most European countries, from England to the Venetian Republic, tried to offset local timber scarcities either by importing planks, masts, and spars from the Baltic[43] or by purchasing sea-going vessels from Dutch shipyards. Another source of supply was found in the New World: following the exhaustion of local forest resources in Biscay where most Spanish and Portuguese ships had been built in the early stages of overseas expansion, shipbuilding developed in the West Indies and Brazil and, from the late sixteenth century, American-built vessels came to handle an increasingly large share of the Atlantic trade;[44] in the later part of the seventeenth century, England, on its part, turned to her North American colonies to meet at least part of her needs for timber and naval stores.

Substitution of new materials for wood occurred, as will be recalled, in construction with the adoption of brick and stone as building materials. More importantly, in some regions peat and coal tended to replace firewood and charcoal as fuel for domestic and industrial uses, with the notable exception of iron smelting. Early examples of the use of coal in industry are provided by the Liège district in the late sixteenth century or by the Cevennes in the next century,[45] but in no other country did the adoption of coal reach the proportions that it did in England. The rise of the coal industry in that country stands as one of the most remarkable developments of the early modern period and has been thoroughly investigated by J. U. Nef. It will be recalled that coal output surged from 200,000 tons at mid-sixteenth century to 3 million tons in the 1690's and that coal provided a timely substitute for firewood and charcoal in a variety of uses thus averting what could have been a near disaster.

[43] H. Waetjen, *Die Niederlaender im Mittelmeergebiet zum Zeit ihrer hoechsten Machtstellung* (Berlin 1900), p. 344.

[44] F. Mauro, *Le Portugal et l'Atlantique au XVIIe siècle* (Paris 1960), pp. 43-5.

[45] E. LeRoy Ladurie, *Les Paysans du Languedoc* (Paris 1966), vol. I, p. 214.

Tapping previously unused or alternative sources of supply was not the only way to meet the rising demand for resource inputs: in a few cases, improved technology helped alleviate the problem by saving scarce resources. The results were no doubt rather limited in scope, but cannot be ignored altogether.

Mining and metallurgy were two fields which benefited from resource-saving techniques. One such technique was the amalgamation process whereby silver was separated from its ore with the use of mercury. Its superiority over the traditional method of cupellation apparently rested on the fact that it saved fuel and ensured a higher yield of pure metal. Probably introduced in the early years of the sixteenth century, it met with remarkable success especially in the Spanish colonies and contributed to the phenomenal increase of silver production there. Another and in the long run more significant case of technological progress was the introduction in the late fifteenth century and the diffusion in the next two centuries of the indirect process of iron smelting; this was made possible by the substitution of the large blast furnace in lieu of older types such as the bloomery and the shaft furnace. As Dr Schubert has brought out,[46] the advantages of the blast furnace were mainly two: fuel inputs per unit of output were considerably smaller; moreover, as inferior ores could now be profitably processed, 'the area of ore resources was widened'. For all this, the blast furnace did not displace more primitive types at once: the heavier investment involved in the construction of a blast furnace and its indispensable complement, the forge, and the larger lumps of working capital required in the indirect process ensured the survival of the older furnaces well into the eighteenth century; moreover, wherever rich ores were available the direct process continued to be quite satisfactory. The point that needs emphasis, however, is that from 1500 onwards the blast furnace did spread from its birthplace in the Low Countries to various parts of Europe — Galicia and Lombardy, Styria and Dauphiné, England

[46] H. R. Schubert, *History of the British Iron and Steel Industry* (London 1957), p. 152.

and Sweden — and thus contributed to the slow, but crucial, expansion of iron production.

Improvements in the means of transportation also led to a more economic use of resources. The adoption of iron tyres, turning front wheels, and a rudimentary system of suspension in carts and carriages in the course of the seventeenth century may have contributed to faster transportation overland thereby reducing to some extent the need for large stocks of commodities, but the actual economic significance of this development still awaits investigation. We are on better ground when we turn to seaborne transportation. We know, of course, that by the opening of the sixteenth century such revolutionary innovations as the marriage of square and lateen sails in ocean-going vessels, the adoption of the stern rudder, and the design of longer, slimmer hulls had already been introduced and successfully tested; and insofar as those innovations increased speed and manœuvrability, they obviously made for a better utilisation of cargo space. We also know that, from 1500 to 1700 no comparable breakthrough occurred in the design and rigging of ships. What did take place in those two hundred years, however, was the diffusion of those earlier innovations from their Iberian homeland to other seafaring nations, their adaptation to local conditions and needs, and their steady improvement as suggested by experience. There was, moreover, some progress in hull design and construction methods which made possible the launching of larger and stouter ships: this is revealed by the increase in the size of ships plying the Atlantic routes from 200 to 600 tons in the course of the sixteenth century; and this must have meant greater seaworthiness and better protection against pirate attacks. But possibly the most significant advance in seaborne transportation was represented by the appearance, late in the sixteenth century, of a new freight carrier, the Dutch *fluyt* or flyboat. Cheaply built, unarmed, shorn of ornaments and heavy suprastructures, equipped with a rather simple sail-plan, the long, flat-bottomed fluyt had the advantage of offering maximum cargo space and of being cheap to operate. The partial loss of speed and the absence of armament prevented its use in the long ocean voyages, but in the North and Baltic seas it proved admirably suited to the transport of bulk cargoes such as salt, grain, and timber.

The efforts to overcome scarcities of resources whether by widening the supply area, introducing substitutes, or adopting resource saving techniques did more than making expansion of output possible; they also had some important indirect effects which should not be ignored. The tapping of new and more distant supply sources, for instance, brought new areas into the orbit of the market economy; by generating fresh purchasing power in those areas, it certainly led to an extension of the market for manufactured goods. The introduction of substitutes and of more sophisticated technology had, on its part, strong backward linkage effects: in the case of iron metallurgy, the indirect smelting process implied heavy outlays in the construction of the blast furnace and the forge; the amalgamation process was responsible for the rapid development of mercury mining in Spain (Almaden) and Istria; the increasing use of coal in England, requiring as it did seaborne transportation from the coal pits of the North, acted as a powerful stimulus on coastal navigation in Tudor and Stuart times.

LABOUR AND TECHNOLOGY

New demands were placed, not only on Europe's resource basis, but on its manpower as well: as traditional industries progressed, however slowly, and new ones were introduced, a larger labour force and a widening spectrum of skills had to be found — unless, of course, some form of inanimate energy or new mechanical devices could be substituted for human efforts and manual dexterity.

Before the eighteenth century, examples of labour-saving techniques and devices are notoriously rare. In iron metallurgy, however, there was a definite tendency to adopt more widely such power-driven machines of late medieval vintage as the large bellows, the tilt-hammer, and the stamping mill for crushing the ore before it was fed into the furnace. A few innovations also made their appearance, and notably the wire-drawing machine, the rolling mill, and the slitting mill.[47] The first was probably invented in Nuremberg before the end of the fifteenth century, but was not widely adopted abroad until the late sixteenth century: it replaced the old, time-consuming, and laborious process of drawing wire by hand; it also made for greater accuracy and more uniform tension, thus improving the quality of wire and its by-products such as nails and needles. The rolling and the slitting mills, on their part, had their birth-place in the Liège area in the early sixteenth century; before the close of the century a number of them was in use outside their native country. The rolling mill was used to turn iron bars into sheets and its superiority over the traditional battery hammer rested on a larger output per hour. In the slitting mill (the *fenderie* for which the Liège metallurgists were justly admired), the iron sheet passed under a grooved cylinder or roller and was cut into rods of equal thickness. By replacing the slow and strenuous method of cutting rods by hand it reportedly enabled 'two men to do the work of a hundred'.

Saving labour became a prime concern in a few other industries as well. Dutch shipyards came to be much admired for their extensive use of mechanical saws and cranes, and also for stockpiling parts that could be easily assembled into cheaply-built freight carriers. Mechanisation made some inroads into the textile sector, too. The ribbon frame, an improved loom which, it was said, raised four-fold the output of the ribbon maker, was slow to gain acceptance (probably in the face of opposition by the guilds), even in Leyden where it originated; by about 1660, however, it had come into use in Lancashire and the Basel area and was a common feature of the peasant house-hold there. The stocking frame, a hand-operated knitting machine of English origin, grew very popular in the Mid-lands early in the seventeenth century and gave rise to an important hosiery manufacture that was soon to over-shadow traditional hand-knitting. In Lombardy an attempt

[47] W. Rees, *Industry before the Industrial Revolution* (Cardiff 1968), p. 610.

to introduce the stocking frame in the late 1660's mis-
carried in the face of local opposition,[48] but in nearby
Venetia it was apparently adopted with little trouble;
before the end of the century, stockings were produced in
that region in considerable quantities and they were said to
be comparable to their English-made counterpart.

Venetia and indeed the whole Po valley must be chiefly
remembered in the seventeenth century for adopting the
power-driven silk mill on a large scale.[49] The mill itself was
possibly the most admired machine at the time due to its
unusually large size and the complexity of its operation
which involved hundreds of spindles and spools. Contemporaries variously estimated its output as the equivalent of
that of 400 to 4,000 spinners, and those wild estimates tell
us more about the way popular imagination was caught by
the sight of those 'wondrous engines' than about the mill's
actual performance. There is no doubt, however, that the
great silk mill (originally built in medieval Bologna, but
jealously guarded for over two centuries as the city's
treasured secret) was one of the most successful labour-
saving devices in pre-industrial Europe. Its diffusion in the
Po valley began early in the seventeenth century; by the
end of the century there were over one hundred such water-
driven machines in operation in that region with an
aggregate output of over one million pounds of high-grade
silk thread (organzine) that was largely exported to the
nascent silk manufactures of southern Germany, Holland,
and England, but above all to the leading centre of the silk
industry at the time, namely Lyons. Before the end of the
century, however, mechanical silk mills had already made
their appearance in the Rhône valley thus heralding their
remarkable diffusion outside Italy and throughout Europe
in the next century.[50]

However significant these and a few other labour saving

[48] E. Verga, 'Le leggi suntuarie e la decadenza dell'industria in Milano',
Archivio Storico Lombardo (1900), p. 95.
[49] D. Sella, 'Contributo alla storia delle fonti d'energia', in *Studi in onore
di A. Fanfani* (Milan 1962), vol. V, pp. 621-31.
[50] Léon, *op. cit.*, p. 44.

devices may have been to a handful of industries and however much they may have helped relieve local shortages of
manpower, the fact remains that in the two centuries we
are surveying manufacturing continued to depend, much
as it had in the past, primarily on man's efforts and skills.
Contemporaries were aware of such dependence: their
emphasis on a plentiful labour supply as a prerequisite for
industrial expansion and the policies aimed at attracting
workers from other countries must be viewed in the light of
an economy in which human energy still played a predominant role and human dexterity could seldom be replaced by the machine.

Immigration from foreign countries was, of course, the
exceptional way to increase the size of the labour force,
although in certain cases, as will be seen, it proved essential
to industrial progress. As a rule, such additional manpower
as a growing industrial sector might require had to come
mainly from the primary sector of the economy. As the
latter comprised an ample majority of the working population, the needs of industry could be met, it would appear,
without any radical redeployment of the labour force.
Moreover, a complete occupational change from the plough
to the loom or the anvil was facilitated by the fact that it
did not necessarily involve the migration and resettlement
of workers from the village to the town: industrial activity
was notoriously carried out in both.

For all that, severe limitations could stand in the way of
an expansion of the industrial labour force: so long as productivity in agriculture was not significantly raised (as apparently it was not, by and large, between 1500 and 1700), a
substantial transfer of manpower from agriculture to industry was bound (once redundant farm labour had been
mopped up) to undercut the output of primary goods, and
notably of foodstuffs, and thus to impair, beyond a certain
point, further industrial progress.

There are good reasons for believing that, in fact, those
limitations were real. No doubt large numbers of rural
people, especially from such relatively overpopulated areas
as the Alps and the Massif Central, did flock to the towns

and while many found employment as domestic servants, petty retailers, or porters rather than as artisans, others certainly came to man the city workshops, smithies, and building yards. It is equally certain that many more switched from agriculture to industry without leaving their ancestral home, for certain industries required a rural, rather than urban, setting. And yet, it is indicative of the delicate balance that had to be struck in the allocation of manpower between primary and secondary production that often enough, and increasingly so in the seventeenth century, the needs of industry were met not by complete occupational transfers, but rather by utilising *in loco* and on a part-time basis rural workers who, while still tending their fields and cattle, were willing to work at the spinning wheel, the loom, or the forge in the slack periods of the agricultural cycle.

Such was the case of the nailmakers in the Verviers region, of the clockmakers in the Black Forest, of the 'rustic, miserable folks' who lived in the Lombard Alps and earned part of their living spinning and weaving wool for the clothiers of the plain; such was also the case of the peasantry of Flanders, Normandy and Switzerland who made linen in their cottages and fed it to the great bleaching centres of Haarlem, Rouen, and Zürich. In Dauphiné, according to a late seventeenth-century report, 'cloth-making is an occupation common among men while the spinning of wool and silk and the sewing of gloves are common among women; this, however, must be understood of the time when farming does not claim their labour.'[51] Similarly, the knitting industry in Yorkshire, cloth-making in the Midlands, iron metallurgy in Normandy and Limburg were chiefly carried out in rural communities in which manufacturing dovetailed with farming and claimed but a portion of the available supply of labour time.

The utilisation of rural labour in industry must obviously have involved some disadvantages: the dispersion of production in widely scattered villages and hamlets, their distance from a marketing centre where goods were to be

[51] Boulainvilliers, *Etat de la France* (London 1737), vol. VI, p. 16.

brought for sale or shipment, the frequent interruptions caused by the demands of agriculture at peak times. Those disadvantages, however, were presumably more than offset in the eyes of the merchant-manufacturer by some important gains. Contemporary sources variously mention lower taxation, freedom from stifling guild regulations, and, above all, lower wages as the chief advantages offered by the countryside over the city. Lower labour costs were probably the most attractive feature of industries employing rural workers who still retained a foothold in agriculture, and understandably so. For those workers, being only partly dependent on wages for their living, could afford to hire themselves out for less; the time they devoted to manufacturing being, in fact, time during which they would have been virtually idle, the supply price of their labour was bound to be appreciably lower than that of the fully specialised urban craftsman and journeyman. For the economy as a whole, on the other hand, the employment of rural labour was no less vital than for the merchant-manufacturer anxious to pare costs: by tapping the reserve of labour time that existed in the countryside industrial production could be expanded very considerably without undercutting food production.

The introduction of a new manufacture as opposed to the expansion of an existing one presented, of course, different problems. In an age in which most work depended on manual dexterity and knowhow rather than on highly sophisticated machinery the recruitment of specialised craftsmen from a more developed area was, as a rule, the first necessary step. Under the circumstances, it is not surprising that in the centuries we are discussing, when all kinds of industrial activity spread into new areas of Europe, migration of skilled personnel was a prominent feature indeed.

We know, for instance, that miners and metal-workers from Saxony, Styria, and Tyrol contributed to the rise and development of 'heavy industry' in France, Italy, and England in the course of the sixteenth century; that Walloon gunfounders and gunsmiths must be largely credited with the creation of the Swedish iron industry, just as others among their fellow-countrymen must be credited with initiating England and the Palatinate to the secrets of the 'new draperies'. The French silk, printing, and glass industries notoriously owed much, during their infancy, to Italian immigrants, while in Geneva clock-making was originally introduced by artisans from Augsburg and Nuremberg. France itself, after being for a century and a half a major recipient of skilled foreign labour, became, in the late seventeenth century at the time of the Revocation of the Edict of Nantes, a source of highly trained manpower for other countries, and notably England, to draw upon.

This enumeration could be prolonged, but unnecessarily so, to stress the vital role played by migrations in Europe's industrial progress. Of greater interest, however, would be to enquire into the forces and motivations behind the individual craftsman's or groups of craftsmen's decisions to leave their homeland and to resettle in a new and often wholly alien society. Of the two mechanisms that are responsible for migration — the 'push' of a hostile homeland and the 'pull' of a more promising future elsewhere — it is the former that is best known. Much has been written about religious and political persecution as a cause of emigration, and the exodus of religious dissidents from the Spanish Low Countries in the late sixteenth century or that of the Huguenots from France in 1685 are two familiar illustrations of that process. The ravages and hardships wrought by war, too, could result in emigration as they did in Italy when the peninsula became the stage and the victim of the long-drawn Habsburg-Valois struggle for supremacy or in Germany during the Thirty Years War. On a smaller scale and in a less dramatic way, the 'push' to emigration could be imparted by a growing tax burden or by stringent and basically obnoxious guild regulations, as apparently was the case in a number of Italian towns during the seventeenth century.

It is much more difficult to tell what made individual workers decide on a specific destination once they had made up their minds about emigrating. We have all heard of

enlightened rulers and ministers enticing artists and craftsmen away from their native land with the promise of high
wages, naturalisation privileges, tax exemption, or dowries
for their brides and nubile daughters, but those induce-
ments were no doubt exceptional, and had prospective
emigrants merely waited for a foreign prince to wave at
them the diffusion of industry in early modern Europe
would have been a very slow process indeed. Most emigrants certainly found out about a suitable destination
through personal contacts and by word of mouth passed
along by relatives or friends who had preceded them and
were in a position to report that in a given area opportunities did exist for a given type of skill. Merchants must have
played an especially useful role in this respect: not only did
they travel a great deal, but, more importantly, by bringing
to a country manufactured goods produced in another, they
created, when successful, a demand for them; and once a
sufficiently large demand had been created, it became
possible and indeed attractive for artisans to come and set
up shop in that area. Thanks to the merchants, in other
words, the artisan's work paved the way to the artisan himself. No doubt, this is largely speculative, but it is no mere
coincidence, for instance, that long before it harboured
refugee silk-makers from Italy and long before it emerged
as a major centre of the silk industry, a city like Lyons had
served as the headquarters of Italian merchants and as the
distributing centre of Italian silk goods in France; nor is it
a mere coincidence that Flemish merchants were very active
in the Baltic area long before Sweden began to attract forge
masters, miners, and gunfounders from the Low Countries.

CAPITAL

While the sources from which the industrial sector of early
modern Europe drew its raw materials, inanimate energy,
and manpower are fairly easy to identify and are often
known with a considerable degree of precision, it is much
harder to be specific about the sources of industrial capital.
Much, of course, is known about the great financiers — the

Fuggers, the Welsers, the Affaitadis, the Ruiz, the Tripps — who built vast fortunes, lent vast sums to impecunious rulers, launched risky commercial ventures, and dominated the money market of Renaissance and Baroque Europe. With some notable exceptions, however, their role in industry was limited: it was mainly confined to providing working capital to certain industries that were heavily oriented towards distant export markets; their main interest was primarily directed at international trade, state finance, and monetary transactions. For their investment needs most industries had thus to turn to sources other than the great banking and financial houses of the time, and more often than not those sources were too small to leave a clear trace in the annals of history. Even in the absence of precise records, however, the historian's task is not entirely hopeless.

We may start by noticing that in early modern times by far the largest group of producing units was represented by the countless workshops, urban hovels, or country cottages where the anvils, the looms, the printing presses, or the ribbon frames were operated by a craftsman and a few assistants or relations. The basic feature of those plants was clearly the diminutive size of the physical capital locked up in them: not only was the building itself often used both as home and as workshop and, as such, represented no additional investment, but the tools and simple machines lodged in it did not amount to very much. What their value may have been is not easy to determine, but it is revealing that innumerable small artisans throughout Europe did own the equipment they used. Poor though they unquestionably were, they provided their own fixed capital; obviously they could do so because that capital itself was small enough to be within their reach. A major source of fixed industrial capital was thus represented by the small investments of the artisans themselves.

A consequence of the puny size of the initial investment was to make entry to most trades relatively easy. To stay in business, however, was often a far more difficult task for the small independent weaver, printer, or nailmaker. His overhead costs might well be negligible, but his own sub-sistence or his wage bill were not; the purchase of raw materials, moreover, could well be beyond his means. This was especially true of the artisan who happened to work for a distant market or had to use expensive raw materials: in one case his limited cash resources could not be stretched to cover the several months that might elapse before his goods were sold; in the other, he might be in no position to purchase his raw materials in advance. These problems were, of course, of old standing and the medieval period, as is well-known, had developed a variety of prac-tices aimed at bridging the gap between the workshop and the market place; those practices carried over into the early modern period and remained normal until the coming of the large factory. Basically, a middleman or merchant commanding both liquid assets and commercial connec-tions relieved the small producer of the burden of a slow turnover or of heavy outlays on raw material purchases; this he could do either by putting out the raw material to the artisan, by paying him wages, or by contracting to buy his goods as soon as they were manufactured.

What particular arrangement was in fact resorted to depended on a number of circumstances. In the linen in-dustry, for instance, where rural artisans generally used flax grown on their own or their fellow villagers' premises, the merchant's chief function was to buy the linen as soon as it was brought to him by peasant producers, thus en-suring the latter a prompt return for their efforts and financ-ing, in fact, the manufacturing process to the extent of reducing the cost represented by a slow turnover. On the other hand, in industries that used imported or expensive fibres, such as fine wool, silk, or cotton, the merchant pro-vided the raw material, handed it over to the weavers with specific instructions as to the type of fabric he expected them to make, and paid them wages. In a similar way, the small, scattered producers of common hardware, while owning their shops and tools, had to depend on a middleman to the extent that either the acquisition of raw materials or the final disposition of their produce involved roundabout, time-consuming transactions. In Normandy, as Jean Vidalenc has brought out in his detailed study of the metal trades in that region, the typical producer was the independent rural craftsman: as long as he confined himself to fashioning inferior local iron into cheap needles, pins, knives, and locks intended for the local market, he remained wholly his own master and was financially autonomous; in the seventeenth century, however, as the industry found new outlets in France itself, in Spain, and in the New World, and as iron increasingly had to be secured from the Rhineland, Burgundy, and Sweden to supplement an inadequate local supply, the small masters came to depend upon the wealthy *négociants* for raw materials, wages, and the marketing of their hardware. Similar examples, could be recited for the nail industry in the Vesdre region, the Auvergne cutlery trades centred around Thiers, or the making of light firearms in the Brescia province. In all such cases industrial production fed on two distinct sources of capital: the artisan's tools and equipment and the merchant's cash.

With a few notable exceptions much the same holds true of the printing industry. Here again was a field of activity where entry was relatively easy for a man who had expertise and ambition: all he needed to get started in business was a couple of rooms, a press, and a good stock of types; the amazing proliferation of tiny, one-press shops manned by a master and two or three assistants throughout Europe from the late fifteenth century onwards is enough evidence of the modest needs for plant and equipment in that industry. To operate an independent book-printing business, however, was a far more arduous game, for the printing of a normal edition (600 to 800 copies) represented a very substantial outlay on paper alone (in fact, one several times the cost of the fixed equipment itself); moreover, the disposal of a newly printed work, given the wide geographical dispersion of its potential readers and the difficulties of transportation, was likely to be a slow process. Under the circumstances, the launching of a book was often beyond the financial ability of a small printer or might wreck him long before he had recovered his investment; outside capital was, in most cases, an absolute necessity. A few fortunate printers might lean on an enlightened patron willing to finance, even at a loss, the production of certain books; others joined in partnership with men of substance and shared with them profits or losses; many more worked on contract for large booksellers or (more rarely) for a wealthier fellow-printer on much the same terms as weavers and nailmakers did for clothiers and ironmongers. This was by far the most common practice: in the printing industry, it has been said, the large bookseller with wide business connections performed the role of a 'banker'.

In a few industries even the provision of fixed capital far exceeded the resources of the average artisan and had to be ensured either by an individual or an institution of unusual financial strength or by the joint effort of several smaller investors. In mining and metallurgy, for example, large landowners continued to play, as they had in medieval times, an important role. In Saxony and Thuringia the manorial lords on whose lands deposits of silver, copper, or lead were found alongside a plentiful supply of timber invested heavily in the exploitation of mineral resources; in Dauphiné the extraction and processing of iron ores continued to prosper, in early modern times, on the estates of the monks of the Chartreuse as well as on those of the old landed nobility; but new pits, furnaces, and forges were opened on the land newly acquired by prominent upstarts such as the Barrals who had climbed to the top of the social ladder through a combination of commercial activities, tax-farming, and public office and were anxious to exploit the resources now in their hands.[52] In Tudor England, peers and upper gentry were active in promoting mining and metallurgy on their estates and invested heavily in coal pits, mining shafts, furnaces, and forges.[53]

At times the large doses of capital needed in mining and metallurgy were supplied by the great merchants and financiers whose fortunes had been built up to heroic pro-

[52] Léon, *op. cit.*, p. 59.
[53] Stone, *op. cit.*, p. 339; also Rees, *op. cit.*, p. 204 n.

portions in long distance trade and state finance. Such were the Chigi, the Pallavicino, the Sauli who, at one time or another, secured the lease of what probably was the largest extractive enterprise in early modern Europe, namely the alumworks of Tolfa in the Papal States, with its workforce of some 800 men;[54] such were the Fuggers and the Welsers who leased and operated copper and silver mines in Saxony, Thuringia, and Tyrol and built impressive refineries (*Saigerhuetten*) for processing the ores.

Investment in large mining and metallurgical enterprises by individual landowners and financiers, however, was probably less common than investment by partnerships in which the merchant, the tax collector, the lawyer, and the nobleman pooled their resources in varying proportions while limiting their risks. In Saxony and Bohemia the mining company (*Gewerkschaft*) derived its life-blood from a wide range of sources — monastic institutions as well as wholesale merchants, titled landlords no less than municipal governments — each holding a number of shares (*Kuxen*). In England the Company of Mines Royal, created in the 1560's to promote the mining of copper, drew on German models for its organisation. It drew on German capital as well: of its original twenty-four shares, eleven were taken up by the great commercial house of Hang, Langnauer, and Co. of Augsburg, the remaining shares being held by Englishmen, among them Sir William Cecil and Robert Dudley, earl of Leicester. The contemporaneous Mineral and Battery Company which combined mining and heavy metallurgy saw its original thirty-six shares subscribed by successful London merchants and prominent peers.[55] A similar pattern obtained in Valsassina, the chief iron mining district in Lombardy: in the seventeenth century the opening and exploitation of new pits was, as a rule, the work of partnerships in which ironmongers and local gentry rubbed shoulders with city patricians and government officials.[56] In Liège and in the regions, such as the Rhineland and

[54] Delumeau, *L'alun de Rome: XVe-XIXe siècle* (Paris 1962), p. 76.
[55] Rees, *op. cit.*, pp. 374, 376.
[56] A. Fanfani, 'L'industria mineraria lombarda durante il dominio

Sweden, where the Liègeois were especially active, a few wealthy families (the Curtius, the De Geer, the Mariotte) managed to build huge industrial empires out of the financial resources they had amassed in trade, real estate speculation, war contracts, and earlier industrial enterprises. Those families, however, were exceptional: in most enterprises capital was initially provided by the joint contributions of local brewers and aldermen, churchmen and ironmasters, most of them merely acting as sleeping partners in the company.

Mining and heavy metallurgy, with their demand for large investments, were clearly fields in which a great landowner, a financial tycoon, or (more commonly) some form of partnership must play a dominant role. In lighter industries, as indicated before, the normal pattern continued to be that of a host of tiny shops owned and operated by individual artisans; only exceptionally did the size of physical plant attain such proportions as to require a generous dose of outside capital. One such exception was the Plantin printing house in sixteenth-century Antwerp: with its 24 presses, over a hundred employees, and an international market to serve, it unquestionably towered in a field where the one or two-press workshop long remained the rule. The rise of that early 'book factory' was basically the work of Christopher Plantin, an artisan of modest means who for years had earned his way by serving as printer and bookbinder in Rouen, Paris, and Antwerp. His success as the leading printer and publisher in Europe, however, was due to his talents and skill as a printer as much as to his ability to find solid partners among the Antwerp bourgeoisie. The glass industry, to quote but another example, remained largely in the hands of small, independent masters, whether impecunious *gentilhommes verriers* of Normandy and Lorraine, expert glassblowers of Murano, or crystal-makers in Bohemia. The introduction of a new process for casting and rolling large glass plate in late

spagnolo', in his *Saggi di storia economica italiana* (Milan 1936), pp. 201, 205.

seventeenth-century France, however, signalled a sharp departure from the traditional pattern: the Royal Plate Glass Company which first adopted the new technique was almost from the start, with several hundred workers on its payroll and an elaborate costly equipment, a large factory. As such, it owed its existence to a partnership formed by four well-endowed financiers.

The industrial partnership, while remaining a sporadic practice in most fields, found nearly universal acceptance in the construction and ownership of merchant ships. Joint ownership of large, ocean-going vessels was, of course, well-known in the late Middle Ages both in the Hanseatic towns and in the Mediterranean seaports; it had been preferred to ownership in severalty basically as a form of insurance for what then was and would long remain a high-risk investment. After 1500, as the size of freight carriers tended to increase and voyages became longer and more hazardous, the practice of joint ownership spread and, if we are to judge from the development of the English shipping partnership, the trend was towards larger numbers of shares and partners.

The decisive role played by the partnership in channelling investments into what was unquestionably one of the fastest growing industries in early modern times seems to be beyond doubt. It was part-owners (*parcenevoli*) who in the sixteenth century made possible the remarkable transformation of the Venetian merchant fleet from one in which oared galleys predominated to one consisting mainly of round ships entirely dependent on their sails. It was the shipping company (*reederij*) in which a dozen individuals (merchants, mariners, patricians, and lawyers) pooled their savings that made possible the spectacular, ten-fold growth of the Dutch commercial fleet between 1500 and 1700. On a smaller scale, what is true of Dutch shipping holds of English shipping too: the creation of what by the Restoration was the second largest merchant marine in the world was the work of innumerable shipping partnerships and of a galaxy of small savers.

Whether provided by individual craftsmen, merchants,

or landowners or through some form of partnership, much new capital thus flowed into industrial undertakings during the sixteenth and seventeenth centuries. Clearly, the expanding market opportunities created by colonisation, urbanisation, and changing patterns of consumption were decisive factors in determining the level and the direction of that flow. Another and no less important factor, however, may have been at work, namely falling interest rates. The evidence for this is still very fragmentary, but it would seem that from the late fourteenth or early fifteenth century onwards, interest rates in western Europe, or at least in its economically most advanced areas, followed a descending trend; by 1700 the cost of loans on good security was probably half of what it had been three hundred years before.[57] The whole phenomenon still awaits, and deserves, further study, and so do its possible causes. Some of its implications, however, can be tentatively read into a number of developments discussed in the preceding pages. The widespread, if not generalised, adoption of such roundabout, capital-intensive techniques as the indirect process of iron smelting and the mechanisation of silk-throwing; the search for, and the working of, new and presumably less accessible mineral deposits outside traditional mining areas; the growing output of consumer goods intended for overseas markets and, as such, dependent on lengthening trade channels and on a slower turnover of capital — these and similar developments are consistent with a significant drop in the cost of capital. They suggest that the downward trend of interest rates had, as we would expect it should, the effect of widening the range of opportunities open to industrial enterprise and of enabling it to respond more effectively to the manifold demands of the early modern world.

---

[57] Cf. S. Homer, *A History of Interest Rates* (New Brunswick, N.J. 1963), part two, for a compendium of the available evidence; C. M. Cipolla, 'Note sulla storia del saggio d'interesse', *Economia Internazionale* (1952) and H. J. Habakkuk, 'The Long-Term Rate of Interest and the Price of Land in the Seventeenth Century', *Econ. Hist. Rev.* (1952) are two of the most significant contributions to the subject.

THE CHANGING GEOGRAPHY OF INDUSTRY

One of the most striking developments that occurred in the first two centuries of the modern age was the spread of industrial activity in areas where, before 1500, such activity had been, if not entirely absent, at least negligible and definitely inferior to that of other and more advanced parts of Europe. Around 1500 the latter included, as is well-known, the southern provinces of the Low Countries, north Italy, and portions of south Germany. In those three main areas manufacturing had attained high levels, in the late Middle Ages, in terms of both the size and the diversity of output: from those 'older industrial countries' came to the rest of Europe the finest cloth, expensive silks and linen, exquisite glassware and ceramics, highly prized incunabula and musical instruments, but also large quantities of fustians, common hardware, arms and armour, leather-goods and writing paper. Admittedly, industry in late medieval times had by no means remained wholly confined to the area roughly comprised between Bruges in the north and Florence in the south: by 1500, for instance, English unfinished cloth already loomed large in international trade; ships built in Zealand and Holland and fish cured and packed in those same provinces were already well-known outside their homeland; the linen industry of Normandy was by then of old standing and an important complement to the rural economy of the region; in the north-west of Spain, to quote one more example, iron mining and metallurgy also had, by the close of the Middle Ages, a long and distinguished record to show. For all this, there is little doubt that the industrial backbone of Europe ran at the time from Flanders to Tuscany; the concentration of industrial enterprise in that narrow corridor had no parallel elsewhere; the rest of Europe depended on that early 'workshop of the world' for its supply of a host of manufactures, while mainly contributing to it farm goods, raw materials, and unfinished goods.

Two hundred years later the old order appeared radically

altered. By that time, as will be recalled, Sweden had emerged as one of the leading producers of iron. The French economy, while still firmly attached to its traditional rural moorings, had gained very considerably in industrial strength: its silks, by then, held sway in Europe, were well-known overseas, and successfully competed everywhere with Italian goods; its linens had captured the lion's share of the Spanish-American market previously controlled by Flemish manufacturers; French glassware, and notably large mirrors, was beginning to displace the products of Venice; in papermaking and printing, too, France had made great strides and, in spite of a serious but temporary crisis in the last quarter of the seventeenth century, could rank among the two or three largest producers of paper and books. Lastly, some progress had been registered in the iron industries of Normandy and Dauphiné, in the woollen industry of Languedoc, and in shipbuilding in Brittany.

Far more remarkable, however, were the gains achieved by the end of the seventeenth century in the northern portion of the Low Countries and in England. In the territory of what in the late sixteenth century had become the Dutch Republic industrial progress was no doubt over-shadowed by the astonishing expansion of the tertiary sector. But even in the field of industry the Dutch could be proud of their record. The old shipbuilding industry continued to be, until the close of the seventeenth century, one of the leading industries of the Netherlands: its size and growth are suggested by the ten-fold increase of Dutch tonnage between 1500 and 1700; at the latter date the Dutch merchant marine, with well over half-a-million tons afloat, was three times as large as its English rival and probably larger than all the European fleets combined.[58] Dutch shipbuilding was thus geared to the growing needs of the largest commercial fleet in the world, but its prosperity was further enhanced by the fact that most other nations — the Spaniards no less than the English, the French no less than the Italians — were partially dependent on Dutch shipyards for their needs. Naturally enough, the

[58] Parry, *art. cit.*, p. 206.

shipbuilding industry was singled out for praise and admiration by contemporary writers and observers of the Netherlands: the size of the industry had no precedent and, moreover, with its many ramifications (the making of sails and cordage, the timber trade, small metallurgy and the casting of anchors) it reached deep into the economic texture of the country and was obviously a major force making for growth and prosperity.

Other industries helped, too. By the mid-seventeenth century, for instance, at a time when the Dutch economy had reached or was near its zenith, the town of Leyden probably ranked as the single largest centre of the wool industry in Europe with an annual output of about 100,000 pieces of cloth. Haarlem, on the other hand, held a commanding position in the linen industry: unfinished linen fabrics from Germany, the Spanish Low Countries, and northern France were brought there to be bleached alongside those made in the town itself or in the surrounding countryside. On a smaller scale, several other industries thrived on Dutch soil: besides such processing industries as sugar refining and distilling in which a nation like Holland, with its world-wide trade connections, enjoyed obvious advantages, there developed a host of manufactures in which the craftsman's expertise was the key to success: silk-making, ceramics, printing, diamond cutting, precision instruments, the making of maps. In spite of their comparatively recent origin, those manufactures, and notably ceramics and printing, soon acquired an international reputation they were to maintain for a long time.

The establishment of a broad spectrum of industrial activities in the Netherlands from the late sixteenth century onwards, had a parallel in England, for here, too, the late sixteenth and, even more so, the seventeenth centuries witnessed the formation of a robust and highly diversified industrial structure. What shipbuilding and the great fisheries had been to the Netherlands in late medieval times clothmaking had been to England: the island's export trade had, in fact, been almost entirely dependent on the shipment of unfinished cloth to the Continent. The surge of cloth exports from 50,000 to 150,000 pieces a year in the first half of the sixteenth century, while unquestionably imparting a powerful stimulus to the whole economy, had also emphasised its traditional, narrowly based character and its vulnerability to the vagaries of foreign demand for a single commodity — a fact painfully brought home by the depression of the 1560's and again by that of the 1620's. Both depressions, however, may have served to quicken a slow process of diversification at the end of which England emerged a strong industrial power.

Mining and metallurgy have already been referred to as fields where progress was especially noticeable. The rise of coal production from 200,000 to 3 million tons in the course of a century and a half is possibly the most impressive and distinct development of the period we are discussing; not only did it enable England to break a dangerous fuel bottleneck, but it also had powerful linkage effects on the rest of the economy as it induced a roughly proportional increase of tonnage in the coastal trade as well as an expansion in the production of tools and implements as were required in coal mining itself. As regards iron mining and metallurgy, information is far less precise, but it would seem that considerable progress was achieved during the sixteenth and the early seventeenth centuries: at the accession of Charles I, that is to say nearly a century after the introduction of the first blast furnace in England, one hundred such furnaces, with an estimated output of 25,000 tons of pig iron a year, were reported in existence; and in the wake of a growing iron output metal trades had made considerable headway in response to the new demand generated by mining, construction, shipbuilding, and armaments. From the Civil War to the early eighteenth century, when output was down to about 18,000 tons, the English iron industry experienced a long period of difficulties and a partial decline that must be largely ascribed to a shortage of charcoal. Industrial progress, however, continued in other fields.

One such field was papermaking where output rose steadily from early Tudor times, although it remained chiefly confined to inferior grades. Another was glass-making: first produced on a substantial scale in the late sixteenth century, English glassware could not compete for a long time with the quality production of continental industries such as those of Italy, Lorraine, and Bohemia; by the early seventeenth century, however, English-made common glassware had captured the domestic market; before the century was over a new English product known as flint-glass had established for itself a solid reputation on foreign markets thanks to its remarkable transparency.

Throughout the period we are discussing woollen textiles continued to hold a major place in English manufactures, although their position relative to aggregate industrial output slowly declined as the whole industrial spectrum grew more diversified.[59] By 1700, moreover, cloth production was markedly different in quality from what it had been in the past: traditional carded fabrics were now dyed and dressed at home rather than abroad; more importantly, as will be recalled, they had been overshadowed by the 'new draperies', that sprawling and ever changing family of worsted fabrics which appealed so much to large classes of consumers.

The industrial awakening experienced by France, the Netherlands, and England since the late sixteenth century had far-reaching consequences for the rest of Europe. The emergence of new, formidable competitors in the north cut deep into existing markets for manufactured goods, confronted long-established industries with unprecedented challenges, and ultimately resulted in the redrawing of the industrial map of Europe.

Spain offers a remarkable illustration of the impact of industrialisation abroad: from the late sixteenth century, in fact, her manufactures lost ground on both the domestic and the colonial markets and the country became an important outlet for French, Dutch, and English goods. True enough, industrial production had never loomed very large in the Spanish economy, and long before the onset of its

[59] R. Davis, 'English Foreign Trade, 1660–1700', *Econ. History Review* (1954).

decay, foreign observers — from Francesco Guicciardini to Jean Bodin — had commented on Spain's meagre industrial performance. Nevertheless, in the early decades of the sixteenth century some progress had been achieved: in the north-west iron mining and metallurgy had expanded very considerably, as had shipbuilding, under the powerful stimulus imparted by colonisation in the New World; in the days of Charles V the making of woollen textiles had experienced a promising, if short-lived, growth in Castile and the silk industry had prospered in Valencia and Granada; in Seville new manufactures had been established, such as pottery, soapmaking and armaments. And yet, what the sixteenth century had begun the seventeenth century proved unable to preserve: increasingly, Spain came to depend on foreign sources of supply for her needs; Dutch built ships, English worsteds and metalware, French and Italian silks, gradually replaced domestic productions and were exchanged for such primary commodities as Spain could offer — raw wool, olive oil, and iron. A similar process of de-industrialisation occurred in Poland. As M. Malowist has brought out, in the course of the sixteenth century, at a time that is when Poland's resources and manpower were being harnessed to large-scale cereal farming and the production of timber, naval stores, and flax in response to a buoyant demand in the west, her handicraft industries were forced out of existence by the inflow of Dutch and English manufactured goods.[60]

Even countries with a glorious industrial past such as Flanders, Germany, and north Italy were bound to suffer severe losses at the hands of their younger rivals and to lose the lead they had traditionally enjoyed in a wide range of activities. One of the fields where losses were highest was no doubt cloth-making: from the late sixteenth century the key centres of the wool industry — Hondschoote, Lille, Florence, Venice — began to feel the pressure of their new competitors; in the following century they all experienced, although in varying degrees, a prolonged and irreversible

[60] M. Malowist, 'L'évolution industrielle de la Pologne du XIVe au XVIIe siècle', in *Studi in onore di A. Sapori* (Milan 1957), pp. 571-603.

decline as their place was taken by the Dutch and English textile industries. Much the same story is written in the records of shipbuilding, iron metallurgy, and silk-making: Italian and other Mediterranean shipyards gave in before the competition of their Dutch counterpart; the old, and once famous, gunfoundries of Flanders, Bavaria, and Lombardy were driven out of business in the face of the superior performance of the English and the Swedes; the silk-makers of Milan and Venice lost ground to those of Lyons and Tours. In all such cases long-established and comfortable supremacies were challenged and toppled as newcomers steadily caught up in field after field and, by dint of greater efficiency, lower costs, or better design, often left the older nations far behind.

Not in every field, however. Insofar as the older industrial countries possessed a comparative advantage either in terms of natural resources or in terms of skills and knowhow which younger economies found hard to imitate, they could still hold their own at least in certain fields. And insofar as in the rising nations of the north, higher incomes meant a larger demand for imports, some room was left in which the older countries could partially recover from the heavy losses suffered in other quarters.

A case in point is provided by the progress of a number of luxury manufactures which catered for the needs of an increasingly affluent and sophisticated international clientele. In the seventeenth century, for instance, the making of tapestries prospered in the Spanish Low Countries;[61] in Nuremberg, no longer a major centre of heavy metallurgy, the manufacture of toys, clocks, and jewellery recovered briskly after the Thirty Years War; Cremona, once an important centre of the fustian industry, achieved world renown in the Baroque age thanks to the incomparable craftsmanship of its Amatis and Stradivaris.

Of greater significance for the welfare of the countries involved was, however, the performance of industries

[61] J. Craeybeckx, 'Les industries d'exportation dans les villes flamandes au XVIIe siècle, particulièrement à Gand et à Bruges', in *Studi in onore di A. Fanfani* (Milan 1962), vol. IV, pp. 411-67.

serving broader and expanding needs. Papermaking was certainly one: in the age of Blaeu and the sugar plantations paper, whether for printing or as wrapping material, came into wider use and its production, as will be recalled, spread from Italy to France, Holland, and England. In the process Italy lost her former supremacy, but in no way was she forced out of the field. By concentrating on quality productions Italian papermills actually managed to retain a very respectable share of a growing market: fine writing paper from the Genoese coast, in particular, was shipped in increasing quantities, in the late seventeenth century, not only to Spain and her colonies, but also to countries such as England and Holland where the paper industry was making headway but was still mainly confined to inferior grades.

Even in the textile sector, where losses were heaviest, the older industrial areas succeeded in retaining a foothold by diversifying or upgrading production, or by seeking new outlets for their goods. In Ghent and Bruges, as J. Craey-beckx has recently shown,[62] a compensation was found for the demise of the traditional cloth industry in the manu-facture of new fabrics variously combining wool, flax, and silk. In Augsburg, after the trials and tribulations of the Thirty Years War, a promising start was made in the pro-duction of light printed cottons. North Italy, as will be recalled, increasingly specialised in the mechanical pro-duction of high-grade organzine that was largely intended for the new silk manufactures then burgeoning abroad; and the Italian silkmakers, if fewer in number than in the past, could still maintain a reputation on world markets with a limited output of elaborately patterned or richly embroidered fabrics. Likewise, the Flemish linen industry owed its survival, in the changing market environment of the seventeenth century, to its ability to turn out fabrics that had few rivals in terms of fineness and workmanship. Predictably enough, much of its production was absorbed by England. And so was that of Bohemia in the late seven-

[62] *Ibid.*

teenth century:[63] traditionally geared to the German market, the linen industry of Bohemia had come close to extinction during the Thirty Years War; its later recovery and prosperity largely reflected its expanding sales to a country where economic progress along a broad front was beginning to make itself felt in higher incomes and new, more sophisticated consumer habits.

[63] A. Klima, 'Industrial Development in Bohemia, 1648-1781', *Past and Present*, no. 11 (1957), pp. 87-99.

Select Bibliography

The student of early modern industrial history will find it worth his while to consult at first such general works on the economic history of Europe as I. Kulischer's (in German), G. Luzzatto's (in Italian), and H. Heaton's (in English). In spite of its title, *An Historical Geography of Europe before 1800* by C. T. Smith (Cambridge-New York 1968) is an excellent, up-to-date introduction to the economic history of continental Europe. Economic histories of individual countries are equally indispensable companions to the student of industry. On England, the massive work by E. Lipson is still useful in spite of its age (1931); the seventeenth century is now fully covered and discussed in the light of recent findings and interpretations in C. H. Wilson, *England's Apprenticeship, 1603-1763* (Oxford 1965). The economic history of France by H. Sée (1927) has yet to find a much needed replacement and the sixteenth century, in particular, still awaits a comprehensive, up-to-date survey; for the seventeenth century C. W. Cole's book on mercantilism previously mentioned and W. C. Scoville's *The Persecution of the Huguenots and French Economic Development, 1680-1720* (Berkeley 1960) contain a wealth of information on the industrial sector; recent, in-depth studies of individual towns and provinces, such as P. Goubert, *Beauvais et le Beauvaisis de 1600 à 1730* (Paris 1960) and P. Deyon, *Amiens capitale provinciale* (Paris-The Hague 1967), mark a new beginning in our knowledge of the French economy in that century. That of Spain is surveyed in J. Vicens Vives' masterly *An Economic History of Spain* (Engl. transl., Princeton 1969); for the early sixteenth century R. Carande, *Carlos V y sus banqueros: la vida economica en Castilla, 1516-1556* (2nd ed., Madrid 1965) is indispensable, and so is for Catalonia, vol. I of P. Vilar's *La Catalogne dans l'Espagne moderne* (Paris 1962). There is no comprehensive work on Italy in the early modern period: G. Luzzatto,

Storia economica, vol. I (Padua 1954) covers the whole of Europe but has some excellent chapters on Italy; A. Fanfani, *Storia del lavoro in Italia dalla fine del secolo XV agli inizi del secolo XVIII* (Milan 1943) is a mine of information on techniques and working conditions; *Crisis and Change in the Venetian Economy in the Sixteenth and Seventeenth Centuries* edited with an introduction by B. Pullan (London 1968), although dealing primarily with Venice, has much to offer on the broader Italian economic context; the course of textile production, papermaking, and the arms industry in north Italy is discussed in D. Sella, 'Industrial Production in Seventeenth-century Italy: a Reappraisal', *Explorations in Entrepreneurial History* (1969). F. Luetge, *Deutsche Sozial-und Wirtschaftsgeschichte* (Berlin 1952) is a valuable introduction to the subject; the vast bibliography on the German economy in the seventeenth century has been discussed in T. K. Rabb, 'The Effects of the Thirty Years' War on the German Economy', *Journal of Modern History* (1962). Much of the literature on the Low Countries and Scandinavia presents to many a student (including the present writer) obvious language problems. Fortunately, on the southern provinces of the Low Countries we have a good compendium in J. A. Van Houtte, *Esquisse d'une histoire économique de la Belgique* (Louvain 1943) and on the northern provinces the older, but still reliable work by E. Baasch, *Hollandische Wirtschaftsgeschichte* (Jena 1927); two recent books in English, C. R. Boxer, *The Dutch Seaborne Empire, 1600-1800* (New York 1965) and C. H. Wilson, *The Dutch Republic* (London 1969), incorporate the latest findings of Dutch economic historiography; lastly the *Acta Historiae Nederlandica* periodically published in Leyden since 1966, are meant to help the English reading public keep abreast of Dutch scholarly production. On Sweden E. J. Heckscher, *An Economic History of Sweden* (Cambridge 1954) is, of course, a classic.

The literature on individual industries is very large, but most of it follows national or regional lines. The few attempts at bringing together, in a European perspective, local historical experiences are all the more noteworthy.

J. U. Nef's pioneer essays on industrial Europe in the sixteenth century and on the comparative growth of industry in France and England have now been conveniently reprinted in book form as *The Conquest of the Material World* (Chicago-London 1964); although written some thirty years ago, they are still worth careful study and consultation. On the iron industry, O. Johannsen, *Geschichte des Eisens* (3rd ed., Düsseldorf 1953) is the chief authority, and so is for the early centuries of printing L. Febvre and H. J. Martin, *L'apparition du Livre* (Paris 1958). Several chapters in vol. III of *A History of Technology* ed. C. Singer are rich sources of information, but the emphasis in them is, of course, on techniques rather than on the economics of industry. The same limitation applies to M. Daumas, *Les instruments scientifiques aux XVIIe et XVIIIe siècles* (Paris 1953) and to J. F. Hayward's remarkably well informed study of small firearms, *The Art of the Gunmaker. 1500-1830* (2 vols., London 1962). The interaction of technological and economic factors, on the other hand, has been carefully and refreshingly explored in two recent books by C. M. Cipolla, *Guns and Sails in the Early Phase of European Expansion, 1400-1700* (London 1965) and *Clocks and Culture, 1300-1700* (London 1967); the sections in the present chapter devoted to armaments and clockmaking are heavily indebted to them. A comparative study by H. Kellenbenz, 'Les industries rurales en Occident de la fin du Moyen Age au XVIIIe siècle', *Annales: Economies, Sociétés, Civilizations* (1963) surveys and discusses the vast literature on the subject.

National and local studies on industrial history are legion, especially in the case of textiles, mining, and metallurgy. As regards textiles, one ought at least to mention, for England, E. Lipson, *A Short History of Wool and Its Manufacture* (London 1953) as a useful introduction to the subject, and B. E. Supple, *Commercial Crisis and Change in England, 1600-1642* (Cambridge 1959) for its thorough discussion of the shift from the 'old' to the 'new draperies'. On the *nouvelle draperie* in the Low Countries the basic work is still E. Coornaert, *Un centre industriel d'autrefois: la draperie-sayetterie d'Hondschoote: XIVe-XVIIIe siècles* (Paris 1930); in *Annales: E.S.C.* (1946) E. Coornaert has also summarised, for the benefit of the non-Dutch reading public, the great work by N. W. Posthumus, *De geschiedenis van de Leidsche lakenindustrie* (The Hague 1933). On the French wool industry the books by Goubert and Deyon mentioned above are most valuable; on the industry in Lille there is an important article by P. Deyon and A. Lattin in *Revue du Nord* (1967). Information on the silk and linen industries is still widely scattered and must be gleaned from secondary sources in which they are often discussed but incidentally; a notable exception is E. Sabbe, *Histoire de l'industrie linière en Belgique* (Brussels 1945).

The study of mining and metallurgy includes such well-known works as J. U. Nef, *The Rise of the British Coal Industry* (2 vols., London 1932), J. Delumeau, *L'alun de Rome: XVe-XIXe siècle* (Paris 1962), H. R. Schubert, *History of the British Iron and Steel Industry from c. 450 B.C. to A.D. 1775* (London 1957), and A. Frumento, *Imprese lombarde nella storia della siderurgia italiana* (2 vols., Milan 1963). Also largely devoted to the iron industry is J. Lejeune, *La formation du capitalisme moderne dans la Principauté de Liège au 16e siècle* (Paris 1939); the next century is covered in J. Yernaux, *La métallurgie liégeoise et son expansion au XVIIe siècle* (Liège 1939). J. Vidalenc, *La petite métallurgie rurale en Haute Normandie sous l'Ancien Régime* (Paris 1946) is especially instructive as a study of the organisation of metallurgy in a rural setting. The history of the iron industry in France at large still awaits investigation.

On shipping and shipbuilding at least two titles must be mentioned in a short bibliographical note such as this: F. C. Lane, *Venetian Ships and Shipbuilding of the Renaissance* (Baltimore 1934) and R. Davis, *The Rise of the English Shipping Industry in the Seventeenth and Eighteenth Centuries* (London 1962). W. C. Scoville, *Capitalism and French Glassmaking, 1640-1789* (Berkeley 1950) and A. Gasparetto, *Il vetro di Murano dalle origini ad oggi* (Venice 1958) are important contributions to a comparatively neglected subject. Papermaking is in even greater need of thorough study. In his book on *The British Paper Industry, 1495-1860* (Oxford 1958) D. C. Coleman has, however, set an example that will hopefully find imitators in other countries.

6. European Trade 1500-1750

Kristof Glamann

THE MERCANTILE ERA

There is scarcely any period in the history of Europe when trade plays so central a role as in the years from 1500 to 1750. Some historians call this the early capitalist age or the age of merchant capitalism, while others term it the mercantile or mercantilist era. Certain of the international conflicts of the period, such as the wars between England and Holland in the seventeenth century and between England and Spain in the first half of the eighteenth, may be ascribed to commercial causes. It was a widely held opinion in those days that the sum of prosperity in the world was constant, and the aim of commercial policy, as expressed in such features as the customs and navigation laws, was to secure for each individual nation the largest possible slice of the cake. On the other hand, compared with factors such as religion and dynastic imperialism, trade ranked only third among the causes of war or conflict in early modern Europe, while allowance should be made for the fact that governments sometimes tried to invent mercantile pretexts for their measures of foreign policy. Many examples testify that trade—meaning first and foremost trade with foreign countries—was imputed to be of vital moment to the prosperity of the nation, and wealth was considered an absolutely essential means of power, just as power was essential as a means of acquiring wealth. Then as now, both wealth and power were ultimate ends of national policy.

Trade was the great wheel driving the whole engine of society, to use a metaphor repeatedly found in economic literature. At first sight it seems curious that an intimate causal relationship should subsist between foreign trade and prosperity in the modern nation-states. Of course the latter were products of the Renaissance and the new age in Europe, and they differed in many respects from the feudal societies of medieval times, but in their demographic and productive aspects they were still agrarian. Most of their inhabitants lived on the land. Apart from a dozen capital cities, European towns resembled large villages, the most usual function of which was to act as a local market for foodstuffs and raw materials. The average production unit was small. Transport links were tenuous. Local regions frequently produced and traded in the same commodities as neighbouring regions. Much everyday business was conducted without the use of money. Many wages were paid in kind. Not a few sectors of public administration were still geared to the economics of barter. Most of the population were too heavily engaged in the struggle for their daily bread, which absorbed about half their budget, to have even the time, let alone the means, to think of enjoying any share of the luxury articles flowing through the channels of international trade. The trade in foodstuffs was on the whole largely a local affair. In relation to total requirements and total consumption, the supply of grain through the channels of international trade (notably by sea) seems to have amounted to barely a few per cent. The conveyance of cloth and household articles was a slow business. House-building was largely based on local materials and labour. Transport costs were determined by the length of the water routes and the layout of the road-system, by the trade winds and other natural obstacles and by the numerous local customs and fiscal barriers that had to be overcome before a commodity could reach its destination. The safety factor —i.e., the physical risks—added a further increment to transport costs. Add to all this the many tribulations, in the shape of war, plague, famine and crop failure, to which sixteenth and seventeenth-century populations were exposed, and it may seem wiser to view the nations of Europe as aggregates of regions or areas whose economic structure and trade were determined not by political boundaries but by geographic, climatic and demographic conditions. Isolation rather than intercourse, then, is the striking feature. Europe so to speak breaks down into an agglomeration of partially autonomous units, whose economies exhibit a

great diversity of evolution and of substance. Where international exchange of goods occurs, it is by virtue of a
marginal or peripheral demand mainly stemming from the
upper classes of the population or from the urbanised areas
of Europe.

On the other hand, when a bird's eye view is taken of the
historical process, it is evident that intercourse between the
regions becomes steadily more regular and that the circle
widens. An analysis of price-movements reveals a certain
unity despite all divergencies, a unity which becomes
stronger as time goes on. This is particularly the case with
maritime trade. Regions linked together by water are more
easily influenced by the same trend than are regions linked
overland—another factor cutting across national frontiers.
International trade is in many cases cheaper and easier to
establish than domestic trade. Socially the strata served by
international trade also widen.

The development of sea-routes is most remarkable, indeed revolutionary. Transoceanic exchange of goods now
supplements coastwise. For the first time in the history of
mankind, an intercontinental trade of regular character is
established. Europe is no longer a continent living its life in
isolation but becomes increasingly a part of a world economy. In particular, the connections between Europe and
the two Americas influenced fundamentally the history of
both continents. These novel features, to which even contemporaries paid lively attention, were not the least of the
characteristics making this the commercial epoch *par
excellence*.

The mercantile era features an economic system in which
fixed capital played a relatively small part, A large part of
non-agrarian wealth consisted of circulating capital, and
the need for ready cash was great. One of the most important objects on which circulating capital was expended
was labour, which represented a high proportion of production costs. In such a context trade attained an importance beyond that of other economic activities. The rapid
turnover yielded a relatively high return, and the merchant
enjoyed a position in which many fields of investment for

his coveted capital were open to him. In addition—the supply of money in general—the monetary system—depended basically upon the flow of bullion, which was determined by the course of foreign trade *inter alia*. How to acquire the largest share of what was commonly seen as a more or less fixed volume of international trade, and how so to manage the national share as to produce a favourable balance of trade and a net import of bullion and precious metals, were the twin tasks to which governments of the day addressed themselves. Monetary and commercial policy were in fact integrated subjects. This too made the merchant a key figure. Thus there were many good reasons for designating this a mercantile age or an age of merchant capitalism.

If we look for a moment at the economic chronology of the mercantile era, we see that it began with the so-called price revolution. Europe experienced in the sixteenth century a continuous inflation of unprecedented proportions. Foodstuffs came under the most violent inflationary pressure while the products of the industrial and handicraft sectors were relatively untouched. Wages did not keep pace, and it is therefore to be presumed that there was an overall drop in the standard of living of wage-earners. The inflation is reflected in business earnings, in the willingness to invest in commercial undertakings, and in an accumulation of mercantile capital. Rising prices stimulated a general business expansion, and the diversity of price-levels within Europe encouraged large-scale trading ventures between one market and another. Part of the explanation of the great upsurge in prices is to be found in the influx of precious metals, especially silver, from the New World: in the second half of the sixteenth century, the international economy was in a phase of silver inflation. But the growth of population, too, in which the growth of towns especially lent impetus to the prolonged and flourishing economic activity that characterised the sixteenth century, must be taken into account, as also must the fact that the total volume of production seems to have been insufficient to satisfy the demand.

In the first half of the seventeenth century the tempo slackened. Prices began to yield. However, production figures do not always run parallel to price movements thus making it rather difficult exactly to state the chronology of the prevailing trend. Lack of sufficient statistical material adds to this difficulty. Obviously the turning points vary from area to area. Presumably the secular trend reversed itself first in southern Europe. In North and Central Italy this happened in connection with the great crisis of 1619-22. In northern Europe the reverse was later, in some places not observable until 1650. From the sparse and heterogeneous population statistics it seems as though the middle years of the seventeenth century ushered in a period of decline or stagnation that lasted for the rest of the century. The century-long rise in food prices came to an end. After reaching a peak in most European countries between 1620 and 1650, grain prices for the next forty years showed a stationary or falling trend. This coincided, too, with an increasing output of vegetable foodstuffs in western and, especially, southern Europe. As a result of this the wage-earning labourer may have enjoyed some increase in real wages. This pre-supposes, however, that he was in employment, which cannot be assumed in an age such as this which is characterised by disturbed economic conditions. Many of the economic writers of the seventeenth century, at any rate, based themselves on the assumption that large-scale under-employment prevailed in their communities. In some areas of Europe the downward trend lasted very long, in others—like England—an upward trend asserted itself before the seventeenth century was over. In Holland the seventeenth century as a whole was marked by growth and prosperity.

Already during the expansive period of the sixteenth century it was clear that the credit system—intimately linked with the network of trade—was very dependent on large bullion reserves. The decennial rate of increase of the arrivals of bullion in Seville reached a peak in the decade 1581-90, and the decreasing supplies of the following century therefore not only meant growing monetary difficulties but also a challenge to the credit system at large. This challenge was most successfully met in the Netherlands, where the seventeenth century was the heyday of international trade reaching a high point around mid-century, when a large part of the total volume of European trade was handled by the Dutch. A vast entrepôt trade was built up in Amsterdam. Many of the great north-west European cities continued to grow, too, at a rate that was actually accelerating in the seventeenth century. London became the centre of a growing trade in re-exports to the Continent; Hamburg expanded its activities considerably; the demands of luxury-loving Paris also stimulated business.

With the eighteenth century, European trade changed its character in certain vital particulars. Geographically the commercial centre of gravity shifted and moved across the Channel. At the same time the colonial trades expanded rapidly. While traffic within the European seas up to the end of the seventeenth century still accounted for the greater part of European trade, the expansion of the extra-European trades becomes really marked in the following period, especially the years after the Treaty of Utrecht, particularly in British foreign trade. The process involves a cheapening of colonial products, which are brought down to a level at which a continuing demand is guaranteed.

Seen from our time, the problems and the changes of the Mercantile Era may well look small and insignificant. Population numbers, production figures, the volume of transport and of trade, even the price revolution itself—all these appear modest when measured against the gigantic standards of the twentieth century. Regarded from afar, the whole tenor of economic life seems rather static compared with the dynamism of our era. The productive forces lacked the potential to overcome certain barriers. Distribution costs remained high. Mass consumption stayed at a relatively low level. From a later industrial point of view it all seems very backward. However, there are many grades of backwardness, everything is relative, and the period should first of all be assessed within the limits of its own dimensions and vitality.

In attempting to do this, we must begin by recognising that 250 years is certainly a long period of time, spanning about nine generations. We start with the Renaissance and the Reformation and conclude with the Enlightenment and the Rococo style. If we observe the course of events from a local standpoint—look at them through the history of a single town or region—it is apparent that the changes could be vast and fateful. Many of the once-flourishing localities around the Mediterranean bore the marks of decay and stagnation by the middle of the eighteenth century. Lisbon, which had quickly reached 100,000 inhabitants—the numbers of a major city—had already levelled off by the mid-sixteenth century and had long been a city in decline when the tragic earthquake of 1755 struck. Seville passed the 100,000 mark in the second half of the sixteenth century, and continued to expand in the seventeenth, but at last, faced with the collapse of the American bubble and the petering out of the bullion flow to Spain, could maintain its position no longer. Until the beginning of the seventeenth century, central and northern Italy constituted one of the most highly developed regions of Europe, with an exceptionally high standard of living. By about 1680, however, Italy had become a backward country—her manufacturing industry collapsed, and her agriculture once again became the dominant sector of her economy. Numerous travellers' accounts bear witness to the poor condition of the Italian towns in the eighteenth century. Venice, the commercial republic supreme, had been reduced to the status of a carnival city. At the other end of the spectrum, Paris, Amsterdam and London were unrecognisable in 1750 by comparison with their status in 1500. In the sixteenth century, Paris and London had already been transformed from cities of wooden buildings into sights of brick and stone. Amsterdam, the wondrous city that in the seventeenth century captured the admiration of all and was christened the Venice of the North, grew from 30,000 in 1530 to 115,000 in 1630, passing the 200,000 mark towards the end of the eighteenth century. London became the greatest of them all, with more than half a million inhabitants by the end of the period. No one had any doubts that the dynamism of Amsterdam and London was intimately bound up with their commerce.

These ups and downs were real enough to the people of the time. They were the products of the interaction of both short-run and long-run changes, and varied sharply in scale from one area to another. Disruption due to war (although the harm done by warfare to population and economic life generally has been exaggerated), crop failures or bumper harvests, plague, famine and monetary speculations, mingled with long-run changes in productive patterns and demand, shifting populations and changing climatic conditions.

In most trades we can distinguish between a permanent and regular traffic and a casual and fluctuating one. The structural changes that lie behind the fluctuations of supply and demand are of special interest in any brief survey of commercial history, which must concern itself particularly with the regular trades and their trends. But let us first look at the most important regions of Europe and the variety of activities that were going on.

AREAS, ROUTES AND TRANSPORT

THE MEDITERRANEAN

Around 1500 the Mediterranean, Europe's classical trading area, was a world of its own, with lively intercourse between its various regions. Within the area, trade cut across the division between Christendom and Islam. From the area, routes went eastwards by land and sea to the Orient and northwards by sea, river or mountain passes to central and western Europe. Land transport was efficient enough in the carrying of spices and manufactured goods to tie south Germany to northern and central Italy. The Adriatic, the Tyrrhenian Sea and the Gulf of Lyons constituted three of its major reservoirs of trade; but a considerable volume of business was transacted in the Aegean and in the Levant as well. Northern Italy was the richest

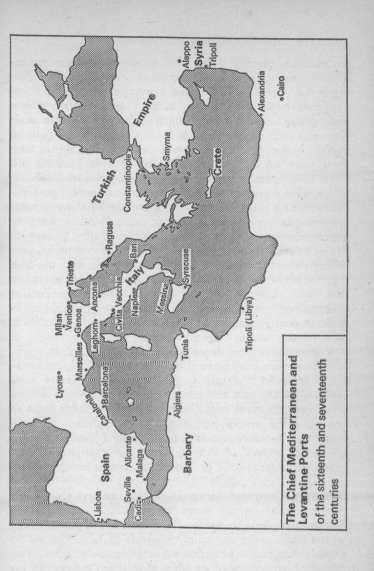

The Chief Mediterranean and Levantine Ports of the sixteenth and seventeenth centuries

of the many regions of the Mediterranean and the one in which the widest range of economic activities was concentrated. Some of the most densely populated urban agglomerations were found here. Florence and Milan were great manufacturing centres; likewise Venice and Genoa, which, in addition, were strong maritime powers and the home ports of great merchant fleets. In the east, too, there were great cities: indeed, the greatest of them all were here, namely, Constantinople and Cairo, both of which were metropolises by European standards. Southern France was a third district with a population densely concentrated in places and a thriving trade. A fair volume of Mediterranean traffic reached the Rhône valley by way of Marseilles. In the extreme west, Andalusia comprised one of the richest districts of the Mediterranean and the one from which in the sixteenth century a trade was inaugurated that quite shattered the old self-sufficient order—Seville and the traffic with America. Cataluña and its great commercial centre, Barcelona, was another trade-generating area of the western Mediterranean.

A great variety of commodities circulated in the area. Mediterranean commerce thus comprised a long-haul seaborne trade in foodstuffs to supplement inadequate local supplies. Grain, salt and victuals preserved in salt, oil and wine were the most bulky commodities, but such items as cheese, dried grapes and sugar were included as well. Sicily was the chief granary of the western Mediterranean, where the supply of foodstuffs was an ever-present and occasionally large-scale problem. Apulia was another grain-producing region supplying such places as Naples. The Nile valley fed Cairo and Alexandria, with plenty to spare; the fertile regions on the shore of the Black Sea furnished Constantinople with foodstuffs. Istria and Sicily together with Cyprus were the chief exporters of salt. The waters around Sicily also provided an abundance of tunny fish, though Mediterranean supplies of salt fish never met the demand. The cities of Italy and Spain in particular used to import fish caught and salted in the Atlantic, a trade in which the Portuguese played a major part. Southern Italy and southern Spain were the principal sources of oil. Cyprus and Crete produced wines that sold all over the Mediterranean; they also, together with Sicily and Andalusia, exported sugar to various parts of the area. As well as the food trade there was trade in raw materials. The Italian cloth industry used fine Spanish wool that was shipped through Malaga, Alicante and Cartagena to Genoa, Leghorn and Venice. It became more and more dependent on these deliveries, especially after the 1570s. Raw silk, a product of many Mediterranean countries, was also extensively traded, one of the chief centres of distribution being Messina. Another important commodity in the Mediterranean trade was cotton. Hides went by shipload from Algeria to Italy, while Spain, another big producer of hides, utilised the whole of her production and more besides in her famous leather manufacture. Among the minerals, copper, tin and lead were old-established items of trade. Copper came largely overland from central Europe and was exported in Venetian ships. England was the chief source of lead and tin. The Mediterranean area itself supplied one mineral that was in international demand—alum—which was used in the textile industry. The various manufactures of the Mediterranean cities also found widespread markets: Italian textiles, Milanese armour and silkwear, Venetian soap and glassware, Genoese paper, Spanish leather goods, to mention the best-known, were in demand both inside and outside the area. The richest trade of all was the famous spice trade, an enterprise of Venetian trade and shipping, but also the Genoese and the Pisans joined them in this lucrative branch of business. Commercial exchanges, beginning in the Far East and ending at Alexandria and Tripoli, brought spices to the Mediterranean world, together with other costly Oriental wares such as Chinese and Persian silks, Indian calicoes, rhubarb and precious stones. From Venice the spices were distributed to northern Italy, across the Alps to south Germany, by sea to Marseilles and France, to the Spanish cities of the western Mediterranean and through the Straits to western and northern Europe.

It is the Italian city-states particularly which, by the vigour of their industry and commerce, represent the dynamic element of the sixteenth-century Mediterranean, forging the links between it and the world beyond, notably the Levant on the one side and western and central Europe on the other. The Renaissance merchant houses of Italy are active in Germany and the Netherlands, their communications with which go either overland via the German cities or Lyons, or right round the Iberian peninsula to London, Bruges and Antwerp. There are links in the reverse direction as well. The Fuggers, greatest merchant dynasty of the sixteenth century, are particularly active in the trade from southern Germany and Hungary to Venice and points beyond in the Mediterranean area, sending out such commodities as copper and silver and bringing back spices, especially pepper, together with great quantities of cotton and other merchandise. The *Fondaco dei Tedeschi* in Venice, at once an hotel, an entrepôt and a market-place for German merchants, is another example of these reverse connections. The discovery of the seaway to the Indies threatened a re-routing of Venice's profitable business of supplying Europe with spices. Portuguese cargoes reached Antwerp in 1501, and Antwerp became thenceforth the chief distribution centre for spices for north-western Europe. The advantages were, however, by no means all on the side of the new Cape route, transportation by sea being at first injurious to the quality of the spices. Political events, moreover, soon favoured the old-established trade, and the Venetians recovered their position as purveyors of spices to a great part of Europe. In the 1580s, the hostilities between Turkey and Persia caused a decline in the Levantine trade, but it was not until the Dutch started importing spices from overseas around the turn of the century that Venetian dominance was finally overthrown.

More serious, undoubtedly, was the fact that in the course of the second half of the sixteenth century, the Mediterranean area manifested an increasing dependence upon the outside world for some of its most essential needs. During that period the grain situation in the western Mediterranean deteriorated. Famines and hunger ravaged the cities; already during the period of the Franco-Spanish wars, 1494-1545, the Italian cities had been hard hit; the troubles continued, however, and other areas were visited. Constantinople later on came in for its share. A general increase of population seems to have been the chief cause of this accelerating shortage, which in fact affected the whole Mediterranean area. This also helps to explain the import of grain, in which Dutch and English vessels were particularly active. During the same half-century, great quantities of barrelled herring from the North Sea began entering the area in Dutch ships. Increasing quantities of hides even began to reach Spain and Italy from Poland, Russia and, especially, the New World. The commercial activity thus set in motion enabled Dutch and English merchants in the seventeenth century to make further inroads into a number of areas of Mediterranean trade, notably the marketing of cloth in the Levant. By these means an enduring link was forged between northern and southern Europe: the Mediterranean ceased to be a world of its own. Economically the centre of power had shifted towards north-western Europe.

CENTRAL EUROPE

Central Europe was another important trading area. It contained many towns and considerable industries, while some of Europe's richest deposits of minerals—especially silver and copper—were located within it or on its margins. It was criss-crossed with a network of roads and rivers, its two greatest waterways, the Danube and the Rhine, being important arteries of trade. The Fuggers' chief seats of operations, Augsburg, Regensburg and, largest in size of population, Nuremberg, controlled the transit trade between the Mediterranean and a considerable part of continental Europe, while themselves participating, by virtue of their own brisk consumption and production, in the international exchange of goods. An example of the extensive business connections of these towns is the great trading company, as it was called, of Ravensburg, which around 1500 had offices in Berne and Geneva, in Lyons, Avignon and Marseilles, in Milan and Genoa, in Barcelona and Valencia, in Antwerp, in Cologne and Nuremberg, in Vienna and in Budapest. Farther towards the north-west lay Frankfurt-am-Main, celebrated for its fairs, and Cologne and Aachen, which were similarly centres of trade and manufacturing, Aachen being noted for its metal-lurgical industries. Starting from Frankfurt, one of the greatest highways of central Europe, the *Hohe Landstrasse* ran eastwards to Erfurt, then on to Leipzig, whence a number of branches proceeded farther east, to Poland for example, which, like Hungary, was a purveyor of food-stuffs to many cities of central Europe. First and foremost, however, it was metals and metal wares on which the great trade of the area was founded. As early as the second half of the fifteenth century an expansion was occurring that was based on German silver production. Its orientation was from south Germany towards north Italy and the Low Countries, especially Brabant. This expansion con-tinued into the sixteenth century, now with copper as its driving force. The market became focused more and more upon Antwerp, whose prosperity rested upon a com-mercial alliance between Portuguese spices, German silver and copper, and precious metals from the New World. Sundry other commodities were drawn into the inter-national market in the wake of these: cloth, canvas, linen, hops and grain. Overland traffic between the Low Countries and Italy expanded.

This combination of transcontinental trade and maritime expansion characterises the sixteenth-century commercial capitalism that centred on Antwerp. Here was the meeting-point of the south German merchant houses, the agents of the Portuguese king, the English merchant adventurers, the traders of Italy and the Hanseatic league. By degrees, how-ever, the maritime element in the expansion takes the lead. Transcontinental trade loses ground; the volume of business transacted at the fairs in Brabant falls off during the middle third of the century: the German economy suffers under the effects of the religious wars; in the last quarter of the century Italian industry begins to feel the weight of the direct Dutch and English commercial assault on the Mediterranean. Thus weakened on the landward side, the fate of Antwerp was sealed when the city was captured by Parma in 1585 and the Dutch blockade of the Scheldt established. So ends a brief but hectic chapter in the history of international trade. It had lasted little more than three-quarters of a century.

THE BALTIC

It has been said of the Baltic that it is a Mediterranean in miniature. Many of the geographical features of each bear a likeness to the other's. But the Baltic area does not enjoy the same degree of self-sufficiency. It is one component of a larger north European grouping embracing the territory from the northern coast of the Netherlands across the North Sea via Kattegat and the Belts to the Baltic Sea. In this area we can distinguish between two trades, one seaborne, one overland, both of them in bulky goods for everyday use. The first of these comprises grain, salt and salt fish, woollen cloth and furs, together with commodities like timber and other forest products such as potash, pitch and tar, as well as flax, hemp, iron and copper. Salt and cloth and, from about the middle of the sixteenth century, herring moved from west to east: the other goods went in the opposite direction. The second category of trade comprises only a single commodity with the unusual characteristic that it could transport itself: cattle. These went from north to south.

The Baltic itself was the granary of northern Europe. It was also, at the beginning of the sixteenth century, the chief northern source of another vital food, viz. salt herring. The principal fisheries were those of Skanör, at the southern tip of Sweden, and off the island of Rügen. The necessary salt came either from Lüneburg in north Germany, supplied by way of Hamburg or Lübeck, or from the Biscay coast of France. In the course of the first half of the century these fisheries declined, mainly because of the disappearance of herring from the Baltic, to be replaced by large-scale herring fisheries that developed on the Dogger Bank and in other parts of the North Sea.

Two groups of ports competed in the seaborne trade of northern Europe, those of the north German Hanse and those of the Netherlands. In the Middle Ages, Hanseatic traders had predominated in the Baltic trade and in the trade to Scandinavia and Iceland, as well as on the North Sea, but changes in trade routes and trade relations tended to favour the Dutch at German expense. The sea-route from the North Sea around the Skaw, through the Sound and into the Baltic was pioneered by the Dutch and soon came to surpass the old overland route from Hamburg to Lübeck. The Danish Sound Toll Register in the 1490s shows Dutch ships to be already a majority of the vessels passing the Sound. The proportion increased steadily in the following century and a half. Amsterdam became in fact the principal grain market for the whole of Europe. The grain trade and the fisheries were keystones of the imposing Dutch trading empire of the seventeenth century. In the carriage of both bulk and mixed cargoes the Dutch were unrivalled, and by the end of the seventeenth century the whole carrying trade between France and northern Europe, and most of the corresponding English trade, were in Dutch hands. Not until the eighteenth century were the English and other nations able seriously to challenge the Dutch lead in the trade of northern Europe.

The Dutch, however, were not the only competitors of the Hanse merchants. The transcontinental trade between the Low Countries and Italy also reduced the volume of business done by the Hanse towns in the west, where their old staple city of Bruges became overshadowed by Antwerp, while the Fuggers' carriage of copper from central Europe to Antwerp via Poland and the Baltic curtailed their activities in the east. The Scandinavian lands, too, joined in these strivings to carve off a slice of the Hanseatic trade. English merchants did the same. In the end the new trade-routes created tension within the Hanseatic league itself.

The merchants of Danzig and the other eastern Hanse ports found it advantageous to co-operate with the Dutch. The Wendish towns, headed by Lübeck, became isolated. Hamburg went its own way and became a great metropolis. It is symptomatic that in 1611 the English merchant adventurers fixed their German headquarters at Hamburg, where they remained until the nineteenth century. Thus it is an exaggeration to think of the Hanse towns as decaying. They lost ground relative to the Dutch dynamo in the west, but some of them were able to adapt themselves and reap advantages from the new commercial patterns of northern Europe.

The north European overland traffic in cattle went from northern Jutland, the Danish islands and Skåne down through Schleswig-Holstein to the Elbe, where the principal market for cattle was located and from whence the cattle were distributed to the towns of north Germany (especially Lübeck and Hamburg), of the Rhine as far as Cologne, and of the Netherlands (especially Amsterdam). As in the case of grain, the key to this trade is to be found in the demand generated by the growing population of western Europe, especially the Netherlands. The population of the Netherlands doubled between 1500 and 1650, and a large proportion of this increase occurred in the towns, which in the province of Holland itself accounted for no less than half the total population. With the exception of northern Italy, Europe's densest concentration of population was in this north-western corner. During the second half of the seventeenth century, population figures in western Europe became stationary. At the same time output of farm produce increased (England, for instance, became an exporter of grain) with the result that the demand for both grain and cattle began to fall. Even the southern European demand for grain was waning in the second half of the seventeenth century. The decline in traffic, particularly in grain, had a critical effect upon the economic life of the Dutch commercial republic, where the recession was not offset by prosperity in other trades. Even up to 1730, Dutch trade played an important part in international business. Then it was finished. Dutch commercial capital transferred itself into government bonds and other securities. The dynamic centre moved to the other side of the Channel.

THE ATLANTIC

The Atlantic coastline stretching from the Straits to the Channel may be considered a fourth European trading area. Between its many coastal and riverine harbours a port-to-port trade was carried on that was equal in variety and possibly also in volume to either the Mediterranean or the northern sectors. Again we find that this trade was overwhelmingly of bulk character, consisting of everyday commodities like wool, wine and salt. There were lively connections between the Atlantic area and the Mediterranean and northern areas. They were perhaps most conspicuous in the case of salt, where the connection between the Atlantic area and northern Europe was so intimate that in this field it is meaningless to differentiate between the two. Here France and Portugal were the two competing suppliers of sea-salt and the lands bordering the North Sea and Baltic were the consumers. The growing shortage of bread grain in Portugal and Spain caused grain to move in the opposite direction. These two commodities indeed occupied a key position in the international maritime traffic of the sixteenth century. For a long time the carrying capacity of a ship was measured simply by stating the number of lasts of grain and salt it could take. A bigger volume of salt passed through the Sound from west to east than of any other commodity. The customs officers at the Sound, in fact, classified the shipping traffic into the Baltic into two main groups: ships in ballast and salt ships from France, Portugal and Spain. It was the merchants of the northern area who were the most active in the exchange of goods between the Atlantic and north European coasts. At first the Hanse merchants and the Dutch were particularly active; later on Dutch carriers completely dominated the traffic, yielding some share to English, Scottish and Scandinavian shipowners only towards the end of the

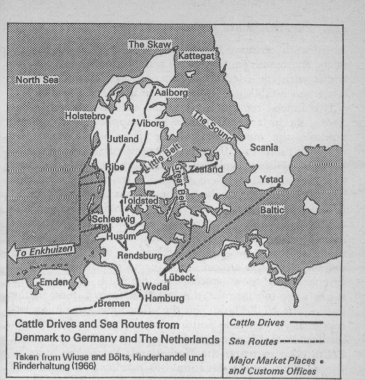

Cattle Drives and Sea Routes from Denmark to Germany and The Netherlands

Taken from Wiese and Bölts, Rinderhandel und Rinderhaltung (1966)

Cattle Drives ———
Sea Routes ----------
Major Market Places •
and Customs Offices

seventeenth century. Russia, too, appeared on the scene in the eighteenth century as an active trader in salt. As the traffic with the Mediterranean increased, a salt-carrying route was established from there to northern Europe.

It is indeed remarkable that the exchange of goods between, for instance, Lisbon, which supplied not only salt but also the much sought-after spices, and Danzig, the principal market for the equally highly prized bread grain, became a Dutch speciality. It has been asserted in regard to Portugal that overseas expansion made such demands upon ships, men and other resources that there was nothing left over for traffic with the north. Of greater moment, undoubtedly, is the geographical position of the two commercial centres in relation to the seasonal fluctuations of the markets. The new harvest arrived on the Danzig corn market every year almost simultaneously with the arrival at Lisbon of the 'new' spices from the East. However, the spices were too late for the last fleet from Lisbon to the Baltic. The Netherlands, on the other hand, was in an exceptionally favourable position to gain control of this intermediate trade. It was possible for both Lisbon spices and Polish corn to reach the Netherlands before the onset of winter. This central location was excellent for exploiting the markets at the two termini, while the merchants of the terminal stations were too far apart to be able to make their dispositions on the basis of information received from the other end. The central situation also permitted a quicker turnover of trading capital.

THE TRANSOCEANIC TRADES

The Atlantic coastal area was also, however, the point of departure for the most spectacular trade of the age, viz. the transoceanic trade, with its two main streams, the Asian and the American. In both these trades the Iberian nations made pioneering contributions. Throughout the century, the Portuguese in particular had penetrated west, south and north into the Atlantic in a mixture of exploration, fishing and colonisation. The urge to trade, too, especially along the coast of Africa, was a motivating force. At last in 1497, the movement culminated with the opening of the sea-route to India via the Cape of Good Hope. The Portuguese monopoly of oceanic traffic to the East lasted for about a hundred years before various countries of the north European area—the Netherlands, England, France, Denmark and Norway—appeared as rivals on the scene. Dutch trade in particular attained an impressive volume and range in the seventeenth century, covering the whole of maritime Asia from Japan in the east and across Taiwan (Formosa) to various stations in south-east Asia, with Batavia on the island of Java as its Asian headquarters; thence extending across India, Ceylon, Persia and Arabia to South Africa in the west.

A common feature of all the European trade with Asia is its concentration on imports. The purpose of the trade was not to find new markets for European products but to furnish Europe with those coveted wares that titillated the palate and adorned the body—the luxury articles so condemned by contemporary pedants. Except for weapons and ammunition, the only 'commodity' that could be disposed of in the East was bullion. The composition of the import list reflects the changes in European demand. In the sixteenth century it is dominated by spices, especially pepper, but during the course of the seventeenth century the selection of merchandise widens and spices lose ground in step with those changes in European eating habits that brought about a reduction of the former heavy consumption of meat, for the preserving of which spices had been heavily used. The successor to spices as the dominant category of imports into Europe is Indian textiles. Around 1700, these account for over 40 per cent of the Dutch East India Company's imports. Later on, during the 1720s and 1730s, coffee and tea, especially the latter, emerge as commodities very much in demand; by 1740 they account for about a quarter of the Company's imports.

As imports rose, prices fell. Tea ceased to be an expensive drug on the chemist's shelf and became, instead, a popular drink steaming deliciously in pots and cups. The tea trade

opened a new chapter in the history of European trade with
Asia. The latter had formerly been characterised by
steadily increasing protection costs and a highly complicated procedure for assembling the return consignments for
Europe, some items being available only to those taking an
active part in the Asian country trade; but tea cargoes were
nearly all obtained by voyaging direct to Canton in China,
where the Imperial functionaries fixed the conditions of
trade for Europeans. All European nations had free admission, thus rendering illusory the old companies' exclusive right of navigation east of the Cape of Good Hope.
The direct trade to China encouraged interloping. New
European trading partners with Canton made their appearance: Ostend, Hamburg, Copenhagen and Gothen-
burg. From the point of view of the small European
countries, this trade had the great advantage of not being
burdened with the usual expensive colonial overheads. The
entry of new participants into the trade intensified competition. The benefits soon manifested themselves in the
shape of bigger turnover with smaller profit-margins and
faster transport. Thus European trade with Asia was of two
sorts: a traditional, slow and high-cost trade versus a trade
that was direct, fast and cheap. And so the company form
of mercantile enterprise was undermined.

The Atlantic ocean trade differs from the Asian trade
primarily by virtue of the colonisation that takes place in
the New World. The forms of colonisation range from the
pure colonies of settlement established by the English and
French in North America, through the plantation-type
colonies of the southern states of North America, the West
Indian islands and Portuguese Brazil, to the mixed types of
colonisation found in the Spanish colonies of Mexico and
Peru. Only in the less hospitable regions of South America,
where the geographic and demographic conditions render
settlement on a major scale impossible, do we find a
'factory' system reminiscent of that in Asia. The acquisition
of land and its exploitation by means of local or imported
labour characterise the intercourse between the Old and
the New Worlds. The most spectacular feature is of course

the exploitation of the New World's deposits of precious metals—the stream of American treasure flowing from the Spanish-owned mines of Central America to Seville and Cadiz, whence it finds its way to the rest of Europe. The effects of this upon the European economy are momentous. Later on Brazilian gold adds itself to the stream, entering into circulation via Lisbon. Bulkier items in the traffic from the New World to the Old, and just as vital from a purely commercial standpoint, are Brazilian timber, sugar, tobacco and cotton. The cod fisheries of Newfoundland and the North American trade in hides, too, contribute to the range of articles in international trade making heavy demands on shipping space. The seventeenth century sees sugar and tobacco, like tea in the beginning of the eighteenth century making the downward leap from the price-level of exclusive luxuries towards that of mass-consumption items. These two articles are vital to the whole of the entrepôt trade developed by Holland and England in the second half of the seventeenth century, in which the re-export of colonial goods accounts for a steadily rising proportion of foreign trade.

In the reverse direction, exports from Europe to the two Americas are quite varied and reflect the needs of the colonial communities, which range from cloth, household furniture and implements to wine and other consumer goods. Towards the end of the period particularly, the demand of the rapidly growing North American colonies for manufactured goods of all kinds was of great importance to England, whose foreign trade, concerned for centuries chiefly with the export of cloth, had lost its one-sidedness by about 1700 and become a more diversified business of supplying the wants and re-exporting the products of the colonies.

An additional element was the export of people across the Atlantic. The efforts to encourage the immigration of women from Spain and Portugal into the colonies were a rather specialised affair. But the conveyance of manual labour swiftly became systematised into a dominant feature of the traffic. No question of conscience was involved.

Portugal in fact, was a slave-owning country before she became a colonial power. Negro slavery spread with sugar cultivation from Portugal to the Atlantic islands and to Brazil and the New World. The slave trade from Africa to Brazil and the West Indies formed part of what is now and then called the Atlantic system of trade. This system was at its zenith in the seventeenth and eighteenth centuries, and one of its features was the variety of forms of triangular trade that it embraced, e.g., between Europe, Africa and the West Indies; or between the North American colonies, Africa and the West Indies; or—without slaves—between northern Europe, North America and southern Europe. (In the last-mentioned case manufactured goods were exchanged for fish, meat, timber and grain, which in turn were exchanged for wine and southern fruits.) The furnishing of Negro labour to the New World was a trade that was marked by fierce international rivalry in the latter half of our period. Eight European nations were competing in the seventeenth century for territory in West Africa. A particularly bitter struggle developed over the *asiento*, as it was called—the exclusive right to supply labour to the Spanish colonies. After having been in Portuguese and French hands this was ceded at the Peace of Utrecht to the English, who exploited it to such effect that Spanish America in the eighteenth century was more of an English trading colony than a Spanish.

There were a few links between the two great ocean trades described above. Metals knew no frontiers: they moved all round the world, some of them using the back door as it were, viz. moving from Acapulco on the Pacific coast to Manila in the Philippines, whence they entered the Asian market. Among Indian textiles were the so-called *guinees*, cheap loin-cloths for Negro slaves named after Guinea in Africa. Cowries—mussel shells fished up from the blue waters of the Indian Ocean around the Maldive Islands—were also in demand in the African slave trade, since they were used as currency in parts of Africa. The chief market for cowries was Amsterdam, the chief supplier, the Dutch East India Company, and the chief buyers the

West Indian Companies and other traders with Africa. Neither was there any lack of schemes for linking the East and West Indian trades together. Interloping individuals, particularly, with their dreams of breaking the monopolies of the great companies, felt the attractions of such projects —which remained on paper, however.

On the other hand it is evident that overseas trade, although generally fragmentary, does possess coherence in certain respects. The records show that there was competition between products on the principal European markets. This might be between alternative products, such as East Indian and European textiles:—between identical products from different regions enjoying similar climates, e.g., sugar from Java and Bengal, sugar from Madeira and São Tomé, and Brazilian and West Indian sugar; or between products grown in different climatic regions, as in the case of tobacco, which is cultivated in tropical, subtropical and temperate climates. Chinese, Persian and Italian silk; Japanese, Hungarian, Swedish and West Indian copper; the spices of Asia, Africa and America; coffee from Mocha, Java and the West Indies: all these competed. Study of the volume of trade and the movement of prices at selected locations reveals numerous instances of uniform trends. For example, the passage of vessels through the Sound to and from the Baltic, the traffic to and from the New World via Seville, and the trade statistics of Lisbon or of Manila in the Philippines, all indicate the state of international trade. The best barometer, however, is represented by the prices on the commodity exchange of Amsterdam. The yearly prices of colonial goods in this, the most important market place of northern Europe, mirror global trade conditions. This is a novel and momentous phenomenon seen in relation to the coastwise and more sporadic exchange of goods that typified earlier days. Now we see a regular flow of traffic through an immense network of trade routes that are linked together to form a European system of redistribution with Antwerp, Amsterdam, London and Hamburg constituting some of its most important centres. The beginnings of an international division of labour are established, or in the words of an English economist, Dudley North, in 1691: 'The Whole World as to Trade, is but as one Nation or People, and therein Nations are as Persons.'

MEANS OF TRANSPORT

Against this background it scarcely comes as a surprise to find the total volume of European shipping increasing steadily during the period, especially on the Atlantic and North Sea coasts. The volume of Dutch shipping increased nearly tenfold in 200 years. In its heyday in the second half of the seventeenth century, the volume of Dutch-owned shipping considerably exceeded Spanish, Portuguese, French, English, Scottish and German combined. The preponderance of Dutch-built shipping was even greater. While the gunned ship as it was developed by Atlantic Europe played an important part in European overseas expansion, the Dutch must take the credit for making a distinction between the functions of the warship and those of the merchant carrier. They achieved this by developing the *fluyt*, a cheaply constructed, specially designed, unarmed merchant ship with increased carrying capacity in relation to her dimensions and therefore relatively low operating costs. The introduction of the *fluyt* is traditionally assigned to the year 1595, but it was of course the outcome of a long process of experiment and modification. Its roots went back to the types of vessels used by the Hanseatic league. The general proportions of the *fluyt* ship in fact became the standard for cargo carriers down to the introduction of iron hulls. This specialisation of function could not be carried through in all trades, but in northern Europe and the Atlantic, at least, the Dutch used the *fluyt* as their principal form of transport. Under war conditions it was necessary to provide convoys, and where the voyage took place in flotillas, as was the case in the East, *fluyts* would be interspersed. This specialisation was carried further still. In Dutch shipyards, the proportions of the *fluyt* were varied according to the trade in which it was to be employed. Ships for the Bergen timber trade could stand two or three more feet of draught than could the grain ships plying to the Baltic rivers. With their round tucks and flat bottoms these ocean-going vessels were equally capable of manœuvring up a river estuary or on a river or canal. Ships of war also underwent modifications. As early as the sixteenth century, the single-masted was giving way to the three-masted ship, which permitted the use of a variety of sails for specialised functions. This change was accompanied by a lengthening of the vessel in relation to its beam. The ship of 1450 rarely had a keel more than twice as long as the beam, whereas in 1600 a ratio of three to one was becoming common in northern Europe. The general effect of these improvements was to increase manœuvrability and shorten voyage times. The most important improvement from the commercial standpoint, however, was the reduction of crew sizes, for the cost of sea transport at this time was basically the cost of paying and feeding a crew, and in this respect the *fluyt* showed the best results.

In the sphere of land transport, too, this era displays much inventiveness, particularly in the design of carts and wagons. Towards the close of the sixteenth century, the 'fifth wheel', or turning-front carriage, and the use of iron tyres were both discovered in Germany. Increased carrying capacity resulted, and for many commodities land and water transport competed in many parts of Europe. Both expanded steadily and traffic alternated between the two. In both cases, costs were determined not only by technical and geographical but also by political factors, among which the exaction of tolls weighed particularly heavily, as well as by the state of general security and of war or peace. A particular coastal or inland waterway might be obstructed by so many hindrances that a parallel land-route became a cheaper alternative.

It is clear, however, that for very heavy and bulky goods water transport was the most economical under all circumstances. Only in the carrying of live cattle was sea transport dearer than land transport. To the question which branches of trade demanded the most tonnage and thus contributed most to the expansion of the shipping industry, the answer is that the brilliant, storied ocean-going trade takes second place to the short-distance traffic in homely, everyday commodities such as timber, coal, grain, salt, fish, flax and hemp. In 1699-1701, the tonnage of shipping required for English imports totalled 359,000 tons (yearly average), whereof northern Europe accounted for 208,000 tons, of which latter in turn 178,000 tons comprised the transport of timber. The East Indian trade accounted for a modest 5,000 tons. On the export side, the export of coal from England to nearby Europe absorbed 108,000 out of a total of 182,000 tons.

THE COMMODITY TRADE

Trade normally involves the transfer (geographically and in time) of a number of commodities. It is conducted by means of a variety of instruments, is organised by one or more persons and is accompanied by a settlement of account in one form or another. Which commodities? What distances? What payment? Who trades? How is it organised? In what follows an attempt is made to give a bird's eye view of some of the important trade flows and especially to deal with the changes in the nature, direction and volume of the commodities selected. These account in the aggregate for a substantial proportion of the total volume of European trade. At bottom trade is the expression of a supply and a demand. The more profound changes in the character of trade reflect changes in the structure of society itself. Regarded thus, trade becomes a mirror in which to catch glimpses of the production and consumption patterns which form the human environment of an age—its good years and its bad, its crises and its economic trends.

THE GRAIN TRADE

The importance of grain in the development of European trade can scarcely be exaggerated. This commodity is fundamental to the standard of life of the people. Wheat and rye are the principal ingredients of the daily bread. In northern Europe, barley forms the basic ingredient in the brewing of ale, and ale is equally as important an item of everyday fare in this part of Europe as is bread, in rather the same way as wine in southern Europe. Finally, oats must be added to the list as a food both for people and for livestock. In an age when the horse is indispensable as a draught and riding animal both in the peaceful everyday round and in time of war, the supply of oats must be as vital a matter as that of other species of grain.

The trade in grain is an ancient phenomenon. Everywhere there is movement of grain from producer to consumer, whether the distance is long or short—to and from the mill at least, if nothing else. Locally grain moves from countryside to town in wagons and sacks, along the coast or by river in smacks and barges. Its uniformity makes it suitable for being transported, but it is heavy; over long distances, therefore, it is best carried by sea. A Venetian secretary of state, Marc Ottoborn, when he was in Poland in 1590-91, trying to secure the supply of bread grain for the 'Queen of the Adriatic,' worked out how expensive it was to transport grain overland: he found that grain bought in Cracow and conveyed to Venice by land-routes would quadruple in price. Only dire need and a full treasury would justify undertaking transport by such means. The grain trade was subject to very severe ups and downs. This is reflected in its prices, which are the most widely fluctuating of all commodity prices. The trade is characterised by its capriciousness, stemming not only from see-sawing harvests that transformed grain-exporting regions into importing regions but also from speculation and the often arbitrary vagaries of governmental regulations and exactions. It may also be noted that despite the continual movement of grain from regions of surplus to regions of shortage, no effective adjustment ever emerges. Famine and periods of high prices are not avoided. This is clearly apparent in the Mediterranean region in the sixteenth century, when the supply situation deteriorated, especially in the towns, which were the grain trade's biggest customers.

We can distinguish several phases in this crisis, which begins in the west, afflicting first Portugal, then Spain and later Italy. Portugal, an exporter of grain in the Middle Ages (supplying places as far off as England) switches the emphasis of its agriculture from grain to olives and wine, but seeks to compensate for it by taking advantage of its overseas expansion and establishing grain cultivation in Morocco, in Madeira and the Azores. These new sources, however, are inadequate to meet the country's needs. Portugal becomes increasingly dependent on supplies from external sources—from Andalusia, Castile and Sicily, and from Flanders in the north, where trade with Bruges and later with Antwerp is well established. This is already happening in the first half of the century. In the second half, Spain too runs into a supply crisis that is particularly acute in the 1560s and 1570s. Andalusia, formerly an exporter of grain, can now cover its consumption only by importing foreign grain. A grain crisis affects Italy as well around mid-century. Even more serious is the series of crop failures that hit Italy from 1586 onwards. In 1590-91, the situation is desperate. The rains pour down, and northern Italy is threatened with food shortage. The Grand Duke of Tuscany establishes contact with Danzig (Gdansk) to the north. Venice does the same, and in 1592-93 the first big shipments arrive. Leghorn, a week's voyage from Gibraltar, is the port chosen to receive large consignments of grain in the succeeding years—whole flotillas from Danzig, Holland and England. This ushers in a new phase, for from now on the consignments are large and regular. How long the crisis in Italy continues is difficult to say. Deliveries from the north decline after 1608, and Sicily, the granary of the Mediterranean, resumes its place as the chief supplier.

Turning northwards next, we find here too that it is chiefly the towns, especially those in the densely populated province of Flanders, that generate the demand which sets shipments into motion and determines (at least partially) their rhythm. The population growth made greater demands upon local food marts than they could satisfy. A whole series of years of high prices and food scarcity, characteristic of the Netherlands, testify to this. The high prices of 1491 in Amsterdam supported a Baltic trade on a major scale, causing an increasing number of merchants from Holland, Zeeland and Brabant to enter the grain trade. In 1501, Amsterdam obtained from Philip the Fair the right of free trade in grain. Antwerp was granted a similar privilege by an ordinance of 1521, but until at least the early 1530s it remains unclear whether Antwerp or Amsterdam is the most advantageous market for the disposal of grain shipments from the Baltic. Later, however, the Amsterdam grain market gains dominance over the whole Netherlands area; indeed, it is no exaggeration to say that in the seventeenth and eighteenth centuries, the celebrated corn exchange of the Dutch metropolis fixes the grain prices of Europe. The ups and downs of the Baltic grain trade conform to the pattern of economic fluctuations in general in the Netherlands. The Netherlanders themselves were quite clear about this. They called the Baltic trade the 'mother of trades' or even the 'soul of trades'; the grain trade in particular was characterised as 'the source and root of all trade in this country'. The axis of this vital traffic lies between the cities of Amsterdam and Danzig.

An essential condition for Amsterdam's imposing role as the commodity exchange of western Europe appears to have been provided by the protectionist line the city followed in its maritime policy during the second half of the fifteenth century. In accordance with this, all shipmasters arriving from the Baltic who were citizens of Amsterdam were required to call at the city. The same applied to Amsterdam citizens co-owning a vessel with a non-citizen skipper. The rule, which is a navigation law in embryo, was aimed against Lübeck and against the direct traffic from the Baltic to Flanders, especially Bruges. It had its counterpart in the rule of the Hanseatic league compelling members to use Bruges as their staple. But this navigation law intensified the struggle for control over the staple commodities from the Baltic region. Even at an early stage it is noticeable that freights outward (many of them in ballast) are less in volume than return cargoes. Traffic with the

Baltic goes either from Amsterdam to the Baltic and back or from Amsterdam to one of the western commercial centres (e.g., to Brouage to collect salt), then straight to the Baltic, and finally back to Amsterdam. The latter is termed a '*door-gaende reyse*' (through voyage). Salt was the only bulky commodity sent to the Baltic. The return cargoes of grain and timber, on the other hand, were both bulky.

At the other end of the west-east axis of the grain trade, viz. Danzig, we find several analogies to Amsterdam. Danzig, too, could boast a site well protected from the open sea, hidden as the town was behind the Hela peninsula. Danzig also functioned as the economic centre for a considerable hinterland, and foreign trade features prominently in the early history of the city. In the sixteenth and seventeenth centuries, commerce on the Vistula was appreciably greater than Poland's overland foreign trade. The river system seems to have contained a larger volume of water than in our day, since the water-table was higher, thanks to the extensive forests. The Polish lowlands placed few obstacles in the way of river traffic, which operated along a whole network of rivers with the Vistula as the main artery. This means that the Vistula carried grain and timber belonging geographically to other regions. Thus a link was established at Augustow, via the river Narew, with the vast forested areas along the Niemen. Similarly there was a connection with the Pripet forests via the river Bug. The grain of the Warta district was shipped via Ner and Bzura to the Vistula, and at Wloclawek (Leslau) in the seventeenth century there was still a link from the Vistula via its tributaries and across lake Goplo with the rich black-earth region of Kujaw. The supplying districts associated with the Vistula trade were thus in the sixteenth and seventeenth centuries substantially bigger than the 'hinterland' drained by that river alone—which is itself bigger than that of the Rhine. A further factor that helped trade on the Vistula and exports via Danzig to reach their high sixteenth- and seventeenth-century levels was that trade along the river Oder (the nearest rival of the Vistula) was subject to interruptions. Disputes between Stettin and Frankfurt over the Warthe trade led to the Oder's being closed by the former city in 1562; in 1573 the closure was made permanent, and only towards the end of the seventeenth century was regular navigation of the Oder reintroduced.

While the river trade of the fifteenth century was still predominantly in the hands of peasants and urban merchants, as exports over Danzig increased the Polish nobility began to interest themselves in the selling of grain. The merchants became agents of the landowners, and the nobility stationed foreign merchants in Poland. In Danzig itself, which in many respects was a 'western' city, Polish merchants were banned in 1565 from transacting business abroad. Admittedly it was a difficult prohibition to enforce, but it does demonstrate the intention of the Polish nobility. What was fraught with still greater consequences of a social nature was the way in which the nobility coerced the peasantry into a system of large estates involving the abolition of peasant holdings and the consequent introduction of compulsory labour services. This development started as early as 1496. Thus, during the course of the sixteenth century, the nobility had secured for themselves a place in the front rank economically, and towards the end of the century, many peasants had become so impoverished that the dwindling of their demand was felt in the Polish towns, which languished in consequence. The lopsided development of agriculture and forestry under the massive pressure of western demand thus took place in Poland at the expense of native industries and handicrafts—which, moreover, had to compete with not inconsiderable imports of manufactured products from the west. The introduction of villeinage, the abolition of peasant holdings and their consolidation into estates brought general impoverishment in their train. Although the balance of trade was favourable, it was only the nobility and the Danzig merchants who profited from the vast traffic between east and west. Some of the eminent merchants of Danzig acquired estates for them-

The Riverine System of Poland

selves besides, thus reaping a double return from the flourishing grain trade.

Matters were very different in Holland. Here the effects of the grain trade spread like ripples in a pond. The trade with western and southern Europe depended upon the grain from the east, of which something like three-quarters was re-exported. The shipbuilding industry was founded in large measure on the demand created by the import and re-export of grain, as also did a number of industries that supplied ballast wares such as flagstones, tiles and bricks for the traffic to the Baltic. Such was the scale of the grain trade that it provided a great deal of direct and indirect employment. This took the form not only of loading and discharging cargoes, but also of building warehouses—over three-quarters of Amsterdam's warehouses appear to have been devoted to grain—and looking after the grain during storage, especially by regular tossing of the grain to prevent germination and spontaneous combustion. Further secondary industries included the building of lighters and the sewing of sacks.

The Sound Toll Register enables the traffic between west and east to be charted. The tables show more than 400,000 entries into and exits from the Sound during the years 1497-1660, and over 520,000 in the years comprising approximately the second half of our period, viz. 1661-1783. Nearly 60% of the entries in the first half-period were ships from the Seven United Provinces of the Netherlands, while in the second half the Dutch percentage was only 35.5. As regards grain, the total transport of rye and wheat amounted to 4.6 million lasts over the first half-period, i.e. nearly 4 million lasts of rye and 0.6 million of wheat. Over the second—and longer—half, 4.7 million lasts passed the Sound, i.e. 3.3 million of rye and 1.4 million of wheat. Shipments of rye thus fell off absolutely and relatively while those of wheat increased. In the first half-period, the Dutch carried 76.5% of the rye and 77.5% of the wheat; in the second half these figures were 71 and 70 respectively. Right down to 1720 the Dutch managed to maintain their position in the Baltic grain trade. The figures in the Sound

Toll tables further reveal that Danzig is far the most important of the exporting ports. In the first half-period, 70% of rye and 63.5% of wheat came from Danzig. Königsberg, Riga and Latvia-Estonia follows far back in the wake of Danzig as suppliers of rye and of Stettin as a supplier of wheat. In the second half-period Danzig lost a lot of ground as a supplier of rye—its share dropped to 47.2%—but it held and indeed improved its position as a supplier of wheat with just 70%. Königsberg improved its share of both commodities. A shift towards the eastern Baltic seems to have occurred in the course of the eighteenth century.

The long-term characteristics of the Dutch Baltic trade were its great stability and fixity, and the channelling of the flow of grain through Amsterdam. Over shorter periods, on the other hand, there are violent year-to-year fluctuations. These are normally the immediate result of interaction between the wildly fluctuating harvest yields of east and west, but in certain years they are caused by wars and other political factors. Thus, particularly high exports from Danzig coincide with crop failures in western Europe, e.g. in 1562, 1565, 1586 and all through the 1590s, when particularly acute shortages in the Mediterranean countries gave rise to heavy exports. Conversely, Danzig's worst year is 1577, when the king of Poland besieges the city; and the deep depression of the 1620s is associated with the Swedish-Polish war and the Swedish blockade of Danzig in 1626-29.

During the 1620s the Swedes got control of larger territories of the Baltic and its grain-producing hinterland. Danzig was never actually conquered, but when Gustavus Adolphus moved his army into West Prussia the city's trade became subject to Swedish control in such forms as tax imposts. Substantial sectors of the Baltic grain trade fell into Swedish hands or came under Swedish export-licensing regulation. It was in this atmosphere that the idea of establishing a Swedish state monopoly came up. Axel Oxenstierna mooted it as early as 1623. Any such monopoly would also have to embrace the exports of Russian grain that went via Archangel. The latter route was of recent date. In 1627 Gustavus Adolphus sounded the Tsar about the possibility of obtaining grain from Russia and did in fact receive permission to make limited purchases. In 1629, negotiations were renewed and it is plain that Königsberg and Danzig were also interested in the Swedish plans, the purpose of which was partly to maintain the level of prices in Amsterdam by restriction of the supply. Despite such a restriction being introduced, prices in the Dutch metropolis began to decline after 1630, which suggests that the monopoly plan must have been unrealistic.

This episode raises the question of the extent to which prices in Amsterdam were determined by deliveries from the east. Was it supply in the east or demand in the west that was the decisive factor? The autumn crop yields in Poland or the economic situation in Holland and western Europe? Price analyses show that it was not always the autumn crop yields in the Danzig hinterland that determined grain prices in Amsterdam. If the harvest failed in Spain or France, the price-bulge could travel from west to east. The increase in demand was felt in the Netherlands first and was then transmitted eastwards. It must be stressed too that it was not Baltic grain alone that determined the supply on the Amsterdam corn exchange. Large quantities of grain were still being produced in western Europe. How large a surplus there was for export is not known as precisely as in the case of the Baltic, but whatever surplus there was mostly went to Amsterdam. Thus, from the 1630s France exported grain regularly to Holland, since the grain-producing provinces of France were situated nearer to the Dutch market than to the regions of France that simultaneously were suffering from a shortage of grain. From Hamburg, too, grain was exported to Amsterdam. During the second half of the seventeenth century, England once more became a grain-exporting nation, and a substantial proportion of English exports found their way to the great corn exchanges on the other side of the Channel. Some contemporaries asserted that Baltic grain was not in fact indispensable to western Europe, even though in times of shortage long distances were covered—as far as to

Archangel on the White Sea—in order to fetch it. Thus Johann Köstner, a Danzig merchant, pointed out in 1660 that when the war of 1655-60 between Sweden and Poland cut off Danzig's exports again for no less than five years, Holland had managed with grain from elsewhere. He believed that deliveries from the east would lose their importance under peacetime conditions. Only a bad harvest in the west or very low prices in the east would make exports a paying proposition. This interpretation, coupled with the failure of the Swedish monopoly policy of the 1620s, could lead one to conclude that it was prices in Amsterdam that determined to what extent and at what price grain could be exported from Danzig, since it must be added that the Amsterdam prices in turn were themselves determined by the harvest yield and market conditions in Europe as a whole.

There are other indications to suggest that there is a turning-point around 1650 in the great east-west grain trade. The long phase of expansion is about to end. An analysis of the volume of trade and of Amsterdam prices shows that the cyclical fluctuations in the trade through the Sound after the middle of the century differ from those before it. There are more fluctuations after 1650 than before, and the curves show greater turbulence. While the cyclical contractions of western demand before 1650 were unable to bring about any long-lasting reduction in the volume of grain imported, and massive rises in imports from the Baltic in certain years were unable to break price-levels in Amsterdam, the situation changes after 1650.

Southern and western Europe seem now to have become more self-sufficient in grain. Maize, which was introduced in Portugal during the sixteenth century and in Spain at the beginning of the seventeenth, begins to feature in the second half of the seventeenth century as an ordinary article of the people's diet. Rice production in Italy is rising during the seventeenth century, and here too increased cultivation of maize is observable after the plague and famine of the 1630s. These new foodstuffs, in conjunction with stagnating economies and population in most of the former grain-importing regions, undoubtedly contributed to a slackening of demand in southern Europe. But there is also plenty of evidence of an increased production of foodstuffs in western Europe during the second half of the seventeenth century, coinciding with a general stagnation of population. There are reports of increased cultivation of buckwheat in western and central Europe, and we hear of expanded production of grain generally in several regions of western Europe in the second half of the seventeenth century. As already mentioned, protectionist agricultural legislation in England after 1660, exemplified in such devices as export bounties, fosters a grain-exporting trade that continues right up to the middle of the eighteenth century. Thus, both demographic and market factors in western and southern Europe must have tended to reduce the demand for grain from the Baltic. In such a context the interruptions of the Vistula trade consequent upon the mid-century wars were particularly damaging for Danzig and Poland. The second Swedish-Polish war of 1655-60 was the turning-point for Danzig. It dealt a lasting blow to trade on the river Vistula. Exports of grain in the next half-century succeeded only rarely in reaching the 50-60,000 lasts annually that had been the normal exports of the preceding period. The campaign of Charles X went on, with its ravagings and requisitions. The devastation inflicted on town and country alike bears comparison with that of the hard-hit districts of Germany in the Thirty Years War.

What did the east-west grain trade actually signify quantitatively in relation to the aggregate demand for or supply of grain? Exact calculations are impossible, but if the annual transit trade figures, which in the first half of the seventeenth century were around 68,500 lasts, are converted and correlated with the estimated average consumption of grain in western Europe, Baltic grain supplies were equivalent to the annual consumption of about three-quarters of a million people. In relation to the aggregate population of western and southern Europe and its volume of demand, this figure is unimpressive. Now it may be objected that this international business should be viewed in relation not to total populations but only to those districts within the orbit of international trade, which means essentially the urbanised districts. On the other hand each district had a hinterland and a local trade that included grain. Amsterdam itself had a local corn exchange ('de korenbeurs op het water') alongside its international corn exchange, and a local grain trade with 'het binnenland,' the hinterland—i.e., the Rhine, Flanders, northern France, England; where the line is to be drawn, and shipments, from being local in character, become international, is difficult to say. Local and international traffic in grain is inextricably interwoven. It would be wrong in the case of a commodity, like grain, to think in terms of a dual economy with two mutually distinct sectors. If this argument is sound, then supplies from the Baltic were marginal in relation to total demand and total supply. From this it follows that relatively slight changes in the total quantities supplied and/or demanded can produce relatively large changes in that marginal sector where Baltic grain was to be found. The depression in the grain trade in the second half of the seventeenth century, which in the long term came to affect the whole economy of the Netherlands, may therefore be regarded as having been caused by a relatively slight decline in (total) demand and a simultaneous slight increase of grain production in southern and western Europe. This marginal conception is perhaps even more applicable to the case of Baltic grain and the demand from southern Europe. This demand was for wheat, and wheat alone. The proportion of wheat in the total grain traffic through the Sound, as has already been indicated, is not large. In the period prior to 1660 it amounts altogether to 13% of the total shipments of grain. These shipments fluctuate, being more important in some years than in others. It is also clear that southern European demand was a key factor in the establishment of Dutch traffic with the Mediterranean, and that this speculative trade in grain had other important effects, e.g., upon the organisation of trade. But in relation to the number of mouths there were to feed, the quantities involved are infinitesimally small;

no doubt they offered relief in years of food shortage to particular and limited areas—especially to the upper classes—but in the long run they can hardly have formed the basis of a continual flow of goods. In other words, southern European demand for grain towards the end of the sixteenth century opened a trade-route which it became the function of other commodities and other forms of commerce to nourish and extend.

THE TRADE IN CATTLE

The trade in cattle has hitherto been a neglected chapter in the history of European trade. The trade is decidedly rural in character, but often covers long distances and crosses frontiers. Down through the centuries we hear of cattle-droves; they continue right down to our own times, but their heyday is the period from the fifteenth century to the beginning of the seventeenth. When the value of grain exports from the Baltic in the period 1601-20 is compared with that of contemporaneous exports of cattle from Denmark (including Schleswig-Holstein and Skåne), grain is seen to account for an annual average value equivalent to 55,000 kg. silver, while the corresponding figure for cattle is about 30,000 kg. silver. What we are dealing with here, therefore, is a commodity that, even from the standpoint of value, ranks among the most important articles in international trade. As with grain, so with cattle: the merchandise moved towards those markets where prices were high, i.e., from east and north to the west.

The background to this sizeable trade in meat is the high level of consumption observable as early as the fifteenth century and continuing into the sixteenth century. While the demand for grain is quite inelastic, fluctuating *pro tanto* with population numbers, that for meat is elastic. It varies with incomes, and there are indications that the rising real wages of late medieval times were reflected in an increased consumption of meat. Very considerable quantities of wine and beer were consumed as well as meat, perhaps in consequence of the lack of dietary balance. A diet dominated by proteins necessitates large quantities being eaten. We have much evidence from the fifteenth century not only of what was consumed at the rich man's table but also of the enormous helpings of meat on which farm labourers, journeymen, servants and others used to gorge themselves. This is in evidence in the north of Europe whereas the consumption of meat in the south of Europe seems to have been on a much more modest scale. The English Admiralty later on recognised that it was easier to make provision for Spanish and Italian sailors because they contented themselves with bread and olives.

People ate and drank heartily throughout the sixteenth century as well, though, on average, not quite to the same extent as before, since real wages were diminishing. On the other hand the urbanising process that was spreading all over western Europe in the sixteenth century may well have compensated for any lowering in the individual's rate of consumption. The large consuming centres were especially important in the halcyon days of the cattle trade, whether cities, mining districts or the great households of princes and armies. Overseas trading too demanded large quantities of beef. The meat supply on long voyages consisted largely of salt beef. The best results in respect of both keeping qualities and taste were obtained by salting down fine-fibred meat. This was one of the reasons why Danish oxen—especially those from Jutland—were in demand in Dutch towns. In the first half of the seventeenth century over 2,000 cattle, annually, were slaughtered for the victualling of the East Indian fleet alone. The requirements of the great war fleets were of a comparable order of magnitude. Holland's famous poet, Vondel, wrote in praise of Danish oxen, and Dutch masters portrayed them in their still life. Much of Europe's trade in the sixteenth and seventeenth centuries so to speak centred upon filling the belly and slaking the thirst.

The trade in cattle covered large distances. The actual stock-rearing was carried on far away from the towns. During their migration (the drove) the animals lost weight and so had to be fattened up somewhere in the vicinity of the place of consumption. There is therefore a clear geographical distinction between the stock-rearing areas on the one hand, and the fattening areas on the other. The typical stock-rearing zones lay beyond the so-called 'corn-growing zones.' Beginning in the north, the stock-rearing areas extended from Jutland across the Danish islands to Skåne, thence to Poland, Bohemia and Hungary, with parts of Russia and Rumania adjoining. The northern area delivered cattle to the towns of north-west Europe, i.e., to the Netherlands, Hamburg and Lübeck. Some part of these supplies found their way south to Cologne. Frankfurt, on the other hand, was beyond the borderline and was supplied for the most part by the south-eastern European districts.

The Polish sphere embraced the region around Lwow (Lemberg), whence the droves via Cracow and Breslau set off westwards, but Lwow was also itself an assembly point for droves from the Duchy of Moldau. The importance of Moldau as a supplier of cattle to central Europe declined with the expansion of the Turkish dominions, however, since large shipments of both grain and cattle were now directed towards the provisioning of Turkish troops and to Constantinople. The largest of the eastern European stock-breeding areas was Hungary. While it is fairly certain that some of the cattle coming from Hungary to central Europe were transit cattle from Wallachia and Moldau, most of them were reared in Hungary itself, where during the fifteenth to sixteenth centuries cattle were far and away the most important article of export. The destinations were Germany, Austria and northern Italy, especially Venice. Hungarian exports encountered a number of serious difficulties in the sixteenth century, arising partly from the Turkish wars and partly from cattle-plague, especially the large-scale outbreaks of 1518 and the period 1549-59. The epidemic of 1518 was regarded in Nuremberg as something of a catastrophe for Germany, since it was believed that the whole of Germany's meat-store was now cut off. The flow of cattle from Hungary was, however, by no means brought to a lasting halt; in the eighteenth century upper Germany and northern Italy were still being supplied from Hungary. But in the case of central Europe, the difficulties of the sixteenth century led to increased supplies being obtained from Galicia and Poland.

The fattening areas lay in the immediate neighbourhoods of the centres of consumption, in an inner 'pastoral zone' consisting of flood-plains and tracts of meadow. The North Sea marshes and Friesland furnish an example of such a fattening zone that was important to the towns of north Germany and the Netherlands.

The lines of communication between the two zones consisted of the so-called drove-roads along which the droves took place. They followed special tracks, often through thinly populated districts so that traffic on the ordinary commercial routes should not be blocked by the slow-moving animals, which used to cover about two to four miles a day and had to rest on every third day. There was no point in forcing the pace, since the cattle would then lose too much meat and fat. The cattle passed through a series of intermediate stations at frequent intervals during these droves, which were often very long and could extend to over a thousand kilometres. In many cases the intermediate stations were identical with the customs posts, where the droves were registered and dues were paid. A considerable number of people accompanied the animals. The rule was one drover to every twenty cattle, together with a forager, often the son of the merchant. The latter's function was to find inns and overnight accommodation, and hay for the animals, which spent the night in the open air. Numbers of lodging-houses sprang up along the drove-roads to serve the needs of both animals and men.

The animals were sold at some market near the fattening districts, e.g., the famous cattle market at the small town of Buttstädt in Thuringia (north of Weimar), where fairs were held three times a year, on the feasts of St John (24th June), St Michael (29th September) and All Saints (1st November). The cattle sold there came from Poland, Brandenburg and Pomerania. The buyers came to Buttstädt from all over central and western Germany. Another celebrated market was that of Wedel, west of Hamburg. Here Danish exporters met purchasers from Germany and the Netherlands at the great spring fair, which lasted from the middle of March to the middle of April. Most of the cattle traded at this fair came from Jutland. They began moving in February. The trip from Vendsyssel to the Elbe took about thirty days. The animals were not much more than skin and bone by the time they reached Wedel—which was also known, appropriately enough, as the 'lean market.' However, a summer's grazing on Dutch or German meadows was sufficient to prepare them for slaughter. There was an autumn fair at Wedel too, for droves of cattle from the Duchy of Schleswig. These were cattle ready for slaughter.

The production of livestock was not dependent to anything like the same degree as grain upon the vagaries of the weather, and prices were accordingly far more stable. In most places the princes and noble landowners asserted that the rearing of cattle for export was their exclusive privilege. They demanded the right of pre-emption over the peasants' young bullocks, thus enabling prices to be held down and the lords' own profit increased correspondingly. Actual trading operations, on the other hand, were frequently in the hands of middle-class merchants or engrossers. The cattle changed ownership several times before ending up in the pot: from the farmer who undertook the actual rearing (a three- or four-year process, on farms whose capacity was often limited to as few as 2-4 head of cattle) to the lord, who had a monopoly of stabling for export (duration: one winter; capacity: several hundred head of cattle); to the merchant who organised the drove of a month or more with herds numbering twenty, forty or as many as several hundred head of cattle; to the engrosser or slaughterer, who arranged for fattening-up prior to delivery at the slaughterhouse in the autumn.

We are well informed about the trade in cattle in the north-western coastal area, thanks to copious customs data that have survived in very long series. Cattle brought overland from the kingdom of Denmark passed through no fewer than five customs barriers in the Duchy of Schleswig, the last two of which, viz. Gottorp (at the city of Schleswig) and Rendsborg, were the most important, since duty was paid there on each individual head of cattle.

Examination of the secular fluctuations in the transport of cattle as revealed in these records discloses an upward trend from 1483 to 1560. The figures rise from a level of just on 13,000 head of livestock a year in transit to over 40,000. In the next two decades the trend is more or less stationary, but after the 1570s the export figures fall off to low points of 26,000 in 1579 and only 19,000 in 1583. The explanation may well be found to lie in the depressed political and economic condition of the Netherlands. By 1596 the setback has been overcome; and now begins the high-noon of the northern European trade in cattle. For practically every year up to 1625, the customs records at Gottorp-Rendsborg show duty levied on over 30,000 head; in some years there were 40,000 animals, and there was one year (1612) with no fewer than 52,350. Fragments of a customs ledger of 1618 give reason to believe that exports that year were higher still.

This high level is maintained until the 1640s, when market conditions deteriorate in the aftermath of the Thirty Years War. Prices on the Elbe market fall, and one merchant after another abandons the export of cattle. With the fall in prices, the rearing of cattle becomes unremunerative, especially on the smaller estates. Export continues, however, and in the second half of the seventeenth century it amounted normally to about 20,000 head per annum overland, though with numerous interruptions and temporary depressions resulting from the war. Thus, exports were completely broken off from 1658 to 1660 during the Danish-Swedish war; similarly, the Anglo-Dutch war of 1665-67 and Louis XIV's war of aggression left their impress in the form of disappointing Netherlands purchases on the Elbe market. At the beginning of the eighteenth century the Great Northern War created difficulties. So did outbreaks of cattle-plague in 1713 and 1745.

The heyday of the cattle trade coincided with the golden age of the nobility. This is evidenced by the many examples, in Hungary, Poland and Denmark, of large incomes from

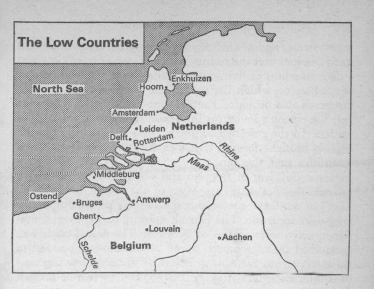

The Low Countries

North Sea

Enkhuizen
Hoorn

Amsterdam

Leiden
Delft
Rotterdam

Netherlands

Rhine

Maas

Middleburg

Ostend
Bruges
Antwerp

Ghent

Louvain

Aachen

Belgium

Schelde

cattle being lavishly dispensed upon the construction of stately homes and the maintenance of great households and a high standard of living. The trade was a firm component of the base on which the rule of the aristocracy rested. But the herds also provided the peasants with their livelihoods, and the customs levies on the trade swelled the treasury of princes. In the case of Denmark, the swift growth of cattle exports brought foreign currency into the country in such quantities that the monetary structure recovered rapidly from the civil war of 1533-36 and was able subsequently to finance the Seven Years War of the North in 1563-70. Last but not least, merchants made their profits out of this long-distance trade. The Danish nobility hardly ever, themselves, acted as exporters of livestock. The actual trade was conducted by merchants. Some of the most important of them were from Flensburg. Before 1630 only a few German or Dutch exporters may be traced, but thereafter foreign engrossers appear on the scene in increasing numbers. The brisk and continuous Dutch demand which brought the Dutch engrossers to the Danish stable-doors, as it were, probably explains why exports went steadily on, even though at a lower level because of reduced German demand.

THE PEPPER TRADE

The categories of foodstuffs entering into international trade include many colonial products, ranging from the vast variety of spices and drugs to commodities such as tea, coffee, tobacco and sugar. The trade in the four last-mentioned items did increase during the seventeenth century, though for the most part it belongs to the subsequent period. But spices enjoyed their heyday in the sixteenth and seventeenth centuries. Foremost among the spices—in both volume and value—was pepper, the most notable speculative commodity of the mercantile era, attracting the attention of the greatest merchants and capitalists of the age.

It is important to understand clearly that pepper was a

bulky commodity, demanding large-scale transport resources by land as well as by water, although, like other spices, it did allow of being divided up into minimal lots, as was normally the practice when sold at retail.

The greatest seventeenth-century importer of pepper, the Dutch East India Company, regarded pepper as constituting a very serviceable form of ballast and a commodity useful for trimming the rest of the cargo because it could be poured into the holds when vessels were being loaded. The Dutch company ordered its pepper in bales (of more than 200 kg.) but sold it by the pound. This divisibility of pepper in conjunction with its durability—especially when compared with other foodstuffs—rendered it an excellent object for speculation. It could be kept for a long time: instances are known of pepper lying in store for over thirty years, which of course did affect the quality, but this could then be improved by an admixture of fresh pepper. The commodity was easy to distribute, and in the retail trade it was sold in such small lots that we are dealing with a commodity that may be presumed to have reached even the poorer levels of the population. In other words, it has the character of an article of mass consumption. A factor contributing to this was the effort on the part of importers to create a uniform product by blending the various grades.

The earliest pepper to reach Europe came from the west coast of India, where the *piper nigrum* bush grew in the forest tracts of Malabar and Travancore. Via Indian and Arabian middlemen, this pepper made its way along the caravan trails to the Levant, where Italian merchants bought up the commodity. We can distinguish two principal routes: from the Persian Gulf overland to Aleppo and Tripoli, or by water through the Red Sea to Cairo and Alexandria. Another pepper-growing region existed within the Indonesian archipelago. From there—and especially from Bantam in West Java—substantial exports of pepper went both to China and also westwards via Malacca to Bengal, the Coromandel coast and other parts of India. Over the years, Indonesian pepper secured an ever stronger position for itself, even in those markets, not only in Europe but also in Asia, that traditionally had been supplied with Indian pepper. It is true that Malabar pepper, at its best, was regarded as being of better quality than Indonesian, but its quality was very variable. And in addition the political deterioration in South India during the second half of the seventeenth century, limited production. The activity of Europeans had its effects too. As soon as the Portuguese arrived, they attempted to secure control of the Malabar coast, the classical pepper region, and to confine its shipment to Europe to the maritime routes. Admittedly, they never managed to get all the Malabar pepper into their hands, but their manœuvres did create temporary disturbances in the Asian pepper trade. Arabian and Indian merchants were looking for alternative supplies, i.e., supplies of Indonesian pepper. When the Dutch, English, French and Danes made their appearance in the producing areas later on, the Portuguese barred them from Malabar, thus leading them to concentrate on purchasing from West Java and Sumatra, thereby contributing to the dissemination of Indonesian pepper.

The alternative purchasing opportunities that were available excluded all possibility of monopolising pepper at the buying stage. The alternative routes by which the commodity could reach Europe did the same. On the other hand the very long transport routes—some of the longest in the history of the commodity trade in this epoch—meant that the supplies were subject to many risks of interruption, natural as well as political. It was therefore difficult to reckon how much pepper would find its way to the European market each year and by which channels. This fundamental uncertainty with regard to the volume of the deliveries and the times of their arrival provided very fertile ground for speculation. In the sixteenth century, numerous interruptions, reductions and reorganisations of supply occurred in consequence of wars by land and sea. The Portuguese were in a more or less permanent state of war with the Turks, who at the beginning of the century had conquered Syria and Egypt, and who, in the 1530s, 1540s and 1550s, conducted a series of campaigns against the Portuguese strongholds along the Arabian coast and the Persian Gulf. The war of 1560-63 between Portugal and Turkey also brought reorganisations of supplies in its train. There were losses by shipwreck as well. It is well-known that Portuguese shipping in the second half of the sixteenth century suffered many misfortunes. Thus, in the period 1586-91, only about 62% of the consignments from Goa reached Lisbon. The wars between Venice and Turkey of 1499-1503, 1537-40 and 1570-73 had similar effects, and also helped to bring other competitors on to the scene.

The seventeenth century likewise offered examples of the interruption of supplies as a result of war; but there was a crucial difference between the sixteenth and seventeenth centuries in that the maritime supply-routes to Europe came to dominate the picture entirely. While 'Mediterranean' pepper (i.e., pepper carried via the Levant) and 'Atlantic' pepper (i.e., seaborne pepper imported at Lisbon) contended for the paramountcy and supplemented one another throughout the sixteenth century, 'Atlantic' supplies held complete pride of place in the seventeenth century, Holland and England being the principal importers. So convincing was the victory of 'Atlantic' pepper that it was even re-exported to the Levant. Political circumstances were not solely responsible for the cessation of the flow of pepper along the caravan routes. Comparative transport costs favoured 'Atlantic' pepper, particularly since steeply rising purchases on the part of the new European buyers had sent production prices soaring at the same time as selling prices in Europe were down. Narrower profit margins meant that the future belonged to whichever method of transport was able to effect the movement of large quantities in a single operation without costly intermediate links.

One can certainly speak of a *European* market for pepper. Price movements exhibit palpable common features. How large the region's aggregate demand was, on the other hand, is difficult to determine. A guess might place it in the vicinity of 3-4 million lbs. a year in the sixteenth century, rising to double that amount during the seventeenth but probably not exceeding 10-12 million lbs. at any point. Demand was evidently increasing, and the new pepper importers of the seventeenth century, the East India companies of north-west Europe, concentrated with particular emphasis on the import of pepper in the first half of the century. Thus the Dutch invested over half of their return-cargo capacity in pepper. Despite the quantitative growth of imports, the proportion represented by pepper in the value of shipments fell heavily during the second half of the century and was only about 11% by 1698-1700. Geographical analysis of the demand discloses that consumption of pepper in the importing countries accounted for only a modest proportion of imports. For Venice and Portugal as well as for Holland and England, pepper was very decidedly an article of re-export. Central and eastern Europe, which lacked direct access to imports, presumably constituted one of the most important destinations for re-exports. Demand was probably also greater in the northern zone of Europe than in the southern, where pepper-plants and other fresh local spices had been articles of diet since ancient times.

While most imports from overseas were paid for by the export of bullion and coin—the East Indian trade was decidedly an import trade with the principal object of satisfying a European demand rather than of finding markets for European products—imports via the Levant presented a rather different face. The worlds of Araby and the Indies coveted a number of articles from the countries of the Mediterranean. Copper was a metal in particular demand and was despatched eastwards from central Europe via Venice. Coral from the fisheries off the Tunisian coast was exported eastwards, some of it by the French *Compagnie du Corail* that operated from Marseilles in the second half of the sixteenth century. Fabrics, quicksilver and saffron, together with opium from Egypt, entered into the stream of goods exchanged between the Mediterranean countries, the Levant and the Indies. This circumstance undoubtedly explains also why the caravan trade did not come to a standstill when the Portuguese found the sea route to the Indies and tried to redirect pepper transport. Trade conditions in the Levant facilitated a greater reciprocity of commodities than was possible in the overseas trade around the Cape.

More detailed study reveals the pepper trade as a sharply fluctuating and in many of its aspects a wealthy trade, displaying attempts at monopoly and cartel agreements as well as periods of fierce competition.

Its inception was very dramatic. The Portuguese success in finding the sea route to the Indies produced a crisis in Venice, the chief mart of the old Mediterranean pepper trade, whence large areas of the rest of Europe had been supplied with pepper and spices, whether overland or by the maritime route in which Bruges and Antwerp were important centres. In 1501, the first Portuguese vessel discharged pepper at Antwerp. From 1503 onwards, shipments arrived regularly. In 1508, the *Feitoria de Flandres* was established as a department of the *Casa da India*. The massive deliveries of overseas pepper produced a heavy fall in prices that undermined Italian sales of the dearer and better Malabar pepper. At the same time, Venice was hit by the failure of supplies from the Levant. The Portuguese triumphed in the northern Netherlands too. They were also selling pepper in England; and, most significant of all, the great German merchant houses, including the Fuggers, began to place their orders with the Portuguese at Antwerp. *Magna Societas* of Ravensburg decided in 1507 to transfer its spice purchases to the Low Countries. In 1512–13 the mercantile community of Vienna complained to the Emperor of the insufficiency of supplies from Venice and requested that the necessary quantities of spices should be ordered from Antwerp, Frankfurt and Nuremberg. Atlantic pepper made progress in France and Spain too, penetrating even into the Mediterranean itself.

The Portuguese offensive reached a climax between 1510 and 1515. Following the naval battle off Diu in 1509, the Egyptian fleet lost control of the seaway to the Indies; next year Goa was taken, and, the year after that, the vital strategic and commercial crossroads of Malacca. Socotra, off Cape Guardafui, also fell into Portuguese hands, thereby furnishing a base that could be used to cut off the consignments of spices to Jeddah and to Cairo/Alexandria. Even more decisive was the conquest in 1515, of Hormuz, at the entrance to the Persian Gulf. With Socotra and Hormuz in their hands, the Portuguese controlled the western end of the Arabian maritime trade network, and with Goa as their main base and smaller stations along the Malabar coast they commanded the corresponding Indian sector of the trade network. In these years, pepper prices at Antwerp dropped to their lowest point. At the same time the Fuggers' shipments of copper to Antwerp reached a peak, while their corresponding shipments to Venice sharply declined. Portuguese pepper was distributed from Antwerp over large areas of Europe. Among the new centres was Lyons, whither a busy pepper trade was established along the Sâone.

Venice did not give up, however. Despite momentary interruptions of deliveries along the caravan routes, the flow via the Levant continued, though on a modest scale. After an absence of some years, the Venetian galleys reappeared in the Scheldt in 1518. In the landward traffic too, Venice began to make some recovery, as in the case of the Alpine route to France, where in 1525-27 Levant spices had won more than half of the Lyons market.

During the 1530s it was plain that Venice was getting its revenge. The Fuggers' consignments of copper to Venice revived. On the Antwerp market, too, Levant pepper again became a factor to reckon with. Thus, pepper prices on the Antwerp market in 1538 reacted in consequence of the difficulties associated with the war against the Turks. The war also gave other intermediaries a chance. Marseilles, previously an important station in the Venetian system of re-exports, obtained by direct treaty between the Sultan and the French king the right of direct sailings to the Levant. Direct imports by France helped to strengthen the position of Mediterranean pepper on the French market, where it competed with Atlantic pepper from Portugal even in such cities as Bordeaux, La Rochelle and Rouen.

Another intermediary to whom the Venetian-Turkish war of 1537-40 gave an opportunity was Ragusa, whence the German houses later sent their own agents to Alexandria. The Fuggers established an import traffic from Alexandria to Fiume in Ragusan bottoms, for instance. Around the middle of the century, the Antwerp market had been substantially reduced, measured against a European yardstick. It was now predominantly a regional market supplying central Germany and the North Sea and Baltic regions. Portuguese pepper was still paramount in this market— even after the closure of the Portuguese factory at Antwerp —but its mastery was not unchallenged.

In Lisbon there was alarm at the successes of the caravan routes. At the beginning of the 1560s, especially during the renewed hostilities between Turkey and Portugal, when the Turks succeeded in confiscating Portuguese pepper destined for Lisbon and redirecting it to Egypt, a shortage of pepper is recorded in Portugal, while at the same time deliveries via the Levant reached a level probably exceeding that prior to the discovery of the sea route. It signalled changing times when the Portuguese ambassador, during the peace negotiations of 1563, tried to obtain the permission of the Porte to send Portugal's Indies pepper up through the Red Sea and thence overland to Cairo/Alexandria or Syria to be sold. Nothing came of this, however. Later, during the Venetian war against the Turks in 1570-73, it was the Queen of the Adriatic's turn to find herself in difficulties. It was not only Ragusa, Ancona and Marseilles, her closest rivals in the Levant trade, that derived advantage from this, but also Lisbon, whose pepper gained ground again.

Thus did the struggle between the two supply arteries for the European market fluctuate, bringing periods of setback, crisis and success for them both. At the century's close, Portugal was on the defensive, partly because of very heavy losses by shipwreck on top of those caused by privateering and the blockade of Lisbon in 1597-98. Prices rose sharply. This gave further encouragement to the growing interloping activities of the northern Netherlands and England that were a feature of the conflict with Spain. Portugal had been bound to Spain by a union of the crowns since 1580, thus finding itself opposed by the same adversaries as the Habsburg dynasty. The capture of Antwerp in 1585 also had caused a disruption of the pepper trade that incited others to fish in troubled waters. Moreover the new partners joining in the contest to bring pepper to Europe operated on both fronts, the Atlantic as well as the Mediterranean. They sought pepper both by sailing south of the Cape and by trading sorties into the Levant.

The years around the turn of the century were marked by much disquiet. Irregular and sporadic supplies, thanks particularly to the activities of the new competitors, caused violent fluctuations in the price of pepper. Raleigh's capture of the Portuguese carrack *Madre de Dios* in the early 1590s brought such a quantity of pepper on to the English market that imports were prohibited for three years in order that the Queen's pepper might be disposed of. When four ships of the newly established East India Company brought home over a million lbs. of pepper in 1603, the English market was again thrown completely off balance. The home market demand—hitherto the determinant of imports into England—was unable to absorb such large quantities. In 1609, all imports of pepper into England other than by the East India Company were forbidden. Soon it was re-exports, and therefore the state of the European market, not the home market, that became the decisive factor in the pepper business of the new East India Company. About 1620 it was clear, too, that the emergence of the Dutch and English on the scene signified a transformation of the international pepper trade, in terms of both quantity and price. The Levant was eventually beaten by the seaborne supplies. Amsterdam became the new mart on whose barometer the state of European trade could be read. Second place was taken by London, while the remainder of Europe's imports were accounted for by the Portuguese, backed up from time to time by the French and the Danes.

The pepper trade of the seventeenth century was characterised by fierce competition, especially between the Dutch and English companies. This was the case during the years of booming sales from 1610 to 1617, when the market was steadily climbing. This is borne out also by prices, which were rising. In the race to assure themselves of pepper consignments for Europe the Asian representatives of the two companies drove prices so high that ultimately an attempt was made to agree on a division of the purchasable supply at Bantam. It was not conspicuously successful, however. After the boom the wheel of fortune turned, and glut became the order of the day. The English company, especially, felt Dutch competition more and more keenly all during the 1620s and early 1630s. The Dutch themselves were trying to steer between Scylla and Charybdis. On the one hand was their desire to prevent their opponents from making purchases in the Orient by pre-empting the market themselves: on the other was their anxiety lest growing stocks in the Netherlands should threaten European prices.

Around the middle 1630s, however, supplies to Europe began to fall off. There were numerous reasons for this. The Dutch East India Company's trade in pepper was conditioned not merely by reference to the European market, but also by the company's trade with its many factories in maritime Asia, from Japan in the east to the Yemen in the west. In the 1630s it was consideration for the trade with Persia, the source of raw silk, that was in view, but the Chinese and Japanese markets too bought significant quantities of pepper. In its endeavours to provide pepper, the Dutch company turned its attention to the Malabar coast, still controlled by the Portuguese. If the company could secure Malabar pepper for its trade in Persia, then the Indonesian pepper supplies might be distributed to China, Japan and Europe. In 1636 the blockade of Goa was started. In fact, the campaign was aimed at the conquest of Malacca, which was achieved in 1641 with very great political consequences for the western part of the Indonesian archipelago. The campaign, however, immediately affected the supplies of pepper to Europe. For nine years the Dutch blockade of Goa caused disturbances in the Portuguese deliveries. English supplies to Europe also suffered, and the English met with the mishap that a ship with a complete cargo of pepper was wrecked in the Thames. The Dutch company's directors in the Netherlands began to get anxious. In December, 1637, they stated that throughout Christendom supplies of pepper were scant, which was the more embarrassing since consumption was increasing. Prices were rising, and there was fear of speculation. Neither in 1638 nor in 1639 did any carracks arrive in Portugal from India, and this undersupply, conjoined to a rumour that the Dutch company's store-rooms were empty, made prices rise at a record pace. The rumour was true. A survey of stocks in March, 1639, showed that there was only a diminutive quantity of pepper, damaged by seawater, in the company's warehouses. As a measure against speculation the Dutch company decided to offer the pepper that arrived during the summer at a fixed price. Buyers were to send their orders in sealed envelopes to Amsterdam. The time for submitting orders was the days from 1st to 10th September. When the orders were counted up, it emerged that the buyers had asked for 380 million Dutch lbs. of pepper while the quantity offered for sale amounted to about 2.4 million Dutch lbs. only. It was impossible to maintain the fixed price in this situation. The price of pepper on the Amsterdam Bourse soared to 175 Dutch florins per 100 lbs.; before speculation started, the level had been around 60 florins per 100 lbs.

The extreme prices of 1639-40 caused a near-doubling of pepper imports to the Netherlands. For the next sixteen years they averaged 4.6 million Dutch lbs. a year. The corresponding English imports were probably about 1.4 million Dutch lbs. annually. In spite of falling prices in the 1640s, the Dutch company did not reduce its orders. These massive supplies reduced pepper prices in Europe to a level different from before. Whereas pepper prices in Amsterdam before the 1640s, though fluctuating widely, were always above the level of 60 florins per 100 Dutch lbs., there were only ten years during the subsequent long period from 1648 to 1732 in which the price of pepper was above the 60 florin level. For some time, however, the increased quantities imported made up for the fall in prices, and the pepper trade was probably a profitable affair for the company. At the beginning of the 1650s, on the other hand, it was obvious that the Dutch company's directors were tired out. They still wanted vast purchases in order to weaken their adversaries, and they stubbornly maintained that they would not give in. But at the same time they requested their headquarters at Batavia not to let pepper occupy shipping space instead of more important return commodities. In 1652 when the price of pepper had been reduced to about 38 florins per 100 Dutch lbs., orders were given to hold off. Europe was glutted with pepper. The Dutch company was able to manage with the stock in hand for three years without any new supplies at all. In the same year the trade from Batavia to the Malabar coast stopped. The Malabar pepper was too expensive, and the warehouses in Batavia were bursting with Indonesian pepper. Large new plantations in the archipelago had brought overproduction. The English company also reduced its imports.

Competition continued throughout the 1660s and 1670s, however. In 1670, the Dutch company imported no less than 9.2 million Dutch lbs. of black pepper from Batavia and Ceylon, which was a record. Although the market fell, and prices as a whole were dull in the 1670s—in 1677-78 they were at their lowest level of the whole seventeenth century—both the Dutch and the English companies continued to import large quantities of pepper, the English East India Company bringing in nearly 4 million Dutch lbs. of pepper annually in the 1670s. It was in fact a trade war, and on some cargoes the importers undoubtedly suffered losses. On the Malabar coast the Dutch had succeeded in displacing the Portuguese, Cochin being conquered in 1663, and they tried to keep the other nations out as well, but in the ancient pepper-purchasing centre of Bantam the Sultan had maintained his sovereignty. He endeavoured to form a barrier against the Dutch by attracting the trade of as many foreign nations as possible. It was the Portuguese, the English and the Danes especially who took advantage of this situation, and large quantities of pepper were shipped from there to Europe. In 1680 the Dutch company struck. Bantam was conquered, and the contest for pepper was thus brought to a provisional conclusion. The exclusion of the English from West Java represented the high point of the Dutch efforts to take the entire Indonesian export of pepper into their hands.

There is scarcely any field in which the spirit of early capitalism reveals itself more clearly than in the further handling of the pepper once it had been brought home. From the very outset, whether it is Atlantic or Levant pepper that is in question, the wealthy merchant houses seek to buy up large lots and form consortia with the aim of maximising profits on the re-sale and distribution of the pepper over Europe. The constellations of interested parties are in continuous flux, and the pepper never stops being manipulated. The state of affairs at the close of the sixteenth century is particularly clearly observable thanks to the brief but well-documented participation of the brothers Philipp Eduard and Octavian Fugger in the international pepper trade.

In Portugal, the crown began by monopolising the trade with the Indies in 1505-6. The royal monopoly meant that the imports were sold *en bloc* or in large lots for the king's account, either in Lisbon or via the factory in the Netherlands. In the early decades of the sixteenth century, the Italian houses of Gualterotti and Affaitadi loomed largest in the purchase of the Portuguese imports to the Netherlands; German merchant houses, and the Portuguese *marranos* even more so, made their entrance later on. The gathering of Portuguese and Venetian sales under a single control was a dream never realised but nonetheless pursued in the sixteenth century. In 1527, the Venetian senate proposed to King John III that Venice should take over all the pepper arriving at Lisbon, save for what was consumed in Portugal itself. In 1585, Philip II of Spain-Portugal offered Venice a contract placing the sale of Portuguese imports in Venetian hands.

In 1577, the Portuguese monopoly was reorganised. Private individuals were now permitted to participate, under the supervision of the crown, in the import of spices from the Indies. From now on a merchant house or a consortium of houses could conclude a contract with the crown for long or short periods. The private *contractadores* had to undertake to furnish vessels and to buy return cargoes in the Indies and convey them to Lisbon for their own account, delivering them to the *Casa da India* at an agreed price plus a sum to cover the costs of the voyage. This was the so-called Asia contract. The sale of the spices delivered was similarly regulated by a so-called Europe contract, whereby a firm or consortium undertook for a one- or two-year period to buy the imports at an agreed price and dispose of them for its own account. The Asia contract was in the nature of a financing agreement inasmuch as the contractor had no control over the disposition of the goods. The actual dealings in the imported pepper were conducted by the second contractor. To some extent there was a conflict of interest between the two contractors. The Asia-contractor would be interested in getting as large an import quota as possible, whilst the Europe-contractor would have to guard against too large a supply of pepper.

There was nothing to stop the two contractors uniting in the same consortium, but this demanded large cash resources. The Asia contract at the close of the sixteenth century was of the order of 200,000 Rhenish guilders a year and the Europe contract 800,000 Rhenish guilders. Konrad Rot, an Augsburg merchant, made the attempt in 1578 with Italian and Portuguese firms as his partners. He divided up the European pepper market into 'provinces' and established price agreements. The Rot cartel had as its headquarters a trading company in Leipzig set up for the purpose by August I, Elector of Saxony. This was to handle sales in the Netherlands, the German Empire, Bohemia, Hungary and Poland. The other territories of Europe were given over to the Portuguese and Italian partners in the consortium. The Elector's brother-in-law, Frederik II of Denmark-Norway, was to furnish vessels for the carriage of the pepper. The plan never came to fruition, however. The parties became disunited. Hamburg and Magdeburg intervened. Uncertainty with reference to the determination of the size of imports from the Levant made it difficult to establish prices, and, last but not least, Rot was unable to raise an advance of 400,000 Rhenish guilders.

The Fuggers began to interest themselves in the Portuguese contracts in 1585. After weighty deliberations they decided to take part in an Asia contract in association with the house of Welser and the Italian merchant house of Rovalesca. From the Asia contract the Fugger brothers were more or less forced into a Europe contract when the Spanish treasury, suffering from chronic shortage of cash and often on the brink of insolvency, threatened the Fuggers with confiscation of their cash resources in Spain-Portugal while demanding that the monies owing to the Fuggers on the Asia contract should be settled in the form of a credit against a Europe contract. So in 1591 the Fuggers joined an international consortium handling the Europe contract. It consisted of Fugger and Welser of Germany, Rovalesca and Giraldo Paris of Italy, Francesco and Pedro Malvenda of Spain, and Andrea and Tomas Ximenes of Portugal. The consortium was represented in numerous European centres but was orientated particularly towards Hamburg, whither the consignments were carried in Hanseatic vessels, which transported corn to Spain and Italy, bringing pepper from Lisbon on the return trip. Of the shipments of 1591, 48% went to Hamburg, 23% to Lübeck (via the Elbe, so as to avoid paying the Sound Toll) and 28% to Amsterdam. Thus for a short time Hamburg inherited Antwerp's position in the European spice market, until Amsterdam and London took over the leadership. Collaboration by the Fuggers in the Europe contract was only brief. As early as 1592, they disposed of their share to Ruy Lopez d'Evora, an in-law of Tomas Ximenes. A factor contributing to this development was that the parties to the contract did not honour the price agreements. Ximenes, who was an old hand at the Portuguese pepper trade, plotted to dump pepper that he still had in store from one of his previous contracts.

Nor did the new East India companies re-export the

imported pepper for their own account; instead they disposed of it to private merchant houses and contractors. Here too we find consortia buying up consignments of a size to bear comparison with the contracts of the sixteenth century. Thus, in 1620, the Dutch company made over all its pepper to a consortium consisting of Elias Tripp, Gerriet van Schoonhoven, Jeronimus de Haze and Philippe Calandrini. In 1622, Gert Direksz: Raedt, Cornelis van Campen, Hans Broers & Co., bought up the entire pepper imports of about 10,000 bales. The company undertook on that occasion not to offer pepper for sale for a whole year. The same consortium took over the pepper of the following year. This contract amounted to 4 million florins. The company's share capital was at that time 6 million florins, so the contract was an evidence of the calibre of Dutch capitalism, the more so since these people also dealt in other commodities. The contract system offered great opportunities for speculation, which showed itself clearly in 1639–40. The events of this year of panic caused the company to give up sale by contract in 1642. Auction sales were introduced as the best safeguard against speculation. In this way the commodities were distributed among a large number of buyers. The English East India Company, too, disposed of its pepper imports by contract in these years, apart from an early period when the pepper was distributed as a dividend to the holders of the joint stock. An example of sale by contract was provided by the making over of a major consignment of pepper in 1627 to the famous government war contractor and City financier, Philip Burlamachi & Co. In 1633, the major part of the East India Company's pepper was sold to a single contractor, Daniel Harvey, and the rest to Sir James Campbell and other Eastland merchants for export to the Baltic.

THE COPPER TRADE

Copper is an interesting commodity to observe in international trade, for a variety of reasons. It had a unique intermediate position between the true coinage metals—the so-called precious metals, gold and silver—and the cheaper metals. By royal privilege, a prince could redeem gold and silver at a price that he himself determined. This right is bound up with the right of coinage itself. In medieval times copper was not a true coinage metal, and for this reason the prince might refrain from making use of that right of pre-emption which in principle he insisted to be immutably reserved to himself even in the case of copper. In the course of the sixteenth century, however, the exercise of the royal right of pre-emption was extended to the cheaper metals, including copper. The latter now began to be employed as a coinage metal at the same time as it was becoming of high strategic significance by virtue of its use in cannon-founding. Further, the princes, irrespective of whether they took advantage of the right of pre-emption, received revenues in copper by way of taxes in kind, such as tithes and tolls, and often operated copper-mines themselves as well. If they could not or would not use the copper themselves then they had to dispose of it either by selling it themselves or by entrusting its sale to merchants. The interest of the princely power in copper was soon reinforced by—and soon at variance with—that of the merchants. On a number of occasions—often at some critical juncture when the need for money was most acute—the right to collect future revenues of metal, whether in the shape of tolls, tithes, pre-emption or self-production, was handed over to capitalist financiers in return for large credits or advances of ready cash. In fact, copper became in this way a key to much of the great-power politics of Europe. In the sixteenth century the Emperor Maximilian and his successors financed their great-power policies by means of central European silver and copper. The Swedish king did likewise in the seventeenth century. Gustavus Adolphus, the champion of Protestantism, sold copper to Catholic Spain via middlemen in Amsterdam—by no means the only example of trade cutting across the religious boundaries that were so strictly drawn in that age. Thus, despite prohibitions without number, a substantial proportion of the Hungarian copper production reached Turkey, the principal antagonist of Christendom. The 'copper purchase,' as it was called, could mean that a fair proportion of the output of an area might fall into relatively few hands. Normally what interested merchants most was trading in copper. They were less eager to take over actual production. But they sometimes found themselves forced to do so, as for instance when a prince could not repay his loans and the creditors accordingly had to foreclose. This happened to the Fuggers. And once involved in production it could be difficult to disengage from it. In the depressed trade conditions of the latter half of the sixteenth century, the Fuggers were unable to find anyone willing to buy their copperworks and mines in the Tyrol. Complete monopoly was never achieved, but from time to time the trade would be characterised by a high degree of regulated marketing. Instances also occur where efforts were made to bring the marketing of the product under state control. A monopoly policy was a common feature of the trading scene, but attempts to keep the prices up by restricting production were comparatively rare.

Copper was produced in various parts of Europe in the fifteenth and sixteenth centuries, but three producing districts stood out as supplying all the copper in international trade, viz., the east Alpine district (Tyrol), the upper Hungarian district (Neusohl, the present Banska Bystrica in Slovakia) and the district around Mansfeld in Thuringia. The combined output of these districts was at a high level in the first half of the sixteenth century, running at between 4,500 and 5,000 tons a year. A sharp decline ensued for the remainder of the sixteenth century. Around 1620, the central European mines were producing about 2,000 tons a year altogether. In the seventeenth century, however, a new large-scale producer emerged on the scene—Sweden. During the first two decades of the century, Swedish production increased fivefold, and as the Thirty Years War proceeded Sweden became the biggest supplier of copper in Europe. Its production peak of 3,000 tons a year was reached in 1650. The level of output remained generally high until 1690, after which date there was a severe fall.

Thus, the production of copper was characterised by wide fluctuations, the product usually of technical or natural causes, and by dramatic geographical dislocations of the supply. However, there was an overall ceiling upon aggregate European output, which barely exceeded 6,000 tons a year at any time.

Copper was in demand for many purposes: for coinage and cast bronze-cannon, for countless articles in industry, handicrafts and the household, for the vats used in brewing and distilling, for cooking and boiling, as a roofing material, in shipbuilding, for a variety of instruments, for kitchen pots and pans, and for sundry decorative purposes (bells, church-doors, bronze statues, fitments and so on). It was also used in making jewellery and trinkets, particularly of the sort that met the needs of the less well-to-do. Copper was the poor man's gold.

Demand did not remain constant. Bronze cannon-founding flourished from the middle of the fifteenth century to the beginning of the seventeenth, the era of the new nation-states with their large armies, their fleets and their wars; these, together with geographical expansion, all added to the demand for cannon, copper and tin. Cast-bronze artillery reached a high state of perfection, especially the German and Flemish pieces, in which there was an extensive trade, while Italian and French production went for local use. Nevertheless bronze artillery lost ground in the course of the seventeenth century to the new and cheaper (though heavier and less perfect) cast-iron pieces in which England and Sweden were specialists. The Swedish statesman Louis de Geer declared in 1644 that iron cannon could be procured for the war fleet at one-third the price of copper cannon, and a survey of the Swedish navy's armament in 1658 shows that there were as many iron cannon as copper. In the subsequent decades iron cannon, now improved to such an extent as to stand comparison with the older ordnance even from the technical standpoint, gained ground everywhere. Naturally this development was bound to affect the demand for copper. But in other fields, too, iron was advancing at the expense of copper, especially among household articles; iron pots and pans were cheaper and cleaner, and, unlike copper, they did not transmit any taste to the food. The increased use of brass afforded some compensation for these changes, but the output of brass was hardly of such proportions as to offset what had been lost to iron elsewhere. The use of copper for coining was an excellent example of a once-for-all demand. Once the circulation was fully supplied with copper coin, it could only absorb further copper to cover wear and tear or any extra need for currency generated by commercial expansion. To exceed these limits was to court inflation. This is precisely what a number of countries, especially Spain, did do. Several countries bought substantial quantities of copper exclusively for minting, but the demand was uneven and indeed probably constituted the demand-side factor most responsible for the ups and downs of the trade cycle. Other short-term fluctuations of demand were induced by business conditions in industries like sugar-refining, brewing, the manufacture of saltpetre, and of course the armaments programmes associated with wars.

Copper sought the nearest route to the sea. This meant that Venice was a principal sales outlet for the Tyrolean and Hungarian portions of the central European output. Despite the ups and downs, the city retained this position right up to the beginning of the seventeenth century. From Venice, copper was traded eastwards to the Levant and thence to India (for it was one of the few commodities with which Europe was able to pay for its imports of spices), and westwards to Majorca and Malaga, the centres of redistribution to Spain and Portugal, whence copper entered into the trade with Africa and the New World. Some of the central European production, however, flowed northwards and westwards, too. While Venice remained the chief market and Germany the subsidiary market for Tyrolean production, in the early decades of the sixteenth century, Hungarian copper was already finding its way via Danzig to Antwerp or via the river Oder to Stettin and thence via Hamburg and Lübeck to the Netherlands. In 1508 the Portuguese factory at Antwerp was founded as a branch of the *Casa da India*, and the Portuguese king bought up considerable quantities of copper each year through his factors. The Antwerp market was of great consequence as an outlet for Hungarian production until the 1570s. Thereafter it was Hamburg that rose to prominence. Germany as a whole constituted an important market for copper, notably that supplied by Mansfeld, with cities like Nuremberg, Aachen (the seat of the largest brass industry in Europe) and Frankfurt acting as the main centres. The biggest buyers of Swedish copper in the sixteenth century were in Lübeck. Later on they were in Hamburg and Amsterdam. Dutch demand was stimulated not only by general business activity but also by the development after 1600 of a considerable copper-working industry in the towns of the Netherlands.

Many were the endeavours that were made over the years to monopolise the copper trade. One of the most notorious of the earlier ones is ascribed to Jakob Fugger, who contracted with Emperor Maximilian in 1490 to purchase the whole output of the Tyrol and followed this up by entering the Hungarian field in 1494. A syndicate was formed in 1498 between Fugger and his nearest rivals in the copper trade, three Augsburg merchant houses. However, Fugger broke the agreement by bringing Hungarian copper on to the Venetian market at dumping prices, and although in so doing he incurred losses himself by virtue of his one-third holding in the Augsburg syndicate, the coup succeeded. His competitors withdrew, and the first European copper monopoly was established. Thereafter the Hungarian share of the output was channelled to the Netherlands and the Tyrolean to Venice. The monopoly was short-lived, although business conditions as a whole were good during the first half of the sixteenth century. At intervals, however, the market showed signs of saturation. This is particularly apparent during the second half of the sixteenth century. In 1546 the Fuggers' interest in the Hungarian Neusohl works ceased, and after some years of state operation these mines were transferred to other Augsburg houses. Hungarian production was restricted drastically in the 1570s, and that

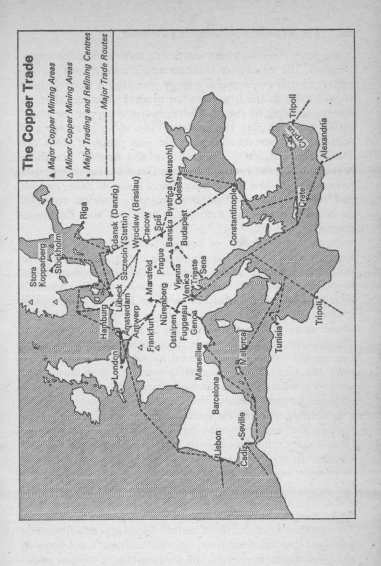

The Copper Trade

▲ *Major Copper Mining Areas*
△ *Minor Copper Mining Areas*
• *Major Trading and Refining Centres*
- - - *Major Trade Routes*

Stora
Kopparberg

Stockholm

Riga

Gdansk (Danzig)

Szczecin (Stettin)

Wyoclaw (Breslau)

Cracow

Spiš

Banska Bystrica (Neusohl)

Odessa

Hamburg

Lübeck

Amsterdam

London

Antwerp

Mansfeld

Frankfurt

Nüremberg

Prague

Vienna

Budapest

Ostalpen

Fuggerau

Venice

Trieste

Sens

Genoa

Marseilles

Barcelona

Mallorca

Lisbon

Seville

Cadiz

Tunisia

Constantinople

Cyprus

Tripoli

Alexandria

Crete

Tunisia

Tripoli

of the other chief suppliers was falling too. During the 1590s, however, the climate of business again took a turn for the better. Dutch commercial energy provided a new element of buoyancy in the international market. Another element was the minting by the Spanish crown of a copper currency, called *vellon*, during the periods 1599-1606, 1617-19, and 1621-26. Copper for this purpose was supplied from the Tyrol and Hungary, especially in the first of the three periods, when the Fuggers and the Genoese banking houses were active, as also was the Augsburg house of Paller, which had the disposal of Hungarian copper. Sweden emerged during this boom as a major supplier of the European market.

Swedish production of copper was rooted far back in time. It was heavily concentrated, being associated with the Falun district of Mälaren in Dalarna, where Stora Kopparberg was the most important location. The Swedish king enjoyed substantial revenues in kind in the form of copper. During the 1570s particularly, when new discoveries of ore were causing output to rise, he showed a growing inclination to control the trade in copper and to manipulate the market to his own financial advantage. From time to time the Crown also sought to establish a monopoly of supply. It used copper as an instrument of Sweden's general commercial policy, one of the aims of which was to establish a direct link with the Netherlands and western Europe, bypassing the north German Hanse towns, and another to control the exchange of goods between Russia and western Europe. In 1595 Sweden was still selling the major share of its production at Lübeck, but in the subsequent period the role of Amsterdam as a market for Swedish copper steadily grew. From about 1600 onwards copper was transported direct from Sweden to Holland.

A further stimulus to Swedish copper production was provided by the indemnity of one million rix-dollars in silver—a gigantic sum in the circumstances of that era—that Gustavus Adolphus had to undertake to pay after the war with Denmark of 1611-13. In 1614 the Swedish king got production going and exercised his right of pre-emption. The effect of pre-emption was to encourage production. Some sales took place in Lübeck and Hamburg, some in the Netherlands. By 1619 the indemnity was paid off, but Swedish state expenditure was rising steeply, and Gustavus Adolphus was looking round for ways of financing it. He found his opportunity with the States General, who for a number of reasons felt it would be advantageous to support Sweden in order to preserve the balance between Denmark-Norway and Sweden in the matter of the Baltic approaches. The Dutch loan was based upon Swedish copper, which in the later decades became the war-winning commodity *par excellence* of the Swedish nation. Large quantities of Swedish copper were shipped to the Netherlands in the years 1616–19. A variety of combinations of great Dutch merchants, including Hugo Muys van Holy, Elias Tripp and Louis de Geer, sought to control the sale of these and subsequent shipments. The Swedes, however, were by no means disposed to yield a monopoly of supply into the hands of any single group but endeavoured to play off the Dutch and German factions against one another. In the 1620s, when prices on the international market were again falling, attempts were made to restrict supply by such measures as the introduction of a copper coinage in 1624, to circulate side by side with the pre-existing silver currency. On the Dutch side the Tripp family was notable for its activity in the copper trade. Around 1632 the Swedish crown was in debt to Elias Tripp to the tune of about a million guilders. By threatening to sell off the Swedish stocks of copper in Amsterdam and thus make Sweden bankrupt, Tripp tried repeatedly to secure for himself a veritable monopoly, as for instance in 1634, when the Dutch and German copper merchants combined to form a company in which the Tripp influence preponderated. The Swedish government, however, refused to have any dealings with them. In the following year, two copper companies were established to divide the market, one of them Dutch-Hanseatic, the other Swedish. The Tripp family, which also ranked at that time among the leading arms merchants of Europe, were principals in the Dutch-Hanseatic enterprise.

This collaboration lasted until 1639. These repeated attempts to gain control of the marketing of the entire Swedish copper production (which dominated the market after the outbreak of the Thirty Years War, when central European production was plagued by extensive disturbances) show that in the seventeenth century too, the copper trade was too large a mouthful for any single group or merchant house to swallow.

In the spring of 1629, Louis de Geer informed his Swedish associates that Japanese copper was beginning to find a market in Amsterdam, where it was causing prices to fall—a fair indication that the European market had again reached saturation point. In the second half of the seventeenth century these imports, for which the Dutch East India Company was responsible, began to reach the European market in significant quantities. Copper had been one of Japan's most important articles of export since ancient times, but in the seventeenth century it achieved clear supremacy over all that country's other exports. Around the middle of the century, Japan was furnishing a large part of maritime Asia with copper for both cannon-founding and for coinage. Even China became dependent on Japanese copper, notably during the early Manchu period—more specifically during the first quarter of the eighteenth century, when Manchu mintings consisted solely of imports from Japan. The Dutch East Indian Company, which had enjoyed exclusive rights to the European trade with Japan since 1623, made a lot of money by negotiating the export of copper from Japan to various parts of maritime Asia. The directors of the company regarded copper from Japan throughout as a commodity reserved primarily for its Asian offices, especially in the Indies. Shipments to Europe were a secondary affair, but they attained regular status in the second half of the seventeenth century. There is little doubt that this new European demand stimulated the company's exports from Japan, particularly in the 1660s. Demand reflected the trend of prices at Amsterdam fairly accurately. When prices were low in the late 1670s and early 1680s, Japanese copper was not wanted. When prices rose again in the 1690s, European demand increased, and shipments went up once more. Japanese copper makes its appearance in the Amsterdam price-currents in 1669, the same year in which another new copper producer—Norway—makes its début. At their peak, Dutch imports from Asia corresponded to between one-third and one-half of the probable Swedish exports of copper and brass.

THE TEXTILE TRADE

Almost everywhere in Europe there was local manufacturing of textiles, but it was mostly inadequate both as to quality and quantity. Additional supplies were brought in from the old-established advanced textile-manufacturing centres in Italy, Flanders, Brabant, the Netherlands, south Germany or England. The finer cloths were luxury articles, but it is important to appreciate the extent to which the social structure of the community, then as now, was defined by differing forms of 'conspicuous consumption,' and that the status value of an impressive attire perhaps was greater politically than was the spoken or written word. To appear in exquisite elegance increased a royal family's prestige and influence of a nobleman's career opportunities. The heavy 'state' costumes of brocade or velvet and silk, inlaid with gold, silver and precious stones, which were worn by princes and potentates in the sixteenth century, could be obtained in most countries and at most of the European courts only as imports.

In the European cloth trade as a whole, however, cloths of superior quality never formed the largest proportion of the total value of the trade. Most of the cloth sold consisted of ordinary cloth or broadcloth, which formed a significant proportion of the total value of the imports of the non-textile manufacturing countries. For example, the general category of 'cloth' constituted more than a third of Sweden's imports in the sixteenth century. In most countries, imported broadcloth had the advantage over the domestic product not merely of being more durable and elegant but also of comparative uniformity of qualities. It was not un-common for wages to be paid, in part at least, in cloth. Mercenaries, in particular, had a traditional claim to be supplied with broadcloth. There were important con-siderations of distinction involved in the provision of parade-dress. It was impossible, as Gustav Vasa is said to have put it, to escape the need to keep up with 'other potentates, caesars, kings and princes, so that we Swedes are no more swine and goats than they.' The lower orders of society likewise demanded textiles that could not be sup-plied by local manufacture. In Russia only the boyars and rich merchants could attire themselves in Flemish or English fabrics, but the middle class made do with cheaper imported goods, from Bohemia for example. Later on, when attempts were made in the eighteenth century to develop manufacture in Russia, it was with a view to re-placing the Bohemian imports. Even those on the lowest rung of the social ladder might in some cases be dressed in materials coming from abroad. The linen industry of Silesia producing a coarse article which at first could only be sold locally, found, thanks to its cheapness, a market in the European plantations of North and South America, clothing the Indian and Negro slaves. The same thing happened with the Indian textile industry, whose cheap cotton fabrics were sent via Europe to Africa and America.

Textiles evolved from heavier to lighter fabrics. Pure woollen goods were mixed with cotton and other materials. In some cases this also made for a cheaper product. The manufacture of these cheaper materials meant that fashion and the change of design it dictated took on a greater im-portance than before. Additional and more intimate items of clothing became articles of commerce. While the manu-facture of woollen fabrics was a speciality of the towns, the production of linen and canvas articles was predominantly a rural craft. We find early on a substantial trade in linen goods alongside that in woollens, notably from south Germany to the Mediterranean countries, where even the Italian cities purchased linen. In the sixteenth century, north German linen also penetrated into Spain and thence to the New World. The Spanish market remained one of the chief outlets for the European linen industry in the seventeenth and eighteenth centuries, its favours being courted by linens from Silesia, Saxony and Bohemia as well as Ireland. Linen was also mixed with other fabrics, the result being the so-called fustian, which was woven of linen warp and cotton weft. The Fuggers had large fustian weaving mills at Weissenhorn.

Probably no country was as dependent upon the textile trade during the fifteenth, sixteenth and early seventeenth centuries as was England. It might be said that the chief function of English foreign trade was to sell English cloth and to export English wool. The general tendency, however, was to divert wool from export in its raw state to an input to the cloth export industry. Wool was exposed to a heavier taxation than cloth exports. English wool was indisputably the best in Europe at this time and therefore in demand on the Continent, especially in the textile industries of the Low Countries, which used this raw material almost exclusively. Under the threats of wool exports being cut off, even Flanders, the textile-manufacturing region of the Low Countries, had been forced to submit in 1470 and allow the sale of English cloth in Bruges. From the beginning of the sixteenth century onwards, English fabrics reigned supreme in the ancient chief market of the north-west European textile trade. Antwerp was a specific cloth rather than a wool market and it was here that the English cloth merchants congregated, first of all the Merchant Adventurers from London. The choice of Antwerp as the 'mart town' for English cloth ranks second only to the establishment of the spice-staple as the reason for merchants being drawn there from all over Europe. Through Antwerp, English cloth reached consumers not only in the Low Countries but also in Germany, Italy and the Levant. The English merchants, however, refrained from committing themselves to using one town alone—especially since they realised that the market for English cloth was expanding towards north Germany. They established staples closer to the German market, e.g., in 1564 at Emden, which was not a Hanse town. Thenceforth they attended the Frankfurt fairs, which were the chief market for German cloth. They ventured even as far as Nuremberg. The Hanse towns capitulated. In 1567, Hamburg granted such favourable terms to the Merchant Adventurers that they moved their staple to that city, which was well situated geographically for exporting via Frankfurt to the central German market and by the overland route to Italy. In 1578, quite certainly under the pressure of the other Hanse towns, Hamburg was obliged to refuse to renew the privileges of the English merchants. Emden and Stade then became the preferred places. But in 1611 Hamburg made its final choice: the Merchant Adventurers returned to the city and remained there from then on.

This English success provoked bitterness on the Continent, especially in Germany, where there was talk of the pride and arrogance of the English. The English merchants' usual manner of dealing with their customers aroused resentment. They had no need to travel from town to town in order to sell their wares: they were able to compel the customers to attend the few places they chose as their staples. For they restricted the number of these precisely in order to be able to exercise control. Even then they did not put their goods on sale continuously but as far as possible, only on certain days of the week—the so-called 'show days' ('toeneeltage' in Dutch), usually held on Monday, Wednesday and Friday each week. On other days the only business that could be done was in items that had been inspected on a 'show day.'

Exportation was based primarily upon the Old Draperies, i.e., unfinished, undyed cloth which, by virtue of easy access to the raw material, English wool, was cheap and competitive. In this cloth, carded yarn contributed both weft and warp. Finishing of the cloth was carried out on the Continent, especially in the Low Countries, where Flanders and Brabant had been since time immemorial the repository of the finest techniques of finishing and dyeing. This was transplanted in the 1530s to Hamburg, when artisans brought in from Antwerp started up the dyeing and finishing of English cloth. The Netherlands too, finished and dyed substantial quantities of English fabric.

The conditions of textile production and marketing in Europe changed decisively as the sixteenth and seventeenth centuries unfolded. English woollen exports rose by two-thirds during the first half of the sixteenth century, the increase being particularly pronounced from the beginning of the 1530s to the beginning of the 1550s and London's export of cloth lying well above the national average. English competition brought adversity upon the traditional cloth manufacture of Flanders and of other areas in the Low Countries so that, in the 1540s particularly, cloth-making ceased in many places. On the other hand, parallel with the decline of the old industry went the rise of a new. Using local raw materials, following locally traditional designs and methods, new fabrics substituted the older heavy-quality woollen products in international trade. Gradually, the so-called New Draperies were introduced, consisting of a variety of lighter articles such as says, bays and fustians. The say industry of Hondschoote prospered. Leiden organised the production of bays. Bruges engaged weavers in order to introduce the new light cloth. The industrial renewal also had a rural aspect, in which linen-weaving was the main element. Flemish linen, bleached in Holland, where Haarlem was the main bleaching centre, was exported under the name of 'Dutch linen' both from Antwerp and Amsterdam.

The collapse of the Antwerp market in the 1550s and the decline of this entrepôt marked a turning-point in London's export trade of traditional cloth. The third quarter of the sixteenth century saw a severe contraction. As an ever-growing portion of the English cloth export had been funnelled through London the difficulties assumed a national magnitude. Restrictionism revived, the rivalry between the Merchant Adventurers and the Hanse flared up, and attempts were made in every conceivable manner to find new markets. The drive to sell English textiles abroad inspired a good many of the famous trading ventures of the Elizabethan Age, from the search for north-east and north-west passages to China to the foundation of the East India Company in 1600. With the opening of the seventeenth century, a further fall in the export of traditional cloth from London occurred. In the early 1620s there is a real slump in this particular trade. The factors of the London merchants reported that a cause of slack markets for English textiles was the making of cloth in Hungary and Silesia. The widespread insecurity and economic breakdown that followed the wars of the early seventeenth century both in the Baltic area and in central Europe favoured the cheaper native industries. There was a growing supply of inexpensive local wool. Moreover, increasing quantities of Spanish wool were reaching the principal manufacturing centres of Europe. For long in demand in Flanders (where Bruges was its main point of entry) wool from Spain was now being sent to Italy, France, the Netherlands and Germany, and it even found a market in England. At the same time a qualitative change was taking place in the English wool supply—possibly as a result of enclosures since the main influence on the nature of wool is the pasturage itself. The new wool was more suited to lighter and thinner kinds of textiles.

Although the English outports in the long run lost ground to London their decline was not a steady one but subject to fluctuations. During the 1550s exports via the outports tended to be more stable than the downturned London exports. The decline in cloth exports also temporarily meant a relative recovery of the wool exports which in some cases was to the advantage of the outports. In the early seventeenth century we have similar examples of short intervals during which the outports fared better than the Metropolis. Many of the south-western ports, exporting cloth to France, Spain and the Atlantic islands, benefited from the cessation of the hostilities with Spain in 1604. In the Londoners' years of depression 1620-24, some of the west-country ports as well as Hull and Newcastle on the east coast, managed fairly well, the great crisis for these ports being the late 1620s. In the 1630s the cloth trade of Hull shifted from the Baltic to the Netherlands, this western outport thus forcing its way into a market previously dominated by London merchants.

England's path of recovery from the depression turned out to be the same as that followed on the Continent, viz., the conversion of her manufacture from the Old to the New Draperies. In this respect the devastations of the 1570s in Flanders had momentous consequences for the whole future of the European cloth industry and trade. In particular, religious persecutions were responsible for textile workers again emigrating from the old centres. Once more they moved northwards and westwards to England and the Netherlands. In the deepest sense these two countries owed their new industries to the expertise that was seeking during these years for new and better working conditions. In England, East Anglia became the focal area of the new manufacture of 'stuffs' and 'mixtures'. Stuffs were worsteds in which both warp and weft consisted of combed wool. Mixtures were fabrics in which the weft was either carded yarn or cotton or silk, while the warp consisted of combed yarn. In both categories the pattern of the weave could still be seen in the finished product.

The Dutch textile industry was dispersed among a number of towns, but its most intensive concentration was at Leiden, which in the seventeenth century constituted the largest single industrial agglomeration in Europe, with an output in the middle of the century amounting to half the total English export of cloth. In this ancient textile centre, too, conversion and external competition are to be observed. In the late sixteenth and early seventeenth centuries, Leiden's range of products is broadly similar to England's, but by degrees the two countries' paths diverge under such influences as competition for markets. A glance at the period 1620-1700 shows that while woollens are in decline in England and worsteds are prosperous, the converse is true of Leiden. The woollens of Leiden, known as *lakens*, do very well in competition with the English product, while England leads in the worsteds group. Much of this was due to the opposition of the powerful Netherlands mercantile interests to any protection of the manufacture of cloth at

Leiden. Imports of Devon cloth from Exeter and Topsham were a particular feature of the Amsterdam cloth trade, as were German linens bleached at Haarlem. Legal restraints upon the export of English and Scottish wool were tightened up in the seventeenth century, and this too hampered Leiden severely. By degrees the Dutch found themselves having to work mostly with Spanish wool. In the second half of the seventeenth century about four-fifths of the raw material came from Spain. Leiden *lakens* became an important export commodity sold in the Mediterranean and the Levant, and even in Africa and the West Indies. Only the English market was closed. There was one product within the worsteds group with which Leiden was also successful—the so-called *greinen*, or camlet. The manufacture of this article began around 1630. A group of Walloon cloth-makers discovered how to blend camel-hair (or Turkish yarn), or goat-hair if desired, into the wool, and later on camel-hair was also mixed with silk. The result was a comparatively light material used particularly for male clothes and sold in France, in the Levant and many other places. In what might be termed the international division of labour that was thus arrived at between the two textile-producing countries of England and the Netherlands, production costs and access to raw materials presumably played a part. One reason for English costs being lower than Dutch was that most English manufacture took place in rural areas while the Dutch was in the towns. Price- and wage-levels in the Netherlands were rising throughout the seventeenth and eighteenth centuries, not least because of the imposition of heavier and heavier taxes on foodstuffs. The English were best at marketing the cheaper fabrics on which profit margins were small. The Dutch did well with articles for which the raw materials were easily available (like camel-hair) and where the finished textile was costly, e.g., because the manufacturing process comprised numerous stages. As has already been noted, it was in finishing and dyeing, particularly, that they had inherited a superior technique.

Both nations made advances in the Mediterranean region

in the seventeenth century at the expense of the Italian, and to some extent French, textiles. The great Italian cloth-producing cities—Milan, Florence, Como—lose ground as the century proceeds. Even the Italian silk industry was hit by the crisis, although the Italian cities did preserve their market for luxury wares such as gold brocades, silks, satins and velvets. Venice struggles longest against the tide, still maintaining in the 1640s, relatively considerable output of textiles, though a decline sets in thereafter. The foreign competition from the north was too stiff. The Levantine markets wanted light, cheap fabrics. The level of costs and the rigidity of the system of production were hindrances. The Venetian cloth industry, one of the oldest and most brilliant in Europe, was mainly based on Spanish wool. The supply of the latter was monopolised, and the price of the finished product rose. To the north, the French textile industry, centred upon Rouen, had made successful attempts to market lighter fabrics in the Levant, but the religious wars undermined the French success. Not until the last quarter of the seventeenth century did France return to the Levantine market with excellent fabrics from the textile towns of southern France.

Leghorn, the port of Pisa and under the rule of the grand dukes of Tuscany, had been made a free port in 1593. It became the favourite port of the English and Dutch and a centre of Mediterranean commerce. It also became the gateway to the Italian market, for not only did the northern textiles displace Italian in the Levant, they actually competed successfully with them at home. Leghorn soon became a flourishing city of cosmopolitan character, with Italian, Dutch, English, Armenian, Persian and even Indian residents, as well as—last but not least—a large and wealthy Jewish community, mainly of Spanish and Portuguese origin. It has been said that it was primarily Leghorn and the Mediterranean market that first helped to rescue the English economy from the disastrous consequences of the decline of the old industry.

The New Draperies continued their triumphal progress, but the era of change was not over, however. The second half of the seventeenth century and the early years of the eighteenth saw the onset of the 'Indian Craze,' especially in the big cities of Europe. 'Now few think themselves well dressed,' wrote John Cary in 1699, 'till they are made up in calicoes, both men and women, calico shirts, neck cloths, cuffs, pocket-handkerchiefs, for the former, headdresses, nightrolls, hoods, sleeves, aprons, gowns, petticoats and what not, for the latter, besides India-stockings for both sexes.' Europe welcomed Indian textiles primarily because of their cheapness and technical excellence, not so much on account of their qualities of design. The Hindu decorative tradition was of little appeal to Europeans, and the success of the East Indian companies depended on getting fabrics specially commissioned according to European needs. This was a highly specialised trade, in which the Dutch and English companies were particularly keen rivals. The companies brought out craftsmen and weavers to teach the Indians how to make cloths that would sell in Europe. Another device was to import semi-manufactured goods and have the finishing done in Europe. Calico-printing was a notable example of this, in which many people became engaged. The linen drapers also benefited from the importing of Indian fabrics. With the spread of the fashion for wearing silks and fine muslin, the demand for Bengal textiles increased rapidly, reaching its peak in the 1690s. In 1697 the Dutch East India Company imported goods from Asia to the purchasing value of 5.4 million guilders, all collected from the company's impressive string of factories from Japan to Mocha in the Yemen. Of this total, Bengal contributed no less than one-third, half of which were Bengal silks and cotton goods.

In Europe, Amsterdam and London were the principal European centres through which this considerable volume of imports was redistributed. Sir Josiah Child, reporting to the Court of Directors in 1681, estimated that four-fifths of the East India Company's imports were re-exported. These re-exports were disseminated far and wide over the Continent, and large quantities reached the Mediterranean, the Levant and the New World. Even if the new textiles did generate much trade and additional employment, the woollen and silk industries, especially in England, nevertheless found that their interests were seriously affected. The woollen industry felt the competition in exports particularly keenly. Dramatic scenes preceded the passing, in 1700, of the act prohibiting calicoes, when weavers' wives invaded the House of Commons threatening those members who had voted against the bill. Soon afterwards a mob of 3,000 weavers assembled to attack Child's mansion, and East India House was also attacked and the Company's treasure nearly seized. Seen from the wider European point of view, however, it was the linen and cotton industries of Europe that were particularly hurt by the competition of Oriental goods.

MONEY AND CREDIT

The progress of trade was dependent upon the monetary situation and credit conditions. Bimetallism was a feature of the European monetary system. Monetary conditions and the movement of treasure depended on a variety of circumstances: balances of trade, levels of internal prices, rates of exchange, duties, treaty arrangements as well as manipulation for fiscal purposes. With both gold and silver coins circulating and each type being valued in terms of the money of account, there were both official mint ratios and market ratios determined by the interaction of demand and supply. So bullion and specie—defying all interdicts—moved across frontiers to take advantage of differences in the ratios. In the long run the relationship between the production of gold and silver was also an important factor. This being so, the discovery of American silver and its influx into Europe meant that the market ratio rose after the middle of the sixteenth century. The various European nations were unable, however, to move in concert to alter the official prices of gold and silver. Violent fluctuations therefore occurred, and from time to time there were heated controversies as to the real values of the national currencies. This could not but have an impact upon trade, in which, in the absence of any more flexible mechanism of settlement, cash payment had to be relied on. Thus, the monetary instability of the first half of the seventeenth century, associated with, *inter alia*, currency depreciations in Germany during the Thirty Years War, had a disastrous effect on the economic prosperity of England.

In the seventeenth century, Amsterdam became the centre of the European trade in precious metals. Spanish silver and, later, Portuguese gold found their way here in payment for the flow of goods from northern Europe. So secure did the position of the metropolis become that the Dutch even permitted the free export of a number of currencies as well as of bullion. Amsterdam held the key, so to speak, to Europe's international payments system. In this system of multilateral trade and payments, transfers of treasure were continually necessary both for trade purposes and for the settlement of the international balance of indebtedness. In trade with regions where the unwillingness of the local populations to purchase goods prevented the trade relationships from being reciprocal, the precious metals had a particularly important role, taking on indeed almost the character of a commodity that could only be exported. Such regions existed both in Europe and elsewhere. Furthermore, precious metals were a necessity whenever trade was conducted under extraordinary circumstances or in times of crisis and war. Such events transformed the pattern of payment, as did interruptions of postal services and business correspondence. Finally, not a few governments and princes required customs tolls to be paid in hard currency, i.e., cash. In this sense the Sound became a terminal point for part of the contents of the Spanish silver fleets. It is understandable, therefore, that the theorists of the age ascribed such importance to the precious metals within a country. Both the Dutch and the English had need of coins and bullion for their trade with such places as Danzig, Königsberg, Russia and Norway. In the second half of the seventeenth century, Amsterdam financed the major share of the trade of north and north-west Europe, including the English trade with the Baltic. The system of payments now developed from bilateral to multilateral, with bills of exchange being increasingly used and settlements being effected by means of a constant movement of bullion between England and the Netherlands. All European nations needed precious metals for their trade with Asia. The stream flowed here from the New World via Europe, supplemented by a subsidiary current crossing the Pacific from Acapulco to Manila. The monetary effect of these transfers could be great at times. The East Indian companies' demands for silver (and in certain situations gold) caused prices to rise. Isaac Newton, Master of the Mint, remarked upon this in 1717. The same phenomenon was observed in Copenhagen, where the Asiatic Company bulked so large compared with the nation's other economic activities that the Danish rate of exchange fluctuated in accordance with the Company's purchases of silver.

An international system of payments associated with transfers of ready money does not by itself explain the growth of European trade. A number of changes occur that are also important from the purely technical standpoint. The sixteenth century is not, of course, characterised by any revolution in this field but by the north-west European assimilation of the Italian achievement. It was chiefly Antwerp that led the way in the adoption of new forms and techniques. These were generally a matter of quantitative rather than qualitative change. These technical improvements were disseminated in the seventeenth century to the rest of Europe. A notable feature is the vigorous expansion of the system of commodity and currency exchange. The familiar bourses of Amsterdam, London, Paris, Hamburg, and Frankfurt were established. The price quotations on the Amsterdam exchange in the seventeenth and eighteenth centuries set the trend of many commodities for the whole of Europe. Speculative trading made its appearance. There had already been speculative trading in grain in Amsterdam in the middle years of the sixteenth century; during the seventeenth century the Amsterdam bourse was the scene of spirited trading in commodity values, which included transactions in options and in futures. 'They invent new ways of trade,' wrote John Cary in 1695, 'great quantities of brandy being disposed of every year, which are never intended to be delivered, only the buyer and seller get or lose according to the rates it bears at the time agreed on to make good the bargains.'

An important innovation of the seventeenth century was the expansion of banking. The Amsterdam Exchange Bank, founded in 1609 and administered under municipal supervision, was the first public bank in northern Europe, and for a long time the greatest. Up to 1683, its activities were confined to exchange and deposit banking. All the great Amsterdam merchants were its depositors. The number of foreign accounts was also considerable. The bank did not lend money to individuals but made advances to the East India Company in the form of short-term loans. The standards of the bank in handling exchange helped to establish Amsterdam as the principal centre for European exchanges. And bills of exchange payable at the bank played a steadily increasing part in international commercial intercourse. Of the other banks with a significant role in European seventeenth-century trade, the Bank of Hamburg was founded in 1618. The European market, however, was everywhere characterised by private merchant houses doing banking business. Here the bill of exchange was an important instrument. Amsterdam again attracts notice for its abundance of capital and low interest rates. The chief employment of the city's capital resources was undoubtedly in trade and activities related thereto. Dutch merchants would allow liberal credit when selling. Later on Hamburg became notable for similar reasons. The readiness of Hamburg merchants to give long credit to their customers successfully maintained their business against competitors, particularly in the northern trades.

THE ORGANISATION OF TRADE

Endeavours to protect and increase business capital, to facilitate and secure long-distance connections, and to spread the risk were among the basic motives underlying the wide variety of forms in which trade was organised.

The simplest and oldest form of trade was when the merchant himself accompanied his wares and personally conducted the buying and selling. The radius of action could be wider when two or more individuals co-operated, with one of them accompanying the goods while the other remained at home. The merchant's representative abroad might be a factor, receiving a salary for his work. But where the representative himself participated in the business on a profit-and-loss basis, then a trading company or partnership was formed. Alternatively, foreign business might be transacted on commission, possibly on a reciprocal basis. In this way the costs would be reduced and a greater local knowledge of the market brought into play. The great advantage of the partnership was that it spread the risk, and it was particularly popular in the north-west European freight markets in the sixteenth and seventeenth centuries. By about 1500, shipmasters engaged in the Dutch carrying trade had already ceased to be proprietors of their vessels. Ownership was now divided into shares, an increasing number of which were held by merchants and shipowners. Amsterdam swarmed with ships' captains, but the merchants were their masters and their status was reduced to that of employees of the shipowners. It is characteristic that shipping interests, maritime commerce and chartering were often united within the same groups of persons and the same partnerships. The division into shares is linked not only with such considerations as the growing size of ships and the increased capital requirement resulting therefrom but also with inheritance, since shipowners fell into two groups, one actively concerned in operating the ship and perhaps also in its freighting, and a passive group that regarded its share as an investment that could be bought or sold, inherited or fragmented. Not until the later years of the seventeenth century, when maritime insurance was gradually becoming a familiar feature, did division into shares decline. Partnership among merchants might also embrace attempts to monopolise the supply. This form of organisation was very characteristic of the Dutch staple market in the seventeenth century.

It was not only merchants but kings and princes too who utilised the services of factors, both in their personal transactions and in attending to the interests of the state. Thus, the Portuguese kings used factors both as purchasing and sales agents who could be sent anywhere and as a sort of official in charge of a factory. The factory system, the keystone of Portuguese commercial organisation, which was first evolved in Flanders, then in Africa, Asia and Brazil, was based upon a blending of public and private interests. The Spanish, the Dutch, the English and the French all adopted the system in their overseas expansions. The factories possessed their own premises. They were a combination of warehouse, market-place, military base and customs post. In new areas buying and selling could be a very complex affair, affected by such circumstances as special coinage, local traditions, shifting banking facilities and trade seasons determined by monsoons. The privileges enjoyed varied from place to place, depending upon the terms accorded by the host country. Thus, the European factories in Japan and China were limited to a very narrow radius of action imposed entirely by the local authorities, while in other parts of maritime Asia and in the New World we find factories whose operations reach up-country to the various producing areas. In Europe too the privileges of the factories varied. To extract goods from distant places also involved a ceaseless game of diplomacy in relations with authorities at several levels. This was so both within and beyond the continent of Europe. Only in exceptional cases were European as well as non-European powers persuaded by treaty to give up part of their sovereignty. The concessions granted to foreign merchants were normally regarded as revocable at the pleasure of the host government.

They consisted of certain privileges such as internal jurisdiction and special regulations concerning the payment of
customs duties. The consular service, originating in the city-
states of the Mediterranean, also played a role with regard
to both protection and jurisdiction. In the Levant trade
of the seventeenth century French organisation suffered
from a conflict between the French commercial community
and the consul, who tended to devote too much of his
attention to his own financial interests. The Dutch were
better placed: their trading activities were always marked
by a close understanding between the merchants and the
States General. The English too avoided such difficulties.

Protection costs always formed a part of the total trading
costs and were particularly significant in overseas trade;
but in European waters they could also play a part, as for
example in connection with the convoy system in time of
war. In Portugal and Spain, expansion was organised by
the state. It was their respective governments that took the
initiative, and the trade was conducted through government offices such as the *Casa da India* in Lisbon and the
Casa de Contratacion in Seville (the latter being founded in
1503 and transferred to Cadiz in 1717). Governments
always reserved one sector of the trade for themselves—that
in precious metals—leaving the rest, together with the
organising of settlement in the colonies, to individual
entrepreneurs. In Holland, England and France, on the
other hand, it was private initiative that predominated.
Official support was secondary, but nevertheless could not
have been dispensed with. The chartered company was the
favoured form of organisation. Chartered companies were
self-governing, and the state as it were yielded up some of
its sovereignty to them, granting them a monopoly of the
trade with some major geographical region. These companies fall into two groups, the regulated and the joint-
stock companies (though there are intermediate types). The
first would comprise a group of merchants operating indi-
vidually and at their own risk but within the framework of
common terms of business and subject to a collective
discipline. A celebrated example is the Company of

Merchant Adventurers, dating back at least to the fifteenth century. By its charter of 1564 this company was given a monopoly of the English cloth trade with the Netherlands and Hamburg. By the middle of the seventeenth century it had 7,200 members. Another was the Eastland Company (trading with the Baltic) of 1579. The second group consisted of permanent trading enterprises with a common capital fund, in which anyone could participate whether a merchant or not. The all-important innovation brought in by the joint-stock companies was the permanence of the capital. In the Dutch East India Company (founded in 1602), the original allotment of shares in the total capital investment was conditional upon a collective agreement whereby the perpetuation of the company in existence depended upon stock being re-subscribed. In 1612, however, the management of the company refused an application for this to take place and advised dissatisfied stockholders to dispose of their shares on the Bourse, where they were negotiable. Other companies made a distinction between fixed and circulating capital, the former constituting a kind of reserve fund while the latter fluctuated with the ebb and flow of business. The joint-stock companies had a large number of passive shareholders who regarded their shares as a capital investment but otherwise neither interested themselves nor participated in trade. The Dutch West India Company (founded in 1621) too, was a joint-stock company, as also were the English East India Company (founded in 1600) and the French companies founded by Colbert. The French companies took the Dutch East India Company—undoubtedly the world's biggest trading company in the seventeenth century—as their model. The English Levant Company was founded in 1581 as a joint-stock company but became a regulated one in 1605.

The large joint-stock companies were the instruments of overseas trade. Attempts were made from time to time, of course, to regulate trade within Europe as well: thus, towards the end of the seventeenth century in Holland, the Directorate of the Dutch Baltic Trade, as it was named, was established. Its life was short and not very brilliant, however. The important Dutch Baltic trade in fact remained without any unifying organisation. Similarly, free and individual shipping and commerce existed on the Dutch routes to Norway, England, France, the Iberian peninsula and every territory within these bounds. Bearing in mind the large membership of the regulated companies and their rather loose organisation, the situation with the other European countries was not very different in practice.

Even though we do find groups of merchants specialising in particular commodities and in trade with particular regions, it was not uncommon for certain of the more energetic merchants of the day to extend their operations into several fields, being active not only in trade and shipping but also investing in the industrial sector and in agriculture. Thus, a number of the individuals in England who established the East India Company were already members of the Levant Company and some were Merchant Adventurers, although Merchant Adventurers did not normally trade outside Europe. Sir Edward Osborne, first governor of the Levant Company, was a prime mover in the foundation of the Eastland Company. In Holland, the Dutch West India Company welcomed members of the East India Company, and in France members of the Compagnie des Indes set up other companies, e.g., for the African trade. It may therefore be concluded that the individual merchant remains important even where he is a member of a company, and that, when all is said and done, the family was the principal unit of enterprise. Family ties —especially when reinforced by religion—sometime sufficed to sustain trade over long distances, as did the seafaring Jews between the Iberian peninsula and Hamburg and between Spain and the Levant; indeed, it was possible for a trade or an account even as far afield as the Indies or the New World to be managed via family channels. The same consideration applied to French, Dutch and Scandinavian Calvinists.

If one examines the class of merchants as a body, a commercial aristocracy can be distinguished from the ordinary or average merchant. The sixteenth century has been termed the century of the Fuggers. The description is apt in the sense that the great south German houses assembled a concentration of capital whose influence on international trade tended increasingly towards the creation of monopolies—copper syndicates, spice contracts, the alum monopoly, and the attempts to gather the international wine and salt trades into a few hands. This concentration of capital also furthered the development of state credit and of deposit banking. And it led to technical innovations, notably in German mining. A seventeenth-century example of a family concern on a giant scale is provided by the Tripp family in the Netherlands. The Tripps were concerned in various branches of trade—iron, copper, armaments (especially cannon)—and they had shipping and stock-jobbing interests as well. Geographically their sphere of activity was almost global, extending not only from Holland itself and the local river trade with Germany onwards to Scandinavia and Russia, but also embracing the Levant trade and a share in the operations of the large East and West Indian companies. This and other efforts of the same sort by family entrepreneurs to establish monopolies were a characteristic practice on the Dutch staple market. The monopolies are generally short-lived and of diverse character. They extend both horizontally and vertically and embrace domestic as well as foreign concessions. The brevity of their existence tends to indicate that they were rather vulnerable: it was difficult to keep competitors out of the market. No doubt, too, these practices provided something of a cushion in the riskier branches of trade. At all events, the facts reveal that the profits from these manipulations were utilised for new investments. In this way, monopoly policies did promote the growth of the Dutch economy. It was the great merchant houses that dominated the joint-stock companies as well. They had seats on the managements and also played an important role as buyers and sellers of goods from and to the companies. An analysis of the Danish Asiatic Company (founded in 1732), for instance, shows that the majority of the commodities in the auction sales were bought by only a very small clientèle.

These same individuals supplied the company with the silver for its outward cargoes. A proposal to prohibit directors from engaging privately in the same trade as the company was flatly turned down: 'Where are, within the walls of Copenhagen, such big capitalists and prosperous merchants to be found as would be willing to serve the Company without being suppliers or commissions merchants and without dealing in Asian goods?'

The small and medium-sized merchants, on the other hand, were by no means excluded. On the contrary, a certain democratising trend can be perceived, for example, in the north European trade expansion of the sixteenth century around Antwerp. Participation in the long-distance trade was no longer the exclusive preserve of those who could afford to travel to the markets or who were members of the closed guilds (the 'corporate trade'). The small merchant had kept his place in the Hanseatic league, and there was room for him also in the regulated companies. If we look again at the Dutch commercial expansion of the seventeenth century, we find a number of trades in which the ordinary merchants participated on a massive scale. Chief of these are the corn trade and the trades in salt, herring, timber and bricks. It was not uncommon, of course, for the small merchants to feel their living to be threatened by the large ones. The dissensions between the outports and London and between the Spanish cities and Seville testify to this.

In his celebrated tract on *England's Treasure by Forraign Trade* (written in the late 1620s and published in 1664), Thomas Mun lists the qualities that are required by a perfect merchant. He ought to be a good penman, arithmetician and accountant, should be familiar with the measures, weights and monies of foreign countries, with customs, tolls, taxes, exchange rates, freights, ship-building and repairing, and navigation. He should also have a command of foreign languages, including Latin. Mun—himself a merchant—declared that no other profession leads to the acquisition of more worldly knowledge. He cites the Italian city-states and the Netherlands in exemplification of this.

Even in those states where merchants are least esteemed, their skill and abilities are often used by their governments. Mun deplores the fact that English merchants receive less encouragement to their profession than in other countries and sees in this the explanation of the readiness of rich merchant families to abandon their calling with such alacrity. The sons bought land and the prestige and security associated with it. But the social status of merchants differed from one country to another. In England there are some instances of financiers reaching the ranks of the peerage, but few merchants pure and simple rise quite so far, Lionel Cranfield, Earl of Middlesex, being one of them. The merchant's place in the social order was lowest, undoubtedly, in the southern European countries (the Italian city-states excepted). It was highest, certainly, in Holland, where the vocation of merchant was highly regarded and where the mercantile interests succeeded in dominating general economic policy. Manufacture and agriculture had to play second fiddle. Merchants received marks of respect, and they were able to marry into the patrician families to whom were reserved the highest offices of the republic and who in many cases would themselves have their children brought up to the profession of merchant. This was in contrast to the south Netherlands, where the Catholic and Spanish conception of an aristocracy that was closed and lacking in social mobility held sway. For the rest, the Continent was dominated by Absolutism, a system that enjoyed its heyday between 1500 and 1750. National monarchy involved a growing national control over finance, commerce and industry. During this process many princes raised middle-class citizens, including merchants, to noble rank, partly as a counter-weight against the old nobility, whose privileges were being curtailed, and partly for fiscal reasons. Princes confronted by critical situations would turn to the large merchants, who lent them money or delivered goods on credit to equip their standing armies or fleets. Thus, creditors of the state played an important part in the introduction of Absolutism into Denmark-Norway in 1660. They accepted crown lands as security and became established in the highest offices of state. If the new upper class performed services for the state and got well paid for doing so, the state went away by no means empty-handed from these changed conditions. It was only exceptionally that the creditors of the state succeeded in securing a place at the top of society for their descendants, and many of them ended their days in penury.

The conception of the economic function of the state differed from place to place. Again Holland stands out from the others. Here the conception is of business welfare working upwards from the merchant community towards a government with minimum powers. In the absolute states of the Continent, we tend rather to find a policy imposed by governments in the interests of the state. These interests coincided with the interests of dynastic power and the regard for fiscal returns—which did not mean, however, that the prince would never employ all his power to promote trade, often doing so both by investing his own resources in it and by coercing noble, ecclesiastical and bourgeois state functionaries into participating. This is particularly true of the furnishing of capital for the trading companies. In England to a higher degree than elsewhere, perhaps, a balance was struck between government and governed. This system of economic nationalism is often called mercantilism. The system is sometimes represented as though it were frozen into a homogeneous whole, but in reality it wore many faces, all fighting with one another for supremacy and modifying themselves according to place and time. On the particular topic of trade, the theorists of those days were particularly interested in the balance of trade and suggested many devices for making it favourable, such as heavy duties on exports of raw materials and imports of manufactured goods, bounties on exports of manufactured goods and imports of raw materials, measures to reduce the use of foreign luxuries and legislation aiming at increasing national shipping so as to retain the profits of the carrying trade.

Perhaps it is the Navigation Laws that reveal most starkly the multifarious motives and ambitions underlying this nexus of ideas and policy. These laws were being elaborated simultaneously with the growth in importance of the new colonial territories. Both private and public interests can be detected at work here. To the merchants, the state was undoubtedly a means, not an end. Their appeals to the state were influenced by practical considerations. Much of the contemporary literature in English is written by merchants who identify the national interest with their own. They had need of the state's help, both military and diplomatic. In their eyes, the state was merely a special form—though a very large and powerful one—of corporate economic enterprise. Later on, towards the end of the early modern period, the merchants felt this form to be burdensome, and they began to favour the liberation of trade and an entirely new style of commercial organisation.

Select Bibliography

THE MERCANTILE ERA. As might be expected there is a comprehensive historical literature on the economic foundations of Early Modern Europe and quite a substantial number of works have been produced in an attempt to give a synthesis of this era. For many years one of the most well-known standard works was Werner Sombart, *Der moderne Kapitalismus* (I-III, 1927-28), which may still be studied with profit. Another classic is Eli Heckscher, *Mercantilism* (I-II, 1931), reviewing the history of mercantilist economic writings and policy. Among contemporary scholars Charles Wilson has studied the character of the age intensively. In *Profit and Power* (1957) he has discussed the interdependence of sea-power and trade during the period of Anglo-Dutch rivalry in the seventeenth century. Among national contributions to the history of foreign trade, G. D. Ramsay, *English Foreign Trade During the Centuries of Emergence* (1957) is one of the best. A very perceptive discussion of the mercantile economy has been presented by B. E. Supple in *Commercial Crisis and Change in England 1600-1642* (1959).

AREAS, ROUTES AND TRANSPORT. One of the most influential of the modern contributions combining the historical with the geographical aspect has been Fernand Braudel, *Le Méditerrannée et le Monde Méditerrannéen a l'Époque de Philippe II* (rev. ed. I-II, 1966). The International Committee on Maritime History regularly publishes papers on routes and transport, e.g., *Les Aspects Internationaux de la Découverte Océanique aux XVe et XVIe siècles* ed. by Michel Mollat and Paul Adam (1966). J. H. Parry, 'Transport and Trade Routes' in *Cambridge Economic History of Europe*, vol. IV (1966) and his *The Age of Reconnaissance* (2nd ed., 1966) are very authoritative.

THE COMMODITY TRADE. Many histories of trade previously dealt more with the externals of trade organisation —the rules and regulations—than with the underlying economic realities. Modern research now centres on business cycles, economic trends and crisis as they reflect changes in production and consumption patterns, trying also to quantify the volume of trade and to chart its directions. This work is in process while research on model-building is still in its infancy, one of the few contributions being F. Mauro, 'Towards an Intercontinental Model: European Overseas Expansion between 1500 and 1800,' *Economic History Review*, 2nd ser., vol. XIV (1961).

A classic on the history of European agriculture and consumption is Wilhelm Abel, *Agrarkrisen und Agrarkonjunktur* (new ed. 1966). W. Achilles, 'Getreidepreise unde Getreidehandelsbeziehungen europäischer Räume im 16. und 17. Jahrhundert,' *Zeitschrift für Agrargeschichte und Agrarsoziologie*, vol. 7 (1959), is an interesting contribution to the history of the grain trade. Indispensable to the study of the Baltic grain trade is Aksel E. Christensen, *Dutch Trade to the Baltic around 1600* (1941). P. Jeannin has used the Sound Toll Registers in an attempt to trace European business cycles, 'Les comptes du Sund comme source pour la construction d'indices géneraux de l'activité économique en Europe (XVIe-XVIIe siècles),' *Révue Historique*, vol. CCXXXI (1964). The same material has been used by J. Faber in his interesting article 'The Decline of the Baltic Grain-Trade in the Second Half of the 17th Century,' *Acta Historiae Neerlandica*, I (1966). Polish historians have also made important contributions to the history of the Baltic trade, thus M. Malowist, 'Les produits des pays de la Baltique dans le commerce international au XVIe siècle,' *Révue de Nord*, vol. XLII (1960).

On the subject of the cattle trade there is a recent monograph by H. Wiese and J. Bölts, *Rinderhandel und Rinderhaltung im nordwesteuropäischen Küstengebiet vom 15. bis zum 19. Jahrhundert* (1966), and on Hungary the authoritative work by Zs. P. Pach, *Die Ungarische Agrarentwicklung im 16.-17. Jahrhundert* (1964).

Fernand Braudel, *op. cit.*, contains much information on the pepper trade of the sixteenth century and so does Frederic C. Lane, 'The Mediterranean Spice Trade: Its Revival in the Sixteenth Century,' *The American Historical Review*, vol. XLV (1940). The European market around 1600 is treated by Hermann Kellenbenz in 'Der Pfeffermarkt um 1600 und die Hansestädte,' *Hansische Geschichtsblätter*, 74 (1956). K. Glamann has dealt with the Dutch East India Company's pepper trade in his *Dutch-Asiatic Trade 1620-1740* (1958), whereas the English Company's imports during the first half of the seventeenth century have been analysed by K. N. Chaudhuri, *The English East India Company, Study of an Early Joint-Stock Company 1600-1640* (1965).

The copper trade has been touched upon by Carlo Cipolla, *Guns and Sails in the Early Phase of European Expansion 1400-1700* (1965) and K. Glamann, 'The Dutch East India Company's Trade in Japanese Copper 1645-1736,' *The Scandinavian Economic History Review*, I (1953). A collection of papers presented at the Third International Colloquium on Economic History at Cologne, 1969, on copper production and copper trade is under way edited by H. Kellenbenz.

Among the contributions to the history of the textile trade *Studier i engelsk og tysk varehandels historie* (1907) by the Danish historian Erik Arup and *Alderman Cockayne's Project and the Cloth Trade*, (1927) by Astrid Friis are both classics and still worth consulting. Charles Wilson, 'Cloth Production and International Competition in the Seventeenth Century,' *Economic History Review*, 2nd ser., vol. XIII (1960) is very interesting for its comparative approach.

MONEY AND CREDIT. Not very many attempts have been made to throw light on this important side of trade history. A classic is K. Ehrenberg, *Das Zeitalter der Fugger* (I-II, 1896). J. G. van Dillen, 'Amsterdam als wereldmarkt der edele metalen in de 17de en 18de eeuw,' *De Economist* (1923) is also indispensable. Among modern works Herman van der Wee in his monumental *The Growth of the Antwerp Market and the European Economy* (I-III, 1963), discusses financial and technical innovations during the early modern period. K. N. Chaudhuri in two articles on 'The East India Company and the Export of Treasure in the Early Seventeenth Century' and 'Treasure and Trade Balances: The East India Company's Export Trade, 1660-1720' (both in *Economic History Review*, 2nd ser., vol. XVI (1963) and vol. XXI (1968)) are also very rewarding.

THE ORGANISATION OF TRADE. Important contributions to the entrepreneurial history of early modern Europe have been made by H. Kellenbenz in *Unternehmerkräfte im Hamburger Portugal- und Spanienhandel 1590-1625* (1954) and *Sephardim an der unteren Elbe* (1958). Reinhard Hildebrandt carries on the learned German tradition of Fugger research in his *Die 'Georg Fuggerischen Erben'* (1966) discussing the social position of the large merchants. A significant contribution to Dutch entrepreneurial history is P. W. Klein, *De Trippen in de 17ᵉ Eeuw* (1965).

7. The Emergence of Modern Finance in Europe, 1500-1730

Geoffrey Parker

INTRODUCTION: EUROPE'S MONETARY STOCK

'What Your Majesty needs is money, more money, money all the time.' Marshal Trivulzio's advice to Louis XII of France as he prepared to invade Italy in 1499 highlighted in a suitably flamboyant way one of the basic problems of life in early modern Europe. During the sixteenth and seventeenth centuries money became of major importance to a rapidly increasing number of people, yet simultaneously ready money became desperately scarce.

There were many reasons for this paradoxical development. In the first place there was the vast growth of the European economy analysed and assessed by other contributors to this series: the rapid rise in population, the emergence of new industries, the intensification of land use, the growth of European trade (both internal and external). All these new or expanded economic activities required money. From the purchase of bread and clothes to the payment of taxes and royal pensions, coins were required in ever greater numbers. Yet the supply of physical money, like the supply of foodstuffs, could not be increased indefinitely. Both were relatively inelastic; both were subject to inexorable limitations.

Europe's monetary stock in early modern times was not large. A recent calculation suggests a total stock in 1500 of about 3,500 tons of gold and 37,500 tons of silver.[1] In the course of the sixteenth century there were, as is well known, very considerable additions to this initial stock. Europe drew upon deposits of gold and silver scattered all over the

1. F. Braudel F. C. Spooner, 'Prices in Europe from 1450 to 1750', *Cambridge Economic History of Europe*, vol. IV (ed. E. E. Rich, C. H. Wilson, Cambridge, 1967), p. 445. All estimates of this kind are, of course, dangerously approximate and must be treated, as the authors are careful to state, with the utmost caution. All tons are 'metric tons'.

world. In Europe itself the silver mines of the Tyrol and Saxony were profitably exploited from the 1450s until the 1620s, with a peak production of around 70 tons a year between 1526 and 1535. Silver was mined in Lorraine too, gold in Hungary, copper in Sweden and the Tyrol. More important, however, were the quantities of gold and silver imported from Africa and America. Between 1485 and 1520 over half a ton of gold arrived in Lisbon every year from Portuguese West Africa, and Europe continued to secure African gold throughout the early modern period – on average rather more than a ton of gold arrived every year from the mines of Monomotapa in Moçambique alone throughout the seventeenth century. This considerable input was dwarfed by the treasure sent to Europe from America. In the decade 1551–60, 43 tons of gold were landed at Seville. Over the whole period 1500–1650, some 181 tons of gold arrived officially in Spain from America while still more was brought in by smuggling, piracy and direct trade. But the chief treasure which America yielded to early modern Europe was silver: 16,886 tons of silver reached Spain officially between 1500 and 1650. In the late seventeenth century it was the turn of gold again: the discovery of rich deposits of alluvial gold in Portuguese Brazil after 1693 initiated a new flow of bullion from America to Europe which lasted for most of the eighteenth century.

These additions to the monetary stock of Europe were impressive. Between 1500 and 1650, according to Professors Braudel and Spooner, the official inflow from America alone increased Europe's total stock of gold by some 5 per cent and the total stock of silver by almost 50 per cent. But these gains were by no means all retained in Europe.

Besides the ordinary loss of coins through hoarding and wear, we know that western Europe in early modern times had a deficit trade balance with two areas – the East Indies and the Levant – and we know that until the 1660s at least the outstanding balances were largely settled in cash, especially in silver. Thus in the 1580s about 1,000,000 Spanish ducats were shipped every year to the Far East by the Portuguese. The drain increased in the seventeenth

century when the English and Dutch also began to send
Spanish silver to the Orient: the English East India
Company exported over £750,000 sterling to the Far East
between 1601 and 1624 – all in Spanish 'pieces of eight':
approximately 2,500,000 ducats – and the company's
bullion exports rose dramatically in the later seventeenth
century, reaching a peak of £703,497 in the financial year
1700-1 alone. The bullion exports of the Dutch East India
Company followed a parallel course, rising from 500,000
ducats exported in the year 1618 to 1,250,000 in 1700.
These totals would have been yet greater had the Dutch not
made skilful use of the silver and gold produced in Japan for
the rest of their Asiatic trade. Scarcely less impressive was the
export of treasure, again largely in Spanish silver coins, to the
Middle East. By the 1590s the annual export of bullion from
western Europe to the Levant was an estimated 1,500,000
ducats. Between 1593 and 1596 Venice alone exported
over 1,000,000 ducats to the Levant, and over 1,500,000
ducats between 1610 and 1614, 84 per cent of it in Spanish
reales. The French port of Marseilles probably exported more.
Taken together, around 1600 Europe's trade with the Near
and Far East probably absorbed about 2,500,000 ducats, or
almost 80,000 kilograms of silver, every year.

To summarise and correlate these very crude figures, it
would seem probable that in each year around 1600 Europe
lost about 80,000 kilograms of silver to the east and a
certain amount in addition in wear and tear on coins.
Against this the mines of central Europe probably still
produced some 20,000 kg. annually while the fleets from
America brought an official cargo of about 220,000 kg. every
year (with yet more carried clandestinely). On balance it
seems safe to assume that Europe's net stock of precious
metals augmented moderately between 1500 and 1580; that
it increased rapidly between 1580 and 1620; and that it
probably declined from the 1620s, when silver mining in
Europe collapsed and the remittances of American silver
fell sharply, until the arrival of the Brazil gold after 1700.

There is no doubt that this growth in the volume of
money available in Europe was extremely important.

Europe's trade in 1700 could clearly not have been carried on with the slender monetary resources of 1500. A crucial question, however, remains: was it enough? Was the net increase in Europe's monetary stock, substantial as it was, equal to the rapidly rising demand for means of payment? There are several indications that it was not, particularly after 1600.

In the first place the letters and papers of merchants and ministers pullulated with laments about the 'scarcity of coin' and the 'want of money'. An English businessman in the 1620s complained that 'the scarcity [of coin] is so great that a man may go into a great many shops in London, of great trade and commerce, before he shall get a 20s. piece in gold . . . changed into silver', while another observed that 'There is great scarcity of money within all the kingdom, so that any man cannot depend upon any payment or receive any money due to him.' It was the same story in Spain, despite the largesse from America. In 1543, and on many subsequent occasions, the great trade fair at Medina del Campo had to be postponed for lack of money, and in the 1580s the *Cortes* of Castile lamented: 'Experience has shown that within a month or two of the arrival of a fleet from the Indies, not a farthing is to be seen.' To some it seemed that 'However much money comes from the Indies, Spain has less' and this impression is supported by the known facts. In 1570 and 1571 some 7,000,000 ducats arrived at Seville from America, but simultaneously all that and more was exported from the city (7,018,000 *pesos* were registered in and 7,049,000 *pesos* were registered out). The same was true of Spain as a whole: she exported more treasure, and often substantially more treasure, than she received, and the drain became worse as time went by.[2]

2. The English quotations come from B. E. Supple, *Commercial Crisis and Change in England, 1600–1642* (Cambridge, 1959), pp. 173 and 175 (pp. 171–8 give an excellent assessment of what contemporaries meant when they spoke of the 'scarcity of coin'); the Spanish quotations come from P. Vilar, 'Les primitifs espagnols de la pensée économique: "quantitavisme" et "bullionisme" ', *Bulletin hispanique*, LXIV bis (1962), pp. 261–84, on pp. 279–80. See also the view of F. C. Spooner, *New Cambridge Modern History*, vol. IV (Cambridge, 1970), pp. 78–86.

'Scarcity of coin' was certainly not a *permanent* problem in many areas of early modern Europe, although the periodic shortages appear to have lasted longer after about 1620. However, with the possible exception of seventeenth-century Amsterdam, every financial centre suffered from *temporary* monetary inanition, causing embarrassment, inconvenience and even bankruptcy to merchants suddenly deprived of their liquidity. This experience, however short-lived, was unpleasant enough to stimulate innovations. Various attempts were made to transact business without resorting to gold and silver at all. Copper currencies were introduced in many countries in the sixteenth and seventeenth centuries, mainly to ease the pressure on gold and silver; but copper was unfortunately only suitable for small denominations (Sweden, which issued a complete range of copper coins, had to strike massive plates weighing 43 lbs. to serve as 10-daler pieces). For larger transactions the only solution was to do without coins altogether, to use credit instruments of one sort or another.

The early modern period witnessed an unprecedented expansion in the use of credit techniques: loans, securities, bonds, credit transfers, bank-money, paper-money and negotiable obligations – all were employed on an increasing scale to avoid the use of precious metals. From being the limited tool of a handful of specialists, mainly Italians and Jews, by 1730 the widespread use of credit was a feature of almost every European country. In some areas, indeed, a sophisticated and interlocking system of multilateral commercial payments, controlled and secure credit, and safe fiduciary money grew up, making it possible to increase the monetary stock of Europe without waiting for new strikes of gold and silver to increase the number of coins in circulation.

The importance of this development was considerable. The establishment of sound financial institutions, of an elastic money supply and of easy and cheap credit were the indispensable preconditions of industrial growth. They were just as crucial in this respect as the changes in agricultural output and technique which occurred during the eighteenth century. It is doubtful whether Europe would have known an 'Industrial Revolution' had a 'Financial Revolution' not preceded it.[3]

PRIVATE FINANCE

Two developments in the field of private finance during the early modern period stand out as crucial: the concentration of credit facilities in a restricted number of large commercial centres and, associated with this, the evolution of an international system of multilateral payments. These developments were neither rapid nor ubiquitous, but they were extremely important. They stemmed in large measure from a change in the popular attitude towards lending money.

LOANS

Amid the uncertainties of daily life in pre-industrial Europe almost everyone needed a loan at some point to tide him over hard times. The failure of a harvest might plunge peasants into debt; a trade recession might throw artisans out of work; a shipwreck or an act of war might destroy a merchant's capital. Only credit could set these innocent victims of misfortune back on their feet. In addition, merchants and noblemen, princes and shopkeepers alike might need a loan if they intended to expand their activity or otherwise increase their expenditure beyond the level of their immediate resources. To serve them, a whole host of individuals and corporate bodies grew up specialising in various forms of lending money, from the licensed pawn-brokers of the Venice ghetto to the Bank of England in Threadneedle Street, London. During the early modern period money-lending, like so many other spheres of economic activity, became the preserve of specialists.

The appearance of professional lenders was longest delayed, as one might expect, in rural Europe. For most of the middle ages the local rich peasant (the *coq de village*),

3. On this vital link see *The Fontana Economic History of Europe*, vol. 3, chap. 4: B. Gille, 'Banking and industrialisation, 1730–1914'.

clergyman or clothier monopolised rural credit. It was only after 1500 that the rising profitability of agriculture encouraged town businessmen to offer loans to local small-holders. In France and Spain between 1530 and 1550 a new credit instrument spread like wildfire, the *rente* or *censo*. This device was a version of the annuities by which most medieval towns raised loans, and it required a landowner (whether large or small) to pledge a piece of his property to a third party (usually a monied man from the nearest town) in return for a capital loan. Interest was paid on the loan by assigning a specified sum from the borrower's revenues (normally payable in cash but sometimes in kind) to the lender. If the payments were not kept up (for instance during a run of bad harvests) the creditor was entitled to seize the property held in pledge. Many did.

If this arrangement seemed too harsh the rural small-holder could turn to his local merchant for credit of a different kind. The practice of selling goods on delayed purchase was commonplace all over Europe, the peasant promising payment in grain from the yield of the next year's harvest; but here too there were obvious dangers of exploitation. It was tempting for the merchant to inflate the price of his goods, exact payment when the grain was cheapest (after the harvest) and then hoard it until it became scarce. When the harvest was poor and the peasant could not pay, his debt was carried over (at interest) and added to whatever he received on credit the following year. In a period of bad harvests this system reduced the small-holders to debt servitude as surely as the *censos* and *rentes*. In Mediterranean Europe the run of harvest failures at the end of the sixteenth century caused widespread rural indebtedness of this sort.

In the towns credit facilities were more diverse and therefore somewhat less oppressive. There were a large number of professional and part-time pawnbrokers and money-lenders willing to advance a sum on the security of a pawn or a written bond. In Italy, Germany and eastern Europe money-lending was largely in the hands of the Jews; elsewhere in Europe native merchants (especially goldsmiths, silversmiths and jewellers) competed with Italian immigrants for business. There was certainly no shortage of clients. All classes of society were deep in debt. In Rome, for example, 5,942 persons – no less than 6 per cent of the city's total population – were imprisoned for debt at some time during the year 1582. The overall number of people actually in debt at this time was naturally far greater.

With such a widespread demand for their services some specialisation developed among the money-lenders. Some, in particular the goldsmiths and jewellers, concentrated on the aristocracy. In Elizabethan England the dukes of Norfolk and Sussex, the earls of Shrewsbury and Essex and many other noblemen pledged their plate and jewels in order to raise cash. In 1642 the total income of the 121 English peers was about £730,000 but their total debts (many at high interest) amounted to around £1,500,000. Small wonder that some merchants abandoned all pretence of trade in order to specialise in lending money at interest. Master Thomas Sutton, the model for Ben Jonson's *Volpone*, lent money to six earls and six other peers and died with nearly £45,000 out at interest. Men of wealth like Sutton had no time for the poor: they were left to raise what they could from smaller but equally rapacious back-street money-lenders – the pawnbrokers. It was to keep the poor out of the hands of usurers, Jewish and Christian, that the remarkable institution of the *monti di pietà* developed.

The first *monte* opened in Perugia in 1462 and by 1509 there were 89 of them, spread all over Italy. Their basic – and often their sole – function was to lend money to the poor at the lowest possible interest to alleviate immediate distress. The *monti* would not, for instance, advance money to permit shopkeepers or artisans to start up or expand a business, and the maximum they would lend to each household was very low (only three ducats at Padua and two at Treviso – and even then only for six months). Most of the *monti* drew their capital overwhelmingly from charitable donations, and their activity was severely restricted by this dependence on private generosity and alms. In some places however they became more adventurous, soliciting deposits from members of the public at 4 per cent interest and lending money to the rich, even to sovereign princes: in 1583 the *monte* of Florence lent 300,000 ducats to Philip II of Spain (at a handsome profit); in the 1620s the *monte* of Verona supplied up to 200,000 at a time to the penurious duke of Mantua. The larger *monti*, several with a working capital of well over 500,000 ducats, acted as savings-banks, safe-deposits and outlets for money seeking a secure investment as well as providing personal loans. However the initial function of the *monti di pietà* as cheap loan-banks for the poor never entirely disappeared and at Rome, Verona and Turin at least the *monti* made small loans entirely free whenever this was possible (although they still demanded pawns from the borrowers).

Yet the *monti* did not put the Jewish and native 'usurers' out of business. The reason was simple: the professional money-lenders offered a better service (albeit at a higher cost). They were prepared to make their loan for longer, they would accept a borrower's written bond instead of insisting on a physical pledge, and they would lend a larger sum. The *monti* therefore did not spread to many countries outside Italy. Proposals by Pieter van Oudegherste, Luis Valle de la Cerda and others in Castile (in 1567, 1576, 1623 and 1627) all failed to produce results; likewise in England the *monti* proposed by Gerard de Malynes in 1622, by Sir Balthazar Gerbier, John Cooke and John Benbrigge in the 1640s, and by Sir Edward Ford and Robert Murray in the reign of Charles II came to nothing.[4] The one concrete attempt, the 'Bank of the City of London' founded by the London Corporation in August 1682, very soon collapsed through mismanagement. It was only in the Netherlands that the Italian *monti* took root.

Loan-banks on the Italian model were founded in a number of the leading towns of the Low Countries during

4. These numerous proposals, all ingeniously (or ingenuously) described in lengthy publications, are discussed in detail by E. J. Hamilton, 'Spanish banking schemes before 1700', *Journal of Political Economy*, LVII (1949), pp. 134–56, and R. D. Richards, *The early history of banking in England* (London, 1929), pp. 12–13 and 93–101.

the sixteenth century and there were many more foundations in the southern Spanish provinces after 1600. Undoubtedly, however, the most famous loan-bank of the Netherlands was the *huis van leening* opened at Amsterdam in 1614 to lend money at low interest to the poor and to small men wishing to expand their business in return for a pledge or pawn. It raised its capital (1,200,000 florins by 1616) solely by issuing bonds and debentures which bore interest. It did not depend on charity. Following the success of the Amsterdam *huis van leening* (or 'Lombard') more were established in other towns and in the 1660s a copy of the loan-bank was set up in Sweden as a department of the *Riksens Ständers Bank*, making loans to the poor and the enterprising on the security of pledges of property, especially land. Some Swiss towns too, Basel for instance, had a public exchange (*stadtwechsel*) which loaned money to the poor as well as to artisans and smallholders who wished to improve their position. A *change publique* was set up in Geneva in 1568 but, as with several *monti*, the fund was grossly mismanaged and it was closed down in 1581. Its function devolved upon individual charities and the parish poor box. All over Europe there were parishes with a 'common stock' of cattle, wool and tools which could be loaned out to the destitute on the brink of starvation. There were also 'improvement funds': trusts established by bequest to provide loans at modest interest to young apprentices so that they could set up for themselves. In England probably 150 young men, almost all from London, benefited from these trusts every year by about 1600.

The *monti di pietà* of Italy and the *huisen van leening* of the Netherlands were 'public banks', that is to say they were rigorously scrutinised, supervised and guaranteed by public authorities. Indeed they were viewed with perhaps excessive mistrust by governments. In particular they were forbidden to allow depositors to 'overdraw' their accounts and this made them practically useless to merchants and businessmen who often required a short-term advance to maintain their liquidity. The trading community therefore turned perforce to private bankers instead.

'Merchant-bankers', businessmen who accepted deposits from their fellows and used the money to finance their own commerce or to make loans to others, had flourished in the Middle Ages. There were 80 separate 'merchant banks' in Florence alone in 1338 and 15 in Bruges in 1369. After 1630 too private banks multiplied, especially in England where they had seldom been seen before. In the first decades of the seventeenth century several London 'scriveners' (sc. notaries) were acting as brokers between those in search of a loan and men with money to invest, and by the 1630s at least thirty scriveners were also accepting deposits and making loans on their own account. They were replaced during the Civil War by the goldsmiths of the City. By 1677, fifty-eight London goldsmiths were involved in banking and the number continued to grow until the crash of 1720. But between these two periods of expansion – the early fourteenth and the later seventeenth centuries – banks everywhere passed through difficult times. In Florence the number of banks fell from 80 in 1338 to 33 in 1460, to only 8 in 1516. The same drastic and prolonged decline took place in Bruges, Venice and the other commercial centres of Europe. In Venice it was asserted in 1585 that of all the 103 private banks which had at some time been established in the city, no less than 96 had gone bankrupt, ruining their clients.

There were several reasons for the failure of so many private banks. In the first place there was flagrant mismanagement. Bankers notoriously employed their clients' deposits in their private ventures to a dangerous degree, thus becoming unduly vulnerable to any shift in the economic conjuncture. In addition many bankers invested heavily in government loans and were therefore ruined if the state declared a moratorium on its obligations (a frequent occurrence as will be seen). But there was also a psychological factor. Bankers worked under the constant stigma of usury, pilloried by the church – both Catholic and Protestant – for 'making money with money'. According to strict theological definition a loan had to be gratuitous; therefore if the lender asked for anything more than the return of the principal of his loan on the agreed date for repayment, he was committing the sin of usury. There were, however, ways of circumventing this definition. Churchmen agreed that a loan which involved any risk of loss or non-repayment entitled the lender to some compensation (the argument of *damnum emergens* or loss arising). It was also admitted that anyone who by lending money missed a chance of making a legitimate profit elsewhere could likewise claim some compensation from the borrower (the argument of *lucrum cessans* or profit ceding). In practice, therefore, the Roman church tolerated a certain amount of interest on certain types of loan. For instance theologians usually accepted the need of the *monti di pietà* to charge interest on their loans and even (though there was considerable criticism of this) to pay interest on deposits made with them. Catholic princes were even less inhibited about permitting usury within certain limits. In 1543 the Holy Roman Emperor Charles V gave his official blessing to merchants lending money at interest in the Netherlands; the practice was already tolerated in Spain.

The situation was not very different in Protestant countries (contrary to the assertions of many historians). Luther bestowed special praise on those who made cheap loans (sc. at under 6 per cent) to farmers, while Calvin tried to ensure that the poor of Geneva could always obtain capital loans at low interest. However the reformers realised that the price of commercial loans could not be artificially depressed. In 1557 Calvin himself bowed to protests from merchants who threatened to transfer their capital to Lyons unless the legal maximum for interest on loans in Geneva was raised from 5 to 6⅔ per cent; in 1568, in similar circumstances, Beza agreed to raise the rate to 10 per cent. In England, after centuries of absolute prohibition on usury, interest of up to 10 per cent was permitted by Parliament and upheld by the Courts in 1545–51 and again after 1571. This did not imply outright acceptance of money-lending by all Protestants however. In the Dutch Republic, citadel of commerce and aggressive capitalism, the general synod of the Calvinist church decreed in 1581 that no banker or his servants should ever be admitted to the communion service, and that his family should be admitted only after they had expressed publicly their distaste for the banker's profession. This stern and self-righteous measure was endorsed by various church assemblies until in 1658, at the command of the States of Holland (the secular arm), it was relaxed.

There can be little doubt that this persistent hostility to the money-lender and his trade in certain parts of Europe dissuaded many people from using their savings, even through a banker, to provide loans for those who needed them. Consequently money was generally available to borrowers only on very expensive terms, especially in the sixteenth century. As Professor Stone has written:

'Money will never become very freely or cheaply available in a society which nourishes a strong moral prejudice against the taking of any interest at all – as distinct from objection to the taking of extortionate interest. If usury on any terms, however reasonable, is thought to be a discreditable business, men will tend to shun it and the few who practise it will demand a high return to compensate them for being generally regarded as moral lepers.'[5]

Nevertheless in the early modern period a more liberal attitude towards money-lending did grow up and it was reflected in what Professor C. M. Cipolla has called 'the revolution in interest rates'. In the main commercial centres of Europe it became possible to borrow money much more cheaply. In the Netherlands, interest on public loans at Antwerp fell from 25 per cent in the 1500s to 9 per cent by 1550, while in the 1660s the government of Holland could borrow in peace-time at under 4 per cent. In Spain tho maximum interest permitted on new *censos* fell from 15 per cent in the early sixteenth century to 7 per cent after 1563 and 5 per cent after 1608. In England, once the ban on usury was lifted in 1571, the maximum interest rate fell from 10 per cent to 8 per cent after 1624, 6 per cent after 1651 and 5 per cent after 1714. Most spectacularly of all,

5. L. Stone, *The Crisis of the Aristocracy, 1558–1641* (Oxford, 1966), p. 529.

the Italian republic of Genoa, already able to borrow at 5 per cent in the 1520s, found itself able to reduce this rate progressively to under $1\frac{1}{2}$ per cent for some years after 1604 and still find lenders!

CREDIT TRANSFERS AND NEGOTIABILITY

From the earliest days of banking in the medieval west clients of a bank had been able to transfer a sum of money from their own account to someone else's by going in person to the bank and dictating to the banker an order to transfer the sum. Any entry in a banker's ledger had the force of law, but at least until the fourteenth century (and in some places until long after) the order had to be given orally. The cheque, a written order to the banker authorising a transfer, did not become common (except in Italy) until the seventeenth century.

Without the cheque it was clearly difficult for a man to transfer money to someone else in a different town. It was therefore a major step forward when, in the fourteenth century, bankers devised the 'bill of exchange'. Derived from the *instrumentum ex causa cambii* of twelfth-century Genoa and used by a number of Italian merchants at the Fairs of Champagne in the thirteenth century, the bill of exchange was a binding written promise to pay a named person a certain sum of money at some future but proximate date in another town. The critical factors were that the bill had to be paid in a different place and (in theory at least) in a different currency from the place and currency of issue. Every bill of exchange involved a short-term loan, possibly at interest: communications in Europe were so slow that even when a bill was payable 'on sight' a considerable amount of time necessarily elapsed while the bill was carried from the place of issue to the place of payment (from Spain or Italy to the Low Countries took between two and four weeks). It was also accepted that for bills involving large sums of money, the person required to pay should be allowed a certain time in which to raise the sum for which he was liable. This further delay, known as *usance* might be

30, 60 or 90 days (it varied from the custom of one town to another) from the day on which the bill was first presented for payment. This meant that if the bill was intended to be a payment for goods received, the merchant who made out the bill enjoyed between one and three months' credit before he had to pay.

Settling a transaction by bill of exchange involved the participation of four persons. First the merchant, A, who wanted to discharge his debt abroad. If he did not possess wealthy business contacts in the foreign country concerned he had to go to a local merchant-banker, B, who did. B wrote out an order, the bill of exchange, to his correspondent in the foreign market, C, authorising payment of the sum concerned to A's creditor, D. A would agree to pay B the sum to be remitted, plus a service charge, and the bill would be sent off to C by the merchants' courier. Some weeks later C would inform D, the beneficiary, of the arrival of his funds and D would be paid in person.

Transfers of credit abroad by private individuals are still performed through a bank in this way (although on the whole rather more quickly). Here is a typical bill of exchange used as an example by the London merchant Gerard de Malynes in his manual of merchant practice, *Lex Mercatoria*, published in 1622:[6]

'Laus Deo. A. D^i 20 August 1622 in London. 500 lb, 34s 6d. At usance, pay by this my first bill of exchange unto A.B. the summe of five hundreth pounds sterling, at thirtie foure shillings and sixe pence Flemish, for euerie pound sterling currant money in merchandise, for the value hereof received by me of C.D. and put it to account, as per aduice. A dio etc.

G.M.

To my loving friend, Master W.C., merchant at Amsterdam. Pa[gate].'

The bill of exchange system was both simple and effective, but it did involve risks. A sudden change in the

6. Gerard de Malynes, *Consuetudo, vel Lex Mercatoria, or the Ancient Law Merchant* (London, 1622), p. 393.

rate of exchange between the two financial centres concerned might create a loss for one of the bankers; either banker might also find that one of the parties to the contract was insolvent or dishonest and that money had been mistakenly paid out which could not be recovered. There were also inconveniences for the payee and the payer (A and D of our simplified scheme): there were the inevitable delays involved in sending the bill by post and waiting for 'usance', delays which would be further increased if banker C refused to honour the bill for any reason (if he 'protested' it, to use the technical term, sending it back to source). Paradoxically, however, these delays were very welcome to some of those who used bills of exchange most frequently. As already noted, every bill of exchange involved a loan as well as a transfer of funds. Loans thus created could usually be prolonged without difficulty simply by instructing banker B's correspondent to take out a new bill of exchange in favour of B for the same value as the one he received, plus a charge for his trouble and costs, and send it back. Once a man had obtained a loan from a banker and agreed to repay him by a bill of exchange issued by another banker in another place and in a different currency, bills could be shuttled back and forth between the two bankers until the debtor was ready to pay. Interest on the loan was concealed in the exchange rates at which the principal was converted from one currency to another. This procedure – known as fictitious, internal or 'dry' exchange in the sixteenth century, and in the seventeenth century with certain modifications as the *ricorsa* exchange – lasted on average for about one year (although it could be much longer) and cost about 12 per cent per year.

Such devious and complicated devices were fortunately unnecessary in countries where lending at interest was not absolutely prohibited. In the Netherlands and England, therefore, the bill of exchange remained restricted to its original role of a credit transfer. Loans in these countries were secured by issuing a simple promissory note, the 'bill obligatory', '*cédule obligatoire*' or '*schulderkenning*', by which the borrower promised to repay a certain sum at a certain date. Such was the popularity of this credit instrument that it was even used to transfer money from one place to another within the same currency area (the 'inland bills' of England) – the exact reverse of the fate of the bill of exchange in Spain and Italy!

In the fifteenth century there is clear evidence that English merchants frequently 'assigned' promissory notes ('bills obligatory') in their possession to their own creditors in order to discharge a debt. Important English clothiers like the Cely family may even have paid as many debts by assigning credit notes as by paying cash. In cases of non-payment the bearer of a promissory note had some legal protection even if he was not named in it: the English Law Merchant recognised the right of any person bearing the bond to sue the debtor (although the Common Law Courts did not permit this until 1704). In the Netherlands, the town of Bruges recognised in 1527 that the bearer of a bond possessed all the rights of the original creditor, and this reform was applied to the whole Netherlands by an Imperial edict of 1537. In 1541 the central government further enacted that the original creditor named in a promissory note became free of all entitlement and liability for its payment when he assigned it to someone else. Thenceforth credit notes circulated freely from hand to hand in the Low Countries and the revised *Customs* of Antwerp issued in 1608 contained a special clause concerning those *schulderkenningen* (bills obligatory) which were assigned in turn 'to four and five persons and even more'.

The bill of exchange took slightly longer to become negotiable. In England at least this development did not take place until the middle years of the seventeenth century. The comprehensive treatise of Gerard de Malynes, the *Lex Mercatoria* published in 1622, contains no mention of the procedure of endorsement by which bills of exchange were normally transferred from one person to another. However the practice was familiarly described in the *Advice concerning bils of exchange* written by John Marius (a scrivener) in 1651. Here the Netherlands were ahead of England in commercial innovation since endorsed bills (sc. with an assignation of the bill to a third party written on the back or *dorse*) became common in Antwerp from the 1570s onwards. In Italy too, where a few remarkable but isolated cases of endorsement date from the fourteenth century, the practice became general in the later sixteenth century (although it remained expressly forbidden in Venice and one or two other financial centres).

Italy was also the first to develop the negotiable cheque (the *polizze*) and again there are scattered examples from the mid-fourteenth century. Although in some places (Venice again for example) bankers long continued to insist upon the physical presence of their client or his attorney in the bank before they would undertake any transaction for him, elsewhere orders in writing came to be accepted. Genuine cheques drawn on a banker by his customer and made out in favour of a third party were common practice by the 1570s and we even find negotiable cheques (called *girata*) like the following:[7]

'Honourable trustees of the *Monte di Pietà* of Naples. Please pay for me to Sir Giovanni Antonio and Sir Domenico Fiorillo 20 ducats of current coin; they are part payment of the 50 ducats which they lent me from the Ravascieri Bank last month. Charge them to my account.

At my house, 2 September 1573,
Your servant, Scipione Fiorillo.

20 – 0 – 0.

Pd 20 ducats, 3 September 1573, C.B.

And for me, Domenico Fiorillo, pay to M° Paulillo the 20 ducats written above. To your (com°), Domenico Fiorillo.'

In time the useful device of the written cheque (although not always negotiable) spread from Italy to most of the rest

7. This example is taken from A. P. Usher, *The early history of deposit banking in Mediterranean Europe* (Cambridge, Mass., 1943), an interesting study but now rather dated. Recent research (in particular by Professor F. Melis) has shown that most of the financial techniques used in the sixteenth century were well known in central Italy at least two centuries earlier.

of western Europe. The first English cheques, known as 'drawn notes', date from the 1660s.

It is surprising that the revival of banking in western Europe during the seventeenth century did not give greater impetus to the spread of the principle of negotiability. Admittedly it was the custom of the Amsterdam and Venice exchange banks and of the London goldsmiths to issue notes to their depositors promising to pay on demand and in cash the amount of money deposited, or a part of it; but only the notes of the Amsterdam bank, the *recipissen*, were fully negotiable, circulating from hand to hand like money. The Venetian authorities resolutely set their faces against all assignment of credit instruments outside the public bank, while in England until the Promissory Notes Act of 1704 the Common Law Courts refused to recognise credit notes as negotiable.

Another relatively late step towards full negotiability was the practice of 'discounting' bills: of selling a credit obligation to a third party before its maturity in return for a sum slightly smaller than the bill's face value. Known in an isolated case from 1536, 'discounting' became common in the Low Countries only after 1550, especially when specie was short. Bill-broking spread to Augsburg by 1576 and Hamburg by 1600, and it became common in most European commercial centres in the seventeenth century, especially in those which possessed a clearing bank. Thus throughout the eighteenth century the Bank of England discounted bills, both inland and foreign, for its customers, at 5 or 6 per cent, while in Venice all bills of exchange – and in Amsterdam all bills for more than 600 florins could only be cashed by paying them in to an account in the city's public bank. It is to the growth of these central clearing banks that we must now turn.

CLEARING: FAIRS OF EXCHANGE AND CENTRAL BANKS

Even without negotiability, Europe possessed relatively efficient methods of transferring debts without transferring the instruments of debt. The time-honoured practice of making a payment 'in bank', whereby a client went to the bank and gave an order for a sum to be transferred to the account of his creditor, could easily be extended if the various bankers in the same town opened an account in each other's bank. Thus the client of one bank could, via the banker, make a payment to an account in another bank in the same town without resorting to cash. In the eighteenth century many London bankers were still operating in this way.

This local clearing organisation was complemented by a precocious superstructure of inter-regional and eventually international clearing systems: the fairs of exchange. Since the major commercial fairs brought together merchants from many different areas, and since it was inconvenient for them to settle all their transactions in cash, it became customary to purchase goods during the fair on credit, noting down all the obligations incurred in the books of any banker who happened to be present. When the fair was over, the 'payments' began. Each banker added up the debits and credits of individual customers, the balance outstanding payable in cash or, from the fourteenth century onwards, by a bill of exchange. It thus became possible for a merchant to buy everything he needed at a fair without bringing any cash with him. Not surprisingly, the system spread fast. First seen at the great Champagne Fairs in the 1190s it spread to the later commercial gatherings at Lyons, Antwerp, Medina del Campo, Frankfurt and the cities of northern Italy.

At some fairs (Lyons for instance) all the merchants present participated in the clearing operations and also in the fixing of exchange rates for bills payable at the fair. Elsewhere these crucial activities were monopolised by a small number of wealthy merchant-bankers – the 'bankers of the fair'. The fairs of Medina del Campo, for example, held for 50 days twice every year, were attended in the mid-sixteenth century by some 2,000 merchants but the clearing and tariff-fixing at each fair was in the hands of a cartel of 14 or 15 bankers. These men settled their clients' obligations by book-transfers between accounts in their own or their colleagues' banks. Financial dealings at the 'Fairs of Besançon', held four times a year at the north Italian town of Piacenza from 1579 until 1622, were even more centralised and involved transfers from all over Europe.[8] Between 1580 and 1620 perhaps 50 million *scudi* changed hands at the 'Fairs of Besançon' every year. They were attended by a maximum of 200 merchants, representing between 100 and 110 firms, and about 50 or 60 merchant-bankers, the *banchieri di conto*, who virtually controlled the fair.

Since the chief aim of these fairs of exchange was, according to many writers, to permit the settlement of accounts worth millions without the transfer of corresponding amounts of specie, the *feraldi* – the merchants who came to the fair – came with much paper but little money. Above all each brought his *scartafaccio*, a bound manuscript volume containing all the bills of exchange and other obligations he had to meet. Everyone worked out the total due on the accepted bills and obligations, and set against it the total due on credit instruments payable; the resulting balance, which was normally small, was settled immediately in gold. Only between 100,000 and 400,000 *scudi* actually changed hands in cash at each fair in Piacenza, even though the total sum involved in the various transactions ran into millions.

This clearing operation ('compensation' as it was called) was of course only a part of the activity of every fair. At 'Besançon' it accounted for a turn-over of no more than 3 or 4 million in total dealings at each fair of between 12 and 16 million *scudi*. The fairs created and prolonged debts as well as settled them. About three-quarters of the business transacted at 'Besançon' concerned the creation or continuation of loans to merchants, mainly it seems by *ricorsa* bills.

8. The 'Fairs of Besançon' began in 1535 when the Genoese merchants at Lyons decided to leave French territory and organise their own fairs. They chose the free city of Besançon in Franche-Comté as their base and the fairs of the Genoese retained the name of 'Besançon' long after they had deserted the city for Italy.

However, the role of the fairs in the economy of western Europe was changing rapidly at this time. As an increasing number of merchants established permanent offices and warehouses at the leading commercial centres they no longer needed or wanted to confine their dealings to the restricted period of the fairs. They were able to trade the whole year round and the erection of an Exchange, *Lonja* and *Bourse* in one town after another (Antwerp 1531, London 1571, Seville 1583, Amsterdam 1611 and so on) provided a permanent forum for dealings in commodities. The fairs lost almost all their commercial importance. The 'Fairs of Besançon', for example, lasted a mere eight days every three months and dealt only in money: no goods were bought or sold at all. Eventually their financial functions died away too, and the great fairs survived only in the shape of the 'quarter-days' on which all outstanding trade balances had to be settled. In Amsterdam during the seventeenth century there were four *rescontre dagen* in the year when a judge, three assessors and a secretary sat down with the *rescontrants* around a special table in the Exchange building to settle the outstanding balances due to them and their clients. The 'Rescounter' system was introduced into England in the 1740s, the settlement days being slightly later than those of the Amsterdam Exchange to allow brokers to take account of Dutch dealings.

The development of commodity wholesale trading all the year round, independent of the fairs, created a pressing need for large, properly regulated banks where merchants could deposit their assets in safety and recover them at an hour's notice. It is doubtful whether the private bankers could have served this need, given their habit of investing clients' deposits in their own commerce, but in any case so many of them disappeared or fell into serious difficulties after 1575 that it was clearly necessary to find an alternative. Many governments solved the problem by adapting or creating a 'public bank', an organism which could receive deposits and make credit transfers but remained guaranteed and closely scrutinised by the public authorities.

In many ways the epitome of the new-style public banks was a new foundation, the Venetian *Banco della Piazza di Rialto*, authorised by the Senate in June 1584 and opened in April 1587, modelled at least in part on the institutions which had long operated in the kingdom of Aragon (a municipal *taula* or bank at Barcelona since 1401, at Valencia since 1408 and others subsequently at Gerona and Saragossa). The Rialto bank was given three main functions to perform. It had to accept and repay deposits, effect transfers between accounts, and credit bills of exchange payable to clients. Deposit and transfer banks of the Rialto type were soon established under government auspices in other Italian cities: the *Banco di San Ambrogio* opened in Milan in 1593, the *Banco del Spirito Santo* in Rome in 1605. Elsewhere, existing banks were allowed to accept deposits from private investors and clear bills of exchange (for instance the *Casa di San Giorgio* at Genoa, which began to accept deposits in 1586, and the united *monti di pietà* of Naples which went public in 1584). Each of these banks immediately became an important centre of credit transactions and each tried to monopolise the clearing operations in its locality.

In northern Europe the great centralising force was the Exchange Bank, or *Wisselbank*, of Amsterdam which was approved by the town council in 1606 and opened in 1609. The activity of the new bank was very similar to that of the Rialto: it could receive money on deposit at interest, transfer money between accounts, and accept, credit and clear bills of exchange payable to clients. Since all bills involving more than 600 florins could only be credited at the bank, almost every merchant was compelled to open an account. In addition the Exchange Bank was allowed to change money and to purchase bullion and foreign coins to mint into legal tender – an activity which brought it considerable profit. As in all the Italian and Aragonese 'public banks', no overdrawing of private accounts was permitted and there were no personal loans to customers (after 1683 the bank issued paper certificates against a customer's deposits of bullion at the bank and these circulated freely, but until 1781 the

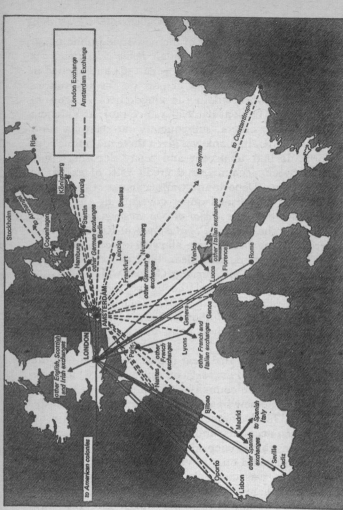

FIGURE I — *The exchange networks of Amsterdam and London, c. 1700.*
Amsterdam clearly surpassed London in its range of direct contacts, particularly with Germany and the

total issue of deposit certificates never exceeded the total bullion held in the bank).

The *Wisselbank* thus proved a sure deposit for the working capital of the business community (guaranteed by the Amsterdam corporation) and an efficient clearing-house for credit notes (a free service until 1683). Other Exchange Banks of the Amsterdam model quickly followed – in Middelburg (1616), Hamburg (1619), Nuremberg and Delft (1621), Rotterdam (1635) and Stockholm (1656) – until by 1697 it was estimated that 25 public banks of one sort or another were in existence in Europe. However few of these later creations could match the power and wealth of the Amsterdam bank: in 1721 it had 2,918 accounts worth a total of 28,886,000 florins. From 1660 until 1710 at least it was the undisputed capital of European trade, the centre of the first multi-lateral payments system in the world.

The secret of Amsterdam's financial ascendancy lay in the ubiquity of Dutch trading concerns. Dutch merchants, Dutch shipping and Dutch investment had acquired a foothold in every major commercial centre of Europe, and in most maritime cities of Asia, America and Africa besides, by 1660. This meant that Amsterdam was in direct trading contact with virtually every other centre, and that it was possible to buy a bill of exchange in Amsterdam which would be honoured almost anywhere in the world. Some trading areas – the Baltic for instance – would only accept bills drawn on Amsterdam. The city's wide commercial contacts and the great influx of bullion and coin from all corners of the globe (Amsterdam was the European capital of the trade in precious metals too) created very stable exchange rates which further consolidated its commanding trading position. Figure 1 illustrates the extent to which Amsterdam had spread its tentacles over Europe by the first decade of the eighteenth century.

Amsterdam's supremacy was only eroded and undermined when the trading contacts and the wealth of the London merchants finally overtook those of Holland. Already in the 1700s, as Figure 1 shows, London's direct contacts were numerous, although during the wars against

Louis XIV England was clearly dependent on the financial services of Amsterdam in order to set her heavy spending on Marlborough's army against her favourable trade balance with France, Holland and Germany. It was chiefly after 1713 that Britain expanded her business contacts, profiting from the exotic commodities which poured in from the New World to establish her own network for distributing them to the rest of Europe. Based soundly on her expanding trade, Britain built up exchange dealings which were as extensive and as far-flung as Amsterdam's.

At the centre of the new prosperity and supremacy was the Bank of England, founded as a joint-stock company in London in 1694. At first the Bank was intended only to handle a government loan and issue bank-notes (known as 'running cash notes') but it soon did much else besides: accepting deposits, trading in bullion (like the Amsterdam *Wisselbank*), transferring money overseas for the government, accepting state securities at par as deposits or for cash payment, handling tax-revenues for the government, accepting and crediting bills of exchange payable to customers . . . By 1698 the Bank had notes in circulation payable on demand worth £1,340,000. By 1720 this total had risen to £2,480,000 (smallest denomination £10) and many other banks in England and Scotland also issued their own notes. In all it was estimated that the total value of paper credits circulating in early eighteenth-century England was about £15,000,000, as against a total coin and bullion stock of £12,000,000. The financial innovations of the later seventeenth century had thus expanded England's total monetary stock by 25 per cent without an equivalent increase in the amount of actual currency.

This achievement was impressive but it was also unique. No other European country managed to create money in this way. The highly valued specie deposit notes of the Amsterdam bank were never allowed to exceed the total of the deposits until 1781; the brief experiments of a paper currency in Sweden (1661–4) and France (1718–20) quickly foundered because notes exceeded cash reserves by too large a margin and could not be redeemed immediately for coin at par. Apart from England and Scotland, banknotes only took hold in the early modern period in North America, where the government of Canada issued 'playing card' notes after the 1670s and a number of English colonies put 'bills of publick credit' into circulation after 1690 – and even then the notes were soon over-issued and ceased to be accepted at their face value. The 'financial revolution' still had its limits.

COMPANY FINANCE

Throughout the early modern period, and far beyond, the commonest species of European entrepreneur was the individual businessman working either on his own or in partnership, formal or informal, with members of his family. In certain overseas ventures, single traders operated under the aegis and according to the rules of a large monopoly – the Hanseatic merchants of Germany and the Baltic, the Staplers or Adventurers of England, the members of the *consulados* of Seville and Burgos in Spain – but still each trader worked for himself selling his own goods and employing his own capital. Often the merchant was unable to accompany his wares to the foreign market in person, and so the practice developed of selling goods through factors (salaried agents in distant trade centres) or through correspondents (merchants resident at a market who would sell goods for others in return for a commission, a percentage of the price or a reciprocal service by the other merchant). Risks for the single operator were high. Many a correspondent or agent proved false; many a ship sank or was captured by pirates; often goods arrived for sale on a market already glutted and had to be disposed of at a loss. It is small wonder that (as today) there was an extremely high rate of failure among small businesses. Few lasted a lifetime.

In the sixteenth century, although this type of merchant continued to thrive and fail, new types of commercial organisation appeared. On the one hand, more very small operators began to participate in seaborne trade thanks to the practice of splitting the cost of a ship and its cargo between a large number of co-owners. This type of marine partnership was common in the Mediterranean (the *loca navis*), in the North Sea (*rederij* in Holland and *reederei* in Germany), and elsewhere. Generally, one partner sailed the ship and sold its cargo while the rest contributed goods and capital and shared in the profit and loss. It made better sense to be part-owner of a number of ships, at a time of high risks and poor insurance, than to be sole owner of one. In contrast to this sub-division of enterprise, the sixteenth century also saw the growth of enormous commercial combines and corporations.

Marine partnerships were normally made for just one voyage or 'venture' but longer partnerships became common in more permanent economic activities such as local retailing, manufacturing and especially banking. In the sixteenth century, as in the Middle Ages, many of these more durable associations were simply enlarged family partnerships. Some were highly centralised, like the company of Anton Fugger of Augsburg which paid agents and branches all over Europe but retained all executive power at the centre; others, like the Affaitidi from Cremona, delegated much power to their local branches, run by junior partners, leaving the parent organisation to fill a role not unlike that of a modern holding company. To increase the working capital of both these types of large company was relatively easy. Every company had a basic capital, the *corpo*, contributed by the partners themselves. Additions to this fund could be made either by accepting deposits at interest from outsiders or by encouraging the partners to make further deposits. This additional capital was known as the *sopracorpo*. The two funds of capital were treated in quite different ways. While those with shares in the *corpo* received shares in the overall profit or loss of the company, those who contributed to the *sopracorpo* received only a limited but guaranteed interest on their deposit which was always paid before the company's profits (or losses) were distributed. This division, evident from the thirteenth century onwards, prefigured the 'shares' and 'bonds' still used by modern companies to raise their capital.

The early modern period saw a number of developments in this binary system of public finance. Most important, and most celebrated, was the growth of the joint-stock company with transferable shares. Partnerships with transferable shares already existed in fifteenth-century Italy (for instance the *Casa di San Giorgio* at Genoa and, in certain cases, the *loca navis*) and in Germany (in some mining enterprises), but they first became widespread and permanent in England and the Netherlands after 1550. The first English joint-stock ventures, to Russia and Guinea, began in the 1550s. It was no accident that both appeared in connection with long-distance trade. Where risks were high and capital running costs (in the shape of factories, convoys or forts) considerable, it made good sense for capital to be pooled and costs and risks equitably spread over the entire venture.

There were about a dozen joint-stock companies in England in 1600, but their organisation was in many ways still primitive. In the trading companies each 'stock' was subscribed for one voyage only and the dividends paid after the 'venture' were made up from capital as well as profit. Further, the companies limited the number of shares they issued (a legacy from the partnership days) and when they wished to call up more capital they asked each shareholder to increase his stake rather than inviting subscriptions from others interested in acquiring a share. In 1569 the Mines Royal, one of the joint-stocks engaged in domestic enterprise, made a new call on its shareholders which raised each individual stake to £850. There were only 24 shares, although many of them were divided into fractions (eighths were not uncommon) and these, like the full shares, were transferable. However in both Holland and England the 'transport' (as it was known) had to be performed in person at the company's headquarters and this in effect restricted dealings in shares to a relatively small group living in the metropolis (London or Amsterdam).

More considerable advances were made in company finance after 1600. In the first place, companies came to regard their capital stock as permanent. The Dutch East India Company decreed in 1612 that its shares could only be cashed by selling them openly on the Exchange; the English company followed suit in 1623. The English East India Company was the first to expand the issue of shares at a fixed nominal value according to its need for capital, instead of making extra calls on existing shareholders, and it was one of the first to distinguish between profits (which it distributed as dividends) and capital (which it usually retained). East India shares at this time were usually units of £50 or above, but other companies pioneered the sale of much smaller denominations (£12.10s. in the Virginia Company of the 1620s). The normal unit for shares in Dutch companies was 3,000 florins (about £300 sterling) throughout the seventeenth century.

The combination of these separate developments had an unexpected consequence: the growth of a complex and unpredictable stock market. At the root of it all lay an insatiable love of gambling. Businessmen (like almost everyone else at that time) laid bets on anything. At Antwerp in the 1560s and '70s there was betting on the safe arrival of ships, on whether and when the king would come to the Netherlands, on the date of a person's birth, marriage or death, and in this highly-charged atmosphere of gamble and risk a lively speculative trade grew up in grain futures. In the seventeenth century, amid a similar atmosphere, the Amsterdam exchange saw speculative 'future' dealings in grain, herring, spices, whale-oil – in all the commodities for which market supplies were unpredictable but demand constant. It was hardly surprising that the fever spread to company shares as soon as these were available. Probably the first clear example came in 1609 when it was discovered that a refugee from Antwerp, Isaac le Maire, had formed a cartel expressly to lower the price of East India shares. By the mid-century there was a regular market in shares, with the stockbrokers and their clients congregating around one of the forty-six numbered pillars in the courtyard of the great Amsterdam Exchange. Every kind of speculation was to be found: time bargains, optional sales and cartels of 'bulls' (who, as today, tried to raise the price of certain shares) and 'bears' (who did the reverse). There were even 'ducat deals' in which small speculators followed the market winning or losing a ducat for every point by which the price of shares went up or down. This mature stock market was described with loving if ironic detail by the exiled Iberian poet and speculator Joseph Penso de la Vega in his book *Confusion de Confusiones*, published in 1688. These refinements came to England a little later but already the 1630s saw a growing trade in stocks and shares in London, together with the introduction of special shares which limited the holder's liability to the company to the face value of his share (no further calls for capital could be made upon him).

Few companies depended solely on share-capital however. Both in England and Holland companies sold 'bonds' (*obligatiën* in Holland) which could be redeemed at short notice. These bonds, descendants of the *sopracorpo* of the medieval Italian trading companies, could be redeemed by investors on demand (unlike shares which could only be sold on the market) and yielded a modest but guaranteed interest. Companies anxious to raise capital found that it was cheaper to sell bonds (with interest of under 5 per cent) than to make a new issue of stock (which yielded on average between 8 and 10 per cent) and bonds were therefore sold in profusion. Thus after 1709 the English East India Company regularly had bonds in circulation worth more than £3 million, although the nominal share-capital of the company was only about £3¼ million. Of course this policy was fraught with danger. In a panic, the bond-holders could and did demand immediate payment *en masse*. In the 'run' of 1682 the English East India Company, which then had bonds in circulation worth only £500,000 or so, was forced to suspend payments for three months.

Panics like these, and lesser fluctuations in response to political or market developments, served to increase the speculative element in stock-buying. In the later seventeenth century the highest and lowest points touched by the shares of most English companies could vary by as much as 140 points in any one year. Naturally speculators were desperate for news, and to satisfy them the price of the leading stocks began to be published in the 1690s in two trade journals:

John Houghton's *A Collection for Improvement of Husbandry and Trade* (1692–1703) and John Castaing's *The Course of the Exchange and Other Things* (first known from 1698; Castaing's list continued after his death, growing by stages into the present 'Official List' of the Stock Exchange). Speculative dealing was increased yet further by the appearance of a large number of new companies, all seeking investors. There were only 11 English joint-stock companies in 1689, but about 100 in 1695 (mainly in the domestic field, thanks to the war with France which blocked investment in overseas trade). Houghton's journal quoted the price of 8 shares and securities in 1692, 52 in 1694 and 64 in 1695; there appear to have been active dealings in almost all, carried on at the tables of a handful of coffee houses crammed into the narrow 'Exchange Alley' which led from Cornhill, near the Royal Exchange, to Lombard Street.

In John Houghton's description of the London market's techniques in the 1690s, as in Joseph de la Vega's description of the Amsterdam market in the previous decade, we may recognise a mature organism. There were share transfers both directly between buyer and seller and indirectly via one of the growing number of stockbrokers; we find forward or option dealings (sc. offers to transfer shares at some future date at a pre-arranged price), 'bulls' and 'bears' (by those names), buying on margin (sc. buying with a small deposit in cash and borrowing the rest by pledging the newly bought stock) and many other sophistications of the modern market. In all, the attitude of both professionals and amateurs towards the newly developed stock markets of London and Amsterdam between 1680 and 1720 had much in common with the dangerous and heady euphoria which characterised Wall Street in the 1920s.

Perhaps surprisingly, however, this intense dealing in stocks and shares was still confined to a relatively small number of people. A new investor seeking an outlet for his money would probably decide against buying company shares for a number of reasons. First, despite the growing number of stockbrokers and the publications of Houghton and Castaing, knowledge of market trends and share prices was often hard to come by; then the transfer of stock had to be performed in person in London, which was inconvenient for country investors; and finally the yield on most shares (around 8 per cent in an average year) was disappointing compared with the risk of loss on its capital value. Investment in shares was therefore confined to a relatively small though extremely active group of City merchants. In 1675, for example, the East India and the Africa companies had a combined stock divided into 741 individual holdings (some held by the same person) worth around £480,000; by 1691 the combined stock had risen to a nominal £850,000 but the number of individual holdings had fallen to 680. Most of these investors lived in London; many had a very large stake (Josiah Childe, the London banker, held £50,000 of India stock in 1691). It was the same story in Holland. Investment in the leading companies was largely concentrated in Amsterdam where in the 1690s over half the stock in both the East and West India companies was held. The greater mobility of shares and the development of a stock market thus does not appear to have attracted notable investment in company shares from new groups outside the traditional merchant community.

The subscription to company bonds, however, was an entirely different story. These had great appeal for all who looked for a steady income from their investment rather than for quick capital gains. The bonds and *obligatiën* issued by the main companies, generally in denominations of £100 (in England) and repayable after 6, 12 or 24 months at the discretion of the lender, were unlikely to depreciate and offered a secure, fixed yield (4, 5 or 6 per cent at this period). They were popular even among the most cautious investors: women, for example, held 20 per cent of all the outstanding bonds of the English East India Company in 1685. Trust managers and chartered institutions also bought bonds as a valuable but safe outlet for their funds. None of these groups would have risked their money in shares.

The bonds of the joint-stock companies did thus attract new money into trade which would otherwise have been sunk in land or some other traditional channel of investment. The growth of private banking furthered this development in England after 1680 since the London bankers were happy to purchase and hold stocks and bonds for their country clients and to collect dividends and interest on their behalf at Company House. After about 1710 the bankers themselves, like the new Insurance Offices in the City of London, began to buy up company bonds for their own use to serve as a liquid cash reserve. Since they were redeemable virtually at an hour's notice, the bonds of the East India and the other great joint-stock companies were an ideal vessel to receive the temporary balances of active merchants, and so throughout the eighteenth century, bonds not only provided the great companies with a large share of their trading capital, they also served as the cash reserve of the City financiers.

Yet as far as the small private investor was concerned, the principal channel of investment in England after 1689 was neither shares nor company bonds but the securities and debentures issued by the government. It is now time to turn to the progress of the 'financial revolution' in the public sector.

PUBLIC FINANCE

THE RISE IN GOVERNMENT SPENDING

There was a considerable overlap between the financial problems which beset the various sovereign states of early modern Europe and those facing the larger commercial concerns within them. Both had to guard against sudden monetary scarcity; both had to take steps to assure their continual financial liquidity; governments, like companies, had eventually to relate their income and resources to expenditure. Here, however, lay the essential difference: state spending increased dramatically all over Europe in the early modern period, but no established mechanism existed to adjust revenues to the new high levels. Bringing the budget of each state into eventual equilibrium was the greatest challenge facing the 'new monarchies' of Europe. Innumerable attempts were made; few succeeded.

There were many reasons for the overall increase in government spending. A great deal of it was caused by the sustained rise in general prices and wages during the same period which forced governments to raise their revenues considerably in order to maintain the same level of activity. But inflation does not explain all the increase. In Spain, for example, general prices appear to have increased about five-fold, government spending nine-fold between 1520 and 1600. Although the chronology was not the same everywhere, state expenditure all over Europe began to rise rapidly from about 1540 onwards and it scarcely stopped until the eighteenth century, the rise continuing whether prices in general moved up or down.

The major factor in the growth in public spending was the greater duration and the rapidly augmenting cost of war. Although it is true that more public funds were channelled into courtly extravagance and conspicuous consumption than ever before, this was just a fraction of total expenditure. In Castile some 70 per cent of the budget of 1574 was accounted for by war and defence; admittedly it was an exceptional year, but 'defence' spending was normally the largest single item of expenditure for most western states in the early modern period.

War also presented a secondary financial problem: not only did a state at war require more money, it required it at once. Raising taxes to the level of expenditure, even if feasible, brought no immediate solution. By the time the new revenues could be collected the troops for whom the money was intended would be in mutiny for their pay. Therefore governments were compelled to borrow on a vast scale in order to meet their wartime needs. In 1574, for example, current revenue accounted for only about half of the money disbursed by the Castilian treasury: the rest was raised in loans.[9] There were of course changes in the taxes

9. For details of the budget of 1574 see G. Parker, 'Spain: her enemies and the Revolt of the Netherlands', *Past & Present*, XLIX (1970), pp. 72–95, on p. 85, with a restatement of the position in *ibid.*, LV (1972),

levied by the various states of Europe between 1500 and 1700, but on the whole they were of a conservative nature: more and heavier taxes of the established type rather than radical new expedients. The fiscal structure continued to be weighted in favour of indirect taxes, in favour of the rich, in favour of decentralising and delegating collection to 'farmers'. The important new initiatives in the field of public finance during the early modern period almost all concerned borrowing and credit.

SHORT-TERM BORROWING

'The use of credit by medieval rulers is at least as old as their possession of regular monetary revenues', wrote Professors E. B. and M. M. Fryde in volume III of the *Cambridge Economic History*. The earliest forms of credit which they describe, forms which survived in certain areas until the nineteenth century, were tax-farming and tax-assignation. Both were important to most governments in early modern Europe. The first practice involved ceding the collection of a tax to a private individual, the 'farmer', who paid a fixed sum of money to the central treasury in return for the right to collect a specified tax from all who were liable to pay it. The tax-farmer did not have to declare what he collected: anything above his fixed 'rent' or 'farm' to the crown was his own private profit, anything below was his loss. 'Assignation' was quite different. Here a creditor of the crown was promised payment from the future yield of a specified revenue, and he was either 'assigned' its collection until his credit was made good – in which case he had to account for every penny received – or else he was authorised to receive from an official government collector all the money produced by a certain tax until the government's debt was paid off.

Both these arrangements involved lending money to the

---

pp. 157–9. The general connection between war and government spending is discussed in G. Parker, *The Army of Flanders and the Spanish Road, 1567–1659* (Cambridge, 1972), pp. 1–21 and 127–38.

crown. The tax-farmer was providing the crown with a regular flow of income in advance while the assignee was consenting to defer payment of his services – perhaps for two or three years – until the tax allocated to him could be collected. Both were in effect *anticipating* revenue to the crown. This was a very valuable service. In England local revenue collectors retained the money they received for up to two years as late as 1820; a tax voted by Parliament might take four years to produce the bulk of its yield in the shape of money in the central treasury. Assignation and tax-farming smoothed out the flow of money into the treasury.

Thus, even in peace-time, governments valued the services of persons prepared to advance them ready cash on the security of the future yield of a source of revenue which was slow to collect. In wartime this need naturally became far more urgent and it could easily develop into deficit borrowing, with the government 'anticipating' more money than the total revenues could be expected to yield. The solution was to mortgage the yield of taxes in years to come. In July 1556, for example, Philip II found at his accession that his Spanish revenues were pledged in full up to and including the year 1561: they had all been 'assigned' to the financiers who had anticipated the revenues to the king. However the system still remained a short-term affair in theory, a 'floating' loan repayable in full on a certain day, even when that day was far in the future. The lender agreed to advance a certain sum to the king at a specified place and time and at an agreed rate of interest.[10] In return he

10. It is often stated that Spanish *asientos* never specifically mentioned interest. This is not true. A large number of *asientos* made with Philip II between 1560 and 1575 specified a rate of interest for the loan. This was normally 7 or 8 per cent per year in the 1560s, rising to 12, 14 or 16 per cent in the period 1572–5 as the government's need for money increased. This open admission of reward for lending money enabled the king to repudiate all his debts for *asientos* on the grounds that they were usurious and therefore invalid. *Asientos* made after 1575 were accordingly more circumspect: as with the bill of exchange, the reward was concealed in the difference between the exchange rates at which the loan was to be paid and repaid.

received a formal promise of repayment at a later date from a specified revenue. This simple contract was known as an *asiento* in Spain and as a *parti* in France.

Very often government borrowing was coupled with the need to send money abroad. The war in the Netherlands after 1572, for example, involved Spain, France and England in considerable and prolonged expenditure outside their frontiers and this led the governments concerned to seek their loans from those who could also transfer it abroad: the great financiers and merchant-bankers with international connections. The government made use of the existing commercial system of credit transfers to make their foreign payments. The financier who made the loan arranged for it to be paid at the government's command by his partners or correspondents abroad on receipt of his bill of exchange. The only difference between the payments on public and private accounts lay in the scale of operation. Spain, by far the largest overseas spender, sent at least 280 million florins to the Netherlands between 1561 and 1610, overwhelmingly by bills of exchange, an average of around $5\frac{1}{2}$ million annually (about £550,000 in the English money of the time). Within this period there were some years of quite extraordinary effort, like the year before the Spanish Armada – 1587 – when 15 million florins were sent. Of course credit transfer operations for governments had arisen before: Louis IX of France used Genoese merchants to remit money on credit to Syria during his crusade (1248–53); Alfonso V of Aragon financed his Italian wars after 1444 with loans paid in Naples and repayable in Aragon – his loan arrangements were almost exactly like those of Charles V and Philip II. Again, the difference lay in the scale. The *asientos* of the Spanish Habsburgs were so enormous that they stimulated a major haemorrhage of treasure from Castile. The king had to permit the export of great stocks of bullion by his bankers, mainly Genoese after 1557, and between 1614 and 1621 $18\frac{1}{2}$ million *escudos* of treasure arrived at Genoa from Spain and 28 million more in 1625–34 (about £7 million sterling).

Queen Elizabeth of England was obliged to use much the

same technique for remitting money to the Netherlands. She persuaded leading merchants with trading links in the Low Countries to send money to the Paymaster of her forces in Holland by bill of exchange, reimbursing them at the Exchequer in London; often much of this money too was shipped out of the country in specie. Between 1585 and 1603 the Queen's Paymaster in the Netherlands received £1,486,026 (almost 15 million florins). The cost of this to England was, of course, much greater: apart from the loss of treasure, the interest on the loans and the cost of the transfer, the business of 'remises' was subject to massive fraud. The total cost of remitting money to the Low Countries, for both England and Spain, could undoubtedly rise above 25 per cent on occasion. One of the most expensive loan-cum-transfers was that arranged by Queen Elizabeth in 1578 with an Italian exile in London, Sir Horatio Pallavicino.[11] In the summer of 1578, Elizabeth formally agreed to lend the States-General £100,000. Unfortunately the Queen's credit abroad was not good and the Dutch were not able to find a banker willing to advance money against her promises. Pallavicino, who had a considerable interest in the alum-workings of central Italy, therefore offered to supply large quantities of alum to the States at a cheap price. The States could then sell it at a profit (alum was crucial for dyeing clothes and there were innumerable cloth-works in the Netherlands) and the total proceeds of the sale would be held to constitute the Queen's loan. Pallavicino's offer was accepted and he promptly dumped alum worth approximately £15,000 on the Dutch, claiming it was really worth £28,757, and sat back to await repayment with interest (at 10 per cent). The years went by, some marked by payment of interest by the Queen, some not, until in 1598 the total interest and capital outstanding stood at £88,901. Pallavicino died in 1600 but repayments and interest charges continued and it was not until 1626 that the matter finally fell into oblivion, £70,000 having been paid by England (the Dutch stubbornly refused to contribute) –

11. The unsavoury saga which follows is based on L. Stone, *An Elizabethan: Sir Horatio Pallavicino* (Oxford, 1956), pp. 65–97.

a profit to Pallavicino of around 450 per cent – over 9 per cent for 48 years – on his original loan of £15,000.

Despite such scandals, when England next went to war in the Netherlands on a grand scale, in the 1650s and after 1689, the Elizabethan techniques were resurrected largely unchanged. London financiers like the goldsmith Edward Backwell remitted government money to Flanders for the Dunkirk campaign in 1658 by bills, and they did the same in the early years of King William's War. The situation only altered substantially with the foundation of the Bank of England in 1694, since the new financial institution was specifically charged with transferring government funds to the English forces abroad. Thus in the eighteen-month period October 1694–April 1696 the Bank organised the dispatch of £1·6 million to the Netherlands on the government's account. The business of 'remises' acquired considerably more sophistication during the war of the Spanish Succession (1702–13). The remittances still involved lending to the government (the Bank 'anticipated' the money) but there was virtually no export of bullion. Since England enjoyed a favourable balance of trade with Holland, France and Germany, and since most of these trading balances were settled through Amsterdam, the Bank was able to set the accumulated cash trading surplus in the Netherlands against the government's need for money there to pay the forces. The Bank's bills of exchange were paid with this surplus. Only when the remittances to the Army rose dangerously high, causing a fall in the rate of exchange for sterling in Amsterdam, did the Bank send English coin. In general, when sterling fell 9 per cent below par the Bank would start exporting bullion; when it fell more than 11 per cent below the Bank authorised the export of large quantities of bullion (in fact this was rarely the case after 1700).

This orderly, rational system of financing foreign wars was unique however. It was but one aspect of the relatively healthy, sound system of public finance (to be discussed in detail below) which distinguished England from most of the other states of Europe. The key-stone of the new English system was the management of the government's long-term debt.

LONG-TERM BORROWING

Without any doubt the pioneers of the basic technique of long-term public borrowing were the west European towns. From the thirteenth century onwards one town after another saved itself from temporary embarrassment by creating a long-term debt. The classic – indeed often the sole – instrument for this was the *annuity*, a single lump sum paid to the town by an investor who in return received annual payments at an agreed rate for a predetermined time. There were three basic types of annuity: perpetual, until redemption by the town, and for the life span of one, two or three named persons. The terms were generous. Redeemable and perpetual annuities could normally be transferred from one person to another and, generally speaking, the annual payment on perpetual annuities was around 5 per cent, between 5 and 10 per cent on redeemable or multiple-life annuities, and 10 per cent or over for single-life ones. These payments were not regarded as usurious by the church because, even in the case of redeemable annuities, they were viewed as an act of sale and purchase. Indeed the church had its own forms of ecclesiastical annuity, known as the *precaria* and *census*. Annuities were therefore sold by towns all over Europe: *renten* in the Netherlands and Germany (where the practice first developed), *rentes* in France, *monti* in Italy and *censos* in Spain.

It was a surprisingly long time before princes were able to emulate their towns. By the end of the fourteenth century only the various dukes and counts of the Low Countries were able to sell annuities on a regular basis. France and Castile followed in the course of the fifteenth century, but only on a very modest scale through lack of demand: investors reckoned (and not without reason) that a town's annuities were safer and more reliable than those of a monarch. It was partly in recognition of this advantage enjoyed by the towns that Francis I of France decided in 1522 to offer government annuities for sale under the aegis of the Paris corporation. The king assigned a number of revenues to the city so that the corporation could sell special annuities, give the proceeds to the king and pay the annual charge out of the assigned revenues. They were known as the *rentes sur l'Hôtel de Ville de Paris*. By 1550 annuities to a capital value of 7 million *livres* had been sold by the towns on behalf of the king. A parallel development took place in Spain during the reign of Charles V. In order to raise money for the wars with France, the government sold annuities at an accelerating pace: by 1556 the capital value of these annuities, known as *juros*, stood at 6 million ducats.[12]

However the direct sale of annuities did nothing to reduce the crushing burden of short-term debt which weighed upon every state, nor were the sums raised by such sales sufficient to diminish the governments' dependence on short-term borrowing. It was for this reason that during the 1550s, a decade of unusually expensive military activity, the financial experts of both France and Spain turned their attention to methods whereby their short-term obligations might be converted or reduced.

In June 1557, as an emergency wartime measure, Philip II of Spain issued a decree which converted all the government's 'floating' debt (unpaid short-term loans, or *asientos*, worth about 7 million ducats) into redeemable annuities (*juros al quitar*) bearing interest at 5 per cent. From the crown's point of view, the decree of bankruptcy not only reduced the rate of interest payable on the debt; more important, it freed those revenues which had been alienated in advance to financiers. The king was therefore at liberty to offer them anew as a pledge for fresh short-term loans.

When the wars were over and the king returned to Castile, a more permanent 'funding' operation was arranged with special revenues set aside to meet the cost of the public

12. In Spain, *juro* was the name given to an annuity issued by the central government; an annuity sold by anyone else, whether in a public or private capacity, was called a *censo*. There was no other material difference.

debt.[13] On 14 November 1560 a new decree of bankruptcy was issued freezing the capital of all loans made to the crown since 1557 and suspending all payments connected with them. The decree of 1557 was also confirmed. All creditors were allowed to exchange their now worthless claims to repayment for new *juro* certificates to the face value of their original loan plus accrued interest. The new *juros* and the old were to bear interest of 5 per cent annually, payable in June and December at the House of Trade (*Casa de Contratación*) in Seville. To meet this charge, some 3,800,000 ducats every year, the *Casa* was allowed to receive and handle the crown's revenues from the Indies, from the mining of copper and silver and from the sale of slaves and other commodities. The *Casa* used the money to pay interest direct to holders of the government bonds (the *juristas*) and to repurchase a number of the redeemable annuities if circumstances allowed.

The *Casa de Contratación* thus began to act in several respects as the National Bank of Spain, servicing the National Debt. Alas, this admirable innovation soon ran into difficulties. The disappointing fall in the quantities of treasure arriving for the king (only 2 million ducats in the quinquennium 1561–5) followed by the enormous increase in government spending after 1566 (with the war against the Turks, the *Morisco* rebellion and the revolt of the Netherlands) depleted the funds set aside for the *juristas*. The later bankruptcy decrees of 1575, 1596, 1607, 1627, 1647 and 1653, which compulsorily consolidated all loans made since the last decree, made no provision for the orderly, centralised payment of interest on the new bonds; instead the financiers whose loans were frozen were forced to accept *juros* in compensation payable from revenues scattered all over the country.

Each decree automatically increased the volume of the funded debt, and therefore the annual interest due. From 3·8 million ducats in 1560 it rose to 4·6 million in 1598 (representing a capital debt of 85 million), to 5·6 million in

13. 'Funding' is simply the appropriation of a specific source of revenue to provide interest payments on a fixed body of long-term debts.

1623 (despite a reduction in the rate of interest from 7 to 5 per cent) and to 9 million in 1667. By this time interest payments had fallen far into arrears. Since the annual charge represented well over half the government's total income (70 per cent in the 1660s), regular payments were simply not possible. The Spanish Habsburgs had borrowed too much for too long. It is doubtful whether any state of the day could have borne a debt equivalent to between ten and fifteen years' full revenue, least of all at a time when revenues were falling and economic activity was in recession as they were in Castile after the 1620s.

French attempts to create a 'funded debt' during the Habsburg-Valois struggle met with even less success. In March 1555 the French government announced that some 4,000,000 *livres* of its short-term debt would be turned into a single, unified sum, to be known as the *Grand Parti de Lyon*, repayable with interest in forty-one equal payments from the royal receipts at Lyons, Montpellier and Toulouse. Each year 1,300,000 *livres* was to be repaid. Unfortunately this sum proved to be too much, on top of the government's other commitments, and in November 1557 the eighth instalment could not be paid. Further repayments were suspended until peace could be concluded with Spain. When this was achieved (April 1559) the government took the idea up again, but it also turned a further 3,000,000 *livres* of short-term debt into a second separate fund, known as the *Petit Parti*. This created a total fund of 11,700,000 *livres* at about 8 per cent interest – roughly a quarter of the crown's total debts (43,000,000 *livres* in 1559). Although revenues to finance the repayments were assigned to the city of Lyons, prospects of amortising the debt were never bright. They were altogether extinguished by the accidental death of Henry II in July 1559. The royal minority, the civil war and the rapid inflation of the 1560s quickly bankrupted the crown so that by 1568 only about 1,800,000 *livres* of capital had been repaid. The creditors never saw another penny. The French government staggered through the civil wars with revenues often 50 per cent below expenditure, bridging the gap by the indiscriminate sale of crown and church lands and by reckless borrowing at extortionate interest, largely from the Italian merchants based on Lyons. Such a legacy could only be liquidated by repudiating a considerable part of the crown's debts. This step was taken by Henry IV in 1599.

Another rational and rather more successful attempt to create a funded debt was made in Italy. As early as 1408 the Republic of Genoa had sponsored the formation of a formal association of its creditors in a sort of joint-stock bank, the *Casa di San Giorgio*. By the 1530s the total debt handled by the *Casa* amounted to more than 40 million *lire* (about 8 million ducats) divided into *luoghi* or paper credit notes worth 100 *lire* each. From 1408 until 1444 and again after 1586 the *Casa* also acted as a deposit bank and this combination of activities, banking and debt-management, was repeated in the *Banco di San Ambrogio*, founded in Milan in 1593, and in the more famous *Banco del Giro* of Venice, founded in May 1619.

Initially the Giro Bank was only allowed to handle part of the Venetian state debt. The bank issued interest-bearing bonds (*partite*) to the value of 500,000 ducats to those who had lent money to the state and the government undertook to make over a fixed sum every month to the bank to pay interest on and amortise the debt. The *partite* proved popular and, guaranteed by the bank and through it by the government, they circulated freely and even at a premium – often 20 per cent above par. Encouraged, the Republic expanded the issue of *partite* until in 1630 the total debt funded at the Giro stood at 2,622,171 ducats. The government paid 80,000 ducats to the bank each month to cover the interest and other charges of management. There was a crisis of confidence in 1630–1 (the result of plague, famine and war in northern Italy) with the *partite* circulating at only 70 per cent of their face value, but the government took the appropriate remedial action and redeemed a large number of bonds until the debt funded at the Giro was reduced to 1 million ducats. The *partite* recovered and retained their premium of 20 per cent for the rest of the century.

The success of the Giro Bank in the public sector encouraged private investors to make use of it, even though at first individuals could make deposits only if they took the money they wished to invest to the state treasury, paid it in there and presented the receipt to the Giro which would then (and only then) issue *partite*. Once an account had been opened in this circuitous way, credit transfers and withdrawals were possible, all in *partite*, and the Giro became so popular that the Rialto Bank lost almost all its business and had to be closed (1638). In 1666 the Giro's role as a bank for ordinary customers was regularised and direct deposits in cash were allowed. About 500,000 ducats were paid in almost at once.

Yet another type of funded debt, completely different from the Italian variety, was developed in the North Netherlands. Although a major public bank existed after 1609 (the Amsterdam *Wisselbank*), it was never used to bolster public credit like the Giro Bank or the later Bank of England (except that after 1624 short-term loans were sometimes made – in complete secrecy – to the Amsterdam corporation). The key to the healthy public credit of the United Provinces lay in the fact that the chief investors ran the government. After 1572, the local estates of each province in revolt against Spain took over responsibility for raising money to pay for the war, the total liability of each province being fixed by the general assembly of all the provinces, the States-General, in their annual estimate of expenditure (the *Staat van Oorlog* or War Establishment). Since the Dutch estates, provincial and general, were made up largely of delegates from the governments of the main towns, and since the towns provided most of the money required for war, it was only natural that the Republic should choose to finance its government by adopting the methods traditionally used by the towns. The estates imposed new indirect taxes (above all excise duties on foodstuffs and other essential goods) and sold life and redeemable annuities in return for cash. The heavy interest charge which the latter imposed was absorbed in the seventeenth century by the expansion in the Dutch population and by the fabulous bonanza in the Republic's trade and industry after 1590, which served to increase the revenues of most towns.

The path of victory was not easy, however. The Dutch did not acquire their awesome financial power in a day. One of the first acts of the States of Holland after their revolt in 1572 was to suspend indefinitely all interest payments on the existing annuities issued in their name. Payments were only resumed in full in 1586. The papers of Johan van Oldenbarneveldt, the leader of the States of Holland, reveal that even the richest province in the Republic continued to experience some difficulty in raising its full quota of taxes and loans until a truce was arranged with Spain in 1607. After this agreement, the Republic's finances quickly improved. Expenditure was reduced and all short-term debts were converted into annuities. The increase in economic activity and the profits of Dutch enterprise caused a flood of money into the Republic which allowed interest rates on government loans to be reduced from 10 per cent in the 1600s by stages to $6\frac{1}{2}$ per cent in the 1630s. In 1640 the official rate was lowered by the States of Holland to 5 per cent and in 1655 to 4 per cent. The last reduction alone diminished the total annual interest payable on Holland's state debt from 7 to 5·8 million florins. Remarkable to relate, each lowering of the rate of interest was decreed voluntarily by the States themselves – that is, by the principal investors in public funds who thus placed patriotic duty (reducing the cost of the public debt) before private profit (maximising investment yields). Patriotism could not brook many further reductions however, and in 1664 and 1667 the States rejected a proposal to lower interest on the debt to 3 per cent. In 1672 a rate of $3\frac{3}{4}$ per cent was agreed under protest, but Louis XIV's invasion later that year prevented the measure from ever taking effect.

The Dutch were not only able to borrow more cheaply than any other government in the seventeenth century (except, for a time, Genoa); they were also able to borrow more. In 1651, at the end of the long war with Spain, the funded debt of the province of Holland alone stood at

140 million florins (mainly in the form of annuities), and there was an additional 13 million incurred by the sale of short-term bonds or debentures (called *obligatiën* like the bonds of the Dutch East India Company). These *obligatiën*, issued above all in wartime, were redeemable at par in cash at all times, although they normally circulated at a premium of between 5 and 7 per cent. There was complete confidence in Dutch public credit. In 1655 a 'Sinking Fund' was established by the States to liquidate part of the public debt, especially the *obligatiën*, but this move was not at all popular with investors since, according to the English ambassador, Sir William Temple: 'When they [the Dutch government] pay off any part of the Principal, those, it belongs to, receive it with Tears, not knowing how to dispose of it to Interest, with such Safety and Ease.' What a contrast with Spain, France and England where the government's creditors would have shed tears of joy to have their money safely returned!

Still, England and France at least were learning some of the techniques of modern finance in the later seventeenth century. Despite the disasters of the *Grand Parti* and the debt repudiation of 1599, the French crown continued to raise long-term loans by selling *rentes* (annuities) guaranteed by the Paris corporation. This was of course inadequate in wartime. In order to finance the almost continuous hostilities, domestic and foreign, which plagued the kingdom from 1619 until 1659, the government solicited short-term loans on all sides (mainly from tax-collectors or large money-lenders) and increased taxes remorselessly to pay for the loans. As in Spain the reckless, unplanned escalation of public expenditure produced serious protests among the tax-payers (with widespread popular revolts, urban and rural, after 1623) and led eventually to a state 'bankruptcy': in November 1648 the French government declared a moratorium on all payments due, froze the capital of all outstanding loans and reduced the interest payable on them from 15 per cent to 6. The decade which followed was a time of almost unbelievable financial chaos and corruption. Instead of openly paying the financiers the 30, 40 or 50 per cent interest which they demanded for their loans, the treasury clerks systematically falsified their accounts (with the full knowledge and approbation of the *surintendant des finances*, Nicholas Fouquet) in order to give lenders their profit without risk of being accused of usury. Often the financiers themselves managed to secure (by purchase) a post in the audit office of the treasury, thus making control of their real interest charges quite impossible. The plunder of the treasury reached such a scale that in 1657 only 20,000 *livres* in cash, out of a total disposable revenue of 42,000,000, actually reached the central coffers.

Only when the Peace of the Pyrenees was signed (1659) could this chaotic structure be reformed. The architect of reconstruction was Louis XIV's principal adviser, Jean-Baptiste Colbert. First a drastic reduction in expenditure was decreed, then taxes were lowered until they would produce just enough to cover essential outgoings. From 1662 until 1671 the French budget was in surplus – the first time since 1610 and the last until after 1789! Even during a major war (1672–8) Colbert refused to raise taxation above 100 million *livres* for fear of its effect on trade. Instead he borrowed. Louis XIV's credit was good at the time thanks to another aspect of the retrenchment of the 1660s. Through forcible conversion and consolidation of some debts and through redemption of others, Colbert reduced the service-charge on the ancient annuities (*rentes*) from 52 million *livres* to 8 million. Then in 1671 he introduced a new issue of *rentes* at 7 per cent which could be cashed for their face value at any time on demand. Interest was paid regularly. In 1674 Colbert established the *caisse des emprunts*, a state deposit bank where private persons could place their money for safe keeping. The depositor received a written certificate (a *promesse de la caisse des emprunts*) for his money, which, since it was payable on demand, soon became fully negotiable and so passed into use as a popular instrument of credit. The deposits themselves earned interest of 5 per cent per year.

Colbert's reforms attracted considerable notice both at home and abroad, and foreign capital flowed into France throughout the 1670s, despite the war. Indeed foreign funds provided the vital reserves which sustained Louis XIV's armies against his enemies. In all, the *caisse des emprunts* received deposits worth 263 million *livres* between 1674 and 1683, and it paid out 227 million. This took place at virtually no cost to the crown and above all without assigning any source of income ·in advance. The tax-collectors and other financiers were no longer needed to mobilise capital for the crown, although Colbert still had to introduce some new expedients, like a stamp duty on paper (the *papier timbré* which provoked a dangerous revolt in Brittany in 1675), during the war-years.

Unfortunately for the health of French finances, Colbert died in 1683. Since Louis XIV rather disdained his minister's professional, 'bourgeois' approach to treasury affairs, and in any case had a strong preference for loans which were repayable at his own pleasure and not when the borrower chose to withdraw his funds, the *caisse des emprunts* was closed down. When war began again in 1689 the king had no alternative but to decree crippling increases in taxation and to seek costly anticipations from the tax-collectors in the time-honoured manner. The only exception occurred between 1701 and 1709 when ·a group of inter-national bankers, notably Samuel Bernard, acquired a preponderance thanks to their ability to anticipate taxes and transfer the proceeds direct to the French armies abroad. Under their auspices, 4 to 5 million *livres* left France every month in the climactic years 1704–8 to refuel the king's forces in Italy, Germany and the Netherlands. In the end, the effort proved too great: Samuel Bernard went bankrupt in 1709.

Louis XIV's borrowing was on an unprecedented scale. In September 1715, the month of his death, the public debt stood at almost 3,000,000,000 *livres*: 2 billion in *rentes* (annuities) costing 86 million in interest every year, 922 million more in floating debt, also bearing interest. To meet these charges there was nothing in the Treasury. The king's revenues, which amounted in theory to 80 million *livres*, were alienated three full years ahead. The only apparent remedy was an enforced reduction of the interest on the debt to 4 per cent, the compulsory consolidation of the floating debt (thus freeing the sources of income pledged in advance to repay the loans) and, where possible, the repudiation of obligations of a dubious or usurious nature (in fact one-fifth of the total debt was written off in this way). This ruthless operation to liquidate the inglorious inheritance of the Sun King was carried out quickly and efficiently in the course of 1716 by a secret committee known as the *Visa*. At the same time the law courts brought to trial about 8,000 persons who had been involved in some way with the finances of the late king's reign: over half of them were convicted and either fined or condemned (to death, prison or the galleys) for fraud and malversation. In this way the personnel of the royal treasury and the structure of its finances were brutally purged and re-organised. But even these draconian measures did nothing to restore the credit and confidence which the state could command on the money market. Here France was at a serious disadvantage throughout the eighteenth century compared with England.

The attempts made in England to rationalise public finance began later than those of Colbert in France but they proved more permanent. The history of the treasury in the early seventeenth century gave little hope for improvement. There was, it seems, no arrangement at all for long-term lending to the crown until the 1690s, and so all borrowing had to be for short periods initially (although these were frequently prolonged) and the interest was correspondingly high. The budget was in almost constant deficit and even in the 1630s and 1680s, when current revenue slightly exceeded current expenditure, no progress was made towards repaying or consolidating the considerable floating debts accumulated in earlier years. Even direct government by Parliament achieved little more success: in 1659, the last full year of the English Republic, government expenditure was estimated at £2,200,000 and revenue at £1,870,000. This was merely the culmination of a series of deficit budgets bridged by prodigal land sales (after the model of the Tudor and Stuart monarchs), by heavy borrowing from the City (especially from the Goldsmiths) and by defaulting on obligations. The public debt in 1659 stood at £2,000,000. As Secretary Thurloe wrote: 'The great want is money, which puts us to the wall in all our business.' By then the Republican government was probably doomed whatever happened to the Protector and his family.

Financially speaking, Charles II was hardly more successful. His budgets, like those of his predecessors, were always in deficit; but there were some constructive attempts to find a solution. A step in the right direction was to abandon the practice of farming the major taxes: direct collection of the customs was resumed in 1671, of the excise in 1683, of the hearth tax in 1684. More promising still, in 1665 a new instrument of credit was introduced: the 'orders of payment', issued by government departments to their creditors in place of cash. The orders constituted a promise by the Treasury to pay a certain sum at a certain date, together (in many cases) with accrued interest. It was possible to assign the orders to a third party (by endorsement) and they were therefore accepted as deposits and payments by the London goldsmith bankers. This scheme, the brain-child of Sir George Downing (Secretary to the Treasury and former ambassador in Holland), was based on a technique of public finance perfected by the Dutch. It was perfectly sound in intention. Trouble only arose at the end of 1671 when there was a panic in the City and all those who held orders of payment seethed around the Treasury demanding immediate reimbursement in cash. The total sum involved was £2,250,000 and the government could not pay. The only solution was to suspend payments (as the goldsmiths themselves had done during the 'run' of 1667) and so on 18 December 1671 the king decreed a moratorium on all the orders not specifically repayable from a fixed future revenue. This move, known as the 'Stop of the Exchequer', affected orders worth about £1,300,000 and it had particularly serious consequences for the handful of leading goldsmith bankers who held almost all the frozen credits. Some of them failed in consequence. Only in 1677 did the bankers reach an agreement with the king by which, although their capital remained frozen, interest of 6 per cent was paid on it.

This clumsy and forcible debt conversion did little to improve the crown's credit. After Charles II's death in 1685 interest payments were suspended and the debt was only officially recognised again in 1705 (when the government promised to pay interest of 3 per cent 'for ever'; even then the principal was never returned). This was a poor precedent for building up a national debt, yet the war which began with France in 1689 made it necessary to borrow large sums to pay the forces overseas. It became desperately important to set public finance on a surer footing.

Even under William III progress towards the 'financial revolution' was surprisingly slow. The king was often absent and, despite his knowledge of Dutch techniques of debt management, he provided little coherent advice. In addition, his ministers were maladroit and inexperienced while the House of Commons had an excessive mistrust of the new ministry and of any financial innovation. Everyone refused to recognise that the war would be long and expensive and that its cost would have to be spread. King William's war was therefore financed by expedients not unlike those of the 1650s. Taxation was increased as much as possible and the proceeds were anticipated by short-term loans. Between 1689 and 1702, government expenditure totalled £72 million, of which £63 million came from taxation and anticipations and only £7 million – under 10 per cent – from long-term loans. The first of these 'perpetual' loans was floated in January 1693 guaranteed by Parliament: £1,000,000 was to be raised by selling life annuities, the annual payments secured on the yield of certain excise duties for the next ninety-nine years. The subscription did not go well (the million had still not been collected a year later) but the life-annuity fund of 1693 did set a crucial precedent. It introduced for the first time the principle of government long-term borrowing into England. Parliament at last recognised that the loan was going to be prolonged (it was called 'a Fund of perpetual Interest') and further long-term loans followed in 1694. In March a lottery was launched to raise £1,000,000 and in April a loan of £1,200,000 was invited at 8 per cent, the subscribers to become incorporated as a joint-stock company entitled 'The Governor and Company of the Banke of England'. This proved to be a great success. The loan was fully subscribed within eleven days and the newly constituted bank went on to raise more loans for the government over and above its original sum. The Bank also agreed to redeem all Exchequer tallies (orders for payment of government debt) presented to it, and it allowed the treasury to issue the Bank's own 'sealed bills' (promissory notes) to pay its debts. After 1697 the Bank also accepted government credit notes as deposits and as subscriptions to new public loans (an operation which almost ruined the Bank but saved the government's credit). The Bank of England's activity as an agent for raising long-term loans carried the ministers of William III through to the Peace of Rijswijk in September 1697.

The English government's financial position proved to be somewhat stronger in the next war which broke out in 1702 and lasted until 1713. First there was a new sovereign: Queen Anne was easier to manage than her predecessor and she found the House of Commons more co-operative and better informed in financial matters. Above all the treasury was now in capable hands: Sidney Lord Godolphin, Lord Treasurer (1702–10), and William Lowndes, the Secretary to the Treasury (1695–1725), were sound and shrewd men who commanded the confidence of the City businessmen and of the Commons. Their financial skill underpinned the great victories of Marlborough and won the admiration of Europe, for Godolphin raised long-term loans worth £8,000,000 between 1704 and 1708 at only 6½ per cent. In all, total government expenditure during the war-years 1702–13 totalled £93,600,000, of which £64,200,000 came from taxation and £29,400,000 (some 31 per cent of the total) by borrowing.

After 1709, however, the government again ran into trouble. Without new victories, and following the long winter and food-shortage of 1708–9, interest rates began to rise and in 1710 a new lottery (the first since 1694) was launched to raise the funds needed for the war. (The proceeds of this lottery were handled by the Bank of England – its first experience as a receiver of public money.) The expedient did not prove particularly happy however, although a new lottery was floated every year until 1714 to raise war-funds. Government paper obligations circulated at an increasing discount and the ministry was defeated in the Parliamentary elections of November 1710.

It was to prevent further depreciation of government stock that Queen Anne's new ministry under Edward Harley decided to create a permanent, guaranteed funded debt, to be quite separate from the Bank of England. In June 1711, therefore, all holders of government short-term obligations automatically became shareholders in a new company, the 'South Sea Company'. Almost £9,000,000 of government paper obligations were affected. Although the company did actually trade to the South Seas (sc. Spanish America) until 1748, its principal purpose was to effect the consolidation of the government's floating debt into a unified, permanent fund. The company had to accept government obligations at face value as deposits to purchase its stock, and stock in the new company was used by the government to pay its creditors and to secure its borrowing.

This intelligent move enabled Britain to emerge from the Peace of Utrecht in 1713 with her credit virtually intact, even though her public debt was enormous. Long-term commitments, some of them secured on revenues up to the 1790s, amounted to £35,000,000 (£10,600,000 in annuities, £11,700,000 in lottery stake money and £10,900,000 in short-term loans funded by the Bank of England in 1697 and by the South Sea Company after 1711) and there were further short-term obligations and debts totalling over £5 million. All bore interest of 6 per cent, a charge of more than £2,500,000 annually. In 1717 the government decided to take steps to reduce this drain on the revenues. A large part of the long-term debt – in fact mainly the Lottery money – was 'consolidated' into a new fund of stock yielding 5 per cent and managed by the Bank of England. The saving in interest charges was to be applied to reducing the overall debt (the 'Sinking Fund') while a separate 'General Fund' was established to pay interest on the newly-constituted stock.

It was the act of a self-confident and competent government. The funding operation of 1717 bore all the hall-marks of a mature financial system. This maturity was also reflected in the sophisticated dealing in government securities which grew up by the side of the existing market in company stocks and shares. And yet the new methods were still very imperfectly understood and precariously rooted in London and the other financial centres of western Europe. The instability of it all was amply demonstrated by the dramatic events which rocked money markets all over Europe in 1719 and 1720 in the first financial crisis of modern times. This catastrophe, as spectacular as the boom and crash in shares during the 1920s, has passed into history as the 'South Sea Bubble'.

CRISIS AND RECONSTRUCTION: THE GREAT CRASH OF 1720 AND BEYOND

The 'Bubble' began in France. Louis XIV's wars, which had swollen the state debt to almost 3 billion *livres*, also caused a massive flight of currency and capital from the country. This, combined with a run of bad harvests and crippling taxation, served to paralyse almost every sector of the French economy. To cap it all, the king died on 1 September 1715 leaving a child of only five years to succeed him. It was a delicate situation, but the new regent, the duke of Orleans, was not dismayed. He turned for advice on how to reactivate the economy to a little-known Scottish exile, John Law. In 1718 and 1719 Law was allowed to establish a complete economic 'system', based on the union of three important state monopolies: a bank which issued notes (the *Banque Royale*), an overseas trading company (the *Compagnie des Indes*) and a collection centre for the yield of indirect taxes (the *Ferme générale des impôts*). The 'system' thus far was basically sound. The only dubious aspect was the over-issue of notes by the *Banque Royale* – notes worth over a billion *livres* were put into circulation in 1719–20 – but there was a real demand for the notes, thanks to the fall in the amount of coin actually circulating in France, and in any case Law's bank, like his trading company, was guaranteed by the yield of the revenues he farmed.

The fatal flaw only appeared in October 1719 when, on top of all his other schemes, Law began to help the government to consolidate its debts. From that date he agreed to accept government securities at their face value as payments towards the cost of a share in his *Compagnie des Indes*. No one holding a government obligation was *forced* to exchange it for company stock, but since almost all paper obligations were worth less than half their face value on the open market, most holders were eager to use them to buy Indies stock where they were accepted at par. As Law had hoped, the rush to buy his stock increased its market price, and the capital gains made by early investors encouraged others to do the same. Even Law had not anticipated the scale of demand, however. Although he created new shares in his company in response to the mounting pressure, the market price of a 500 *livre* share had risen to 18,000 *livres* in January 1720 – a capital appreciation of 3,600 per cent in four months! France's public debt was quickly reduced.

The success of Law's 'system' encouraged the British Parliament to endorse a similar scheme to reduce the public debt. There was already the equivalent of the *Compagnie des Indes* to hand, the South Sea Company, and the government decided to use it to reduce the burden of the long-term annuities created during the war years but unaffected by the consolidating operation of 1717. These annuities represented a capital of £10,600,000, some of them payable until 1808. By the South Sea Act of March 1720 holders of the annuities were to be offered the opportunity of exchanging their investment for a pre-arranged capital sum in the form of South Sea stock. As in France there was to be no compulsion, but the government was confident that the prospect of a rapid appreciation in the price of the stock in addition to payment of dividends would prove more attractive than holding on to the old annuities. Those who accepted the offer would gain more from their original investment, while the state would offload some of the burden of debt without breaking faith with its creditors.

As in France, the response was astonishing. Within a year 80 per cent of the annuities and 85 per cent of other government interest-bearing securities had been converted into South Sea stock. The nominal capital of the company, which stood at £11·7 million in 1719, increased by a massive £26 million during 1720, the government paying interest of 5 per cent to the company for this new transferred public debt. The annuities had cost up to 14 per cent. For the investor, the attraction of exchanging securities for stock lay, as with the parallel French operation, in the rapid increase in the price of the company's stock. On 1 January 1720 it was quoted at 128; on 1 July at 950.

The rise in the South Sea Company's shares encouraged a general stock market boom. A mania for speculation in shares gripped London and spread to Paris, Amsterdam and other European capitals. New companies were floated, some of them obvious swindles although they found gullible subscribers, while existing companies lent money to their shareholders who wished to buy more stock, accepting their own stock as security. Even the Bank of England lent £1 million and more in this highly dangerous way. Land prices too began to climb dramatically as the newly rich investors (including many South Sea Company directors) bought up landed estates at almost any price.

The boom leader was always South Sea stock. Even the hard-headed capitalists of Holland and the Swiss cantons opened their purses to buy the shares of the English growth company (as late as 1723, 587 Dutch investors held £1,560,000 of South Sea stock while 216 Swiss held a further £564,178). The mania was not long in striking the Netherlands itself. In May 1720 the States-General considered creating a company like Law's or the South Sea to reduce the public debt, while 40 new project-companies were advertised in Amsterdam between June and October attracting 'hot money' from home and abroad. Similar speculation was reported from Geneva, Vienna and Hamburg, while a 'Brazil Bubble' was announced from Lisbon in the autumn. No part of western Europe seemed to escape the itch to speculate in stock. Even a financial backwater like Ulster was drained of cash as everyone with money to hand sent it to the London exchange. In July 1720, at the height of the boom, an observer in London lamented the folly of the masses, with 'the world crammed into Change Alley'. It did not last long. By August the masses were cramming the Exchange to demand their money back. The bottom had suddenly fallen out of the market.

The crash, like the boom, began in Paris. The *Compagnie des Indes* declared a derisory dividend of 2 per cent in spring 1720. It was the first warning sign: many sold their holdings at this point, collecting money by the carriage-load from the company's headquarters in the rue Quincampoix, often re-investing the gains in the London or Amsterdam 'Bubbles'. Selling increased in May and Law only managed to prevent a catastrophic fall in share prices by buying up stock himself. In the late summer his efforts were overwhelmed by events in London. In August 1720 the British government suddenly tightened its control on speculative dealings in stock (the so-called 'Bubble Act' was rushed through Parliament) and at exactly the same time, by some coincidence, many investors (particularly the French and the Swiss) decided to sell their holdings and realise their gains (once more partly with the intention of re-investing, this time in the newly-floated Dutch companies). These two independent but simultaneous movements proved fatal to the 'Bubble'. As soon as the price of the 'wonder stock' began to fall, investors clamoured to sell their holdings with the same rash insistence with which they had bought them a few months before. The Great Crash began. The South Sea Company's stock fell from 775 points on the Stock Exchange Index on 1 September to 520 a fortnight later and to 170 on 14 October. At the same time Bank of England stock fell from 227 points on 1 September to 135 on

14 October, East India stock from 345 to 145, African Company stock from 130 to 40.

These events quickly triggered off similar falls in share prices in other financial centres. In Paris the stock of the *Compagnie des Indes* became almost worthless and in October 1720 the notes of the *Banque Royale* ceased to be legal tender. In Amsterdam the new companies crashed; their shareholders were ruined. Coins virtually disappeared from circulation: in London they could only be borrowed at 5 per cent *per month*, while in Ireland ordinary commerce was practically reduced to barter for lack of currency.

The first stock market crash of modern times provided a graphic demonstration of the fragility of the new financial edifice. Reckless euphoria gave way with disturbing rapidity to panic and fears of revolution. Britain had a new monarch of questionable title; France a king only ten years old. In both countries a shaky government had to face public hostility and frustration of unusual intensity. Many observers believed that organised revolt would have been the unavoidable consequence of the ruinous crash but for the self-interest and avarice of the injured parties, who were too busy trying to salvage their own investments to combine with others to subvert the state.

Yet the resilience of the new financial techniques soon appeared. In Holland, France and Britain hard-headed ministers and financiers put through draconian but effective measures to liquidate the inheritance of the 'Bubble Year'. In the United Provinces the retrenchment was simplest because speculative activity there had begun later and finished earlier than elsewhere. The few speculative companies floated in 1720 which had survived the crash were quickly liquidated. In France, John Law fled in December 1720 as a treasury committee of enquiry (known as the second *Visa*) was established to clear up the tangled affairs of his bank, his *Compagnie des Indes* and the mass of paper obligations he had created. First, both organisations were dissolved. France was without a central bank until 1776, and the new *Compagnie des Indes* formed in 1723 had little to do with public finance. Then the *Visa* called in all paper credits and banknotes for compulsory conversion. It was estimated that obligations worth 4,000,000,000 *livres* were in circulation by the end of 1720, but in fact only 2,450,000,000 *livres* were presented to the *Visa* (almost all issued by the late *Banque*). The *Visa* repudiated over 500,000,000 *livres* of this total, and declared all obligations not presented to be void. The approved remainder, 1,640,000,000 *livres*, was converted into government stock at 2 or $2\frac{1}{2}$ per cent interest, an annual charge of only 47,000,000. So France reduced her public debt to manageable proportions, but at an absurdly high price: the memory of the 'system' and of the savings and fortunes lost in the crash scarred French finances for the rest of the eighteenth century, preventing all moves to establish a national bank of issue and discouraging foreign investors from placing their money in French government funds.

In Britain the problems created by the 'Bubble' were equally serious, but the solutions adopted were less savage and, in the long term, more successful. As in Holland, almost all the mushroom speculative companies disappeared by themselves as stock prices crashed. The South Sea Company, however, involved far too much money and far too many people to be simply left to die. Apart from the stock created since the first funding operation in 1711, it was estimated in 1721 that the Company owed £14,000,000 to shareholders and others in sundry claims for dividends, goods supplied, loans and bonds. Against this, the company could lay claim to no less than £80,000,000 owed by people who had bought, or who had promised to buy, stock or bonds but had not yet paid in full. After prolonged debate, Parliament decided in August 1721 to reduce the debts of the company to £8,000,000 by itself taking over liability for the rest. The next step came in October 1722 when the Bank of England was persuaded to take over a further £4,200,000 of South Sea stock, paying cash for it. This stock (which was originally, it will be recalled, government annuities) was to earn 5 per cent interest, paid by the government. The South Sea Company's capital was now reduced to just under £34,000,000 and at the same time the sale of the extra stock to the Bank gave the new Directors some cash which could be used to resume the company's trading operations with Spanish America. In January 1723 South Sea stock was quoted at par for the first time since the crash. In June 1723 it was decided to separate investments seeking a speculative profit from those in search only of a secure income by dividing the company's capital into halves. Half was made into a 'gilt-edged', fixed-interest stock managed by the company, known as the 'South Sea Annuities'; the other half remained as the company's trading capital which was invested for profit and yielded fluctuating dividends.

These measures, together with the proceeds of the fines and confiscations exacted from the company's pre-1720 Directors (which were used to compensate shareholders) substantially reduced the losses of those who had purchased South Sea stock. All the same, those who had bought shares during the boom forfeited almost all their capital outlay, while those who had exchanged their government annuities for South Sea stock lost between 25 and 50 per cent of the annual yield of their original investment. While it is true that the government gained financially by the misfortunes of these investors (the capital and interest of the National Debt were much reduced), as in France the price paid was unacceptably high. Government creditors were ruined or severely impoverished; the government's trustworthiness was temporarily impaired. The South Sea experiment may have been honourable in intention, but its consequences were not significantly different from the state bankruptcies decreed by the Spanish Habsburgs.

But at least the 'Bubble' taught British ministers and merchants a constructive lesson which they never forgot. Never again did the public debt become the plaything of politicians. Interest was paid regularly and promptly thereafter on all government debts, and the restoration of confidence in the public sector helped private investment to regain some of its natural buoyancy. By the 1730s the stock market was again functioning smoothly, and prices were virtually back to their pre-Bubble levels. Thanks to the skill and rectitude of Sir Robert Walpole, holders of English government obligations soon became as reluctant to have them repaid as the holders of Dutch state bonds. Walpole himself was able to write in 1735:

'The high state of Credit, the low rate of Interest of money, and the advanced price of the publick Stocks and Funds above Par, made the great monied Companies and all their Proprietors [sc. shareholders], apprehend nothing more than the being oblig'd to receive their Principal too fast; and it became almost the universal consent of Mankind, that a Million a year was as much as the Creditors of the Publick could bear to receive, in discharge of part of their Principal.'

Even South Sea stock, yielding a steady interest of 4 per cent, was at a premium after 1730! Times had indeed changed.

Such indomitable confidence was, admittedly, far from typical. The prevailing financial condition of most of Europe in the early eighteenth century was very different. In many areas, even in 1730, barter remained the most common commercial arrangement, small transient partnerships and individual enterprises continued to dominate the private sector, and public finance was still confined within the straitjacket of anticipations and tax-farming. But the fact remained that in the north-western corner of Europe a new system of interlocking credit, investment and public finance had been created, a system which was strong enough to survive even a crisis like 1720. Modern finance, the essential prerequisite of industrialisation, had emerged at last.

Bibliography

There is, to my knowledge, no study of the European 'financial revolution' as a whole. The pioneering survey of Richard Ehrenberg, *Das Zeitalter der Fugger: Geldkapital und Creditverkehr im 16. Jahrhundert* (2 vols., Jena, 1896; heavily abridged English translation, *Capital and Finance in the Age of the Renaissance*, London, 1928; more complete French translation, *Le Siècle des Fugger*, Paris, 1955), has never been followed up. Instead the available literature tends to deal only with specific problems or specific countries.

PRIVATE FINANCE: On the growth of private borrowing there is the book of B. Schnapper, *Les rentes au XVIe siècle. Histoire d'un instrument de crédit* (Paris, 1957); the introduction of R. H. Tawney to Thomas Wilson, *A discourse upon usury* (*1572*) (London, 1925; reprinted 1962); and the article of B. Bennassar, 'En Vieille Castille: les ventes de Rentes perpétuelles', *Annales E.S.C.*, XV (1960), 1115–26. There is a good general outline of the growth of the *monti di pietà* by Henri Lapèyre, 'Banque et crédit en Italie du XVIe au XVIIIe siècle', *Revue d'Histoire moderne et contemporaine*, VIII (1961), 211–26; while the magisterial study of Brian Pullan, *Rich and Poor in Renaissance Venice* (Oxford, 1971) has an important section devoted to the various forms of credit available to the poor in the Venetian Republic (Part III). On the 'revolution in interest rates' see C. M. Cipolla, 'Note sulla storia del saggio d'interesse', *Economia Internazionale*, V (1952), 2–18.

There are a number of good studies of banking in the early modern period, most of them based upon the extant archives of the banks themselves. There is an excellent introduction to the character of banking at this time by Raymond de Roover, 'New interpretations of the history of banking', *Journal of World History*, IV (1954), 38–76. This may be followed by the wide-ranging survey of R. D.

Richards, *The early history of banking in England* (London, 1929) and the valuable essays on individual banks in J. G. van Dillen (ed.), *History of the principal public banks* (The Hague, 1934).

The history of bills of exchange, negotiability and clearing operations is also well covered. Again the best introduction is by R. de Roover, *L'évolution de la lettre de change du XIVe au XVIIIe siècle* (Paris, 1953). For the development of 'dry exchange' in Italy there is G. Mandich, *Le Pacte de Ricorsa et le marché italien des changes au XVIIe siècle* (Paris, 1953). For England, see J. M. Holden, *The history of negotiable instruments in English Law* (London, 1955); for the Netherlands see Hermann van der Wee, 'Anvers et les innovations de la technique financière aux XVIe et XVIIe siècles', *Annales. E.S.C.*, XXII (1967), 1067–89, and 'Antwerpen's bijdragen tot de ontwikkeling van de moderne geld en bank-techniek', *Tijdschrift voor Economie*, X (1965), 488–500. There is an important study of the international clearing system in about 1600: J. Gentil da Silva, *Banque et crédit en Italie au XVIIe siècle* (2 vols., Paris, 1969). For the situation a century later, see J. Sperling, 'The international payments mechanism in the seventeenth and eighteenth centuries', *Economic History Review*, XIV (1962), 446–68.

The methods used by merchants and firms to raise capital are less well known. There are some perceptive general remarks in the excellent handbook of Pierre Jeannin, *Les marchands au XVIe siècle* (Bourges, 1957), and for Britain there is the exhaustive compendium of W. R. Scott, *The constitution and finance of English, Scottish and Irish Joint-Stock companies to 1720* (3 vols., London, 1912–13). Interesting information on the financing of Dutch trade is contained in V. Barbour, *Capitalism in Amsterdam in the Seventeenth Century* (Baltimore, 1950) and E. Baasch, *Holländische Wirtschaftsgeschichte* (Jena, 1927). For the south Netherlands in the sixteenth century there is the massive study of H. Van Der Wee, *The Growth of the Antwerp market and the European Economy, 14th to 16th centuries* (3 vols., Louvain, 1963). Beyond this, there are some outstanding studies of individual firms and their financial organisation, for example:

W. Brulez, *De firma Della Faille en de internationale handel van Vlaamse firma's in de 16é eeuw* (Brussels, 1959 – with a long French *résumé*) and H. Lapèyre, *Une famille des marchands – les Ruiz* (Paris, 1955). On the beginnings of the stock-exchange in Holland and England, see Charles Wilson, *Anglo-Dutch commerce and finance in the eighteenth century* (Cambridge, 1941; reprinted 1966); J. G. van Dillen, 'Isaac Le Maire et le commerce des actions de la compagnie des Indes Orientales', *Revue d'Histoire moderne*, X (1935), 5–21 and 121–37; and K. G. Davies, 'Joint-stock investment in the later seventeenth century', *Economic History Review*, IV (1952 – reprinted in E. Carus-Wilson, ed., *Essays in Economic History*, II, London, 1962, 273–90). A contemporary account of the stock-dealing in Amsterdam is also worth consulting: Joseph de la Vega, *Confusión de confusiones: diálogos curiosos entre un philósopho agudo, un mercader discreto, y un accionista erúdito, descriviendo el Negocio de las Acciones* (Amsterdam, 1688; facsimile edition, Madrid 1958; heavily abridged English edition, with a useful introduction by H. Kellenbenz, Boston, Mass., 1957).

PUBLIC FINANCE: Studies of public finance during this period are less common and tend to be tightly confined within national boundaries. Easily the best study of its kind is P. G. M. Dickson, *The Financial Revolution in England: a study in the development of Public Credit, 1688–1756* (London, 1967). An earlier phase of English public borrowing is ably described by R. Ashton, *The crown and the money market, 1603–1640* (Oxford, 1960).

The finances of several leading states of Italy are still somewhat obscure, but for Naples there is the admirable volume of G. Coniglio, *Il viceregno di Napoli nel secolo XVII: notizie sulla vita commerciale e finanziaria secondo nuove ricerche negli archivi italiani e spagnuoli* (Rome, 1955 – see pp. 125–323 for public finance); on the papal states there are numerous references in the vast work of J. Delumeau, *Vie économique et sociale de Rome dans la seconde moitié du XVIe siècle* (2 vols., Paris, 1957–9); for Venice there is only the somewhat antiquated F. Besta, *Bilanci generali della Repubblica di Venezia*

(Milan, 1912 – a number of documents illustrative of Venetian public finance together with a commentary).

Spain has fared rather better with the important articles of F. Ruiz Martín, 'Las finanzas españolas durante el reinado de Felipe II', *Cuadernos de Historia; anexos de la revista Hispania*, 2 (Madrid, 1968), 109–73, and 'Los hombres de negocios genoveses de España durante el signo XVI', in H. Kellenbenz (ed.), *Fremde Kaufleute auf den Iberischen Halbinsel* (Cologne, 1970), 84–99. There are also two excellent articles by A. Castillo, 'Los juros de Castilla: apogeo y fin de un instrumento de crédito', *Hispania*, XXIII (1963), 43–70, and 'Dette flottante et dette consolidée en Espagne, 1557–1600', *Annales, E.S.C.*, XVIII (1963), 745–59. For the earlier period, see the definitive study of Ramon Carande, *Carlos V y sus banqueros* (3 vols., Madrid, 1949–67 – 2nd edn. for the first volume).

The history of public finance in modern France is dealt with competently by M. Marion, *Histoire financière de la France depuis 1715* (6 vols., Paris, 1914; cf. vol. I). There are detailed studies of important earlier periods and problems by R. Doucet, 'Le Grand Parti de Lyon au XVIe siècle', *Revue Historique*, CLXXI (1933), 473–512, and CLXXII (1933), 1–41; by J. Dent, 'An aspect of the crisis of the seventeenth century: the collapse of the financial administration of the French Monarchy', *Economic History Review*, XX (1967), 241–56; and by L. Germain-Martin and M. Bezançon, *L'histoire du crédit en France sous le règne de Louis XIV* (Paris, 1913).

The finances of the Dutch Republic remain only imperfectly known. The works of J. G. Van Dillen, E. Baasch, V. Barbour and C. H. Wilson, cited above, cover only selected aspects of the question; so does D. Houtzager, *Hollands Lijf- en Losrenteleningen voor 1672* (Schiedam, 1950). There is a clear need for a thorough study like Dr Dickson's on England, which will reveal the financial power and organisation which enabled the United Provinces to rise to an unprecedented pinnacle of prosperity despite crushing and continuous taxation for war.

Finally on the 'Great Crash', the best account for England, again, is P. G. M. Dickson, *The Financial Revolution in England*; for France, H. Luethy, *La Banque protestante en France de la Révocation de l'Edit de Nantes à la Révolution* (vol. I, Paris, 1959); for the Low Countries, F. Ph. Groeneveld, *De economische crisis van het jaar 1720* (Groningen, 1940).

Statistical tables to *Rural Europe 1500-1750* ALDO DE MADDALENA (pp. 273-353)

TABLE I: Northern Europe
Yield ratios for cereals (seed sown = I)

Years	Country or district	Wheat	Rye	Barley	Oats	Notes
16th cent.	Northern Europe in general	3·5				General Average
1540-41	Wolfenbüttel, South Hanover, Germany	6·5	7·2	6·6	5·2	Averages
1540-41	Wickensen, South Hanover, Germany	3·6	6·1	5·6	2·3	,,
1546	Falster, Denmark		2·4	2·0	1·5	,,
1550-1600	Germany, France, Denmark, Sweden (general)	3·5				General average
1549-64	Near Weimar, Germany	4·4	4·5	5·5	5·3	Averages
1552-57	Schmatzfeld Harz Germany	3·5	3·7	4·6	3·9	,,
1571	Ostra, Dresden, Germany	7·8	3·5	4·0	4·3	,,
1579-83	Wickensen, South Hanover, Germany	4·9	5·6	5·6	5·3	,,
1579-83	Gandersheim, South Hanover, Germany	5·5	5·5	5·9	5·5	,,
1579-90	Wolfenbüttel, South Hanover, Germany	6·2	6·5	7·2	6·2	,,
1581	Wobeck, Lower Saxony, Germany	4·5	3·8	4·1	4·6	,,
1582	North Zealand, Denmark		3·6	4·1	4·0	,,
1583	Folster, Denmark		2·0	3·6	1·0	,,
1595-99	Lucklum, South Hanover, Germany	3·6	4·1	4·6	4·6	,,
1600-99	Northern Europe in general	3·0-3·5				Most frequent averages

TABLE I

Years	Country or district	Wheat	Rye	Barley	Oats	Notes
1600–99	Ouges, Dijon, France	3·0 } 8·0				Averages on moderate soils / Averages on good soils
1600–06	Lucklum, South Hanover, Germany	2·6	3·6	5·3	3·6	Averages
1600–11	Wolfenbüttel, South Hanover, Germany	5·3	6·6	7·7	5·2	„
1601–02	Mariental, Lower Saxony, Germany	2·5	2·3	6·0	3·0	Averages (spring barley)
1602–09	Gandersheim, South Hanover, Germany	4·5	4·5	4·4	3·4	Averages
1604–06	Walkenried, Lower Saxony, Germany	4·0	2·0	5·5	2·5	„
1608–28	Bahrdorf, South Hanover, Germany	2·9	2·9	4·0	2·2	„
1610	Rundhorf, Schleswig Holstein, Germany	3·7	5·4	6·5	2·3	„
1610	Drillt, Schleswig Holstein, Germany		3·3	4·9	1·8	„
1610–39	Hagelhose, Scania, Sweden		2·2	3·2		„
1610–44	Boringe, Scania, Sweden		1·2	2·5		„
1610–44	Lindholm, Scania, Sweden		1·9	3·4		Averages
1610–59	All Denmark (43 estates)		1·0–2·4	1·5–3·4		Most frequent ratios
1611–37	Hagelose, Sweden		1·9	3·0	1·9	Averages
1612–22	Lucklum, South Hanover, Germany	3·9	5·1	3·6	3·1	„

TABLE I

Years	Country or district	Wheat	Rye	Barley	Oats	Notes
1613–23	Wickensen, South Hanover, Germany	2·9	1·9	2·8	2·5	Averages
1618	Near Nuremberg, Germany		7·9		4·7	,,
1619–32	Hagelöse, Sweden		1·7	2·6	1·9	,,
1619–39	Gandersheim, South Hanover, Germany	5·1	5·3	5·8	3·8	,,
1620–31	Wolfenbüttel, South Hanover, Germany	5·6	7·4	7·1	4·4	,,
1629–60	Søndringholm, Jutland, Denmark		3·4	3·1	2·4	,,
1631–33	Lohmen, Dresden, Germany	4·3	4·7	3·8	3·9	,,
1631–40	Lucklum, South Hanover, Germany	5·2	5·9	3·6	3·0	,,
1632–90	Hedeper, South Hanover, Germany	5·7	6·4	6·6	6·7	,,
1633–34	Selsø, Eskildsø, Zealand, Denmark	0·5	1·5	4·6	1·7	,,
1633–35	Koselan, Schleswig Holstein, Germany	6·6	3·4	5·0	2·8	,,
1634–44	Wickensen, South Hanover, Germany	2·7	3·7	2·7	2·1	,,
1635–45	Cismar, Oldenburg Holstein, Germany		4·2			,,
1635–53	Cismar, Oldenburg Holstein, Germany	5·4		5·8	3·5	,,
1637–48	Bahrdorf, South Hanover, Germany	1·4	2·3	1·6	2·3	,,
1638–53	Skovgaard, Jutland, Denmark		3·2	3·6	2·6	,,
1638–53	Körnick, Oldenburg Holstein, Germany		3·5	4·7		,,
1641–53	Körnick, Oldenburg Holstein, Germany	5·0				,,
1642–46	Near Luléa, Sweden			2·7		,,
1642–47	Lohmen, Dresden, Germany	3·4	5·8	5·4	3·3	,,
1643–61	Gessingholm, Jutland, Denmark		2·8	3·0	2·3	,,

TABLE I

Years	Country or district	Wheat	Rye	Barley	Oats	Notes
1644–59	Lucklum, South Hanover, Germany	2·9	2·3	5·2	4·5	Averages
1649–59	Gandersheim, South Hanover, Germany	7·1	4·7	5·8	5·0	,,
1650–61	Wolfenbüttel, South Hanover, Germany	6·5	5·4	6·9	5·4	,,
1651–53	Gorbitz, Dresden, Germany	4·5	4·7	4·6	3·3	,,
1653–55	Wickensen, South Hanover, Germany	5·2	3·5	3·7	3·2	,,
1658–64	Bahrdorf, South Hanover, Germany		3·9	3·5	1·9	,,
1660	Schmatzfeld, Harz, Germany		3·9	3·5	3·7	,,
1660–66	Lucklum, South Hanover, Germany	4·8	4·8	4·8	5·2	,,
1663	Gorbitz, Dresden, Germany	4·1	5·7	3·6	3·1	,,
1663–64	Wickensen, South Hanover, Germany	3·2	0·6	2·8	3·2	,,
1669–70	Lucklum, South Hanover, Germany	3·4	3·5	4·7	3·8	,,
1670	Schmatzfeld, Harz, Germany	4·4	5·2	4·8	5·2	,,
1670–82	Wolfenbüttel, South Hanover, Germany	6·2	5·1	6·9	7·1	,,
1673	Gorbitz, Dresden, Germany	3·8	4·5	5·9	5·2	,,
1680	Lohmen, Dresden, Germany	9·0	5·0	3·7	3·2	,,
1683	Hackenstedt, Lower Saxony, Germany	3·5	4·0	3·5	2·5	,,
1683	Gorbitz, Dresden, Germany	3·6	3·7	4·0	3·3	,,
1684	Bahrdorf, South Hanover, Germany	2·7	1·7	0·6	1·5	,,
1690	Rundhof, Schleswig Holstein, Germany	2·4	3·3	5·8	3·1	,,
1690	Drillt, Schleswig Holstein, Germany			4·8	5·1	,,
1693	Gorbitz, Dresden, Germany	3·6	3·5	1·7	2·3	,,

TABLE I

Years	Country or district	Wheat	Rye	Barley	Oats	Notes
1694–99	Ostra, Dresden, Germany	6·0	4·4	6·1	3·3	Averages
End of 17th cent.	Angermanland, Sweden			3·0–4·0		,,
c. 1700	Norway (general)					
1700–50	Northern France	3·0–5·0		3·4		Most frequent ratios
1701–05	14 Villages near Lulea, Sweden			1·2–2·6		Min. and max. averages
1712	Rundhof, Schleswig Holstein, Germany	5·0	6·4	5·8		Averages
1712–50	Schleswig Holstein (in general)	7·3				,,
1714–54	Near Geneva, Switzerland	3·0				,,
1720	Ostra, Dresden, Germany	6·3	3·9	3·3	4·0	,,
1724–33	Skarhult, Scania, Sweden		5·0			,,
1725	Rundhof, Schleswig Holstein, Germany		5·4	3·4	3·6	,,
1726–27	Schönhorst, Schleswig Holstein, Germany	5·3	3·6	4·3		,,
1727–30	Schönhorst and Offendorf, Schleswig Holstein, Germany				3·8	,,
1729–40	Bürau, Schleswig Holstein, Germany	7·6	5·7	7·4	7·2	,,
1730	Ostra, Dresden, Germany	9·5	5·6	5·8	3·8	,,
1731–33	Rydboholm, Uppland, Sweden		5·0			,,
1732–33	Oppendorf, Schleswig Holstein, Germany	6·7			5·4	,,

TABLE I

Years	Country or district	Wheat	Rye	Barley	Oats	Notes
1734	Drüllt, Schleswig Holstein, Germany		7·6	6·4	3·3	Averages
1734–39	Lucklum, South Hanover, Germany	4·7	5·7	6·8		,,
1734–43	Skarhult, Scania, Sweden		3·9			,,
1734–43	Rydboholm, Uppland, Sweden		4·8			,,
1735	Rundhof, Schleswig Holstein, Germany	8·5	5·7	3·4	2·9	,,
1735	Drüllt, Schleswig Holstein, Germany	8·5		5·4	3·9	,,
1735–36	Schönhorst, Schleswig Holstein, Germany		6·0		4·2	,,
1735–44	Schönhorst, Schleswig Holstein, Germany		6·3			,,
1735–44	Offendorf, Schleswig Holstein, Germany	7·8			4·9	,,
1736–41	Offendorf, Schleswig Holstein, Germany			5·2		,,
1736–42	Offendorf, Schleswig Holstein, Germany	5·6 ⎫				,,
1737–40	Schönhorst, Schleswig Holstein, Germany	5·0 ⎭	3·0	3·0	2·0	Average low yields
1738–52	Henmelmark, Schleswig Holstein, Germany	7·0	9·0	10·0	5·0	Average high yields
1740–45	Lucklum, South Hanover, Germany	3·9	5·4	8·0	5·8	Averages
1741–43	Schönhorst, Schleswig Holstein, Germany	4·9		5·5		,,
1742–44	Offendorf, Schleswig Holstein, Germany	6·7			5·5	,,
1742–51	Bürau, Schleswig Holstein, Germany	8·6	7·4			,,
1744–50	Skarhult, Scania, Sweden		6·6			,,

TABLE I

Years	Country or district	Wheat	Rye	Barley	Oats	Notes
1744–50	Rydtoholm, Schleswig Holstein, Germany		5·3			Averages
1746	Rundhof, Schleswig Holstein, Germany	6·0	7·4	8·5	3·4	,,
1746	Drüllt, Schleswig Holstein, Germany		6·6		4·0	,,
1746–49	Bürau, Schleswig Holstein, Germany			7·2		,,
1749–50	Offendorf, Schleswig Holstein, Germany	7·0	10·0			,,
1749–50	Schönhorst, Schleswig Holstein, Germany		7·0			,,
1750	Ostra, Dresden, Germany	6·5	6·4	3·5	4·8	,,
1750	Rurdhof, Schleswig Holstein, Germany		8·3	7·5		,,
1750	Drüllt, Schleswig Holstein, Germany		7·7	6·2	4·1	,,
1750	Bürau, Schleswig Holstein, Germany				10·0	,,
1750	Offendorf, Schleswig Holstein, Germany				5·0	,,
1750	Schönhorst, Schleswig Holstein, Germany				5·5	,,

TABLE 2: Eastern Europe
Yield ratios of cereals (seed sown = 1)

Years	Country or district	Wheat	Rye	Barley	Oats	Notes
1548	Riga, Latvia		1·4	0·9		Averages
1549–51	Riga, Latvia		2·5			,,
1550–1695	East Prussia	3·1–5·0	3·0–4·1	2·3–5·5	1·9–3·7	Min. and max. annual averages
1552–53	Murány, Gömör, Hungary	1·9				Averages
1552–55	Murány, Gömör, Hungary					,,
1552–73	Sieradz, Poland	2·9–6·0	2·9–4·4	3·2–6·2	1·4–3·8	Min. and max. annual averages
1559–60	Vistula fens (3 estates), Poland			3·4		Averages
1561	Knyszyn, Poland	2·8	7·1	4·0	3·2	,,
1563–64	Palatinate of Lublin, Poland	5·0	5·9	6·8	5·3	,,
1563–64	Palatinate of Masowsze, Poland	6·7	5·7	7·6	5·7	,,
1564	Korkczyn, Poland	4·9	4·4	5·5	4·9	,,
1564	Zator-Oświeçim, Poland	8·0	9·0		3·1	,,
1564	Sochaczew County, Poland	5·1–11·0	6·9–10·6	5·5–15·0	4·1–7·8	Min. and max. averages
1564	Near Osiek, Poland	5·7–11·1	6·6–10·0	6·7–9·3	4·7–12·8	Min. and max. averages
1569	40 'réserves' in Masovia, Poland	6·4				Averages
1569	Korkczyn, Poland	4·3	4·5	5·5	5·1	,,

TABLE 2

Years	Country or district	Wheat	Rye	Barley	Oats	Notes
1569	Szatmar, Hungary (3 districts)	2·6		2·7	2·7	Averages
1569–72	Tokaj, Zemplén, Hungary					"
1570	Sochaczew County, Poland	3·8–9·6	4·6–6·1	8·6–12·3	2·6–8·3	Min. and max. averages
1570–71	Vistula fens (3 estates)			3·4		Averages
1571	Szatmar, Hungary (3 districts)	1·3			1·7	"
1577	Szatmar, Hungary (3 districts)	5·4		5·3	2·8	"
1582–92	Latvia (3 cistricts)		4·7	2·6		"
1584–86	Lusatia, Saxony, Germany		3·3			"
1584–94	Lusatia, Saxony, Germany		3·7			"
1585	Latvia (3 districts)		3·3	3·7	2·0	"
1586–88	Vistula fens Laski, Poland	0·3–3·5		4·2	4·9	Min. and max.
1590	4 districts, Hungary					Averages
1590	Szatmar, Hungary	1·1		2·8	2·8	"
1590	Tokaj, Zemplén, Hungary					"
1592	Volokolamsk, North Moscow, Russia		2·9	5·0	2·8	"
1597	Near Kobryz, Poland		2·8	3·1	2·3	"
End of 16th cent.	Poznan, Poland	5·2	4·2	5·7	2·9	"
End of 16th cent.	Masovia and Inner-Poland		4·5–5·0			"

TABLE 2

Years	Country or district	Wheat	Rye	Barley	Oats	Notes
17th cent.	Hungary (general)	3·5				Est. average for century
Begin. of 17th cent.	Archbishop Gniezno and Poznan estates, Poland		4·0			Average
1602	Palatinate di Sandomierz, Poland	2·8–5·0	1·7–3·9	2·5–9·3	1·7–6·0	Min. and max.
1603	County of Sochaczew, Poland	2·2–5·4	2·8–3·7	3·2–5·7	1·9–3·6	Min. and max.
1609	Samokleski, Poland		3·0			Averages
1614	Gniezno (4 estates), Poland		2·7			,,
1615	Palatinate di Sandomierz (45 estates), Poland	3·8	3·6	4·7	3·9	,,
1615	Korczyn, Poland	3·7	3·4	4·1	5·0	,,
1615–17	Grzegorzew, Poland (4 estates)		3·8			,,
1616	Masovia, Poland	6·8				,,
1616	Duchy of Oświęcim, Poland	7·0	4·7	7·6		,,
1617	Opatowek, Poland		4·8			,,
1617	Near Kobryn, Poland		4·0	3·7	1·5	,,
1620	Sochaczew, Poland	6·4–10·0	3·3–6·0	5·0–7·5	3·8–8·7	Min. and max.
1620–50	District of Tjumen', Siberia, Russia		3·0–10·0		7·0–8·0	Min. and max.
1623–26	Tomsk, W. Siberia, Russia	3·4	3·4		2·7	Averages
1624	Districts of Wolmar and Wenden, Latvia		1·3–3·5	1·5–3·3		Min. and max.
1624	Cesis Valmeria, Estonia		2·5			Average

TABLE 2

Years	Country or district	Wheat	Rye	Barley	Oats	Notes
1628	Verchotur'e, Siberia, Russia		8·0		10·0	Averages
1630	Sochaczev, Poland	5·2–11·0	4·4–6·0	5·0–7·5	3·3–9·0	Min. and max.
1630–31	Eastern Germany		10·0–12·0			Most frequent averages
1630–49	Turinsk, Siberia, Russia		8·0		6·0	Averages
1631–32	Purschwitz, Lusatia, Germany		2·3	1·5		,,
1633–36	Körmend, Hungary	3·8				,,
1636	Kluki, Tu·kowice and Csowa, Poland		4·0			,,
1637	Kuckau ard Panschwitz, Lusatia, German		3·0	1·8		,,
1638–44	Németujvár (5 farms), Hungary	1·8–3·1	1·8–2·1			Min. and max. annual averages
1639–44	Körmend, Hungary	3·5				Averages
1640	Moscovy, Russia		10·0	5·6		,,
1642	Zdnińska, Poland		4·2			,,
1646	Kunzelow, Poland		4·0			,,
1648–57	Gauszig, Lusatia, Germany		2·5	3·1		,,
1649–56	Németujvár, Hungary	3·3–3·8	2·6–3·8		1·3–4·2	Min. and max. annual averages

TABLE 2

Years	Country or district	Wheat	Rye	Barley	Oats	Notes
1650–99	Latvia (general)		3·0			Averages
1651–53	Ösel (17 estates), Estonia		3·7	3·5	3·7	,,
1651–1700	Krumlov, Bohemia		2·7–3·0	3·9	2·3	50-year average
1653	Kloister of Kostroma, Russia				1·7	Averages
1653	Gniezno, Poland		3·8			,,
1653	Kuckau, Lusatia		4·4	3·0		,,
1654	Ösel, Estonia	3·4				,,
1654	Cesis, Valmeria, Estonia		3·2			,,
1657–58	Cloister of Kostroma, Russia		2·0			,,
1658	Districts near rivers Lena, Angara, Ilim, Siberia		9·5	0·8–3·3	2·6–5·9	Min. and max.
1658	Uniejow, Poland		3·7			Averages
1659–64	Viljandi, Estonia		3·8	3·2	2·8	,,
1660	Duchy of Oświęcim, Poland	1·5	2·1	3·0		,,
1660	Masovia, Poland	2·8				,,
1660	Korczyn, Poland	3·2				,,
1660–61	Nižnij, Novgorod, Arzamas, Russia		2·4–5·2		2·4–5·2	Min. and max.
1660–84	Several estates, Estonia		4·5	3·5		Averages
1661	Tomsk, W. Siberia, Russia		4·7		2·5	,,
1661	Duchy of Oświęcim, Poland				3·7	,,
1661	Sochaczew, Poland	2·0–4·0	2·2–4·5	3·0–5·2	2·0–4·4	Min. and max.

TABLE 2

Years	Country or District	Wheat	Rye	Barley	Oats	Notes
1664	Ziakowie, Poland		3·2			Average
1666–1700	Lovosice, Bohemia	4·1	4·0	3·6	3·6	35-year average
1667	Panschwitz, Lusatia, Germany		2·9			Averages
1667	Rjazan, Razsk, Tver, Russia		3·0–4·0		7·0	,,
1674–93	Villages of Lower Dvina, Russia		7·2			,,
1675	Vistula fens, Laski and Kaldowo, Poland			3·5		Average for the two places
1675	Poland (in general)	2·1	3·0–4·0	3·0–4·0	4·0–4·5	Most frequent averages
1675	Near Moscow, Russia		3·0		2·5	Averages
c. 1675	District of Tot'ma, Russia	4·0–4·5	2·5–3·0		3·0	Most frequent yields
c. 1675	Arzamas, Slopin, Russia		5·0		5·0	Averages
1677	Several districts (18 estates), Hungary	3·6	3·7	3·8	2·9	,,
1678	Troice-Gled-nski, Lower Dvina, Russia	1·0–10·0			1·5–3·0	Min. and max.
1678	Velikij, Ustj.ng, Lower Dvina, Russia		2·0–6·5	4·0–5·0	3·8	Min. and max.
1679	Districts near rivers Lena, Angara, Ilim, Siberia		2·4			Averages
1680–87	8 estates, Estonia		3·2–4·8	2·8–5·5	1·9–3·2	Min. and max. annual averages

TABLE 2

Years	Country or district	Wheat	Rye	Barley	Oats	Notes
1681–85	Haiba, Hageri, Estonia	2·9				Average
1681–85	Lihula, Estonia	5·5				,,
1681–90	About 180 estates, Estonia		3·5–4·6	3·5–4·6	2·3–3·6	Min. and max. annual averages
1682	Troice-Gledenski, Lower Dvina, Russia	2·0–3·0				Most frequent yields
1682	Velikji, Ustiung, Lower Dvina, Russia		1·5–5·0	3·0–4·0	2·0–4·0	Min. and max.
1682–87	Vizdeme, N.W. Latvia		4·7	5·4	3·6	Averages
1685	Zduńska Wola, Poland		4·0			,,
1685	Zeakowie, Poland		3·3	4·0		,,
1685	Opotowek and Kluki, Poland		2·0			,,
1685	Cloister of Cholmogorsk, Russia		5·0	4·0		,,
1687	Districts near rivers Lena, Angara, Ilim, Siberia		3·6		4·1	,,
1688–92	Giersdorf, Silesia, Germany		3·4	2·9	3·6	Averages
1690	Districts of Wolmar and Wenden, Latvia		4·3	4·1	3·8	,,
1693	Poland (in general)	1·4–2·0				Most frequent averages

TABLE 2

Years	Country or district	Wheat	Rye	Barley	Oats	Notes
1699–1700	Giersdorf, Silesia, Germany	1·9				Average
18th cent.	Eastern Germany (general)		10·0–12·0			Most frequent yields
18th cent.	Lithuania (general)		3·0		3·0–3·5	Most frequent yields
18th cent.	Latvia (general)		3·1 and 5·0			Yields on poor and good soils
1701	6 districts near rivers Angara and Lena, Siberia		6·2–10·8		2·1	Min. and max. and averages
1701–09	Giersdorf, Silesia, Germany	3·3	3·2	2·4	2·2	Averages
1701–50	Krumlov, Bohemia	3·8	3·2	3·8	2·5	,,
1701–50	Lovosice, Bohemia	3·6	2·6	3·3	2·8	,,
1706–12	Szentmihaly, Kendermezö, Transilvania, Hungary					,,
1708–10	Szalard, Bihar, Hungary	4·2	4·6			,,
1710	Troice-Gledeaskij, Lower Dvina, Russia		7·0	5·6	2·6	,,
1710	Velikij, Ustiurg, Lower Dvina, Russia	2·0–7·0	4·0–10·0	5·0–9·0	3·0–4·0	Min. and max.
1712	Giersdorf, Silesia, Germany		4·5	3·4	3·1	Averages
1712–44	Sárospatak, Zemplén, Hungary				1·5–2·7	Min. and max. 5-year average

TABLE 2

Years	Country or district	Wheat	Rye	Barley	Oats	Notes
1712–44	Regéc, Abaúj, Hungary (3 allodial tenures)				0·9–3·8	Min. and max. frequent averages
1713	Kuckau and Panschwitz, Lusatia, Germany			4·2		Averages
1715–18	Kuckau and Panschwitz, Lusatia, Germany	1·5–3·4	3·4–4·2			Min. and max. annual averages
1715–29	Sárospatak, Zemplén, Hungary	2·8–3·9				Min. and max. 5-year averages
1715–39	Regéc, Abaúj, Hungary (3 allodial tenures)	2·2–4·0		1·7–3·5		Min. and max. 5-year averages
1716–20	Sárospatak, Zemplén, Hungary		4·7			Averages
1716–42	Regéc, Abaúj, Hungary (one allodial tenure)		3·4–5·7			Min. and max. 5-year averages
1719–24	Németújvar, Vas, Hungary	3·5				Averages
1726–50	Trébon, Bohemia	3·5	2·7	3·6		,,
1729	Cloister of Cholmogorsk, Russia		7·0	4·5	2·6	,,

TABLE 2

Years	Country or district	Wheat	Rye	Barley	Oats	Notes
1735–39	Sárospatak, Zemplén, Hungary	2·1		2·0		Averages
1740–44	Sárospatak, Zemplén, Hungary			1·4		,,
1746	Rammenau, Lusatia, Germany		3·8	3·3		,,
1748	Rammenau, Lusatia, Germany		3·3	1·4		,,
1748	Demesnes in South Wolhynia, Russia		1·8		1·8	,,
c. 1750	Russia (general)	3·0				Most frequent yields
c. 1730	Estonia (general)	5·0				Most frequent yields
c. 1750	Poland (general)	2·0				Most frequent yields
1751	Rammenau, Lusatia, Germany	2·8	3·7	3·6		Averages
1751–60	Giersdorf, Silesia, Germany		3·7	3·2	3·2	,,
1765	Korczyn, Poland	3·2				,,
1766	4 estates in Upper-Lusatia, Germany	3·3–4·9	2·6–3·4	3·0–5·4	2·2–2·3	Min. and max.

TABLE 3: Atlantic Europe
Yield ratios of cereals (seed sown = 1)

Years	Country or district	Wheat	Rye	Barley	Oats	Notes
	(a) *The Netherlands, Belgium*					
1570–73	Hitsum, Friesland	10·3		7·5–9·0		Averages winter and spring barley
1571	Hitsum, Friesland				3·0	Averages
1573	Hitsum, Friesland				5·0	,,
1586–1602	Lier	10·9				,,
1601	Overijssel		5·0–8·0			,,
1604	Het Bildt, Friesland	14·1		7·0		,,
1608	Het Bildt, Friesland	4·8		5·8		,,
1617	Het Bildt, Friesland	6·4				,,
1765	Friesland	15·0–20·0	20·0–24·0	20·0–30·0	30·0	High yields on rich soils
	(b) *Great Britain*					
1504–37	Hurdwick, Devon	6·6			4·5	Averages
1562	Heighton St. Clair, Sussex	3·0	8·1	2·8	3·2	,,
1571–80	Cuxam, Oxon	8·0		2·0–3·0		Average barley yield 3·0 is for drage
c. 1583	Walton, Somerset	8·0		6·6	4·0	Expected yields

TABLE 3

Years	Country or district	Wheat	Rye	Barley	Oats	Notes
1604–17	Nibley, Gloucestershire	4·7		4·3		Averages
1607	Arburg, Warwickshire	8·0		6·2	3·5	,,
1612–20	Harwell, Berkshire	11·6		7·1		,,
1618	Kampsford, Gloucestershire	5·4				,,
1625–26	Kampsford, Gloucestershire	3·6		4·3	2·0	,,
1627–31	Kampsford, Gloucestershire					,,
1630–31	Kampsford, Gloucestershire			2·7	2·2	,,
c. 1655	England, al over	6·0–8·0				Most frequent averages
1768	Great Britain: 13 districts	8·7				Averages
1768	,, ,, 11			7·6	7·3	,,
1768	,, ,, 12					,,
1770	,, ,, 70	10·0				,,
1770	,, ,, 29		12·3			,,
1770	,, ,, 72			10·2	8·3	,,
1770	,, ,, 73					,,
1771	,, ,, 46	8·9				,,
1771	,, ,, 9		9·7			,,
1771	,, ,, 45			9·3	8·9	,,
1771	,, ,, 40					,,
1771	Leicestershire	12·0		8·0–9·0	8·0	,,

TABLE 3

614 *Appendix*

Years	Country or district	Wheat	Rye	Barley	Oats	Notes
	(c) *France: Atlantic regions*					
16th cent.	Haut Poitou	4·0–5·0				Most frequent averages
1672–77	Beauvaisis: 3 districts	5·0–6·0				Most frequent averages
End of 17th cent.	France (general)	4·5 / 5·5 / 10·0 / 15·0				Averages on poor, good, rich and very rich soils
1716	District of Soissons and Amiens	3·0–4·0 / 6·0–7·0 / 8·0–10·0				Most frequent averages on poor, good and rich soils
1716	Soissonais		5·0–6·0			Averages on moderate and rich soils
1716	Pas de Calais		10·0 / 13·0–16·0			Averages on very rich soils
1728–31	Fontmorigny, Cher	3·4				Averages
1732–35	Noisy – Le Grand, Brie	4·8	8·8	4·6	7·0	„

TABLE 3

Years	Country or district	Wheat	Rye	Barley	Oats	Notes
1732–40	Fontmorigny, Cher	3·3				Averages
1741–42	Fontmorigny, Cher	0·8				,,
1742–43	Fontmorigny, Cher	11·0				,,
1743–45	Fontmorigny, Cher	2·5				,,
c. 1750	Berry	8·0				Averages on good soils
c. 1750	Poitou	9·0				Averages on good soils
c. 1750	Gâtinois	5·0			5·0	Averages
1776–78	Bretagne (general)	5·0	8·0		9·0–10·0	Most frequent averages

TABLE 4: Mediterranean Europe
Yield ratios of cereals (seed sown = 1)

Years	Country or district	Wheat	Rye	Barley	Oats	Notes
1st half 16th cent.	Chieri, Piedmont, Italy	5·0–6·0				Most frequent averages
16th cent.	Lombardy, Veneto, Emilia, Italy	3·5–6·0	4·0–5·0	5·0–6·0	4·0–7·0	Max. and min.
1533–48	Catalonia, Spain	3·0–4·0				Most frequent averages
1540	Low Provence, France (4 districts)	3·0–4·0				Most frequent averages
1540	Low Provence, France (7 districts)	7·0–10·0				Yields on very good soils
1540	Caussols, Alpes Maritimes, France	5·0				Averages
1545–54	Imola, Romagna, Italy	6·3		4·6		,,
1550–1600	Campagna Romana, Italy	c. 8·0	c. 8·0	c. 8·0	c. 8·0	Yields probably too high
1555–64	Imola, Romagna, Italy	5·2		5·5		Averages
1565–74	Imola, Romagna, Italy	6·0		7·4		,,
1570	Districts of Siena, Tuscany, Italy	4·0				,,
1585–94	Imola, Romagna, Italy	5·6		5·4		,,
1595–1604	Imola, Romagna, Italy	5·1		9·3		,,

TABLE 4

Years	Country or district	Wheat 3·0-5·5	Rye 3·0-5·0	Barley 5·0-5·5	Oats 5·0-6·0	Notes
17th cent.	Lombardy, Veneto, Emilia, Italy					Min. and max. of the most frequent averages
1603	Cuna, Tuscany, Italy	4·5 and 9·0	4·5 and 9·0	6·0 and 12·0		Yields on mod. and high soils
1605-14	Imola, Romagna, Italy	6·4		3·9		Averages
1615-24	Imola, Romagna, Italy	5·4		4·8		,,
1625-34	Imola, Romagna, Italy	5·6		7·5		,,
1635-44	Imola, Romagna, Italy	5·7		7·1		,,
1640	Districts of Siena, Tuscany, Italy	5·0	5·2	5·2		,,
1645-54	Imola, Romagna, Italy	4·9		5·5		,,
1649-50	Montaldeo, Piedmont	less than 1				,,
1655-64	Imola, Romagna, Italy	5·5		5·8	3·2	,,
c. 1664	Alessandria, Piedmont	c. 6·0				,,
1665-74	Imola, Romagna, Italy	6·6		7·6		,,
c. 1672-74	Montaldeo, Piedmont	2·2				,,
1674	Lodève, Languedoc, France	5·0	5·0	4·0	6·0	,,
1675-84	Imola, Romagna, Italy	6·0		5·1		,,
1676	District of Siena, Tuscany, Italy	5·1	6·3	6·3		,,
1677-78	Montaldeo, Piedmont, Italy	2·4				,,

TABLE 4

Years	Country or district	Wheat	Rye	Barley	Oats	Notes
1681	Montaldeo, Piedmont, Italy	1·8			3·0	Averages
1682	Montaldeo, Piedmont, Italy				3·2	,,
1683	Montaldeo, Piedmont, Italy	3·0–6·0				Min. and max.
1685	Montaldeo, Piedmont, Italy				3·5	Averages
1685–88	Montaldeo, Piedmont, Italy	1·0–3·3				Min. and max.
1685–94	Imola, Romagna, Italy	6·6		6·7		Average
1686	Montaldeo, Piedmont, Italy				less than 1	,,
1692–95	Montaldeo, Piedmont, Italy	2·0				,,
1694	District of Siena, Tuscany, Italy	5·4				,,
1695–1704	Imola, Romagna, Italy	5·8		8·1		,,
1697–1700	Montaldeo, Piedmont, Italy	1·5				,,
1700–1750	Lombardy, Veneto, Emilia, Italy	4·0–6·5	5·0–8·0	6·0–8·0	6·0–9·0	Most frequent averages
18th cent.	Spain (general)	3·0–4·0				Most frequent averages
1702–09	Montaldeo, Piedmont, Italy	3·1				Averages
1705–14	Imola, Romagna, Italy	5·8		7·9		,,
1714	Montaldeo, Piedmont, Italy	2·8				,,
1715–24	Senigallia, Marche, Italy	c. 3·0				,,
1715–24	Imola, Romagna, Italy	6·4		7·6		,,

TABLE 4

Years	Country or district	Wheat	Rye	Barley	Oats	Notes
1716	Montaldeo, Piedmont, Italy	1·6				Average
1718	Montaldeo, Piedmont, Italy				less than 1	,,
1720	Montaldeo, Piedmont, Italy	4·2				,,
1722–28	Montaldeo, Piedmont, Italy	2·3–3·9				Min. and max.
1725–34	Imola, Romagna, Italy	5·5		7·2		Averages
1730–34	Montaldeo, Piedmont, Italy	0·6–3·0				Min. and max.
1735–44	Imola, Romagna, Italy	5·9		7·3		Averages
1738	Montaldeo, Piedmont, Italy	4·9				,,
1745–54	Imola, Romagna, Italy	5·8		5·0		,,
1747	Lodeve, Languedoc, France	4·0				,,
c. 1750	Northern Italy (many districts)	6·0–7·0	7·0–9·0	8·0–9·0	9·0–11·0	Most frequent averages
c. 1750	Lombardy, Italy	15·0–20·0				Yields on very good soils
c. 1750	Lazare, Languedoc, France	3·0–3·5				Averages
1758	Lodeve, Languedoc, France	4·0		4·0		,,
1759–61	Villabianca, Sicily, Italy	5·0–6·0				Most frequent averages
1764	Districts of Siena, Tuscany, Italy	6·4	6·5	6·5		Averages
c. 1768	Sicily, Italy	6·0–8·0				Most frequent averages

TABLE 5: Weight per Head of Livestock (Kilograms)

Years	Country or district	Ox and bull	Cow	Calf	Pig	Sheep	Notes L.W. = Live weight D.W. = Dead weight
16th cent.	Schleswig Holstein, Germany				42–48 35–40		{ L.W. { D.W.
2nd half 16th cent.	Lombardy, Italy	290–310	200–230	40–50	55–90		L.W. calf 6–8 months old
17th cent.	Denmark				35–40	20–25	D.W.
1618	Ostra, Saxony, Germany	{ 325 { 175	{ 250 { 100		16		{ L.W. { D.W.
c. 1650	Heilsbronn, Germany	163·5–225		24			L.W. calf up to 6 months old
1660	Montaldeo, Piedmont, Italy					19·5	L.W.
1663	Montaldeo, Piedmont, Italy					17·7	L.W.
1663–66	Montaldeo, Piedmont, Italy				85·5		Average of annual live weights
1668	Montaldeo, Piedmont, Italy					24	L.W.
1669–70	Montaldeo, Piedmont, Italy				73·2		Average of annual L.W.
1673	Montaldeo, Piedmont, Italy				56·9		L.W.
1674	Schleswig Holstein, Germany				{ 30 { 15		{ L.W. { D.W.

TABLE 5

Years	Country or district	Ox and bull	Cow	Calf	Pig	Sheep	Notes
1675	Montaldeo, Piedmont, Italy	146·5 215·0 255·5					L.W. animals 3 years old L.W. animals 4 years old L.W. animals 5 years old
1679	Montaldeo, Piedmont, Italy				51·7		L.W.
1680	Montaldeo, Piedmont, Italy					20·7	L.W.
1683	Montaldeo, Piedmont, Italy			79·9			L.W. calf 1/2 years old
1683–90	Montaldeo, Piedmont, Italy					79·2	Average of annual L.W.
1684	Montaldeo, Piedmont, Italy	149·5		32·5			L.W. ox 2½ years old Calf 5 months old
1686	Montaldeo, Piedmont, Italy	108·5 214					L.W. animals 2 years old L.W. animals 3½ years old
1688	Montaldeo, Piedmont, Italy	260					L.W. animals 4 years old
1690	Montaldeo, Piedmont, Italy			58·5			L.W. animals 1 year old
1694	Montaldeo, Piedmont, Italy				50·4		L.W.
1695	Montaldeo, Piedmont, Italy				58·6		L.W.
1698	Montaldeo, Piedmont, Italy					22·8	L.W.
c. 1700	Hanover, Germany	360 220	225–275				L.W.
18th cent.	Schleswig Holstein, Germany				62·5–100		L.W. D.W.

TABLE 5

Years	Country or district	Ox and bull	Cow	Calf	Pig	Sheep	Notes
18th cent.	Normandy, France	400					L.W.
18th cent.	Norfolk, England		254				L.W. Hereford cattle
18th cent.	Norfolk, England		317				L.W. Scotch cattle
18th cent.	Scottish Lowlands		250–300				L.W.
18th cent.	Scottish Highlands		150–200				L.W.
18th cent.	Picardy, France		200			20	L.W.
1701	Montaldeo, Piedmont, Italy				63·0		L.W.
1710	Montaldeo, Piedmont, Italy				94·7		L.W.
1718	Montaldeo, Piedmont, Italy					24·4	L.W.
1718–19	Montaldeo, Piedmont, Italy				79·3		Average of annual L.W.
1722	Montaldeo, Piedmont, Italy				77·3		L.W.
1725	Montaldeo, Piedmont, Italy	206					L.W. animals 4 years old
1728	Montaldeo, Piedmont, Italy					26·8	L.W.
1737	Montaldeo, Piedmont, Italy	146·5		64·7			{ L.W. ox 3 years old / Calf 1 year old
1772	Montaldeo, Piedmont, Italy				81·3		L.W.

Notes on the Authors

CARLO M. CIPOLLA

is professor of Economic History at the University of Pavia and at the University of California at Berkeley. Born in 1922 at Pavia, Italy, he graduated from Pavia University, then proceeded to Paris and London where he continued his studies from 1945 to 1948. Since 1949 he has lectured at various European and American Universities on economic history. His publications in English include *Money, Prices and Civilisation* (1956), *The Economic History of World Population* (1962), *Guns and Sails in the Early Phase of European Expansion* (1965), *Clocks and Culture* (1967), *Literacy and Development in the West* (1969) and *Cristofano and the Plague* (1973).

ROGER MOLS

was born in 1909 and entered the Society of Jesus where he was ordained in 1938. Since 1954 he has taught Church History, Religious Sociology and Demography at the Faculté Saint Albert, Egenhoven, Louvain. He is Vice-Chairman of the Belgian Society of Demography and among his best known publications are *Introduction à la Démographie des villes d'Europe du XIVe au XVIIIe siècle* 1954–56, 3 vols; *Démographie et paternité responsable* 1969; and *La periphérie bruxelloise* 1970.

WALTER MINCHINTON

has been Professor of Economic History at the University of Exeter since 1964. Born in London in 1921, he was educated at Queen Elizabeth's Hospital, Bristol, and the London School of Economics. From 1948 to 1964 he taught at the University College of Swansea. He has published books on *The British Tinplate Industry: a history* (1957), *The Trade of Bristol in the Eighteenth Century* (1957), *Politics and the Port of Bristol in the Eighteenth Century* (1962), *Industrial South Wales,*

1750–1914: essays in Welsh economic history (1969), *Mercantilism: system or expediency?* (1969), *The Growth of English Overseas Trade in the Seventeenth and Eighteenth Centuries* (1969) and *Wage Regulation in Pre-industrial England* (1972).

HERMANN KELLENBENZ

was born in Württemberg in 1913. He studied at the universities of Tübingen, Munich and Kiel, reading History, Philosophy, Literature and Art History. His Ph.D. thesis *Holstein-Gottorp, eine Domaine Schwedens 1657–1675* was published in 1940.

After the war he taught at Regensburg and Würzburg, was a Rockefeller Fellow, at Harvard 1952–3 and a member of the Ecole Pratique des Hautes Études in Paris 1953–4. From 1960–70 he held the chair of Economic and Social History at the University of Cologne, moving in 1970 to the same chair at the University of Erlangen-Nürnberg. His publications include *Unternehmekräfte in Hamburger Portugal und Spanienhandel 1590–1625* (1954); *Sephardim an der unteren Elbe* (1959); and *Die Fuggerache Maestragopacht 1538–1542* (1967); *Fremde Kaufleute auf der Iberischen Halbinsel* (ed.), 1970.

ALDO DE MADDALENA

was born in 1920 and studied at the University L. Bocconi in Milan. He was Professor of Economic History at the University of Genoa and Parma from 1951–68 and now holds that position at the University of Turin. He has contributed to several Italian and foreign journals, and among his publications are studies on: *Prices and the Market in Milan in the Seventeenth Century; Agriculture and Property in Lombardy in the Sixteenth and Seventeenth Centuries; The Economic Development of the Provinces of Novara and Mantua in the Nineteenth and Twentieth Centuries; The Foreign Commercial Policy of the United States (1789–1812)*, etc.

DOMENICO SELLA

was born in Milan in 1926 and studied at the University of Milan, Notre Dame University, the University of Venice and the London School of Economics. He has been teaching at the University of Wisconsin in Madison since 1960 and is currently Professor of History there. In 1966–67 he was Visiting Lecturer at Bocconi University in Milan. Among his publications is *Commerci e industrie a Venezia nel secolo XVII* (Venice-Rome, Istituto per la Collaborazione culturale, 1961).

KRISTOF GLAMANN

is professor of history at the University of Copenhagen. He is President of the International Economic History Association, editor of *The Scandinavian Economic History Review* and member of the board of the Scandinavian Institute of Asian Studies. Professor Glamann is the author of *Dutch-Asiatic Trade 1620–1740* (1958) and *A History of Prices and Wages in Denmark 1660–1800* (1958 with Astrid Friis). He has also written a history of the Danish brewing industry (1963), edited Otto Thott's Tract on Commerce (1966) and presented several other contributions to the study of modern history.

GEOFFREY PARKER

is lecturer in modern history at the University of St Andrews. Born in Nottingham, England, in 1943, he was successively student, research student and fellow of Christ's College, Cambridge, until 1972 when he moved to St Andrews. He has written two books and a number of articles on the history of early modern Europe, of which the best known is *The Army of Flanders and the Spanish Road (1567–1659): the logistics of Spanish victory and defeat in the Low Countries' Wars* (1972).

Index of Persons

(The names of modern writers have not been included)

Index of Places

Note: Detailed references to certain countries have been omitted (e.g. England, France, Germany, Netherlands, etc.) because their number is so great as to have little use to the reader.

General Index